Beginning SQL Server 2000 for Visual Basic Developers

Thearon Willis

054785

Apress™

Beginning SQL Server 2000 for Visual Basic Developers

Credits

About the Author

Thearon began his career in computers in 1980 as a computer operator. During the fall of 1980 he took a course in BASIC programming using the Radio Shack TSR-80 computer and has been hooked on programming ever since.

After learning the BASIC language Thearon moved on to learn COBOL and began writing programs to help automate some of his daily tasks as a computer operator. Advancing his career, Thearon became an Operations Analyst and learned several other languages to assist in his job.

In 1989 Thearon moved into Systems Programming and started programming in S370 ASSEMBLER language. He coded batch programs in ASSEMBLER language and then moved on to code CICS programs. The Help Desk and Network Operations used these batch and online programs to perform some of their daily tasks, such as monitoring CICS printers and polling sales. During this time he started working with relational databases on the mainframe and immediately saw the benefits that relational databases provided.

Between the years of 1988 and 1993 Thearon learned several more programming languages, which include QBASIC, PASCAL, and C++. Thearon decided that he enjoyed programming so much that he switched his career path and became a developer full time.

The first application that Thearon worked on was written in ASSEMBLER language and included over 70 ASSEMBLER programs. To help automate some of the tasks that were performed by the department that used this application, he wrote several programs in Visual Basic. One of these programs read and processed data from message queues that were populated from the mainframe, and performed automated balancing.

Thearon first began working with Visual Basic in version 3.0. After version 4 was released he switched his career from the mainframe to client-server development. He still enjoys working with relational databases and uses SQL Server as the back-end to all of his applications that store and retrieve data.

Thearon currently works as a senior consultant and develops intranet/Internet and business-to-business applications. He lives with his wife Margie and daughter Stephanie in Charlotte, North Carolina.

I would like to thank some of the folks at Wrox Press for making this book possible. Thanks go to Dominic Lowe for getting this project started, to Dianne Parker for her invaluable insight and technical editing skills, to Ben Egan for his hard work, and to Cilmara Lion for coordinating the work.

I would like to thank my wife Margie for her faith in me and the patience she has shown while I write one book after another. It is to her and my daughter Stephanie that I dedicate this book.

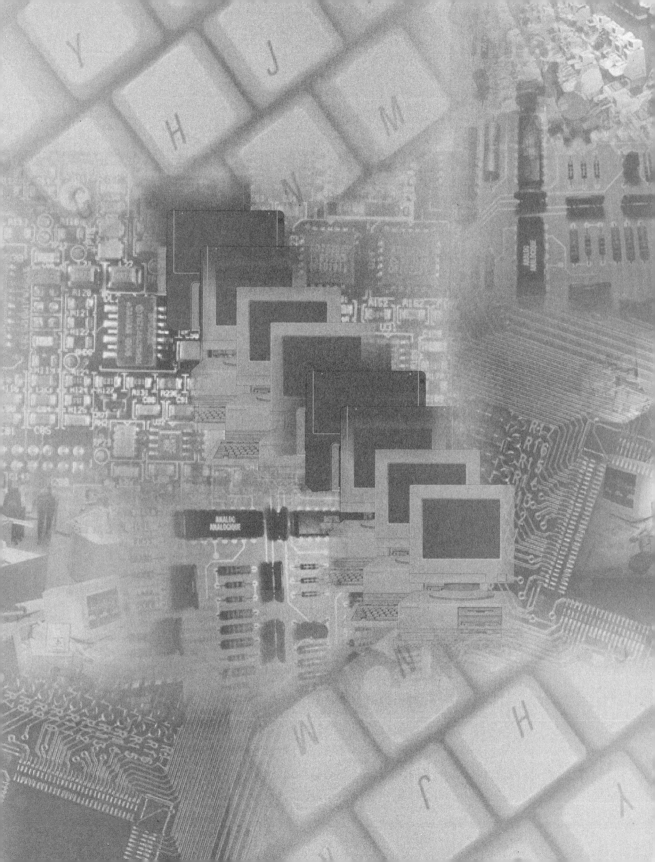

Table of Contents

Table of Contents

Table of Contents

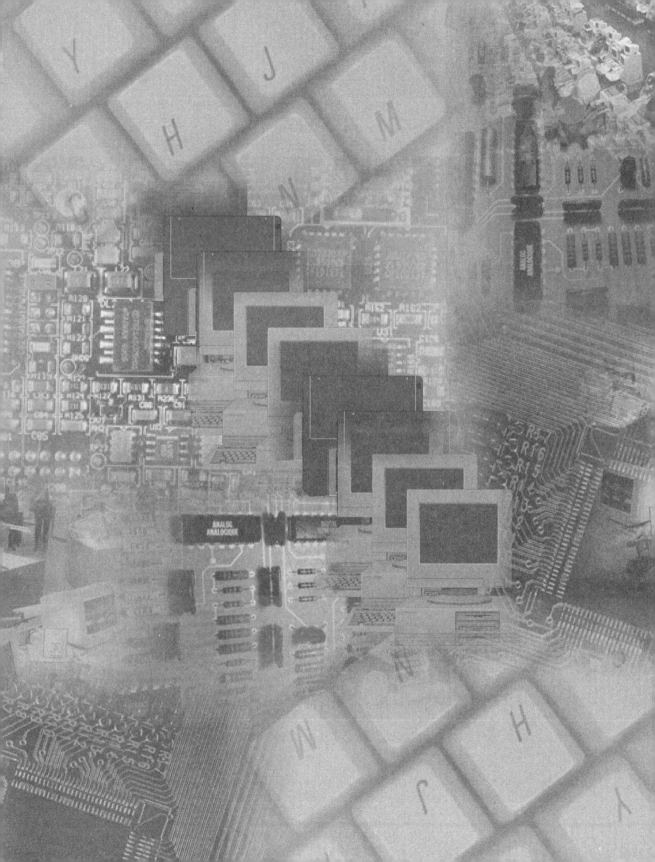

Introduction

Everywhere you look these days Microsoft SQL Server is there. You hear about dotcom companies running SQL Server and accessing terabytes of data, and applications that need to be scaled up from Access to use SQL Server. You just can't seem to escape the presence of SQL Server in the workplace.

SQL Server 2000 is the latest release and, because of performance enhancements and new features, this is a great time to learn how to use SQL Server and how to incorporate it into your applications.

Whether you are building VB applications (front-end or back-end) or web applications, if you need data access to SQL Server 2000 this book can help. While most of the book covers accessing SQL Server 2000 from VB, the same principles can be applied to Active Server Pages using VBScript and ADO (ActiveX Data Objects). This book covers the use of in-line SQL statements and stored procedures, and how to use both in your VB programs and web applications.

The new XML features of SQL Server 2000 are also covered – you will learn how to execute queries and stored procedures in the URL of a web browser to retrieve XML data from the database. XML templates, XSL stylesheets, and XML schemas are also covered, and we show you how to format your XML data into a presentable format for display in a browser.

SQL Server 2000 includes many useful tools. For example, English Query is a powerful tool for building applications that allow users to access the data without understanding query languages or the structure of the database. This book will step you through creating your own English Query application.

What This Book Is About

This book will introduce you to SQL Server 2000, starting with the basic concepts and working through the features that are most commonly used by VB developers. We start by introducing the core components of a SQL Server database, such as tables, primary keys and foreign keys, indexes, and stored procedures.

We cover the installation of the Personal Edition of SQL Server 2000 and show you how to install multiple instances of SQL Server 2000 on the same machine. We then move on and discuss relational database design, and help you get off on the right foot by walking through the design and normalization of the development database that will be used throughout this book.

We discuss SQL Server security and show you how to grant access to the various database objects to users and roles that we set up. We also cover database connections and how to create DSN and DSN-less connections from VB using both Windows authentication and SQL Server authentication.

One whole chapter has been set aside to cover the details of the Query Analyzer. This is a powerful tool that you as a developer will use to write and debug queries and stored procedures. This tool also allows you to view and manage the objects in your database, such as tables and stored procedures.

Creating and using stored procedures is covered in depth and we walk you through building a sample application that uses stored procedures to select, insert, update, and delete data. As you progress from one chapter to the next you will be building upon the previous chapter's content to increase the functionality of the sample application. By the time you get to the end of the book, not only will you have gained a better understanding of SQL Server and stored procedures, but you will also have a complete application that serves as an example for future reference and use.

The last chapters in this book deal with the XML features of SQL Server 2000. The first of these gets you up to speed with XML and covers some simple formatting of XML data using XSL stylesheets. The second walks you through the process of creating XML reports that are displayed in a web browser.

The case study, split into two parts, introduces you to English Query and shows you how to build and deploy an English Query application. English Query is a separate product that ships with SQL Server 2000 – it allows you to build an application that your end users can use to ask natural English questions to query the database. These questions are translated into SQL statements behind the scenes and are executed, returning the data that the user has asked for.

How This Book Is Organized

This section provides a summary of each chapter, showing how we start with the basics and work our way up to more complex topics.

Chapter 1 – Introduction to SQL Server 2000

This chapter covers an overview of SQL Server 2000 and all of the objects that make up a database. We cover databases, transaction logs, tables, indexes, and constraints. We also introduce you to data access with ADO, XML support in SQL Server 2000, English Query, and Analysis Services.

Chapter 2 – Installing the Personal Edition of SQL Server 2000

This chapter covers the various SQL Server 2000 editions and the prerequisites for installing the Personal Edition of SQL Server 2000. After covering the installation of the Personal Edition we introduce you to the various tools that are installed with SQL Server, including the Enterprise Manager.

Chapter 3 – Designing and Creating the Development Database

This chapter covers relational database design and will walk you through the design and normalization of the development database that will be used throughout the rest of the book. We also cover some suggested naming standards that can be used. We create, step-by-step, the development database and show you how to view and modify the database.

Chapter 4 – SQL Server Security

This chapter covers the two types of security modes in SQL Server: Windows authentication and SQL Server authentication. We show you how to use both, and we will continue to do so as we progress through the book. Database security is also covered and, after we discuss how this works, we show you how to grant permissions on the database objects that you create.

Chapter 5 – SQL Server Query Analyzer

This chapter introduces you to the features of the Query Analyzer. You get first hand experience with this powerful tool as we walk through its features and learn how to use them. The Object Browser is covered in depth as you learn how to view and manipulate the objects in your database and discover how to use this feature to your benefit.

Chapter 6 – Database Connections

This chapter covers connecting to SQL Server from your VB program using both DSN and DSN-less connections with Windows authentication and SQL Server authentication. We build a login form that gives you a choice of which mode and type of connection to use. We also show you how to create a DSN to be used in a DSN connection.

Chapter 7 – Introduction to Stored Procedures

This chapter begins your introduction to stored procedures as we cover stored procedure input and output parameters and return values. We walk through simple examples showing you how to build these stored procedures as well as call them from your VB programs. This chapter includes a look at some useful methods of the ADO `Recordset` object, to retrieve multiple results sets and to work more efficiently with static data.

Chapter 8 – Stored Procedures versus SQL Statements

Having had an introduction to stored procedures, this chapter shows a side-by-side comparison of using stored procedures and in-line SQL statements in VB. You will come to realize what can and cannot be accomplished using in-line SQL statements, and also the power and flexibility that stored procedures provide. Ways of optimizing in-line SQL statements are also demonstrated.

Chapter 9 – Selecting Data

This chapter covers creating stored procedures that select data. We cover simple `SELECT` statements and then progress to more complex `SELECT` statements that use joins. The various types of joins are discussed and used in our stored procedures. This chapter introduces the Hardware Tracking application that will be expanded on in the following chapters.

Chapter 10 – Inserting Data

`INSERT` stored procedures are covered in this chapter and we introduce topics such as conditional processing logic and error handling in your stored procedures. The stored procedures start to become more complex at this stage and these stored procedures are incorporated into the Hardware Tracking application.

Chapter 11 – Updating Data

This chapter covers `UPDATE` stored procedures and shows you how to use logic in your stored procedures to validate data if needed. We also introduce transactional processing in stored procedures, allowing you to create stored procedures that use transactions.

Chapter 12 – Deleting Data

This chapter not only covers stored procedures that delete data but it also covers triggers. We will walk you through the process of creating triggers that can be used to delete data. Along with this we also cover cascading referential integrity constraints. We show you exactly how they work and also show you how to create and use them.

Chapter 13 – Working with Text Data

This chapter shows you how to work with text data in SQL Server 2000. This chapter covers more advanced topics regarding SQL Server data types and processing, as well as ADO. We use the `GetChunk` and `AppendChunk` methods in ADO to manage large amounts of data. We show you how text data is managed in SQL Server and how to work with it efficiently. This chapter completes the Hardware Tracking application that is written in VB.

Chapter 14 – Installing Internet Information Services (IIS)

This chapter helps you prepare for the next chapter and for the case study by walking you through the process of installing IIS and setting up a virtual directory that will be used for your intranet web site. We also walk through the steps to set up a virtual directory for SQL Server that will allow us to query the database directly from the URL of a web browser.

Chapter 15 – SQL Server and XML

This chapter introduces you to the XML features of SQL Server 2000. We explore how to query the database through the URL of the web browser using both SQL statements and stored procedures. We also cover XML templates, XSL stylesheets, and XML schemas. We display raw XML data in the browser and, through the use of XSL stylesheets, display formatted XML data in the browser.

Chapter 16 – XML Web Reports

This chapter continues your study of XML by showing you how to create XML reports that are displayed in the browser. We take a more in-depth look at XML templates and XSL stylesheets to create sophisticated web reports. We cover the use of scripts in both XSL and HTML to format, display, and manipulate data.

Case Study part 1 – Building an English Query Application

This part of the case study introduces you to English Query and walks you through the steps of installing it. We then proceed to build an English Query application using our development database as the source. We learn how to use entities and relationships effectively to build a powerful application for our users.

Case Study part 2 – Deploying an English Query Application

The second part of the case study shows you how to deploy your completed English Query application over the web. We walk through the steps of creating the web pages that will host your English Query application. When we are done, you will have deployed your English Query application over the intranet.

Appendix A – SQL Server and VB Data Types

Appendix B – ADO 2.6 Object Model

Appendix C – SQL Server Functions

Appendix D – Building the Hardware Tracking Framework

Appendix E – Creating the Hardware Tracking Business Server Component

Appendix F – References

Appendix G – Support, Errata, and forums.apress.com

Who This Book Is For

Since this is an Apress Beginning series book, it is our goal to teach you everything you need to know to get up to speed using SQL Server 2000 from the ground up. This book is aimed at experienced Visual Basic developers who want to increase their knowledge and skill set by using an enterprise relational database.

Although experienced VB developers with little or no knowledge of databases should be able to learn all of the basics needed, there are two types of VB developers for whom this book is ideal:

❑   Experienced developers who are making the transition from Access to SQL Server 2000

❑   Experienced developers who are making the transition from some other type of enterprise relational database, such as Oracle or Sybase

This book assumes you are an experienced Visual Basic developer and as such will not teach you how to code Visual Basic, but instead will teach you how to create SQL Server stored procedures and call them from your Visual Basic programs and web pages.

A basic understanding of relational database concepts will be helpful but is not assumed, as this topic is covered in the first few chapters of this book. It is also not assumed that you have any experience working with ADO, but again it will be an advantage if you have.

What You Need To Use This Book

You will need a copy of SQL Server 2000 to install the Personal Edition on your workstation. Your workstation can be Windows 98, Windows NT 4.0, or Windows 2000 (Professional or Server). If you cannot get a copy of SQL Server 2000 to install on your workstation, you can use an edition of SQL Server 2000 (Standard or Enterprise) installed on your network. If you will be using a network-installed edition of SQL Server 2000, consult with your database administrator about creating the sample database for you, and have them grant you database administrator rights to that database.

Since this book is about learning how to use SQL Server 2000, we will step you through installing the Personal Edition on your workstation.

You will need Visual Basic 6.0 installed in order to develop and try the examples in this book. You will also need the Windows NT 4.0 Option Pack if your workstation is running Windows 98 or Windows NT 4.0, in order to try out the web-based examples.

All code and samples in this book were developed and tested on workstations running Windows 2000 Professional and Server editions.

Conventions

To help you understand what's going on, and in order to maintain consistency, we've used a number of conventions throughout the book:

When we introduce new terms, we **highlight** them.

> **These boxes hold important information.**

Advice, hints, and background information comes in an indented, italicized font like this.

Try It Out

After learning something new, we'll have a Try It Out section, which will demonstrate the concepts learned, and get you working with the technology.

How It Works

After a Try It Out section, there will sometimes be a further explanation, to help you relate what you've done to what you've just learned.

Words that appear on the screen in menus like the File or Window menu are in a similar font to what you see on screen. URLs like http://www.apress.com are also displayed in this font.

Keys that you press on the keyboard, like *Ctrl* and *Enter*, are in italics.

We use two font styles for code. If it's a word that we're talking about in the text, for example, when discussing `functionNames()`, `<Elements>`, and `objects`, it will be in a fixed pitch font. If it's a block of code that you can type in and run, or part of such a block, then it's also in a gray box:

```
<html>
  <head>
    <title>Simple Example</title>
  </head>
  <body>
    <p>Very simple HTML.</p>
  </body>
</html>
```

Sometimes you'll see code in a mixture of styles, like this:

```
<html>
  <head>
    <title>Simple Example</title>
  </head>
  <body>
    <p>Very simple HTML.</p>
  </body>
</html>
```

In this case, we want you to consider the code with the gray background, for example to modify it. The code with a white background is code we've already looked at, and that we don't wish to examine further.

Downloading The Source Code

As we move through the chapters there will be copious amounts of code available for you, so that you can see exactly how it works. We'll also be stopping frequently and trying it out, so that you can not only see how things work, but make them work yourself.

The source code for all of the examples is available for download – more on that in a while. You might decide that you prefer to type all the code in by hand. Many readers prefer this because it's a good way to get familiar with the coding techniques that are being used.

Whether you want to type the code in or not, we have made all the source code for this book available at our web site, in the Downloads section at the following address:

http://www.apress.com

If you're one of those readers who likes to type in the code, you can use our files to check the results you should be getting – they should be your first stop if you think you might have typed in an error. If you're one of those readers who doesn't like typing, then downloading the source code from our web site is a must!

Either way, it'll help you with updates and debugging.

Tell Us What You Think

We've worked hard to make this book as relevant and useful as possible, so we'd like to get a feel for what it is you want and need to know, and what you think about how we've presented things.

If you have anything to say, let us know at:

http://www.apress.com

Errata & Updates

We've made every effort to make sure there are no errors in the text or the code. However, to err is human, and as such we recognize the need to keep you informed of any mistakes as they're spotted and amended.

More details on finding out about errata and providing us with feedback can be found in Appendix G.

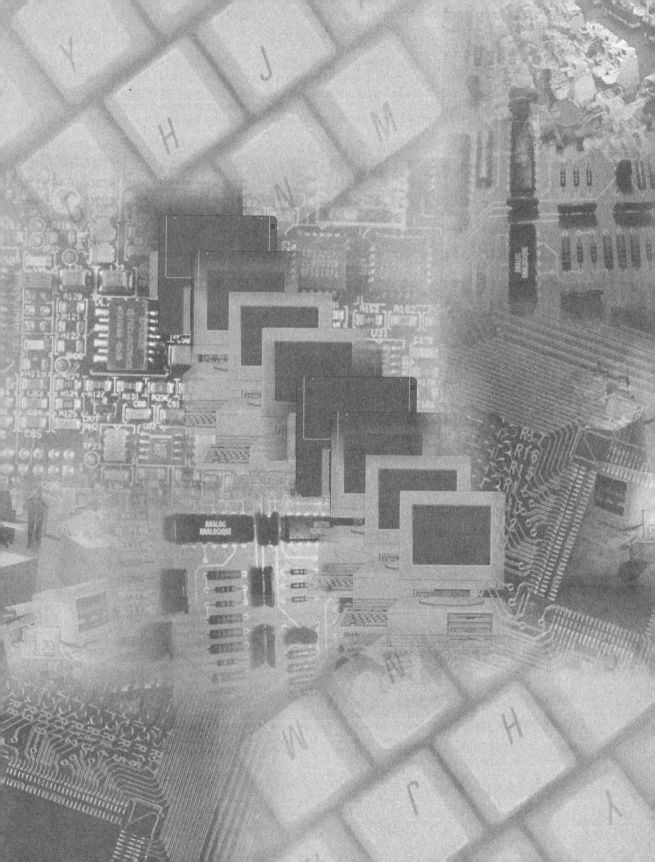

Introduction to SQL Server 2000

SQL Server 2000 is the latest release of SQL Server and it brings about a lot of changes to the user interface, as well as performance enhancements in the underlying database engine. If you are new to SQL Server this product will amaze you with its richness of features and ease of use. If you are upgrading from a previous version of SQL Server you will find that SQL Server 2000 has many new features to offer developers.

This chapter focuses on the core concepts and features of SQL Server 2000 from a developer's standpoint. We will discuss the basic concepts of databases in SQL Server 2000 and some of the additional features that SQL Server 2000 has to offer.

In this chapter we will introduce:

- ❏ SQL Server 2000
- ❏ SQL Server databases and database objects
- ❏ OLE DB, ODBC, and ADO
- ❏ XML
- ❏ English Query
- ❏ Analysis Services, Meta Data Services, and DTS

SQL Server 2000

Most people think of SQL Server as solely a relational database. However, SQL Server 2000 is actually a family of separate, but inter-related product components – these include the Relational Database Engine, Replication, Data Transformation Services (DTS), Analysis Services, Meta Data Services, and English Query. We will discuss these in a little more detail later in this chapter.

The **Relational Database Engine** is at the heart of SQL Server and provides the majority of the services that we will be dealing with in this book. The database engine is highly scaleable – it can perform optimally on a single computer running the Windows 2000 Professional operating system, or can be scaled up to function on a cluster of servers running Windows 2000 Datacenter Server. We will cover all of the operating systems that SQL Server 2000 can run on in the next chapter.

The database engine can also dynamically tune itself. That is, it can acquire and release system resources as the need arises. For example, if the system is running with 50 concurrent users and 50 more users log onto the system, SQL Server will automatically acquire the resources necessary. Likewise, if your transaction log fills up and you have it set to automatically grow, SQL Server will allocate it more space so the database will keep running. We will discuss transaction logs in more detail later in this chapter.

Not only does SQL Server provide the database engine, but it also provides many robust user interfaces. Among these are the **Enterprise Manager**, which allows us to perform administrative tasks on SQL Server databases, and the **Query Analyzer**, a most useful tool for developers. The latter assists the developer in writing and debugging queries and stored procedures. We will cover both of these user interfaces in more depth in later chapters, as well as learning what queries and stored procedures are.

As we progress through this and the next several chapters you will come to realize what a powerful database application SQL Server 2000 is, with easy-to-use interfaces and many powerful features.

SQL Server Instances

SQL Server 2000 introduces a new feature called **named instances**. An instance is just an installation of SQL Server 2000, whether it is the first installation on a machine or a subsequent installation on the same machine. The first installation of SQL Server 2000 on a machine, with no previous versions installed, is considered the **default instance**. This operates and is addressed like previous versions of SQL Server. For example, the default instance of SQL Server 2000 installed on a computer named SProd1 would be addressed as SProd1.

The named instance feature allows you to install SQL Server 2000 on a computer already running a previous version of SQL Server or a default instance of SQL Server 2000. Each additional instance of SQL Server 2000 installed on the same machine must be given a unique **instance name**. These names are limited to 16 characters and are not case sensitive. So if we install a second instance of SQL Server 2000 on SProd1 and give it an instance name Client1 then we would address that instance of SQL Server as SProd1\Client1.

Each instance of SQL Server is isolated from the rest. This means that if, for example, your organization were a service provider, you could install multiple instances of SQL Server 2000 on the same machine and install additional service packs without affecting the settings of the other copies. The only shared components between instances are the tools, search services, and the English Query application. Put simply, everything that is installed in the Microsoft SQL Server program group (for example the Enterprise Manager, Query Analyzer, and Books Online) is shared between instances and everything else is isolated. Clients can connect to any instance of SQL Server on a single machine, providing they have the correct access permissions.

We will explore named instances in more depth in the next chapter when we actually walk through the procedure for installing SQL Server 2000.

SQL Server Databases

SQL Server 2000 consists of many **databases**. Indeed, it even uses databases to store information about itself! Each database consists of multiple objects, with the database itself also considered an object.

The objects contained in each database are as follows:

- Tables
- Keys
- Indexes
- Constraints
- Stored procedures
- Views
- Triggers
- Defaults
- User-defined functions
- User-defined data types
- Users
- Roles
- Rules

We will cover these objects in this and subsequent chapters.

As we mentioned earlier, SQL Server provides a tool known as the Enterprise Manager – this allows us to manage all of the databases created in SQL Server from one window. The Enterprise Manager is the main user interface to SQL Server and allows us to view and manipulate the various objects in our databases. Using the Enterprise Manager, we can connect to other SQL Servers installed on the network and administer them all from the same window, as long as we have the appropriate permissions. We will be covering the Enterprise Manager in the next chapter after we have installed SQL Server.

The user who creates a database is considered the **owner** of that database. Only that user and the database administrator will initially have access to the database. (The database administrator is usually defined as the person or persons who have access to the system administrator login, sa.) This is part of the security features of SQL Server; all objects are secure until the appropriate permissions are granted. Chapter 4 will discuss SQL Server security in greater detail and demonstrate how to grant permissions on various database objects to other users. The database owner or the database administrator must explicitly grant **permissions** on the database to other users before they can access or work with the database. Once this is done the other users can then create objects in the database, such as tables, stored procedures, and views, depending on the permissions they have been granted.

Database Files

A SQL Server database is organized into logical objects that are visible to the user, such as tables, indexes, and stored procedures. Behind the scenes a SQL Server database is actually implemented as two or more physical files on the file system. The first file is the **data file** and contains all of the information that makes up a SQL Server database. The second file is called a **transaction log file** and contains the transaction logs, which are records of changes made to the database. Transaction logs will be covered in more detail in the next section.

A **primary data file** is the first data file created when you create your database. Primary data files for a database are created with the .mdf file extension by default. You can change this, but it is not recommended for the sake of consistency. As your database grows and you run out of room on the hard drive in which the primary data file was placed you can create one or more **secondary data files**. These are usually created with the `.ndf` file extension by default. Again, you can use whatever file extension you want but to be consistent with others you should use the default. It also helps to maintain consistency within your SQL Server installation and aids the quick identification of database files. Creating secondary files on different drives of your computer will spread the workload of your database across other drives and thus improve the performance of your database.

Log files are used to hold all of the information needed to recover your database, either from a system failure or from accidental or purposeful destruction of data. These log files are kept separate from the data files so that, although they may reside on the same physical volume, they are *never* created in the same physical file. Log files are created with the default extension of `.ldf` and, again, you should not change this. Wherever possible your log files should be created on separate physical drives to protect against drive failure.

You can create SQL Server data and log files on either FAT or NTFS file systems. You cannot, however, create a data or log file on a compressed volume in these file systems. **FAT** stands for **File Allocation Table** and is a file system that has been around since DOS. Windows 95/98 and, optionally, Windows NT/2000 use the FAT file system. **NTFS** is an acronym for **NT File System** and is used exclusively by Windows NT/2000. This file system provides security and recovery features not available in the FAT file system.

The following diagram shows the implementation of the logical database that you see into the physical database that SQL Server uses. The logical database is the database that you see in the Enterprise Manager and the physical database is the group of files that make up the database on your hard drive. **Database A** contains a primary data file that has been populated to capacity, meaning there is no more space available in this file. Therefore a second data file was created for this database with a file extension of `.ndf`, indicating that it is a secondary database file. Each database in the diagram has its own transaction log file, which is used to record the transactions that occur in the database. **Database B** in the diagram only contains a primary data file and a transaction log file:

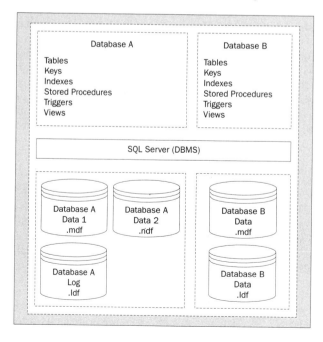

SQL Server as the **database management system** (**DBMS**) actually resides in the middle, as shown in the diagram, managing the physical implementation of the database in the file system and also the logical database that users interact with. It uses various programs to manage the physical database files, such as the relational database engine and the storage engine. It also uses various programs to manage the logical database, such as the Enterprise Manager and the Query Analyzer.

As a developer you shouldn't be too concerned with the physical implementation of the database files but it helps to understand the big picture. An understanding of what goes on behind the scenes is useful when you need to design databases and communicate with the database administrator. However, what you are really concerned with is the logical implementation of the database, such as tables, keys, and indexes. These are the things that you can control to optimize the way your database performs. For clarity, the objects listed at the top of the diagram represent only a partial list of the objects that make up a database.

Chapter 3 will help you to better understand how databases are implemented in SQL Server, as we step through creating our own development database.

Transaction Logs

As we mentioned above, each database that you create has its own transaction log. The transaction log contains details of transactions that have been applied against your database. A **transaction** is the execution of a group of **SQL** statements as one logical unit of work.

SQL is an acronym for **Structured Query Language**. Any application that accesses SQL Server does so through the use of SQL statements, which perform such actions as selecting data, and creating and modifying the structure of your database.

SQL Server automatically manages transactions within the transaction log and will record a "before and after" picture of the data in a table that has changed. This means that if you execute an update query to revise a row of data, SQL Server will log a record of the data before and after it was changed. This allows for both backward and forward recovery of the data in your database, should the need arise.

- ❑ **A forward recovery** means that if you have a hardware failure, you can restore your database from the last backup, and then apply the transaction logs to recover the transactions from the point of the last backup.

- ❑ A **backward recovery** means that if your stored procedure or business component implements transactions, and somewhere in the processing your code decides that it needs to back out of those transactions, the transaction log will be used to recover the data to the state the data was in before the changes began.

SQL Server manages transaction logging automatically. You can, however, use transactions in your queries and stored procedures to perform automatic recovery of the data that you changed. Transactions will be covered in depth in Chapter 11 where we will show you how they work and also how to implement them in your stored procedures.

Incremental backups of your transaction logs should be performed on a regular basis, and the database administrator normally handles these. Incremental backups can be used to recover transactions that were processed since the last time your database was backed up. This is useful when you need to restore and recover your database after a hardware failure. Performing incremental backups also serves to clear the transaction log file, making room for new transactions.

You can **truncate** the transaction log to remove old records that are no longer needed. SQL Server will automatically truncate the transaction log when a backup of the log is performed. It also automatically truncates the file when a checkpoint is processed and the Truncate Log On Checkpoint option is turned on for the database. With this option turned on you could potentially lose transaction records if the log is truncated without first backing it up.

A **checkpoint** is used to minimize the amount of data in the transaction log that must be processed to recover the database. When a checkpoint of the log is taken, it writes unsaved changes to disk, making them a permanent part of the database. SQL Server will store as many transactions in memory as it can before writing them to disk – this is just one way that SQL Server optimizes performance. When this process is completed, the pages of the transaction log are free to be used by new transactions. SQL Server automatically performs checkpoints on the log and uses the blocks that have been freed up. A checkpoint is automatically performed, based on the *number of records* in the log and not based on the *time* since the last checkpoint.

Tables

Databases contain many different types of objects but the **table** is perhaps the most fundamental of these. A table is an object in your database that contains information. You could create a table that contained data about employees and this table would represent information about each employee in your organization. Each table that you define is made up of **columns** and **rows**. Each column represents an attribute about the information that is stored in your table, such as an employee's title and first or last name. Collectively, the columns form a row in your table that represents a single occurrence of the information that the table represent, which in this case is a single employee.

The following partial table is taken from the Employees table in the sample Northwind database that is installed with SQL Server. Notice how each column represents an attribute of the employee being defined and each row represents a single employee:

	Column 1	Column 2	Column 3	Column 4
	EmployeeID	LastName	FirstName	Title
Row 1	1	Davolio	Nancy	Sales Representative
Row 2	2	Fuller	Andrew	Vice President, Sales
Row 3	3	Leverling	Janet	Sales Representative

Each database in SQL Server contains a collection of tables. These include multiple **system tables**. SQL Server creates these system tables when we initially create a database and they are used to manage information about the database. As users we create one or more **user tables** that contain the information that we want to store in the database, such as products and suppliers. These tables contain data that is related in some way, such as a supplier who supplies parts to manufacture a product. This is part of what makes up a relational database – the relationship of objects. We'll be discussing the concept of relational database design in more detail in Chapter 3.

A table can contain up to 1,024 columns but it is highly unlikely that we would have that many columns. We usually **normalize** our database and end up with more tables and fewer columns. Normalization is the process of eliminating duplicate data and providing a fast efficient search path to the data, which will also be covered in detail in Chapter 3.

Each column in a table must have a unique name within that table, but you can use the same column name in multiple tables. Along the same lines, each table in a database must have a unique name but, again, you can have the same table name in different databases.

As we mentioned earlier, each table you create is secure and no other user can access it until you grant them **permission**. There are different levels of permissions that can be granted on a table to each user or **role**. A role is assigned a unique name, and defines a group of users who have the same permissions. You can, for example, allow one group of users to select data, while allowing another user to both select and insert data, by placing them in different roles. Object level permissions and roles will be discussed in detail in Chapter 4 when we look at SQL Server security.

Each table in a database can contain one or more objects, such as constraints, triggers, or defaults. These objects help to preserve and enforce **data integrity** within your tables. Data integrity ensures that each column in a table contains the correct data values. These topics will be covered later in this chapter.

Each table in a database usually has a special column, called an **identity column**, which uniquely identifies each row of data. Generally, this column contains a sequential number that is automatically incremented by SQL Server, although other values are possible, as will be discussed in more detail in Chapter 3.

Identity columns are typically used in SQL Server to assign a unique number to each row in a table, which will ensure the uniqueness of that row's data. This column is also typically used as the primary key column, although it can alternatively be used in the index. We will be discussing primary keys and indexes next.

Primary Keys, Foreign Keys, and Referential Integrity

A **primary key** identifies the column or columns whose values uniquely identify a row of data in the table. No two rows in a table can contain the same primary key and SQL Server enforces this rule. This is why primary key columns are often defined using an identity column, where each row has a unique value automatically generated for it. Primary keys may also contain other non-numeric values, such as an employee's employee number, which could consist of alphabetic and numeric characters. Also, primary key columns cannot contain **null values**. A null value is one that is missing, in other words the data does not exist.

When a primary key is created on a table, SQL Server automatically creates a unique index for the primary key on the table. This ensures that no two primary keys can be the same. Indexes are covered in more detail in the next section. For now it is enough to know that using an index on the primary key column provides a fast, efficient path to the data when the primary key is used for data access.

If a primary key consists of data from multiple columns, the individual columns can contain duplicate values but, when taken as a whole, the reference must be unique. In other words, if a primary key consists of data from column A and column B, column B can contain duplicate values or column A can contain duplicate values. However, the combination of columns A and B must be unique within each row of the table.

Foreign keys are keys that point to the primary key in another table. A foreign key in one row of a table points to an exact row of data in another table. A foreign key value cannot be inserted into a table if the row of data that it is pointing to in another table does not exist. This is just one of the constraints that are placed on foreign keys which help to ensure **referential integrity**.

Consider the following diagram as an example. We can have more than one employee sharing the same title, so we have moved the `Title` column into a separate table. This reduces the amount of duplicate data, and then the two tables are joined using a foreign key. The following figure shows how the foreign key, `TitleID`, in the `Employees` table, points to the primary key in the other table. This approach provides more efficient storage of the data, as we need only store a foreign key pointing to one row of data in the `Title` table.

This example also demonstrates referential integrity; suppose we had not inserted the second row of data in the `Title` table. The foreign key constraint would not allow us to insert a value of 2 in the `TitleID` column of the `Employee` table for the second employee.

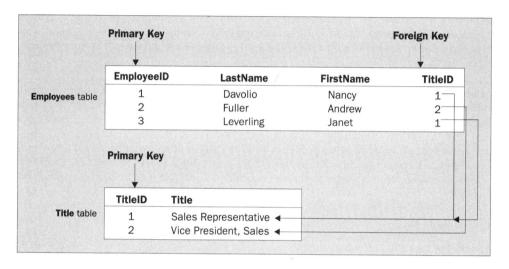

Referential integrity enforces the defined relationship of data between tables, and is automatically applied to foreign keys. Just as we cannot insert a foreign key value for a row of data that does not exist in another table, referential integrity prevents us from deleting a row of data that is referenced by a foreign key. In order to delete a row of data that is referenced by a foreign key, we must first delete the row of data containing the foreign key or update the column using a null value. Then we are able to delete the row containing the primary key.

Referential integrity is based on the relationship between foreign and primary keys and it ensures that key values are consistent across all tables. Referential integrity is automatically enforced by SQL Server, and prevents a user from updating a primary or foreign key that would break the integrity of the data. Also, as we mentioned earlier, SQL Server prevents you from inserting a foreign key that does not reference a valid primary key, and additionally prevents you from deleting a primary key that is being referenced by a foreign key.

Cascading Referential Integrity Constraints

Cascading referential integrity constraints is a feature of SQL Server 2000 that allows you to decide what action, if any, SQL Server should take when a user updates or deletes data that is referenced by a foreign key in another table. There are two cascading constraints available: ON UPDATE and ON DELETE.

The ON UPDATE cascading constraint specifies what action should be taken on the foreign keys that reference the primary key in the table when the primary key is *updated*. NO ACTION, which is the default when this constraint is not specified, will cause SQL Server to take no action. In this case an error is raised when a user tries to update the primary key column that is referenced as foreign keys in other tables. CASCADE specifies that an update to the primary key should be cascaded to all foreign keys that reference this primary key.

Let's look at an example of ON UPDATE CASCADE and use the tables shown in the previous figure. Suppose we updated the value for the column TitleID from 1 to 100 in the Title table. This change would then be cascaded to the Employees table and all employees who had a TitleID of 1 would now have a TitleID of 100, as shown in the following figure:

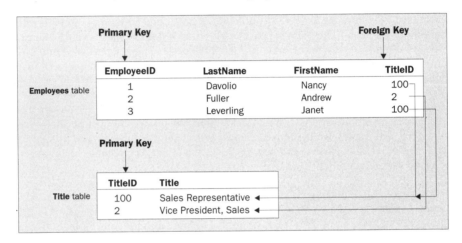

Cascading updates are useful in situations where the primary key requires changing.

The ON DELETE cascading constraint specifies what action should be taken on the foreign keys that reference the primary key in the table when the primary key is *deleted*. Again, NO ACTION is the default, and will cause SQL Server to take no action. Just as with ON UPDATE, an error is raised when a user tries to delete the primary key column that is referenced as foreign keys in other tables. CASCADE specifies that the deletion of the primary key should be cascaded to all foreign keys that reference this primary key. In other words, all rows that have foreign key references to the primary key are deleted.

Using our previous example, if we deleted from the Title table the row of data in the TitleID column that now contains a value of 100, all rows in the Employee table that have a foreign key reference to this deleted primary key would also be deleted.

This is useful in situations where related items should be deleted, such as for tables of suppliers and their products. If you deleted the supplier, you would also want to delete the products they supplied.

Indexes

An **index** is an object that is associated with tables and is built using one or more columns from a table. Just like an index in a book, it provides a means for looking up specific data. Indexes store information from columns (usually primary and foreign key columns) along with the exact location of the associated data within the table. Using an index to access information in a table is very efficient as SQL Server makes use of the index to find the exact location of the row of data that you want retrieve or update.

There are two different types of indexes in SQL Server – clustered and non-clustered.

Clustered indexes sort the data in the table rows by key. You can think of a clustered index as being like a phone book. The columns that define the index (for example, the phone owner's last name then their initial) are used to sort the table rows. This provides a very efficient means to access data in the table. However, since a clustered index *sorts* the data in the table, there can be only one clustered index for each table.

A clustered index actually stores the data rows of the table in the bottom leaf of the index. This means that the index consists of the index entries pointing to each row of data, and the data rows are stored at the end of the index.

Non-clustered indexes store the keys of the table in the index and contain **pointers** to where the data actually resides in the table. The pointer in a non-clustered index is called a **row locator** because it actually locates the row of data in the table. If the table does not have a clustered indexed defined, the row locator in a non-clustered index contains a pointer to the row of data in the table. If a clustered index is defined on a table, the row pointer contains the clustered index key. You can define as many non-clustered indexes on a single table as you see fit.

Indexes can either be unique or not. Indexes that are unique do not allow duplicate keys (keys that contain the same data value), while indexes that are not defined as unique may contain duplicate keys. Index keys should not be confused with primary keys in a table. Any column in a table can be used as the key column for an index.

Regardless of type, simply placing an index on your tables for the columns that are used to access data will generally confer a speed advantage. This is true whether the access is by means of SELECT, UPDATE, or DELETE statements. However, when you define an index on a table, SQL Server must maintain the entries within that index and this requires extra overhead. This is usually offset by the increased efficiency the index provides, especially for larger tables with thousands of rows or more. Each INSERT, UPDATE, and DELETE statement performed against a table must also be used to update the index. SQL Server automatically takes care of keeping the index in sync with the table.

When designing indexes for your tables, you should consider what types of SQL statements are going to be used to select, insert, update, and delete data in your tables. You will usually want to define indexes on columns that are specified in the WHERE, ORDER BY, and GROUP BY clauses. These will be covered in detail later, for now an example of a SELECT statement that uses a WHERE clause is:

```
SELECT FirstName, LastName
    FROM Employees
    WHERE EmployeeID = 4
```

In this case we only select the first and last name from the Employee table where the EmployeeID has a value of 4. If the EmployeeID column were defined as the index key, the SELECT operation would be more efficient.

We will be working with indexes in Chapter 3 when we design and build our database. Actually creating the indexes will help you to gain a better understanding of how to use and create them.

Defaults

Defaults are values that are automatically placed into a column when a new row of data is inserted and no value has been specified for that column. In order to have a default value inserted, you must first define the default and specify the columns to which it should apply. Default definitions are commonly used to specify a zero for numeric columns, instead of having a null value inserted into them, as this prevents problems when carrying out sorting operations, comparisons, or calculations.

Each column in a table can be assigned only one default. Identity columns cannot have defaults applied to them nor can columns that contain the Rowversion data type, as the Rowversion data type is a database-wide unique number.

A default value can be any constant or an expression that evaluates to a constant. For example, expressions could be mathematical formulae or SQL Server functions, such as GETDATE() that returns the current date and time.

When a column in a table does not allow null values and no default has been defined for that column, you must specify a value for it when inserting data into the table or you will receive an error.

You can specify a default value for a column when a table is created, or you can alter the table and add a default at a later date. However, if you apply a default to an existing table it is only applied to *new* rows that are added – the *existing* rows are unaffected. You can also create a default as an object in the database and share it between many tables. When created this way you can bind a default to multiple columns in multiple tables.

Stored Procedures

A **stored procedure** is a group of T-SQL statements stored under a unique name and executed as a unit. A stored procedure can have multiple T-SQL statements to perform such tasks as selecting data from one table and updating data in another table.

As we mentioned earlier, SQL is an acronym for Structured Query Language. **T-SQL** is an acronym for **Transact Structured Query Language**. SQL complies with the **American National Standards Institute** (**ANSI**) SQL standards, while T-SQL is Microsoft's version of SQL that is based on ANSI SQL. The latest version of ANSI SQL is referred to as SQL-99. Remember, any application that accesses SQL Server does so through the use of SQL statements, which perform such actions as selecting data, and creating and modifying the structure of your database.

Stored procedures should not be confused with **queries**, as queries are not stored in the database and cannot be accessed by other applications. Queries are simply ad hoc T-SQL statements that you write and execute in the Query Analyzer. They can be saved, but only as a file on your computer – SQL Server does not know anything about them.

Stored procedures increase application performance. Firstly, there are less SQL statements to be transmitted across the network as you only need to send the name of the stored procedure and any parameters it requires. Secondly, stored procedures are parsed and optimized when they are created and are compiled on the first execution, so they require less processing.

Stored procedures are similar to functions in other languages, as they can contain both input and output parameters and can return values. They use logic to control the flow of processing, and there are numerous functions and T-SQL statements that can be used in stored procedures.

You can use stored procedures to execute routine functions such as selecting, inserting, updating, and deleting data. A single stored procedure can be executed by multiple applications, thus providing code reuse. Stored procedures can also be used to perform database functions, such as backing up your database and transaction log. A simple stored procedure is listed in the following code fragment:

```
CREATE PROCEDURE up_parmsel_employee (@EmployeeID INT) AS

SELECT LastName, FirstName, Title
   FROM Employees
   WHERE EmployeeID = @EmployeeID
```

Each stored procedure contains the CREATE PROCEDURE keywords to instruct SQL Server to create the stored procedure. Then a name is assigned to the stored procedure, and any parameters it expects are declared. The example listed here shows a name of up_parmsel_employee, and an input parameter of @EmployeeID.

This is followed by the T-SQL statements and functions that are to be performed in the stored procedure. In this example, the stored procedure will accept one input parameter, the employee ID, and then select the employee's first name, last name, and title from the Employees table where the value in the EmployeeID column matches the value in the @EmployeeID input parameter.

Stored procedures can be used to shield the complexities of the database from the users. All they need to know is what stored procedure to execute and what parameters (if any) it expects, in order to get the results they need. They do not need to know the relationship of the tables or even what tables exist in the database.

SQL Server caches the stored procedure's execution plan in memory when the stored procedure is executed. The **cache** is an area of memory that SQL Server uses to keep objects. Subsequent executions of the stored procedure are executed using the copy in cache, thus optimizing the performance of your application and SQL Server. SQL Server does a lot to optimize stored procedures, and using them has many performance advantages over in-line SQL statements. In-line SQL statements are coded directly into your program as a string and then sent to SQL Server for execution.

Chapter 7 will introduce stored procedures in more detail, and Chapter 8 explores the performance benefits of using stored procedures over in-line SQL statements. We will learn how to create stored procedures in SQL Server and then call them from our Visual Basic programs.

Triggers

Triggers are a special class of stored procedures and also contain T-SQL statements. However, instead of executing a trigger like you would a stored procedure, a trigger is defined to execute *automatically* when certain actions (insert, update, delete) are performed against a table. For example, you can define a trigger that is to be executed when a DELETE statement occurs on a particular table. Then, when the DELETE statement is processed, the trigger is executed by SQL Server. This trigger can perform such actions as logging the record deleted and the user who performed the deletion.

Triggers are most often used to enforce the business rules and complex constraints that are defined by your business requirements. Triggers can be used to create an audit record of the changes made to a row of data, along with details of the user who made the changes. We will see this in action in Chapter 12 when we create our own triggers.

You can have multiple triggers for one table as long as each trigger has a unique name. Triggers can also cause other triggers to be fired when an action is performed on another table that has a defined trigger, thereby increasing their effectiveness and scope. Because triggers can contain complex processing logic using T-SQL statements and functions, they are often used to help enforce data integrity. This is especially true when one trigger calls another to delete related data. You can nest up to 32 levels of triggers, having each perform an action that causes another to be executed, and so on.

Views

A **view** is like a virtual table containing data taken from one or more other tables. It is stored in the database as the actual T-SQL statements that define the view, just like a stored procedure. When the view is referenced, the virtual table is then created using the T-SQL statements contained in the view.

Views are generally used to let users see data from multiple tables all at the same time, thereby giving the illusion that the data exists as a single table or group of data. The benefits of this are that it provides the user with the illusion that all of their data is in one table, and hides the complexities of the database from them. It also provides a security mechanism as we can grant users access to the view but not to the actual tables from which it is derived, thereby limiting their access to only the data they are authorized to see.

Views can also be defined to be updateable. That is, they can actually update data that resides in multiple tables. There are strict guidelines that must be adhered to in order for a view to update data in the underlying tables. The view cannot use any **aggregate functions** in the SELECT list. Aggregate functions are functions provided by SQL Server that perform calculations on the values in a column from multiple rows, and return a single result. Also views cannot contain the TOP, GROUP BY, UNION, or DISTINCT clauses that allow you to control how data is returned.

Views are flexible in that they allow you to execute other views and stored procedures to achieve the end results. However, this flexibility only goes so far and there are some restrictions that are imposed on views. For example, you cannot use the ORDER BY, COMPUTE, or COMPUTE BY clauses or the INTO keyword. These will be defined in later chapters – they affect how data is returned and manipulated.

It is also not possible to use **temporary tables** within views. These tables are very similar to permanent tables except they are stored in the TempDB database and are automatically deleted by SQL Server when your session ends. Populating a temporary table is usually done using the INTO keyword within a SELECT statement. As this keyword is not permitted in views, the temporary tables that depend on them cannot be used either. We will cover temporary tables in detail later in this book.

OLE DB, ODBC, and ADO

Our VB and web applications do not communicate directly with SQL Server. We must use a data access method such as ADO together with an **Application Programming Interface** (**API**) such as **OLE DB** or **ODBC** that is designed specifically to access and expose the features of the various data stores. For example, we might use an OLE DB for SQL Server driver or, if using Access, we could use an ODBC for Access driver.

The following diagram illustrates how these technologies fit in with SQL Server:

Let's take a look at each of these types of API in turn.

Open Database Connectivity (**ODBC**) is an API that allows lower-level languages, such as Visual C++, to access various databases. ODBC is a high performance API used by tools, utilities, and system level applications. It is an older technology that has been built upon by many database vendors and third party suppliers of ODBC drivers.

ODBC is a complex API that even VC++ developers find hard to master. Given this, Microsoft built several objects that reside on top of ODBC to make it more user-friendly. These include the **Microsoft Foundation Classes** (**MFC**), **Data Access Objects** (**DAO**), and **Remote Data Objects** (**RDO**). These provide an easier-to-use interface when compared with using ODBC directly, and most developers will have used these objects at one time or another.

As time progresses, so does technology, and **OLE DB** (**Object Linking and Embedding DataBase**) entered the scene. OLE DB is a low-level **COM** (**Component Object Model**) API that is used to access information from just about any type of data store, not just databases. SQL Server ships with Microsoft's version of the OLE DB API. This API provides high performance access to SQL Server and supports the SQL-92 syntax, which makes it compliant with the OLE DB 2.0 specification. Tools, utilities, and system-level development also use this API when high performance is needed.

While OLE DB provides an API that is easier to use than ODBC, it isn't ideal for every developer because of its complex API interface. So **ADO** (**ActiveX Data Objects**) has been created as a COM object to provide an interface with OLE DB. ADO provides an easy to use, lightweight COM object suitable for general business applications. ADO is considered lightweight because of the size of its DLL (Dynamic Link Library) when compared to those of DAO and RDO.

ADO has evolved from DAO and RDO, providing an interface that is easier to learn and use. It also provides a feature set that most applications need to access data, whether that data resides in a flat file, a database, or on the Internet. Because ADO is a COM object it can be used by any programming language and technology that supports COM, for example Visual Basic, Visual C++, and ASP scripting languages.

Chapter 6 provides a general overview of the ADO object model, and a more detailed introduction to ADO and how it can be used to enable database access from our VB and web applications.

XML

SQL Server 2000 provides native support for **Extensible Markup Language** (**XML**), a markup language that is used to describe structured data. Not only can an XML document provide data but, through the use of descriptive tags, it can also indicate the structure of that data. SQL Server 2000 provides native support for this, meaning that you can select data from a table in SQL Server and have the results returned as XML data. SQL Server 2000 also provides a useful utility to set up a **virtual directory** in **Internet Information Server** (**IIS**) that allows the user to access a SQL Server database through the **Universal Resource Locator** (**URL**) of a web page. A virtual directory provides the necessary association between IIS and SQL Server.

What does all this mean? It means that you can query data in your database through the URL of a web page. Take a look at the following URL:

```
http://LOCALHOST/NORTHWIND?SQL=SELECT+*+FROM+EMPLOYEES+WHERE+EMPLOYEEID+=+1+FOR+XM
L+AUTO,ELEMENTS
```

This URL specifies a virtual root of NORTHWIND, which has been set up to point to the Northwind database in SQL Server. The SQL SELECT statement selects a specific employee (with EmployeeID = 1) from the Employees table and returns the results. Notice all the plus signs in the URL. This is a special character used to represent a space, as spaces are not allowed in a URL. This SELECT query produces the following results:

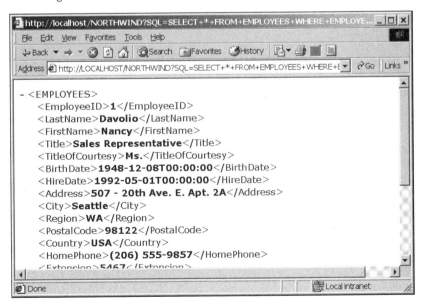

As part of the native support for XML, SQL Server 2000 also provides a new keyword for the SELECT statement called FOR XML. This new keyword returns data from the SELECT statement as XML documents instead of the standard rows that we are used to.

This new keyword allows us to write queries and stored procedures that return data as XML. We can then use these queries to return XML to our web pages and VB programs. In the previous example we used an XML mode of AUTO. The mode determines the shape of the XML tree returned by SQL Server. We also used the ELEMENTS argument, which specifies that columns in the table be returned as sub-elements in XML. You can also define your own XML **stylesheets**, for example to display the data returned from a SELECT statement in tables on your web page. These topics will be covered in more depth in Chapter 15, where we'll take a closer look at the syntax and use of each of these features.

English Query

English Query is a separate product that ships with SQL Server 2000. It provides an environment for creating applications that allow users to ask questions in natural English, instead of writing a SQL query to retrieve the data they want to see. This makes the database accessible to even the most non-technical end users, by concealing its underlying structure and negating the need to be conversant with SQL grammar.

For example, suppose a user wanted to know the title of Andrew Fuller in the Employees table of the Northwind database. Instead of creating a SQL query to retrieve the information, they could simply ask the question "*What is Andrew Fuller's Title?*". The English Query application would then build and execute the appropriate SELECT query behind the scenes to retrieve the information and display it to the user.

English Query works best with normalized databases, so you should ensure that your database design has been normalized. You must also ensure your database contains data so you can build, test, and train your English Query application. It can then be published using Visual Basic or the Web, meaning that you can deploy your English Query application though VB if your target audience is small, or use an intranet or the Internet if your audience is great, or spread over multiple locations.

The case study (parts 1 and 2) provides an in-depth look at creating and deploying an English Query application over the Web.

Analysis Services

Analysis Services, formerly known as **OLAP**, is a service that builds multidimensional cubes of data retrieved from **data warehouses** (large databases that contain historical data about your business). These multidimensional cubes contain both dimension and summary data held in cells, each addressed by a set of coordinates that specify a position within the structure's dimensions. For example, imagine you wanted to track sales of a number of components over a period of time – you could build a cube to represent this data. In this case the dimensions would be component, sales, and time. The data would be pulled from the data warehouses to build the results.

The data is used for analysis, and can be viewed from Microsoft Excel using the **PivotTable** service. If you don't want to use Excel, you can also use **ADO Multidimensional extensions** to access the data. Cubes of data can also be write-enabled so users can perform different scenarios on the data.

Because of the complexities of Analysis Services, SQL Server provides a number of wizards to help you work with and build these data structures. There are wizards available to help you build the cubes of data and also to create shared dimensions for use by other cubes.

Analysis Services was built as a technology to allow client applications efficient access to data stored in data warehouses. It provides a multidimensional model making it easy for the user to navigate and select information. You can use it to create views of data using ad hoc calculation functions, and to view complex business data relationships.

You can process data from various data warehouse databases, such as SQL Server and Oracle (using OLE DB). In fact, any database that supports OLE DB can be used as a data source for Analysis Services.

Part of Analysis Services functionality is a feature called **Data Mining**. It allows you to perform data analysis and prediction within Analysis Services. Data Mining can be used to perform analysis of both relational and multidimensional data. It provides the means to build **Data Mining Models**, which contain predictive analysis of relational or multidimensional data.

Meta Data Services

Meta Data Services is a replacement for the Microsoft Repository found in earlier releases of SQL Server. This new service actually builds on and expands the former version and provides an object oriented repository technology that can be used by applications and systems that process meta data.

So what exactly is **meta data**? Meta data is information about data. That is, it provides property information such as the type and length of the data in a column. It can also specify the structure of the data or the design of objects, such as the cubes used in Analysis Services.

The Meta Data Services provides a way for you to store and manage meta data. SQL Server provides a browser that allows you to view the data in the repository. This can be run from within the Enterprise Manager or as a snap-in to the MMC console.

DTS

DTS (Data Transformation Services) is a component of SQL Server that provides graphical tools and programmable objects enabling you to consolidate data from multiple sources into a single source. Not only are you able to consolidate data, you are also able to extract and transform the data from multiple sources prior to consolidation.

DTS is based on the OLE DB architecture and allows you to copy and transform data from Oracle to SQL Server using native OLE DB providers. For data sources that do not support OLE DB, SQL Server's OLE DB provider can use ODBC to copy and transform data. SQL Server itself uses DTS to copy and transfer data and objects from one SQL Server installation to another.

Summary

This chapter has introduced SQL Server 2000 at a high level. We have covered the basics of SQL Server 2000 and have found that it is actually a family of products that combine to make up a very powerful and rich relational database, loaded with features.

We have also explored databases in SQL Server and now know that they are made up of several different objects, such as tables, keys, and indexes. Having explored the various database objects, we can now see how they all work together to help provide secure and reliable data. Through the use of primary and foreign key constraints, SQL Server can enforce the rules of referential integrity, which helps to ensure that our data is reliable and consistent.

We took a quick look at how our applications communicate with SQL Server, and learned that ADO provides an easy-to-use object model that simplifies this communication process.

Having briefly covered some of the other features of SQL Server 2000, such as XML support, English Query, Meta Data, and Analysis Services, we can see that SQL Server 2000 has a lot to offer through additional complementary features and services.

We saw how the XML features of SQL Server 2000 allow us to access data residing in our databases over the Web, or through VB programs. We also discovered that SQL Server provides native support to return the data in XML format straight from the database.

To summarize, you should:

❑ Understand SQL Server databases and transaction logs at a high level

❑ Be aware of the various objects that make up a SQL Server database

❑ Understand tables, keys, and indexes

❑ Know that we can use stored procedures and views to extract data for viewing

❑ Be aware of the existence of data access technologies, such as ADO

❑ Know that SQL Server 2000 provides native support for XML

❑ Know that we can use English Query to build a simple user-friendly interface that allows users to query our database by asking questions in natural English

In the next chapter we will install the Personal Edition of SQL Server 2000 and cover some of the tools that are available. This will help set the stage for the chapters that follow, as you become familiar with the user interfaces of SQL Server 2000.

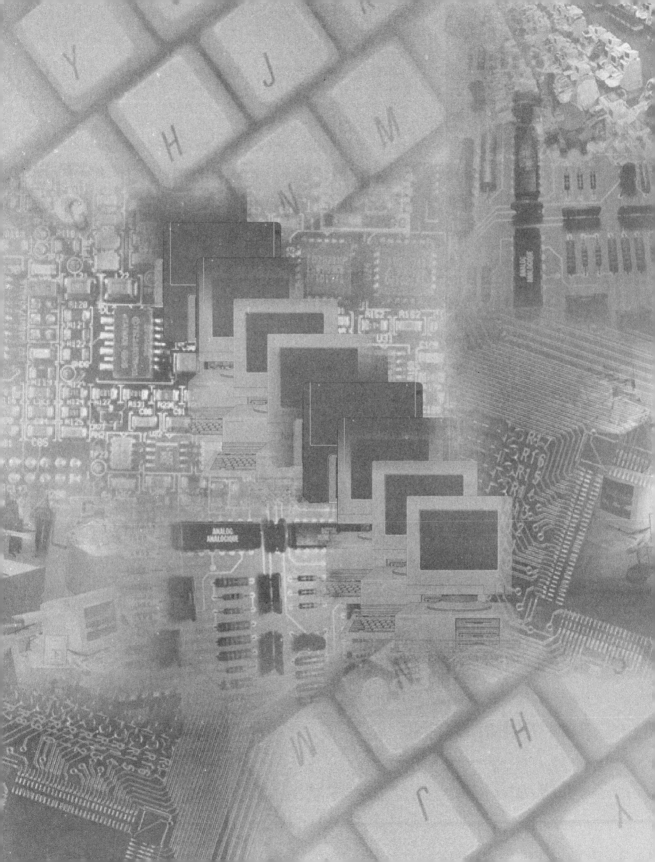

Installing the Personal Edition of SQL Server 2000

Having just had an overview of SQL Server 2000, you are probably ready to install this product and begin working with it. This chapter will help you do just that.

SQL Server 2000 comes in several different editions, each designed to meet a specific need. And while we will briefly cover each of these editions, our main focus will be on the *Personal Edition* of SQL Server 2000. This edition provides most of the features available and allows us to install it on our workstations.

We will cover the supported platforms for each edition and the prerequisites for installing the Personal Edition. We will then go through the installation process, explaining each step.

Once our installation has been completed, we will take a tour of the Enterprise Manager to acquaint you with the features of this tool. This is the main user interface used to administer databases in SQL Server. We will also take a brief look at some of the other tools and wizards that come with SQL Server, which help to simplify various administrative tasks.

In this chapter, we will:

- ❑ Discuss the differences in the SQL Server 2000 editions and suitable platforms
- ❑ Cover SQL Server 2000 prerequisites
- ❑ Step through installing SQL Server 2000 and SQL Server instances
- ❑ Tour the Enterprise Manager
- ❑ Preview the Query Analyzer and SQL Profiler
- ❑ Preview common wizards

SQL Server Editions and Platforms

As we mentioned above, SQL Server 2000 comes in many editions. This section will examine some of the high level features of each edition and identify the platforms that each will run on. While this list will not be exhaustive, it should serve to give you a good idea of the supported features in each edition. In addition, this list will also let you know what editions are available should you need to identify a suitable edition for your business.

Enterprise Edition

We start with the **Enterprise Edition**. This is a full-featured edition of SQL Server 2000, and scales to meet the demands of the largest web sites and data warehousing applications. The Enterprise Edition of SQL Server 2000 is the edition that most companies would run in an environment where SQL Server needs to be clustered and the volume of transactions is high. You would most likely find this edition installed at dotcom-type companies where there is a high volume of online transactions.

This edition contains features such as Full-Text Search, Multiple Instance Support, Log Shipping, and Failover Clustering.

Full-Text Search is a feature of SQL Server that allows you to search for words or phrases in a character column of a table. Multiple Instance Support means that multiple named instances of SQL Server can be installed on the same machine. Log Shipping is a feature that allows you to have transaction logs automatically shipped to a SQL Server installed on another machine and recorded. This provides a hot standby machine in case the primary SQL Server machine fails. Failover Clustering provides a means of having SQL Server failover onto another SQL Server on a cluster of machines should a hardware failure occur on the node that SQL Server is running on.

The Enterprise Edition runs on server operating systems only:

❑   Windows NT 4.0 Server

❑   Windows NT 4.0 Server Enterprise Edition

❑   Windows 2000 Server

❑   Windows 2000 Advanced Server

❑   Windows 2000 Datacenter Server

Similar to the Enterprise Edition is the **Enterprise Evaluation Edition**. This is a full-featured evaluation edition of SQL Server 2000 that will expire after 120 days. The Enterprise Evaluation Edition will run on the same operating systems as the Enterprise Edition. You can download this evaluation edition for free at http://www.microsoft.com/sql/.

Developer Edition

The next edition available is the **Developer Edition**. This edition of SQL Server 2000 has all of the functionality and features of the Enterprise Edition but is licensed only for development and testing. You cannot legally run this edition of SQL Server in a production environment. This edition will run on:

❑   Windows 98

❑   Windows NT 4.0 Workstation

❑   Windows NT 4.0 Server

- ❑ Windows NT 4.0 Server Enterprise Edition

- ❑ Windows 2000 Professional

- ❑ Windows 2000 Server

- ❑ Windows 2000 Advanced Server

- ❑ Windows 2000 Datacenter Server

If running this edition on Windows 98, the **Desktop Engine** is used, which provides less functionality (for example, no Full-Text Search). The Desktop Engine will be covered shortly.

Personal Edition

The **Personal Edition** of SQL Server was primarily designed for mobile computing users. This edition of SQL Server is also ideal for applications that need a standalone installation of SQL Server on the client machine. This edition will run on:

- ❑ Windows 98

- ❑ Windows NT 4.0 Workstation

- ❑ Windows NT 4.0 Server

- ❑ Windows NT 4.0 Server Enterprise Edition

- ❑ Windows 2000 Professional

- ❑ Windows 2000 Server

- ❑ Windows 2000 Advanced Server

- ❑ Windows 2000 Datacenter Server

The Full-Text Search and Multiple Instance features are supported in this edition, however the Full-Text Search features are not available when running Windows 98.

Standard Edition

For small workgroups and departments SQL Server **Standard Edition** fits the bill, and should provide all the functionality needed by these groups of users. This edition runs on server operating systems only:

- ❑ Windows NT 4.0 Server

- ❑ Windows NT 4.0 Server Enterprise Edition

- ❑ Windows 2000 Server

- ❑ Windows 2000 Advanced Server

- ❑ Windows 2000 Datacenter Server

This edition also supports the Full-Text Search and Multiple Instance features.

Desktop Engine

The Desktop Engine is the redistributable database engine for SQL Server 2000 and is freely distributable with your applications. The Desktop Engine is a replacement for the **MSDE** (Microsoft Data Engine), which you may be familiar with if you have used previous versions of SQL Server. This edition will run on:

❑ Windows 98

❑ Windows NT 4.0 Workstation

❑ Windows NT 4.0 Server

❑ Windows NT 4.0 Server Enterprise Edition

❑ Windows 2000 Professional

❑ Windows 2000 Server

❑ Windows 2000 Advanced Server

❑ Windows 2000 Datacenter Server

The only feature supported by this edition of SQL Server is Multiple Instances.

Windows CE Edition

The **Windows CE Edition** runs on handheld devices running Windows CE. This edition supports the essential database functionality of SQL Server 2000 and provides replication features, so the database can stay in sync with SQL Server 2000 Standard and Enterprise editions. This edition requires less than 1 MB for installation and does not include any GUI tools. The only feature supported by this edition of SQL Server 2000 is Multiple Instances.

If you are tasked with finding the right SQL Server edition for your company, use this list as a starting point and then consult **SQL Server Books Online** (the SQL Server online help). SQL Server Books Online provides a comprehensive list, by edition, of all the features supported.

SQL Server Prerequisites

Since we will be installing the Personal Edition of SQL Server 2000, let's expand on the requirements for this edition.

You will need a computer that has at least a 166 MHz processor and 32 MB of RAM. More is always better, as most developers know from experience. Along with the processor and memory requirements, you will need at least 65 MB of free disk space for a minimum installation, and 180 MB of free disk space for a full installation. A full installation is recommended, so that you may explore all of the features of SQL Server 2000.

Different operating systems have different prerequisites so let's go through each one.

It should be noted here that users must have at least a minimum of Internet Explorer 5.0 installed *before* installing SQL Server 2000. SQL Server 2000 uses some of the components that are installed with Internet Explorer 5.0 for the **Microsoft Management Console** (**MMC**) and for the **HTML Help** used by SQL Server Books Online. It should also be noted that Internet Explorer 5.0 does not have to be your default browser.

❑ **Windows 98** requires Windows 98 Service Pack 1 and Internet Explorer 5.0 be installed

❑ **Windows 98 Second Edition** requires no prerequisites as it ships with Internet Explorer 5.0 and it is installed during system setup

❑ **Windows NT 4.0** users must have Windows NT Service Pack 5 installed and Internet Explorer 5.0

❑ There are no prerequisites for **Windows 2000** operating systems

Installation

Once you have determined that your hardware meets the minimum requirements and you have installed all the necessary prerequisites, you are ready to begin the installation.

Ensure you have the CD for the Personal Edition of SQL Server 2000, or that this software is on a shared network drive available for installation.

SQL Server Instances

As we mentioned in the last chapter, SQL Server 2000 provides **named instances**. That is, you can install multiple instances of SQL Server 2000 on the same machine, each running its own database engine. If you have SQL Server 6.5 or SQL Server 7.0, you can leave these versions installed, and additionally install a named instance of SQL Server 2000.

The first installation of SQL Server 2000 on a machine with no other SQL Server version installed is considered to be the **default instance** of SQL Server.

The second and subsequent installations of SQL Server 2000 on a machine already running SQL Server 2000 are installed as a named instance. During the installation process you must provide an **instance name** for the new installation. We will cover providing an instance name during the installation of SQL Server 2000.

There is a 16-character limit for instance names, and the first character of an instance name must be a letter, an ampersand (&), an underscore (_), or a pound sign (#). Subsequent characters can be any of the above and numbers. You cannot embed a space in the instance name. Instance names are not case sensitive. They cannot be named using any SQL Server reserved system names, such as *default*, *Temp*, or *MSSQLServer*.

When installing a default instance of SQL Server 2000 on a computer running SQL Server 6.5 you must use **version switching** to switch between the two versions of SQL Server. SQL Server 2000 will then install the utilities to switch between the different versions of SQL Server.

You cannot install a default instance of SQL Server 2000 on a computer running SQL Server 7.0. It is necessary to upgrade the version 7.0 installation, or install a named instance of SQL Server 2000.

You cannot install a named instance of SQL Server 2000 on a computer running SQL Server 6.5 unless you also have SQL Server 7.0 installed. If SQL Server 7.0, and optionally SQL Server 6.5, are installed, you can switch between SQL Server 2000 and SQL Server 7.0 without using the version switching utility. You cannot, however, switch between SQL Server 2000 and SQL Server 6.5.

When installing a named instance of SQL Server 2000, leaving the version 7.0 installation intact, the tools and utilities will be upgraded to the ones used by SQL Server 2000. This means that tools such as the Enterprise Manager, Query Analyzer, and utilities such as the SQL Server Service Manager, will be upgraded to the SQL Server 2000 version and shared between both versions of SQL Server.

Installation Procedure

1. To begin the installation, insert the SQL Server 2000 CD. If AutoRun is not enabled or if you are installing from the network, double-click on the AutoRun.exe program in the root of the CD or installation folder to start the installation process. The following screen appears:

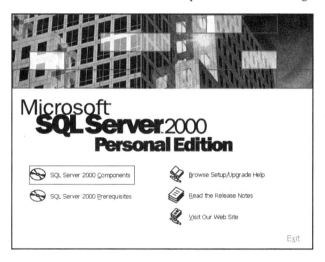

The SQL Server 2000 Prerequisites option will install the Common Controls Library Update for Windows 95. This allows Windows 95 computers to connect to SQL Server 2000 on the network.

2. We will choose the SQL Server 2000 Components option. Once you click on the SQL Server 2000 Components option, you will progress to the next screen of the menu:

This screen shows the components that are available, and we want to choose the Install Database Server option. Notice the additional components that can also be installed.

We briefly touched on the Analysis Services in Chapter 1, and if at a later date you wish to install this option this is where you would come to do it. The English Query option can also be installed from this menu. We will cover this later, in the first part of the case study that deals with English Query.

3. So at this point click on the Install Database Server option to proceed to the next step, which is the Welcome screen. This lets you know what the Installation Wizard will allow you to do:

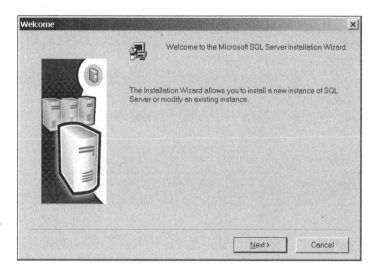

4. Click Next to proceed to the next step, which verifies where you want to install SQL Server. By default, the Local Computer option is checked and your computer name is displayed in the box above the option buttons. Since this is where we want to install SQL Server we will accept the defaults on this screen:

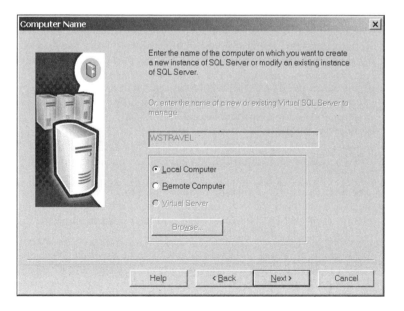

The Installation Wizard will also allow you to install SQL Server on another machine. However, you must be logged onto the local computer with a user account that has administrative authority on the remote machine onto which you wish to install SQL Server. Also, both machines must be running Windows NT or both machines must be running Windows 2000.

If the machine onto which you are installing SQL Server is a clustered computer, the Installation Wizard will automatically detect this and enable the Virtual Server option.

5. Accepting the defaults for this screen, click the Next button to proceed. This next step of the Installation Wizard will automatically detect previously installed versions of SQL Server and display the appropriate options:

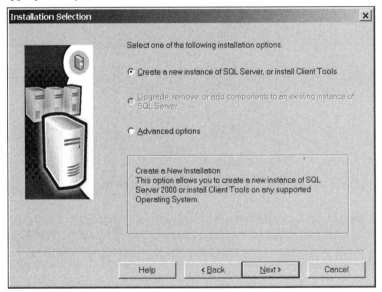

For example, if no other version of SQL Server is installed on the computer, the second option (Upgrade ... SQL Server) should be grayed out. If a previous version of SQL Server is detected, then this option will be available so that you may upgrade a previous version.

If you select the Advanced options button, an additional dialog is presented that allows you to create an initialization file for unattended SQL Server 2000 installations, to rebuild the registry entries for a corrupted installation, or to make changes to a SQL Server installation on a clustered setup.

6. We'll accept the default on this screen, so click the Next button to proceed.

7. The next screen (not shown here) allows you to validate your name and company. These fields are pre-filled with information read from the registry. If they are not correct, you can change them. When you are satisfied that the information is correct, click Next to proceed.

8. The next screen that you will see (also not shown here) is the screen for the license agreement. Read the license agreement and if you agree with the terms click **Yes** to proceed.

9. The next screen of the Installation Wizard allows you to choose what type of installation you want. There are three options on this screen:

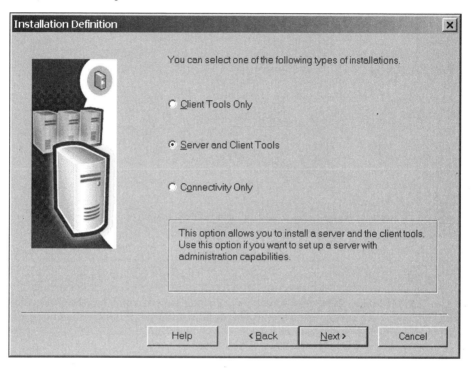

The first option, **Client Tools Only**, allows you to install the tools necessary to manage a SQL Server installation on the network, and tools such as the Enterprise Manager and Query Analyzer will be installed. These are the tools that you need to manage and work with SQL Server, no matter where SQL Server has been installed.

The next option, **Server and Client Tools**, will install the SQL Server and its tools and utilities on your machine.

The last option on this screen, **Connectivity Only**, will only install the Microsoft Data Access Components (MDAC) and the Net Libraries needed to connect to SQL Server. Net Libraries will be discussed in more depth shortly, but briefly they are the protocols used by SQL Server to communicate with clients and other SQL Server installations on your network.

10. For our purposes, we want to choose the **Server and Client Tools** option, which is the default. Click the **Next** button to proceed.

11. As in previous steps, the Installation Wizard automatically detects any installed versions of SQL Server on the machine. If this installation will be the first instance of SQL Server installed, the next screen will have the Default checkbox checked and the Instance name textbox grayed out, as shown:

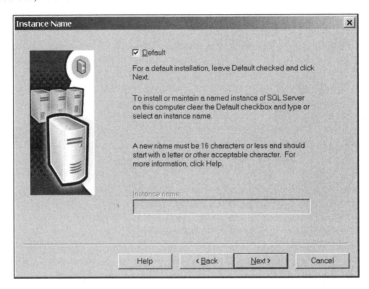

If, however, a previous version of SQL Server exists and you did not choose the upgrade option earlier, then you will see the following screen, which has the Default checkbox grayed out and the Instance name textbox available for input. In this installation I have chosen to give this named instance of SQL Server 2000 a name of SQL2000 because SQL Server 7.0 was already installed on my machine:

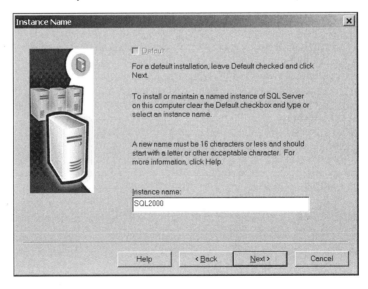

Remember that an instance name can only be up to 16 characters in length and that it must begin with a letter, an ampersand (&), an underscore (_) or a pound sign (#).

12. Once you have chosen the appropriate option for your installation, click the Next button to proceed. The next step of the Installation Wizard allows you to choose the type of setup that should be performed:

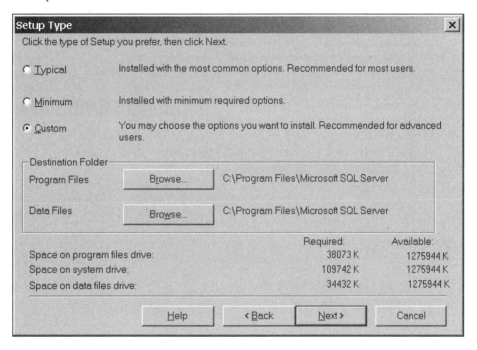

Again, there are three options, the first being a Typical installation. This is the option recommended for most users. This type of installation installs SQL Server 2000 with the default installation options. This option will not install any code samples and will only install the debugger as part of the development tools.

The second option, Minimum, will perform a minimum installation of SQL Server 2000. This is the option recommended for users who have little disk space available but need SQL Server 2000 installed on their machine. This option will not install any upgrade tools, client management tools, Books Online, development tools, or code samples.

The last option, Custom, allows you to pick and choose what options to install. This is the route we will take to enable us to explore the various options available.

This step of the Installation Wizard also allows us to change the folder that the program files will be installed in, as well as the folder that the data files will be installed in. This release of SQL Server has finally followed the standards set by Microsoft by having the default folder specified as the Program Files folder. Change the installation folders if necessary to install SQL Server 2000 on different drives. For example, if your software is installed on a drive other than C then you will need to select a different drive. Also, if you have more room on another drive for data files then you should choose that drive here.

13. To continue, check the Custom option and click on the Next button.

SQL Server 2000 comes with more options than have been available in previous releases. This next screen allows you to select various components, and sub-components for each component:

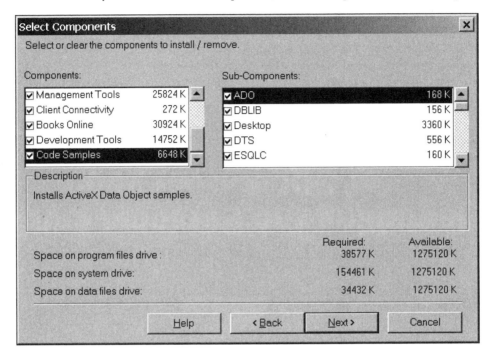

There are six separate components that can be installed and we will take a look at each in turn.

Server Components

Starting at the top of the list is Server Components. This component has several sub-components:

❑ SQL Server – when this sub-component is checked, it installs the database engine and core tools, for example, Bulk Copy Program (BCP).

❑ Upgrade Tools – this option installs the Upgrade Wizard, which is used to upgrade SQL Server 6.5 databases. This sub-component is not available for Windows 98 users.

❑ Replication Support – this option installs the necessary files needed to support database replication. Replication allows you to schedule replicating database tables from one SQL Server to another.

❑ Full-Text Search – installs the Microsoft full-text search engine. This feature allows us to define full-text indexes on character columns in our database. We can then perform full-text searches for keywords or phrases in character column data. This sub-component is not available for Windows 98 users.

❑ Debug Symbols – checking this sub-component will install the debug symbols.

❏ Performance Counters – these are the performance counters used by the Performance Monitor to monitor SQL Server installations. Again, this sub-component is not available for Windows 98 users.

Choose the appropriate sub-components to be installed. If you are new to SQL Server, I suggest that you check all of these sub-components. This way you can explore them at your leisure.

Management Tools

The next component in the list is Management Tools. There are also several sub-components for this component and we will take a look at each one in turn:

❏ Enterprise Manager – we have talked about this tool before and it is mainly used to administer your database and SQL Server.

❏ Profiler – this tool is used to monitor and record activity against SQL Server databases.

❏ Query Analyzer – the main tool used by developers. This tool aids the developer in writing and debugging queries and stored procedures.

❏ DTC Client Support – allows you to extend transactions across servers.

❏ Conflict Viewer – allows you to view and change synchronization conflicts. This is grayed out, indicating that it is a required sub-component.

Client Connectivity

The next component is Client Connectivity. This component has no sub-components and installs the components necessary to provide connectivity between clients and SQL Server. These components include MDAC and the Network Libraries.

Books Online

The Books Online component provides one option: Books Online on Disk. Choosing this sub-component will install the Books Online on your hard drive. No CD will be required to view the SQL Server documentation.

It is recommended that if you have the available space on your hard drive that you check the Books Online on Disk option. This allows fast access to the documentation when needed.

Development Tools

Next in the list of components is Development Tools. There are four sub-components for this component:

❏ Headers and Libraries – will install the include files and library files for Visual C++ developers. These files allow VC++ developers to create applications that use OLE DB and ODBC. VB developers do not typically use this sub-component because these libraries are used behind the scenes in VB.

❏ MDAC SDKs – will install the MDAC (Microsoft Data Access Components) and XML software development kits.

❏ Backup/Restore API – will install header files, sample programs, and documentation needed by developers to create applications that backup and restore SQL Server databases.

❏ Debugger Interface – will install the interface that is used to debug stored procedures.

Code Samples

Code Samples is the last component in the list. This component has many sub-components and they all install an executable file that will install the samples when run. Since the list of sub-components is long, we will forego listing them all. Suffice to say, you should probably install all of these samples and you can then view them at your leisure.

The code samples get installed to the following directory, assuming of course that you accepted the default directory for the installation of the program files, and the drive that SQL Server is installed on is C:

```
C:\Program Files\Microsoft SQL Server\80\Tools\DevTools\Samples
```

The samples provided include such items as ADO samples, Desktop Engine samples, and samples for the XML features of SQL Server 2000.

14. Once you have made the appropriate choices, click the Next button to proceed. This next step of the Installation Wizard allows you to specify the account for the SQL Server and SQL Server Agent services. Note that this step is not available for Windows 98 users.

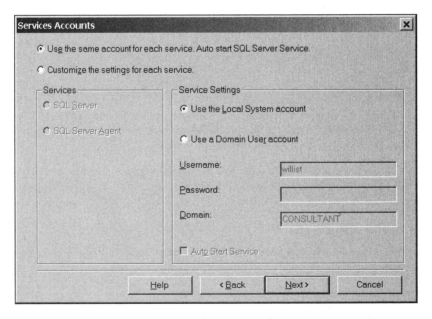

You have the option of specifying a separate account for each service or specifying the same account for both.

You also have the option of using the Local System account or choosing a Domain User account. The choice you make depends on your company's standards.

It is recommended that you choose the Local System account and Use the same account for each service. This will alleviate any problems that may be encountered with a domain user account because the password was reset, or the account was accidentally deleted.

15. Click the Next button to continue. The next step is very important, as it deals with the **authentication modes** that SQL Server will support, and the security of the local system account.

The authentication modes supported by SQL Server allow a Windows Authentication Mode only, or a Mixed Mode (Windows and SQL Server).

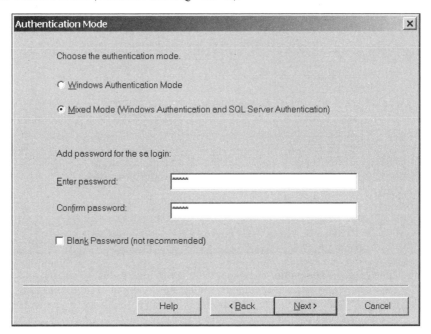

Windows authentication mode will use your domain user account to validate that you have the appropriate permissions to access SQL Server. SQL Server authentication mode will prompt you for your SQL Server Login ID and Password when you try to connect to SQL Server. These are maintained in SQL Server. These two modes of authentication will be discussed in depth in Chapter 4.

You should choose the Mixed Mode option for authentication. This allows us to explore both options and how they are handled in SQL Server.

This step of the Installation Wizard also prompts you for a password for the SQL Server system account (sa) if you chose the Mixed Mode option. You should provide a password at this point and ensure the password is something you will remember. This will be the password that will be used by the SQL Server services, and also the password that you will use to gain access to SQL Server.

16. Once you have made the appropriate selections and entered a password, click the Next button to proceed to the next step, which deals with the **collation settings** of SQL Server. Collation refers to a set of rules that determine how data is compared and collated within SQL Server.

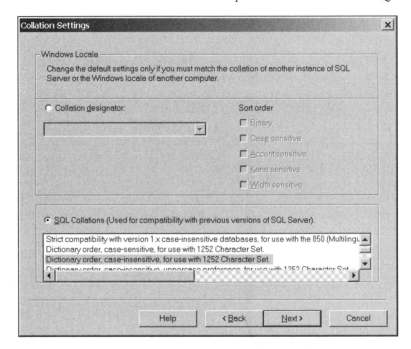

The Collation designator corresponds to the Windows locale setting, and should reflect the Windows locale setting on your computer. For example, if your computer were set up to use the Latin locale then you would choose the Latin collation, or if you were using Traditional Spanish on your computer you would use the Traditional_Spanish collation. Once you select a specific collation designator then the check boxes to the right become available and you can choose how SQL Server will sort data.

The second option on this screen is used to specify the SQL Collations, and it is the default option that is checked. The setup program will automatically detect the appropriate locale setting on your computer, and select the appropriate SQL Collations setting. Therefore, unless you need to override the SQL Collations, you can accept the default on this screen. If you wanted your data sorted in a different manner other than the default, such as using case-sensitive sorting, you would choose the appropriate option here.

17. Click the Next button to proceed to the next step of the Installation Wizard, which deals with the various **network libraries** that can be installed. There are various network libraries to choose from, and we will explain each one in turn.

SQL Server uses network libraries to pass network packets of data between SQL Server and its clients. SQL Server can listen for packets from clients using multiple protocols. By default, SQL Server is set to listen for these packets on the Named Pipes shown in the following figure. This option is only available and is required on Windows NT and Windows 2000. These options can be changed after installation.

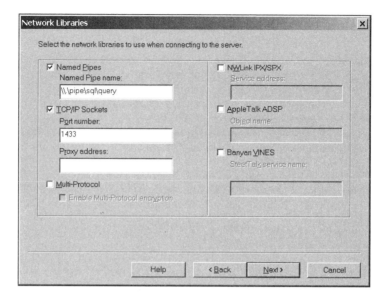

If you are installing a named instance of SQL Server, the instance name is inserted, as shown in the figure below:

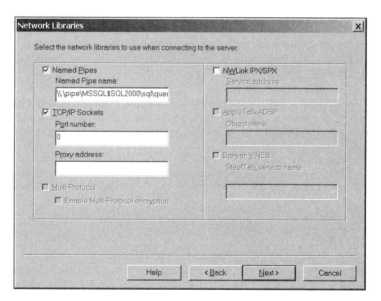

The Named Pipes option is not supported on Windows 98.

The TCP/IP Sockets net-library allows SQL Server to communicate using standard Windows sockets. Windows 98 uses this protocol by default. The port number of 1433 is the default port number for SQL Server. A default port number of 0 is automatically specified for named instances of SQL Server, as shown in the second Network Libraries figure. If you choose to have SQL Server listen for client packets on Microsoft Proxy Server, then you need to enter the server address in the remote Winsock Proxy address box.

The Multi-Protocol option uses the Windows **Remote Procedure Call** (**RPC**) facility. You can choose to have SQL Server encrypt data and passwords if you check the Enable Multi-Protocol encryption checkbox.

The Enable Multi-Protocol encryption option is not supported on Windows 98, thus encryption cannot be performed on this platform.

If you choose to use the IPX/SPX net-library you can check the NWLink IPX/SPX checkbox and supply the Novell Bindery Service address.

If you choose to use the Apple Talk ADSP net-library, check the checkbox and enter the Apple Talk server Object name.

Apple Talk ADSP is not supported on Windows 98.

Check the checkbox for Banyan VINES if this net-library is to be used and supply the StreetTalk service name.

Banyan VINES is not supported on Windows 98.

---

18. Once you have chosen the appropriate options, click the Next button to continue to the next step. This is the last step of the Installation Wizard before the installation of the files begins. If you are satisfied with the choices you have made, click the Next button to begin the actual installation of the files:

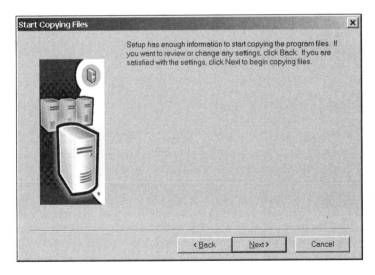

The first part of the installation of files is to install the Microsoft Data Access Components. This is automatic, and installs ActiveX Data Objects version 2.6.

If you chose to have the Full-Text Search feature installed, this is installed next, followed by the actual SQL Server programs and files.

The last step of the Installation Wizard informs you that the installation has been completed. Windows 98 and Windows NT 4.0 users will have to restart their computers. The Installation Wizard will prompt you for this and perform the restart for you.

Windows 2000 users do not need to restart their computers. However, before you can continue, you must start the SQL Server services. You can do this by performing the following steps:

1. Start the Service Manager by navigating to the **Microsoft SQL Server** program group and selecting the **Service Manager**.

2. Select **SQL Server** in the **Services** combo box and then click on the **Start/Continue** button.

3. Select **SQL Server Agent** in the **Services** combo box and then click on the **Start/Continue** button.

4. Select and start any other services that were selected for installation, such as Microsoft Search and Distributed Transaction Coordinator.

For all operating systems, all SQL Server services will be started when your machine reboots and the **SQL Server Service Manager** will be started and displayed in the system tray. (If they are not started automatically you can start them manually and choose to have them auto-started by checking the **Auto-start service when OS starts** checkbox for each service.)

Installing Additional Instances

For each additional instance of SQL Server that you want to install, you must follow and complete the installation steps outlined above. Remember to keep your instance names unique, and remember that they are limited to 16 characters.

SQL Server 2000 supports up to 16 named instances on a single machine.

Installation Wrap-Up

After the installation of SQL Server is complete, you will find a program group called **Microsoft SQL Server**. This program group contains SQL Server tools and utilities, and is shown in the figure below. We will describe each of these tools and utilities so you will know what is available.

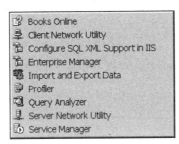

❑ The first option in this program group is Books Online. This is SQL Server's help documentation and provides a wealth of information. This is an HTML help file and thus is one of the reasons that Internet Explorer 5.0 is required.

❑ The next entry in this program group is the Client Network Utility. This utility allows you to reconfigure how SQL Server communicates with clients and allows you to change your network libraries.

❑ Next in line is Configure SQL XML Support in IIS. This utility configures a virtual directory in IIS so you can access a SQL Server database through the URL of a web page. This option will not run on Windows 98 computers, even if PWS is installed.

❑ The Enterprise Manager is one of the main tools that we will be using in this book and is listed next in the program group. We will cover this tool in the *Tools Overview* section of this chapter.

❑ The next entry, Import and Export Data, invokes the Data Transformation Import/Export Wizard. This wizard assists you in importing and exporting data into and out of SQL Server.

❑ Profiler is next in the program group and is a graphical tool that allows you to monitor and collect SQL Server events. The SQL Server Profiler can be used to trace events in SQL Server and help diagnose problems. This tool will be highlighted later in this chapter.

❑ Next is the Query Analyzer, which is used for developing and debugging queries and stored procedures. This tool will be discussed in the *Tools Overview* section of this chapter.

❑ The next entry in the program group is the Server Network Utility. This utility allows you to view and change the network libraries that SQL Server uses.

❑ The last entry in the program group is the Service Manager. This utility allows you to start, stop, and pause SQL Server components such as MSSQLServer (the database server), SQLServerAgent (an agent that runs scheduled tasks), MSSearch (the full-text search engine) and MSDTC (the Distributed Transaction Coordinator).

Tools Overview

This section covers the major tools installed with SQL Server 2000. We will cover the Enterprise Manager, Query Analyzer, and the SQL Profiler. From a developer standpoint, these are the main tools that we will be using to build and test our database solutions.

After covering the tools mentioned above, we will touch on some of the more useful wizards that will help simplify setting up and administering your databases. In the coming chapters, we will be using these tools and wizards to build, test, and administer our development database.

Enterprise Manager

Before we get started explaining the features and functions of the Enterprise Manager, we should start it up. Click on the Enterprise Manager in the Microsoft SQL Server program group.

The Enterprise Manager is built as a snap-in to the **Microsoft Management Console** (**MMC**). Any developer who has used Microsoft Transaction Server, Internet Information Server, SQL Server 7.0, or Windows 2000 should already be familiar with the MMC. The MMC is the user interface and framework for Microsoft BackOffice server management and administrative tools in Windows 2000. The MMC is a host container that contains management programs. This user interface is very similar to Windows Explorer as it provides a tree pane on the left side of the console and a details pane on the right side.

If you expand the Microsoft SQL Servers group in the Enterprise Manager and then expand the SQL Server Group, you will see that during the installation process the setup program registered your new SQL Server installation. For a default installation of SQL Server, the name of your SQL Server installation is the name of your computer, as shown in the following figure:

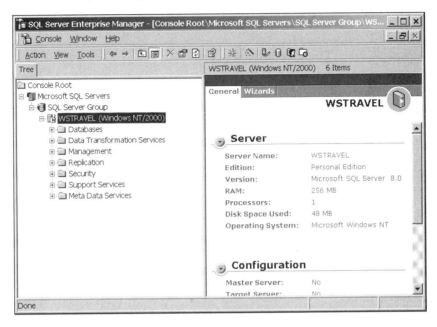

For a named instance installation of SQL Server, the name of your SQL Server installation is the name of your computer then a backslash and the instance name, as shown in next figure. Here, the instance name of SQL Server is SQL2000:

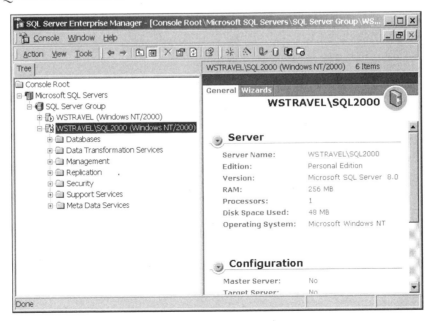

These installations were performed on a machine running Windows 2000 Professional. Notice how SQL Server reports the operating system SQL Server was installed on as Windows NT/2000 in the tree pane, but in the details pane it reports the operating system as Microsoft Windows NT. Some programs detect the version number of Windows 2000 as Windows NT 5.0, just as SQL Server reports its version as SQL Server 8.0, which is the version number of SQL Server 2000.

Taking a quick look at the menus and toolbar icons, we notice that there are actually two levels of menus. The top-level menus are used to manage the MMC windows. You can open and switch between console windows using the top-level menus.

The second level menus are used to manage SQL Server. The Action menu allows you to perform such tasks as registering a new SQL Server, changing the properties of a SQL Server that is already registered, or deleting a registered SQL Server.

The View menu allows you to change the view in the detail pane. You will find entries here similar to what you would find in Windows Explorer (for example, Large Icons, Small Icons, List).

The Tools menu lists the various tools, utilities, and wizards available in SQL Server.

The icons on the toolbar will change according to what is being viewed in the detail pane. However, there is a standard set of icons on the right of the toolbar that remain constant, and provide services such as running a wizard, creating a new database, and adding logins.

If you haven't already done so, expand the instance of SQL Server 2000 that you have just installed. We will continue by reviewing the function of the groups within the named instance group.

Databases

The Databases group is where we will spend most of our time, and is the place where we will create and maintain our databases. We can view all objects associated with our database in this folder. We will be exploring the Databases group in more depth in the next chapter.

If we expand the Databases group in SQL Server, we see that there are several databases, which are shown in the next figure:

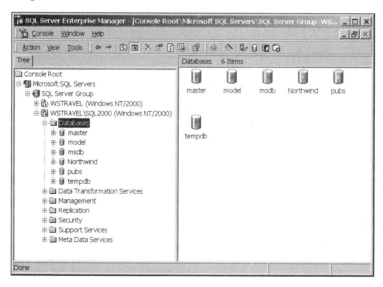

These are the databases that are installed with SQL Server. The Northwind and pubs databases are sample databases provided for learning and testing.

The master, model, msdb, and tempdb databases are **system databases**, and are used by SQL Server to manage the installation and maintenance of SQL Server itself.

The master database is used to record all system level information for SQL Server. It contains all login accounts and system configuration settings, and also contains information about all user-defined databases.

> **Important: you should never edit or modify the master database.**

The model database is used as a template when you create a new database. When a new database is created the model database is used to populate the new database with default tables, views, stored procedures, and roles. We will see this in the next chapter when we create our own database.

The SQL Server Agent uses the msdb database for scheduling alerts and jobs, and recording operators.

The tempdb database holds all temporary objects in SQL Server, such as temporary tables and temporary stored procedures. The tempdb database is re-created every time SQL Server starts and uses the model database as a template for creating this database.

Data Transformation Services

When we expand the Data Transformation Services (DTS) group we see three items, Local Packages, Meta Data Services Packages, and Meta Data:

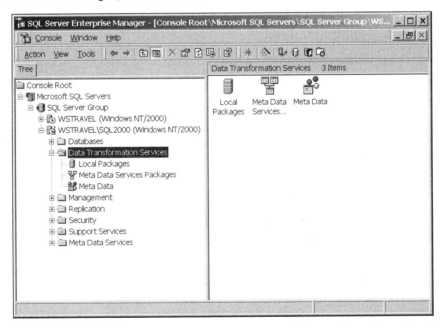

DTS provides a set of tools and utilities to import, export, consolidate, and transform data between heterogeneous data sources using an OLE DB provider. DTS also allows you to transfer database objects between SQL Servers running on different machines on the network.

Local Packages allows you to create and maintain local DTS packages. If versioning of DTS packages is maintained, you may also view the version history of a DTS package.

Meta Data Services Packages allows you to save all DTS packages and even maintain versions of the DTS packages. You can view and open any version of a DTS package stored here.

The Meta Data option allows you to view the meta data stored in the SQL Server Meta Data Services. Meta data describes the *structure* of the data – it does not actually contain data itself.

Management

The Management group provides a set of tools and utilities to manage your SQL Server installation, such as managing your backup devices, maintenance plans, and scheduling jobs.

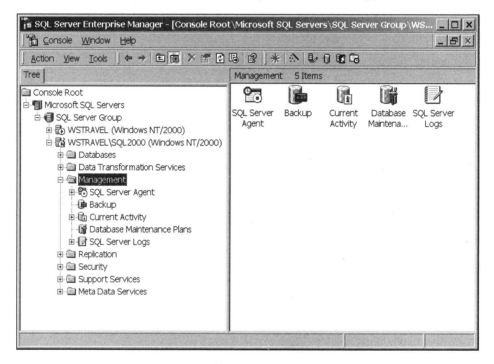

SQL Server Agent provides features that allow you to schedule activities and to provide notification events to problems that occur in SQL Server. Although not shown here, SQL Server Agent provides three further options: Alerts, Operators, and Jobs. **Alerts** can be used to define actions to be taken when a specific error or event occurs. Alerts can send mail or run jobs to correct the error. **Operators** are people identified as someone who can respond to alerts to fix the errors. Operators can be notified through e-mail, pager, and a net send network command. **Jobs** can define objects that contain one or more steps to be performed. These jobs can be scheduled to execute at specific times and perform such actions as automatically backing up your database and transaction logs.

The Backup option allows you to create new backup devices and perform database and transaction log backups. You can schedule a one-time backup or a recurring backup here.

Current Activity comprises three further options (Process Info, Locks/Process ID, and Locks/Object), which allow you to view the volume and general activities being performed against SQL Server. **Process Info** displays what processes are running, who the owner of each is, and what database the process is being run against. You can kill a long running process in this window or send a message to it. The **Locks/Process ID** option shows what processes have locks applied. Clicking on a specific lock will show general information about the lock. The **Locks/Object** option displays the locks applied to the different database objects. Clicking on an object here will display what process ID has a lock on the object, general information, and the specific lock type applied.

Database Maintenance Plans displays information about the current maintenance plans. Here you can view the history of a plan or even set up a new database maintenance plan using the Database Maintenance Plan Wizard.

SQL Server Logs are like the Event Log in NT and are not related to transaction logs. Here you can view the current log or any archived logs. Detailed information is contained in each log about what processes SQL Server has performed. Along with each message are a date and time stamp, indicating when the event happened, and the source of the event.

Replication

The Replication group provides two options, Publications and Subscriptions. This group of options allows you to set up and maintain both publications of and subscriptions to data from other SQL Servers.

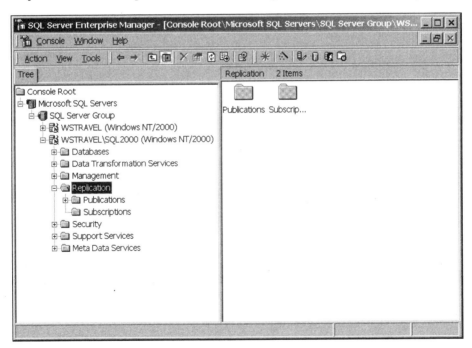

The Publications option allows you to set up SQL Server to publish data from this SQL Server to other SQL Servers on your network. This option provides a useful wizard, which will help you set up new publications and even filter the data to be published.

The Subscriptions folder allows you to subscribe to published data from other SQL Servers. Again, a wizard is provided, which can help you subscribe to published data and even help you create initialization and synchronization schedules.

Security

The Security group provides options that let you manage the security features of SQL Server. You can manage individual Logins or Server Roles. It is also possible to manage security for Linked Servers and Remote Servers.

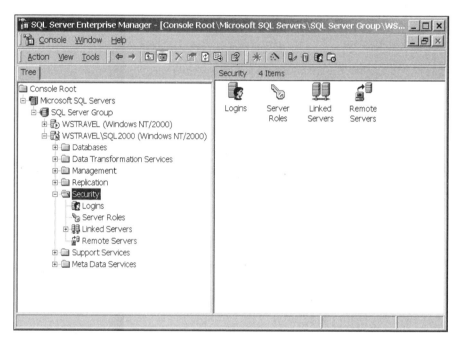

Logins lists all login IDs that have access to SQL Server. Here you can add, delete, and update logins. SQL Server requires that you supply a login before allowing access to SQL Server or any of its databases. Each login can have access to one or more databases.

Server Roles contains several pre-defined roles with permissions that cannot be granted to user accounts. A **role** is a security group that a user login is assigned to. You then assign the role permissions to the various objects in your database. If a user requires the permissions that a server role has, you must add their login to that server role. This will be covered in detail in Chapter 4 when we discuss SQL Server security in depth.

Linked Servers allow SQL Server to execute commands against other OLE DB data sources on different servers. You can link to an Oracle database or another SQL Server, and execute a query to select or update data on that database.

Remote Servers allow a user connected to one SQL Server to execute a stored procedure on another SQL Server, without establishing another connection. This feature is provided for backward compatibility and has been superseded by Linked Servers. Linked Servers provides all of the functionality of Remote Servers plus a lot more.

Support Services

The Support Services group provides just that, supporting services to SQL Server. This includes the Distributed Transaction Coordinator, Full-Text Search, and SQL Mail.

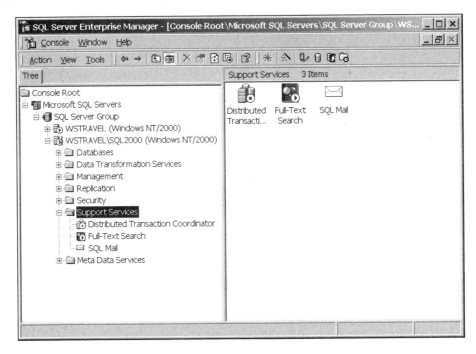

The Distributed Transaction Coordinator (DTC) is a transaction manager that allows you to execute transactions in the current SQL Server database and on other SQL Server databases on the network. It ensures that each transaction completes as a whole unit of work, or that none of that transaction completes. You can start and stop the DTC service from this option.

The Full-Text Search option allows you to manage the Full-Text Search features of SQL Server. You can start and stop the Full-Text Search service from this option.

SQL Mail allows SQL Server to send and receive e-mail by establishing a client connection to Microsoft Exchange Server or a POP3 Server. Using SQL Mail you can mail-enable your stored procedures and triggers.

Meta Data Services

Meta Data Services supports browsing meta data through the **Meta Data Browser**, which is an add-in component, installed with SQL Server. The Meta Data Services is an object-oriented repository technology. Meta Data Services is normally used in conjunction with the Analysis Services.

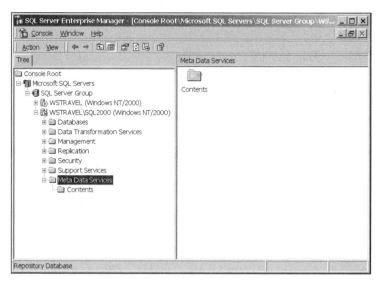

We have now briefly covered all of the groups in the instance of SQL Server 2000 – many of which we'll be investigating further later in the book.

Query Analyzer

The **Query Analyzer** is probably one of the most valuable tools for developers. It provides a number of tools and features that will aid you in writing, running, and debugging queries and stored procedures. It also provides shortcuts to wizards found in the Enterprise Manager that will aid you in optimizing your database for query and stored procedure execution.

To start the Query Analyzer, you can navigate to the Microsoft SQL Server program group and click on Query Analyzer, or you can choose SQL Server Query Analyzer from the Tools menu in the Enterprise Manager.

The following figure shows the Query Analyzer after the execution of a query:

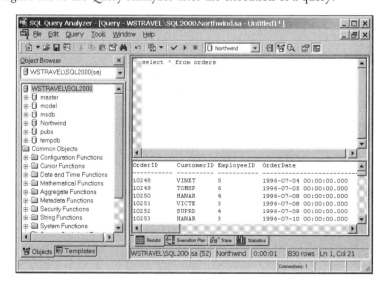

The tabs at the bottom of the results pane will only be displayed if the appropriate options are turned on before the query is executed. We will cover this in detail in Chapter 5.

Notice that we can view the execution plan by clicking on the Execution Plan tab. This is the plan of execution that was carried out by SQL Server to execute the query. This plan shows what indexes were used to execute the query, and any other actions that SQL Server took to execute the query.

The Trace tab, which is also shown in the results pane, shows the impact of the execution of the query on the server. The trace shows what statements were executed and the duration and CPU time spent on those statements.

The Statistics tab shows the impact of the execution of the query on the client side. It shows various application, network, and time statistics.

Notice that on the left-hand side of the window there is an Object Browser. This allows you to browse the various database objects as well as common T-SQL functions. (Remember from Chapter 1 that T-SQL stands for Transact Structured Query Language, which is Microsoft's version of SQL, and is used to perform actions such as creating and modifying the database.) At the bottom of the Object Browser is a Templates tab. This tab provides common templates to help you create queries, tables, views, and stored procedures. You can even add your own custom templates.

We will cover the Query Analyzer in more detail in Chapter 5.

SQL Server Profiler

The **SQL Server Profiler** is a tool that allows you to monitor the events for a particular instance of SQL Server. This tool is fully customizable, and provides filters to allow you to capture only the events that you want to see. You can capture the events of a SQL Server instance to a file or database table, and then replay those events. This can be particularly useful in situations where you are troubleshooting and tuning.

You can start the SQL Server Profiler from either the Enterprise Manager Tools menu or by navigating to the Microsoft SQL Server program group and clicking on Profiler.

The next figure, overleaf, shows just some of the information available from a trace. Notice that when you click on the stored procedure that was executed, the SQL Server Profiler shows the details of the stored procedure that was executed in the detail pane at the bottom of the screen:

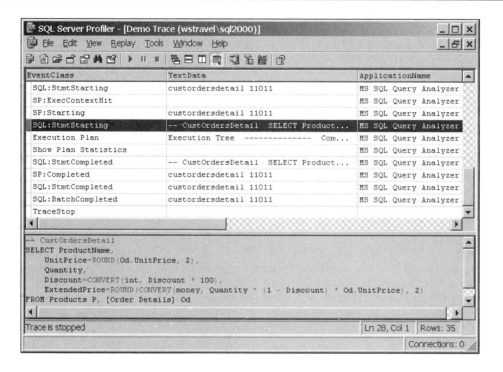

Wizards

SQL Server 2000 provides many useful wizards that help to simplify the administration tasks of creating and maintaining a database. There are literally dozens of wizards and we will just highlight some of the more useful ones here. As we progress through the book we will be using some of these and other wizards to perform administrative tasks on our database.

Register SQL Server Wizard

When you installed SQL Server and started the Enterprise Manager, the installation process had already created a SQL Server Group and registered the instance of SQL Server that was installed. However, you are not limited to displaying only the SQL Server instances installed locally. You can register and access other SQL Server installations on your network.

This wizard's job is to help you do just that. It will walk you through a series of steps that will help you locate and register a new SQL Server instance.

It should be noted here that this and all other wizards in SQL Server display a Welcome screen that will explain what functions the wizard will help you perform.

Create Database Wizard

When you are new to a sophisticated software product, it can sometimes be intimidating and seem overly complex. You may find that you are presented with a dialog with multiple tabs, each tab having multiple options. This can be the case when you try to manually create a database in SQL Server.

The Create Database Wizard helps simplify the process of creating a new database by breaking down the process into multiple steps. Each step of the wizard explains what needs to be done, and also allows you to navigate forwards and backwards.

The wizard will also display a summary of the actions that SQL Server will perform and give you a chance to finish the process or cancel the process.

Create Index Wizard

Creating indexes on your tables is probably one of the most important tasks you can perform to help optimize your database. Creating the appropriate indexes on a table will help to optimize and speed up the execution of your queries and stored procedures, and will have a dramatic effect on your application's performance.

The Create Index Wizard assists you in creating indexes on your tables. This wizard steps you through the process, allowing you to choose the table on which the index should be created, and also showing you the existing indexes for that table. It then steps you through the options for an index, allowing you to specify the column or columns to be included in the index.

Create Login Wizard

Creating logins for your database can sometimes be a daunting task, especially in the light of all of the security features available in SQL Server.

The Create Login Wizard helps simplify the process of creating a login for your database and walks you through a series of steps asking for the authentication mode and then displaying the appropriate steps after that. It also allows you to assign the new login to one of the predefined system roles and then lets you choose which databases the login should have access to.

Like all the other wizards, this wizard also displays a summary step informing you what actions will be taken to create the login. This gives you a chance to go back and make changes if necessary.

Full-Text Indexing Wizard

The Full-Text feature of SQL Server is a very powerful and useful feature that allows us to efficiently perform searches on character data in a column. Unfortunately, as with most powerful features, it can be somewhat complex to set up.

The Full-Text Indexing Wizard helps simplify the process of defining a full-text index for a column in a table. It steps you through the process of creating the full-text index and all of the options needed to make this feature work.

Wizard Summary

Most wizards can be invoked by selecting Wizards from the Tools menu in the Enterprise Manager. This will invoke the Select Wizard dialog and display a list of available wizards by category. Some wizards can even be invoked from within the Query Analyzer, and some from the context menus within the Enterprise Manager.

We will be exploring the wizards mentioned here and more wizards in the coming chapters.

Summary

We have accomplished a lot in this chapter. We have discussed the various editions of SQL Server 2000 and the various platforms that these different editions run on. You should be able to determine which edition suits your purposes.

Having covered the prerequisites for the installation of the Personal Edition of SQL Server on the supported platforms, we walked through the installation process, explaining the various options along the way. Where it was appropriate, we made recommendations for various installation options. We also covered SQL Server instances and, where appropriate, pointed out the differences of a named SQL Server instance versus a default instance during the installation process.

After the installation we took a tour of the Enterprise Manager to acquaint you with the available features of this tool. While we will not use many of the features, it is important to know that they exist, so you know where to find them should you need them in the future. We will be working with the Enterprise Manager more in the next few chapters.

The Query Analyzer and SQL Server Profiler were introduced, and we will be working with the Query Analyzer more in Chapter 5.

We touched briefly on some of the more useful wizards from a developer's standpoint. We will also be working with these and more wizards in the next few chapters.

To summarize, you should know:

❑ What SQL Server editions exist and what platforms they run on

❑ What prerequisites must be met for each platform before installing SQL Server 2000

❑ How to install SQL Server 2000 Personal Edition

❑ What features are available in the Enterprise Manager

❑ That wizards can assist you in the more complex administrative tasks

In the next chapter we will go through the design and creation of the development database that we will be using in the rest of the book. Once you have completed the next chapter, you should be fairly intimate with the Enterprise Manager.

Designing and Creating
the Development Database

In the last chapter we took a look at all of the features available in the Enterprise Manager. This chapter will expand on that, as we drill down into the details of the database that we will create. Before we can do so, we must first walk through the process of designing and creating the development database, which we will do in this chapter.

Database object naming standards are vital, and help to ensure consistency in the code that is written. This chapter will cover some suggested naming conventions that could be used. Using standards in your database design and throughout your coding of stored procedures, views, and triggers helps to ensure that any developer can pick up your code and know exactly what is going on. The stored procedure code and database naming conventions that we will use throughout the rest of this book will be written to the standards presented in this chapter.

This chapter will also go through the process of relational database design and normalization. Normalization is the process of eliminating duplicate data, providing a fast and efficient search path to the data. After we have designed and normalized our database, we will step through the procedures for creating the database and the various database objects (such as tables, indexes, and constraints).

In this chapter we will:

- ❑   Study relational database design
- ❑   Learn about normalization
- ❑   Cover suggested naming conventions
- ❑   Create the development database
- ❑   Create the database objects (for example tables, constraints, indexes)

Project Scope

Before we get into the details of this chapter, we should take a minute to talk about the project scope. This book will step you through the development of one complete project. A lot of books have a different approach and sometimes have a separate project in each chapter. You do not always know how or if the project from one chapter relates to another. This is especially true when each chapter has totally independent projects with different tables and data.

In this book we will develop one project, and each chapter will build upon the last and integrate a new piece of functionality. By the time you reach the last chapter you will have a fully functional and comprehensive project.

The project that we will develop in this book will be a hardware tracking application. This simple application will track the computer hardware in an organization. You can choose to enter data for your own company or use a fictitious one. This application will have a Visual Basic front-end, a Visual Basic business server component, and web-based reports.

The front-end program will provide data presentation, while the business server component will provide the business logic and data access for our front-end. The web browser will provide the data presentation for our reports, and Active Server Pages will provide the business logic and data access for our web pages. The following diagram illustrates how this application will function in an n-tier configuration:

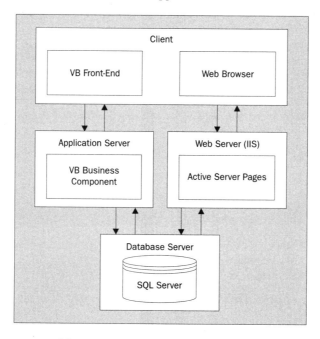

To some readers this may seem like a complicated project. However, we'll keep things as simple as possible, and rest assured that we will carefully step you though the process of creating the entire project. For our purposes here, all components will be running on one machine.

With all that being said, let's get started by designing our database.

Relational Database Design

A relational database contains tables, rows, and columns that are related to one another through the use of constraints and business rules. A relational database that has been properly normalized will have more tables that contain fewer columns, rather than a few tables each containing lots of columns. A normalized relational database actually improves storage efficiency and performance, even though there are physically more tables. We will be discussing normalization in the next section.

Each table in the database represents an **object** within your business, and each column in a table represents an **attribute** of the object that the table represents. A row in the table represents a unique entry for the object that the table defines.

To design a relational database you must first identify all of the objects that will make up your database. We use the term object to represent a group of information. We can also use the term **entity** in place of object. An entity is an object that refers to a person, place, or thing.

We know that we will be building an application that tracks computer hardware in our organization. So first we identify what objects make up the computer hardware, and who the hardware will be assigned to. For this example, computer hardware is an object and employee is an object. We will also track what software is installed on a computer, so we know that software is also an object.

Next, we want to identify what attributes make up the hardware, software, and employee objects. The following tables illustrate the attributes that have been identified for these objects:

Hardware Attributes	Description
Manufacturer	Computer manufacturer
Model	Model number of the computer
Processor Speed	Processor type and speed
Memory	Amount of installed memory
Hard Drive	Size of installed hard drive
CD	What type of compact disc is installed (for example CD, CDR, DVD)
Sound Card	Type of installed sound card
Speakers	Type of speakers that come with the system
Video Card	Type of video card installed and amount of memory on the card
Monitor	Type and size of monitor that comes with the system
Serial Number	Serial number of the computer
Lease Expiration	If this is a leased machine, when the lease expires

Software Attributes	Description
Software Name	Name of the installed software
Software Category	Category of the software (such as OS, Office, Tools)

Employee Attributes	Description
Employee Name	Name of the employee
Phone Number	Employee's phone number
Location	Where is the employee located (for example building and office/cube)

Now that we have identified all of the attributes for these objects, we must identify the tables that these attributes will be assigned to. We can begin defining the tables that will go into our database, as shown in the following figure. Notice that we have separated the employee's name into two separate fields. This allows us to select and order the employees by first or last name.

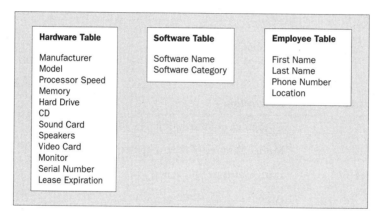

Looking at the previous tables, we see that we have the information we need, but there is no relationship between the various items of data. Therefore, we need to create another table that will tie the information from these tables together. Let's call this new table System Assignment. This will allow us to assign hardware and software to an employee (identified as an Employee in the System Assignment table).

The next figure shows a new table, which will form the relationships between the earlier tables. Since there will be more than one piece of software loaded on a computer, we have added five fields for software:

This is the start of our relational database design. At this point our database design is relational because the tables relate to one another; however, our design is not yet complete. To complete our database design we must first normalize it.

Normalization

Normalization is the process of using formal methods to eliminate duplicate data, and to separate data into multiple related tables. A normalized database will actually have improved database and application performance over a database that is not normalized, and one that has been over-normalized. A normalized database also leads to more efficient data storage, as we will eliminate repeating groups of data. Normalization will also help to make your tables easier to maintain.

As normalization increases so will the number of **joins** that are required to access the data; however, SQL Server is optimized to handle normalized databases that require multiple joins. Joins are a logical relationship between two tables that allow you to access data in both tables from the same query. Joins are usually defined in the form of foreign key constraints.

Normalizing a logical database design involves using formal methods to separate the data into multiple, related tables. Each method is usually referred to as a **normal form**. There are three normal forms for a normalized database: first normal form, second normal form, and third normal form. An over-normalized database will be normalized to the fourth and fifth forms, and is rarely considered practical in relational database design.

We'll be looking at an example of the first, second, and third normal forms next, but briefly:

- ❏ **First normal form** eliminates repeating groups of data in a table. We create a separate table for each set of related data, and identify each table with a primary key, which uniquely identifies each row of data.

- ❏ **Second normal form** creates separate tables for sets of values that apply to multiple records, and relates these tables with foreign keys.

- ❏ **Third normal form** eliminates columns that do not depend on the primary key.

First Normal Form

We want to apply the rules of normalization to our database design. In the first normal form we need to eliminate repeating groups of data, and create separate tables for each set of related data. We must also identify each table with a primary key.

The previous table, the System Assignment table, had repeating groups of data so this table is a prime candidate for the first normal form. To eliminate the repeating groups of data (such as Software 1, Software 2) we have created a relationship table between the System Assignment table and the Software table, and called it System Software Relationship. This allows us to enter as many software titles as are installed on a single machine. This table provides a many-to-one relationship to the System Assignment table as we have many rows of data in the System Software Relationship table that relate to one row of data in the System Assignment table. This table also provides a many-to-one relationship to the Software table.

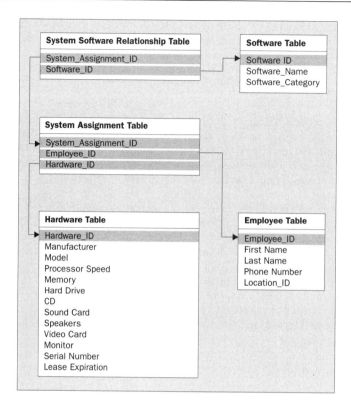

All tables must have a primary key assigned and we have done this, as shown in the figure. Notice that the `System Software Relationship` table contains the primary keys from the `System Assignment` and `Software` tables. These keys will be used in this table as both the primary keys and foreign keys. We will discuss this further shortly.

Notice that all primary keys end with the suffix of `_ID`. This suffix will identify all primary keys and we will use an identity column for the primary key. An identity column automatically generates a sequential number for each row of data that is inserted. You could use any other unique value, but I prefer to keep the primary keys non-intelligent. This allows for table changes without affecting the primary and foreign keys. (Intelligent primary keys tend to leave themselves open to change. Thus if a primary key needs to be changed, all foreign key references to that primary key must also be changed.)

Second Normal Form

The rule of second normal form indicates that we must create separate tables for sets of values that apply to multiple records, and relate these tables with foreign keys.

Starting with the `Software` table, we know that the `Software Category` column could relate to multiple rows. An example of this would be the Operating Systems category. We could have a `Software Name` of Windows 98, Windows NT, or Windows 2000. All of these are operating systems and the category would be duplicated. So, following the rules of second normal form, we create a separate table for `Software Category` and relate this new table to the `Software` table with a foreign key. This provides a one-to-many relationship where we have one row in the `Software Category` table relating to multiple rows in the `Software` table.

The next table that we want to examine for the rules of second normal form is the Employee table. We could have multiple rows of employees who are located in the same location. Therefore, we want to remove Location from the Employee table and create a separate table called Location. We then relate this new table to the Employee table through the use of a foreign key. This relationship also provides a one-to-many relationship, as we have one row of data in the Location table relating to many rows of data in the Employee table.

The last table we want to examine is the Hardware table. This table requires some thought and discretion. First, we could have multiple manufacturers that are the same. We have to determine whether or not it is worth creating a separate table for Manufacturer. We will forego creating a separate table for this column, thereby not fully normalizing our database. However, when we look at the CD column, we can determine very quickly that there are industry standard CD drives. What we really want in this column is an indication of whether a system has a CD, CD-R, or DVD installed. Therefore we will create a separate table for these entries and relate this new table to the Hardware table with a foreign key. This will also create a one-to-many relationship between the CD table and the Hardware table. There are other columns in this table that could be removed and placed in a separate table. You must use your discretion, and your knowledge about the project, to determine whether a column is a prime candidate for a separate table.

So, with the addition of these new tables, our database design looks like this:

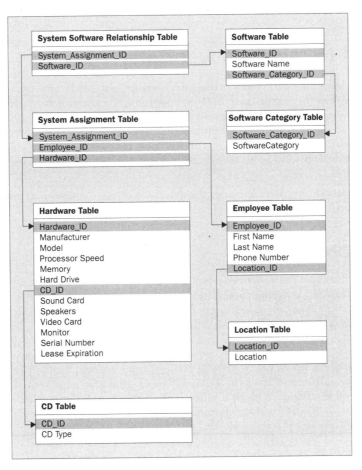

Third Normal Form

The rules of the third normal form indicate that we eliminate columns that do not depend on the primary key. Given our database design, we have no columns that match this description. All columns in all tables depend on the primary key to uniquely identify each row.

The figure below shows a table that this rule applies to. In this example, `City` does not depend on the primary key of `Address_ID` as a city could relate to more than one address:

The normalization of our database design has yielded three key points. First, we have more narrow tables than wide tables. Second, because of the normalization we are better able to maintain data integrity, because we eliminated duplicate and repeating data. Last, because our database design is normalized, this database will perform optimally in SQL Server.

Suggested Naming Conventions

Standards are an important part of any organization, and help to control the look and feel of applications, as well as the maintenance of those applications. The **database naming standards** suggested here are just that – *suggested*. If your organization already has database standards in place, then feel free to use them instead. But if your organization has none, then this section can be used as a guideline in developing some. All of the examples in this book adhere to these standards, so you need to be aware of them, even if you don't plan to adopt them when developing your own databases.

> *The naming standards suggested here use suffixes. This is a personal preference, as prefixes could be used just as well.*

Identifying Objects

In Chapter 1 we discussed the various objects that make up a database, for example tables, views, and stored procedures. When assigning names, each object should be suffixed with the first letter of the object (or, where more than one object shares the same first letter, a suitable alternative). An example for the `Employee` table in our database would be `Employee_T`.

Suffixing each object will help to quickly identify what the object is. This is especially useful when dealing with the code in stored procedures, as distinguishing between data retrieved from a *table* named `Employee` and a *view* named `Employee` can be confusing and time-consuming for someone who did not write the stored procedure. Without a suffix appended to the object, you have to go through the list of tables and views in the database to determine what the object is.

Tables

Table names can be up to 128 characters in length and should be as descriptive as possible. The first letter of each word in a table name should be capitalized, and an underscore character should separate each word. Abbreviations should be avoided wherever possible. Using upper and lower case letters, as well as underscore characters, helps to make object names easier to read. An example of a suitable name for the `System Assignment` table name is `System_Assignment_T`.

Columns

Column names can also be up to 128 characters in length, and should follow the same naming conventions as tables. All column names should be suffixed with the *data type* of the column, according to the following table. An example of a column containing the last update date and time of a table would be `Last_Update_DT`.

Suffix	Data Type
BI	Big Integer
BN	Binary
BT	Bit
CH	Char
DT	DateTime
DC	Decimal
FL	Float
IM	Image
IN	Integer
MN	Money
NC	NChar
NT	NText
NV	NVarChar
RL	Real
SD	SmallDateTime
SI	SmallInteger
SM	SmallMoney
SV	SQL Variant
TX	Text
TS	TimeStamp
TI	TinyInt
VB	VarBinary
VC	VarChar

Using a suffix on each column will help other developers working with these columns in a stored procedure. They will know at a quick glance what type of data they are dealing with, according to the suffix of the column name.

Primary and Foreign Keys

All columns that are primary keys should end with a suffix of _ID and should have the same name as the table. This will help anyone looking at stored procedures and views to know what the keys are, and to what tables they belong. If you are using more than one column to make up the primary key, you could suffix the column names with _PK. All primary and foreign keys are usually Integer data types but can be other data types as well.

Indexes

When you create a table that contains a primary key, SQL Server will automatically place an index on that column using a name of PK_table_name where table_name is the name of the table. An index on the primary key column for the Employee_T table created by SQL Server would look like this: PK_Employee_T.

In keeping with this, when we create additional indexes on a table, they should be prefixed with IX_ followed by the table name. Thus, if we wanted to create an additional index on the Employee_T table, our index name would look like this: IX_Employee_T.

If you create more than one index on a table, you can suffix each index with _n where n would represent the number of indexes added by you.

Views

View names can be up to 128 characters in length, and should follow the same naming conventions as table names. All views should be suffixed with _V.

Triggers

Trigger names can also be up to 128 characters in length, and follow the same naming conventions as tables. All triggers should be suffixed with _G.

Stored Procedures

Stored procedures are at the heart of our development efforts, and therefore naming standards are even more important here. The database administrator can create stored procedures that can be used enterprise-wide and which can be placed in your database. Developers also create stored procedures in the database. Therefore, a naming standard here is especially important, and takes a different twist to what we have observed so far. The stored procedure naming standard that follows is one that I personally find useful, and I'll explain why after we review the standard:

❑ All stored procedures created by the *database administrator* should be *prefixed* with SP_

❑ All stored procedures created by *developers* should be *prefixed* according to the following table:

Prefix	Description
up_parmdel_	up_ indicates a user stored procedure, in other words one created by a developer. This stored procedure accepts parameters and will delete data.
up_parmins_	This stored procedure accepts parameters and will insert data.
up_parmsel_	This stored procedure accepts parameters and will select data.
up_parmupd_	This stored procedure accepts parameters and will update data.
up_select_	This stored procedure selects data but does not have parameters.

We will be covering each of these types of stored procedures in the upcoming chapters. A medium to large database can have hundreds of stored procedures. If no naming standard has been implemented, a new developer will not know what each stored procedures does. Likewise, even the developers who wrote the stored procedures will have a difficult time finding the correct stored procedure to modify.

Using the suggested naming standard above serves three purposes. Firstly, it lets you know at a quick glance what the purpose of each stored procedure is. Secondly, all of the stored procedures are grouped together, which makes a stored procedure that, for example, accepts parameters and updates information, easier to find in the list of hundreds of stored procedures. Lastly, the stored procedures that are prefixed with SP_ indicate those created or owned by the database administrator (DBA), which are used enterprise-wide. This gives a clear differentiation between stored procedures created by the DBA and the developer.

Now that we have described the naming convention, let's complete our database design according to these standards. This will serve two purposes; it will identify all data types for our columns, and it will give us a final design to work from when we create our development database.

The following figure shows our completed database diagram:

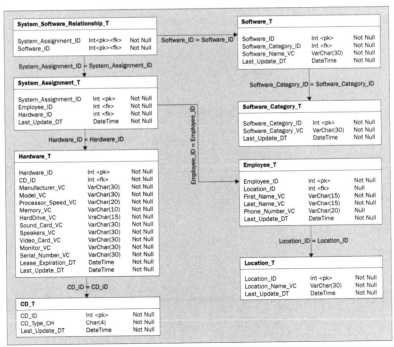

Notice that we have added the appropriate standards to the column names, and have also identified the data types for each column (Appendix A lists all of these SQL Server data types). Also, for each column we have identified whether or not the column will allow null values. A null value is a column that has the value of Null inserted and no data. We have used the symbols of <pk> to identify the primary keys for the tables and the symbol of <fk> to identify foreign keys.

Each table has also had the standards applied to the table name, and an extra column added to keep track of the last date and time the row was modified. This will provide an audit trail should you ever need to know when a row of data was modified. It also keeps the folks in Internal Auditing happy. The only table that did not get this new column was the System_Software_Relationship_T table. This is because this is a relationship table that provides a many-to-many relationship, where all entries are foreign keys to other tables and there is no data to update.

Try It Out – Creating the Development Database

Having gone through the process of creating and normalizing our relational database design, and having applied the naming standards to our design, we are ready to actually create the database.

1. Start by opening the Enterprise Manager.

2. Expand the **Microsoft SQL Servers** group, the **SQL Server Group** group, and then the instance of SQL Server 2000 that you installed. Lastly, expand the **Databases** group.

3. There are two ways we can use the Enterprise Manager to create a new database. First, we can right-click on the **Databases** group and choose **New Database** from the context menu. Once you have created a couple of databases and are comfortable with other techniques, this will be the way to go. For now, we are going to use the Create Database Wizard.

   To start the wizard, click on the **Tools** menu and choose **Wizards**. Then expand the **Database** group in the **Select Wizard** dialog, and click on **Create Database Wizard**, as shown in the next figure. Click **OK** to proceed and to invoke the wizard.

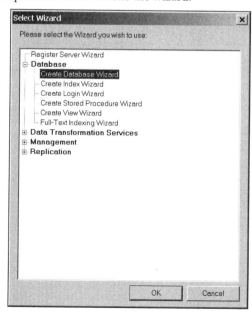

4. The first step of the Create Database Wizard is the Welcome screen. All wizards in SQL Server 2000 provide a Welcome screen that informs you what actions will be performed. Click Next to proceed to the next step of the wizard.

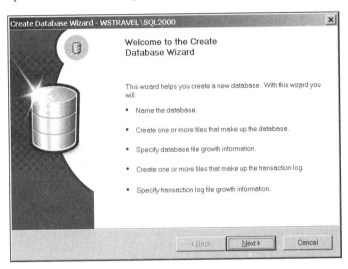

5. The next step of the wizard allows you to name the database, and specify the location of the database file and transaction log file. Remember that in Chapter 1 we said that the transaction log is a file that records all transactions performed against your database, and can be used for either forward or backwards recovery.

Notice in the following figure that, since I am working with a named instance of SQL Server 2000, the file path has the instance name in it, as specified by $SQL2000. The dollar sign is used as a separator and SQL2000 is the name of my instance of SQL Server.

You normally do not have to change the path of the database file and transaction log unless you want them created in a different directory. For our purposes, we will take the default path for these files. We do, however, want to change the database name to Hardware Tracking, as shown:

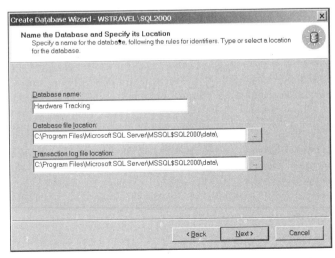

6. Click the Next button to proceed. This step of the wizard allows us to change the database file name and the initial size of our database. It is recommended that you take the default file name, as all database files are created using the database name plus the word Data. The default size is always one megabyte and we want to change this default size. We will specify a default size for our database of five megabytes, which should be more than enough. Setting the appropriate size now prevents fragmentation of the database file, thus improving performance.

There is no magical formula for determining database size. This is experience that you gain over the years when working with SQL Server. However, if the size we have specified is not enough, the next screen will allow us to specify what SQL Server should do if we were to run out of space in our database.

Change the default database size to 5 megabytes and then click the Next button to proceed.

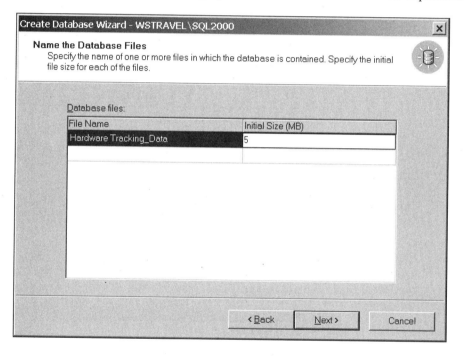

7. The next step of the wizard specifies how SQL Server should handle file growth of our database file. By default, SQL Server will automatically expand our database should we run out of room in the disk partition (or volume) in which it is located. We can manually handle file growth ourselves, but this requires constant monitoring of the database. We want SQL Server to handle this, so we will accept the default for this.

This screen also allows you to specify how file growth should occur for your database; by percentage or megabytes. It also allows you to specify a maximum file size for your database, or to let it grow unlimited.

We will accept all defaults on this screen, so click the **Next** button to proceed to the next step.

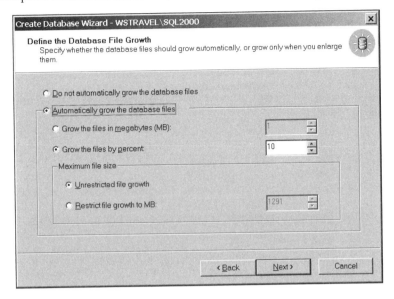

8. The next step of the wizard deals with the file name and size of the transaction log file. The default name and size are acceptable. If you wanted to change the file name or size you could. If your database was required to handle a lot of transactions, as would be the case in, say, a data entry system or an e-commerce web site, then you would probably want to increase the initial size of the transaction log.

    For our purposes, however, the defaults are fine so click the **Next** button to proceed to the next step.

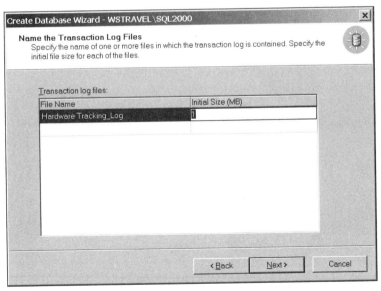

9. The next screen in the wizard is a duplicate of the screen dealing with database file growth. However, this screen deals with the file growth of our *transaction log*. All defaults on this screen are acceptable, so click the Next button to proceed.

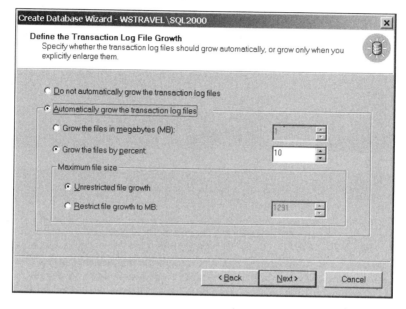

10. The summary step of the wizard summarizes what actions it will perform for you. **Review these actions carefully**. If you want to make any changes, click on the Back button to go back and make any necessary changes. If you want to proceed, click the Finish button and SQL Server will proceed and create your database for you.

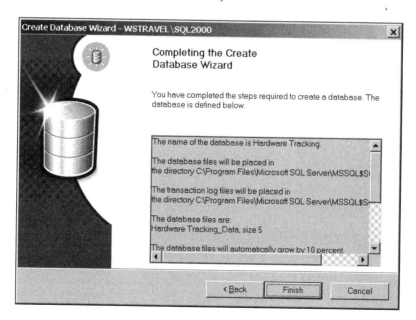

11. Once SQL Server has finished creating the database, it will display a dialog message indicating that it has successfully created the database:

Once you click the **OK** button, you will be prompted with another dialog asking if you want to create a database maintenance plan. Clicking **Yes** on this dialog would invoke the Database Maintenance Plan wizard, which would guide you through creating a maintenance plan that will perform integrity checks, update database statistics, perform backups, and ship your transaction logs to another SQL Server.

We do not want to perform these tasks, so click the **No** button. You can run the Database Maintenance Plan wizard at any time by right-clicking on your database in the Enterprise Manager, choosing **All Tasks**, and then choosing **Maintenance Plan**. Maintenance plans are outside the scope of this book.

This completes the creation of our database files. However, we still need to create the tables and constraints in our database. Before we do that, we should point out that there is a quick way to view space usage of your database. Click on the **Hardware Tracking** database in the Enterprise Manager and scroll to the bottom of the detail pane. (You may need to select **View | Taskpad** to see this view.) Here you can view the space usage of your database and transaction log files:

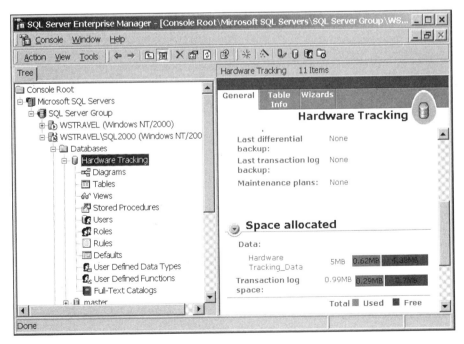

Once you have created and populated some tables in your database, you can view space usages by table when you click on the Table Info tab at the top of the detail pane.

Creating Tables

There are no wizards to assist you in creating tables in your database. However, this is a fairly simple task that we will walk through here. If you expand the Hardware Tracking database and then click on Tables in the tree pane, you will see that 19 system tables have already been added to the database. These tables are used by SQL Server to manage various aspects of our database, such as foreign keys and indexes.

> **WARNING: feel free to look at these tables, but do not amend them in any way.**

In the last chapter we talked about the model database. If you take a look at that database you will see that our database contains the same 19 tables. That's because SQL Server uses the model database to create other databases.

Try It Out – Add Tables to the Database

1. To start creating tables in the Hardware Tracking database you need to click on Tables in the tree pane. You can then either click on the Action menu before selecting New Table, or you can right-click on Tables in the tree pane and choose New Table from the context menu. Once you have chosen a method and executed it, an empty table is displayed in design view:

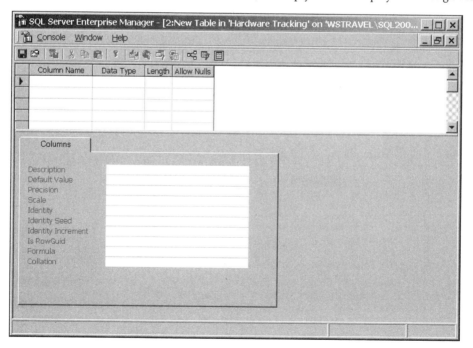

2. It does not matter what table we start with, so let's start creating tables from the top left of our completed database diagram shown earlier in this chapter. This is the `System_Software_Relationship_T` table and contains only two columns, `System_Assignment_ID` and `Software_ID`. We enter the **Column Name** and **Data Type**, which is int for both columns (the default length of 4 will be fine for these, and for other `Integer` columns in our database), and then ensure we uncheck the **Allow Nulls** checkbox, because both of these columns do not allow null values.

Notice at the bottom of this screen is a **Columns** tab. Here we can change various attributes for the column that we are working with. You can assign a description to the columns that you add and, depending on the data type, change the various attributes for that data type.

3. Since both of these columns combined make up the primary key to this table, as shown earlier in our database diagram, we want to select the first column and then, while holding down the *Shift* key, select the second column. Next, click on the **Set primary key** icon to set the primary key for this table. A key will appear in the row selector for both columns. The final table should look like the one shown:

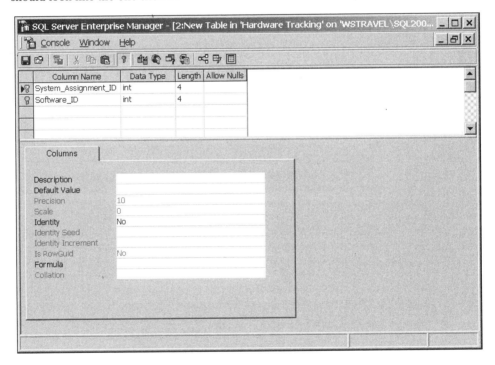

4. To save the table, click on the **Save** icon and enter the name System_Software_Relationship_T. When you save the table, SQL Server will create the table and an index on the primary key(s) that you have defined. Close the design view for this table by clicking on the second (lower) **X** in the upper right-hand corner.

5. The next table that we want to create is the `System_Assignment_T` table. Again, either click on **Tables** in the tree pane, then click the **Action** menu followed by **New Table**, or right-click on **Tables** in the tree pane and choose **New Table** from the context menu.

6. The first column that we want to add to this table is the System_Assignment_ID column. This column is an `Integer` data type (int), and we do not want to allow null entries so we uncheck the Allow Nulls checkbox. This column, in addition to being the primary key, will also be an identity column. An identity column is one that is maintained by SQL Server and will automatically have an incremental value inserted into it by SQL Server.

7. In the Columns tab at the bottom of the screen we want to change the value for Identity to Yes. The Identity Seed is the initial value that this column will have. Thus, if you entered 10 in this field, the value for the first row inserted into this table would be 10. The Identity Increment is self explanatory, as it increments the value of the identity column. A value of 1 in both of these fields is fine for our purposes.

8. Go ahead and enter the rest of the columns for this table, as shown in the following figure.

The primary key for this table only consists of one column, System_Assignment_ID. Click on this column and then click on the Set primary key icon to make this column the primary key. Save the changes to this table and enter a name of System_Assignment_T. The completed table in design view is shown:

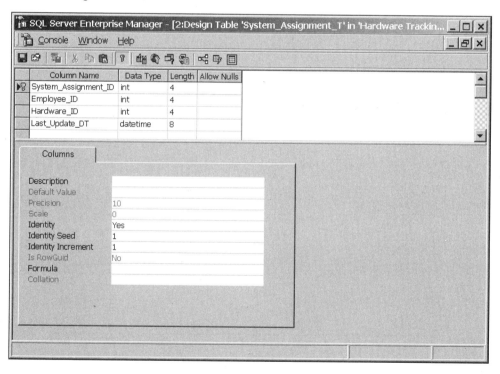

9. The next table to be created is the `Hardware_T` table, and is the largest table in our database. Again, either click on Tables in the tree pane and select New Table from the Action menu, or right-click on Tables in the tree pane and choose New Table from the context menu.

The first column in this table, Hardware_ID, is an identity column and the primary key. Ensure you uncheck the Allow Nulls checkbox and set Identity to Yes. Also, set this column to be the primary key for this table by clicking on the Set primary key icon.

Complete the rest of the table as per the following diagram:

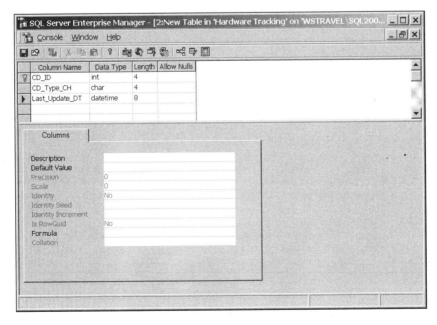

10. The next table that we want to create is the CD_T table. This table has only three columns and the first is both a primary key and an identity column. Every column in this table is required, and thus we need to uncheck the **Allow Nulls** checkbox for all columns. The completed table is shown in the next figure. Take note that the **CD_Type_CH** column is a char data type. A Char data type is a fixed length data type, and in our case has a length of four. Hence, any value inserted into the column will be padded with spaces. If you try to insert more than four characters you will receive an error indicating that the value you are trying to insert is too long.

11. Starting at the top right of our completed database diagram (shown earlier in the chapter), the next table we want to create is the `Software_T` table. The first column is again both the primary key for the table and an identity column, so set the attributes for this column appropriately. The completed table is shown:

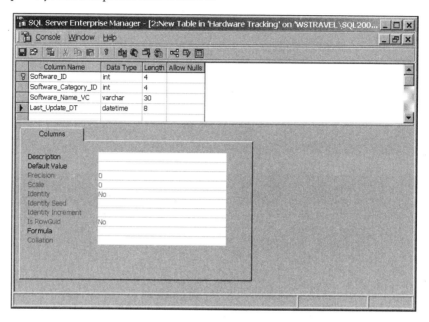

12. The next table that we want to create is the `Software_Category_T` table. Once again, the first column is both the primary key and an identity column, and thus requires that the appropriate attributes are set. The completed table is shown here:

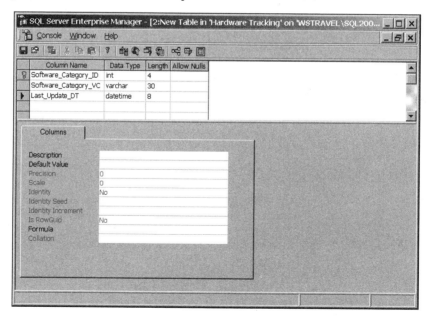

13. The next table to be created is the `Employee_T` table. Once again, the first column is both the primary key for this table and also an identity column. Take note that the **Location_ID** and **Phone_Number_VC** columns both allow null values. This is because an employee could be hired and entered into the system, but not assigned a location. The completed table is shown in the following figure:

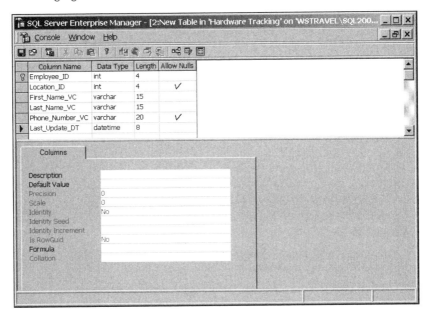

14. The last table that we need to create is the `Location_T` table. The first column is both the primary key for this table and an identity column. The completed table is shown in the next figure:

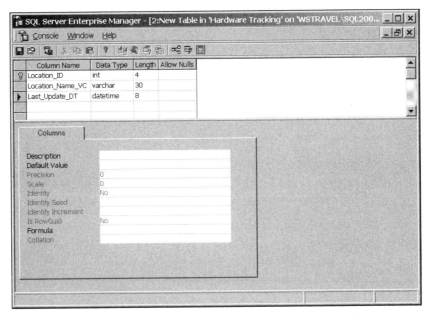

To view the tables you have just created, click on Tables in the tree pane. By default, all tables are sorted by name, thus you will see some User created tables and also some System created tables all intermingled. You can bring all of your tables to the top of the list by clicking twice on the Type header in the detail pane. The first time you click Type it sorts all tables by type, but System comes before User, so we click it again to sort the list of tables in descending order.

Creating Foreign Key Constraints

A foreign key is a key in one table that points to a primary key in another table. A foreign key constraint enforces the rules of referential integrity between the two tables, preventing the deletion or changing of the primary key in a table that is being referenced through a foreign key in another table.

There are several ways to create foreign key constraints. One is to create the constraint when the table is created. When using this method, the table that the foreign key points to must already exist. Another way is to modify the table in design view, and then create the constraint. However, by far the easiest way to create the foreign key constraints is graphically, which we will demonstrate here.

To create the foreign key constraints in our database, we need to create a **database diagram**. A database diagram is a graphical representation of the tables in your database. This graphical representation allows you to modify the table structures, indexes, and constraints graphically.

Try It Out – Create a Database Diagram

1. To create a database diagram, either click on Diagrams in the tree view, and then click on the Action menu followed by New Database Diagram, or right-click on Diagrams in the tree pane and choose New Database Diagram from the context menu. This will invoke the Create Database Diagram Wizard. The first step of the wizard is a Welcome screen, which explains what actions the wizard will perform:

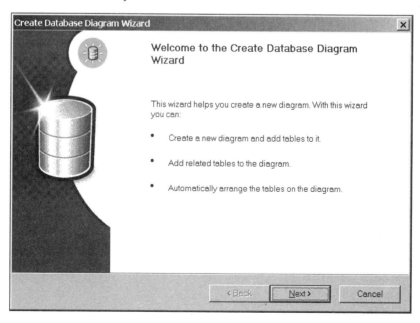

2. Click the **Next** button to proceed to the next step, which allows you to choose the tables to be added to the diagram. Notice that the **Available tables** list box contains both system and user tables. Click on each of the eight user tables that we created and then click the **Add** button to have the table(s) added to the **Tables to add to diagram** list box.

It should be noted here that this is a standard list box that allows multiple selections. Therefore, you can selectively choose tables by clicking on a table name, and then holding down the *Ctrl* key while selecting another table name. Likewise, you may choose a range of table names by clicking on the first table and then, holding down the *Shift* key, selecting the last table name.

The **Add related tables automatically** checkbox will automatically add tables that have existing foreign key constraints. Since we have not added any constraints yet, this checkbox does not apply to us. When the checkbox is checked, it allows you to choose how many levels of tables to add.

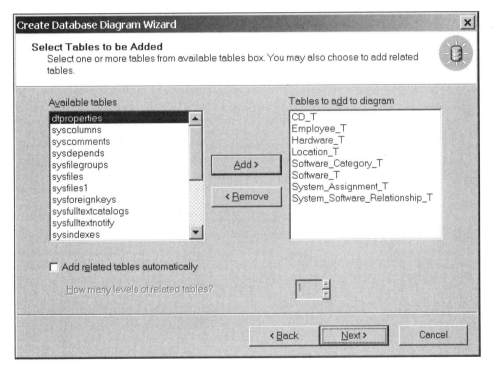

3. Once all user tables have been added, click on the **Next** button to proceed to the next step. This is the summary step – it explains what actions will be performed and summarizes your selections. View this screen carefully, clicking the **Back** button should you need to make any changes.

If you are satisfied with the selections you have made, click the Finish button to have the wizard complete the process.

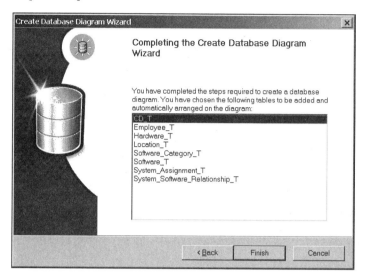

4. The wizard will add the tables selected to the database diagram and arrange them so they fit on the screen. When complete, the database diagram is displayed and the view is usually rather small. I like to increase the view by clicking on the Zoom icon and zooming in until I can read the table names. I then arrange the tables to my satisfaction, for example to match the completed database diagram that was shown at the start of this chapter. Go ahead and arrange your tables – the following figure shows how I arranged the tables in my diagram:

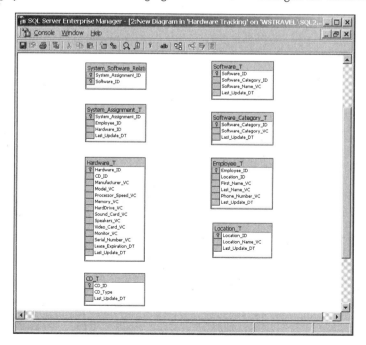

5. At this point we want to save our database diagram, so click on the Save icon. You can choose any name you wish, but it should be something descriptive. I chose the name Constraints for my database diagram.

Try It Out – Creating Foreign Key Constraints

Once you have the tables arranged to your satisfaction, you are then ready to create the foreign key constraints.

1. To begin, click on the System_Software_Relationship_T table, click on the row selector for the System_Assignment_ID column, and drag it to the System_Assignment_T table. When you release the mouse button the Create Relationship dialog appears:

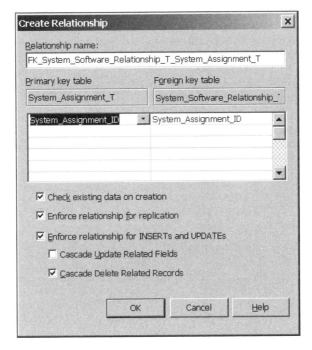

This dialog confirms the foreign key relationship with the closest match that it can determine. Unless you have multiple foreign keys all with different names, this dialog does a good job of making the correct match. If the dialog did not make the correct match in the relationship for you, you can choose the appropriate columns in the combo boxes for the Primary key table and Foreign key table.

You can change the name of the relationship if you so desire, but it is recommended that you accept the default names. This allows for consistency in your foreign key relationship names.

There are several checkboxes on this dialog, the first of which is Check existing data on creation. When this checkbox is checked, the dialog will ensure any existing data conforms to the constraints that will be created. If any existing data does not meet the rules of this constraint, an error message will be displayed.

The Enforce relationship for replication checkbox will enforce the rules of referential integrity if this table is replicated and the checkbox is checked. Replication is a method used to copy and distribute data to SQL Servers installed across your network.

The Enforce relationship for INSERTs and UPDATEs checkbox will enforce the rules of referential integrity on the foreign key table when this checkbox is checked. Along with this is the Cascade Update Related Fields checkbox. When checked, any changes made to the primary key value will be propagated to the foreign key table. This will not be an issue for us, as we have chosen the primary keys in all our tables to be identity columns. If you had a primary key that consisted of a phone number, then you would want this checkbox to be checked as the phone number could change. The last checkbox in this dialog is the Cascade Delete Related Records. When checked, SQL Server will delete all foreign key rows that reference the primary key that was deleted. We want to check this checkbox to cascade the deletes from the System_Assignment_T table to the System_Software_Relationship_T table.

2. Click the OK button to close this dialog. Once the dialog is closed, you will see that the constraint has been created and is represented by a line between System_Assignment_T and System_Software_Relationship_T tables.

3. The next foreign key constraint that we want to create is between the System_Software_Relationship_T table and the Software_T table. Click on the row selector for the Software_ID column in the System_Software_Relationship_T table, and drag it onto the Software_T table. Again, the Create Relationship dialog is displayed, with the appropriate information filled in:

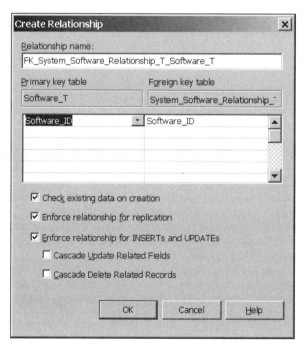

4. Click the OK button to close the dialog.

5. The next constraint to be created is in the `System_Assignment_T` table. Click on the row selector for the **Employee_ID** column and drag it onto the **Employee_T** table. If we delete an employee, we want to delete the system assignment for that employee, so we need to check the **Cascade Delete Related Records** checkbox. This will allow the deletion of an employee from the `Employee_T` table to cascade so that it also deletes the related row in the `System_Assignment_T` table.

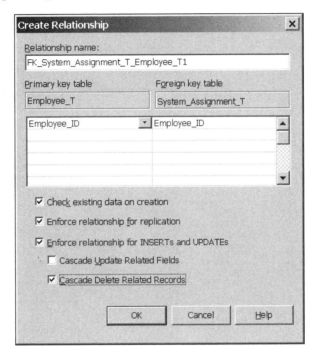

6. Click OK to close the **Create Relationship** dialog.

7. The next constraint that we want to create is between the `System_Assignment_T` table and the `Hardware_T` table. Click on the row selector for the **Hardware_ID** column in the **System_Assignment_T** table and then drag it onto the **Hardware_T** table. We do not want to cascade any deletes or updates, so just click on the **OK** button in the **Create Relationship** dialog.

8. The next constraint is between the `Hardware_T` table and `CD_T` table. Click on the row selector for the **CD_ID** column in the **Hardware_T** table and drag it onto the **CD_T** table. Accept all defaults in the **Create Relationship** dialog and click the **OK** button to close the dialog.

9. The next constraint to be created is between the `Software_T` table and the `Software_Category_T` table. Click on the row selector for the **Software_Category_ID** column in the **Software_T** table and drag it onto the **Software_Category_T** table. Accept the defaults in the **Create Relationship** dialog and click the **OK** button to close the dialog.

10. The last constraint to be created is between the `Employee_T` table and the `Location_T` table. Click on the row selector for the **Location_ID** column in the **Employee_T** table and drag it onto the **Location_T** table. We do not want to cascade any updates or deletes, so click the **OK** button to close the **Create Relationship** dialog.

Your completed database diagram should look similar to the one shown:

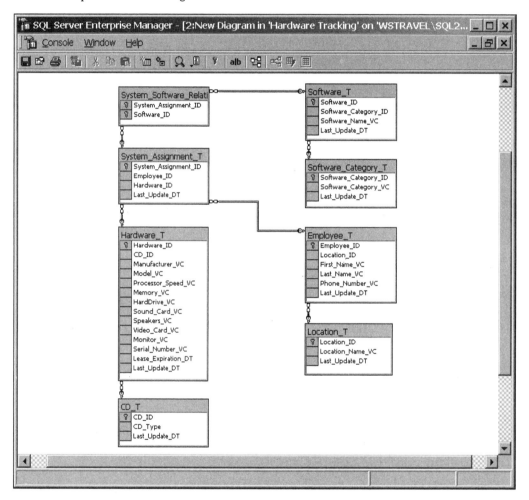

11. Save the changes you have made to the diagram. When you click the Save icon, SQL Server will prompt you with a Save dialog. It informs you that it will save the changes you have made graphically in the database diagram to your tables, in essence creating the foreign key constraints.

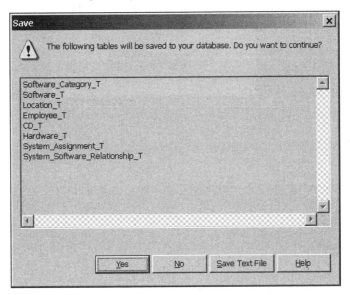

12. Click the Yes button to allow SQL Server to make these changes.

Clicking the No button will discard all changes that you have made, and no tables will be updated. Clicking the Save Text File button will allow you to save the tables that will be affected to a text file for later viewing, though it is not necessary that you actually do this. Once you save the changes to a text file you are returned to this dialog and must choose Yes or No (again, remember that you will lose the changes that you've made if you select the No option). An example of the contents of the text file is shown in the next figure:

```
/*
    Tuesday, May 30, 2000 12:32:29 PM
    User: sa
    Server: WSTRAVEL\SQL2000
    Database: Hardware Tracking
    Application: MS SQLEM - Data Tools
*/

Software_Category_T
Software_T
Location_T
Employee_T
CD_T
Hardware_T
System_Assignment_T
System_Software_Relationship_T
```

13. You can close the database diagram window by clicking the second (lower) X in the upper right-hand corner.

Additional Indexes

There are two more indexes that we want to create in our database. Looking back towards the start of this chapter at our completed database diagram, we see that we may need to select and sort data from the `Employee_T` table by first and last name. We may also want to select and sort data from the `Hardware_T` table by manufacturer. Placing indexes on these columns will speed up the process of selecting and sorting data from these tables.

We could have created these indexes when we created the tables, but this way gives you the opportunity to modify an existing table. There are several ways to create additional indexes on a table, and we will walk you through two different ways here.

Try It Out – Adding an Index to a Table

1. To create an additional index on the `Employee_T` table, click on **Tables** in the tree pane, right-click on the **Employee_T** table, and choose **Design Table** from the context menu.

2. Click on the **Table and Index Properties** icon and then click on the **Indexes/Keys** tab in the **Properties** dialog.

3. Next, click on the **New** button to create a new index. Notice that the new index has been given a default name of **IX_Employee_T**. You can change this name, but for consistency we will leave it as it is.

4. We want to choose the columns and sort order of the columns that we want indexed. Since most queries will probably want a list of employees sorted by last name first and first name last, we will select the **Last_Name_VC** column and leave the sort order for this column as **Ascending**. We also want to include the **First_Name_VC** column in this index, so we select it on the second row of the **Column name/Order** grid, as shown in the figure:

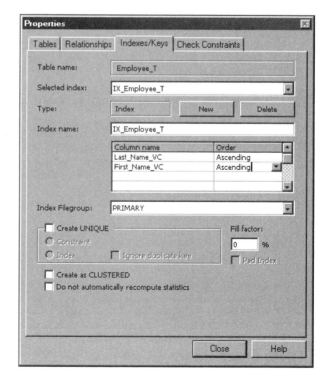

5. Since a clustered index sorts the data in the table by the key of the clustered index, we want this index to be clustered. This will keep the data rows sorted by last name and first name, providing a fast efficient search path to our data. However, when SQL Server created the index on our primary key, it created a clustered index on it. We can only have one clustered index per table, because the actual table rows are sorted, so we must modify the index on the primary key.

Select the PK_Employee_T index in the Selected index combo box, and uncheck Create as CLUSTERED at the bottom of the Properties dialog. Now, reselect the IX_Employee_T index and check the Create as CLUSTERED checkbox. Your new index should look like the one shown:

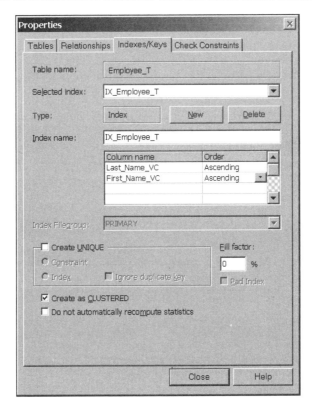

The Create UNIQUE checkbox allows you to create a unique index where there are no duplicate entries. When this checkbox is selected, the other options become available. If you were creating a constraint, you would select the Constraint option button, while you would select the Index option button to create an index. The Ignore duplicate key checkbox will ensure each index entry is unique.

Fill factor specifies how full an index page can be. By leaving this entry set to 0, SQL Server will manage this for us.

The Do not automatically recompute statistics checkbox provides an option to not automatically re-compute the statistics on our table and index. Since we have not populated this table, we can ignore this checkbox.

6. Click on the Close button to close the Properties dialog and then click on the Save icon to save the changes to our table. You will be prompted with the Save dialog informing you that changes to the Employee_T and System_Assignment_T tables will be made. This is because we have a foreign key relationship between System_Assignment_T and Employee_T and we have modified the primary key index. Click Yes to close this dialog. Then close the design view of the Employee_T table.

7. To create the additional index on the Hardware_T table, right-click on the Hardware_T table, choose All Tasks, then choose Manage Indexes.

8. In the Manage Indexes dialog, click on the New button and enter the name IX_Hardware_T in the Index name textbox.

9. The Column that we want in this new index is the Manufacturer_VC column, so check this column in this dialog.

Notice that the Clustered index checkbox is grayed out in this dialog. That's OK in this instance, as we do not want to create a clustered index on manufacturer name. The reason here is that there could be dozens of rows for each manufacturer, and the overhead of having SQL Server inserting and reordering the index to keep it clustered would not be worth it.

There are a few additional options on this dialog that were not present on the Properties dialog shown for the previous method. They are the File group checkbox and combo box, which lets you specify the **file group** in which the index should be created. This is an advanced feature to be used when you have multiple file groups. Briefly, a file group is a way to manage multiple physical database files in a single group. The Pad index checkbox leaves free space on each node of the index, and the Drop existing checkbox indicates that SQL Server should drop an existing index with the same name before creating this one.

10. Click OK to close the **Create New Index** dialog and then click Close on the Manage Indexes dialog.

At this point the creation of our database is complete. We have created the appropriate tables, SQL Server created the indexes for the primary keys for us, and we have created the foreign key constraints. We then created two additional indexes that will allow us to query the `Employee_T` and `Hardware_T` tables more efficiently.

We will be building functionality into our database in subsequent chapters as we create users and stored procedures.

Summary

This chapter has covered a lot of ground from the design and normalization of our database, to actually creating the database's tables, constraints, and indexes.

As we went through the development of our database design, you saw at first hand how important it is to follow the process of normalization. During this process, we weeded out repeating groups of data and duplicate data (data that applied to more than one row). You saw how the process of normalization created a greater number of narrow tables versus the few wide tables that we started with.

As we stepped through the wizard to physically create our database, you saw how important wizards in SQL Server can be. They introduce themselves with a Welcome screen defining what actions they perform, and then summarize the options you select prior to acting on them. They also give you a chance to go back and change any options before applying them. We saw this with the Create Database Wizard and the Create Database Diagram Wizard.

When we created our tables, we learned how we could create primary keys and change the attributes for a specific column, as we set the identity attribute for our primary key columns. We also know that SQL Server automatically creates the indexes for our primary key columns when it creates our tables.

We learned how to use the database diagram to graphically alter our tables, when we created the foreign key constraints for our tables. We also explored two different methods for creating additional indexes on tables.

To summarize, you should know how to:

- ❑ Create a relational database design
- ❑ Normalize the database design
- ❑ Create a database using the Create Database Wizard
- ❑ Create tables
- ❑ Create foreign key constraints
- ❑ Create additional indexes

In the next chapter we will explore SQL Server security features as we step through the process of adding logins and users to SQL Server and granting them authority to our database.

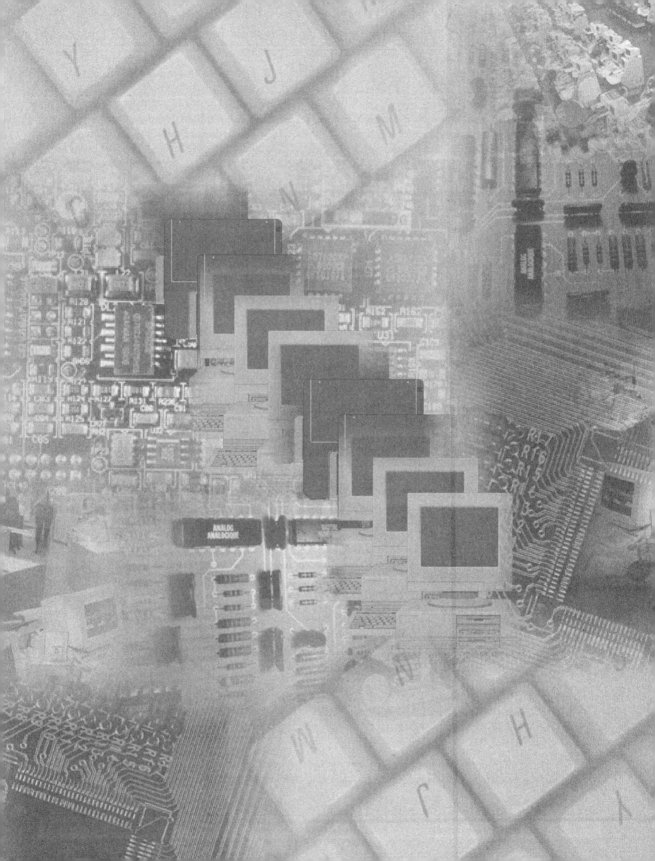

SQL Server Security

If you look at recent events, you will see that hackers have violated many systems worldwide and have caused major damage and downtime. **Security** is of importance to everyone, especially people in the technology industry. We want to do everything possible to secure our systems and data from access by unauthorized persons. This includes both malicious and accidental unauthorized access. Security is not only used to prevent unauthorized access to our database – it is also used to prevent the accidental destruction of data. How many times have you been cleaning up your hard drive and accidentally deleted a file that you wanted to keep?

SQL Server provides security features that will help to ensure that only authorized people have access to view, change, and delete data. In this chapter we will explore the security features of SQL Server 2000. These security features can restrict access to not only the different databases, but also the various database objects, such as tables, views, and stored procedures.

In this chapter we will cover:

- ❑ General security overview
- ❑ Windows authentication and SQL Server authentication
- ❑ Roles and logins
- ❑ Database security
- ❑ Database object security

General Security Overview

As we just mentioned, security is not only used to prevent unauthorized access to your data but is also used to prevent accidental destruction of your data. You may want the administrators or power users of your application to have full access, which would allow them to read, insert, update, and delete data in your database. You may want to grant the general populous read-only access to your data, so that they are able to use the data to make informed business decisions but not actually change the data. There may even be users whom you want to have insert and update permissions for data entry without being able to view or delete existing data.

SQL Server provides various levels of security, as shown in the following figure. At the top level are **logins**, the user IDs that you use to log into SQL Server and access the database. Each login can be assigned to one or more **roles**, which are the next level of security. The login is assigned permission to access one or more databases and does not have to be assigned to a role.

A role is a security group in SQL Server that has various permissions to the database in which it is defined and to database objects. A role can contain one or more users and other roles.

The bottom level of security is **permissions**. Permissions can be granted on one or more database objects that allow functions such as selecting or inserting data to be performed. Each database object has different permissions that can be assigned. We will cover this in more detail later in the chapter.

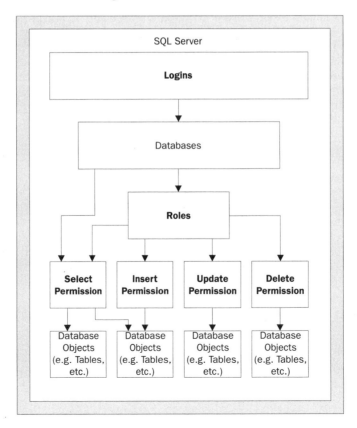

Authentication

Authentication is the method used by SQL Server to validate that your user ID and password are valid. Each login defined in SQL Server uses one of two methods of authentication: **Windows authentication** or **SQL Server authentication**.

When we walked through the installation process of SQL Server in Chapter 2, one of the options was to select the authentication mode that would be supported by SQL Server. One mode was Windows authentication mode and the other was mixed mode (Windows and SQL Server authentication). We chose to use mixed mode because not all readers will be developing on a Windows NT or Windows 2000 platform.

We will demonstrate both authentication modes in this book, so that you are aware of how to connect to SQL Server using either mode. However, our focus will be on the Windows authentication mode and this will be used in most of our examples. It is recommended that you use Windows authentication if possible as it provides the best security.

Let's take a closer look at each one of these authentication modes.

Windows Authentication

When SQL Server uses Windows authentication to validate your login, it performs a call to the Windows security features to validate that your user account information is valid and that you have logged into a Windows NT/2000 domain. It also validates that your login has permissions to log into and access SQL Server. When using this type of login, you do not have to specify a user ID or password; SQL Server will determine this from the security features of the operating system.

> **Windows authentication mode is not available on SQL Server running on Windows 98.**

What are some of the benefits of using Windows authentication? First, there is no separate user ID and password to remember; you simply need to be logged onto the network in order to gain access to SQL Server. Having only one ID/password combination is easier for the user and the administrator. Second, you get all of the benefits of Windows accounts, some of which are discussed next.

Password Expiration

Most organizations automatically expire passwords after 30 or 60 days. This will force you to change your password to minimize the security risk of someone else gaining access to your password. Passwords are usually restricted; not allowing common words and names, and not allowing you to use a specified number of previous passwords.

Account Lockout

Account lockout is also another viable security feature of Windows. It will usually lock out your user account if a user tries unsuccessfully to log onto the system with your user ID. Once an invalid password is supplied a certain number of times, the account is locked out. This helps to prevent unauthorized access to the system.

Auditing

Auditing can also be used to expose potential security threats from a user account that repeatedly tries to access data or resources for which they do not have authorization. When auditing is turned on for user accounts, you can select the types of audit actions that are to be logged, such as failed log on attempts and attempts to access sensitive data.

User Groups

User groups can also be set up in Windows and these groups can be given access to a specific database within SQL Server. For example, this would allow a department to have access to their departmental database, and as users come and go they can be added and deleted from the Windows group. No actions would be required in SQL Server.

SQL Server Authentication

SQL Server authentication uses logins (user accounts) defined in SQL Server itself. It manages these accounts internally and keeps track of passwords and permissions. Logins defined in SQL Server operate independently from those of the operating system. The user logs onto the operating system using one user ID and password, and then to gain access to SQL Server they must enter another user ID and password – one that is defined and managed in SQL Server. Benefits of using SQL Server authentication include the fact that users don't have to be part of a domain group, and it is easier to programmatically administer user information.

> **SQL Server refers to a user account as a login, whereas Windows refers to a user account as a user ID.**

Another way of managing security using SQL Server authentication is to define one user ID and password for a group of users. All users of that group can then use the same user ID and password to gain access to SQL Server. This is not recommended, and would only really be suitable for small non-mission critical applications. Note also that this is not valid for distributed applications using MTS/COM+, as they use database connection pooling. This is, however, beyond the scope of this discussion.

Roles

A role is a group that has specific permissions to perform various tasks. Logins added to a role automatically inherit the permissions of that role; you do not have to specifically grant permissions to a login. There are three types of role in SQL Server: **server roles**, **database roles**, and **user-defined database roles**. Server roles and database roles are *fixed* roles, that is, you cannot modify these roles in any way. User-defined database roles are roles that are created in a specific database and you have full control over these roles.

Let's take a look at each of these types of role and then create our own user-defined database roles.

Server Roles

There are several server roles that are defined in SQL Server. These roles allow you to perform specific administrative tasks in SQL Server, such as creating databases or configuring SQL Server settings. To view these roles, start the Enterprise Manager, expand the **Microsoft SQL Servers** group, expand **SQL Server Group** and your instance of SQL Server, expand the **Security** group, and then click on **Server Roles**:

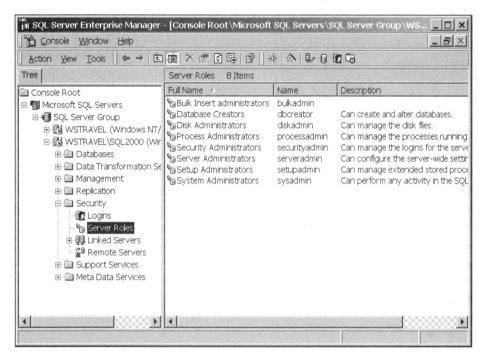

Each server role has a full name, a short name, and a description, as shown in the previous figure. The following table summarizes the server roles:

Role	Nature
bulkadmin	This role has permissions to execute the BULK INSERT statement. The BULK INSERT statement is used to copy a file into a table in your database.
dbcreator	This role is limited to creating, altering, and dropping databases.
diskadmin	This role manages disk files (which filegroups database files are assigned to, attaching and detaching databases, etc.). A filegroup is a name assigned to a group of database files and is used for administration purposes.
processadmin	This role has the capability to manage processes running in SQL Server – members of this role can kill long running processes if necessary.

Table continued on following page

Role	Nature
`securityadmin`	This role is very handy for logins that you create specifically to manage logins, read error logs, and to have `CREATE DATABASE` permissions. In many ways, this one is the classic system operator role – it can handle most of the day-to-day tasks, but doesn't have the kind of global access that a truly omnipotent super-user would have.
`serveradmin`	This role can set server-wide configuration options or shut down the server. It's rather limited in scope, yet the functions controlled by members of this role can have a very significant impact on the performance of your server.
`setupadmin`	This role is limited to managing linked servers and startup procedures.
`sysadmin`	This role can perform any activity in SQL Server. Anyone with this role is essentially an `sa` for that instance of SQL Server. The creation of this server role provides Microsoft with the capability to one day eliminate the `sa` login – indeed, the Books Online refers to `sa` as being legacy in nature.
	It's worth noting that the local NT administrators group on the SQL Server is automatically mapped into the `sysadmin` role. This means that anyone who is a member of your server's administrators group also has `sa`-level access to your SQL data. You can, if you need to, remove the NT administrators group from the `sysadmin` role to tighten that security loophole.

Database Roles

Each database in SQL Server has a set of fixed database roles. SQL Server predefines these roles and you do not have to do anything special to get them. Let's take a look at these roles in the Enterprise Manager.

Expand the Hardware Tracking database and then click on Roles. You should see the same roles as those shown in the following figure:

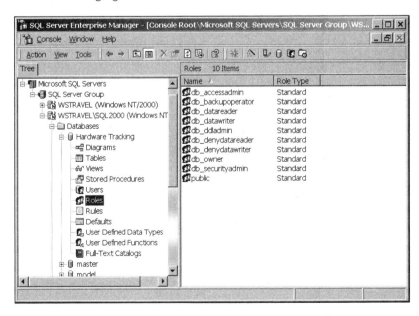

The following table summarizes each of these database roles:

Role	Nature
db_accessadmin	This role performs a portion of the functions similar to the securityadmin server role, except that this role is limited to the individual database to which it is assigned, and the creation of users (not individual rights). It cannot create new SQL Server logins, but members of this role can add NT users and groups as well as existing SQL Server logins into the database.
db_backupoperator	This role can back up the database and also issue DBCC and CHECKPOINT statements.
db_datareader	This role can issue a SELECT statement on all user tables in the database.
db_datawriter	This role can issue INSERT, UPDATE, and DELETE statements on all user tables in the database.
db_ddladmin	This role can add, modify, or drop objects in the database.
db_denydatareader	This role provides the equivalent of a DENY SELECT on every table and view in the database.
db_denydatawriter	This role is similar to db_denydatareader, only it affects INSERT, UPDATE, and DELETE statements.
db_owner	This role performs as if it were a member of all the other database roles. Using this role, you can create a situation where multiple users can perform the same functions and tasks as if they were the database owner.
db_securityadmin	This role is the database-level equivalent of the securityadmin server role. This database role cannot create new users in the database, but does manage roles and members of database roles, as well as managing statement and object permissions in the database.
public	This role is a generic role that all logins belong to.

Both server roles and database roles are designed for administrative tasks. The roles we are more interested in are user-defined database roles. These are roles that we can control and set up to perform specific actions on the data in our database.

User-Defined Database Roles

User-defined roles can be broken down into two types. First there is the **standard** role in which we can add users. The second type of user-defined role is an **application** role. This is where users can only access the database through an application, and the application must provide a password that we have chosen. This prevents direct user interaction with the database objects, and the only information users can retrieve or update is what has been specified in the code of the application.

As you can see, this is a secure method of controlling the integrity of the data, as long as you have a well-written application. You do not and cannot specify users in an application role because any user that has access to the application will have access to the database. Security within your application becomes really important at this point if your application accesses sensitive information or updates information to the database.

We want to deal with standard roles, so this is where we will be focusing our attention in this book.

Try It Out – Create a User-Defined Database Role

Given our database design, we want to create one role that has complete access to all objects in our database. The developers of the application, as well as the main users of the application, will use this role. For generic access to our application we will use the db_datareader database role.

To create the new role in our database:

1. Start the Enterprise Manager, expand the Microsoft SQL Servers group, expand the SQL Server Group group, and then expand the Hardware Tracking database.

2. Click on Roles in the tree pane, click on the Action menu, and then New Database Role. Alternatively, right-click on Roles in the tree pane and choose New Database Role from the context menu.

3. Give the new role a name of Hardware Users as shown in the following figure. Notice that the Permissions button is grayed out. We will have to come back after the role has been created to grant the appropriate permissions for this role.

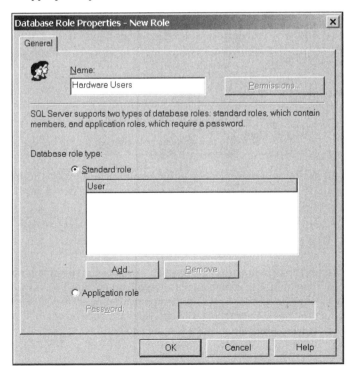

4. We have not created any users (logins) yet, so we just need to click on the OK button to close the Database Role Properties dialog.

When you have completed the steps above, you should be able to see your newly created role in the Enterprise Manager, as shown here:

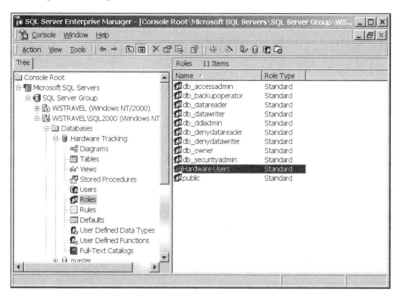

5. We want to modify the permissions on this new role, so either click on the Hardware Users role in the detail pane, click on the Action menu, and click on Properties, or right-click on the Hardware Users role and choose Properties from the context menu.

6. Click on the Permissions button to see the various database objects that we can grant permissions on.

There are two option buttons on this next dialog, as shown in the following figure. The first option button, List all objects, will list all database objects in our database. As we want to be able to see what objects are available we select this option. We do this so that we can see which permissions to grant for this role. The second option button, List only objects with permissions for this role, will only list the objects that this role has permissions to. You would use this option button if you just wanted to see what objects this role has permissions for.

The objects that we are interested in are the tables that we have created in the last chapter, and they are listed at the top of the dialog. Each table has several checkboxes and we will look at what each one means.

❑ The SELECT checkbox, when checked, means this role has permissions to select data from this table using the SELECT SQL statement.

❑ The INSERT checkbox, when checked, means that this role has permission to insert data into the table using the INSERT SQL statement.

❑ The UPDATE checkbox, when checked, means this role has permission to update data in the table using the UPDATE SQL statement.

❑ The DELETE checkbox, when checked, means this role has permission to delete data from this table using the DELETE SQL statement.

❑ The EXEC permission checkbox will be addressed later.

❑ The DRI (Declarative Referential Integrity) checkbox, when checked, allows this role to check the data integrity of this table. We'll discuss this in a little more detail later in the chapter.

7. We are only interested in allowing this role to select, insert, update, and delete data from tables, so check those checkboxes for all of the eight tables that we have created:

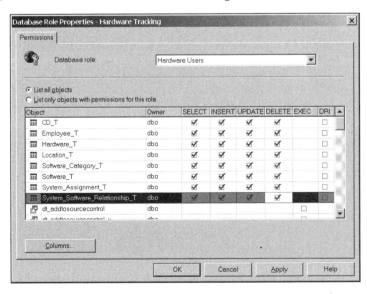

8. Click the Apply button to have these permissions applied to this role and then click OK to close the Database Role Properties dialog.

Creating Logins

As we discussed earlier, user accounts in SQL Server are called logins and contain a user ID and password. Each login in SQL Server can be granted access to one or more databases and system- or database-defined roles. For our application, we want to create three logins.

The first login will be for us as the developers, the second login will be for the main user of your application, and the third will be the login that is used to access this application from the Web, which we will be using later in Chapters 14 and 15.

There are several ways to create a new login and since we have three logins to create, we will explore three different ways to do this.

Try It Out – Create a New Login Using Windows Authentication

The first login that we want to create is our own login, which will use Windows authentication mode. Since we are the developers of this application, we will need to have special access to the database and be able to create any database objects that we need (stored procedures, views, etc.). Thus, when we create our login we will assign it to the database role db_owner in addition to the hardware users role.

> **Those readers who are using Windows 98 should review the next Try It Out section first, to see how to create a login that uses SQL Server authentication.**

To create this new login:

1. Expand the Security group in the Enterprise Manager and click on Logins in the tree pane, as shown in the following figure:

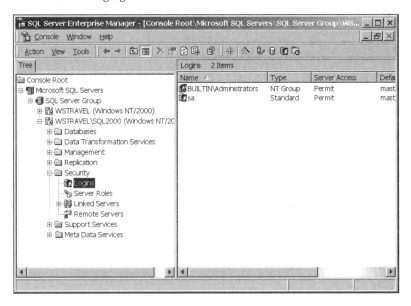

2. Either click on the Action menu and then click on New Login, or right-click on Logins in the tree pane and select New Login in the context menu.

3. This login will use Windows Authentication – this mode is already checked. Enter your login name in the Name textbox, or click on the browse button (...) and select a login name.

4. Select your domain in the Domain combo box.

5. Select the Hardware Tracking database in the Database combo box.

6. Select the appropriate language in the Language combo box.

There are two option buttons that allow you to grant or deny access to logins that are set up using Windows authentication mode. This allows you to temporarily deny a user access to SQL Server without removing their login from SQL Server. If this login was set up to use SQL Server authentication then these options would be grayed out.

The Server Roles tab in the SQL Server Login Properties dialog lists all the server roles that are available, and will allow you to select the appropriate server role that this login should be added to. We are not going to add this login to any server roles.

7. Click on the Database Access tab and then check the Permit checkbox next to the Hardware Tracking database.

Once you check a checkbox for a database, the database roles for that database are displayed in the list box at the bottom of the dialog.

8. Since we want to add this login to the db_owner database role, check the checkbox next to db_owner.

The Properties button at the bottom of the screen will allow you to add other users and user-defined roles to the db_owner database role.

9. We also want to add this login to the hardware users role, so scroll down to the bottom of the Database roles list and check the checkbox next to Hardware Users.

10. Click the OK button to have the login added to the database with the appropriate permissions.

Once the login has been added to SQL Server, you will see it listed under Logins, as shown in the next figure:

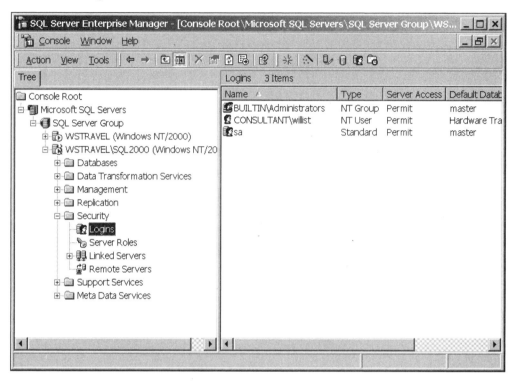

When this login was added, it was added with the appropriate permissions already granted because we added it to existing roles that had the permissions applied. This means that this login inherits the permissions of the roles to which it was assigned.

Try It Out – Create a New Login Using SQL Server Authentication

Let's assume that several people will be using our application. However, we are only going to set up one login, so let's choose a name and create a new login that will use SQL Server authentication. When we create this login we will be doing so from within our database. This is the second method that can be used to create a new login.

To create this login:

1. Expand the Databases group and then expand the Hardware Tracking database. Click on Users.

2. Either click on the Action menu and then click on New Database User, or right-click on Users in the tree pane and choose New Database User from the context menu.

3. In the Database User Properties dialog, select <new> for the Login Name. This will invoke the SQL Server Login Properties dialog.

4. Enter the login name that you want to assign to this user. You can choose any name that you want; it can be up to 128 characters long and can include digits and symbols. I chose to use Stephanie.

5. Select SQL Server Authentication and then enter a password for this user. The password I entered was stephanie.

6. Select the Hardware Tracking database in the Database combo box and select the appropriate language in the Language combo box.

When you have entered this information, your dialog should look similar to the one shown in the next figure:

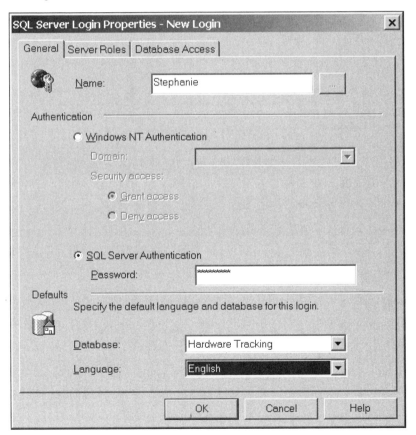

7. Click on the Database Access tab and check the checkbox next to the Hardware Tracking database.

8. The database roles for the Hardware Tracking database will then be listed in the listbox at the bottom of this dialog. Scroll to the bottom of the list and check the Hardware Users role.

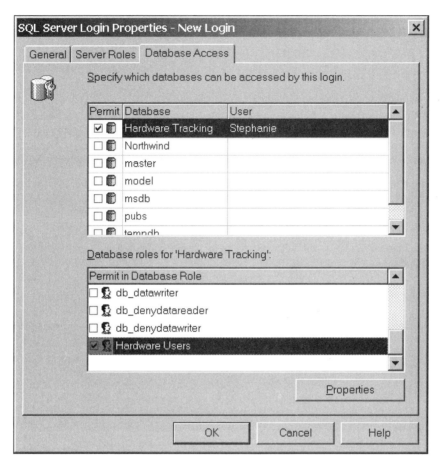

9. Click the OK button. You will then be prompted with the Confirm Password dialog.

10. Re-enter the password for this new login and then click the OK button.

11. Click the Cancel button to cancel the Database User Properties dialog. (The login was created for us in the SQL Server Properties – New Login dialog, so we just need to cancel out of this dialog.)

You should now see three users listed in the Users group in your database, as shown in the following figure. The login CONSULTANT\willis is the Windows account that was added when I added a login that uses Windows authentication. You should see your own login here, with the domain that you are logged into and your Windows user account.

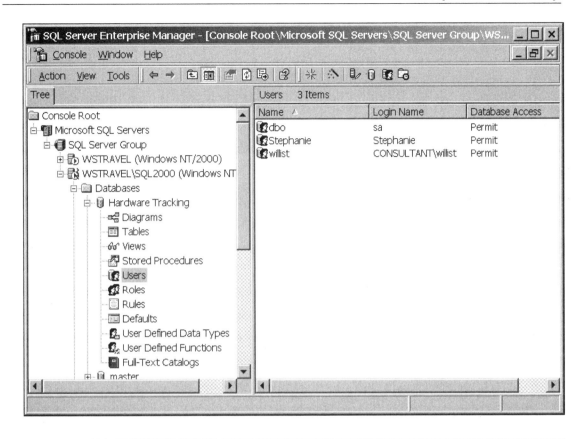

Try It Out – Create a New Login Using the Create Login Wizard

The last login that we want to create in our database is the login that will be used by our web pages that we will develop later in the book. This login will only have SELECT access to the tables, as our web pages will be used for reporting only.

To create this login:

1. On the Tools menu select Wizards.

   Ensure that you have either clicked on the named instance of SQL Server or any node below it in the tree pane. Otherwise, the Select Wizard dialog will only display the Register Server Wizard.

2. In the Select Wizard dialog, expand the **Database** group, click on the **Create Login Wizard**, and then click the **OK** button:

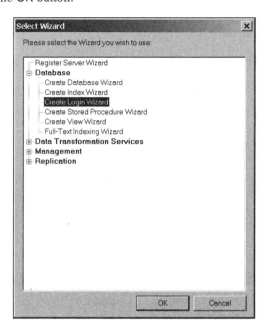

3. Like the other wizards that we have worked with so far, this wizard also provides a **Welcome** screen that informs you what actions it will perform. Click the **Next** button to proceed to the next step.

4. For this login we want to choose SQL Server authentication mode, so click this option, as shown in the next figure. Then click the Next button to proceed to the next step.

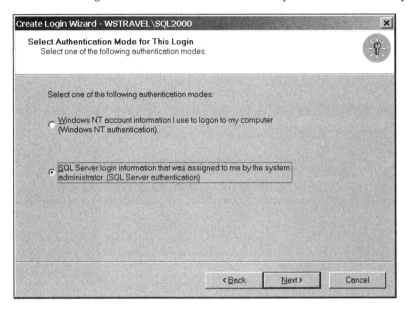

5. The next step of the wizard allows us to choose a Login ID and Password for this new user. Since this login will be used exclusively by our application, and not an individual user, I chose to assign a name HardwareApplication in the Login ID field. I chose a password of hardware and placed it in the Password and Confirm Password fields. Once you have completed the fields, click the Next button to proceed.

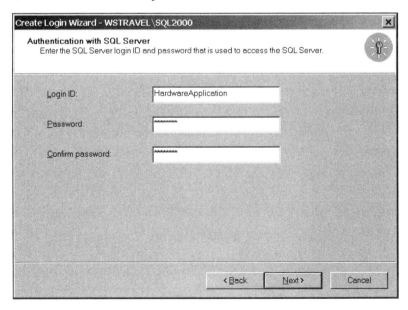

6. The next step of the wizard allows us to place this new login in one or more **Server roles**. Since we do not want to grant this login this type of permission, do not select anything on this screen, simply click the **Next** button to proceed.

7. The next step of the wizard will list all available databases. We can choose one or more databases that this new login should have access to. Since we only want this login to have access to the **Hardware Tracking** database, we just need to check the checkbox next to this database. Click the **Next** button to proceed to the next step.

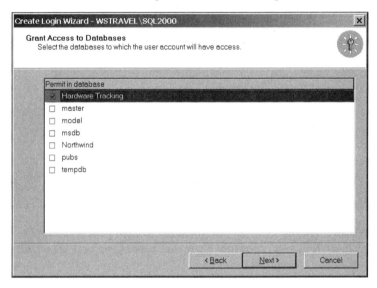

8. The last step of the wizard summarizes what actions it will take. Review these actions and click the **Back** button if you want to change any of your options. Otherwise, click the **Finish** button to have the wizard create the login.

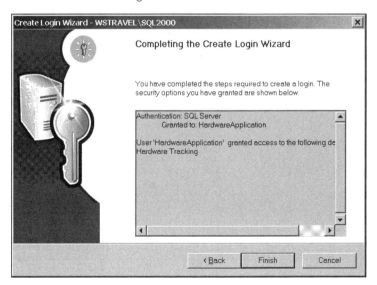

120

9. Once the wizard has completed creating the new login, it will display the Wizard Complete dialog as shown next. Click the OK button to finish this process.

It should be noted that creating a login this way does not give us the opportunity to assign this login to any database roles or user-defined roles during the creation process. We must do this manually, which we will cover next.

Try It Out – Assign the New Login to a Database Role

Since this login will be used by our web pages to produce reports, this login needs read-only access to our data. A database role already exists for this purpose (db_datareader), so we will use this role instead of creating a new one.

To assign this new login to the db_datareader database role:

1. Expand the Databases group in the Enterprise Manager, expand the Hardware Tracking database, and then click on Roles in the tree pane.

2. Click on the db_datareader role in the detail pane and either click on the Action menu and then click on Properties, or right-click on db_datareader and then choose Properties from the context menu.

3. Click on the Add button to display a list of all logins and roles defined in our database, as shown in the Add Role Members dialog in the following figure.

4. Click on the HardwareApplication login and then click the OK button to have this login added to the role:

5. Click the OK button in the Database Role Properties dialog to complete the addition of this login to the role:

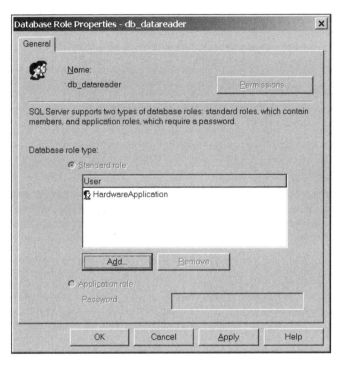

This takes care of adding all roles and logins to our database. We have created a user-defined role and logins, and have assigned these logins to various roles in our database. This allows us to grant permissions to a few roles instead of trying to maintain permissions at the login level. This simplifies the task of administering security in our database.

Database Security

When we add a new login to SQL Server, it does not mean it automatically has access to our database. When we set up a login, we grant the login permission to see our database and to be a user of our database. Any further permissions within the database are not automatically granted.

When we add a login to a role, the login inherits the permissions of that role. However, we must also grant that role security permissions to the various objects in our database, as we did when we created the hardware users role earlier.

SQL Server implements security at the object level. That is, SQL Server controls the security level for each individual object. This means that each table, view, trigger, and stored procedure that we define is secure. We can grant a user access to one table but not to another. We can also grant a user SELECT permissions to one table while granting them INSERT permissions to another. We can even grant users and roles column level permissions in a table, allowing them to select data from one column but not another.

Object Security

As we discovered in Chapter 1, a database contains many objects, such as tables, indexes, views, and stored procedures. Knowing that security in SQL Server is implemented at the object level, we also need to be aware that each object has different permissions that can be set. For example, tables have security permissions that can be set for SELECT, INSERT, UPDATE, and DELETE operations, as we saw earlier in this chapter. Stored procedures on the other hand, implement security permissions that allow a user to execute the stored procedure; as such there are no SELECT, INSERT, UPDATE, or DELETE permissions for a stored procedure.

The next few sections will discuss the various objects and security permissions that can and will be set for use in the rest of this book.

Table Security

Security can be implemented on table objects at various levels and can be implemented for logins and/or roles. Object security applies to individual table objects – each table has permissions that must be set before logins or roles can access data in that table. You can implement security on a table object at the column level or at the table level. We will be implementing security at the table level in our exercises.

The various permissions that we can grant users are SELECT, INSERT, UPDATE, and DELETE, as well as DRI, which is outside the scope of this book. Briefly, DRI (Declarative Referential Integrity) is a constraint that checks and alters the data integrity for a specific table, such as adding a new foreign key constraint. If we grant a user SELECT permissions to a table, they have the appropriate authority to select data, for read-only purposes, from all rows in our table. INSERT permissions allow users to insert new data into our tables, while UPDATE permissions allow users to update the existing data in our tables. When we grant DELETE permissions to a login, they can delete rows of data from our table.

Column Security

Each table contains one or more columns of data. When we grant permissions on a table, we can drill down even further to the column level. This allows us to grant access to the data in one column while denying access to data in another column. This could be useful if you had a payroll table, and you needed one user to be able to select data from all columns except the Salary column.

When dealing with column level security, there are two levels of security that can be granted for each column in a table. The first is SELECT permission, which only allows a user to select data from this column. The second is UPDATE permission, which allows a user to perform any action (such as insert, update, delete) on a column. Of course, if you did not check any permissions for a column, then the user would not be able to access the data in that column at all.

View Security

If you recall our discussion from Chapter 1, a view is a virtual representation of data from one or more columns from one or more tables. The code for a view is stored as it would be for a stored procedure, in that the actual SQL statements that get executed to open the view are stored in the database. The virtual table is built when the view is executed. View security is implemented in the same manner as security for tables, thereby also allowing you to drill down to the column level. Each view represents an object in the database, and can have the same permissions granted to it as could be for a table.

Stored Procedure Security

A stored procedure is a group of Transact-SQL (T-SQL) statements that are stored in the database. Stored procedures can be coded to select data, insert data, update data, and delete data, or can provide a combination of these services. Since stored procedures return rows of data and do not actually contain data themselves, security is implemented on stored procedures a little differently from how it is on tables and views.

Security is still implemented at the object level and each stored procedure is considered an object. However, since stored procedures do not actually contain data, the only permissions that can be granted are EXECUTE permissions. This allows a user to execute the stored procedure and retrieve the data returned.

We will cover more on stored procedure security in the upcoming chapters when we start creating stored procedures. When we create a stored procedure we will need to grant permissions on that stored procedure before other users can execute it, and we will cover this in the chapters that deal with stored procedures.

Summary

This chapter has taken a detailed look at the security features of SQL Server. We have taken a look at how SQL Server implements security at different levels, starting with authentication modes. We have explored logins and the various methods by which they can be created, as well as user-defined roles, server roles, and database roles.

We have also taken a look at object-level security and know that each database object implements various security features. For example, we know that tables implement security by allowing us to specify SELECT, INSERT, UPDATE, and DELETE permissions, while stored procedures allow us to specify EXECUTE permission.

Each object that is created in the database is secure. In other words, you must specifically grant permissions in that object to the various roles and/or logins before they can access that object. This is an important security feature of SQL Server.

In summary, you should know:

❑ The difference between Windows authentication and SQL Server authentication

❑ What logins are, and how to create them

❑ What roles are, how to use them, and how to create user-defined roles

❑ The importance of using roles to simplify the administrative tasks of maintaining security

❑ How object-level security is implemented

The next chapter will take a detailed look at the Query Analyzer and its features. This invaluable tool aids developers in writing and executing queries and stored procedures.

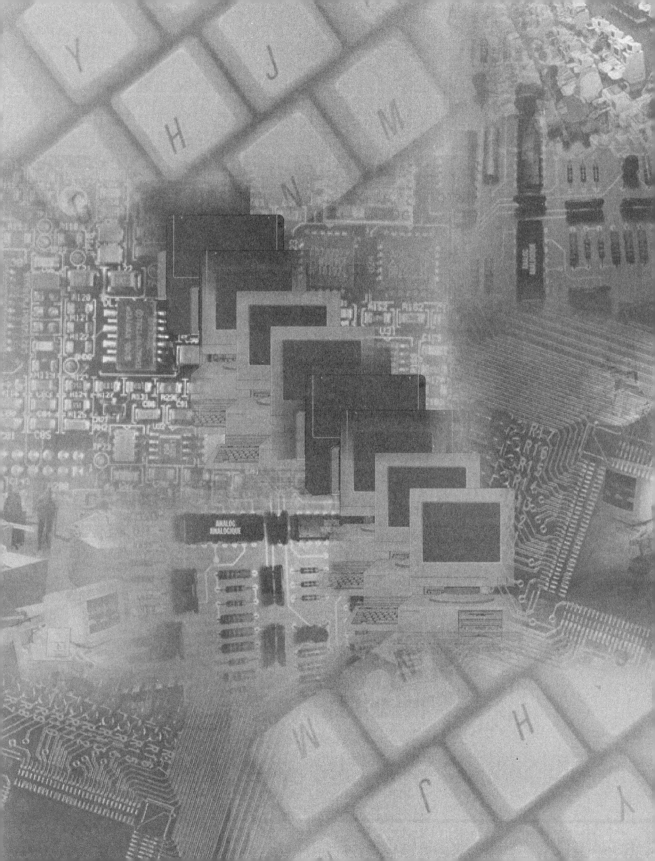

SQL Server Query Analyzer

The last chapter dealt with SQL Server security and, during the process of creating new logins and roles, you got a chance to explore more of the features and functionality of the Enterprise Manager. You should now be pretty familiar with that tool.

This chapter expands on SQL Server tools by taking a detailed look at the **Query Analyzer**, a tool that can aid developers in creating and debugging queries and stored procedures. From a developer stand point, this will be the main SQL Server tool that you use when developing a database application.

The Query Analyzer is a powerful tool that has lots of features. While we do not have space in this chapter to cover every feature of the Query Analyzer, we will cover most of them and certainly the more important ones. As we progress through this chapter we will also be introducing some T-SQL statements that will be covered in more depth in the remainder of the book.

So, this chapter will cover:

- ❑ An overview of the Query Analyzer
- ❑ Connections to SQL Server
- ❑ The SQL Server Object Browser
- ❑ `SELECT`, `INSERT`, `UPDATE`, and `DELETE` T-SQL statements
- ❑ Queries and debugging
- ❑ Templates

Query Analyzer Overview

As we have mentioned several times, the Query Analyzer is a tool that aids developers in writing and debugging queries and stored procedures. So what exactly is a query? A **query** is one or more T-SQL statements that will interrogate and/or manipulate data in your database. (Remember, T-SQL is the language used to communicate with SQL Server.) Queries are not stored in the database, but you can save query scripts to a file and open them later to re-execute them.

Stored procedures are very similar to queries and sometimes they even start out as queries. However, stored procedures are stored in the database as objects. These stored procedures can then be executed in the Query Analyzer or from your VB programs or Active Server Pages.

Where do stored procedures and queries differ? Queries are written and executed from within the Query Analyzer and do not accept or return parameters. Stored procedures, on the other hand, can accept and return parameters, and they can be executed from the Query Analyzer, VB programs, or Active Server Pages. Because queries are not stored in the database, they are usually used for one-off checks of the data, or simple checks carried out infrequently.

Some of the tasks the Query Analyzer can be used for are:

- ❏ Creating and debugging queries
- ❏ Creating and debugging stored procedures
- ❏ Creating database objects using T-SQL statements and predefined templates
- ❏ Monitoring and debugging query and stored procedure performance
- ❏ Inserting and updating data in your tables graphically

The Query Analyzer is also fully customizable in that you can add buttons to the toolbar and also create your own shortcut keys. You can also add your own menu items to the Tools menu to execute programs, command files, and batch files.

Starting and Connecting

There are a couple of ways to start the Query Analyzer. First, you can start it from the Enterprise Manager by clicking on the Tools menu and then clicking on SQL Query Analyzer. Using this method will start the Query Analyzer and use the login that was used to register the instance of SQL Server that you are working with, which in most cases is the sa login.

You can also start the Query Analyzer by navigating to the Microsoft SQL Server program group and clicking on Query Analyzer. Using this method, the Query Analyzer will start and prompt you for your login, as shown in the following figure:

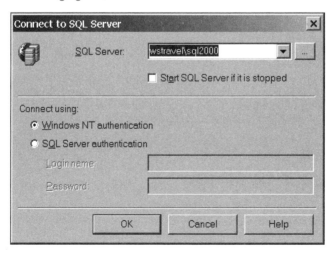

If your login was set up in SQL Server to use Windows authentication, then all you need to do is click the OK button. If, however, your login was set up in SQL Server to use SQL Server authentication then you must select the **SQL Server authentication** option button and specify your Login name and Password.

You can use the browse button to search for the instance of SQL Server you want to connect with, and if that SQL server is not currently running, it can be started from this dialog.

If you are using the first method to start the Query Analyzer, be aware that the connection made from the Query Analyzer to SQL Server uses the login from the Enterprise Manager. In most circumstances this is OK, but any objects that you create (for example, stored procedures) will be prefixed with the login that is used in the Query Analyzer. Thus, if you started the Query Analyzer from the Enterprise Manager and you registered your instance of SQL Server in the Enterprise Manager using the sa login, then your stored procedures will have a user prefix of dbo (database owner). We will cover more on stored procedure user prefixes in Chapter 7. It does not matter which way you start the Query Analyzer, but you should ensure you are using the correct login. This can be verified by looking in the title bar to see if your login or the sa login is being displayed. If your login is not being displayed then close the current query window, choose the Connect menu item from the File menu, and specify your login details.

The following figure shows the various windows in the Query Analyzer. Notice that on the left of the Query Analyzer is the **Object Browser** and to the right are the **query window** and **results pane**. Note that the Query Analyzer allows you to have multiple query windows opened, and each query window can use a different connection. We will be exploring this feature in much greater detail later in this chapter.

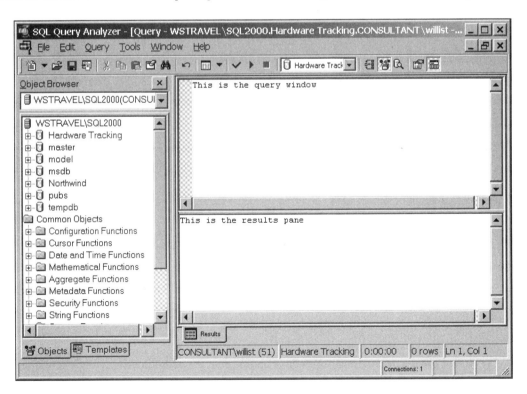

Menus

The Query Analyzer provides several key menu items that contain important features and functionality, so let's review the menus and menu items in this tool. As with any well-behaved Windows application, the Query Analyzer will disable menu items that are not available for the task you are performing.

File Menu

Starting with the File menu, there are various items available. Most should already be familiar to you but let's cover them all, as they perform slightly differently in the Query Analyzer than they do in other applications.

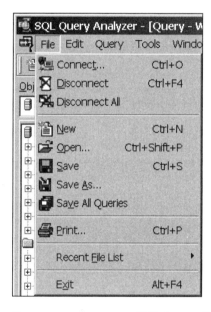

❑   The Connect menu item allows you to connect to SQL Server. Clicking this menu item will invoke the Connect to SQL Server dialog that was shown earlier in the chapter. The Query Analyzer allows you to open multiple query windows and each query window can be connected using a different login. Once you connect, a new query window is opened with that connection.

❑   The Disconnect menu item will disconnect the login in the current query window and close the current window. If you have a query in that window, the Query Analyzer will prompt you to save your changes.

❑   As you might have already guessed, the Disconnect All menu item will disconnect all connections and close all query windows, again prompting you to save all unsaved queries.

❑   The New menu item opens a new query window using the login and connection associated with the currently displayed query window.

❑   The Open menu item will allow you to open any previously saved queries or query results.

❑   The Save menu item allows you to save a query or the results from an executed query or stored procedure. It also allows you to save custom templates that you create. A template is a saved file that contains T-SQL statements that can be reused and executed again and again. Templates will be covered at the end of this chapter.

- ❏ The Save As menu item will allow you to save a new or previously saved query, query results or template to a new file.

- ❏ The Save All Queries menu item will save all queries in all windows. If the queries have not been previously saved, you will be prompted for a name to save each query as.

- ❏ The Print menu item allows you to print a query or query results. To print a query, position the cursor in the query window and then click this menu item. To print the results of a query, position the cursor in the results pane and then click this menu item.

- ❏ The Recent File List menu item will display a sub-menu of recently opened and saved files.

- ❏ The Exit menu item will close all query windows and shut down the Query Analyzer. You are prompted to save any unsaved queries.

Edit Menu

Moving on to the Edit menu, shown in the following figure, we see that there are many items that we have come to expect in all Windows applications. Since most of these menu items are common and standard (such as Cut, Copy, and Paste) we will not cover them here. We will, however, cover the non-standard Edit menu items.

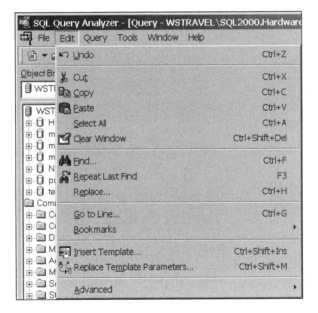

- ❏ The Clear Window menu item will clear the contents of the current query window. Thus, if you have an existing query and want to quickly remove it so you can enter another query, this menu item will do the trick.

- ❏ The Go to Line menu item will display a dialog allowing you to enter a line number in your query. When you click the OK button, the line that was specified will be highlighted and your cursor will be placed at the beginning of that line.

- ❏ The Bookmarks menu item displays a sub-menu that allows you to set, navigate, and clear bookmarks in your query.

❑ The Insert Template menu item will open any existing template in a query window and allow you to modify it.

❑ The Replace Template Parameters menu item will invoke the Replace Template Parameters dialog, which lists any and all parameters in a query created from a template. This allows you to replace the default values for parameters in the template with the values of your choosing. We will cover this in more depth in the section that discusses templates.

❑ The Advanced menu item displays a sub-menu that will allow you to change selected text to lower case or upper case. You can also increase and decrease indents, and comment and uncomment sections of code.

As you can see, the Edit menu provides some very powerful and useful features.

Query Menu

Moving on to the Query menu, we can see there are a lot of features in this menu too:

❑ The Change Database menu item allows you to switch to another database. This will change the database that the query in the current query window will execute against.

❑ The Parse menu item will parse your query for errors. This can be especially useful when you have large queries. This menu item will only parse the query for syntax and does not validate any database objects such as tables or column names.

❑ The Execute menu item will execute the query or stored procedure in the current query window.

❑ The Cancel Executing Query menu item will stop an executing query. This can be a lifesaver for queries that get hung up in a loop.

❑ The Display Estimated Execution Plan menu item will display the execution plan that SQL Server is most likely to execute when it runs your query. An execution plan is a graphical representation of the T-SQL statements that were executed and the resources that SQL Server used to execute those statements.

❑ The Index Tuning Wizard menu item will invoke the Index Tuning Wizard. This wizard will examine the current indexes on your tables and recommend any new indexes that will help improve performance.

❑ The Results in Text menu item will display the results of your query or stored procedure as text in the results pane. This is the default for executed queries and stored procedures.

❑ The Results in Grid menu item will display the results of your query or stored procedure in a grid in the results pane. This enables you to save the results and then open them using Microsoft Excel, where the data will then automatically be placed in columns and rows in the spreadsheet.

❑ The Results to File menu item will send the results of your query or stored procedure directly to a file.

❑ The Show Execution Plan menu item will display the actual execution plan that was carried out by SQL Server when your query or stored procedure was executed. It should be noted here that if you want to see the execution plan, this menu item has to be checked *before* you run your query.

❑ The Show Server Trace menu item will show all statements executed by SQL Server to complete your query. Information such as duration, reads, and writes is available for each statement. Like Show Execution Plan, if you want to utilize this option, then this menu item must be checked *before* you run your query or stored procedure.

❑ The Show Client Statistics menu item is very similar to Show Server Trace, except that it shows client statistics, such as the number of SELECT statements executed and the number of rows affected by the statement. Again, if you want to see these results, you must check this item *before* running your query or stored procedure.

❑ The Current Connection Properties menu item displays the connection properties for the current connection. All of the various connection properties, such as Set ansi_nulls and Set quoted_identifier, are displayed and you can change the options for the current connection. This menu item is particularly useful for turning off the row count message and limiting the number of rows that a query or stored procedure returns.

Tools Menu

The Tools menu, while small, provides some big features, which we will cover here. The following figure shows the available items for the Tools menu:

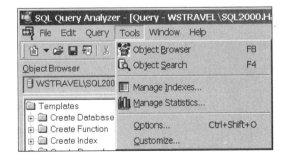

❑ The Object Browser menu item, which is usually checked by default, hides and shows the Object Browser in the Query Analyzer. The Object Browser allows you to view and manage the objects in your database such as tables, columns, and stored procedures.

❑ The Object Search menu item will invoke the Object Search function – this allows you to search for database objects. If a resulting match is found, the database name of the object is returned along with the object owner, object name, and object type.

❑ The Manage Indexes menu item will invoke the Manage Indexes dialog. You can create and edit indexes for the current or any other database in SQL Server.

❑ The Manage Statistics menu item allows you to create and edit statistics on columns in your tables. SQL Server uses these statistics to estimate the processing cost in terms of resources used when executing queries.

❑ The Options menu item invokes the Options dialog, which allows you to set and change various options within the Query Analyzer, such as editor, fonts, and scripting options.

❑ The Customize menu item allows you to set up and define your own shortcut keys and menu items on the Tools menu. This menu item allows you to customize the Query Analyzer to make it more productive for you to use.

Window Menu

While most of the menu items in the Window menu are standard, there are a few that deserve some discussion. All available items in the Window menu are shown in the following figure, but we will only be discussing the first three:

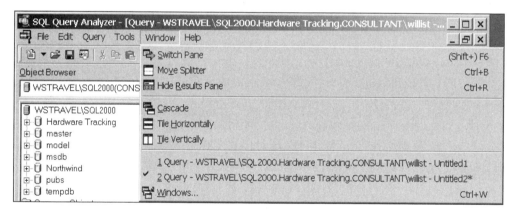

❑ The Switch Pane menu item will switch the cursor from the query window to the results pane or from the results pane to the query window.

❑ The Move Splitter menu item will highlight the splitter bar and allow you to move the splitter bar up or down, increasing or decreasing the query window and results pane.

❑ The Hide Results Pane will hide the results pane. Note that this menu item simply hides the results pane – it does not clear the contents of the results pane. When this menu item is clicked, it is replaced with the Show Results Pane menu item.

Help Menu

Like the Window menu, the Help menu provides some standard menu items in addition to a few special ones, which we will discuss here. The complete Help menu is shown in the next figure:

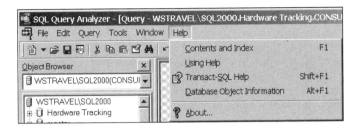

❑ The Transact-SQL Help menu item will open the SQL Server Books Online and display the index and help topic for the keyword on which the cursor is currently positioned. If there is more than one topic for the keyword identified then that keyword will be listed in the index and you can choose the topic to display. If your cursor is not on a particular keyword, then the keyword closest to the cursor will be used.

❑ The Database Object Information menu item will display information about the currently highlighted database object. Note that the database object (such as table name or column name) must be highlighted.

Toolbar

As with any other Windows application, the toolbar displays some of the same icons found in the various menus, and provides a one-click shortcut to using the corresponding menu items. Each toolbar icon provides a tool tip that can be viewed if you hover your mouse pointer over it. Some toolbar icons also have a down arrow next to the icon indicating that multiple options are provided.

The following figure details the toolbar icons and lists their corresponding menu items:

Icon	Name	Corresponds to
	New Query	Corresponds to File>New
	Load SQL Script	Corresponds to File>Open
	Save Query/Results	Corresponds to File>Save
	Insert Template	Corresponds to Edit>Insert Template
	Cut	Corresponds to Edit>Cut
	Copy	Corresponds to Edit>Copy
	Paste	Corresponds to Edit>Paste
	Clear Query Window	Corresponds to Edit>Clear Window
	Find	Corresponds to Edit>Find
	Undo	Corresponds to Edit>Undo
	Execute Mode	Corresponds to six Query menu items
	Parse Query	Corresponds to Query>Parse
	Execute Query	Corresponds to Query>Execute
	Cancel Query Execution	Corresponds to Query>Cancel Executing Query
	Database Combo Box	Corresponds to Query>Change Database
	Display Estimated Execution Plan	Corresponds to Query>Display Estimated Execution Plan
	Object Browser	Corresponds to Tools>Object Browser
	Object Search	Corresponds to Tools>Object Search
	Current Connection Properties	Corresponds to Query>Current Connection Properties
	Show Results Pane	Corresponds to Window>Show Results Pane

135

Selecting a Database

When you first start the Query Analyzer and log in using the `sa` login, the `master` database is the database that you are connected to by default. If you log in with your own login, the database that your login is associated with is the database that you will be connected to. As we mentioned earlier when we were exploring the menu options, you can select a different database to perform a query against. You can do this either from the Query menu or from the change database combo box on the toolbar. You can select a different database for each query window.

You can select any database you want, but you will only be able to run queries against the databases for which you are authorized. If you try to run a query against a database for which you do not have the appropriate permissions, you will receive an error message.

To change the database for the current window, select the appropriate database in the change database combo box from the toolbar. Alternatively, the database can be set in the Select Database dialog when using the Query Change Database menu item. Once you have changed the database for the current window, you can then execute your queries against that database.

You can switch back and forth between databases in the same query window, but the query you are executing must contain the objects defined in that database. Otherwise you will receive an Invalid Object Name error message because the objects do not exist in that database. For example, you can execute a query against the `CD_T` table in the `Hardware Tracking` database and then select the `Northwind` database. However, the `CD_T` table does not exist in the `Northwind` database, so you must change your query to reflect the objects that do exist in that database.

Object Browser

The Object Browser contained in the Query Analyzer is much different from the Object Browser contained in VB. This Object Browser provides information about the objects contained in your databases (such as tables, views, stored procedures) and is therefore a particularly powerful feature of the Query Analyzer. It allows you to drill down on each object and get details about that object.

Looking at the following figure, we can see that we can drill down to the column level of the tables in our database, and the data type for that column, as well as whether or not the column allows null values, will also be displayed:

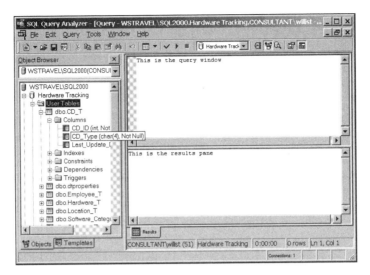

We can also drill down into the details of our stored procedures and examine what parameters each stored procedure expects, as well as the data type for each parameter, and the parameter's direction. We will explore this more later, starting in Chapter 7.

In addition to providing information about our database objects, the Object Browser also displays helpful information about the **common objects** defined in SQL Server. This includes information about common T-SQL functions that we can use in our queries and stored procedures, as well as SQL Server data types.

The following figure shows the details of the string function CHARINDEX. When you hover your mouse over a function, the Query Analyzer will display a tool tip for that function giving a brief explanation of what actions that function performs. As you can see in the next figure, you can also drill down into the details of that function to determine what parameters it expects, as well as the data types for those parameters:

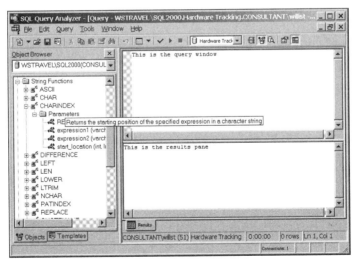

Notice that at the bottom of the Object Browser there are two tabs. The first is the Objects tab, which is the one that we have been working with so far. The second tab is the Templates tab, which we will cover towards the end of this chapter.

Query Analyzer Color Coding Scheme

When you enter code in the query window, the Query Analyzer will color code the various statements, just like the VB IDE does. Once you have a feel for the color-coding scheme you will know when you have misspelled a keyword or function name.

The following table outlines the colors used by the Query Analyzer:

Color	Definition
Red	Indicates a character string has been coded. All strings must be enclosed in single quotes. Example: `'This is a character string'`
Dark Red	Indicates a system stored procedure is being used. Example: `EXEC sp_helplogins`
Green	Indicates a system table is being used. Example: `SELECT Text FROM Syscomments`
Dark Green	Indicates a comment has been coded. Example: `-- This is a comment`
Magenta	Indicates a system function is being used. Example: `PRINT GETDATE()`
Blue	Indicates a T-SQL keyword has been coded. Example: `SELECT`
Gray	Indicates an operator for a function, such as the parentheses in a system function. Example: `PRINT ASCII('A')`

Saving Queries and Query Results

In this section we are going to briefly explore saving queries and query results. As we do this, we are going to use some of the features of the Query Analyzer that we explored when we covered the menu items.

You can create queries and save them for later use and you can also save the results of the execution of a query. Saving queries can be a time saver, because you only need to write the query once. This can become especially useful when you have to write a fairly complex query. You save the query to a file and then you can open that query at any time and run it.

Try It Out – Writing and Saving a Query

As mentioned previously, we want to use as many of the features of the Query Analyzer as possible. This serves two purposes. Firstly, it will acquaint you with these features through first hand experience, and secondly, it will identify the features that are most useful for developers.

The query we want to write will select data from the Software_Category_T table in our database.

To write a new query:

1. Ensure that you are on the Objects tab in the Object Browser and then expand the Hardware Tracking database.

2. Expand User Tables, expand the Software_Category_T table, and then expand Columns:

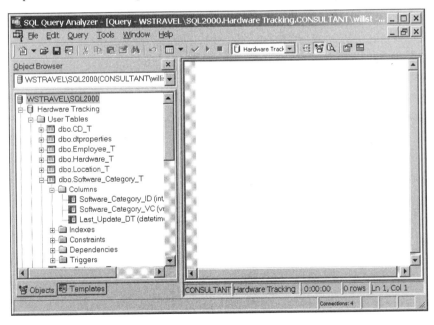

As we can see from the figure above, we have three columns in the Software_Category_T table.

3. Enter the following query in the query window. We will explain the full details of this query in the *How It Works* section.

```
SELECT Software_Category_ID, Software_Category_VC
    FROM Software_Category_T
    ORDER BY Software_Category_VC
```

> **Tip: you can drag column names and table names from the Object Browser and drop them into the query window, instead of typing them by hand.**

4. To check your query syntax, click on the Query menu and then click on Parse. Alternatively, click the Parse Query icon on the toolbar. If you do not remember what the Parse Query icon looks like, hover your mouse pointer over each icon for a tool tip.

If your query contained no errors, you will receive the message: The command(s) completed successfully in the results pane.

5. Before executing your query, we want to select the Results In Text menu item from the Query menu, or click the down arrow on the Execute Mode icon and choose the Results In Text menu item on the drop down menu.

6. To execute your query, click on the Query menu and then click on Execute, or click the Execute Query icon on the toolbar.

We have no records in our table, so the execution of the query will return zero rows. However, the query does return the column names that we selected in our query, as shown in the following figure:

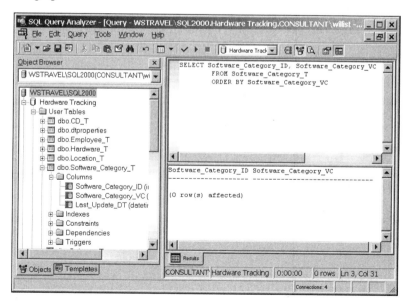

7. To save the query we have just entered, ensure your cursor is in the query window, click on the File menu, and then click on **Save** or **Save As**. Since we have not saved this query yet, both menu items will perform the same task. Alternatively you can click on the **Save Query/Results** icon on the toolbar.

8. The Save Query dialog is invoked and you need to specify the folder you want to save the query in. This can be any folder that you want. Specify a name for the query, giving it something descriptive. An example is shown in the following figure. When you have specified the folder and name of the query, click on the **Save** button to save the query:

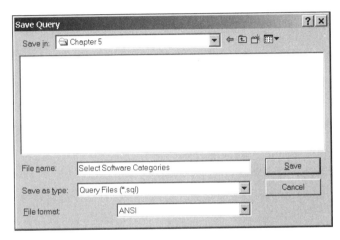

The query is now saved and can be retrieved at any time.

How It Works – Writing and Saving a Query

Before we explain exactly what our query is doing, let's take a look at the syntax for the SELECT statement. The complete syntax for the SELECT statement is quite complex, so the basic syntax is shown:

```
SELECT select-list
    FROM table-name
    WHERE search-condition
    ORDER BY order-by-expression [ASC | DESC]
```

The *select-list* argument is a list of columns each separated by a comma, or the argument can be an asterisk (*), which specifies that all columns should be selected. This argument is required.

The *table-name* argument is the name of the table that data should be selected from. This argument is also required.

The WHERE clause is optional, and the *search-condition* argument of the WHERE clause will limit the number of rows returned by searching only for rows that match the *search-condition*. We will see this clause used in the upcoming chapters.

The ORDER BY clause is also optional and orders the data returned. The *order-by-expression* argument is one or more columns that determine the sort order of the data returned. The ASC and DESC keywords are optional, and represent ascending and descending order. ASC is the default and does not have to be specified.

The query that we entered previously uses the SELECT statement to select data from the Software_Category_T table. We have specified the specific columns that we wanted to select data from to limit the number of columns selected. If we wanted to select all columns in the table, we could simply specify SELECT * instead of the SELECT statement shown in the following code fragment:

```
SELECT Software_Category_ID, Software_Category_VC
    FROM Software_Category_T
    ORDER BY Software_Category_VC
```

> **Tip: it is always better to specify the specific column names that you want returned in your select list instead of using a SELECT * statement. This prevents unwanted data from being returned and also helps to keep your queries optimized.**

The ORDER BY clause specifies how the data returned should be sorted, and since we have specified the Software_Category_VC column in this clause the data will be sorted by the name of the software category. Had we specified the Software_Category_ID column in the ORDER BY clause, the data returned would be returned sorted by the primary key.

Try It Out – Inserting Data

Since we had no data in the Software_Category_T table, our query did not return any rows. Let's write a simple query to insert some data into this table. This query will use the INSERT T-SQL statement, which we will explain in detail in the *How It Works* section.

To insert data into the Software_Category_T table:

1. Open a new query window either by clicking on the File menu and then clicking on New, or by clicking on the New Query icon on the toolbar. If using the menu, you will also need to choose Blank Query Window.

2. Enter the following query:

```
INSERT INTO Software_Category_T
    (Software_Category_VC, Last_Update_DT)
    VALUES('Operating Systems',GETDATE())
```

3. Parse the query for errors by either clicking on the Query menu and then clicking on the Parse menu item, or clicking on the Parse Query icon on the toolbar. You should receive the message: The command(s) completed successfully in the results pane.

4. Execute your query by clicking on the Query menu and then clicking on the Execute menu item, or by clicking on the Execute Query icon on the toolbar. When your query has executed, you will see a message in the results pane like the one shown in the next figure:

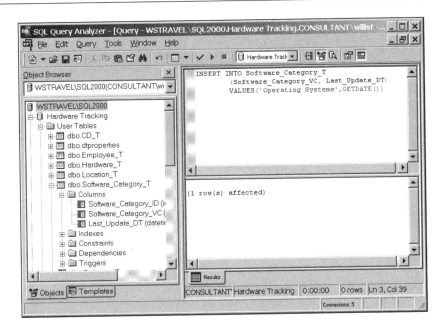

5. We want to enter another row of data into this table, and also want to demonstrate the Clear Window feature.

> **Tip: since this is basically the same query you can select the query text, copy it to the clipboard, and then paste it in the next step. Then you need only change the values that are inserted.**

To clear the query window, click on the Edit menu and then click on Clear Window, or click on the Clear Query Window icon on the toolbar. The query in the query window should now be cleared.

6. Enter and execute the following query:

```
INSERT INTO Software_Category_T
    (Software_Category_VC, Last_Update_DT)
    VALUES('Office Suites',GETDATE())
```

7. Enter and execute the following queries to insert the rest of the data into the Software_Category_T table:

```
INSERT INTO Software_Category_T
    (Software_Category_VC, Last_Update_DT)
    VALUES('Office Tools',GETDATE())
```

```
INSERT INTO Software_Category_T
        (Software_Category_VC, Last_Update_DT)
        VALUES('Development Tools',GETDATE())


INSERT INTO Software_Category_T
        (Software_Category_VC, Last_Update_DT)
        VALUES('BackOffice Software',GETDATE())
```

How It Works – Inserting Data

We have executed a number of queries to insert data into the `Software_Category_T` table. As you have probably already noticed, the basic query did not change, only the values that were inserted. Let's take a look at the basic syntax of the INSERT statement:

```
INSERT [INTO] table-name
        (column-list)
        VALUES(value-list)
```

The INSERT statement has an optional keyword, which is INTO. Using this keyword is not essential, but it helps to add to the readability of the INSERT statement.

The *table-name* argument is required and specifies the name of the table that data is being inserted into.

The *column-list* argument is optional and specifies which columns that data is being inserted into. A comma separates each column name. If you do not specify a *column-list*, then you must insert data into every column and the values of the data inserted must be in the same order as the columns are defined in your table. It is a good habit to always specify the *column-list*, as it also helps the readability of your INSERT statement.

> **You do not have to specify an identity column in the column-list. SQL Server will automatically insert the correct value in an identity column.**

The *value-list* is required and specifies the values that are to be inserted. The value-list should be in the same order as the *column-list*, with a comma separating each value. Notice that our string values have been enclosed in single quote marks ('). SQL Server requires us to enclose all string values in single quote marks.

Now, let's take a look at the INSERT query that we ran. In the first line of the query we have specified the INSERT statement followed by the INTO keyword and the table name that we are inserting data into.

On the second line of our query, we have specified the column list of the columns that we want to insert data into. This list must be enclosed in parentheses and each column must be separated by a comma:

```
INSERT INTO Software_Category_T
        (Software_Category_VC, Last_Update_DT)
        VALUES('Operating Systems',GETDATE())
```

The last line of our query specifies the VALUES keyword and the value list. Again, notice that we have enclosed the string value of Operating Systems in single quotes. The last value in our value list is actually a T-SQL function that returns the current date and time. This date and time will be inserted into the Last_Update_DT column of our table.

Try It Out – Executing a Saved Query

Now that we have some data in the Software_Category_T table, we execute our SELECT query to see the data that we have inserted.

To execute the saved query:

1. Click on the File menu and then click on the Open menu item, or click on the Load SQL Script icon on the toolbar.

2. Navigate to the folder where you saved your query earlier, click on the file name, and then click on the Open button:

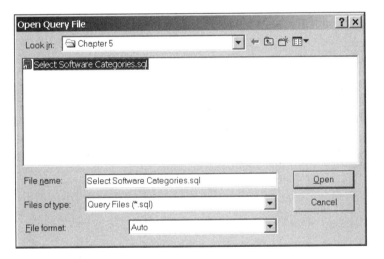

Your saved query should now be loaded in the query window.

3. To execute your query, click on the Query menu and then click on Execute, or click the Execute Query icon on the toolbar. The results you see should be similar to the ones shown in the figure overleaf:

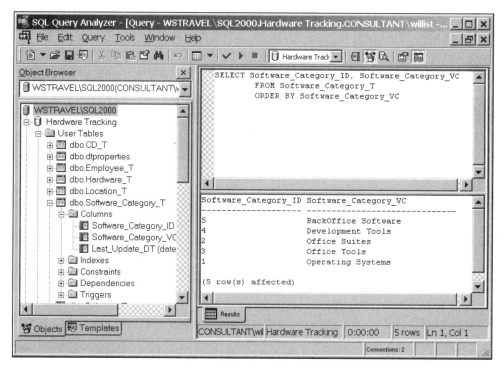

Notice that the results returned are ordered by the `Software_Category_VC` column. This is not the same order in which we entered the data, but is the order that we have specified by the `ORDER BY` clause in our `SELECT` statement.

Try It Out – Save the Results of a Query

Not only can we save the actual query itself to a file, but we can also save the results of the query. When we save the results of a query, we can also open that file at a later date in the query window.

To save the results of the execution of our query:

1. Click in the results pane to place your cursor there.

2. Click on the File menu and then click either the Save or Save As menu items. Alternatively, you can click on the Save Query/Result icon on the toolbar.

The Save Results dialog is invoked and you need to specify the folder in which you want the results saved and the name of the file. The Save as type is already specified for you as Report Files (*.rpt). This is because you clicked in the results pane before invoking the Save Results dialog.

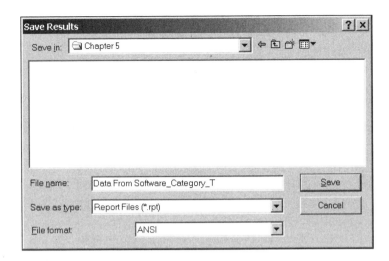

3. Once you have specified the appropriate information, click on the Save button to have the results saved and to close the Save Results dialog.

4. You can now open the saved query results using the Open Query File dialog and selecting the All Files (*.*) file type in the Files of type combo box. Then locate your saved file that has a file extension of .rpt.

Update and Delete Statements

In the last few *Try It Out* exercises we covered the SELECT and INSERT statements. This section completes the core T-SQL statements to manipulate data in our tables by covering the UPDATE and DELETE statements.

We will be working with the same table that we have been working with in the past few *Try It Out* exercises. However, the existing data that we have inserted is good, so let's leave that data alone and insert one more row into the Software_Category_T table. We will then use this new row of data to practice with while we explore the UPDATE and DELETE statements.

Using the following query, insert a new row of data into the Software_Category_T table:

```
INSERT INTO Software_Category_T
    (Software_Category_VC, Last_Update_DT)
    VALUES('Test Data',GETDATE())
```

Update Statement

Like the other T-SQL statements that we have examined so far, the UPDATE statement is a complex statement that has a lot of optional keywords. We are going to cover the basic syntax of the UPDATE statement here. We will expand on this T-SQL statement in the upcoming chapters.

The basic syntax of the UPDATE statement is as follows:

```
UPDATE table-name
    SET column-name = expression [,...n]
    WHERE search-condition
```

The *table-name* argument is the name of the table in which we want to update columns.

The *column-name* argument is the name of the column to be updated and the *expression* argument is the expression or data that is being placed into the column. The *...n* argument can be other columns in the table, with each column being separated by a comma.

The WHERE clause is an optional clause and, when present, the search condition is specified to limit the number of rows that get updated. When the WHERE clause is not specified, all rows in the specified table are updated.

Try It Out – Updating Data

In this exercise we want to update the row of data that we just inserted and change the value in the Software_Category_VC column to another value.

Since we do not want to update all of the rows of data in our table, we must first determine the row of data that we want to update. There are two columns of data in the Software_Category_T table that we could specify in the WHERE clause of our UPDATE statement.

One is the Software_Category_VC column and since we know the value that we want to update, Test Data, we could go ahead and build the UPDATE statement. However, this is not an indexed column and if we had thousands of rows of data, this query could take a while.

The other column that we can use is the Software_Category_ID column. This is the primary key to our table and this column is indexed, which makes a query using this column in the WHERE clause very efficient. This is the column that we are going to use.

However, before we can specify this column in the WHERE clause of our query, we must first determine the value of the Software_Category_ID column of the row that we want to update. Therefore, we need to execute our saved query again.

Open the query that you saved, and execute it to find the value in the Software_Category_ID column for the row of data that we inserted a few minutes ago. The value in the Software_Category_ID column for the row of data that I inserted is 6.

To update this row of data:

1. Open a new query window either by clicking on the File menu and then clicking the New menu item, or by clicking on the New Query icon on the toolbar.

2. We want to replace the value of Test Data with Update Query. We also want to update the Last_Update_DT column with the current date and time. Enter the following query, ensuring you insert the value of the row of data that matches the row of data in your table:

```
UPDATE Software_Category_T
    SET Software_Category_VC = 'Update Query',
    Last_Update_DT = GETDATE()
    WHERE Software_Category_ID = 6
```

3. Parse the query for errors either by clicking on the Query menu and then clicking on Parse, or by clicking the Parse Query icon on the toolbar.

4. Execute the query either by clicking on the Query menu and then clicking on the Execute menu item, or by clicking on the Execute Query icon on the toolbar.

   After executing your query you should see the following message: (1 row(s) affected).

5. To see the results of the execution, switch to the query window containing the query that we saved earlier, for example by clicking on the Window menu and choosing the appropriate query window.

6. Before we execute this query again, click on the Query menu and then click on Results in Grid. Alternatively, click on the down arrow on the Execute mode toolbar icon and then click on Results in Grid. This will place the results of the execution in a grid.

7. We also want to take a look at the execution plan that SQL Server uses. To do this, click on the Query menu and then click on the Show Execution Plan menu item, or click on the down arrow on the Execute mode toolbar icon and then click on Show Execution Plan.

8. Re-execute the saved query to see the results of the UPDATE query. You should see results similar to those shown in the next figure:

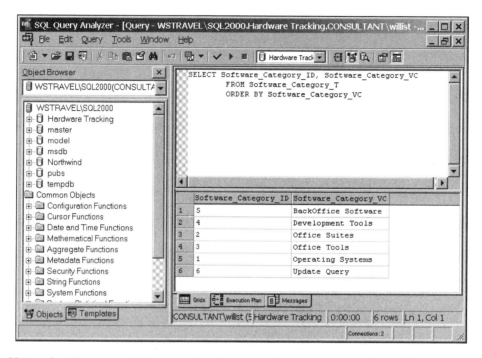

Notice that the results of the execution of our saved query are now in a grid. If you switch to the Execution Plan tab, you see the actual execution plan that SQL Server used to execute the query, as shown in the next figure:

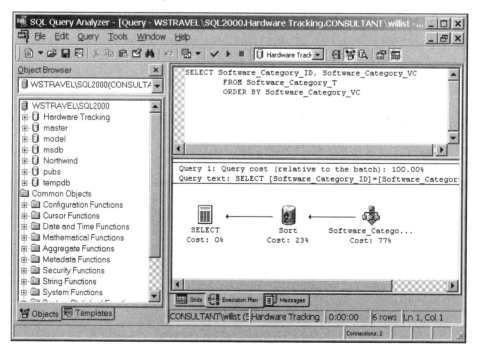

The SELECT icon in the execution plan shows the cost of selecting the data that was specified by the SELECT statement. The Sort icon shows what the cost was to sort the data as specified by the ORDER BY clause. The Index Scan icon shows the cost of scanning the index for the data that we wanted to retrieve. Cost is relative to the query optimizer and is determined to be a combination of the total cost of CPU time and the total cost of I/O time that was spent executing the query.

We can get more detailed information by hovering the mouse pointer over each icon, as shown in the next figure:

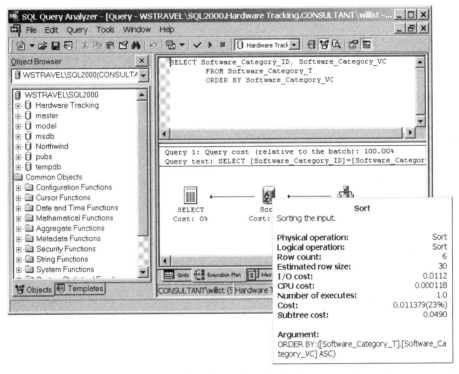

In this figure, the tool tip that has popped up shows detailed information about the sort operation performed by SQL Server, including such information as Row count and the I/O cost.

The information shown in these tool tips can help you tune your queries and stored procedures. If you find that the total cost of the sort is high because most of your SELECT statements order data from a specific table on columns that are not indexed, then you know that an index is needed. You will be able to see this and know that you should place an index on the columns used in the ORDER BY clause to help improve the performance of your stored procedures or queries.

How It Works – Updating Data

Let's take a closer look at our UPDATE query. The first line of the query contains the UPDATE T-SQL statement and the table name that we want to update.

The second line of our query contains the SET keyword and the first column that we want to update, along with the new value that we want in the column. Notice that we have a comma at the end of the second line. This is because we are updating more than one column in this table.

The third line of this query specifies the `Last_Update_DT` column and again we are using the `GETDATE` function to insert the current date and time in this column.

The `WHERE` clause of the `UPDATE` statement specifies the exact row that we want to update – we have specified the `Software_Category_ID` column and a value of 6:

```
UPDATE Software_Category_T
    SET Software_Category_VC = 'Update Query',
    Last_Update_DT = GETDATE()
    WHERE Software_Category_ID = 6
```

> **If we did not specify the WHERE clause, then *all* rows in our table would be updated and they would all have a value of 'Update Query'.**

Delete Statement

The `DELETE` statement allows us to delete one or more rows of data in a table, and it is also a very powerful T-SQL statement that has a complex syntax. Therefore, we are only going to show the basic syntax for the statement:

```
DELETE [FROM] table-name
    WHERE search-condition
```

The `FROM` keyword is an optional keyword in the `DELETE` statement. I always include it because it helps the readability of the statement.

The `table-name` argument specifies the table that you want to delete data from.

The `WHERE` clause is an optional clause and, when present, the `search-condition` is specified to limit the number of rows that get deleted.

> **When the WHERE clause is not specified, *all* rows in the specified table are deleted.**

Try It Out – Deleting Data

For this exercise we are going to delete the row of data that we inserted and updated a few minutes ago. The `DELETE` statement that we will use is very simple, and will use the `Software_Category_ID` column in the search condition of the `WHERE` clause. Therefore, it is very important that you have the correct value before continuing.

To delete a row of data:

1. Open a new query window either by clicking on the File menu and then clicking the New menu item, or by clicking on the New Query icon on the toolbar.

2. Enter the following query, ensuring that you have specified the correct value for the `Software_Category_ID` column:

```
DELETE FROM Software_Category_T
    WHERE Software_Category_ID = 6
```

3. Parse the query for errors by either clicking on the Query menu and then clicking on Parse, or clicking the Parse Query icon on the toolbar.

4. Execute the query by either clicking on the Query menu and then clicking on the Execute menu item, or by clicking on the Execute Query icon on the toolbar.

5. After successful execution of your query, you should see the message (1 row(s) affected). You can verify the deletion of data by switching to the window containing your saved query and re-executing it. You should now have only five rows of data.

How It Works – Deleting Data

Our `DELETE` query is very simple as we are only deleting data from one table. The first line of our query specifies the `DELETE` statement followed by the `FROM` keyword. Remember that this keyword is optional, but does help improve the readability of our query. The table that we want to delete data from follows the `FROM` keyword.

The second line of our query specifies the search condition for our query. If we had not specified this line, then all rows in the `Software_Category_T` table would have been deleted, without warning. The search condition specifies the column and the value in the column that should be found. If no matches were found, then we would have received the message: (0 row(s) affected).

```
DELETE FROM Software_Category_T
    WHERE Software_Category_ID = 6
```

> It is very important that you always specify a search condition unless you want all rows of data in your table to be deleted.

Debugging

Previously when we created our queries we checked them for errors using the Parse function in the Query Analyzer. Of course, our queries were simple and we had no errors, but what if we did? This section demonstrates finding and resolving errors in the queries and stored procedures that you develop.

When an error occurs in your query, an error message is displayed in the results pane. The error message displayed depends on the type of error received. Not all errors are caught by the parser in the Query Analyzer. The parser validates SQL syntax in your query; it does not validate database objects.

When an error does occur and a message is displayed in the results pane, you can double-click on the error message and the offending line of code in your query will be highlighted.

Try It Out – Debugging a Query

The query that we will use for this exercise is the SELECT query that we saved and have been using in the previous exercises. While this exercise is simple, it should serve to give you an idea of how to debug queries. We will also be covering debugging in subsequent chapters as we write more complex queries and stored procedures.

1. To debug a query, switch to the window that contains your saved SELECT query, or open the saved query if it is not already opened.

2. We want to cause an error on purpose, so delete the letter O from the word ORDER on the third line of your query.

3. Parse the query for errors either by clicking on the **Query** menu and then clicking **Parse**, or by clicking the **Parse Query** icon on the toolbar. You should receive the error message shown in the next figure:

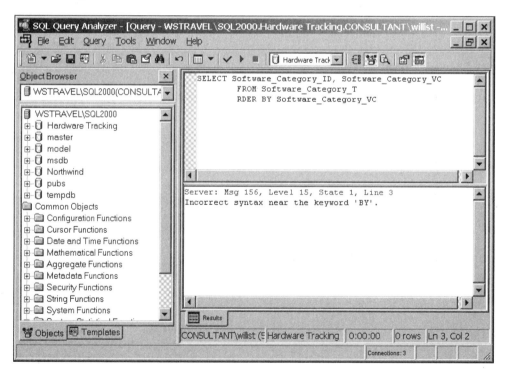

If we did not know where in the query the error existed, we could simply double-click on either line of the error message and the offending line of code would be highlighted, as shown in the next figure:

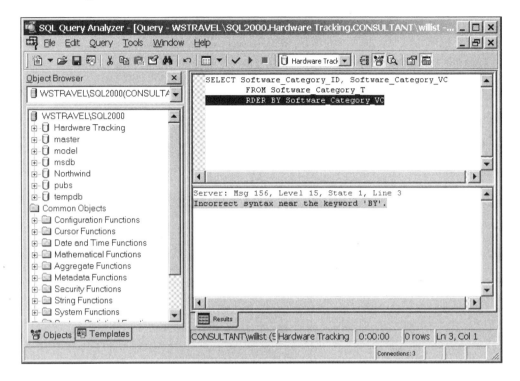

6. Correct the error and then parse the query to verify that the error was corrected.

The Query Analyzer does not always point out the exact position of the error. In these cases we need to look closer at our query, and examine the database objects (such as tables and column names) that we have specified.

7. To cause an error related to a database object, delete the letter S from the word Software on the third line of the query.

8. Run the parser and you should receive the message: **The command(s) completed successfully.** The parser checked the SQL statements in our query but has not validated the database objects.

9. Run the query to see what type of error message is displayed.

10. Double-click on the error message to see which line of code is highlighted. The following figure shows how the debugger has interpreted the error in our query:

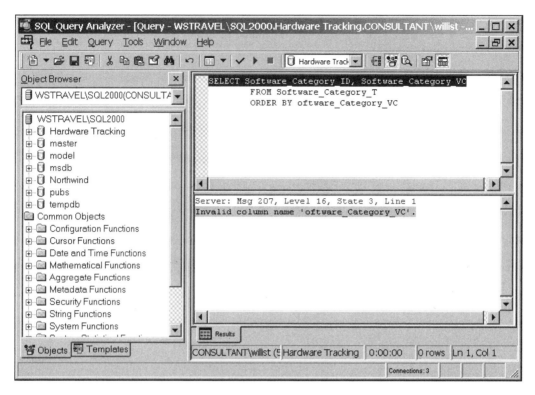

Preventing these types of errors is where the Object Browser can help. If you drag and drop the database objects needed into your query, the chances of you receiving an error message due to a bad database object name is slim to none.

As we mentioned earlier, we will cover more on debugging in subsequent chapters.

Templates

Now that you have a feel for writing queries in the Query Analyzer, let's take a look at how **templates** can assist you in writing queries. Templates are actually saved query files that contain T-SQL statements that will assist you in writing common queries. They save time and avoid typos. So let's switch to the second tab in the Object Browser, Templates.

As you can see in the following figure overleaf, there are multiple categories that contain predefined templates. These same categories appear when we create a new query, using either the File | New Query menu option or the dropdown arrow of the New Query toolbar icon.

If we expand the Create Database category, we see that there are multiple templates in this category. Double-clicking on a template will place the T-SQL statements for that template in the query window, or you can drag and drop a template into an empty query window.

The figure shows what is displayed when we double click on Create Database Basic Template:

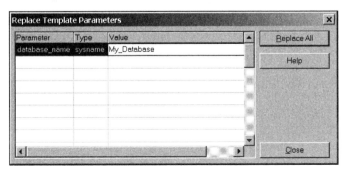

The first three lines of the T-SQL statements of this query are **comments**. Comments in SQL Server can be defined in one of two ways. The first method, shown here, is where we use two consecutive dashes. Comments defined in this way can appear anywhere on a line and apply to only one line. This means that for each line that you want a comment on you must place two consecutive dashes.

The second method of defining comments in SQL Server will allow you to span multiple lines without placing the comment characters on each line. This is where we use the beginning comment characters of /*, and on the last line of the comment we end the comment with the characters */. This is the same method of defining comments as in C++.

If you look closely at the T-SQL statements, you can see that there are some **parameters** contained in the template, as indicated by the opening (<) and the closing (>) brackets. We can manually edit these parameters in our template code, or we can do this automatically by clicking on the Edit menu and clicking on the Replace Template Parameters menu item.

This invokes the Replace Template Parameters dialog and lists all of the parameters contained in the template that we are working with, as shown in the following figure:

We can replace the value for each parameter and then click the **Replace All** button to have this dialog replace the default template values with the values that we have specified. Once this is complete, our code will look similar to that shown in the following figure:

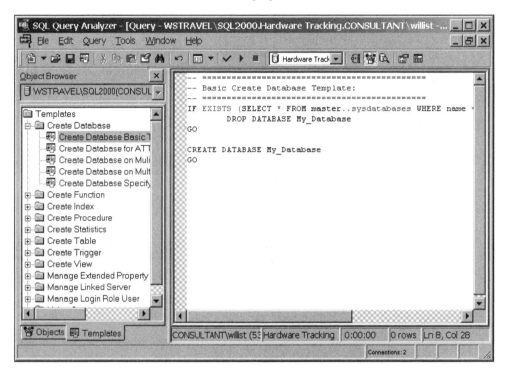

It should be noted here that these templates are not designed to handle filenames that contain spaces. It is therefore recommended that you use names that contain underscores in place of spaces, as we have done in this demonstration. Alternatively, enclose the name that you supply in square brackets, as shown in the next figure. SQL Server uses square brackets to delimit names that contain spaces.

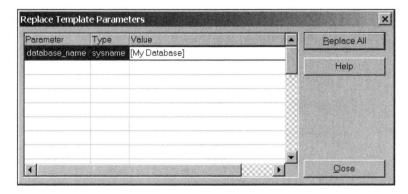

The Query Analyzer also allows you to create your own templates. The templates you create can be as simple or as complex as you want. They can also specify parameters or not, as the case may be. Before we walk through creating our own templates, let's discuss how these templates get into the Query Analyzer Object Browser.

All templates in the Object Browser are actually stored on your hard drive as files and folders. For example, the **Create Database** category is actually a folder on your hard drive and all of the templates are files in that folder.

The location of these files and folders is the `C:\Program Files\Microsoft SQL Server\80\Tools\Templates\SQL Query Analyzer` folder, assuming your installation of SQL Server is on your `C` drive and you did not change the default installation folder when you installed SQL Server.

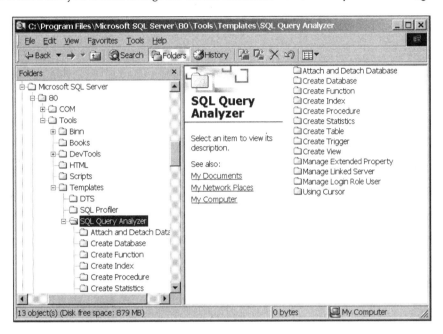

Try It Out – Create Your Own Template

Let's create a simple template to select data from the `Software_Category_T` table in our database. When we create this template, we will also want to create a new category for our template. You can place your own custom templates in any of the pre-existing template categories or you can create a new category, as we will demonstrate here.

To create this template:

1. Clear the existing query window by clicking on the **Clear Query Window** icon on the toolbar. (Or click on the **Edit** menu and then click on the **Clear Window** menu item.) Make sure that the **Hardware Tracking** database is selected.

2. Enter the query shown in the next figure. This query will allow us to select the specified columns from the `Software_Category_T` table in our database.

Notice that when creating template parameters for our query, we have to specify three parts and enclose the parameter in tags (`<>`). The first part of our template parameter is the parameter *name*, while the second part of our parameter is the *type*. This is the data type of the parameter that we are defining. In this instance, the data type of the parameter is an `Integer`

159

data type because `Software_Category_ID` in our table is an `Integer` data type. The last part of our parameter is the *default value*, which is set to 1 in this case. The users of our templates will replace this value using the **Replace Template Parameters** dialog.

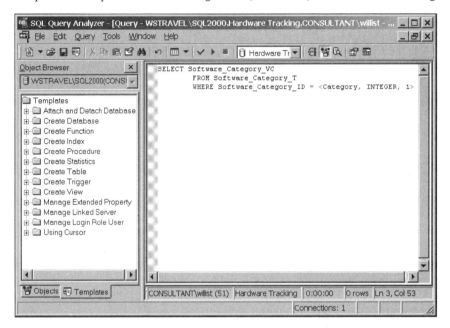

3. We want to save the query that we have entered, as a template query. We can do this by clicking on the **Save** icon on the toolbar. Since we have not saved the query in the query window before, the **Save** icon will invoke the **Save Query** dialog, which will allow us to specify the **File** name and **Save as type**.

4. Navigate to the `C:\Program Files\Microsoft SQL Server\80\Tools\Templates\SQL Query Analyzer` folder and then click on the **Create New Folder** icon at the top of this dialog. Give this new folder a name of **Hardware Tracking**. This will identify this category in the Object Browser using this name, and will indicate that the templates in this category belong to the **Hardware Tracking** database.

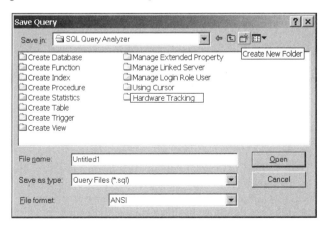

5. Open this new folder and give the template a File name of Select Software Category. Choose the Template SQL Files (*.tql) as the Save as type. Click on the Save button to save this template:

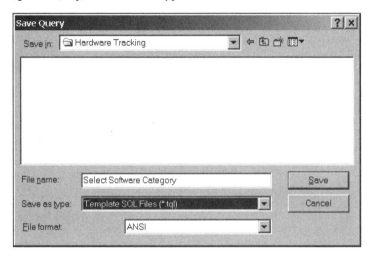

6. The template is now available in the Object Browser, but before we can see it we must refresh the list of templates and categories in the Object Browser. Right-click on **Templates** in the Object Browser and choose **Refresh** from the context menu.

Our new template is now ready for use, as shown in the following figure:

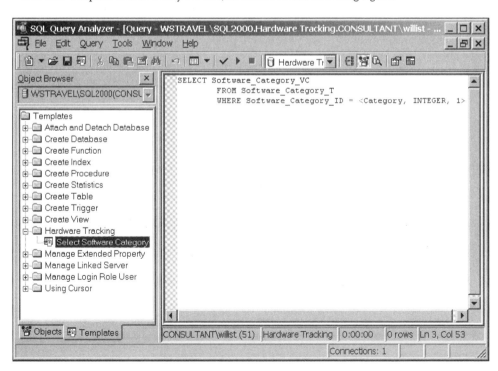

Try It Out – Use Your New Template

To use your newly created template, perform the following steps:

1. Double-click on the Select Software Category template. The template is then displayed in a new query window, as shown in the previous figure.

2. Click on the Edit menu and then the Replace Template Parameters menu item. This will invoke the Replace Template Parameters dialog.

3. Change the value of 1 to a value of 5 and then click on the Replace All button:

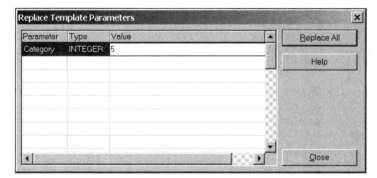

The Replace Template Parameters dialog will then replace the template parameter value with the new value that we have specified. The resulting query will look like the one shown in the following figure:

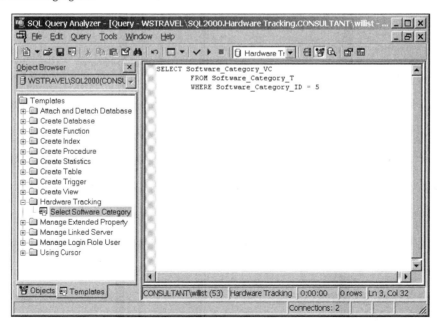

4. This query is now ready to execute. Execute the query by clicking on the Execute Query icon on the toolbar. You will see the results of the execution in the results pane. You have just successfully created and executed your own custom template.

> Tip: if you see the error *Server: Msg 208, Level 16, State 1, Line 1, Invalid object name 'Software_Category_T'* then you will need to change the database selected to the `Hardware Tracking` database. To change the database, click on the **Database** combo box on the toolbar and select the **Hardware Tracking** database.

As you can see from these exercises, creating your own custom templates is a very simple process. Using the templates provided or using your own templates can be a time saver. Building your own custom templates provides you with queries that are specific to your database and you can perform any processing in a template that you would normally perform in a query.

Summary

This chapter has taken a detailed look at most of the available features in the Query Analyzer. Having toured and used the menus and menu items, as well as the toolbar icons, you should now be fairly familiar with the features and functions that the menus and toolbar icons provide.

You should also be familiar with connections in the Query Analyzer and how to select other databases. You should also now know that you can establish a new connection or change the database for each query window that you open.

Having covered the Object Browser in some depth, you should be aware of what a powerful tool this is. You should now be able to navigate the various folders in the Object Browser to find the information that you need. You should also be aware of how useful the templates provided are, and how useful creating your own templates can be.

As we went through the basics of the SELECT, INSERT, UPDATE, and DELETE statements you saw how easy it is to work with these T-SQL statements. As we progress through the book, we will be introducing more of the basic syntax of these statements.

You now know how to save and open a query and saw first hand what a time saver this can be. You can write complex queries and then save them for later use. You also saw how to save the results of an executed query.

To summarize, you should know how to:

❏ Establish a connection to SQL Server in the Query Analyzer

❏ Switch databases and execute queries in them

❏ View the various objects in your database using the Object Browser

❏ Find the system functions and know what parameters they expect using the Object Browser

❏ Write simple INSERT, SELECT, UPDATE, and DELETE queries

❏ Save and open a query

❏ Debug a query

❏ Use and create templates

In the next chapter we will explore the various ways to establish a connection to SQL Server from Visual Basic – exploring DSN and DSN-less connections.

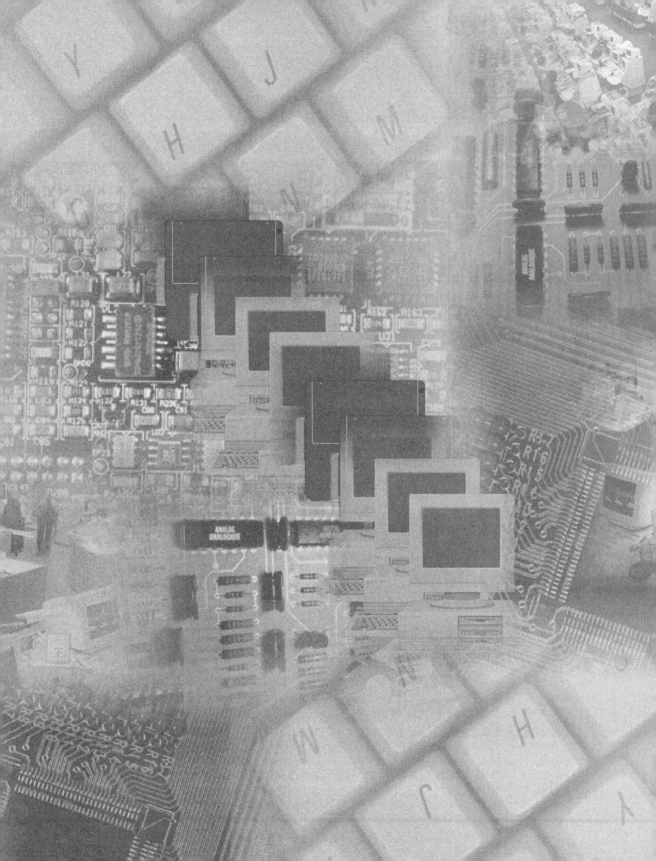

Database Connections

In the last chapter we saw how to use Windows authentication and SQL Server authentication to connect to SQL Server from the Query Analyzer. Following along those same lines, this chapter will take a look at establishing a connection from your VB programs to SQL Server, using both modes of authentication.

Before we can execute even a single stored procedure or in-line SQL statement (those SQL statements stored in our VB code) from our VB programs, we must establish a **connection** to SQL Server. As well as deciding whether to use Windows authentication mode or SQL Server authentication mode, we must also decide whether to use a **DSN** (**Data Source Name**) or DSN-less connection.

This chapter will dispel the mystique surrounding these connections, and provide tips as to when each method is most useful. However, before we cover connections we need to explore the **ADO** (**ActiveX Data Objects**) objects that are available for establishing a connection to SQL Server. So, given this, we need to explore the ADO object model at a high level.

This chapter will cover the following topics:

- ADO object model
- ODBC versus OLE DB
- Setting up a Data Source Name (DSN)
- Using DSN connections and DSN-less connections

Connections

Before we begin discussing database connections, let's recap on our discussion from Chapter 1. We saw how our VB applications use ADO (ActiveX Data Objects) to connect to the database. When we establish our connection to the database using ADO, we have two choices of which application programming interface (API) that we want to use, OLE DB or ODBC.

While OLE DB is certainly the better choice, for reasons discussed in Chapter 1, we sometimes may need to use ODBC. This chapter takes a look at both methods, and provides working examples for both. If we take a look at the following diagram we can see where ADO, OLE DB, and ODBC fit into the picture:

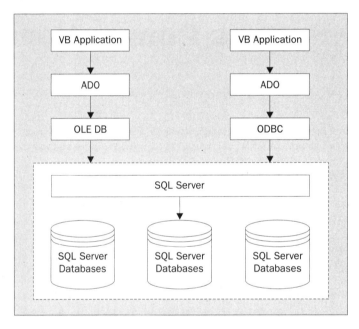

Once we begin working with the ADO `Connection` object, you will see at first hand how the pieces come together as shown above.

ADO Object Model

As we briefly discussed in Chapter 1, ADO is part of the **Microsoft Data Access Components** (**MDAC**), which also include **Remote Data Services** (**RDS**), **OLE DB**, and **Open Database Connectivity** (**ODBC**). These components together make up Microsoft's **Universal Data Access** (**UDA**) strategy that allows access to relational and non-relational data across the enterprise.

ADO provides a lightweight object model with high-performance access to data. Designed to provide access to any type of data store, ADO has replaced **Data Access Objects** (**DAO**) and **Remote Data Objects** (**RDO**) as the preferred data access method. ADO, initially created for web access, was designed to be easy to learn and use, as is evident from its programming model. It can be used throughout your n-tier and client-server applications, and in your web applications.

When we installed SQL Server, part of the installation performed by the setup program was to install MDAC, which includes ADO version 2.6. The ADO 2.6 object model is summarized in the following diagram:

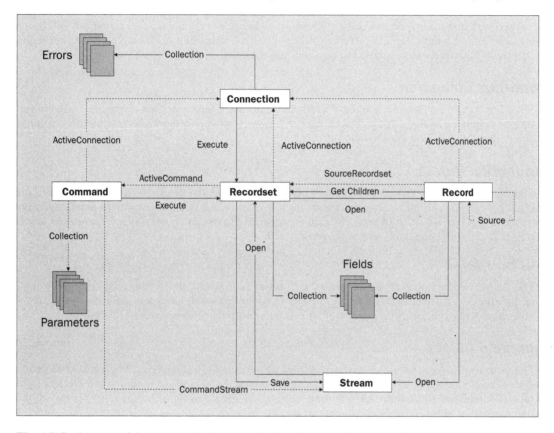

The ADO object model consists of **objects** and **collections**. At the root of the objects is the Connection object, which also contains the Errors collection. The Command, Recordset, and Record objects all require an active connection from the Connection object in order to perform any activity against the database. Associated with the Command object is the Parameters collection, while the Fields collection is associated with the Recordset and Record objects. The Stream object is used in a similar fashion to the Recordset object, except that it uses binary or text data from files on your computer or network.

Each of the objects in the previous diagram has an associated Properties collection, which is not shown. The Properties collections represent the various properties of each object.

ADO Objects and Collections

Most developers are familiar with object-oriented programming and the ADO object model, having worked with it at some time or another. However, to be sure everyone is up to speed, we will cover the major objects at a high level. We will be getting into the details of most of these objects in subsequent chapters when we use these objects to perform various tasks.

Properties Collection

The Properties collection is applied to all ADO objects. Each object has a Properties collection, which is made up of Property objects. Each Property object represents a characteristic of an ADO object that is defined by the provider.

Connection Object

The Connection object is at the very heart of the model and allows you to connect to the data store. We'll be studying this object in greater detail in this chapter. All other objects in the model incorporate the Connection object to provide the active connection to the database. Once a connection is made, it is used to execute commands and transactions.

Errors Collection

The Errors collection is associated with the Connection object, as all errors are returned from the underlying data store or from OLE DB to ADO. This collection contains any errors returned (as Error objects) as a result of executing a method or setting a property of any of the ADO objects.

Command Object

The Command object executes stored procedures and in-line SQL statements. We'll see much more of this in the next chapter. The Command object is an optional object in the model as not all data sources support command execution. The Command object can execute stored procedures and in-line SQL statements that return records and those that do not.

Parameters Collection

Associated with the Command object is the Parameters collection, which allows you to add parameters that are required for a stored procedure or in-line SQL statements.

Recordset Object

The Recordset object should be familiar to everyone who has done database programming with ADO before. The Recordset object supports the Record object (introduced in ADO version 2.5), which makes programming with the Recordset object easier. The Record object is covered next, but basically represents a row of data in the Recordset object. While the Recordset object represents the entire collection of records from a table or as the result of executing a stored procedure or SQL statement, you can only access one row of data in the Recordset object at a time. Various methods are supported for moving between rows in the recordset.

Fields Collection

The Fields collection contains all the information about each field in the recordset, such as the field name in the database, the data type, attributes, and the actual value of the field. A field in the Recordset object corresponds to a column in the database.

Record Object

The `Record` object represents a row of data in a `Recordset` object, a file, or a directory in a file system, or folders and messages in an e-mail system. For example, using the `Record` object you can represent each directory on your computer as a parent `Record` and each file within the directories as a child `Record`. You can then manage these files on your computer by using the `CopyRecord`, `MoveRecord`, and `DeleteRecord` methods. As one might imagine, this can be a powerful tool when working with the VB TreeView control, which provides parent and child nodes. Using the `MoveRecord` method of the `Record` object we could move parent and child nodes around in the TreeView control, providing a very flexible control for the users.

As with the `Recordset` object, the `Record` object also contains the `Fields` collection.

Stream Object

The `Stream` object (also introduced in version 2.5) represents a stream of text or binary data. When used in conjunction with the `Record` object, the `Stream` object can be used to open, read, and write data, and then close a file represented by the `Record` object.

The complete ADO 2.6 object model is listed in Appendix B along with the methods and properties of each object.

Connection Object

Now that we have had a quick look at all of the objects in the ADO object model, let's turn our attention back to the object that is the focus of this chapter – the `Connection` object. The `Connection` object establishes a connection to the database so we can access and manipulate data using the other objects in ADO.

Before calling any of the methods of this object, a valid `Connection` object needs to be defined, such as:

```
Dim g_objConn as New ADODB.Connection
```

This type of declaration uses the `New` keyword, which enables implicit creation of the `Connection` object. The first time this object is referenced a new instance of the object will be created.

An alternative way to create the `Connection` object would be to use the following statements:

```
Dim g_objConn As ADODB.Connection
Set g_objConn = New ADODB.Connection
```

This type of declaration is usually specified in multiple places in your code. The `Connection` object is usually declared in the general declarations section of a form, module, or class. The `Set` statement is usually used in a procedure or function to actually set a reference to the object, which creates a new instance of the object. This method allows for greater control of resources, as you only actually create the object when it is needed. Using this method we can create and destroy the object as many times as is needed in our program.

This is the preferred method to use, and we will be using this in our exercises.

We use the `Open` method of the `Connection` object to actually establish and open the connection to SQL Server. The `Open` method has the following syntax:

```
g_objConn.Open ConnectString, UserID, Password, Options
```

The `ConnectString` parameter contains the information that is used to establish a connection with the database. It can contain information such as the ODBC driver, OLE DB provider, or the Data Source Name being used (all of which will be covered shortly). `UserID` and `Password` are self-explanatory, and contain a valid login to SQL Server and an associated password. The `Options` parameter specifies whether the connection should be returned asynchronously or synchronously. A **synchronous connection** is when the method being executed must complete before the next method can be executed. An **asynchronous connection** allows your code to perform other tasks while the method is executing. When this parameter is not specified, a synchronous connection is established by default. This will satisfy the majority of your programming needs, and is the method that we will be using in all of our exercises.

Once all processing has been completed, we close the database connection using the `Close` method of the `Connection` object:

```
g_objConn.Close
```

You should always close your `Connection` object as soon as you are done with it to free up system resources, and release the connection to SQL Server. This also reduces the number of concurrent users connected to SQL Server.

We'll be using the `Connection` object later in the chapter, but first we will look in more detail at the connection information required and the methods for providing it. The two methods we will consider are using a DSN, and hard coding the information in the connection string (that is, a DSN-less connection).

ODBC versus OLE DB

Before we can proceed and explain how DSN and DSN-less connections work, we must first understand what a DSN is. **DSN** is an acronym for **Data Source Name** and defines the name of the data source that contains the information to establish a connection from your VB program to SQL Server. All the connection information for a DSN is stored in the registry, and when the DSN is specified the information is retrieved and used to establish a connection to the database.

As we mentioned in Chapter 1, ODBC is an older technology than OLE DB, but as we will see later in this chapter, the ODBC Data Source Administrator uses this technology to create DSNs. We have no choice but to use ODBC when using a DSN. The DSN that we will define provides all of the functionality that we will need for the exercises in this book. However, there will be circumstances where the functionality provided by ODBC is not sufficient, and you will need to use OLE DB instead. This is the preferred technology, although you should ensure you know how to use ODBC in case you run across it in the workplace.

What exactly is a DSN-less connection? A DSN-less connection is where we able to specify all of the parameters required to establish a connection to SQL Server without using a DSN. We must still specify all of the information that is provided when we set up the DSN, but instead of doing it through the DSN administrator, we supply the information within our code – in the connection string, or as properties of the `Connection` object.

We need to specify such properties as the driver to use, the server the database resides on, and other basic information such as the database name, login, and password.

Setting Up a DSN

In order to create a DSN, we must invoke the ODBC Data Source Administrator dialog. This dialog provides a series of steps that walk you through setting up a DSN. It can be found in the Control Panel under the name of Data Sources (ODBC) on Windows 98 and Windows NT systems. On Windows 2000 systems, you must go to the Control Panel and then double click on the Administrative Tools icon – the Data Sources (ODBC) icon can then be found in this folder.

Try It Out – Create a DSN

1. Locate the Data Sources (ODBC) icon and double click on it to invoke the ODBC Data Source Administrator dialog.

   There are three types of DSN, the first of which is the **User DSN**. This tab allows you create a DSN that is local to the currently logged on user. This type of DSN is not accessible to anyone else who logs onto your machine. You would use this type of DSN to access your own personal databases.

   The second type of DSN is the **System DSN**, and this is the type of DSN that we will be creating. A System DSN is local to the machine on which it is defined, but all users who log onto the machine will have access to it. Both User and System DSNs are stored in the registry.

   The last type of DSN is the **File DSN**. This DSN is similar to the System DSN in that all users logged onto the machine on which it is defined can access it. This type of DSN, however, is written to a file instead of the registry. This makes porting this type of DSN easier, as we simply need to copy the DSN file to another machine and place it in the correct directory.

2. Click on the System DSN tab as this is the type of DSN that we want to create:

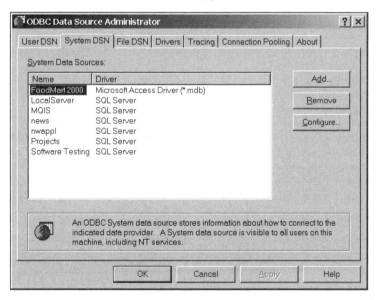

There are three buttons on the right of this dialog. The Add button allows you to add a new DSN, while the Remove button allows you to delete an existing DSN. The Configure button enables you to configure the current properties of an existing DSN, by allowing you to change properties such as the database, user ID, or password.

The four buttons at the bottom of the dialog allow you to manage the dialog itself. Clicking the OK button dismisses the dialog, saving any changes you have made, whereas clicking on the Cancel button will dismiss the dialog, cancelling any changes you have made. The Apply button will apply any changes you have made and leave the dialog open. The Help button displays context help for the current screen displayed in the dialog.

3. We want to create a new DSN, so click on the Add button. You will be presented with a list of all available drivers installed on your machine, similar to that shown in the next figure:

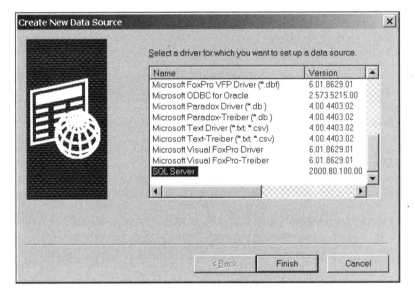

4. We want to choose the SQL Server driver. Click the Finish button to invoke the Create a New Data Source to SQL Server wizard, which will allow us to enter connection settings specific to the chosen driver.

5. The first screen of this wizard prompts us for the Name of the DSN as well as the Server the database resides on. The Description text box is an optional field on this step of the dialog. Let's give the DSN a Name of HardwareAppl, a suitable description, and select the Server (machine name) on which you installed SQL Server. If SQL Server is installed on your local machine then you should specify local in the Server combo box.

If you installed a named instance of SQL Server, you must specify the machine name followed by a backslash and then the instance name of SQL Server, as I have done in the following figure:

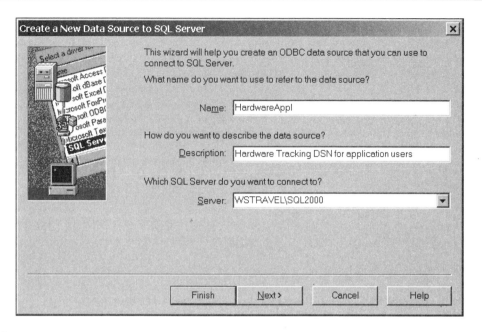

6. Click the Next button to proceed.

The next step of the wizard provides you with the option of using Windows authentication or SQL Server authentication, just as we saw in the last chapter when we connected to SQL Server from the Query Analyzer.

Experience has shown that the best method to use for authentication is SQL Server authentication. This provides the most secure of DSN connections. If you use Windows authentication and your login ID is set up for Windows authentication in SQL Server, then anyone using your machine while you are logged on can access SQL Server with your login. Even if the user specifies another login ID and password, Windows authentication will override it. For this reason, and to provide a more secure DSN, use SQL Server authentication wherever possible.

The Client Configuration button allows you to change how the DSN will communicate with SQL Server. This is an advanced option that should only be changed when instructed by the SQL Server Database Administrator or Network Administrator.

7. Check the With SQL Server authentication ... option button and enter the Login ID and Password of the second user that we set up in Chapter 4. Click the Next button to proceed.

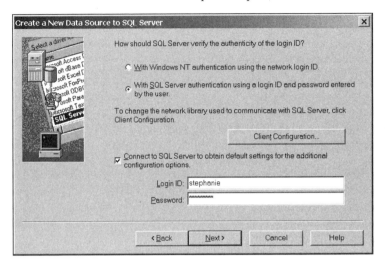

Note that with the 'Connect to SQL Server to obtain default settings...' check box selected, the SQL Server named instance specified on the previous page of the wizard has to be started, or you will receive an error message. You will not be able to continue past this step until you have started it or cleared the check box.

8. The next step of the wizard (see next figure) allows you to set the default database for the login that you specified in the last step. This is useful when the login that you are using has access to multiple databases. Since the login that we are using only has access to the one database we do not need to change this, as our database is already displayed in the default database combo box. We want to accept all other defaults on this screen, so click the Next button to proceed.

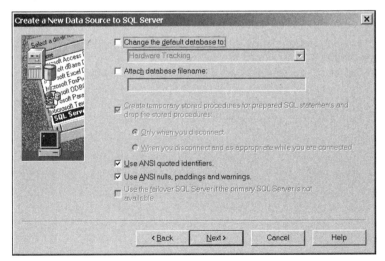

The Attach database filename option allows you to specify the name of the primary file for an attachable database.

The Create temporary stored procedures... option specifies that the ODBC driver should create temporary stored procedures to support the SQLPrepare *ODBC function. This option only applies to older versions of SQL Server and does not apply in our case.*

The Use ANSI quoted identifiers option specifies that the ODBC driver should set the QUOTED_IDENTIFIER option to true. This option specifies that double quotation marks (") can only be used to delimit identifiers (such as table names that contain spaces) and single quote marks (') must be used to enclose character string data.The Use ANSI nulls, paddings, and warnings option specifies that the ODBC driver should set the ANSI_NULLS, ANSI_PADDINGS, and ANSI_WARNINGS options to true. The ANSI_NULLS option, when set to true (on) returns a value of UNKNOWN for comparisons against null values. The ANSI_PADDING option, when turned on, specifies that trailing blanks on VarChar *fields are not automatically trimmed. The ANSI_WARNINGS option, when set to true, allows SQL Server to issue warning messages for conditions that violate ANSI rules but do not violate the rules of Transact-SQL. The Use the failover SQL Server if the primary SQL Server is not available option specifies that the connection will automatically attempt to connect to the alternative server if the connection to the primary server is lost.*

9. We want to accept all defaults on the next screen of the wizard, so click the Finish button to proceed.

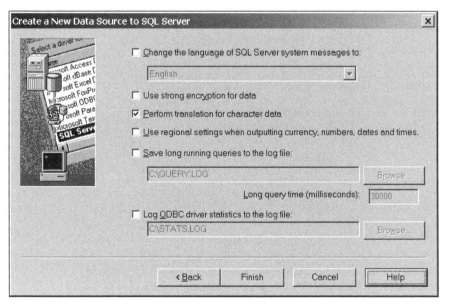

The Change the language of SQL Server system messages to option specifies the language of the messages returned by SQL Server. The language set in this option is set according to the language specified in your login or, if no language option was set, the default language of SQL Server.

The Use strong encryption for data option specifies that data be encrypted when sent and received from SQL Server.

The Perform translation for character data option, when checked, specifies that the ODBC driver should convert, using Unicode, ANSI strings sent between the client computer and SQL Server.

The Use regional settings when outputting currency, numbers, dates and times option specifies that the ODBC driver is to use the regional settings of the client computer for formatting currency, numbers, dates, and times in character output strings.

The Save long running queries to the log file option specifies that the ODBC driver log any query that takes longer than the Long query time value. The Log ODBC driver statistics to the log file option specifies that statistics are to be logged. It should be noted that when this option is turned on, you will experience poor performance in your applications. This option should only be turned on for debugging purposes and then turned off when no longer needed.

10. The wizard displays a dialog box, informing you of the options that will be used to create your DSN. You can click the Cancel button to return to the wizard and then click the Back button to go back and change your options. You can also click the OK button to have your DSN created. However, it is always good practice to test your DSN by clicking the Test Data Source button, so do this now.

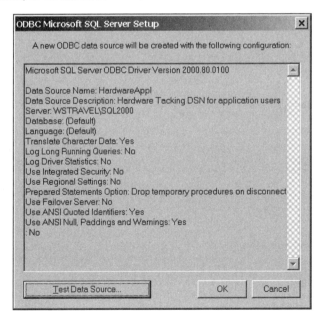

11. Once your DSN has been successfully tested, you will receive a confirmation dialog like the one shown next. Click the OK button to return to the previous step.

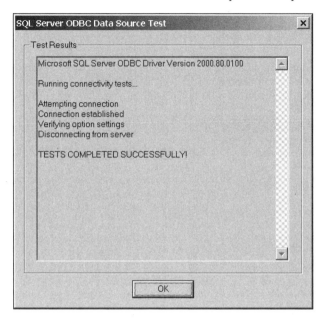

Tip: if your test failed, check to ensure that SQL Server is actually started. If you are
using SQL Server installed on your network check with your DBA to ensure SQL
Server is running. Also retrace your steps to ensure you have specified all the options
correctly.

12. Click the OK buttons in the SQL Server ODBC Data Sources Test dialog and the ODBC Microsoft SQL Server Setup dialog to return to the ODBC Data Source Administrator dialog, and then click the OK button to close this dialog.

We have now successfully created a DSN that we can use in our VB programs. When we do so, we must specify the `UserID` and `Password` parameters as part of the parameter set required by the `Open` method of the `Connection` object. You may be wondering why we must specify these parameters if we had to enter them when we set up the DSN.

The reason for this is that these parameters are not stored with the information about the DSN. They were used so the ODBC Data Source Administrator could connect to SQL Server to gather information about the login, such as what database the login had access to, and what language the login was defined with.

If we take a look at the information that *is* stored as part of the DSN, we see that it only contains the last user who used the DSN. This information can be viewed in the system registry.

Try It Out – Viewing the DSN Registry Information

1. To start the registry editor, click on the Windows Start button and then select Run.

2. Enter RegEdit in the combo box and then click on the OK button.

3. Navigate to the HKEY_LOCAL_MACHINE hive and expand it, expand the SOFTWARE group, the ODBC group, and finally the ODBC.INI group. Click on the HardwareAppl key to view the values. The values for this DSN are shown in the following figure:

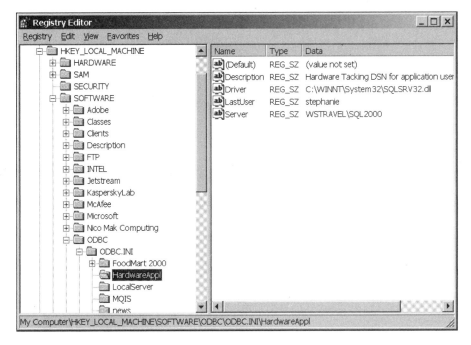

As you can see, this confirms that the DSN only stores the last user. As UserID and Password parameters are not stored, we need to specify these when calling the Open method of the Connection object.

In later sections we will cover the intricacies of using both a DSN and a DSN-less connection. Each section will also cover using Windows authentication and SQL Server authentication with these connections. To allow us to expand our options and use various options in subsequent chapters, let's create a login form that will allow us to choose what type of login to use. We can then use this form in subsequent exercises as the login form for our projects.

Creating the Login Form

The basic functionality of this form is to allow you to experiment with the various ways of connecting to SQL Server. We can choose a DSN or DSN-less connection and also choose between Windows and SQL Server authentication modes.

Try It Out – Creating a VB Login Form

1. To create the sample project start a new VB project and choose the Standard EXE project type:

2. The first thing we want to do in our project is set a reference to ADO. Open the References dialog by clicking on the Project menu and then clicking on References. Scroll down the list of available references and set a reference to the Microsoft ActiveX Data Objects 2.6 Library:

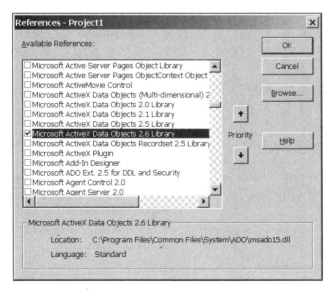

181

3. Next, change the Name of the form to frmLogin and the Name of the project to Login:

4. Since this is going to be a login form, we want to change the BorderStyle property of the form. Let's set it to **3 – Fixed Dialog**. This gets rid of the Minimize and Maximize buttons, and only leaves us with the Close button on the form's title bar.

5. We want to change the form's Caption property to Login, which is more appropriate than Form1. We also want to get rid of the form's icon, so delete this by double-clicking on the word (Icon) in the Icon property and then pressing *Delete*. This will change the word (Icon) to (None) and the icon on the form will disappear. To have the form centered on its parent form when it starts up, change the StartUpPosition property to **1 – CenterOwner**.

6. We want this form to provide robust functionality for the rest of the projects in this book and allow us to choose the options we want to use to logon with. The following table summarizes the controls that we want to include on this form.

Control	Name	Properties
Frame	Frame1	Caption = DSN
OptionButton	optDSN(0)	Control Array, Caption = DSN, Value = True
OptionButton	optDSN(1)	Caption = DSN-Less, Value = False
TextBox	txtDSN	Text = HardwareAppl
Frame	Frame2	Caption = Authentication Mode
OptionButton	optMode(0)	Control Array, Caption = Windows Authentication, Value = True
OptionButton	optMode(1)	Caption = SQL Server Authentication, Value = False
Label	lblLogin	Caption = Login Name, Enabled = False
TextBox	txtLogin	Text = nothing, Enabled = False, BackColor = &H80000000&
Label	lblPassword	Caption = Password, Enabled = False
TextBox	txtPassword	Text = nothing, PasswordChar = *, Enabled = False, BackColor = &H80000000&
CheckBox	chkConnectString	Caption = Make the UserID and Password Part of the Connect String
CommandButton	cmdOK	Caption = OK, Default = True
CommandButton	cmdCancel	Caption = Cancel

Place these controls on the form according to the figure shown:

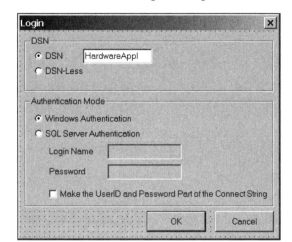

7. The code presented in the *How It Works* section should be added to your form (frmLogin).

8. Save your project in the directory of your choice.

How It Works – Creating a VB Login Form

The first option button on our form deals with the DSN type that we will be using, so let's start with the code for this option button.

We made this option button a control array, so VB has added an Index parameter to the Click event for this option button. This lets us know which button in the control array was clicked. The indexes for all control arrays are zero based, meaning that the first option button in the control array is zero.

We want to add the following code to the optDSN_Click event. The first thing we do in this event is to check to see if the Index parameter is 0, which would indicate that the first button in the control array was clicked.

If it is, then we want to enable the DSN textbox (txtDSN) and then set the BackColor property of the textbox to the color constant of vbWhite. This sets the background color of the text box to white. Notice that we are using the color constant from the ColorConstants enumeration. You can view the constants of the ColorConstants enumeration in the Object Browser.

```
Private Sub optDSN_Click(Index As Integer)
    If Index = 0 Then
        'If DSN then enable fields
        txtDSN.Enabled = True
        'Use ColorConstants enumeration
        txtDSN.BackColor = vbWhite
```

If the second option button (DSN-Less) in the control array was clicked, then we want to disable the DSN textbox and set its BackColor constant to gray. Since the color of gray on forms in Windows 2000 is a different shade of gray from the color of gray on forms in Windows 98 and Windows NT, I have chosen to use a color constant that will reflect the correct color on *any* system. The vbInactiveCaptionText constant is taken from the SystemColorConstants enumeration, which can also be viewed using the Object Browser.

```
    Else
        'If DSN-Less then disable fields
        txtDSN.Enabled = False
        'Use SystemColorConstants enumeration
        txtDSN.BackColor = vbInactiveCaptionText
    End If
End Sub
```

That is all the code we need to manage the DSN option buttons. The next set of controls that we want to take a look at is the set of option buttons for the authentication modes. The code that we will use here is very similar to the code we just examined.

Again, we check to see which button in the control array was clicked. If it was the first option button then we disable the labels, textboxes, and checkbox for SQL Server authentication. Again we are using the SystemColorConstants to ensure a consistent color of gray across all platforms:

```
Private Sub optMode_Click(Index As Integer)
    If Index = 0 Then
        'If Windows Authentication then disable fields
        lblLogin.Enabled = False
        txtLogin.Enabled = False
        'Use SystemColorConstants enumeration
        txtLogin.BackColor = vbInactiveCaptionText
        lblPassword.Enabled = False
        txtPassword.Enabled = False
        'Use SystemColorConstants enumeration
        txtPassword.BackColor = vbInactiveCaptionText
        chkConnectString.Enabled = False
```

If the user clicked the option button for SQL Server authentication, we want to enable all of the labels, textboxes, and checkboxes associated with SQL Server authentication. Here we are using the ColorConstants to set the background color of the textbox to white:

```
    Else
        'If SQL Server Authentication then enable fields
        lblLogin.Enabled = True
        txtLogin.Enabled = True
        'Use ColorConstants enumeration
        txtLogin.BackColor = vbWhite
        lblPassword.Enabled = True
        txtPassword.Enabled = True
        'Use ColorConstants enumeration
        txtPassword.BackColor = vbWhite
        chkConnectString.Enabled = True
    End If
End Sub
```

Once all of the required options have been checked and the textboxes filled with information where appropriate, the user would either press the *Enter* key or click the OK button. Either way, the cmdOK_Click event will be fired. This is because we set the Default property for the OK button to True. So, if a user presses the *Enter* key VB interprets it the same as if the user had actually clicked on the OK button.

Since the EstablishConnection function returns a Boolean value, we can execute that function and use it in an If...Then statement at the same time, as shown in the next code fragment. Because the EstablishConnection function accepts so many parameters, we are actually going to specify the parameter names in the execution of this function. We do this by specifying the parameter name followed by a colon and then the equal sign. Then we follow the parameter name with the actual parameter data from our form. Using this method helps any developer looking at this code to quickly identify what parameters the function accepts without having to look at the actual function itself.

```
Private Sub cmdOK_Click()
    'Establish connection to SQL Server
    If EstablishConnection(blnDSN:=optDSN(0).Value, _
        strDSN:=txtDSN.Text, _
        blnWindowsAuthentication:=optMode(0).Value, _
        strLogin:=txtLogin.Text, _
        strPassword:=txtPassword.Text, _
        blnConnectString:=chkConnectString.Value) Then
```

If the EstablishConnection function returns a value of True, then we display a message indicating that the login was successful. This message box displays the Information icon along with the OK button.

If the value returned by the EstablishConnection function was False, then we display a message box indicating that the login failed. This message box displays the Critical icon along with just the OK button:

```
        MsgBox "Login Successful!", vbInformation + vbOKOnly, "Login"
    Else
        MsgBox "Connection Failed", vbCritical + vbOKOnly, "Login Failed"
    End If
```

After we display the appropriate message box, we terminate the connection. This code is simply here for testing purposes. This allows you to establish a connection using one connection type and mode, and then experiment with another connection type and mode. We will remove this code in the next chapter:

```
    'Close connection
    Call TerminateConnection
End Sub
```

The last piece of code contained in our form is for the Cancel button. When the Cancel button is clicked, we want to close and unload the form. We use the Unload statement for this and pass the reference of Me as the object to unload. We could just as well explicitly specify the form name for the object to be unloaded. Using the Me keyword makes code maintenance easier in case someone comes by later and changes the form name.

```
Private Sub cmdCancel_Click()
    Unload Me
End Sub
```

We now have created a generic form that we'll use later in the chapter as we add the functionality to connect to the database using each of the connection and authentication methods.

DSN Connections

This section will walk you through the steps of adding the functionality to the login form to support using a DSN connection with both SQL Server authentication and Windows authentication. We will code and test each authentication method separately so that you are aware of the distinct differences between the two methods.

SQL Server Authentication

The first DSN connection method that we want to explore is a connection using SQL Server authentication. We can pass the UserID and Password as part of the connection string or as separate parameters. To prove our point, we will demonstrate both methods.

Try It Out – DSN SQL Server Authentication

1. Open up the login form project and add a standard module. Set the module's **Name** property to modConnect.

2. We will be adding code to this module in the rest of the exercises in this chapter. The code that pertains to this option is presented in the *How It Works* section that is discussed next. Once you've entered the code, go ahead and save your project.

3. Then let's execute this project, and enter the second user login that we created in Chapter 4. Remember, this login was set up to use SQL Server authentication. So when you run the project, you will need to click on **SQL Server Authentication** and enter the **Login Name** and **Password** that you personally created in Chapter 4. Then click the **OK** button. You should see the results shown in the following figure:

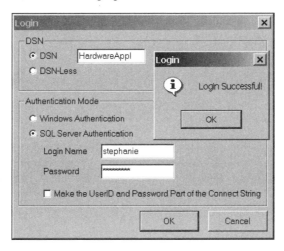

4. Accept the message and click the **Cancel** button to end the program, then let's take a look at the EstablishConnection function.

5. We want to set a break point in the following line of code in the modConnect module. (If you're not familiar with the VB debugging features, refer to the VB Help.) This will allow us to examine the strConnectString variable before we execute the Open method of the Connection object.

```
'Open the Connection object
If blnConnectString Then
```

6. Once you have set the break point, run the project again. Select **SQL Server Authentication**, and enter the **Login Name** and **Password**, and then click the **OK** button or press *Enter*.

7. When the break point is reached, we can examine the contents of the strConnectString, strLogin, and strPassword variables. There are two ways you can do this. By far the easiest method is to hover your mouse pointer over these variables; their values will then be displayed as a tooltip. The second method is to interrogate the variable in the **Immediate** window by typing a question mark followed by the variable name, and then pressing *Enter*. The sample shown in the next code fragment demonstrates this and the results returned:

```
?strConnectString
DSN=HardwareApp1;
```

8. Now, step through the next few lines of code to see which branch your code takes. You should see the code in the Else condition being executed. This code uses the strLogin and strPassword as separate parameters of the Open method. Hit **Run** and let the code finish executing.

9. For our second test, we want to check the **Make the User ID and Password Part of the Connect String** checkbox so that the login name and password are actually built as part of the connect string, and not passed as separate parameters to the Open method.

10. Leaving all data as it is on the form, check the **Make the User ID and Password Part of the Connect String** checkbox and then press *Enter* or click the **OK** button. When your code gets to the break point, examine the strConnectString variable. Notice that the login name and password are actually part of this variable. When you step through the next few lines of code you will see that the statement immediately following the If statement is executed. This statement does not pass the strLogin and strPassword variables as parameters to the Open method.

11. Go ahead and let your code run and complete. Then click on the **Cancel** button to end the program.

How It Works – DSN SQL Server Authentication

The variables that we define in this module must be public because we will establish a connection to SQL Server from the login form and then control will be passed to the main form for the projects that we code in later chapters. The code in the other forms will need to be able to access a Connection object that is opened and available.

To that end we need to define the following public variables in the modConnect module:

```
Option Explicit

'Declare public objects
Public g_objConn As ADODB.Connection
Public g_objError As ADODB.Error
```

We have defined two ADO objects, one for the Connection object and one for the Error object.

We now need to write a function that will establish a connection to SQL Server. This function will accept the appropriate parameters to allow for a DSN or DSN-less connection as well as Windows authentication or SQL Server authentication.

We use a function instead of a subroutine so we can return a Boolean value indicating success or failure. Let's start this function by defining the parameters that it should accept:

```
Public Function EstablishConnection( _
    ByVal blnDSN As Boolean, _
    ByVal strDSN As String, _
    ByVal blnWindowsAuthentication As Boolean, _
    ByVal strLogin As String, _
    ByVal strPassword As String, _
    ByVal blnConnectString As Boolean) As Boolean
```

Using the fields on the form as a guide to the parameters that this function should expect, we know that we need to accept a Boolean value indicating the type of DSN mode that we should create and this is the first parameter that we have defined. For now, we are focusing on a DSN connection.

The next parameter is a string value that contains the DSN if a DSN type connection was requested.

The third parameter determines whether we are using Windows authentication or SQL Server authentication. Along with this are the parameters that are required for SQL Server authentication, strLogin and strPassword.

The last parameter determines whether or not the login and password should be added to the connect string or passed as separate parameters to the Open method of the Connection object.

Notice that this function returns a Boolean value, which will let us know whether or not an error occurred while trying to connect.

The first thing we want to do in this function is to set up our error handling. Should there be any errors, we want to handle them gracefully. So, the next step is to declare the local variables for this function. The strConnectString variable will contain the final connect string that we use in the Open method of the Connection object.

```
'Setup error handling
On Error GoTo EstablishConnection_Error

'Declare local variables
Dim strConnectString As String
```

Now we need to set a reference to the ADO `Connection` object:

```
'Set a reference to the ADO Connection object
Set g_objConn = New ADODB.Connection
```

Next, we want to actually start building the connect string. At this point we are only focusing on a DSN type connection, so this is all our code will handle at the moment, but we will expand this section of code later. Here, we are setting the `strConnectString` variable to contain the text `DSN=` plus the value contained in the `strDSN` variable. Notice that we are using a semicolon after each argument in the connect string. This delimits the various arguments.

```
'Build the DSN or DSN-Less part of the connect string
If blnDSN Then
    strConnectString = "DSN=" & strDSN & ";"
End If
```

We want to check to see whether the user ID and password should be part of the connect string or if they should be passed as separate parameters to the `Open` method. If you want the user ID and password to be part of the connect string, then this is where they are set:

```
'Add the User ID and Password to the connect string
If blnConnectString Then
    strConnectString = strConnectString & _
        "User ID=" & strLogin & ";" & _
        "Password=" & strPassword & ";"
End If
```

The connection string is now set up, so we can now invoke the `Open` method of our `Connection` object. Again, we need to check whether the user ID and password are part of the connect string or whether they should be specified as separate parameters. If they should be specified as separate parameters then the second part of our `If` statement is executed and we pass the `strLogin` and `strPasswords` variables as parameters to the `Open` method:

```
'Open the Connection object
If blnConnectString Then
    g_objConn.Open strConnectString
Else
    g_objConn.Open strConnectString, strLogin, strPassword
End If
```

We want to ensure our connection is opened and ready, so we check the `State` property of the `Connection` object. The `State` property returns a `Long Integer` that indicates the state of the connection. The `ObjectStateEnum` enumeration contains a list of all possible return values for this property. You can view the `ObjectStateEnum` enumeration in the Object Browser in VB by clicking on the **View** menu and then clicking on the **Object Browser** menu item, or by clicking on the **Object Browser** icon on the toolbar.

Once in the Object Browser click on the **ObjectStateEnum** item from the **Classes** list. The following figure shows the available items for this enumeration:

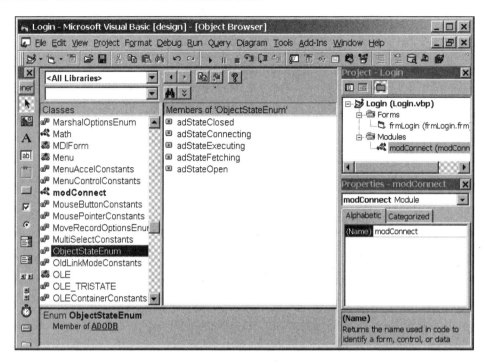

If the `State` property is not equal to `adStateOpen`, we want the `EstablishConnection` function to return a value of false, so we set the function's value to `False`. Otherwise, the `State` property indicates that the connection state is fine and we set the function's value to `True`:

```
'Check connection state
If g_objConn.State <> adStateOpen Then
    EstablishConnection = False
Else
    EstablishConnection = True
End If
```

At this point, everything is fine and we want to exit the function:

```
'Exit function
Exit Function
```

The next piece of code in this function is our error handling routine, where the code will branch should an error occur.

This section of code declares a string variable that will contain the error number and description of the errors that were received. Then we enumerate each error in the ADO `Errors` collection. Remember that the `Errors` collection is a collection of the `Connection` object as was shown in the ADO object model diagram earlier in this chapter.

We add each error in the `Errors` collection to the `strError` variable. Notice that after we add an error to this string variable, we include two `vbCrLf` constants so that each message is separated, preventing all of the messages from being strung together on the same line.

Once all errors have been added, we display the `strError` variable as the message for our message box. The `MsgBox` function has five arguments, the first of which is the `Message`. The second is the `Buttons` argument, and will display buttons only or an icon and buttons. We set the `vbCritical` constant to display the Critical icon in the message box and we also set the `vbOKOnly` constant so that only the OK button is displayed for the `Buttons` argument. The `Title` argument is next, and we have set the title of our message box to Login Error. The fourth and fifth arguments are for the help file and context number of the help topic. Since we do not have a help file or help topic, we have omitted these arguments:

```
EstablishConnection_Error:
    'Connection failed, display error messages
    Dim strError
    For Each g_objError In g_objConn.Errors
        strError = strError & g_objError.Number & " : " & _
            g_objError.Description & vbCrLf & vbCrLf
    Next
    MsgBox strError, vbCritical + vbOKOnly, "Login Error"
End Function
```

We now have a complete function that will allow us to establish a connection to SQL Server using SQL Server authentication. Remember that we will be expanding this code to include more functionality in the coming exercises. Once a connection has been established, we need a method to terminate that connection.

The next section of code that we want to create is a procedure to terminate the connection that we have established. This code does not have to return any values, so we can create a standard procedure to perform this task.

The `TerminateConnection` procedure is shown in the following code fragment. The first thing we do in this procedure is to turn on error handling. We don't care if any errors occur at this point because we are closing the database connection and removing any references to the ADO objects held.

Next we close the database connection by executing the `Close` method of the `Connection` object. Then we release our references to the ADO objects by setting them to `Nothing`. This frees up the memory held by these objects.

```
Public Sub TerminateConnection()
    On Error Resume Next
    g_objConn.Close
    Set g_objConn = Nothing
    Set g_objError = Nothing
End Sub
```

Windows Authentication

Now that we are able to connect to SQL Server from our VB programs using SQL Server authentication, we need to explore connecting to SQL Server using Windows authentication. This method allows for a more secure connection because SQL Server actually uses your Windows network login to validate your access. This means that if you have not logged onto the network then you will not be able to gain access to SQL Server.

Just a reminder for those readers who have installed SQL Server 2000 on Windows 98, this feature is not supported on this platform. You can follow along, but you will be unable to test these features.

Try It Out – DSN Windows Authentication

Using the same project, we need to slightly modify the code in the `EstablishConnection` function. These modifications will allow us to use Windows authentication. You could actually use Windows authentication with your code as it is, but the second `Open` method will be executed and an empty login and password will be sent to SQL Server. When SQL Server sees this it will then try to authenticate you using Windows authentication. This is not as efficient as using the required authentication method at the first attempt.

What we will do in this exercise is to actually clean up the code a little bit and make our code take the appropriate branch when we choose Windows authentication.

The only code that needs to be modified in our project is the code in the `EstablishConnection` function in the `modConnect` module:

```
'Add the User ID and Password to the connect string
If Not blnWindowsAuthentication And blnConnectString Then
...
'Open the Connection object
If blnWindowsAuthentication Or blnConnectString Then
```

How It Works – DSN Windows Authentication

This one simple modification will make the code branch appropriately. All we are doing here is checking to see if the Windows authentication option was selected on the form. That value is being passed to this function in the `blnWindowsAuthentication` parameter, which is a Boolean value.

Performing this check simply prevents the code from passing an empty login and password to SQL Server. This way SQL Server knows immediately that it needs to use Windows authentication to validate our login and grant us access.

You can now thoroughly test the functionality of using a DSN connection using either Windows authentication or SQL Server authentication. If you use SQL Server authentication, you can have the login and password passed as separate parameters to the `Open` method or as part of the connect string.

DSN Connections Summary

We are now able to connect to SQL Server using a DSN type connection using either Windows authentication or SQL Server authentication. Remember, however, that when you use a DSN connection to connect to SQL Server, you are using ODBC.

While ODBC is an older technology, it is still supported and distributed by Microsoft even in their newest products (such as Windows 2000 and SQL Server 2000). This type of connection should only be used to support legacy systems.

When you create new applications and systems, you should use OLE DB. This is the newer technology for MDAC and provides many features not supported by ODBC. I have personally found that when working with Text fields in SQL Server and AppendChunk and GetChunk methods in ADO, OLE DB is required in order for the operations to successfully complete. Therefore you should always use OLE DB for your new applications and systems.

DSN-less Connections

As we just mentioned, OLE DB is a newer technology that provides many features not supported in ODBC. In order to use OLE DB you must use a DSN-less connection, a connection that does not use a DSN. This type of connection requires that you pass all of the information normally provided by a DSN to the Connection object, either through the Connection object's Properties collection or as part of the connect string.

This section explores using a DSN-less connection with both SQL Server authentication and Windows authentication.

Try It Out – DSN-less SQL Server Authentication

The project that was created in the first exercise is the foundation for all of the connection types covered in this chapter. This allows us to use either a DSN (ODBC) or a DSN-less (OLE DB) connection. We then have a choice of either Windows authentication or SQL Server authentication when working with either type of connection.

This exercise will cover modifying the code in our login project to provide the functionality to use a DSN-less connection that uses SQL Server authentication.

No changes need to be made to the login form or code within that form. We simply need to modify a little bit of code in the EstablishConnection function in the modConnect module.

1. Make the following modifications to your code. Substitute your machine name in the Data Source argument and if you are using a named instance of SQL Server then specify that also.

```
'Build the DSN or DSN-Less part of the connect string
If blnDSN Then
    strConnectString = "DSN=" & strDSN & ";"
Else
    strConnectString = "Provider=SQLOLEDB;" & _
                       "Data Source=WSTRAVEL\SQL2000;" & _
                       "Initial Catalog=Hardware Tracking;"
End If
```

193

2. At this point we are ready to test, so save your project. If you cleared your break point from the previous exercise, you'll need to set it again. The next code fragment specifies the point in the `EstablishConnection` function where we want this break point set:

```
'Open the Connection object
If blnWindowsAuthentication Or blnConnectString Then
```

3. Run your project and choose a **DSN-Less** connection and **SQL Server Authentication**. Specify the **Login Name** and **Password** and either press *Enter* or click on the **OK** button.

4. When the break point has been reached, examine the `strConnectString` variable to see what information it contains. You should see the code that we just entered in this variable, and can step through the next few lines to see which `Open` method is executed. Let your project finish running and you should then see that you have successfully logged in, as shown in the following figure:

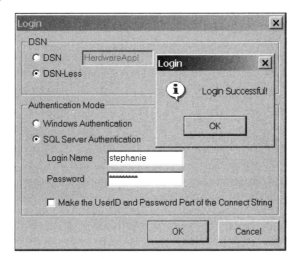

5. To perform the second test, check the **Connect String** checkbox and then click the **OK** button or press *Enter*. Examine the `strConnectString` variable when you reach the breakpoint and then step through the next few lines of code to see which `Open` method gets executed.

As you can see, this section of code performs the same way as using a DSN connection with SQL Server authentication.

How It Works – DSN-less SQL Server Authentication

In order to use a DSN-less connection, we need to specify the basic information that is supplied in the DSN. This information includes the type of driver to use, the server that the database resides on, and the database name.

To do this, we have added an `Else` clause to our `If` statement that checks whether or not we wish to use a DSN connection. Within this `Else` clause we have added code to build a connection string containing the appropriate information to establish a DSN-less connection.

Let's take a look at the information that is being specified. When we created our DSN at the beginning of this chapter, we had to select a driver to use. The appropriate drivers were listed and we selected the SQL Server driver. Just like a DSN connection, a DSN-less connection needs to know what type of driver to use. Since we are connecting to SQL Server and want to use OLE DB, we have specified the SQLOLEDB driver as the Provider:

```
Else
    strConnectString = "Provider=SQLOLEDB;" & _
                       "Data Source=WSTRAVEL\SQL2000;" & _
                       "Initial Catalog=Hardware Tracking;"
```

We also specified the server that SQL Server was running on when we set up our DSN and thus we must also provide that information here as the Data Source. Since I am using a named instance of SQL Server 2000, I need to specify the server name as well as the instance name of SQL Server. If you have installed a default instance of SQL Server, then you need only provide the name of the server where you installed SQL Server.

The last piece of information that we need to provide is the database name, and this is specified here as the Initial Catalog.

This basic information is needed by the SQLOLEDB driver to establish a connection to SQL Server. The Login and Password are needed to authenticate your login, and are passed in the code that we have already written.

Try It Out – DSN-less Windows Authentication

The code to establish a DSN-less connection to SQL Server using SQL Server authentication was pretty simple. We merely had to add the appropriate connect string to accomplish the task. Establishing a DSN-less connection to SQL Server using Windows authentication requires a bit more code due to the complexities of using OLE DB and Windows authentication.

To establish a DSN-less connection using Windows authentication we must specify and set some properties that are specific to the SQLOLEDB provider. These properties are set in the Connection object's Properties collection and then passed on to the SQLOLEDB driver.

Given this, we need to add code that will specifically check for a DSN-less connection and Windows authentication mode. This section of code will handle this type of connection, while the rest of the code that has been entered will handle the other connection types and modes.

1. Add the following code to the EstablishConnection function:

```
'Set a reference to the ADO Connection object
Set g_objConn = New ADODB.Connection

If Not blnDSN And blnWindowsAuthentication Then

    g_objConn.Provider = "SQLOLEDB"
    g_objConn.Properties("Data Source").Value = "WSTRAVEL\SQL2000"
    g_objConn.Properties("Initial Catalog").Value = "Hardware Tracking"
    g_objConn.Properties("Integrated Security").Value = "SSPI"
```

```
        g_objConn.Open

   Else

        'Build the DSN or DSN-Less part of the connect string
        If blnDSN Then

...existing code

    End If

        'Check connection state
        If g_objConn.State <> adStateOpen Then
```

2. It is now time to save your project and test the latest functionality. This time we want to set a new break point, because the existing code will not be executed for this test. Set a break point on the first line of code that we added which is shown in the following code fragment:

```
   If Not blnDSN And blnWindowsAuthentication Then
```

3. Run your project and choose a **DSN-Less** connection and **Windows Authentication**. Press *Enter* or click the **OK** button. When your code reaches the break point, step through the new section of code. As you can see, the `Provider` property of the `Connection` object is set, followed by the various properties of the `Properties` collection. Then we execute the `Open` method to establish a connection with SQL Server.

How It Works – DSN-less Windows Authentication

What we have done here is to check specifically for a DSN-less connection that uses Windows authentication. Both of the conditions must be met in order for this section of code to execute. If the conditions are not met, then we branch to the `Else` statement and execute the existing code that we have built in the last three exercises:

```
   If Not blnDSN And blnWindowsAuthentication Then
```

The first thing we do in this section of code is to set the `Provider` property of the `Connection` object. This will let ADO know what provider is being used so it can pass on the properties that we set in the `Properties` collection to that provider.

Then we set the first property in the `Properties` collection specifying the name of `Data Source` for that property and assign it a value of `WSTRAVEL\SQL2000`. This should look familiar to you as we specified the `Data Source` property in the connect string in the last exercise. Remember that if you have installed a default instance of SQL Server you need only specify the server that SQL Server is installed on.

Next, we set the `Initial Catalog` property as we also did in the last example, by including it in the connect string. This property contains the database name that we want to connect to.

The last property in the `Properties` collection that we want to set is the `Integrated Security` property. This property instructs the provider on the type of authentication to use. We have specified a value of `SSPI`. **SSPI** is an acronym for **Security Support Provider Interface**. This interface allows the `SQLOLEDB` provider to call the appropriate security provider in the operating system to gain access to our login name and then use that login name to allow SQL Server to validate our access.

After the properties have been set in the `Properties` collection, we call the `Open` method of the `Connection` object, with no parameters, to establish a connection with SQL Server:

```
g_objConn.Provider = "SQLOLEDB"
g_objConn.Properties("Data Source").Value = "WSTRAVEL\SQL2000"
g_objConn.Properties("Initial Catalog").Value = "Hardware Tracking"
g_objConn.Properties("Integrated Security").Value = "SSPI"

g_objConn.Open

Else
```

DSN-less Connections Summary

This wraps up the section on DSN-less connections. We have seen how easy it is to use either connection type and what extra steps are required to provide a DSN-less connection. We now know that we must provide the same basic information for a DSN-less connection that we supply to the wizard when we set up a DSN.

Which Connection Method to Use

Which type of connection mode is best? That entirely depends on the circumstances but, as a general rule, the DSN-less connection is best. Why? Because it allows you to use OLE DB, which is not available using a DSN connection. Also, you can compile your component and move it from server to server without recompiling or worrying about having to set up a new DSN on each server that you move your component to. It also allows you to create VB front-ends that establish connections to SQL Servers and to distribute your client-server application to customers without having to set up a DSN on each customer's workstation.

Which authentication mode is the best one to use? Again, this depends on the circumstances but, as a general rule, using Windows authentication mode provides the best security. This also allows you to distribute a client-server application to your customers and then grant various customers different access rights within SQL Server. For business components this requires a little more thought, as no user is logged onto the server on which the component is running so there is no Windows network login for SQL Server to validate. In this case, a generic login could be created in SQL Server for this purpose and the component would use SQL Server authentication.

Summary

At the beginning of this chapter we took a brief look at the ADO object model and highlighted the various objects. If you weren't already familiar with the ADO object model you should be by now. You should also be fairly familiar with the `Connection` object, having used it in the exercises in this chapter. We will explore and use one more method of the `Connection` object in the next chapter, as well as various other ADO objects.

As we walked through the steps to create a DSN, you saw what information was required and then used some of the same information to create a DSN-less connection. You can see how these two types of connection modes are very similar. You should now be familiar with setting up a DSN.

Having created a login form that will be used in subsequent chapters, you saw at first hand how to use both DSN and DSN-less connections in your VB programs. Along with this, you now know what is needed to establish either type of connection and also what is needed to perform Windows or SQL Server authentication.

As we talked about ODBC and OLE DB throughout the chapter, you should have gained a better feel for these access methods. You should now know which method to use and when.

To summarize, you should:

❑   Know how to use the `Connection` object to connect to SQL Server

❑   Be able to connect to SQL Server using DSN and DSN-less connections

❑   Know how to use Windows and SQL Server authentication with both connection modes

❑   Be able to set up a DSN

❑   Be more familiar with the ADO object model

As we introduce stored procedures in the next chapter we will be exploring the ADO object model in more depth. We will be using various ADO objects to manage the execution of stored procedures from VB programs.

Introduction to Stored Procedures

By working with the Query Analyzer in Chapter 5 we saw how to use the basic SELECT, INSERT, UPDATE, and DELETE statements in the queries that we wrote. While writing queries in the Query Analyzer is great for ad hoc queries and reporting, they cannot be accessed from our VB programs and distributed to the users of our applications. This is where stored procedures come in; we can access them from our VB programs, and they are available to all users of our applications.

This chapter covers the details of stored procedures as we begin to work with them and explore their functionality and uses. We will examine such details as stored procedure performance, user prefixes, stored procedure parameters, and return values.

We covered the ADO Connection object in the last chapter and saw how to use its Open method to establish a connection to SQL Server from within our VB programs. This chapter expands on the ADO object model as we cover the Connection object in more depth, as well as the Command object and the Recordset object. We can use all of these objects to execute our stored procedures, as we will discover in this and subsequent chapters.

This chapter will explain:

- ❑ Stored procedure performance
- ❑ User prefixes and security
- ❑ Stored procedure parameters
- ❑ SELECT, INSERT, UPDATE, and DELETE stored procedures
- ❑ Various useful Recordset object methods

Stored Procedure Basics

What exactly is a **stored procedure**? A stored procedure is a database object that contains T-SQL statements that perform a unit of work. When the stored procedure is first executed, SQL Server compiles it into an **execution plan,** and keeps that execution plan in its procedure cache (an area of memory in SQL Server). Subsequent executions of that stored procedure are then executed from the procedure cache.

Stored procedures provide a way to *share* code, in much the same way that a server component can be shared among multiple programs and applications. Multiple users and programs can execute the same stored procedures, thus providing code reuse. Maintenance becomes easier because we can change one stored procedure and the change immediately becomes effective for all users and programs.

Stored Procedure versus Transact-SQL Performance

When executed from a program, stored procedures are more efficient than **in-line SQL statements**. In-line SQL statements are actually part of your VB code and get compiled with your program. The reason that stored procedures are more efficient was mentioned above: when the stored procedure is executed, SQL Server creates and saves an execution plan. Subsequent executions of the stored procedure are then executed using the execution plan that was saved in the procedure cache. In addition, the amount of network traffic is reduced, because the T-SQL statements for the stored procedure are stored in the database. Thus you also reduce the amount of time the user has to wait for a response, in other words there is a shorter time delay between clicking a button to execute a stored procedure and actually seeing the data.

SQL statements executed from your programs, however, are not as efficient. Each time the SQL statements are executed by your program, your program must send all of the SQL statements across the network to SQL Server, then SQL Server must compile and optimize them into an execution plan before they actually get executed. While this performance decrease is not that noticeable for small numbers of SQL statements, or on your personal computer running the Personal Edition of SQL Server, it becomes more evident on a large-scale SQL Server system with multiple databases and hundreds of concurrent users.

If you must execute SQL statements from your program and you are executing the same SQL statements in a loop, then ADO can help. The ADO `Command` object provides a property called `Prepared` which, when set to `True`, will instruct SQL Server to compile and save a copy of your SQL statements in cache. After you execute the SQL statements the first time, subsequent executions are executed from the SQL Server cache. While this will help *subsequent* executions of your SQL statements, you still take a performance hit on the first execution.

As you can see from this scenario, you can gain some benefits if you use ADO to help optimize your SQL statements. Using stored procedures, however, will provide the greatest performance benefit overall. We'll be covering the subject of performance comparisons in much more depth in the next chapter.

User Prefixes and Security

When a user creates a stored procedure, the user's login is used to uniquely identify the stored procedure, and actually becomes part of the stored procedure itself. The user who created the stored procedure is considered to be the owner of that object. No other users (except the database owner, dbo) are allowed to execute or modify that stored procedure until the user who created it grants them access to that object.

The next figure shows how two different users, dbo and Stephanie, have created stored procedures that have the same name, in this case up_select_software_categories. The user prefix is actually part of the object name and each stored procedure is considered unique within the database:

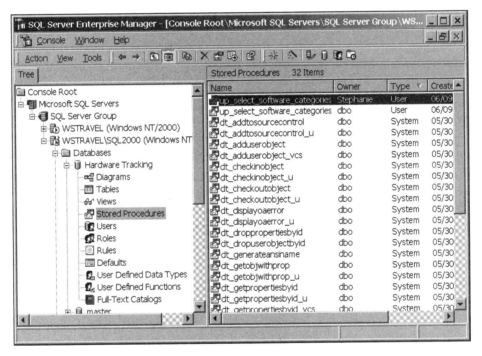

The sa (system administrator) login has the dbo (database owner) user prefix and is the ultimate owner of all objects in SQL Server. When SQL Server was installed, the setup program used the sa login to create all of the databases and objects in SQL Server. This is why you see the user prefix of dbo on all database objects.

When we execute stored procedures that have the dbo prefix, we do not have to do anything special because this is the default prefix. Assuming that we had the appropriate permissions to execute the stored procedure listed above, which contained the dbo user prefix, we would simply specify the stored procedure name as shown here:

```
EXEC up_select_software_categories
```

Note: the use of the keyword EXEC is not required if this is the only statement you are executing.

203

If we wanted to execute the stored procedure that has a user prefix of `Stephanie`, we would actually need to specify the user prefix as part of the stored procedure, as shown in the next code fragment:

```
EXEC stephanie.up_select_software_categories
```

How can we avoid all of this confusion and have all stored procedures created with a `dbo` user prefix? We can specify the `dbo` user prefix when we actually create the stored procedure, as shown in the following code fragment:

```
CREATE PROCEDURE dbo.up_select_hardware_categories AS
    SELECT * FROM software_category_t
```

Of course, in order to do this we need to be part of the `db_owner` database role, which we are in our sample database. When we created our login in SQL Server, we specified that our login should be assigned to the database role of `db_owner`.

By specifying the `dbo` owner prefix as part of the stored procedure name, as shown in the code above, we can create all of our stored procedures with a `dbo` user prefix. Of course, no users can execute the stored procedures we create until we have granted them the appropriate permissions. When we create a stored procedure, only users who belong to the `db_owner` role can access those stored procedures. We must grant the appropriate permissions to the users who are not part of the `db_owner` role before they can access them.

Let's take a quick look at how this is done. You don't have to actually create the stored procedure, just follow along, as we will be covering this again later in the chapter when we create our own stored procedures that we will execute from our VB program. To allow other users in our database to execute our stored procedure, we must grant them execute (**EXEC**) permission to our stored procedure, as shown in the following figure:

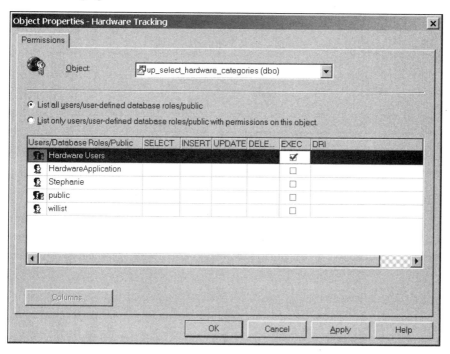

Since we have chosen to define and use roles in our database, we simply need to grant EXEC permission for this stored procedure to the role that we have defined. All logins that have been assigned to the role will inherit the permissions of the role. This simplifies the administrative tasks that we need to perform in our database.

We will cover the exact steps required to grant permissions on our stored procedures later in this chapter.

Create Procedure Syntax

Let's take a look at the syntax for creating a stored procedure before we actually dive in and start creating them. As with most other T-SQL statements in SQL Server, the syntax for creating a stored procedure is complex, so we'll take a look at the basic syntax here:

```
CREATE PROCEDURE procedure-name
      @parameter-name data-type [=default] [OUTPUT]
      [,...n]
      AS
      SQL statements
```

The *procedure-name* argument names the stored procedure and it is required. A stored procedure name can be up to 128 characters in length.

Stored procedures can contain one or more parameters, and each parameter name is specified starting with the "at" sign (@) followed by the *parameter-name*. The "at" sign identifies parameters and variables in your stored procedure. Each parameter name can also be up to 128 characters in length.

Each parameter must contain a data type, such as Integer or VarChar, as specified by the *data-type* argument.

For each parameter you can specify a default value, as represented by the *=default* argument in the syntax above. This is especially useful for numeric data types as you can specify a default value of zero if the parameter was not passed.

The OUTPUT keyword identifies the parameter as an output parameter. By default, all parameters are considered to be INPUT parameters unless the optional OUTPUT keyword is specified.

The *,...n* in the syntax specifies additional parameters as required.

The T-SQL statements that are contained in your stored procedure are specified after the AS keyword.

Select Stored Procedures

We now have data in the Software_Category_T table, so let's build a set of stored procedures to select, insert, update, and delete data from the Software_T table. Remember that this table has a foreign key reference to the Software_Category_T table and the data in that table will be used when we insert data into the Software_T table. We will also be creating a VB front end to act as the user interface for our stored procedures.

All of our stored procedures will be created in the Query Analyzer. This allows us to take advantage of the Object Browser in the Query Analyzer and also the debugging capabilities of this tool.

Try It Out – Create a Select Stored Procedure

We want to create a stored procedure that will select all software from the `Software_T` table (where software is a column in the `Software_T` table). We also want to select the software category name that the software belongs to, so we will need a second stored procedure.

To create these stored procedures:

1. Start the Query Analyzer and follow the login procedures outlined in Chapter 5.

> **Tip: you can hide the Object Browser so you have more room in the query window by clicking on the Object Browser icon on the toolbar. You can then show the Object Browser again at any time by clicking on the Object Browser icon on the toolbar.**

2. Change the database to the Hardware Tracking database and enter the following stored procedure:

```
CREATE PROCEDURE dbo.up_select_software AS

SELECT Software_ID, Software_Name_VC, Software_T.Software_Category_ID,
    Software_Category_VC

    FROM Software_T

    JOIN Software_Category_T on Software_T.Software_Category_ID =
        Software_Category_T.Software_Category_ID

    ORDER BY Software_Name_VC
```

3. Parse the stored procedure for errors, either by clicking on the Query menu and then clicking the Parse menu item, or by clicking the Parse Query icon on the toolbar.

4. Create the stored procedure by clicking on the Query menu and then clicking the Execute menu item, or by clicking on the Execute Query icon on the toolbar.

5. To grant permissions for other users to execute this stored procedure, start the Enterprise Manager. Expand the Hardware Tracking database and then select the Stored Procedures group.

6. Right-click on the up_select_software stored procedure, choose All Tasks, and then choose Manage Permissions from the submenu.

7. We want to grant execute permission to the Hardware Users role so check the checkbox in the EXEC row:

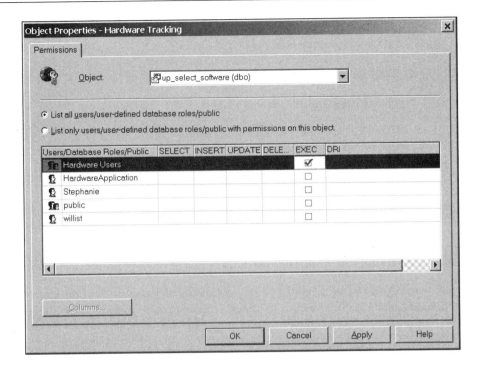

8. Click OK to dismiss the Object Properties dialog.

9. The next stored procedure we will create will select all category names.

   In the Query Analyzer, clear the current query window by clicking on the Clear Query Window icon on the toolbar, or open a new query window by clicking the New Query icon on the toolbar.

10. Enter the following stored procedure:

```
CREATE PROCEDURE dbo.up_select_categories AS

SELECT Software_Category_ID, Software_Category_VC

    FROM Software_Category_T

    ORDER BY Software_Category_VC
```

11. Parse the stored procedure for errors, either by clicking on the Query menu and then clicking the Parse menu item, or by clicking the Parse Query icon on the toolbar.

12. Create the stored procedure, by clicking on the Query menu and clicking the Execute menu item, or by clicking on the Execute Query icon on the toolbar.

13. Again, we want to grant permissions on this stored procedure to the Hardware Users role. In the Enterprise Manager, right-click on the Stored Procedures group and choose Refresh from the context menu.

14. Right-click on the up_select_categories stored procedure, choose All Tasks, and then choose Manage Permissions from the submenu.

15. Check the EXEC checkbox on the line for Hardware Users.

16. Click OK to dismiss the Object Properties dialog.

How It Works – Create a Select Stored Procedure

Let's start by taking a look at the code for the first stored procedure we created. This stored procedure will select all software titles and their respective software categories.

The first line of our stored procedure specifies that a stored procedure should be created with the name given. Notice that we have prefixed the stored procedure name with the dbo prefix. This will identify this stored procedure as being owned by the database administrator.

```
CREATE PROCEDURE dbo.up_select_software AS
```

The SELECT statement in our stored procedure is selecting the Software_ID, Software_Name_VC, and Software_Category_ID columns from the Software_T table. Notice that we have prefixed the Software_Category_ID column with the table name. This is because this column exists in both of the tables that we are selecting data from. We must let SQL Server know from which table the data for this column should be extracted. We will discuss this further in the next chapter.

The last column in the select list is Software_Category_VC. This column will be selected from the Software_Category_T table.

```
SELECT Software_ID, Software_Name_VC, Software_T.Software_Category_ID,
    Software_Category_VC
```

Next we specify the FROM clause and specify the Software_T table as the primary table that we want to select data from. Then we join the Software_Category_T table on the Software_T table. We will cover joins in the next chapter and will defer discussing the details of this JOIN statement until then. Basically a join allows us to select data from multiple tables, and provides a means for us to identify which row in the second table we want to manipulate.

```
FROM Software_T

JOIN Software_Category_T on Software_T.Software_Category_ID =
    Software_Category_T.Software_Category_ID
```

The last clause in our SELECT statement is the ORDER BY clause. This clause will order (sort) the results of the data selected. Here we have specified that we want the results ordered by the Software_Name_VC column:

```
ORDER BY Software_Name_VC
```

The next stored procedure that we created was the up_select_categories stored procedure. This stored procedure selects all rows from the Software_Category_T table. We have specified the Software_Category_ID and Software_Category_VC columns in our select list, and have specified that we want the results ordered by the Software_Category_VC column:

```
CREATE PROCEDURE dbo.up_select_categories AS

SELECT Software_Category_ID, Software_Category_VC

    FROM Software_Category_T

    ORDER BY Software_Category_VC
```

Using the Recordset Object to Return Results

Next we are going to create the VB portion of this exercise. This program will use the login form that we created in the last chapter to provide a login to the database. We will then create a simple form that will execute the two stored procedures that we just created, and display the results in combo boxes.

We will be using the Open method of the ADO Recordset object to return the results of our stored procedure. Let's take a look at the Open method syntax:

recordset-object.Open Source, ActiveConnection, CursorType, LockType, Options

The recordset-object represents a valid ADO Recordset object.

The first parameter of the Open method is the Source parameter and this specifies a table name to be opened, in-line SQL statements, or the stored procedure to be executed.

The ActiveConnection parameter lets the Open method know how it should access the database. This parameter can be in the form of a Connection object or a connection string.

The CursorType parameter specifies what type of **cursor** the database should use when opening the recordset. A cursor controls how the recordset is navigated and how the data is updated in the recordset. There are four different types of cursors that we can use: Dynamic, Keyset, Static, and Forward Only.

❑   A Dynamic cursor allows you to fully navigate the recordset, and all additions, changes, and deletions by other users are visible using this type of cursor.

❑   A Keyset cursor also allows full navigation of the recordset; however, you cannot see additions by other users, and deleted records are inaccessible.

❑   A Static cursor, as its name implies, is a static copy of the data. This type of cursor also allows full navigation; however, you cannot see any additions, changes, or deletions of records by other users.

❑   The last type of cursor, the Forward Only cursor, only allows navigation of the recordset in a forward motion. You cannot see any additions, changes, or deletions of records.

LockType specifies what type of **locking** the database should use on the recordset when editing of records occurs. There are four different lock types: Optimistic, Batch Optimistic, Pessimistic, and Read Only.

❑   An Optimistic lock specifies that the provider (SQL Server) should only lock the record when you execute the Update method of the Recordset object.

❑ A `Batch Optimistic` lock is used for batch updates and is like the `Optimistic` lock.

❑ A `Pessimistic` lock specifies that the provider should lock a record when editing occurs. This means that as soon as you start editing a record it will become locked.

❑ Finally, the `Read Only` lock type specifies that the record in the `Recordset` object can only be read.

The last parameter of the `Open` method is the `Options` parameter. This tells the database how it should interpret the `Source` parameter.

Now that we understand the syntax, let's get on and use it in our VB project.

Try It Out – VB to Process the Select Stored Procedure

1. To create the VB program start a new Standard EXE project.

2. Add a reference to the Microsoft ActiveX Data Objects 2.6 Library.

3. Set the Project Name to Software.

4. Set the Name property of the form to frmSoftware, the MaxButton property to False, and the Caption property to Software.

5. Add the following controls to the form:

Control	Name	Properties
Label	Label1	Caption = Software Title
ComboBox	cboSoftware	Style = 0 – Dropdown Combo
Label	Label2	Caption = Software Category
ComboBox	cboCategory	Style = 2 – Dropdown List
CommandButton	cmdSelect	Caption = Select
CommandButton	cmdExit	Caption = Exit

Your form should now look like this:

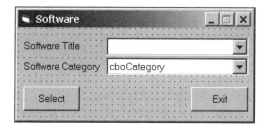

6. Add the login form (frmLogin) that we created in the last chapter.

7. Add the modConnect module that we also created in the last chapter.

8. The code that needs to be added to the project is listed in the *How It Works* section below. Save the project in a folder of your choice before proceeding.

9. After entering the new code for the login form and the first two procedures for the software form you can test the modifications that you have made. Save your project and then run it. You will see the Login form displayed. Choose a connection mode and authentication mode and then click the OK button.

10. When you have successfully logged in to SQL Server, the Login form will close and the Software form will be displayed. At this point you have successfully tested that the login form is working correctly, so end the program and continue adding code to the module and software form.

11. Once you've finished adding code, save your project. Before we can run the program, we need to insert at least one entry into the Software_T table. Since we have not yet covered INSERT stored procedures (this will be covered next), we will use the Query Analyzer to insert a row of data into the Software_T table.

Start the Query Analyzer if it is not already running. Once you log in, ensure the Hardware Tracking database is selected in the Database combo box on the toolbar. In the Object Browser in the Query Analyzer, expand the Hardware Tracking database and then expand the User Tables. Then expand the Software_T table and then the Columns for this table.

12. We can now see the columns that are contained in this table, and we see that we need to insert a value into the Software_Category_ID column. Before we can insert a value for this column, we need to know what values are available.

Let's execute the up_select_categories stored procedure in the Query Analyzer to see what data we have in this table. Simply enter the stored procedure name in the query window and click on the Execute Query icon on the toolbar. The following figure, overleaf, shows the results of the execution:

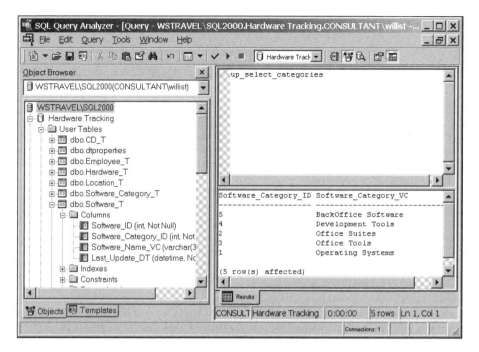

13. Let's use the **Operating Systems** category for the data that we will insert into the Software_T table. So what we need here is the Software_Category_ID for this entry, which is 1.

Enter and execute the following query in the Query Analyzer:

```
INSERT INTO Software_T
    (Software_Category_ID,Software_Name_VC,Last_Update_DT)
    VALUES(1,'Windows 2000 Professional',GETDATE())
```

This is a simple INSERT statement that inserts the data needed into the Software_T table. Remember that we do not insert a value for the Software_ID column, as this is an identity column that SQL Server will insert a value into.

14. We are now ready to run our program and test the newest functionality that we have added. Run your program and, as expected, the **Category** combo box has been loaded with data. Notice that **Operating Systems** is the last entry in the combo box.

15. Click on the Select button to have the Software Title combo box loaded. You now have one entry in the Software Title combo box. If you select that entry, the corresponding software category will be selected in the Software Category combo box, as shown in the figure opposite:

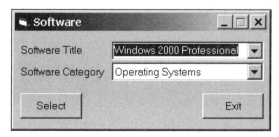

How It Works – VB to Process the Select Stored Procedure

The first thing that we want to do is to modify the login form (frmLogin) that we have added to our project. In the cmdOK_Click procedure, remove the MsgBox function that informs us that the login was successful, and change the If statement to include the Not keyword, and also remove the Else keyword from the If clause.

Since this procedure now only displays a message if the connection failed, we also want to add the End statement. This will cause our program to end should an error occur.

Next, remove the call to the TerminateConnection procedure and add the Unload statement. This will unload the form once we have established a successful connection.

Your complete code for this procedure should now look like this:

```
Private Sub cmdOK_Click()
    'Establish connection to SQL Server
    If Not EstablishConnection(blnDSN:=optDSN(0).Value, _
        strDSN:=txtDSN.Text, _
        blnWindowsAuthentication:=optMode(0).Value, _
        strLogin:=txtLogin.Text, _
        strPassword:=txtPassword.Text, _
        blnConnectString:=chkConnectString.Value) Then

        MsgBox "Connection Failed", vbCritical + vbOKOnly, "Login Failed"
        End
    End If

    Unload Me
End Sub
```

Now when we establish a successful connection to SQL Server, our login form will close and return to the form that called it.

If the user clicks the Cancel button on the login form we want to end the program. Modify the cmdCancel_Click procedure in the login form by removing the line Unload Me and replacing it with the VB End statement. Your procedure should now look like the following code:

```
Private Sub cmdCancel_Click()
    End
End Sub
```

In order to invoke the login form, we need to add some code to the Form_Load event of the software form (frmSoftware). Add the following code to your software form:

```
Private Sub Form_Load()
    'Display the login form
    frmLogin.Show vbModal
End Sub
```

When we close the software form we want to terminate the connection to the database. Add the following code to the Form_UnLoad event:

```
Private Sub Form_Unload(Cancel As Integer)
    'Terminate database connection
    Call TerminateConnection
End Sub
```

Since we are going to use the connection module (modConnect) in this and subsequent exercises, let's add an ADO Recordset object to this module to use when we open a recordset. This way we do not have to keep adding one to every project we create.

Add the following Recordset object declaration to the general declarations section of the module:

```
'Declare public objects
Public g_objConn As ADODB.Connection
Public g_objError As ADODB.Error
Public g_objRS As ADODB.Recordset
```

Since we have added a declaration for this object, we need to add some code to close it and dereference it. In the TerminateConnection procedure add the following code:

```
On Error Resume Next
g_objRS.Close
Set g_objRS = Nothing
g_objConn.Close
Set g_objConn = Nothing
Set g_objError = Nothing
```

That takes care of the Recordset object, so now let's add the code to the software form (frmSoftware) to load the **Category** combo box. This combo box will list all available software categories. Given this, we want to add some code in the Form_Load event of the software form. Note that error handling has been omitted from this and the following exercises in this chapter. The next chapter will introduce ADO error handling.

After the code to display the login form, we add some code to set a reference to the ADO Recordset object:

```
'Display the login form
frmLogin.Show vbModal
```

```
'Set a reference to the ADO recordset object
Set g_objRS = New ADODB.Recordset
```

We want to execute our stored procedure that we created earlier to return all categories. We do this by using the Open method of the Recordset object. As you can see from the following code we specified for the Source parameter the stored procedure that we created to select all categories. Then we specified the Connection object, g_objConn, for the ActiveConnection parameter. This object was activated by the login form and has an open connection to the database.

Since we only want to read the records in one direction we have specified the adOpenForwardOnly constant for the CursorType parameter. This constant is from the CursorTypeEnum enumeration and can be viewed in the VB Object Browser.

The adLockReadOnly constant has been specified for the LockType parameter, as we only want to read these records. This constant is from the LockTypeEnum enumeration and can also be viewed in the Object Browser.

The Options parameter has been set using the adCmdStoredProc constant from the CommandTypeEnum enumeration. This constant informs the provider what type of command we are trying to execute. Go ahead and insert this code into your project:

```
'Open the recordset object
g_objRS.Open "up_select_categories", g_objConn, adOpenForwardOnly, _
    adLockReadOnly, adCmdStoredProc
```

After our recordset has been opened, we want to loop through the recordset and populate the **Software Category** combo box. We start a Do loop and will perform the loop until an end-of-file condition has been reached on the recordset:

```
'Loop through the recordset and load the category combo box
Do While Not g_objRS.EOF
```

The first thing we do in the loop is to add the software category name to the combo box using the AddItem method of the combo box. For the combo box item we have specified the field name, Software_Category_VC, in the Recordset object. There are several ways to specify the field name in the Recordset object. The method shown below is one that I personally like. You could also specify the field name as g_objRS![software_category_vc] or as g_objRS("software_category_vc").

```
'Add the category name
cboCategory.AddItem g_objRS!software_category_vc
```

Next we add the software category ID. This is the primary key of the software category that we have just added to the combo box. We are using the ItemData property of the combo box to keep track of the primary key of each software category that we add to the combo box. This will be used when we select the data for the software titles later. Using the NewIndex property of the combo box we are able to add the software category ID to the ItemData property in the correct location so that it matches the List property of the software category just added:

```
'Add the category id
cboCategory.ItemData(cboCategory.NewIndex) = g_objRS!software_category_id
```

The last thing we do in the loop is to move to the next record in the Recordset object. We do this using the MoveNext method of the Recordset object. Then we loop back to the top, and start all over again.

```
'Move to the next record
g_objRS.MoveNext
Loop
```

Once an end-of-file condition has been reached on the Recordset object, we close the Recordset object and remove our reference to it:

```
'Close and dereference the recordset object
g_objRS.Close
Set g_objRS = Nothing
```

The next piece of code that we want to add is the code to end the program when you click on the **Exit** button. To do this, add the following code to the cmdExit_Click procedure:

```
Private Sub cmdExit_Click()
    Unload Me
End Sub
```

At this point you can run your project and the software category combo box will be populated. Congratulations on the execution of your first SQL Server stored procedure from Visual Basic!

To complete this exercise, we need to execute the first stored procedure that we created. This stored procedure will select all software titles, and the categories to which they belong.

The up_select_software stored procedure will return all software titles and their categories. When we load the software titles in the **Software Title** combo box and close the recordset, we will have no way to know what category the software title belongs to. To alleviate this problem, we will declare a one-dimensional array to keep track of the ID of the software category. Add the following code to the general declarations section of the software (frmSoftware) form:

```
'Declare variables
Dim arrSoftware() As Integer
```

When we click on the **Select** button in the software form, we want to execute the stored procedure, to select all software titles and have them loaded into the **Software Title** combo box. We want to add this new code to the cmdSelect_Click procedure.

The first thing we do in this procedure is to set a reference to the ADO Recordset object and then open our Recordset object. Notice that the Open method of the Recordset object is now executing our up_select_software stored procedure. Also notice that we have specified the adOpenStatic constant for our CursorType parameter. This type of cursor allows us to navigate and search the recordset. We need to move to the last record in the recordset, so that we can get an accurate count of how many records were returned in our recordset. A static cursor allows us to do this and then navigate backwards to the first record.

```
Private Sub cmdSelect_Click()
    'Set a reference to the ADO recordset object
    Set g_objRS = New ADODB.Recordset

    'Open the recordset object
    g_objRS.Open "up_select_software", g_objConn, adOpenStatic, _
        adLockReadOnly, adCmdStoredProc
```

Once the recordset is open, we move to the last record. Then we redimension our array using the `RecordCount` property of the `Recordset` object to determine the dimension of the array. An array by default is zero based (that is, its first index number is zero, not one), as is the `ListIndex` property of a combo box. The `RecordCount` property of a recordset returns the exact number of records so we subtract one from the number returned. Then we want to move to the first record in the `Recordset` object to prepare for reading it:

```
'Move to the last record so we can get an accurate count of the
'number of records in the recordset object
g_objRS.MoveLast

'Redim the software array to the correct number of entries
ReDim arrSoftware(g_objRS.RecordCount - 1)

'Now move to the first record to prepare for reading
g_objRS.MoveFirst
```

It is possible that we will be selecting data more than once during our testing. To that end, we don't want to end up with duplicate data in our **Software Title** combo box. Using the `Clear` method of the combo box, we can clear all existing entries using this one statement:

```
'Clear any existing entries
cboSoftware.Clear
```

Next, we loop through the `Recordset` object loading the combo box. This code is very similar to the code that we used to load the **Software Category** combo box. The one line that is different here is the line to load the array. We are using the `NewIndex` property of the `cboSoftware` combo box to determine the index position in the array into which we want to insert our data. This keeps the `ListIndex` of the combo box in sync with the `Index` of the array. We place the ID of the software category that the software title belongs to into the array. This provides an efficient lookup in the array to find the software category ID. We will see this in use shortly.

```
'Loop through the recordset and load the software combo box
Do While Not g_objRS.EOF
   'Add the software name
   cboSoftware.AddItem g_objRS!software_name_vc
   'Add the software id
   cboSoftware.ItemData(cboSoftware.NewIndex) = g_objRS!software_id
   'Add the software category id to the software array
   arrSoftware(cboSoftware.NewIndex) = g_objRS!software_category_id
   'Move to the next record
   g_objRS.MoveNext
Loop
```

After our combo box has been loaded, we close the `Recordset` object and remove the reference to it:

```
'Close and dereference the recordset object
g_objRS.Close
Set g_objRS = Nothing
End Sub
```

When we click on a software title in the **Software Title** combo box, we need to look up the corresponding software category and select it in the **Software Category** combo box. To do this we need to add some code to the click event for the cboSoftware combo box.

The first thing we want to do in the cboSoftware_Click procedure is to declare our local variables:

```
Private Sub cboSoftware_Click()
    'Declare local variables
    Dim intIndex As Integer
```

We want to loop through the entries in the cboCategory combo box, so we set up our loop using the ListCount property of the cboCategory combo box as the ending number in our loop. Since the ListCount property contains the actual number of entries in the combo box and the ListIndex property is zero-based, we specify ListCount - 1 to get the correct number of items:

```
    'Loop through the category combo box until a match is found
    For intIndex = 0 To cboCategory.ListCount - 1
```

Within the loop we check the ItemData property to see if it is equal to the entry in the array. The ItemData property and the array entry both contain the software category ID. We use the intIndex variable to check the specific entry in the ListIndex property of the cboCategory combo box and the currently selected entry in the cboSoftware combo box, to point to the corresponding entry in the array.

If a match was found, we set the ListIndex property of the cboCategory combo box using the intIndex variable, which will select that entry. We then exit the For loop using the Exit For statement.

If no match was found, we restart the loop using the next number:

```
        If cboCategory.ItemData(intIndex) = arrSoftware(cboSoftware.ListIndex) Then
            cboCategory.ListIndex = intIndex
            Exit For
        End If
    Next
End Sub
```

We are now able to *select* data from the Software_T table, and display the software title along with the corresponding software category. Let's now focus our attention on programmatically *inserting* data into the Software_T table.

Stored Procedure Parameters

Stored procedures are similar to funtions in programming languages in that they can accept and return parameters and can also return values. Stored procedures contain T-SQL statements; T-SQL is the programming language that your applications use to interface with SQL Server databases to manipulate data. Using T-SQL, you can write stored procedures that contain logic, can perform conditional branching in the code, and can also perform loops. These topics will be introduced in subsequent chapters.

We just mentioned that stored procedures are able to accept and return parameters, so let's take a look at these. Stored procedures can have either **input** and **output** parameters, or none at all. Input parameters allow you to pass data to a stored procedure, just as you can pass data to a procedure or function in your VB program. Output parameters allow the stored procedures to pass data back to the caller. We will examine the input parameter in more depth later in this chapter and the output parameter in more depth in the next chapter.

Return values are like return codes in VB. A stored procedure can return a value to indicate the success or failure of the execution. In fact, stored procedures return a return value of zero by default. You can specify the value that you want a stored procedure to return. All return values must be a SQL Server `Integer` data type. An `Integer` data type in SQL Server can contain a value in the range of –2,147,483,648 to 2,147,483,647. SQL Server data types are detailed in Appendix A.

It is important to note that stored procedures do not have to contain any parameters at all. Let's take a look at the code for the following stored procedure, also shown earlier. (You do not need to code the examples listed in this section.)

```
CREATE PROCEDURE up_select_software_categories AS

SELECT Software_Category_ID, Software_Category_VC
    FROM Software_Category_T
```

This stored procedure simply selects all data from the `Software_Category_T` table and contains no parameters. Notice that we are using the standards defined in Chapter 3 for our stored procedure name. That standard specified that we should prefix our stored procedure name with `up_select` to indicate a stored procedure that selects data and accepts no parameters.

So, what if we wanted to select specific data from the `Software_Category_T` table? We could create the following stored procedure:

```
CREATE PROCEDURE up_parmsel_software_categories
    @Category_ID INT AS

SELECT Software_Category_VC
    FROM Software_Category_T
    WHERE Software_Category_ID = @Category_ID
```

This stored procedure also uses our naming standard from Chapter 3, and specifies that this stored procedure selects data and accepts parameters. Notice that we have specified an input parameter of `@Category_ID` and that this input parameter is an `Integer` data type. Notice the abbreviation of the data type name.

The `SELECT` statement will select the `Software_Category_VC` column from the `Software_Category_T` table where the `Software_Category_ID` matches the input parameter.

Since this stored procedure would only return one column, `Software_Category_VC`, we could return this column as an output parameter. Let's take a look at the same stored procedure that has been modified to return this column as an output parameter:

```
CREATE PROCEDURE up_parmsel_software_categories
    @Category_ID INT,
```

```
        @Category_Name VARCHAR(30) OUTPUT AS

SELECT @Category_Name = Software_Category_VC
    FROM Software_Category_T
    WHERE Software_Category_ID = @Category_ID
```

What we have done here is to define an output parameter called `@Category_Name`. Notice that we have specified the data type as well as the `OUTPUT` keyword. We have also used this parameter in the `SELECT` statement, assigning the value of the `Software_Category_VC` column directly to this parameter.

Suppose that in addition to an output parameter we also wanted a return value indicating success or failure. We could modify the stored procedure above to include a return value, which is shown in the next code fragment:

```
CREATE PROCEDURE up_parmsel_software_categories
    @Category_ID INT,
    @Category_Name VARCHAR(30) OUTPUT AS

SELECT @Category_Name = Software_Category_VC
    FROM Software_Category_T
    WHERE Software_Category_ID = @Category_ID

IF @@ERROR <> 0
    RETURN 1
ELSE
    RETURN 0
```

Using the built-in system function `@@ERROR`, we check the last error number. This function returns the error value for the last T-SQL statement executed. If no error occurred, then this function returns zero, otherwise it returns the last error value. Keep in mind that this function only returns the error number of the last executed T-SQL statement.

Next, by using a little conditional logic, we check the value contained in the `@@ERROR` function to see if the error number is not equal to zero. If it is not we return a value of one, otherwise we return a value of zero.

The `IF...ELSE` statement in SQL Server is very similar to the `IF...ELSE` statement in VB. However, this statement does not contain the `THEN` keyword nor does it contain the `END IF` keyword. Using the `IF...ELSE` statement we can execute a single T-SQL statement or a block of T-SQL statements. If we wanted to execute a block of T-SQL statements we would have to enclose the block of T-SQL statements, using the control-of-flow keywords `BEGIN` and `END`. We will cover more on this in Chapter 10.

So our stored procedure above will now accept one input parameter, return one output parameter, and also return a value indicating success or failure.

It's time to put this newfound knowledge to use as we demonstrate creating `INSERT`, `UPDATE`, and `DELETE` stored procedures using practical hands-on exercises.

Insert Stored Procedures

Insert stored procedures will take data passed from your program and insert it into the appropriate tables. As expected, these types of stored procedures will require us to declare some input parameters when we build them.

We know from the INSERT statement that we ran a few minutes ago what type of data we will need to pass to this stored procedure. We need the ID of the software category, along with the name of the software title. We will not pass the date as a parameter as we will let SQL Server take care of inserting the current date and time using the GETDATE function.

Try It Out – Create an Insert Stored Procedure

To create this stored procedure:

1. Start the Query Analyzer and log in, if you don't still have it open.

2. Enter the following stored procedure.

> Tip: you can quickly create this stored procedure by dragging the table name and column names from the Object Browser to the query window.

```
CREATE PROCEDURE dbo.up_parmins_software
    @Software_Title_VC VARCHAR(30),
    @Software_Category_ID INT AS

INSERT INTO Software_T
    (Software_Name_VC, Software_Category_ID, Last_Update_DT)
    VALUES(@Software_Title_VC, @Software_Category_ID, GETDATE())
```

3. Parse the stored procedure for errors, by either clicking on the Query menu and then clicking the Parse menu item, or clicking the Parse Query icon on the toolbar.

4. Create the stored procedure, by clicking on the Query menu and clicking the Execute menu item, or by clicking on the Execute Query icon on the toolbar.

5. To grant permissions for other users to execute this stored procedure, start the Enterprise Manager.

6. Expand the Hardware Tracking database and then expand the Stored Procedures group.

7. Right-click on the up_parmins_software stored procedure, choose All Tasks, and then choose Manage Permissions from the submenu.

8. We want to grant execute permission to the Hardware Users role, so check the EXEC checkbox in this row.

9. Click OK to close the Object Properties dialog.

How It Works – Create an Insert Stored Procedure

The first line of our stored procedure should look familiar, as we have specified the CREATE PROCEDURE T-SQL statement followed by the stored procedure name:

```
CREATE PROCEDURE dbo.up_parmins_software
```

The next two lines of our stored procedure are the input parameters. Remember that unless we specify the OUTPUT keyword, all parameters are input parameters. For each parameter that we specify, the parameter name is prefixed with an "at" sign (@). This is the syntax required by SQL Server when specifying user variables and parameters. Next, we identify each parameter's data type. The first parameter has a VarChar data type, and can contain up to 30 characters. The second parameter is an Integer data type.

```
@Software_Title_VC VARCHAR(30),
@Software_Category_ID INT AS
```

The INSERT statement specifies the table name that we want to insert data into. Remember that the INTO keyword is optional, but does help the readability of the statement. Next, we specify the column names that we want to insert data into. These column names can be in any order; they do not have to appear in the same order in which they are defined in the table.

The last line of the INSERT statement contains the values that we want to insert, preceded by the VALUES keyword. These values must be in the same order as the column list in the preceding line. The first two values are our input parameters and the last value is the GETDATE function, which returns the current date and time:

```
INSERT INTO Software_T
    (Software_Name_VC, Software_Category_ID, Last_Update_DT)
    VALUES(@Software_Title_VC, @Software_Category_ID, GETDATE())
```

Try It Out – VB Code to Process Insert Stored Procedure

The VB portion of this exercise will use the existing software project that we created in the last exercise. We merely want to add a command button to allow us to execute the code to insert a row of data into the Software_T table.

To modify the Software.vbp project:

1. Start Visual Basic, and open the Software.vbp project from the last exercise.

2. Add a command button to the Software form (frmSoftware) and set its Name property to cmdInsert and its Caption property to Insert. The following figure shows the placement of the command button on the form:

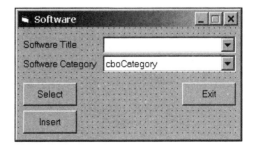

3. Add the code to execute this stored procedure, as discussed in the *How It Works* section.

4. We are now ready to test our new code, so save your project before you begin. Run your project and choose the connection mode and authentication mode of your choice. Click on the Select button and then examine the contents of the Software Title combo box; we only have one entry.

5. Now, enter a value in the Software Title combo box and choose the appropriate software category in the Software Category combo box. I chose to insert the value of Office 2000 as the software title and selected Office Suites as the category. Then click the Insert button.

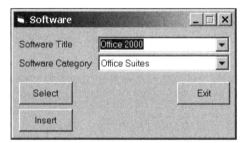

6. Click on the Select button again, and then examine the contents of the Software Title combo box and select your new entry. The appropriate category should now be selected in the combo box.

How It Works – VB Code to Process the Insert Stored Procedure

In our VB code, we want to add code to the `cmdInsert_Click` procedure in the Software form (`frmSoftware`). When you click on the Insert button this procedure is fired, and is the logical choice for our code to execute our `INSERT` stored procedure.

The first thing we want to do in this procedure is to validate the data. The first validation is performed against the Software Title combo box. Since this combo box has its `Style` property set to allow both inputting data and selecting data, we need to validate the `Text` property of the combo box.

Here we are validating that some data exists by checking the length of the `Text` property. We also use the `Trim` function to remove any spaces, just in case a user enters a space by pressing the space bar. If the length of the `Text` property is zero, indicating that no text exists, then we display a message using the `MsgBox` function. Remember that the `MsgBox` function accepts the message as a string, followed by the optional icon and buttons to display, followed up by the message box title.

We have specified the message, and have then specified the `vbInformation` constant from the `VbMsgBoxStyle` enumeration to display the Information icon, plus the `vbOKOnly` constant to display only the OK button. Last, we have specified the title of the message box.

After control is returned from the message box, we set the focus to the control that is in error, in this case the Software Title combo box (`cboSoftware`). Then we exit the procedure.

```
Private Sub cmdInsert_Click()
    'Validate software title was entered
    If Len(Trim(cboSoftware.Text)) = 0 Then
```

223

```
      MsgBox "You must enter a software title to add.", _
          vbInformation + vbOKOnly, "Software Insert"
      cboSoftware.SetFocus
      Exit Sub
  End If
```

The next validation that is performed is the validation of a selection of a category. The **Category** combo box (cboCategory) has its Style set to 2 – Dropdown List, which means that this combo box will display a list, from which we can select entries only. We cannot enter data in this combo box.

Given this, we need only to validate the ListIndex property of the combo box. If the ListIndex property is equal to –1, then no selection has been made. Therefore, we check to see if the ListIndex property is –1, and if it is we display a message using the MsgBox function.

Then we set focus to the control in error and then exit the procedure:

```
  'Validate software category was selected
  If cboCategory.ListIndex = -1 Then
      MsgBox "You must select the appropriate software category.", _
          vbInformation + vbOKOnly, "Software Insert"
      cboCategory.SetFocus
      Exit Sub
  End If
```

If all data has been validated, then we find ourselves ready to execute our INSERT stored procedure to insert data into the Software_T table.

First, we declare an ADO Command object. There are several methods that we can use to execute our INSERT stored procedure, including another variation of the Command object, as well as using the Connection object. We will explore all of these methods as we progress through this chapter. However, this method is by far the easiest. The Command object provides the most reliable method of inserting data without errors.

Next, we set the properties of the Command object. The ActiveConnection property is set to an active connection. This can be an active Connection object, as in our case, or it can be a connection string. If you did not already have a Connection object defined and opened, you could use a connection string.

Then we set the CommandText property, which can contain the name of a stored procedure, in-line SQL statements, or the name of a table.

Last, we set the CommandType property. This property specifies what type of command we are executing. The values for this property can be found in the CommandTypeEnum enumeration. Since we are executing a stored procedure, we have specified the adCmdStoredProc constant.

```
  'Declare and set a reference to the Command object
  Dim objCmd As New ADODB.Command

  'Set the command object properties
  Set objCmd.ActiveConnection = g_objConn
```

```
        objCmd.CommandText = "up_parmins_software"
        objCmd.CommandType = adCmdStoredProc
```

We have two parameters that we need to pass to this stored procedure. Here we are using the
Parameters collection of the Command object. We append a parameter to the Parameters collection
using the Append method of the Parameters collection. In order to create the parameter, we use the
CreateParameter method of the Command object.

The CreateParameter method accepts five parameters: Name, Type, Direction, Size, and Value.

- ❏ The Name parameter is a string value that represents the name of the parameter. This is a
  name that you can choose, and can be used to access the parameter in the Parameters
  collection by name.

- ❏ The Type parameter is a value from the DataTypeEnum enumeration. This is the data type
  of the parameter in your stored procedure.

- ❏ The Direction parameter expects one of the constants from the
  ParameterDirectionEnum enumeration and specifies the direction of the parameter in
  your stored procedure.

- ❏ The Size parameter specifies the length of the parameter that your stored procedure expects.

- ❏ Finally, the Value parameter is the value that is to be passed to your stored procedure parameter.

> **Tip: the parameters in the Parameters collection must be specified in the same
> order as the parameters in your stored procedure.**

The first parameter that we have appended to the Parameters collection is the software title, and we
have given this parameter a name of Software. We have specified the data type for this parameter as
adVarChar. This is the data type of the parameter in SQL Server, not VB. The differences in the data
types are outlined in Appendix A. We specify that this parameter is an input parameter by using the
adParamInput constant. Then we specify the size of the parameter, as was specified in our stored
procedure. Finally, we specify the value of this parameter. We are getting the value from the **Software
Title** combo box's (cboSoftware) Text property.

The second parameter that we have specified is the software category ID. This parameter is a SQL
Server Integer data type, and we are getting the value of this parameter from the cboCategory
combo box's ItemData property. Remember that we set the ItemData property to the
Software_Category_ID, which is the primary key of the category that we have selected in this
combo box. Notice that we have not specified a size. This is because we do not have to specify the size
of numeric data types, as they are represented by fix values. For example, a SQL Server Integer data
type has a storage size of 4 bytes.

```
        'Append the parameters to the parameters collection
        objCmd.Parameters.Append objCmd.CreateParameter("Software", _
            adVarChar, adParamInput, 30, cboSoftware.Text)
        objCmd.Parameters.Append objCmd.CreateParameter("Category", _
            adInteger, adParamInput, , cboCategory.ItemData(cboCategory.ListIndex))
```

Before we explain this next section of code, it should be noted again that error handling has been omitted. This will be covered in the next chapter.

We execute the command object using the `Execute` method. This will in turn execute our stored procedure in SQL Server and insert our data into the `Software_T` table.

The last line of code in this procedure removes the reference to the `Command` object:

```
    'Execute the command object to insert the data
    objCmd.Execute

    'Remove the reference to the command object
    Set objCmd = Nothing
End Sub
```

We can now select and *insert* data into the `Software_T` table from Visual Basic using stored procedures. Let's move on and examine how we can *update* this data. The INSERT stored procedure that we have just created is a very simple stored procedure and does not check for duplicate data. We will address this issue later when we start building more complex INSERT stored procedures.

Update Stored Procedures

At some point the data we have inserted into our database will become outdated. Most of the time we will be able to update some or all of the columns in the table to keep the data up to date. This allows the data to serve a useful purpose, and allows the users of our system to make informed decisions based on the data in our tables.

When we look at updating data there is one thing to keep in mind. We do not want to update the primary key for the data. There are two reasons for this, the first of which is that the data in the table could be referenced as a foreign key in another table. Also the rules of foreign key constraints will prevent this and cause an error. As a general rule, you never want to update the primary key of a table.

However, there are exceptions to this. Suppose our primary key were not defined as an `Integer` data type and an identity column, but instead as some combination of numbers and letters. Suppose also that we had set up this column to automatically cascade updates to the primary key. Under these circumstances it would be all right to update the primary key.

Try It Out – Create an Update Stored Procedure

There are two columns that we want to be able to update in the `Software_T` table, the software title and the software category. So, we know that we will need to create parameters in our stored procedure for these two columns.

But how do we identify which row in the `Software_T` table to update? If we think about this for a second, we realize that we also need to make the primary key a parameter to our update stored procedure. Given this, we want to set about creating our update stored procedure.

To create this store procedure:

1. Start the Query Analyzer and log in if you don't still have it open.

2. Enter the following stored procedure:

```
CREATE PROCEDURE dbo.up_parmupd_software
    @Software_ID INT,
    @Software_Title_VC VARCHAR(30),
    @Software_Category_ID INT AS

UPDATE Software_T
    SET Software_Name_VC = @Software_Title_VC,
    Software_Category_ID = @Software_Category_ID,
    Last_Update_DT = GETDATE()
    WHERE Software_ID = @Software_ID
```

3. Parse the stored procedure for errors, by either clicking on the Query menu and clicking the Parse menu item, or clicking the Parse Query icon on the toolbar.

4. Create the stored procedure, by clicking on the Query menu and clicking the Execute menu item, or by clicking on the Execute Query icon on the toolbar.

5. To grant permissions for other users to execute this stored procedure, start the Enterprise Manager.

6. Expand the Hardware Tracking database, and then expand the Stored Procedures group.

7. Right-click on the up_parmupd_software stored procedure, choose All Tasks, and then choose Manage Permissions from the sub menu.

8. We want to grant execute permission to the Hardware Users role, so check the EXEC checkbox in this row.

9. Click OK to close the Object Properties dialog.

How It Works – Create an Update Stored Procedure

Having identified the parameters needed for this stored procedure in an earlier discussion, the parameters shown should come as no surprise. The first parameter in our stored procedure will identify the row of data that we want to update in the Software_T table. The second and third parameters were also used in the last stored procedure, and contain the software title and the primary key of the software category.

```
    @Software_ID INT,
    @Software_Title_VC VARCHAR(30),
    @Software_Category_ID INT AS
```

We saw the syntax of the UPDATE T-SQL statement in Chapter 5, and also saw how this statement worked. Our stored procedure uses the same syntax for the UPDATE statement and the first line of this statement contains the table that we want to update.

The next line of the UPDATE statement contains the keyword SET followed by the first column in the Software_T table to be updated. We use the input parameter, @Software_Title_VC, as the value that we want updated in the Software_Name_VC column. The next two lines of the UPDATE statement update the Software_Category_ID and Last_Update_DT columns.

The WHERE clause of the UPDATE statement specifies the search condition to be used when updating the data in our table. This limits the update to one row of data, where the value in the Software_ID column is equal to the value in the @Software_ID input parameter.

```
UPDATE Software_T
    SET Software_Name_VC = @Software_Title_VC,
    Software_Category_ID = @Software_Category_ID,
    Last_Update_DT = GETDATE()
    WHERE Software_ID = @Software_ID
```

Try It Out – VB Code to Process the Update Stored Procedure

We are now ready to create the VB portion of this exercise. Once again, we will use the same project that we have been working with in this chapter.

1. Open the Software.vbp project and perform the following steps.

2. As in the last example, we want to add one command button to the Software form (frmSoftware). Add the new command button, set its Name property to cmdUpdate and its Caption property to Update. The adjacent figure illustrates the placement of the command button on the form:

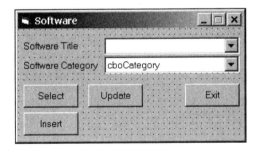

3. Enter the code for this new command button, listed in the *How It Works* section.

4. We are now ready to test our update functionality. Save your project and then run it. Choose the DSN and authentication mode of your choice and click the OK button on the Login form.

5. Click the Select button on the Software form to populate the Software Title combo box. Choose a software title in this box, and then change the name of the software title, the software category, or both. Then click on the Update button to process the update.

6. To verify your changes, click on the Select button again to repopulate the Software Title combo box and select the item that you changed:

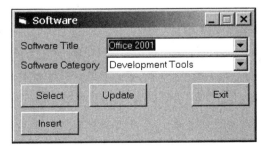

228

How It Works – VB Code to Process the Update Stored Procedure

In our VB code, we need to discuss the behavior of the combo box before we proceed. We know from the stored procedure that we just created that we will be able to update the software title and the category to which it is assigned. This brings up the point of the **Software Title** combo box's (cboSoftware) behavior. When we select an entry in the combo box, the ListIndex property is set to the item number selected. Keeping in mind that this is a zero-based index, if we select the second item in the combo box, the ListIndex property is set to 1.

So, we have selected the second item in the combo box and the ListIndex property is set to 1. However, if we attempt to change the software title, the ListIndex is set to −1 because the Style property is set to allow us to select items or enter items.

This behavior is fine when we select an item or insert a new item because we are looking at either the ListIndex or the Text property. However, when we want to update an item in this combo box, we want the values for both the ListIndex and Text properties. The ListIndex property allows us to retrieve the correct ItemData property, which contains the primary key of the software title that we want to update.

Given this, we need to declare a variable in the general declarations section of the **Software form** (frmSoftware) to keep track of the correct software ID for the item selected in the **Software Title** combo box:

```
'Declare variables
Dim arrSoftware() As Integer
Dim lngSoftwareID As Long
```

Next, we want to add a line of code to the cboSoftware_Click procedure to save the value in the ItemData property of the cboSoftware combo box. Add this line of code at the end of this procedure:

```
    'Save the key
    lngSoftwareID = cboSoftware.ItemData(cboSoftware.ListIndex)
End Sub
```

Now that we have saved the value that was contained in the ItemData property we can move on and examine the code in the cmdUpdate_Click procedure. This is the code that gets executed when you click on the **Update** button.

As was done in the cmdInsert_Click procedure, the first thing we want to do is validate the data. Here we are validating that something was entered for the software title, and that a category was selected. These are the same validations that were performed in the cmdInsert_Click procedure.

```
Private Sub cmdUpdate_Click()
    'Validate software title was entered
    If Len(Trim(cboSoftware.Text)) = 0 Then
        MsgBox "You must enter the new software title.", _
            vbInformation + vbOKOnly, "Software Update"
        cboSoftware.SetFocus
        Exit Sub
    End If
```

```
    'Validate software cateogry was selected
    If cboCategory.ListIndex = -1 Then
        MsgBox "You must select the appropriate software category.", _
            vbInformation + vbOKOnly, "Software Update"
        cboCategory.SetFocus
        Exit Sub
    End If
```

Next, we declare and set a reference to the Command object and declare an ADO Parameter object:

```
    'Declare and set a reference to the Command object
    Dim objCmd As New ADODB.Command

    'Declare the Parameter object
    Dim objParm As ADODB.Parameter
```

We set the Command object's properties, just as we did in the cmdInsert_Click procedure. This time however, we have specified the up_parmupd_software stored procedure for the CommandText property:

```
    'Set the command object properties
    Set objCmd.ActiveConnection = g_objConn
    objCmd.CommandText = "up_parmupd_software"
    objCmd.CommandType = adCmdStoredProc
```

We mentioned earlier that we would demonstrate different methods for executing stored procedures. This is the next method that we wish to demonstrate. Again, we are using the Command object and the Parameters collection. However, this time we have declared a Parameter object, and will set the various properties of the Parameter object, and then will append the Parameter object to the Parameters collection.

This is the method that you would need to use if you had numeric data types that contained decimal values. You would then need to set the NumericScale property of the Parameter object to indicate how many digits were to the right of the decimal. You would also use this method for SQL Server Text data types, and would need to set the Attributes property of the Parameter object to specify that a long VarChar data type was being passed.

We are using simple data types just to demonstrate this method, and do not need to specify any other properties of the Parameter object other than those we specify here.

The first parameter in our stored procedure is the parameter that contains the primary key of the row of data to be updated. We set a reference to the ADO Parameter object and then proceed to set the various properties of the Parameter object. The first property that we set is the Name property. Again, this is the name that you would use if you wanted to access this parameter in the Parameters collection by name. Since this parameter contains the primary key of the row to update, we set the Type property to the adInteger constant.

An Integer data type in SQL Server is equal to a Long data type in VB. SQL Server data types are detailed in Appendix A with a comparison of the differences between SQL Server and VB data types.

Next, we set the `Direction` property using the `adParamInput` constant and then set the `Value` property to the `lngSoftwareID` variable. This was set using the saved data from the `ItemData` property of the `cboSoftware` combo box.

Once all of the properties of the `Parameter` object have been set, we append the `Parameter` object to the `Parameters` collection:

```
'Set a reference to the ADO Parameter object and then set
'the Parameter's properties
Set objParm = New ADODB.Parameter
objParm.Name = "Software ID"
objParm.Type = adInteger
objParm.Direction = adParamInput
objParm.Value = lngSoftwareID

'Append the Parameter to the Parameters collection
objCmd.Parameters.Append objParm
```

We repeat the process of setting the next two parameters that are input to our stored procedure. The next parameter contains the software title and its `Value` property is set using the `Text` property of the `cboSoftware` combo box. The last parameter contains the primary key of the software category that this software title is associated with, and its `Value` property is set using the `ItemData` property for the currently selected item in the `cboCategory` combo box.

```
'Set a reference to the ADO Parameter object and then set
'the Parameter's properties
Set objParm = New ADODB.Parameter
objParm.Name = "Software Title"
objParm.Type = adVarChar
objParm.Direction = adParamInput
objParm.Size = 30
objParm.Value = cboSoftware.Text

'Append the Parameter to the Parameters collection
objCmd.Parameters.Append objParm

'Set a reference to the ADO Parameter object and then set
'the Parameter's properties
Set objParm = New ADODB.Parameter
objParm.Name = "Category ID"
objParm.Type = adInteger
objParm.Direction = adParamInput
objParm.Value = cboCategory.ItemData(cboCategory.ListIndex)

'Append the Parameter to the Parameters collection
objCmd.Parameters.Append objParm
```

After all parameters have been created and appended to the `Parameters` collection, we execute the `Command` object to have our update stored procedure executed:

```
'Execute the command object to update the data
objCmd.Execute
```

Then we remove our references to the objects declared in this procedure:

```
    'Remove the references to the ADO objects
    Set objParm = Nothing
    Set objCmd = Nothing
End Sub
```

Now that we are able to select, insert, and update data, all we have left to do is create a method to allow us to *delete* data. This is covered in the next section.

Delete Stored Procedures

At some time or another the data in your database will outlive its usefulness. The time will then have come to remove the data from the database, so it stays up to date. This is where the delete stored procedure comes into play.

This stored procedure will allow us to delete a specific row of data in a table. The stored procedure is really simple but can be very dangerous. When we delete data, it is gone. The only way to recover the data is from the transaction logs, or from a backup of our database. It is therefore extremely important that only the correct users have access to stored procedures that delete data.

Try It Out – Create a Delete Stored Procedure

The delete stored procedure that we are going to create will delete only one row of data from the Software_T table. Therefore, we need to specify an input parameter that specifies the row of data to delete.

To create this stored procedure:

1. Start the Query Analyzer and log in if you don't still have it open.

2. Enter the following stored procedure:

```
CREATE PROCEDURE dbo.up_parmdel_software
    @Software_ID INT AS

DELETE FROM Software_T
    WHERE Software_ID = @Software_ID
```

3. Parse the stored procedure for errors, by either clicking on the Query menu and clicking the Parse menu item, or clicking the Parse Query icon on the toolbar.

4. Create the stored procedure, by clicking on the Query menu and clicking the Execute menu item, or by clicking on the Execute Query icon on the toolbar.

5. To grant permissions for other users to execute this stored procedure, start the Enterprise Manager.

6. Expand the Hardware Tracking database and then expand the Stored Procedures group.

7. Right-click on the up_parmdel_software stored procedure, choose **All Tasks**, and then choose **Manage Permissions** from the sub menu.

8. We want to grant execute permission to the **Hardware Users** role, so check the **EXEC** checkbox in this row.

9. Click **OK** to close the **Object Properties** dialog.

How It Works – Create a Delete Stored Procedure

Our delete stored procedure only accepts one parameter, the ID of the primary key of the row of data to be deleted:

```
CREATE PROCEDURE dbo.up_parmdel_software
    @Software_ID INT AS
```

The DELETE statement specifies the table that we want to delete data from, in this case the Software_T table. Notice that we have also specified the optional keyword FROM. Again, this just helps to improve the readability of our code.

```
DELETE FROM Software_T
```

The WHERE clause in our DELETE statement specifies the search condition that must be matched before a delete can occur. Again, we are specifying that the value contained in the Software_ID column must match the value contained in the input parameter @Software_ID:

```
WHERE Software_ID = @Software_ID
```

Try It Out – VB Code to Process the Delete Stored Procedure

To create the VB portion of this exercise, we will once again use the same project that we have been working with in this chapter.

1. Open the Software.vbp project and perform the following steps.

2. Add a command button to the **Software** form (frmSoftware) and set its **Name** property to **cmdDelete** and its **Caption** property to **Delete**. Use the following figure as a guide for the placement of this command button on the form:

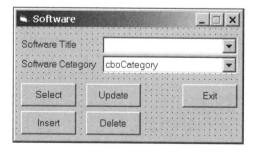

3. Enter the code listed in the *How It Works* section.

4. At this point, save your project and then run it. Use any DSN mode and authentication mode to log in with, and then click the **OK** button on the **Login** form.

5. Populate the Software Title combo box by clicking on the Select button. Choose an item in the Software Title combo box to delete, and then click on the Delete button:

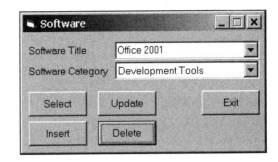

6. To confirm the deletion of the item, click on the Select button again to repopulate the Software combo box and then look for the deleted item.

How It Works – VB Code to Process the Delete Stored Procedure

The only code that we need to add to our VB project is contained in the `cmdDelete_Click` procedure. The first thing we want to do in this procedure is to validate that an item was selected in the Software Title combo box.

In order to do this, we validate that the `ListIndex` property of the `cboSoftware` combo box does not equal -1, which indicates that no entry has been selected. If this is true, then we display a message using the `MsgBox` function:

```
Private Sub cmdDelete_Click()
    'Validate software title was selected
    If cboSoftware.ListIndex = -1 Then
        MsgBox "You must select the software title to delete.", _
            vbInformation + vbOKOnly, "Software Delete"
        cboSoftware.SetFocus
        Exit Sub
    End If
```

The next method of executing a parameterized stored procedure that we want to demonstrate does not use the `Command` object. Instead, we use the `Connection` object that was set and opened in the login form. Using this method for stored procedures that accept simple parameters is quick and easy.

The first thing we need to do now that our data has been validated is to declare a local string variable that will contain the SQL statement to be executed:

```
    'Declare local variables
    Dim strSQL As String
```

Then we build the SQL string, setting it to the name of our stored procedure and the parameters the stored procedure expects, in this case just one parameter:

```
'Build the SQL string
    strSQL = "up_parmdel_software " & cboSoftware.ItemData(cboSoftware.ListIndex)
```

Finally, we use the `Execute` method of the `Connection` object to execute our SQL string:

```
    'Execute the SQL string
    g_objConn.Execute strSQL
End Sub
```

Stored Procedure Summary

At this point we have created stored procedures to select, insert, update, and delete data. We have executed these stored procedures from our VB program to manipulate the data in the `Software_T` table. You have seen several different methods of executing these stored procedures from VB using the ADO `Recordset`, `Command`, and `Connection` objects. We have pointed out the preferred method of executing stored procedures that accept parameters, but at the same time have demonstrated alternatives.

As we progress through several of the following chapters, our stored procedures will become more complex as we introduce topics like joins, start adding logic to our stored procedures, and use more of the built-in T-SQL functions of SQL Server in our stored procedures.

In order to prepare the `Software_T` table for the next chapter, we need to add some more data to this table. We want to add at least one row for each of the different categories. You can use the table below as a guide, or enter your own software titles:

Software Title	Category
Windows NT 4.0	Operating Systems
Windows 98 SE	Operating Systems
Windows ME	Operating Systems
Office 2000 Standard	Office Suites
Office 2000 Professional	Office Suites
Office 2000 Premium	Office Suites
Office 2000 Small Business	Office Suites
Access 2000	Office Tools
PhotoDraw 2000	Office Tools
CorelDraw 9	Office Tools
Adobe Photoshop 5.5	Office Tools
Visual Studio 6.0	Development Tools
Visual Studio Installer 6.0	Development Tools
RoboHelp Office 2000	Development Tools
InstallShield 2000	Development Tools

Table continued on following page

235

Software Title	Category
Rational Rose	Development Tools
SQL Server 2000	BackOffice Software
Internet Information Server	BackOffice Software
Microsoft Transaction Server	BackOffice Software

Once you have inserted this data using your program, you can view this data in your program or by running the up_select_software stored procedure in the Query Analyzer, as shown in the following figure. This allows you to see the data that you have inserted; you can only view the data, you cannot change it.

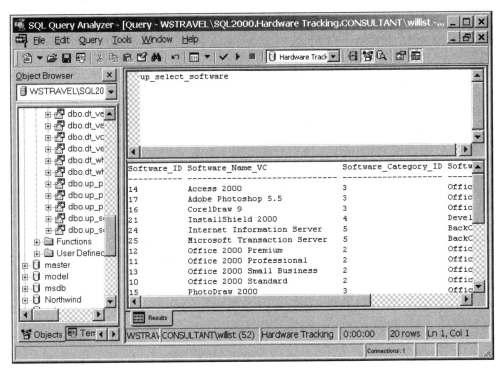

The other way to view the data from within the Query Analyzer is to expand the Hardware Tracking database in the Object Browser and then expand the User Tables group. Right-click on the Software_T table and then choose Open from the context menu.

The contents of the table will be displayed and you will be able to edit the data in the columns. The next figure illustrates what opening the table would look like:

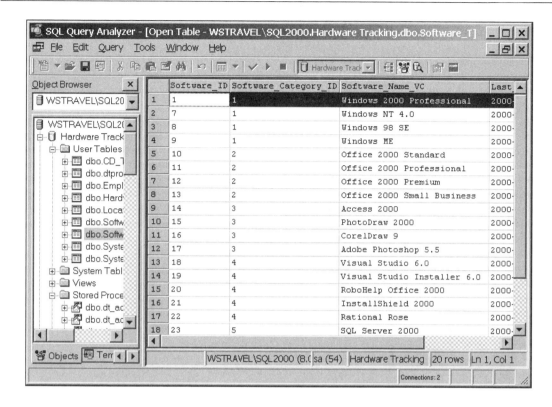

Recordset Methods

Let's expand on the ADO `Recordset` object that we saw earlier in the chapter. This section takes a look at some `Recordset` methods that may prove useful to you in the future. During our examination of these methods we will also look at doing something new with stored procedures, so let's get started.

We have seen in this chapter that we can use the `Recordset` object to open a recordset, and this can be done by executing either in-line SQL statements or stored procedures. When we executed the `Open` method of the `Recordset` object it returned a single recordset.

Let's now examine executing the `Open` method of the `Recordset` object and returning *multiple* recordsets in the same `Recordset` object. We will look at creating a stored procedure to handle the task.

Try It Out – Processing Multiple Recordsets

Firstly we will look at creating a stored procedure that returns two separate recordsets.

1. Start the Query Analyzer, if it is not already running, and log in.

2. Earlier we created a stored procedure named `up_select_software` to select all software titles in the `Software_T` table. Execute this stored procedure now in the Query Analyzer to see the data that it returns.

You can execute this stored procedure using one of two formats:

```
up_select_software
```

or:

```
EXEC up_select_software
```

3. The other stored procedure that we created was the `up_select_categories` procedure. Execute this stored procedure, using one of the formats shown already, by substituting this stored procedure name for the one previously listed. Notice the data that this stored procedure returns.

4. Now execute both of these stored procedures within the same query window. You will need to use the format shown below to execute both simultaneously:

```
EXEC up_select_software
EXEC up_select_categories
```

5. Notice the results that you get. After the first stored procedure completes, the second is executed, and you get two different sets of data, as shown in the following figure:

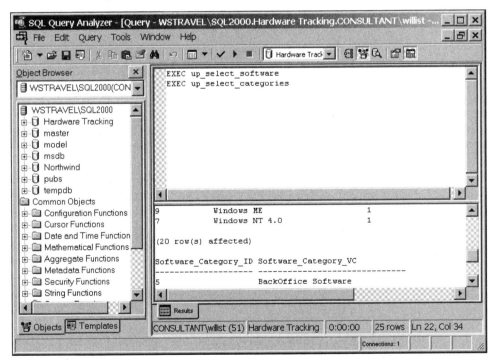

6. This is what we wanted to do: return two separate results sets from one stored procedure. You already have the core of the stored procedure that we want to create. All that is left is to actually make this into a stored procedure. Add the following code in the query window:

```
CREATE PROCEDURE dbo.up_select_software_and_categories AS

EXEC up_select_software
EXEC up_select_categories
```

7. There's no need to parse this code for errors, as we have already tested it. To create this new stored procedure, click on the **Execute Query** icon on the toolbar.

8. Start the Enterprise Manager, if it is not already running, and expand the **Hardware Tracking** database, then click on the **Stored Procedures** group.

9. Right-click on the up_select_software_and_categories stored procedure, choose **All Tasks** from the context menu, and then choose **Manage Permissions**.

10. Grant EXEC permission to the **Hardware Users** role and then click OK to close the dialog.

You have just created a stored procedure that performs two tasks: firstly, this stored procedure executes other stored procedures; and secondly, it returns multiple results sets.

Now we want to create a VB program that will execute this stored procedure and process both of the recordsets it returns. The program that we create here will also be used in future exercises, so we will be adding all of the controls and functionality now that we will need in the subsequent examples.

Try It Out – Process Multiple Results Sets

For this exercise, the program will execute the stored procedure that we just created and process both recordsets returned to load a pair of list boxes on the form.

1. Start a **Standard EXE** project and set a reference to the **Microsoft ActiveX Data Objects 2.6 Library**.

2. Set the project name to **RecordsetMethods** and the form name to **frmRecordsetMethods**. Set the **Caption** property on the form to **Recordset Methods** and set the **MaxButton** property to **True**. If you want, change the **StartupPosition** property to 2 – CenterScreen.

3. Using the following table, add the required controls to the form. Some of the buttons on the form will not be used until the exercises in the next chapter.

Control	Name	Properties
Label	Label1	Caption = Software
Label	Label2	Caption = Categories
ListBox	lstSoftware	
ListBox	lstCategories	
CommandButton	cmdClearLists	Caption = Clear Lists

Table continued on following page

239

Control	Name	Properties
CommandButton	cmdOpenDoubleRecordset	Caption = Open Double Recordset
CommandButton	cmdSaveRecordset	Caption = Save Recordsets
CommandButton	cmdOpenSavedRecordset	Caption = Open Saved Recordsets
CommandButton	cmdExit	Caption = Exit

Your form should look like this:

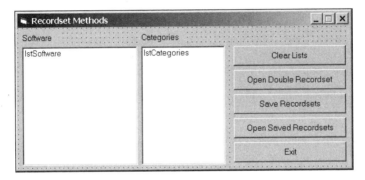

4. We want to add the login form (frmLogin) from earlier in this chapter to our project, so go ahead and add it. (If you saved the changes made to the login form in the last example as a different form then use the new login form.)

5. Add the connect module (modConnect) to the project. Again, if you saved the changes from the last example to a new connect module then use the latest version.

6. Add the code presented in the How It Works section that follows.

7. At this point you should save your project in the directory of your choice. Run your program and log in.

8. Click on the Open Double Recordset button and the Software and Categories lists should be populated. If you click on the Clear Lists button both lists should be cleared. You can click on the Open Double Recordset button again to have the lists populated again. The results that you see should be similar to the following:

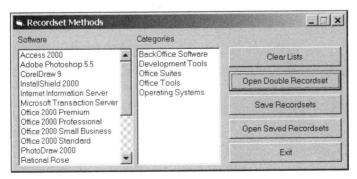

How It Works – Process Multiple Results Sets

The first thing we want to do in this project is to display the login form so we can establish a connection with SQL Server. Add the following code to the `Form_Load` event of the `frmRecordsetMethods` form:

```
Private Sub Form_Load()
    'Display the login form
    frmLogin.Show vbModal
End Sub
```

Having established a connection with SQL Server, we also need a means to terminate that connection. Add the following code to the `Form_Unload` event:

```
Private Sub Form_Unload(Cancel As Integer)
    'Termination of the database connection
    Call TerminateConnection
End Sub
```

There is a lot of code that will be used in this and the next exercise, so we want to place that code into different procedures that we can then call, to simplify the design. The first of these is the `ADOError` procedure that was used in previous exercises.

There is some new code in this procedure, as we now check to see if the error came from ADO or VB. This is done using the `IsEmpty` function to see if the `strError` variable is empty. If the variable is empty then we know that the error came from VB. We want to display the error number and description from the VB `Err` object, as this can be useful to know.

```
Sub ErrorHandler()
    'Declare local variables
    Dim strError

    'Loop through the errors collection and display all errors
    For Each g_objError In g_objConn.Errors
        strError = strError & g_objError.Number & " : " & _
            g_objError.Description & vbCrLf & vbCrLf
    Next

    'Ensure this is an ADO error
    If IsEmpty(strError) Then
        MsgBox "Error " & Err.Number & vbCrLf & vbCrLf & Err.Description, _
            vbCritical + vbOKOnly, "VB Error"
    Else
        MsgBox strError, vbCritical + vbOKOnly, "ADO Error"
    End If
End Sub
```

The next procedure that we want to create is the `GetSoftwareAndCategories` procedure. This will open a `Recordset` object and execute the `up_select_software_and_categories` stored procedure.

The first thing that we want to do in this procedure is to set up our error handling. Then we set a reference to the global `Recordset` object `g_objRS`:

```
Sub GetSoftwareAndCategories()
   'Setup error handling
   On Error GoTo GetSoftwareAndCategories_Err

   'Set a reference to the ADO recordset object
   Set g_objRS = New ADODB.Recordset
```

Next, using the standard Open method that we have used before, we execute the up_select_software_and_categories stored procedure. Notice that this recordset is opened as read-only and we can only navigate the Recordset object in a forward direction.

Once the Recordset object is open, we exit the procedure:

```
   'Open the recordset object
   g_objRS.Open "up_select_software_and_categories", g_objConn, _
      adOpenForwardOnly, adLockReadOnly, adCmdStoredProc

   Exit Sub
```

Our error handling procedure calls the ADOError procedure, which will display any errors in a message box:

```
GetSoftwareAndCategories_Err:
   'Call the error routine
   Call ErrorHandler
End Sub
```

The next procedure that we want to code is the LoadSoftware procedure. This procedure uses the global Recordset object to load the **Software** list (lstSoftware):

```
Sub LoadSoftware()
   'Loop through the recordset and load the software list box
   Do While Not g_objRS.EOF
      'Add the software title
      lstSoftware.AddItem g_objRS!Software_Name_VC
      'Move to the next record
      g_objRS.MoveNext
   Loop
End Sub
```

Since we have a procedure to load the **Software** list, it makes sense to create a procedure to load the **Categories** list. Thus, we want to create the LoadCategories procedure to do this, as shown in the following code:

```
Sub LoadCategories()
   'Loop through the recordset and load the categories list box
   Do While Not g_objRS.EOF
      'Add the software category
      lstCategories.AddItem g_objRS!Software_Category_VC
      'Move to the next record
      g_objRS.MoveNext
   Loop
End Sub
```

Since we have coded a procedure to open the global `Recordset` object we also need a procedure to close it. The `CloseRecordset` procedure listed below will close and remove our reference to the global `Recordset` object:

```
Sub CloseRecordset()
    'Close and dereference the recordset object
    g_objRS.Close
    Set g_objRS = Nothing
End Sub
```

The first button on our form is **Clear List** which, when clicked, should clear the lists on the form. The code in the `cmdClearLists_Click` procedure will clear both list boxes:

```
Private Sub cmdClearLists_Click()
    'Clear the list boxes
    lstSoftware.Clear
    lstCategories.Clear
End Sub
```

The next button on the form will open the `Recordset` object that contains multiple recordsets within one object. The `OpenDoubleRecordset_Click` procedure shown next contains the code to open and display the data residing in the `Recordset` object.

The first thing we want to do in this procedure is to set up our error handling. This is the standard error handling that we use throughout this chapter.

Then we call the `GetSoftwareAndCategories` procedure that will open the global `Recordset` object:

```
Private Sub cmdOpenDoubleRecordset_Click()
    'Setup error handling
    On Error GoTo cmdOpenDoubleRecordset_Err

    'Open the recordset
    Call GetSoftwareAndCategories
```

We call the `LoadSoftware` procedure to load the software list on the form. That procedure will loop through the `Recordset` object until an end-of-file condition occurs:

```
    'Load the software list
    Call LoadSoftware
```

The next statement is a method of the `Recordset` object that we have not met before. The `NextRecordset` method will clear the current `Recordset` object and advance to the next recordset within the `Recordset` object. This will clear all properties of the `Recordset` object and reset them. Thus, the `EOF` property that is currently set to `True`, because an end-of-file condition was reached in the previous procedure, will be cleared and set to `False`.

Notice that we use the same `Recordset` object when calling this method. We could alternatively have declared and set a reference to another `Recordset` object and set that `Recordset` object to the contents of the global `Recordset` object.

```
    'Get the next recordset
    Set g_objRS = g_objRS.NextRecordset
```

After we have moved to the next recordset in the global `Recordset` object we want to load the **Categories** list by calling the `LoadCategories` procedure:

```
    'Load the categories list
    Call LoadCategories
```

The last thing we do is to call the `CloseRecordset` procedure to close and remove our reference to the global `Recordset` object. Then we exit the procedure.

The code at the bottom of this procedure is for our error handler. This is the same error handler that we have used in previous exercises:

```
    'Close and dereference the recordset object
    Call CloseRecordset

    Exit Sub

cmdOpenDoubleRecordset_Err:
    'Call the error routine
    Call ErrorHandler
End Sub
```

We are not going to provide any code for the **Save Recordsets** and **Open Saved Recordsets** buttons in this exercise, so we want to skip to the **Exit** button. Add the following code to the `cmdExit_Click` procedure:

```
Private Sub cmdExit_Click()
    Unload Me
End Sub
```

In this exercise we used a single `Recordset` object and called the `NextRecordset` method to handle multiple results sets. This is a great method to use when you need to load multiple combo boxes or lists on a form and do not need to keep a `Recordset` object open. You save the extra overhead of opening, processing, closing, and referencing multiple `Recordset` objects, as you can do all of this processing with just one `Recordset` object.

There is one little drawback to this method; you cannot use it for client-side recordsets. This means that you cannot set the `CursorLocation` property of the `Recordset` object to the `adUseClient` constant.

This should not be a problem for VB client-server applications but could be a problem if you want to use this type of processing from a web page. The reason for this is that when dealing with web pages you really don't want to hold a database connection open any longer than necessary, due to concurrent usage by other users.

I'm sure you'll find some use for this type of processing somewhere down the line.

Saving and Opening a Recordset

Sometimes you have static data in a table that rarely, if ever, changes. In these cases it would seem prudent that this data be loaded from a local source, instead of making a call to SQL Server and using up machine resources and bandwidth on the network.

The Save method of the Recordset object allows you to save the data in the current recordset to a file on your hard drive. You can then open that recordset file using the Open method of the Recordset object. Opening a saved recordset file does not require a connection to SQL Server and does not involve any network traffic.

Before we proceed with the next exercise, let's take a look at the Save method of the Recordset object. The format for the Save method is shown here:

```
recordsetobject.Save destination, persistformat
```

Both *destination* and *persistformat* are optional parameters to the Save method, and *recordsetobject* represents a valid opened Recordset object to be saved.

The *destination* parameter specifies the complete path and file name that should be used to save the file. If you do not specify this parameter, the file name will be derived from the Source parameter that was used to open the Recordset object. You should at least specify the file name, so that you control the file name and extension used to save the recordset.

The *persistformat* option is also optional and specifies one of two constants from the PersistFormatEnum enumeration. The first constant in this enumeration is the adPersistADTG constant and will save your Recordset object in the Microsoft Advanced Data TableGram (ADTG) format. This constant is the default when *persistformat* has not been specified, and saves your data as a normal recordset in binary format. The second format constant is adPersistXML which will save the Recordset object in XML format. (XML, or Extensible Markup Language, will be introduced in Chapter 15, but essentially it is a way of describing the structure of data which aims to simplify data transfer between applications.)

> *Note: two limitations apply when saving hierarchical recordsets (data shapes) to XML format. You cannot save to XML if the hierarchical recordset contains pending updates, and you cannot save a parameterized hierarchical recordset. A hierarchical recordset is like a tree view that represents parent-child relationships. A single row and column in the recordset can represent more rows and columns.*

Suppose we had a Recordset object named objRS and wanted to save the contents of the recordset to the Temp folder on the C drive using a name of Software.rs. We would specify the Save method as shown:

```
objRS.Save "C:\Temp\Software.rs", adPersistADTG
```

Now that we have an idea of how this works, let's put it into use by saving the recordsets that we retrieved in the last exercise.

Try It Out – Saving and Opening a Recordset

1. We will be using the same project from the last exercise (`RecordsetMethods`) and the code to be added will be listed in the *How It Works* section.

2. Once you've entered all the code, you will want to save your project again before we start testing. Run your program and log in. Once you have logged in, click on the **Save Recordsets** button. This will open a `Recordset` object that executes the `up_select_software_and_categories` stored procedure and then saves each of the recordsets in this `Recordset` object to your hard drive.

3. You can verify the saved recordset files by either navigating to the directory where your project is running using Windows Explorer, or by clicking on the **Open Saved Recordsets** button. This will cause the saved recordsets to be opened and the **Software** and **Categories** lists to be loaded:

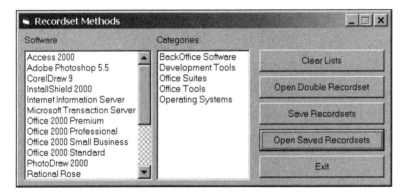

How It Works – Saving and Opening a Recordset

The code we want to add first is for the `cmdSaveRecordset_Click` procedure. This procedure is executed when you click on the **Save Recordsets** button.

The first thing we do in this procedure is to set up our error handling. Then we call the `GetSoftwareAndCategories` procedure to open the `Recordset` object that contains two recordsets:

```
Private Sub cmdSaveRecordset_Click()
    'Setup error handling
    On Error GoTo cmdSaveRecordset_Err

    'Open the recordset
    Call GetSoftwareAndCategories
```

Next, we execute the `Save` method of the `Recordset` object and specify a file name of `Software.rs`. Since we have not specified a path, the file will be saved in the current directory where your project is running. Even though we do not have to specify the `persistformat` parameter, we do so anyway to make our code readable and to quickly identify which format the recordset will be saved in:

```
'Save the software recordset
g_objRS.Save "Software.rs", adPersistADTG
```

> **Note: the current directory where your project is *running* is usually `C:\Program Files\Microsoft Visual Studio\VB98`. This should not be confused with the directory where your project files are *saved*.**

After we have saved the first recordset in the `g_objRS` Recordset object, we get the next recordset in that object by executing the `NextRecordset` method. Notice that we do not have to process any records from the `Recordset` object before executing the `NextRecordset` method.

Next, we save the categories in the `Recordset` object to a file called `Categories.rs`:

```
'Get the next recordset
Set g_objRS = g_objRS.NextRecordset

'Save the categories recordset
g_objRS.Save "Categories.rs", adPersistADTG
```

After we have finished saving our recordsets, we want to close the global `Recordset` object `g_objRS`. We do this by calling the `CloseRecordset` procedure. Then we exit the procedure, as we have completed the operation of saving our recordsets:

```
'Close and dereference the recordset object
Call CloseRecordset

Exit Sub
```

The error handler in this procedure is the same as in the previous exercises in this chapter:

```
cmdSaveRecordset_Err:
    'Call the error routine
    Call ErrorHandler
End Sub
```

Now we have a procedure to *save* recordsets on our hard drive, we need a method to *open* those recordsets. When you click on the **Open Saved Recordsets** button the `cmdOpenSavedRecordset_Click` procedure will be executed.

Again, the first thing we do is to set up our error handler. Then we set a reference to the global `Recordset` object `g_objRS`:

```
Private Sub cmdOpenSavedRecordset_Click()
    'Setup error handling
    On Error GoTo cmdSaveRecordset_Err

    'Set a reference to the ADO recordset object
    Set g_objRS = New ADODB.Recordset
```

Using the Open method of the Recordset object, we open our saved recordset file. Notice that we have not specified any parameters, not even a Connection object. That's the beauty of using saved recordsets. You don't have to establish a connection to the database in order to open and read the saved recordsets.

When we opened the initial recordset that executed the up_select_software_and_categories stored procedure, the recordset was opened using a forward-only cursor, meaning we could only move in a forward direction in this recordset. This was the recordset that we used to save the recordset to a file.

Now, when we open the saved recordset we can navigate both forward and backwards using the MoveFirst, MoveLast, MovePrevious, MoveNext, and Move methods. As you can see, there are quite a few benefits from using saved recordsets.

After we open the saved recordset we call the LoadSoftware procedure to load the **Software** list, using the saved recordset as the source. If the recordset is not in the same directory as the program, you can enter a fully qualified path name, such as C:\Data Files\Software.rs.

Once an end-of-file condition has been reached on the saved recordset, we close the Recordset object using the Close method:

```
'Open the saved software recordset
g_objRS.Open "Software.rs"

'Load the software list
Call LoadSoftware

'Close the current recordset
g_objRS.Close
```

We repeat the process using the saved Categories.rs recordset. We open the saved recordset, call the LoadCategories procedure to load the **Categories** list and then close the saved recordset:

```
'Open the saved categories recordset
g_objRS.Open "Categories.rs"

'Load the categories list
Call LoadCategories

'Close and dereference the recordset object
Call CloseRecordset
```

Once all processing has been completed, we exit the procedure. The error handling routine is the same one that we have used throughout this chapter:

```
    Exit Sub

cmdSaveRecordset_Err:
    'Call the error routine
    Call ErrorHandler
End Sub
```

There is one word of caution here: you can only save the recordsets to a file *once*. The Save method does not overwrite any existing files, and you will receive an error if you try to save the recordsets again. You will need to delete the files before you can save them again. This can be done manually or programmatically depending on your situation.

Summary

This chapter started with a discussion on stored procedure performance, as we looked at why stored procedures perform better than in-line SQL statements. Having studied this topic, you should have a better understanding of why stored procedures perform so well, and having completed this chapter, you should also know that creating and executing stored procedures from your VB programs is easy.

We also covered stored procedure user prefixes, and have learned how each user creating a stored procedure has their login prefixed to the stored procedure name. We also examined how we could execute a stored procedure belonging to another user, and also how to create stored procedures containing a dbo user prefix, so that the database administrator owns the stored procedure.

Having gone through the steps of creating a stored procedure, we also went through the steps of granting execute permissions to the hardware users role, so that the users in that role have access to execute our stored procedures. We know that when any database object is created it is secure, and no other user has permissions to access that object until the appropriate permissions are granted to them or to their role, allowing them access to the object.

Stored procedure parameters go a long way in making stored procedures robust and very functional for almost every task that we need to perform against our tables. We have learned that stored procedures accept both input and output parameters and can also return values. Having explored input parameters and used them in most of the stored procedures created in this chapter, we now have a good understanding of how these work. In the next few chapters we will expand on this by using output parameters and return values.

We covered each of the basic SQL statements in our stored procedures: SELECT, INSERT, UPDATE, and DELETE. We created a stored procedure for each of these basic SQL statements, and executed these stored procedures from our VB program. You now know just how easy it is to execute stored procedures from your VB programs. We also covered the various ADO objects that can be used to execute these stored procedures, and you should now be more familiar with these objects.

This chapter has also further explored the functionality of the Recordset object, and we have seen some useful methods that we can implement. Returning multiple recordsets within a single Recordset object is a very useful feature that can be exploited to our advantage. This is especially so when all we need to do is simply load combo boxes and lists on a form without keeping a recordset open.

We have also seen how we can use the Save method to save a recordset to disk and then, using the Open method, open and use the saved recordset. This is a really useful feature for data that does not change very often and it can be a time- and resource-saver for applications. This allows you to open a saved recordset without establishing a connection to SQL Server.

To summarize, you should know:

- ❏ That stored procedures are more efficient than in-line SQL statements
- ❏ How to grant execute permissions on a stored procedure to a role or login
- ❏ How to use input parameters in your stored procedures
- ❏ How to execute stored procedures from your VB program

- ❑ How to return and process multiple recordsets in a single `Recordset` object
- ❑ How to save a recordset
- ❑ How to open a saved recordset

The next chapter explores stored procedure performance versus in-line SQL performance in greater detail. We will also expand our knowledge of the ADO `Command` object as we cover stored procedure output parameters and return values.

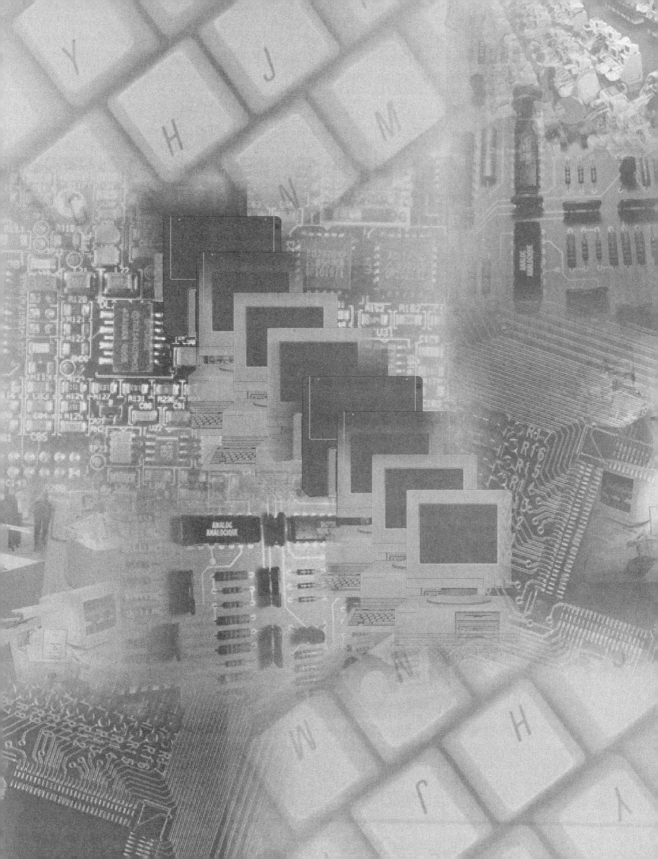

Stored Procedures versus SQL Statements

In the last chapter we talked about stored procedure performance, and explained why stored procedures perform better than in-line SQL statements. This chapter expands on that discussion by using side-by-side comparisons of stored procedures and in-line SQL statements. We will show and demonstrate that stored procedures offer more robust functionality and easier maintenance than in-line SQL statements.

While we demonstrate that stored procedures offer more functionality and better performance than in-line SQL statements, we also recognize that in-line SQL statements have their place. Given this, we will show you how to make the most of in-line SQL statements, and how ADO and SQL Server can help optimize the execution of in-line SQL statements.

As we go through this chapter we will be expanding our knowledge of both ADO and stored procedures, while becoming more familiar with the functionality of the Command object. We will be exploring more of the properties and methods of this ADO object.

In this chapter we will:

- ❑ Perform side-by-side comparisons of stored procedures and in-line SQL statements
- ❑ Take a detailed look at stored procedure output parameters and return values
- ❑ Optimize in-line SQL statements

Side-by-Side Comparisons

In the last chapter we examined stored procedure performance, and saw that SQL Server optimizes your stored procedures by compiling them and placing them in the procedure cache in SQL Server. This allows for fast and efficient retrieval for subsequent executions of previously executed stored procedures.

Now we want to examine why stored procedures provide robust functionality that cannot be surpassed by in-line SQL statements. Remember that we said in-line SQL statements are SQL statements that are stored as part of your VB code and get compiled with your program.

First and foremost in this examination is the fact that when you compile your VB code the in-line SQL statements that are hard coded in your program are set. They cannot be changed without having to recompile and redistribute the program to your clients. Using stored procedures we can make any necessary changes and save the stored procedure in the database; it will then be immediately available to all clients that use the stored procedure. These could be VB clients, web clients, or both. Any program that calls the amended stored procedure will execute the new copy the next time it executes the stored procedure. We will cover changing stored procedures in a subsequent chapter but you should be aware of the impact of adding or changing the parameters of a stored procedure that is being used by a production program. This has the same impact as changing the parameters to a function in VB.

The next thing we want to examine is the fact that stored procedures offer more robust functionality than in-line SQL statements. We will see this as we walk through the exercises in this chapter. Why do stored procedures provide more robust functionality? Because stored procedures use T-SQL statements (which, if you recall, is Microsoft's version of SQL for SQL Server) but when we code in-line SQL statements in our VB programs we must use ANSI (American National Standards Institute) SQL, also known as SQL-99. SQL Server performs better with T-SQL as this language is built into and is optimised for SQL Server.

Performance issues aside, let's begin our examination of functionality in a side-by-side comparison of stored procedures versus in-line SQL statements.

Select Comparison

We start our comparison with a SELECT stored procedure – we will be using the CD_T table for this and all comparisons in this chapter. The SELECT statements that we will be using in our stored procedure and in-line SQL will be simple SELECT statements. That is, they contain no joins or WHERE clauses. This will give you an idea of the comparison between a simple SELECT stored procedure, and in-line SQL statements that select data. You will be able to expand these examples on your own if you so desire.

The VB project that we will create in this exercise will form the foundation for the next few exercises. We will build a form that contains options that will allow us to choose between stored procedures and in-line SQL statements. We'll create these in the subsequent exercises. As we work through the various exercises we will be adding more functionality to the program.

Try It Out – Select Stored Procedure

We need to start with the stored procedure to select data from the CD_T table. This stored procedure will simply select the CD_ID and CD_Type_CH columns from this table, and order the results using the CD_Type_CH column.

To create this stored procedure:

1. Start the Query Analyzer and log in.

2. Select the Hardware Tracking database and enter the following stored procedure in the Query Analyzer:

```
CREATE PROCEDURE dbo.up_select_cd_types AS

SELECT CD_ID, CD_Type_CH
    FROM CD_T
    ORDER BY CD_Type_CH
```

> **Tip: use the drag and drop features to drag the column names and table name from the Object Browser to the query window.**

3. Parse the code for errors by clicking on the Parse Query icon on the toolbar, and then create the stored procedure by clicking on the Execute Query icon on the toolbar.

4. Start the Enterprise Manager if it is not already running. Expand the Hardware Tracking database, and click on the Stored Procedures group. If the Enterprise Manager is already running you may need to refresh the list of stored procedures. This can be done by right-clicking on the Stored Procedures group and choosing Refresh from the context menu.

5. Right-click on the up_select_cd_types stored procedure, choose All Tasks from the context menu, and then choose Manage Permissions.

6. Grant EXEC permission to the Hardware Users role and then click OK to close the dialog.

How It Works – Select Stored Procedure

This is a very simple SELECT stored procedure, and you should feel comfortable with what we have done here.

This stored procedure has no parameters, as we will be selecting all rows of data from the CD_T table. The name of the stored procedure, which follows the standards outlined in Chapter 3, reflects that it will select all data in the table:

```
CREATE PROCEDURE dbo.up_select_cd_types AS
```

The SELECT statement is selecting two columns from the CD_T table, and is sorting the results using the CD_Type_CH column, as indicated by the ORDER BY clause. Notice that the CD_Type_CH column has the CH suffix. This indicates that this column contains fixed character data. In this particular case, the length of the data was set to four characters when we designed the table.

```
SELECT CD_ID, CD_Type_CH
    FROM CD_T
    ORDER BY CD_Type_CH
```

Try It Out – VB for Comparing Stored Procedures and In-line Statements

To create the VB portion of this exercise:

1. Start a new Standard EXE VB project and add a reference to the Microsoft ActiveX Data Objects 2.6 Library.

2. Set the project name to Comparison and the form name to frmComparison.

3. Set the form properties as shown in the table:

Property	Value
Caption	Side-by-Side Comparisons
MaxButton	False
StartUpPosition	2 - CenterScreen

4. Add the controls listed in the following table to the form:

Control	Name	Properties
Label	Label1	Caption = CD Types
ComboBox	cboCDTypes	Style = 0 – Dropdown Combo, Text = nothing
Frame	Frame1	Caption = Execution Mode
OptionButton	optExecution(0)	Control Array, Caption = Select Stored Procedure, Value = True
OptionButton	optExecution(1)	Control Array, Caption = Select In-Line SQL, Value = False
OptionButton	optExecution(2)	Control Array, Caption = Insert Stored Procedure, Value = False
OptionButton	optExecution(3)	Control Array, Caption = Insert In-Line SQL, Value = False

Control	Name	Properties
OptionButton	optExecution(4)	Control Array, Caption = Update Stored Procedure, Value = False
OptionButton	optExecution(5)	Control Array, Caption = Update In-Line SQL, Value = False
TextBox	txtSQL	Text = nothing, MultiLine = True, ScrollBars = 2 – Vertical
CommandButton	cmdPreview	Caption = Preview SQL
CommandButton	cmdExecute	Caption = Execute
CommandButton	cmdExit	Caption = Exit

This figure shows the placement of these controls on the form:

5. Add the login form (`frmLogin`) that was modified in Chapter 7.

6. Add the connect module (`modConnect`) that was also modified in Chapter 7.

7. The code for the comparison form will be shown and explained in the *How It Works* section. After entering all of the code, you'll want to save your project in the directory of your choice. We are now ready to test this program. However, keep in mind that we have not inserted any data into the CD_T table, so you will not get any records returned in the Recordset object. However, we can test the general functionality of this program at this point and exercise most of the code.

Run your program and connect to SQL Server using the connection mode and authentication mode of your choice.

8. The Select Stored Procedure option button is selected by default, and this is the code that we have added so we do not need to select a different option. However, to fully test the selection of different options, you can select any option listed, and then select the Select Stored Procedure option. This will test the code that sets the intExecutionMode variable.

257

9. To preview the stored procedure that will be executed, click on the **Preview SQL** button. The stored procedure name will then be displayed in the SQL text box at the bottom of the form, as shown:

10. We can click on the **Execute** button to test most of the code that will execute this stored procedure. However, since there is no data in the CD_T table, we won't have any data displayed in the **CD Types** combo box.

How It Works – VB for Comparing Stored Procedures and In-line Statements

The controls that we added to the comparison form (frmComparison) will allow us to perform the various comparisons that will be covered in this chapter. We will only add the code for this comparison and add the rest of the code in later exercises. As we walk through the explanation of the code, enter the code in your own form.

We want to start with the code in the general declarations section of the comparison form. We have declared two variables that will be available to all procedures in this form. The first variable, intExecutionMode, will be used to determine which execution mode is selected in the frame on the form. This variable will be used in several places in our code.

The second variable, lngCDID, will be used to hold the CD_ID value that will be placed in the ItemData property of the cboCDTypes combo box. We will use this variable when we update the CD types.

```
'Declare variables
Dim intExecutionMode As Integer
Dim lngCDID As Long
```

Moving on to the Form_Load event, the first thing we want to do is to establish a connection to the database so we can execute the various stored procedures and in-line SQL statements. To that end, we have added the code to show the login form so we can establish a connection to SQL Server.

The second part of the code in this event will set the default value for the `intExecutionMode` variable. The default mode is the first option in the `optExecution` option buttons array:

```
Private Sub Form_Load()
    'Display the login form
    frmLogin.Show vbModal

    'Set default execution mode
    intExecutionMode = 0
End Sub
```

Because we have opened a connection to SQL Server, we want to terminate that connection when we close the form. To that end we call the `TerminateConnection` procedure in the `modConnect` module in the `Form_Unload` event. This event is fired when the form is about to be unloaded.

```
Private Sub Form_Unload(Cancel As Integer)
    'Termination of the database connection
    Call TerminateConnection
End Sub
```

The next section of code that we want to take a look at is contained in the `optExecution_Click` procedure. This is the procedure that is executed when you click on an option button. The `Index` parameter in this procedure contains the number of the option button in the `optExecution` array that was selected.

Using a `Select Case` statement, we check to see which option was selected and then set the `intExecutionMode` variable to that option. This variable will be used in other procedures.

```
Private Sub optExecution_Click(Index As Integer)
    'Save the option chosen
    intExecutionMode = Index
End Sub
```

The next section of code that we want to look at is the code behind the **Execute** button, which is contained in the `cmdExecute_Click` procedure. We set up a `Select Case` statement to examine the `intExecutionMode` variable. This variable tells us which execution mode has been selected, and allows us to execute the appropriate selection.

If the first option, **Select Stored Procedure**, were chosen we would want to execute the `SelectStoredProcedure` procedure. The other modes will be deferred until later. However, for clarity we have inserted the comments for these modes:

```
Private Sub cmdExecute_Click()
    Select Case intExecutionMode
        Case 0
            'Execute Select Stored Procedure
            Call SelectStoredProcedure
        Case 1
            'Execute Select SQL String
        Case 2
            'Execute Insert Stored Procedure
        Case 3
```

```
            'Execute Insert SQL String
        Case 4
            'Execute Update Stored Procedure
        Case 5
            'Execute Update SQL String
    End Select
End Sub
```

Let's take a look at the SelectStoredProcedure procedure next. The first thing we want to do in this procedure is to set up our error handling. We have defined a label at the bottom of this procedure, called SelectStoredProcedure_Err, and the code will branch to this label should an error occur.

Next, we set a reference to the global Recordset object that is defined in the modConnect module. We have decided to use a global Recordset object to reduce the number of Recordset objects that need to be defined and referenced.

```
Private Sub SelectStoredProcedure()
    'Setup error handling
    On Error GoTo SelectStoredProcedure_Err

    'Set a reference to the ADO recordset object
    Set g_objRS = New ADODB.Recordset
```

Next, we open the recordset using our stored procedure as the Source parameter of the Open method, and the global Connection object, g_objConn, as the ActiveConnection parameter. Since we are only interested in *reading* this recordset to load the combo box, we have specified the adOpenForwardOnly constant for the CursorType parameter and the adLockReadOnly constant for the LockType parameter. The Options parameter has the adCmdStoredProc constant specified, to indicate that this is a stored procedure that we are executing.

```
    'Open the recordset object
    g_objRS.Open "up_select_cd_types", g_objConn, adOpenForwardOnly, _
        adLockReadOnly, adCmdStoredProc
```

Because we can execute multiple options that load the **CD Types** combo box, we want to clear it of any existing entries to prevent duplicate entries. Using the Clear method of the cboCDTypes combo box, we remove all existing entries that may exist in the combo box:

```
    'Clear the combo box of any previous entries
    cboCDTypes.Clear
```

We want to loop through the Recordset object and load the cboCDTypes combo box. Using the data contained in the CD_Type_CH field of the Recordset object we load the combo box. The value contained in the CD_ID field is set in the ItemData property of the combo box.

Then we move to the next record in the `Recordset` object and start the loop all over again:

```
'Loop through the recordset and load the cd combo box
Do While Not g_objRS.EOF
    'Add the cd types
    cboCDTypes.AddItem g_objRS!CD_Type_CH
    'Add the cd id
    cboCDTypes.ItemData(cboCDTypes.NewIndex) = g_objRS!CD_ID
    'Move to the next record
    g_objRS.MoveNext
Loop
```

Once we have reached an end-of-file condition on the `Recordset` object, we close and remove the reference to it. Then we exit the procedure:

```
'Close and dereference the recordset object
g_objRS.Close
Set g_objRS = Nothing

Exit Sub
```

Our error handler simply calls another procedure that will handle all errors for our project:

```
SelectStoredProcedure_Err:
    'Call the error routine
    Call ADOError
End Sub
```

The `ADOError` procedure, coded in the form module, gets called any time an error occurs in one of our procedures that accesses SQL Server. This procedure declares a string variable that will be used to hold all errors returned in the `Errors` collection:

```
Sub ADOError()
    'Declare local variables
    Dim strError As String
```

Then we iterate through the `Errors` collection, and add the error number and error description from the `Errors` collection to the string variable. It should be noted that the `Errors` collection contains more information than we are displaying here. The `Errors` collection contains a collection of `Error` objects and each `Error` object contains the following properties:

❑ `Description` – contains a description of the error

❑ `HelpContext` – contains the help context ID of a help topic

❑ `HelpFile` – contains the path and file name of a help file.

❑ `NativeError` – contains the provider-specific error code

❑ `Number` – contains the error number from ADO or SQL Server

❑ `Source` – contains the source of the error

❑ `SQLState` – indicates the SQL state for the error

```
      'Loop through the errors collection and display all errors
      For Each g_objError In g_objConn.Errors
         strError = strError & g_objError.Number & " : " & _
            g_objError.Description & vbCrLf & vbCrLf
      Next
```

After we have added all errors to the `strError` variable, we display the errors in a message box using the `MsgBox` function:

```
      MsgBox strError, vbCritical + vbOKOnly, "ADO Error"
   End Sub
```

The next procedure that we want to take a look at is the `cmdPreview_Click` procedure. This is the code that gets executed when you click on the **Preview** button. What we want to do here is display the code that will be executed. This will give you a quick glance at what stored procedure or SQL string will be executed without having to dig into the code. This can be very useful further down the road when you come back and revisit the code that you create here today.

Again, we are using the `intExecutionMode` variable to determine which execution mode was chosen. And also once again, we will only add the code that is relevant to the exercise at hand. For this exercise we are displaying the stored procedure name that is being executed in the `SelectStoredProcedure` procedure. This text is displayed in the SQL text box on our form.

```
   Private Sub cmdPreview_Click()
      Select Case intExecutionMode
         Case 0
            'Display Select Stored Procedure
            txtSQL.Text = "up_select_cd_types"
         Case 1
            'Display Select SQL String
         Case 2
            'Display Insert Stored Procedure
         Case 3
            'Display Insert SQL String
         Case 4
            'Display Update Stored Procedure
         Case 5
            'Display Update SQL String
      End Select
   End Sub
```

The last code we have for this exercise is the code to end the program. This code is contained in the `cmdExit_Click` procedure, which is executed when you click on the **Exit** button. It simply unloads the form, thereby ending the program:

```
   Private Sub cmdExit_Click()
      Unload Me
   End Sub
```

Try It Out – Select In-line SQL Statement

Now that we have the foundations laid and the code built to handle multiple selections, it's time to add the code to execute another **Execution Mode** option in the **Comparison** form. This time we want to execute the companion in-line SQL statements to select data from the CD_T table. The SQL statements that we use here will duplicate the functionality of the up_select_cd_types stored procedure.

1. The code for the SelectSQL procedure is listed below and will be explained in the *How It Works* section. Go ahead and add the code to your comparison form (frmComparison):

```
Sub SelectSQL()
    'Setup error handling
    On Error GoTo SelectSQL_Err

    'Declare local variables
    Dim strSQL As String

    'Build SQL string
    strSQL = "SELECT CD_ID, CD_Type_CH " & _
        "FROM CD_T " & _
        "ORDER BY CD_Type_CH"

    'Set a reference to the ADO recordset object
    Set g_objRS = New ADODB.Recordset

    'Open the recordset object
    g_objRS.Open strSQL, g_objConn, adOpenForwardOnly, _
        adLockReadOnly, adCmdText

    'Clear the combo box of any previous entries
    cboCDTypes.Clear

    'Loop through the recordset and load the cd combo box
    Do While Not g_objRS.EOF
        'Add the cd types
        cboCDTypes.AddItem g_objRS!CD_Type_CH
        'Add the cd id
        cboCDTypes.ItemData(cboCDTypes.NewIndex) = g_objRS!CD_ID
        'Move to the next record
        g_objRS.MoveNext
    Loop

    'Close and dereference the recordset object
    g_objRS.Close
    Set g_objRS = Nothing

    Exit Sub

SelectSQL_Err:
    'Call the error routine
    Call ADOError
End Sub
```

2. There are a couple of modifications to make to existing code. In order to have the above code executed, we need to modify the `cmdExecute_Click` procedure. Modify the procedure as shown here:

```
Private Sub cmdExecute_Click()
    Select Case intExecutionMode
        Case 0
            'Execute Select Stored Procedure
            Call SelectStoredProcedure
        Case 1
            'Execute Select SQL String
            Call SelectSQL
```

3. To display the SQL string that will be executed, we click on the **Preview SQL** button, so we need to modify the `cmdPreview_Click` procedure. Modify this procedure as shown in the following code fragment. The SQL string that we are using is taken from the `SelectSQL` procedure. We have added a carriage return line feed character after each line of the SQL statement, so it is formatted for displaying in the SQL text box on the form:

```
Private Sub cmdPreview_Click()
    Select Case intExecutionMode
        Case 0
            'Display Select Stored Procedure
            txtSQL.Text = "up_select_cd_types"
        Case 1
            'Display Select SQL String
            txtSQL.Text = "SELECT CD_ID, CD_Type_CH " & vbCrLf & _
                "FROM CD_T " & vbCrLf & _
                "ORDER BY CD_Type_CH"
```

4. Save your project and let's test this new code. Of course, we still have no data in the `CD_T` table but we will be able to execute most of this code.

Run your program, and then select the **Select In-Line SQL Execution Mode** option. You can click the **Execute** button to run through the code, but no data will be returned. Click on the **Preview SQL** button to see what SQL statements will be executed to select data:

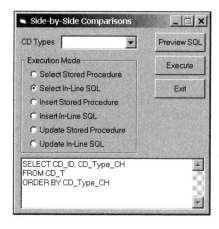

How It Works – Select In-line SQL Statement

We added the SelectSQL procedure to the comparison form (frmComparison). The first thing we do in this procedure is to set up our error handling, and declare a string variable to hold the in-line SQL statements that we will build:

```
Sub SelectSQL()
    'Setup error handling
    On Error GoTo SelectSQL_Err

    'Declare local variables
    Dim strSQL As String
```

Next we set the in-line SQL statement to the string variable strSQL. A closer look at the following SELECT statement reveals that this is the same SELECT statement that was used in the up_select_cd_types stored procedure. What this example is revealing to us is that there is no difference, other than performance, between the SELECT stored procedure and the in-line SQL statement.

```
'Build SQL string
strSQL = "SELECT CD_ID, CD_Type_CH " & _
    "FROM CD_T " & _
    "ORDER BY CD_Type_CH"
```

Next, we set a reference to the Recordset object and then execute the Open method of the recordset object to execute our in-line SQL. Notice that for the Options parameter of the Open method, we have specified the adCmdText constant, since we are executing a text string:

```
'Set a reference to the ADO recordset object
Set g_objRS = New ADODB.Recordset

'Open the recordset object
g_objRS.Open strSQL, g_objConn, adOpenForwardOnly, _
    adLockReadOnly, adCmdText
```

The next section of code is the same code that was contained in the SelectStoredProcedure procedure. We still have the same fields in the Recordset object, and we still want to load the cboCDTypes combo box with this data:

```
'Clear the combo box of any previous entries
cboCDTypes.Clear

'Loop through the recordset and load the cd combo box
Do While Not g_objRS.EOF
    'Add the cd types
    cboCDTypes.AddItem g_objRS!CD_Type_CH
    'Add the cd id
    cboCDTypes.ItemData(cboCDTypes.NewIndex) = g_objRS!CD_ID
    'Move to the next record
    g_objRS.MoveNext
Loop
```

The last part of code in this procedure closes and removes the reference to the `Recordset` object:

```
'Close and dereference the recordset object
g_objRS.Close
Set g_objRS = Nothing

Exit Sub
```

The error handler for this procedure will call the `ADOError` procedure should an error occur:

```
SelectSQL_Err:
    'Call the error routine
    Call ADOError
End Sub
```

Select Comparison Summary

Even though we have no data in the `CD_T` table as of yet, we were still able to see how the SQL statements in the select stored procedure and the in-line SQL statements matched. In fact, we actually used the same SQL statements for both the stored procedure and in-line SQL statements.

Of course, these were simple `SELECT` statements and we did not return any output parameters or a return code from our stored procedure. As your `SELECT` statements and stored procedures become more complex, you will notice more difference between the SQL statements in your stored procedures and the in-line SQL statements in your program.

Insert Comparison

Our insert comparison starts with a stored procedure that will insert a new entry into the `CD_T` table, and return the identity value (that was inserted as the primary key) as a return value from the stored procedure.

We will then move on to duplicate this functionality using in-line SQL statements. As you will soon see, there are some features of stored procedures that cannot be duplicated using in-line SQL statements, such as returning a return value.

Try It Out – Insert Stored Procedure

The `INSERT` stored procedure that we want to create will insert a new CD type and the current date and time into the `CD_T` table. The stored procedure will then get the identity value that was inserted into the `CD_ID` column by SQL Server, and return that value as a return value from the stored procedure.

This will afford us two opportunities. First, we get to see first hand how to handle and query a return value from a stored procedure using the `Command` object. Second, we get to see how to handle this functionality of the stored procedure using in-line SQL statements, which will be shown in the next exercise.

To create this stored procedure:

1. Start the Query Analyzer if it is not already running, and log in.

2. Enter the following stored procedure:

```
CREATE PROCEDURE dbo.up_parmins_cd_type
    @CD_Type CHAR(4) AS

INSERT INTO CD_T
    (CD_Type_CH, Last_Update_DT)
    VALUES(@CD_Type, GETDATE())


RETURN @@IDENTITY
```

> **Tip: to see input and output parameters and return values from T-SQL functions, expand the Common Objects in the Object Browser in the Query Analyzer, then expand a category and a T-SQL function. For example, to see the return value of the GETDATE T-SQL function, expand Common Objects, Date and Time Functions, GETDATE, and finally Parameters. When you hover your mouse pointer over a parameter, a tooltip will be displayed specifying information about the parameter or return value.**

3. Parse the stored procedure for errors by clicking on the Parse Query icon on the toolbar, then create the stored procedure by clicking on the Execute Query icon on the toolbar.

4. If the Enterprise Manager is not running, start it. Then expand the Hardware Tracking database and click on Stored Procedures. Right-click on the up_parmins_cd_type stored procedure, choose All Tasks from the context menu, and then choose Manage Permissions.

5. Grant EXEC permission to the Hardware Users role and then click OK to close the dialog.

6. Add the following procedure to the comparison form (frmComparison):

```
Sub InsertStoredProcedure()
    'Validate CD type data
    If Len(Trim(cboCDTypes.Text)) = 0 Then
        MsgBox "You must enter a CD type to add.", _
            vbInformation + vbOKOnly, "Insert Stored Procedure"
        cboCDTypes.SetFocus
        Exit Sub
    End If


    'Setup error handling
    On Error GoTo InsertStoredProcedure_Err


    'Declare and set a reference to the Command object
    Dim objCmd As New ADODB.Command
```

```
'Set the command object properties
Set objCmd.ActiveConnection = g_objConn
objCmd.CommandText = "up_parmins_cd_type"
objCmd.CommandType = adCmdStoredProc

'Append the parameter to the parameters collection
objCmd.Parameters.Append objCmd.CreateParameter("RC", _
    adInteger, adParamReturnValue)
objCmd.Parameters.Append objCmd.CreateParameter("CD Type", _
    adChar, adParamInput, 4, cboCDTypes.Text)

'Execute the command object to insert the data
objCmd.Execute

'Display the Identity value that was inserted for this entry
txtSQL.Text = "The Identity value that was inserted using" & vbCrLf & _
    "the up_parmins_cd_type stored procedure" & vbCrLf & _
    "is " & objCmd.Parameters.Item("RC")

'Remove the reference to the command object
Set objCmd = Nothing

Exit Sub

InsertStoredProcedure_Err:
    'Call the error routine
    Call ADOError
End Sub
```

7. In order for this code to be executed, we must modify the `cmdExecute_Click` procedure as shown:

```
Case 1
    'Execute Select SQL String
    Call SelectSQL
Case 2
    'Execute Insert Stored Procedure
    Call InsertStoredProcedure
```

8. In order to display the SQL for this selection, we need to modify the `cmdPreview_Click` procedure as shown in the next code fragment:

```
Case 1
    'Display Select SQL String
    txtSQL.Text = "SELECT CD_ID, CD_Type_CH " & vbCrLf & _
        "FROM CD_T " & vbCrLf & _
        "ORDER BY CD_Type_CH"
Case 2
    'Display Insert Stored Procedure
    txtSQL.Text = "up_parmins_cd_type"
```

9. At this point you should save your project so that we can make a test run. Run your program and select the connection and authentication mode of your choice to login. Then select the Insert Stored Procedure option and enter **CD** in the **CD Types** combo box. Next, click on the Preview SQL button to view the SQL statement that will be executed.

Finally, click on the Execute button to have this CD type inserted. Notice the message that is displayed in the SQL text box at the bottom of the form:

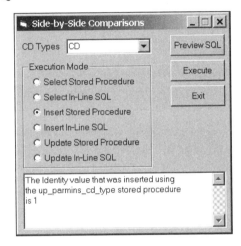

10. At this point you can fully test the Select Stored Procedure and Select In-Line SQL options. Select one of these options, click on the Execute button, and then examine the contents of the CD Types combo box. Test both options and also preview the SQL code by clicking on the Preview SQL button.

How It Works – Insert Stored Procedure

Once again, let's start with the stored procedure that we have created. This stored procedure accepts one parameter, the CD type to be inserted. Notice that this input parameter is a Char data type that contains four bytes of data. Remember that a Char data type in SQL Server is a fixed data type, and will always contain the number of characters specified in the argument of the data type.

```
CREATE PROCEDURE dbo.up_parmins_cd_type
    @CD_Type CHAR(4) AS
```

The INSERT statement specifies that we want to insert data into the CD_T table. Then we specify the column list containing the columns that we want to insert data into.

> Remember that we do not have to specify the columns in the column list in the same order that they are defined in the table.

Next, we specify the values that we want to insert. We start by specifying the input parameter, which contains the CD type to be inserted. Then we specify the GETDATE T-SQL function which will insert the current date and time.

```
INSERT INTO CD_T
      (CD_Type_CH, Last_Update_DT)
      VALUES(@CD_Type, GETDATE())
```

The last line of the stored procedure specifies that we return the identity value that was inserted into the CD_ID column by SQL Server. The @@IDENTITY function, or global variable, is a T-SQL function that will return the last identity value that was inserted into a table. Using the RETURN T-SQL statement, we return the identity value that was inserted:

```
RETURN @@IDENTITY
```

How It Works – VB Code to Process the Insert Stored Procedure

Switching to our VB code, we want to take a look at the new procedure that we have entered. This procedure starts by validating that some data has been entered into the cboCDTypes combo box.

We are using the Text property of the combo box to validate that data has been entered, and the Trim function to trim any spaces that may exist. Then we use the Len function to determine the length of the data. If the length of the Text property is zero, then no data was entered and we display a message using the MsgBox function. Once the message has been displayed and dismissed, we set focus to the combo box and then exit this procedure:

```
Sub InsertStoredProcedure()
    'Validate CD type data
    If Len(Trim(cboCDTypes.Text)) = 0 Then
        MsgBox "You must enter a CD type to add.", _
            vbInformation + vbOKOnly, "Insert Stored Procedure"
        cboCDTypes.SetFocus
        Exit Sub
    End If
```

If the validation of data has succeeded, then we set up the error handling for this procedure. We declare and set a reference to the ADO Command object:

```
    'Setup error handling
    On Error GoTo InsertStoredProcedure_Err

    'Declare and set a reference to the Command object
    Dim objCmd As New ADODB.Command
```

We want to set the Command object's properties next. We set the ActiveConnection property to the global Connection object, g_objConn. Then we set the CommandText property to the stored procedure we want executed, and set the CommandType property using the adCmdStoredProc constant from the CommandTypeEnum enumeration:

```
    'Set the command object properties
    Set objCmd.ActiveConnection = g_objConn
    objCmd.CommandText = "up_parmins_cd_type"
    objCmd.CommandType = adCmdStoredProc
```

Our stored procedure only accepts one input parameter but it also returns a value. Therefore, we append two parameters to the Parameters collection.

> **Whenever a stored procedure returns a value, you must append a parameter for the return value as the first parameter in the Parameters collection. This is because the stored procedure always returns its return value as the first parameter.**

The first parameter we append to the Parameters collection is to hold the return value, and we have given this parameter a name of RC. Remember that the Name parameter of the CreateParameter method is the name that we will use later to access this parameter in the Parameters collection.

Notice that we have specified the adInteger constant as the Type parameter of the CreateParameter method. This is because the Return T-SQL function always returns an integer value. We have then specified the adParamReturnValue constant for the Direction parameter. Since this is a return value, we do not have to specify the Size and Value parameters of the CreateParameter method.

The next parameter that we append to the Parameters collection is the input parameter going to our stored procedure. Notice we have specified the adChar constant for the Type parameter of the CreateParameter method, and a size of 4 for the Size parameter. Our Value parameter gets its data from the Text property of the cboCDTypes combo box:

```
'Append the parameter to the parameters collection
objCmd.Parameters.Append objCmd.CreateParameter("RC", _
    adInteger, adParamReturnValue)
objCmd.Parameters.Append objCmd.CreateParameter("CD Type", _
    adChar, adParamInput, 4, cboCDTypes.Text)
```

Now that all of our parameters have been appended to the Parameters collection, we can execute the Command object:

```
'Execute the command object to insert the data
objCmd.Execute
```

We make our SQL text box on the form perform double duty as we also use this text box to return messages as a result of the INSERT stored procedure. Here we are displaying a message indicating the identity value that was inserted into the CD_T table for this entry.

Notice in the following code how we are accessing the return value from our stored procedure that was returned in the Parameters collection. We specify the Command object that we have defined, followed by the Parameters collection, and specify which Item in the Parameters collection we want to access. We access the parameter by name, which is RC.

```
'Display the Identity value that was inserted for this entry
    txtSQL.Text = "The Identity value that was inserted using" & vbCrLf & _
        "the up_parmins_cd_type stored procedure" & vbCrLf & _
        "is " & objCmd.Parameters.Item("RC")
```

Each parameter in the `Parameters` collection has its own set of properties, the default of which is `Value`, so we do not have to specify it. We could have fully qualified this statement as `objCmd.Parameters.Item("RC").Value`, or used the short cut method and accessed the parameter by its ordinal position such as `objCmd(0)`. This method does not specify the `Parameters` collection as it is the default collection of the `Command` object.

Given all of the different ways to access the return code, the best method is the one we have shown below, as it fully identifies the return code as a parameter from the `Parameters` collection and does not leave the code up to individual interpretation. This code will display the return value from the stored procedure, which contains the identity value that we previously inserted.

The last thing we have to do in this procedure is to remove our reference to the `Command` object by setting its value to `Nothing`:

```
'Remove the reference to the command object
Set objCmd = Nothing

Exit Sub
```

Our error handler for this example is the same as the one we used in the previous two exercises.

Now that we can insert data into the `CD_T` table using an `INSERT` stored procedure, we want to examine the equivalent SQL statements to perform the same tasks. Remember that not only did our `INSERT` stored procedure insert data into the `CD_T` table, it also returned the identity value that was inserted into the `CD_ID` column by SQL Server.

We used the `@@IDENTITY` T-SQL function to get the identity value that was inserted and the `RETURN` T-SQL statement to return the identity value. Since these statements and functions are specific to T-SQL, we know that they are not available to us when we use in-line SQL in our programs. We cannot execute T-SQL functions from our program; we can only execute them in SQL Server, or through the Query Analyzer.

Try It Out – Insert In-line SQL Statement

1. We need to add the following procedure to the comparison form (`frmComparison`):

```
Sub InsertSQL()
    'Validate CD type data
    If Len(Trim(cboCDTypes.Text)) = 0 Then
        MsgBox "You must enter a CD type to add.", _
            vbInformation + vbOKOnly, "Insert SQL"
        cboCDTypes.SetFocus
        Exit Sub
    End If

    'Setup error handling
    On Error GoTo InsertSQL_Err

    'Declare and set a reference to the Command object
    Dim objCmd As New ADODB.Command
```

```
'Set the command object properties
Set objCmd.ActiveConnection = g_objConn
objCmd.CommandText = "INSERT INTO CD_T " & _
    "(CD_Type_CH, Last_Update_DT) " & _
    "VALUES('" & cboCDTypes.Text & "', '" & Now & "')"
objCmd.CommandType = adCmdText

'Execute the command object to insert the data
objCmd.Execute

'Set a reference to the ADO recordset object
Set g_objRS = New ADODB.Recordset

'Open the recordset
g_objRS.Open "SELECT MAX(CD_ID) AS 'CD_ID' FROM CD_T", _
    g_objConn, adOpenForwardOnly, adLockReadOnly, adCmdText

'Display the Identity value that was inserted for this entry
txtSQL.Text = "The Identity value that was inserted using" & vbCrLf & _
    "in-line SQL statements is " & g_objRS!CD_ID

'Close and dereference the recordset object
g_objRS.Close
Set g_objRS = Nothing

'Remove the reference to the command object
Set objCmd = Nothing

Exit Sub

InsertSQL_Err:
    'Call the error routine
    Call ADOError
End Sub
```

2. In order for this procedure to be executed, we must add some code to the `cmdExecute_Click` procedure. The next code fragment shows the code to be added to this procedure:

```
Case 2
    'Execute Insert Stored Procedure
    Call InsertStoredProcedure
Case 3
    'Execute Insert SQL String
    Call InsertSQL
```

3. To display the SQL statements that have been, or are yet to be, executed we must add the following code in the `cmdPreview_Click` procedure. Notice that we have included all the SQL statements that are executed, so the results will look similar to those of our INSERT stored procedure. Also, once again we are using carriage return line feed characters to separate our SQL statements onto separate lines for easier reading:

```
Case 2
   'Display Insert Stored Procedure
   txtSQL.Text = "up_parmins_cd_type"
Case 3
   'Display Insert SQL String
   txtSQL.Text = "INSERT INTO CD_T " & vbCrLf & _
      "(CD_Type_CH, Last_Update_DT) " & vbCrLf & _
      "VALUES('" & cboCDTypes.Text & "', '" & Now & "')" & vbCrLf & _
      vbCrLf & "SELECT MAX(CD_ID) AS 'CD_ID' FROM CD_T"
```

4. At this point save your project and run your program. Select the connection and authentication mode of your choice to login with.

Select the Insert In-Line SQL option and enter CDR in the CD Types combo box. To preview the SQL statements that are about to be inserted, click on the Preview SQL button.

To have this text inserted, click on the Execute button. You should see a message similar to the one shown:

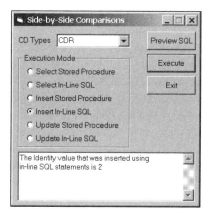

You can now use one of the Select options on the form to select all the data from the CD_T table.

How It Works – Insert In-line SQL Statement

Again, we want to validate the data in the cboCDTypes combo box before we proceed any further in our procedure. This is the same code that we examined in the InsertStoredProcedure procedure:

```
Sub InsertSQL()
   'Validate CD type data
   If Len(Trim(cboCDTypes.Text)) = 0 Then
      MsgBox "You must enter a CD type to add.", _
         vbInformation + vbOKOnly, "Insert SQL"
      cboCDTypes.SetFocus
      Exit Sub
   End If
```

Next we set up our error handling and declare and set a reference to the ADO Command object:

```
'Setup error handling
On Error GoTo InsertSQL_Err

'Declare and set a reference to the Command object
Dim objCmd As New ADODB.Command
```

We want to set the properties of the Command object next. Notice in the code below that we are not using parameters for this in-line SQL. We are building the CommandText property using both SQL statements and values from the controls on our form. Notice this is basically the same INSERT SQL statement that we used in our stored procedure, except that we are passing the values as part of the SQL statement.

Here, we have specified the Text property of the cboCDTypes combo box as the value for the CD type. As CD type is a string value, we must enclose it in single quote marks. In our stored procedure in the last exercise, we used the GETDATE T-SQL function to insert the current date and time. Since that is a T-SQL function, it is not available to us when we use in-line SQL statements. So we must use the VB Now function, which returns the current date and time. Again, we need to enclose this value in single quote marks.

Notice that since we are executing in-line SQL statements, we have specified the adCmdText constant for the CommandType property of the Command object:

```
'Set the command object properties
Set objCmd.ActiveConnection = g_objConn
objCmd.CommandText = "INSERT INTO CD_T " & _
    "(CD_Type_CH, Last_Update_DT) " & _
    "VALUES('" & cboCDTypes.Text & "', '" & Now & "')"
objCmd.CommandType = adCmdText
```

Next we execute the Command object, which will insert the data into the CD_T table.

We must now execute another SQL statement to get the identity value that has been inserted into the CD_ID column. Since this SQL statement will return data, we must use the Recordset object, so we set a reference to the global Recordset object g_objRS:

```
'Execute the command object to insert the data
objCmd.Execute

'Set a reference to the ADO recordset object
Set g_objRS = New ADODB.Recordset
```

We open the Recordset object and pass it a SQL string as the Source parameter of the Open method. This SQL statement selects the maximum value in the CD_ID column and specifies the name of the field that should be returned. This is achieved through the use of the aggregate function Max. An **aggregate function** is a function that returns a single value from a group of values. As it only returns a value, and not the column name, we have compensated for this by specifying a column alias of CD_ID, which will represent a field name within the returned recordset that can be addressed to retrieve our data.

275

For the `Options` parameter of the `Open` method we have specified the `adCmdText` constant because we are executing a SQL string.

```
'Open the recordset
g_objRS.Open "SELECT MAX(CD_ID) AS 'CD_ID' FROM CD_T", _
    g_objConn, adOpenForwardOnly, adLockReadOnly, adCmdText
```

We display a similar message to the one displayed in the last example, except this time the identity value is coming from the `CD_ID` field in the recordset:

```
'Display the Identity value that was inserted for this entry
txtSQL.Text = "The Identity value that was inserted using" & vbCrLf & _
    "in-line SQL statements is " & g_objRS!CD_ID
```

The last thing we do in this procedure is to close and dereference our `Recordset` object and dereference our `Command` object. Then we exit the procedure:

```
'Close and dereference the recordset object
g_objRS.Close
Set g_objRS = Nothing

'Remove the reference to the command object
Set objCmd = Nothing

Exit Sub
```

The error handler is the same as for our previous exercises, so we have not repeated it here.

Insert Comparison Summary

This comparison has shown that we need to use more SQL statements and ADO objects to accomplish the same task that is performed by our stored procedure. Why? This is because stored procedures are becoming progressively more complex and are now able to implement a great many T-SQL functions and statements that do not have ANSI-SQL equivalents.

As we start to build more complex stored procedures we need to execute more and more SQL statements, and use more ADO objects, to obtain the same results. This comparison makes a good case for the use of stored procedures in your production applications, as you will definitely receive better performance, execute fewer SQL statements, and use fewer ADO objects.

Update Comparison

Now that we have shown some of the differences between `SELECT` and `INSERT` stored procedures and in-line SQL statements, we want to wrap up the section with a comparison between an `UPDATE` stored procedure and in-line SQL statements. Once again, the stored procedure that we develop will be more complex than our previous stored procedures.

Try It Out – Update Stored Procedure

We want to create a stored procedure to update the CD_T table. This stored procedure will accept two input parameters and return one output parameter. The input parameters will contain the primary key of the row to be updated and the new CD type that it should be updated with. The output parameter will return the return code for the stored procedure.

To create this stored procedure:

1. If the Query Analyzer is not already running, start it and log in.

2. Enter the following stored procedure:

```
CREATE PROCEDURE dbo.up_parmupd_cd_type
      @CD_ID INT,
      @CD_Type CHAR(4),
      @Return_Code INT OUTPUT AS

UPDATE CD_T
      SET CD_Type_CH = @CD_Type,
      Last_Update_DT = GETDATE()
      WHERE CD_ID = @CD_ID

SET @Return_Code = @@ERROR
```

> **Tip: you can drag and drop T-SQL functions from the Object Browser to the query window in the same fashion that you can for table and column names.**

3. Parse the stored procedure for errors by clicking on the Parse Query icon on the toolbar.

4. Create the stored procedure by clicking on the Execute Query icon on the toolbar.

5. If the Enterprise Manager is not running, then start it. Expand the Hardware Tracking database and click on the Stored Procedures group.

6. Right-click on the up_parmupd_cd_type stored procedure, choose All Tasks from the context menu, and then choose Manage Permissions.

7. Grant EXEC permission to the Hardware Users role and click OK to close the dialog.

8. Switching to our VB code, we want to add some instructions to the cboCDTypes_Click procedure on the comparison form:

```
Private Sub cboCDTypes_Click()
    'Save the ID of the CD type in case we need it
    If cboCDTypes.ListIndex > -1 Then
       lngCDID = cboCDTypes.ItemData(cboCDTypes.ListIndex)
    End If
End Sub
```

9. Add the following procedure to the comparison form (`frmComparison`):

```
Sub UpdateStoredProcedure()
    'Validate CD type data
    If Len(Trim(cboCDTypes.Text)) = 0 Then
        MsgBox "You must enter a new CD type to update.", _
            vbInformation + vbOKOnly, "Update Stored Procedure"
        cboCDTypes.SetFocus
        Exit Sub
    End If

    'Setup error handling
    On Error GoTo UpdateStoredProcedure_Err

    'Declare and set a reference to the Command object
    Dim objCmd As New ADODB.Command

    'Set the command object properties
    Set objCmd.ActiveConnection = g_objConn
    objCmd.CommandText = "up_parmupd_cd_type"
    objCmd.CommandType = adCmdStoredProc

    'Append the parameter to the parameters collection
    objCmd.Parameters.Append objCmd.CreateParameter("CD ID", _
        adInteger, adParamInput, , lngCDID)
    objCmd.Parameters.Append objCmd.CreateParameter("CD Type", _
        adChar, adParamInput, 4, RTrim(cboCDTypes.Text))
    objCmd.Parameters.Append objCmd.CreateParameter("RC", _
        adInteger, adParamOutput)

    'Execute the command object to insert the data
    objCmd.Execute

    'Display the return code
    txtSQL.Text = "The return code from the up_parmupd_cd_type" & vbCrLf & _
        "stored procedure is " & objCmd("RC")

    'Remove the reference to the command object
    Set objCmd = Nothing

    Exit Sub

UpdateStoredProcedure_Err:
    'Call the error routine
    Call ADOError
End Sub
```

10. We need to modify the `cmdExecute_Click` procedure in order to have the code above executed. The next code fragment shows the necessary modifications:

```
Case 3
    'Execute Insert SQL String
    Call InsertSQL
Case 4
    'Execute Update Stored Procedure
    Call UpdateStoredProcedure
```

11. In order to display the SQL statements that will be executed, we need to modify the `cmdPreview_Click` procedure, as shown in the following code fragment:

```
Case 3
   'Display Insert SQL String
   txtSQL.Text = "INSERT INTO CD_T " & vbCrLf & _
      "(CD_Type_CH, Last_Update_DT) " & vbCrLf & _
      "VALUES('" & cboCDTypes.Text & "', '" & Now & "')" & vbCrLf & _
      vbCrLf & "SELECT MAX(CD_ID) AS 'CD_ID' FROM CD_T"
Case 4
   'Display Update Stored Procedure
   txtSQL.Text = "up_parmupd_cd_type"
```

12. This is all of the code that we need for this exercise, so save your project, then run your program and log in. Once logged in, choose one of the Select options and click the Execute button to populate the CD Types combo box.

13. Select the Update Stored Procedure option and then select the CDR entry in the CD Types combo box. Change the entry to CD-R, and then click the Execute button to have this entry updated. Notice that you receive a message in the SQL text box at the bottom of the form indicating that the stored procedure returned a return code of zero (which implies that no SQL Server errors were encountered), as shown in the following figure:

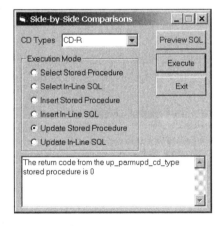

How It Works – Update Stored Procedure

This UPDATE stored procedure accepts two input parameters. The first, @CD_ID, will contain the primary key of the row of data to be updated. The second input parameter, @CD_Type, will contain the new CD type that should be updated in the table. The @Return_Code parameter is an output parameter specified by the OUTPUT keyword:

```
CREATE PROCEDURE dbo.up_parmupd_cd_type
       @CD_ID INT,
       @CD_Type CHAR(4),
       @Return_Code INT OUTPUT AS
```

This is a simple UPDATE statement that you have seen before. We are updating the CD_T table and specifying the columns to be updated. The WHERE clause limits this update to a specific row where the value in the CD_ID column matches the value in the @CD_ID input parameter:

```
UPDATE CD_T
      SET CD_Type_CH = @CD_Type,
      Last_Update_DT = GETDATE()
      WHERE CD_ID = @CD_ID
```

The @@ERROR T-SQL function returns the return code from the last executed T-SQL statement, in this case the UPDATE statement. Here, we are setting the @Return_Code output parameter to the value returned by the @@ERROR function. This method demonstrates using the @@ERROR function to set the return code in the stored procedure.

```
SET @Return_Code = @@ERROR
```

How It Works – VB Code to Process the Update Stored Procedure

The cboCDTypes_Click procedure will set the lngCDID variable using the ItemData property of the cboCDTypes combo box for the item selected. We only want to set the lngCDID variable if an item has actually been selected, so we first check the ListIndex value of the combo box to ensure it is greater than –1:

```
Private Sub cboCDTypes_Click()
    'Save the ID of the CD type in case we need it
    If cboCDTypes.ListIndex > -1 Then
       lngCDID = cboCDTypes.ItemData(cboCDTypes.ListIndex)
    End If
End Sub
```

The first thing that we want to do in the new procedure is to validate that some data has actually been entered in the Text property of the cboCDTypes combo box. This is the same validation procedure that we have seen in the last two exercises:

```
Sub UpdateStoredProcedure()
    'Validate CD type data
    If Len(Trim(cboCDTypes.Text)) = 0 Then
       MsgBox "You must select and change a CD type to update.", _
          vbInformation + vbOKOnly, "Update Stored Procedure"
       cboCDTypes.SetFocus
       Exit Sub
    End If
```

Then we want to set up our error handling for this procedure, and declare and set a reference to the ADO Command object:

```
    'Setup error handling
    On Error GoTo UpdateStoredProcedure_Err

    'Declare and set a reference to the Command object
    Dim objCmd As New ADODB.Command
```

We then set the Command object's properties. Notice that we have specified the adCmdStoredProc constant for the CommandText property, as we are executing a stored procedure:

```
'Set the command object properties
Set objCmd.ActiveConnection = g_objConn
objCmd.CommandText = "up_parmupd_cd_type"
objCmd.CommandType = adCmdStoredProc
```

The up_parmupd_cd_type stored procedure has three parameters: two input parameters and an output parameter.

> **We must add these parameters to the Parameters collection in the same order as they are specified in the stored procedure.**

The first parameter that we need to append to the Parameters collection is the parameter that contains the primary key of the row that we want to update. This parameter has its Value property set using the lngCDID variable. Remember that this was one of the first variables declared in the general declarations section of the form at the beginning of this chapter.

We set this variable in the cboCDTypes_Click procedure when you select an entry in the cboCDTypes combo box. This variable gets set using the ItemData property of the cboCDTypes combo box.

The second parameter that we want to append to the Parameters collection is the parameter containing the new CD type. We are getting this information from the Text property of the cboCDTypes combo box. Notice that we have specified the RTrim function for the parameter.

When we add a CD type to the CD_T table, it gets padded with spaces (provided the length of the added text is less than the length of the data type) because the CD_Type_CH column in the CD_T table is a Char data type. Char is a fixed length data type and we have set it to four bytes. Thus, when we get this column returned from our SELECT stored procedure or in-line SQL statement, this field in the recordset will always be exactly four bytes in length.

If we made any changes to the length of the CD type, we want to get rid of any trailing spaces in it before we attempt to add it. Otherwise, we will get an error that we are using a value of the wrong type. This is something that you should watch out for in a production application. You will want to ensure that the input data for all inserts and updates of columns that contain a Char data type do not exceed the assigned length. For example, our column has a fixed length of four bytes. When we insert data we could validate that the user has not entered more than four characters. Likewise, when we update the column we would also want to ensure that the value to be inserted is not greater than four characters, hence we trim the blank spaces.

The last parameter that we are appending to the Parameters collection is the output parameter. Remember that this parameter will contain the return code from our stored procedure. Since this is an output parameter, we do not have to specify the Value property for it in the CreateParameter method.

```
'Append the parameter to the parameters collection
objCmd.Parameters.Append objCmd.CreateParameter("CD ID", _
    adInteger, adParamInput, , lngCDID)
objCmd.Parameters.Append objCmd.CreateParameter("CD Type", _
    adChar, adParamInput, 4, RTrim (cboCDTypes.Text))
objCmd.Parameters.Append objCmd.CreateParameter("RC", _
    adInteger, adParamOutput)
```

Once we have appended all of the parameters to the `Parameters` collection, we execute the `Command` object to have the entry updated in the `CD_T` table:

```
'Execute the command object to insert the data
objCmd.Execute
```

Remember we talked about the various ways to access a parameter in the `Parameters` collection. Here we are using the short cut method to access the parameter just for demonstration purposes. The preferred method is the method that we used in the `InsertStoredProcedure` procedure. The `RC` parameter was the output parameter that we specified above.

Again, we are using the SQL text box on the form to display a message about the status of our execution. This time, however, instead of returning the identity value that was inserted, we are displaying the return code from our stored procedure:

```
'Display the return code
txtSQL.Text = "The return code from the up_parmupd_cd_type" & vbCrLf & _
    "stored procedure is " & objCmd("RC")
```

The last thing that we want to do in this procedure is to remove our reference to the `Command` object. Then we exit the procedure. The error handling code at the bottom of this procedure is the same error handling code that we have used in all of these exercises in this chapter:

```
'Remove the reference to the command object
Set objCmd = Nothing

Exit Sub

UpdateStoredProcedure_Err:
    'Call the error routine
    Call ADOError
End Sub
```

The last comparison that we want to examine is the in-line SQL statements that will provide the same functionality as the up_parmupd_cd_type stored procedure.

As you might imagine, we cannot duplicate the return code in the output parameter of the stored procedure. Thus, while we can update the data, we cannot return a return code. We must rely on our error handling in the procedure that executes the in-line SQL to deal with a non-zero return code.

1. Add the following code to the comparison form (`frmComparison`):

```
Sub UpdateSQL()
    'Validate CD type data
    If Len(Trim(cboCDTypes.Text)) = 0 Then
        MsgBox "You must select and change a CD type to update.", _
            vbInformation + vbOKOnly, "Update SQL"
        cboCDTypes.SetFocus
        Exit Sub
    End If

    'Setup error handling
    On Error GoTo UpdateSQL_Err

    'Declare local variables
    Dim strSQL As String

    'Build the SQL string
    strSQL = "UPDATE CD_T " & _
        "SET CD_Type_CH = '" & RTrim(cboCDTypes.Text) & "', " & _
        "Last_Update_DT = '" & Now & "' " & _
        "WHERE CD_ID = " & lngCDID

    'Execute the SQL string
    g_objConn.Execute strSQL

    'Display the Identity value that was inserted for this entry
    txtSQL.Text = "Update Complete"

    Exit Sub

UpdateSQL_Err:
    'Call the error routine
    Call ADOError
End Sub
```

2. In order for this procedure to be executed, we need to modify the `cmdExecute_Click` procedure. The following code fragment shows the necessary changes:

```
Case 4
    'Execute Update Stored Procedure
    Call UpdateStoredProcedure
Case 5
    'Execute Update SQL String
    Call UpdateSQL
```

3. To display the SQL statements that we will be executing, we need to modify the `cmdPreview_Click` procedure. The next code fragment details the changes that need to be made to this procedure. Notice that we have once again added a carriage return line feed character to make our SQL readable in the SQL text box on the form.

```
Case 4
    'Display Update Stored Procedure
    txtSQL.Text = "up_parmupd_cd_type"
Case 5
    'Display Update SQL String
    txtSQL.Text = "UPDATE CD_T " & vbCrLf & _
        "SET CD_Type_CH = '" & RTrim(cboCDTypes.Text) & "', " & vbCrLf & _
        "Last_Update_DT = '" & Now & "' " & vbCrLf & _
        "WHERE CD_ID = " & lngCDID
```

4. We are ready to run this program for our final test. Save your project and run it, choosing the connection and authentication mode of your choice to log in.

To view the existing entries, execute one of the Select options. So far, we have two entries in the CD Types combo box: CD and CD-R.

5. We want to add one more entry, so choose an Insert option and enter dvd in the CD Types combo box before clicking on the Execute button.

6. Now we want to repopulate the CD Types combo box, so choose another Select option and execute it.

7. We now want to update the dvd entry in the CD Types combo box, so choose that entry. Change it all into upper case and then select the Update In-Line SQL option. Before you update the entry take a look at the SQL string that will be executed, by clicking on the Preview SQL button. The SQL string to be executed will then be displayed in the SQL text box, as shown:

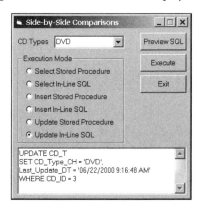

8. Now go ahead and update this entry by clicking on the Execute button. Notice a message is returned in the SQL text box indicating the update procedure worked correctly, as shown in the next figure:

How It Works – Update In-line SQL Statements

The first thing that we want to do here is validate the data in the CD Types combo box. This is the same validation routine we have used in the previous exercises:

```
Sub UpdateSQL()
    'Validate CD type data
    If Len(Trim(cboCDTypes.Text)) = 0 Then
        MsgBox "You must enter a new CD type to update.", _
            vbInformation + vbOKOnly, "Update SQL"
        cboCDTypes.SetFocus
        Exit Sub
    End If
```

Next, we set up our error handling and declare a string variable for our SQL string:

```
    'Setup error handling
    On Error GoTo UpdateSQL_Err

    'Declare local variables
    Dim strSQL As String
```

We can use the same UPDATE statement that we used in the UPDATE stored procedure. We have, however, substituted the input parameters with the actual values retrieved from the controls on our form and our form variables.

Notice that we once again use the RTrim function to trim all trailing spaces from the entry contained in the Text property of the cboCDTypes combo box. Also notice that we have enclosed the value using single quote marks.

We use the Now function to get the current date and time passed to the stored procedure so the Last_Update_DT column can be amended. We have also enclosed this value in single quote marks.

The WHERE clause in our UPDATE statement uses the value contained in the lngCDID variable (remember that the value of this variable gets set via the cboCDTypes_Click procedure).

```
'Build the SQL string
strSQL = "UPDATE CD_T " & _
    "SET CD_Type_CH = '" & RTrim(cboCDTypes.Text) & "', " & _
    "Last_Update_DT = '" & Now & "' " & _
    "WHERE CD_ID = " & lngCDID
```

After our SQL string has been built, we can execute it using the Connection object. That's right, we are using the Execute method of the Connection object to execute our SQL string. We could have used the Command object, but for executing simple SQL strings this way uses less resources and we do not declare and set a reference to an additional ADO object.

```
'Execute the SQL string
g_objConn.Execute strSQL
```

Since we cannot return a return code in our SQL statements, we simply display a message that the update has been completed. We assume that if we get to this point, the update has been successful. If an error had occurred we would have fallen into the error handling routine within the procedure.

```
'Display the Identity value that was inserted for this entry
txtSQL.Text = "Update Complete"

Exit Sub
```

Again, we are using the same error handling routine as in the previous exercises.

Update Comparison Summary

In the insert comparison, we found that more in-line SQL statements and ADO objects were needed to achieve a result than were required in a stored procedure. Also, the UPDATE stored procedure could provide functionality that simply wasn't available using in-line SQL statements.

We could not duplicate a return code in an output parameter using in-line SQL statements. Instead we had to assume that if our in-line SQL statement completed then our update had been made. Otherwise, we relied on our error handling to return an error number for the problem.

This comparison fell short of duplicating the exact functionality of our stored procedure. So what we have seen during all of these comparison tests is that we can duplicate *most* but not *all* of the functionality of stored procedures.

These comparisons should give you a good idea that stored procedures provide functionality over and beyond the in-line SQL statements that can be coded into your program.

Optimizing In-line SQL Statements

We know from previous discussions that stored procedures execute faster and provide superior performance when compared with in-line SQL statements. Of course, by preparing your in-line SQL, although the first time will not be fast, any subsequent calls will be. In-line SQL statements do have their place, and we must sometimes use them. For example, suppose you created a form that allowed a user to pick and choose fields to query on. You could then build a dynamic SQL string into your code and execute it.

So, what can you do to maximize the performance of in-line SQL statements? This depends entirely upon the use of the statements that you write. For a one-time execution of in-line SQL statements there is nothing that can be done. However if you are planning on executing the in-line SQL statements several times over in your program, or running through them repeatedly in a loop, you can use the Command object's Prepared property. This property will instruct SQL Server to compile the statements before they are first executed. While this slows down the first execution of those SQL statements, subsequent executions are carried out using the compiled version stored in SQL Server's cache, resulting in an increase in performance. When SQL Server compiles the SQL statements, it optimizes them to use the appropriate indexes to ensure the most efficient execution. Once this is done it stores the compiled version of your SQL statements in the SQL Server cache, which allows for fast and efficient execution of those SQL statements.

So, how do we use the Command object's Prepared property? We simply set this property to True before executing the in-line SQL statements. The following code fragment shows how this can be done:

```
'Set the command object properties
Set objCmd.ActiveConnection = g_objConn
objCmd.CommandText = "SELECT Software_Category_ID, " & _
    "Software_Category_VC " & _
    "FROM Software_Category_T"
objCmd.CommandType = adCmdText
objCmd.Prepared = True

'Execute the command object to insert the data
objCmd.Execute
```

To get an idea of how this property works, let's perform a little speed test.

Try It Out – Speed Test

We can write some in-line SQL statements and use the Command object's Prepared property to have SQL Server compile and optimize the execution of these statements. But, without anything to compare it with we would not actually know what performance gains have been accomplished. To that end, we will write two sets of in-line SQL statements to select data.

So, let's get started and create a new VB project. To create this project:

1. Start a new Standard EXE VB project.

2. Set a reference to the Microsoft ActiveX Data Objects 2.6 Library.

3. Change the name of the project to SpeedTest.

4. Change the name of the form to frmSpeedTest. Change the Caption property of the form to Speed Test and set the MaxButton property to False. Change the StartUpPosition property to 2 – CenterScreen.

5. Using the following table and figure, add the following controls to the `frmSpeedTest` form:

Control	Name	Properties
Label	lblNonPrepared	Caption = Non Prepared
Label	lblPrepared	Caption = Prepared
CommandButton	cmdRun	Caption = Run
CommandButton	cmdExit	Caption = Exit

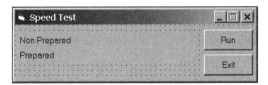

6. Add the code to this form, as presented in the *How It Works* section.

7. We will need to establish a connection to SQL Server, so we add the login form (frmLogin) and the connect module (modConnect) to this project.

8. At this point save your project. Before we can run the test and get true results, we must reboot our workstation. The reason behind this is that SQL Server caches all stored procedures and SQL statements that it executes. Thus if you developed these SQL statements using the Query Analyzer and were then to run these SQL statements from your program, SQL Server will recognize that the SQL statements are in the cache and execute them from there.

After you reboot your workstation and there is no activity (disk activity or CPU activity associated with loading Windows) you can run your project. Choose the connection and authentication mode of your choice and log in. Once logged in, click on the Run button to perform your tests.

You should see results similar to the ones shown in the next figure. There are a lot of factors that will affect the results that you see, such as CPU speed, memory and, if you are running SQL Server across the network, network traffic and concurrent users.

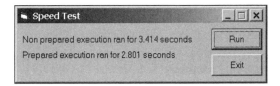

How It Works – Speed Test

In the `Form_Load` event of the speed test form we want to show the login form so we can establish a connection to SQL Server. Add the following code to your project:

```
Private Sub Form_Load()
    'Display the login form
    frmLogin.Show vbModal
End Sub
```

Since we have added code to establish a connection to SQL Server, we also want to add code to terminate that connection when the form unloads. We accomplish this with the following code in the `Form_Unload` event:

```
Private Sub Form_Unload(Cancel As Integer)
    'Termination the database connection
    Call TerminateConnection
End Sub
```

When we click on the Run button we want our speed test to be performed. Therefore, we want to add the bulk of our code in the `cmdRun_Click` procedure.

The first thing we want to do in this procedure is to declare and set a reference to two separate `Command` objects. One `Command` object will execute our in-line SQL statements for the unprepared test and the other will execute our in-line SQL statements for the prepared test:

```
Private Sub cmdRun_Click()
    'Declare command object for unprepared execution
    Dim objCmd1 As New ADODB.Command

    'Declare command object for prepared execution
    Dim objCmd2 As New ADODB.Command
```

In order to keep track of the starting and ending times, we want to set up two separate variables. Both of these are declared as a `Single` data type. A `Single` data type is a single-precision, floating-point variable, meaning that it can hold a value that contains a decimal point and a number of digits to the right of that decimal point.

We declare the variable to be used as the loop counter as an `Integer` data type.

```
    'Declare variables to hold the start and end times
    Dim sngStart As Single
    Dim sngEnd As Single

    'Declare variable for loop counter
    Dim intLoop As Integer
```

The first SELECT statement in our test will select data from the `Software_Category_T` table. This table should contain about five rows of data. The SELECT statement shown next is selecting data from the `Software_Category_ID` and `Software_Category_VC` columns.

We set the `ActiveConnection`, `CommandText`, and `CommandType` properties of the `Command` object. Since we are using in-line SQL statements, we set the `CommandType` property using the `adCmdText` constant from the `CommandTypeEnum` enumeration.

> **Tip: you can develop and test your SQL statements using the Query Analyzer before placing them in your code.**

```
'Set the first command objects properties
Set objCmd1.ActiveConnection = g_objConn
objCmd1.CommandText = "SELECT Software_Category_ID, " & _
    "Software_Category_VC " & _
    "FROM Software_Category_T"
objCmd1.CommandType = adCmdText
```

We save the start time in the `sngStart` variable using the `Timer` function. This function should not be confused with the `Timer` control. The `Timer` function will return a `Single` data type containing the number of elapsed seconds since midnight. The number of seconds returned also includes the fractional portion of a second thus giving us an exact number for testing.

After we have saved the starting time, we execute the `Command` object in a loop. We will perform this loop 1000 times. Once the loop has completed, we save the ending time, again using the `Timer` function:

```
'Save the start time
sngStart = Timer

'Execute the loop
For intLoop = 1 To 1000
    objCmd1.Execute
Next intLoop

'Save the end time
sngEnd = Timer
```

We display the results of the execution, subtracting the starting time from the ending time to give us the total number of seconds and fractions of a second that this loop took to execute. Using the `Format` function, we format the results of our time to include the number of seconds and the fractions of a second.

The results are displayed in the `lblNonPrepared` label.

```
'Display the results
lblNonPrepared.Caption = "Non-prepared execution ran for " & _
    Format(sngEnd - sngStart, "#0.000") & " seconds"
```

The SQL statements for the second part of our test will also select data from the `Software_ID` and `Software_Name_VC` columns of the `Software_T` table. This table should contain at least three times as much data as the table used in the previous `SELECT` statement. This means that this `SELECT` statement will have more data returned than the previous `SELECT` statement. Using a table that returns more data will really prove that using the `Prepared` property speeds up the results.

Again, we set the Command object's properties. This time we have included the Prepared property. Remember that when we set this property to True, SQL Server will compile and optimize the SQL statements before it executes them.

This only happens for the first execution. Thus, the first time in the loop, the SQL statements will be compiled in SQL Server and subsequent executions in the loop will use the compiled SQL statements in SQL Server. This slows down the first execution of our SQL statements, but subsequent executions are executed using the compiled SQL statements in SQL Server's cache.

```
'Set the second command object's properties
Set objCmd2.ActiveConnection = g_objConn
objCmd2.CommandText = "SELECT Software_ID, Software_Name_VC " & _
    "FROM Software_T"
objCmd2.CommandType = adCmdText
objCmd2.Prepared = True
```

We save the starting time and then perform this loop 1000 times, executing the Command object. Once the loop has been completed, we save the ending time:

```
'Save the start time
sngStart = Timer

'Execute the loop
For intLoop = 1 To 1000
    objCmd2.Execute
Next intLoop

'Save the end time
sngEnd = Timer
```

Once again, we subtract the starting time from the ending time and display the formatted results. This time we display the results in the lblPrepared label:

```
'Display the results
lblPrepared.Caption = "Prepared execution ran for " & _
    Format(sngEnd - sngStart, "#0.000") & " seconds"
```

The last thing we want to do in this procedure is to remove our references to the Command objects:

```
'Dereference command objects
Set objCmd1 = Nothing
Set objCmd2 = Nothing
End Sub
```

The last piece of code that we need to add to this project is for the Exit button. We want to unload the form when we click on the Exit button:

```
Private Sub cmdExit_Click()
    Unload Me
End Sub
```

The bottom line here is that the SQL statements that were executed using the Prepared property of the Command object executed faster. Even though SQL Server had to compile and optimize the SQL statements before it executed them, and even though this SQL statement returned more data, the prepared version ran faster. This will much more noticeable when running this test across the network on a SQL Server table that contains thousands of rows of data and multiple concurrent users in a real production environment.

Now you have an idea of how to optimize in-line SQL statements that get executed several times in your program. This method should only be used if you are executing the SQL statements more than once, as you will see no performance gains from a single execution of in-line SQL statements.

Summary

Once again, we have touched briefly on stored procedure performance. However, the main focus of this chapter has been to show how stored procedures provide functionality above and beyond what can be achieved using in-line SQL statements. We have seen that while we can duplicate most of the functionality of stored procedures, it does cost us in the long run through the use of extra ADO objects and in-line SQL statements.

In-line SQL statements do have their place and we have shown how you can maximize the performance of your in-line SQL statements using the Command object's Prepared property. We have seen that by using this property we can have SQL Server compile and optimize our SQL statements before they are executed. This allows subsequent executions of these SQL statements to use the compiled and optimized version in SQL Server.

To summarize, you should know:

❑   How to use return values from a stored procedure and how to retrieve them from the Command object

❑   How to use an output parameter in a stored procedure and how to retrieve the value from the Command object

❑   The value of using stored procedures in your applications

❑   How to optimize your in-line SQL statements

In the next chapter we will look in more detail at SELECT stored procedures. We will cover topics such as joins, table aliases, and column aliases.

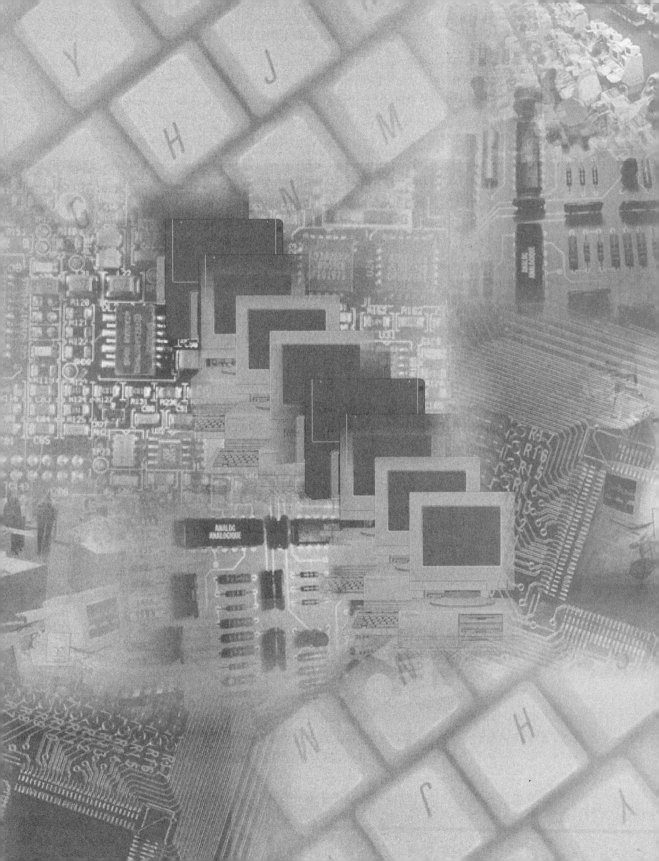

Selecting Data

In the past several chapters we have seen how to select data using in-line SQL statements and simple SELECT stored procedures. This chapter picks up the pace for SELECT stored procedures as we introduce topics such as joins, table aliases, and column aliases. These terms will be explained in depth shortly.

As our data needs become more complex, so do the complexities of our stored procedures. We start to introduce more T-SQL functions, statements, and clauses in our stored procedures in order to return the data that is required. This chapter introduces these T-SQL functions, statements, and clauses that allow you to write more complex stored procedures.

As we cover these topics we will be creating more and more complicated stored procedures. This chapter also sees the start of the VB application that was discussed in Chapter 3. As we progress through the next several chapters we will be expanding the functionality of the Hardware Tracking application.

This chapter will cover:

- ❑ Complex SELECT stored procedures
- ❑ Joins
- ❑ Column and table aliases
- ❑ Temporary tables

Prior to trying out this chapter's exercises, you will need to have the framework set up for the Hardware Tracking VB application. This is available in the code download, but if you prefer to step through and create it for yourself you should refer to Appendix D – *Building the Hardware Tracking Framework*.

Table Preparation

Before we can begin discussing the topics that this chapter covers, we need to insert some more data into our tables. Because we have not yet covered the various INSERT stored procedures we will manually insert the data using the Query Analyzer.

Inserting a couple of rows of data now will serve several purposes. Firstly, it allows you to become more familiar with the structure of our database. Secondly, it gives us some data to test our complex stored procedures with.

When we code simple stored procedures that select some or all data from a single table, you can visualize the data that will be obtained, because you have specified the column names in the select list and you know that data will be returned. As we write more complex stored procedures, where we start joining other tables and using compound expressions, we need to actually see the data returned to ensure the results we are getting are what we expected. So, each time we run a complex stored procedure we will run an appropriate SELECT query to verify that our procedure has worked correctly.

> *Compound expressions are expressions that can be used in the select list to specify which data is selected based on certain criteria, or can be used to join one table to another. We will be exploring them in more depth when we create temporary tables later in the chapter.*

If you review the database diagram from Chapter 3, repeated opposite, you can see that, because of the foreign key relationships, we must insert data into the tables in a certain order. For example, we cannot insert data into the System_Assignment_T table before we have inserted data into the Hardware_T and Employee_T tables. If you attempt to insert data into the System_Assignment_T table that does not reference a valid entry in the Hardware_T table, you will receive an error message that the insert statement conflicted with a foreign key constraint. This is because the System_Assignment_T table contains a foreign key reference to both the Hardware_T and Employee_T tables:

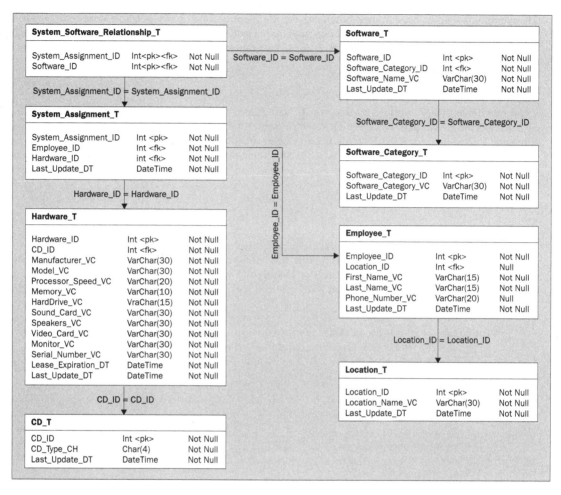

So let's insert some data into our tables. The values that are being inserted using the INSERT statements that follow can be substituted with your own values. Values that need to be verified will be noted, as will those that cannot be substituted.

The first table that we want to insert data into is the Location_T table. This table contains the locations of the employees who are listed in the Employee_T table. You can use any value that you want for the Location_Name_VC column.

In the Query Analyzer, enter and execute the follow INSERT statement:

```
INSERT INTO Location_T
   (Location_Name_VC, Last_Update_DT)
   VALUES('HOME OFFICE',GETDATE())
```

Remember, we don't have to specify a value for the identity field in any of these tables – SQL Server takes care of that. Once the data has been inserted, select the data from this table in order to find the identity value that was inserted by SQL Server. You can use a simple SELECT statement as shown:

```
SELECT * FROM Location_T
```

The next table that we want to insert a row of data into is the Employee_T table. The first value that is being inserted is the identity value that was inserted into the Location_T table. If the value that was inserted into your Location_T table is not 1, then substitute the identity value that was inserted into your table. The rest of the values in this INSERT statement can be substituted with your own values:

```
INSERT INTO Employee_T
    (Location_ID, First_Name_VC, Last_Name_VC, Phone_Number_VC, Last_Update_DT)
    VALUES(1,'Thearon','Willis','123-456-7890',GETDATE())
```

The next table that we want to insert data into is the Hardware_T table. The following INSERT statement may look intimidating but it merely lists all of the columns that we want to insert data into, followed by the values that are to be inserted. Verify the values already in the CD_T table and choose the appropriate value for the entry you want inserted. All other values can be the values of your choice.

> **Tip: instead of running a SELECT query to query the values in the CD_T table, you can expand the Hardware Tracking database in the Object Browser and then expand User Tables. Right-click on the CD_T table and choose Open from the context menu to view the data in this table.**

```
INSERT INTO Hardware_T
    (CD_ID, Manufacturer_VC, Model_VC, Processor_Speed_VC, Memory_VC,
        HardDrive_VC, Sound_Card_VC, Speakers_VC, Video_Card_VC,
        Monitor_VC, Serial_Number_VC, Lease_Expiration_DT,
        Last_Update_DT)
    VALUES(3,'Dell','Dimension XPS B800','800 MHZ','256 MB',
        '40 GB Ultra ATA','Turtle Beach Montego II A3D',
        'Altec Lansing ACS-340','32 MB nVIDIA AGP','17" P780 Triniton',
        '123-980A','12/30/00',GETDATE())
```

In order to perform some testing on one of the more complicated stored procedures that we will create later in this chapter, we need to insert one more row of data into the Hardware_T table. This hardware has not been assigned to anyone at this point. Use the same INSERT statement that was just used, change some or all of the values, and execute it.

Now that we have inserted data into the Employee_T and Hardware_T tables we can insert data into the System_Assignment_T table. The values that are to be inserted into this table contain the identity values that were inserted into the Employee_T and Hardware_T tables. Verify those values before running this INSERT statement:

```
INSERT INTO System_Assignment_T
    (Employee_ID, Hardware_ID, Last_Update_DT)
    VALUES(1,1,GETDATE())
```

The `System_Software_Relationship_T` table has a **many-to-one relationship** to the `System_Assignment_T` table. That is, there can be many entries in this table associated with only one entry in the `System_Assignment_T` table. You will need to identify the `Software_ID` values that you want inserted, from the `Software_T` table. You also need to know the identity value that was inserted into the `System_Assignment_T` table.

Using the following INSERT statements as a guide, pick and choose what software you want to be installed on the hardware that you inserted:

```
INSERT INTO System_Software_Relationship_T
    (System_Assignment_ID, Software_ID)
    VALUES(1,1)

INSERT INTO System_Software_Relationship_T
    (System_Assignment_ID, Software_ID)
    VALUES(1,12)

INSERT INTO System_Software_Relationship_T
    (System_Assignment_ID, Software_ID)
    VALUES(1,18)

INSERT INTO System_Software_Relationship_T
    (System_Assignment_ID, Software_ID)
    VALUES(1,19)

INSERT INTO System_Software_Relationship_T
    (System_Assignment_ID, Software_ID)
    VALUES(1,24)

INSERT INTO System_Software_Relationship_T
    (System_Assignment_ID, Software_ID)
    VALUES(1,25)

INSERT INTO System_Software_Relationship_T
    (System_Assignment_ID, Software_ID)
    VALUES(1,23)
```

We are now ready to proceed with discussions about new SQL Server functions, statements, and clauses.

Joins

A **join** is a condition that allows us to logically join two tables together so that we can select data from both tables. Joins are typically based on a logical relationship between two tables. This allows two tables to be joined based on the common value of the primary key in one table and a foreign key in the other.

Using a primary and foreign key is the logical choice for joins as this provides for great efficiency. This is because the primary key that the foreign key refers to is indexed. In fact, SQL Server is optimized internally to handle joins based on primary and foreign key relationships. This means that we can efficiently use one or more joins in our queries and stored procedures.

Of course, joins don't always have to join tables using a primary and foreign key relationship. Any columns in both tables that contain the same data can be used. For example, you could join two tables based on a column that contains a date value.

When we join tables there are several **logical operators** that can be used. For instance, we can use the equal (=) operator to specify that the data in both tables must be equal in order to be included in the join, or we can use the not equal (<>) operator to specify that the data must not be equal. We can also use such logical operators as less than (<), greater than (>), less than or equal to (<=), greater than or equal to (>=) and others, to provide even greater flexibility.

The logical operator that we use to join tables specifies the data that will be included in the results set, as we mentioned above. Suppose we want to list all employees at a specific location. Using the Employee_T as the primary table, we could join the Location_T table on the Location_ID, as shown in the following sample code:

```
SELECT First_Name_VC, Last_Name_VC
    FROM   Employee_T
    JOIN Location_T ON Employee_T.Location_ID = Location_T.Location_ID
    WHERE Location_Name_VC = 'HOME OFFICE'
```

This SELECT statement will select all employees from the Employee_T table who are located in the home office. We use the Employee_T table as the primary table because this is where most of the data is that we want to select. We then join the Location_T table using the foreign key Location_ID in the Employee_T table, and specify that it should equal the primary key Location_ID in the Location_T table. We only want to see the results where the Location_Name_VC column in the Location_T table contains the value of HOME OFFICE.

Inner Join

The join that we used in the previous example is also known as an **inner join** and can be specified as JOIN or INNER JOIN. An INNER JOIN, which is the default for JOIN, returns rows from the joined table whose values in the column or columns match the values in the table to which it is joined. This is the type of join we will be using most often, and is the most common type of join. The SELECT statement that was shown above could also be coded as shown below, specifying INNER JOIN instead of JOIN:

```
SELECT First_Name_VC, Last_Name_VC
    FROM   Employee_T
    INNER JOIN Location_T ON Employee_T.Location_ID = Location_T.Location_ID
    WHERE Location_Name_VC = 'HOME OFFICE'
```

There are several other types of join available in SQL Server and they are discussed next. Each type of join has its purpose and you will probably find a use for them all sooner or later.

Cross Join

A CROSS JOIN returns each row from both tables as one results set, in what is know as a **Cartesian product**. If you have five rows in table 1 and five rows in table 2, the results you will see are 25 rows of data (the rows in table 1 multiplied by the rows in table 2). A CROSS JOIN does not use a logical relationship between the tables, as all rows from both tables are returned. Each row in table two is returned for one row in table 1. The following code shows how a CROSS JOIN works:

```
SELECT Software_Name_VC, Software_Category_VC
    FROM Software_T
    CROSS JOIN Software_Category_T
    ORDER BY Software_Name_VC
```

If the Software_T table has 20 rows of data and the Software_Category_T table has five rows of data, multiply the two together and 100 rows of data are returned.

Left Outer Join

A LEFT OUTER JOIN is used to return all **left outer rows** even where there is no matching data in the joined table. Left outer rows are the rows in the table on the left side of the JOIN statement. Using this type of join ensures that, even if no data exists in the right outer table, the data in the left table is returned. We will be exploring the LEFT OUTER JOIN later in this chapter, but a brief example is shown here:

```
SELECT Manufacturer_VC, Model_VC, System_Assignment_ID
    FROM Hardware_T
    LEFT OUTER JOIN System_Assignment_T ON Hardware_T.Hardware_ID =
        System_Assignment_T.Hardware_ID
```

Remember that we inserted two rows of data into the Hardware_T table but only one of the systems was assigned. Using the SELECT statement above, we select both systems but only the System_Assignment_ID column for the system assigned returns data. The system that was not assigned returns a null value in this column. Using this type of join ensures all data is returned even if SQL Server has to place a null value in a column in order to return the data.

Right Outer Join

A RIGHT OUTER JOIN is similar to a LEFT OUTER JOIN except it returns all right outer rows even if there is no match, in which case it returns null. A RIGHT OUTER JOIN returns all rows in the second table regardless of whether there is matching data in the first table. An example of a RIGHT OUTER JOIN is shown:

```
SELECT Manufacturer_VC, Model_VC, System_Assignment_ID
    FROM Hardware_T
    RIGHT OUTER JOIN System_Assignment_T ON Hardware_T.Hardware_ID =
        System_Assignment_T.Hardware_ID
```

This example returns only the rows in the right outer table (System_Assignment_T) and execution of this SELECT statement will only yield one row of data.

Full Outer Join

A FULL OUTER JOIN is similar to a CROSS JOIN except that is uses a logical relationship to join the tables and does not produce a Cartesian product. All rows from both tables are returned. When no match is found in either the left outer row or the right outer row a null value is returned. An example of this type of join is shown:

```
SELECT Manufacturer_VC, Model_VC, System_Assignment_ID
    FROM Hardware_T
    FULL OUTER JOIN System_Assignment_T ON Hardware_T.Hardware_ID =
        System_Assignment_T.Hardware_ID
```

Executing this SELECT statement will return two rows of data, with one of the System_Assignment_ID columns containing a null value.

Now that we have had a look at some of the different types of join let's build some stored procedures that use them.

Try It Out – Employees and Locations Select Stored Procedures

If we take a look at the data needed for the **Employees** page of frmMain in our VB project, as discussed in Appendix D, we see that we need not only the employee's name and phone number but also their location. But what we actually want here is a list of *all* employees and a list of *all* locations. That way, when we display an employee, we can select their location in the **Location** combo box and display it.

Since this is a Win32 (Windows 32-bit) client-server application and our target audience is small, we will establish a connection to the database and hold it open until the application ends. If this were an intranet or Internet application we would be more concerned about open connections and would open and close our database connections as quickly as possible. Internet applications are typically more heavily used, as the target audience is greater. Therefore we need to be more concerned about database connections in this type of application and want to free up all resources as soon as possible.

Given this, let's create three stored procedures. The first will select all pertinent data about our employees, the second will select location information, and the third will implement the multiple recordsets feature that we explored in Chapter 7, by returning both employees and locations within one Recordset object.

1. Start the Query Analyzer and log in.

2. To create the employee stored procedure, enter the following:

```
CREATE PROCEDURE dbo.up_select_employees AS

    --
    --    Select data from the Employee_T table
    --
        SELECT Employee_T.Employee_ID, Employee_T.First_Name_VC,
            Employee_T.Last_Name_VC, Employee_T.Phone_Number_VC,

    --
```

```
--    Select data from the Location_T table
--
    Location_T.Location_ID, Location_T.Location_Name_VC,
--
--    Select data from the System_Assignment_T table
--
    System_Assignment_T.System_Assignment_ID
--
--    From
--
    FROM Employee_T
--
--    Join the Location_T table
--
    LEFT OUTER JOIN Location_T ON Employee_T.Location_ID =
        Location_T.Location_ID
--
--    Join the System_Assignment_T table
--
    LEFT OUTER JOIN System_Assignment_T ON Employee_T.Employee_ID =
        System_Assignment_T.Employee_ID
--
--    Sort the results
--
    ORDER BY Last_Name_VC, First_Name_VC
```

3. Parse the stored procedure for errors by clicking on the **Parse Query** icon on the toolbar.

4. Execute the code to create this stored procedure by clicking on the **Execute Query** icon.

5. Start the Enterprise Manager and expand the **Hardware Tracking** database.

6. Click on the **Stored Procedures** group and then right-click on the **up_select_employees** stored procedure. Choose **All Tasks** and then **Manage Permissions** from the context menu. Grant **EXEC** permission to the **Hardware Users** role and then click **OK** to close the dialog.

7. The next stored procedure that we want to create is the stored procedure to select all locations. To create this stored procedure, clear the current query window by clicking on the **Clear Query Window** icon on the toolbar, or open a new query window by clicking on the **New Query** icon on the toolbar.

8. Enter the following stored procedure:

```
CREATE PROCEDURE dbo.up_select_locations AS

SELECT Location_ID, Location_Name_VC
    FROM Location_T
    ORDER BY Location_Name_VC
```

9. Parse the query for errors, and then create it by clicking on the **Execute Query** icon on the toolbar.

10. Grant permissions on this stored procedure to the hardware users role.

11. The last stored procedure that we want to create is the stored procedure that will execute both of the previous procedures. This will allow us to execute one stored procedure and have two results sets returned. Clear the current query window or open a new one, and enter the following stored procedure:

```
CREATE PROCEDURE dbo.up_select_employees_and_locations AS

EXEC up_select_locations
EXEC up_select_employees
```

12. There is no need to parse the code for errors, but you can if you want. Create this stored procedure by clicking on the **Execute Query** icon on the toolbar.

13. Grant permissions on this stored procedure to the hardware users role.

How It Works – Employees Select Stored Procedure

The up_select_employees stored procedure may look a little complicated but this really isn't the case. There are lots of comments within the procedure to help anyone looking at it identify what each line is doing.

The first line creates the stored procedure and specifies the procedure name, prefixed with the dbo user prefix:

```
CREATE PROCEDURE dbo.up_select_employees AS
```

The SELECT statement in this stored procedure is selecting data from three different tables. We actually only need a few columns from a couple of tables to populate the **Employee** tab on the form in our program, but we want to maximize the use of this stored procedure and the data it returns. We have therefore included the System_Assignment_T table. This allows us to also use the data returned to populate the **Employee** combo box on the **System Assignment** tab, which we'll discuss later.

The comment on the next line of our stored procedure tells us from which table the data in the select list is coming. Notice that we have specified the table name as a prefix for each column; this also helps identify from which table the data is coming:

```
--    Select data from the Employee_T table
--
SELECT Employee_T.Employee_ID, Employee_T.First_Name_VC, Employee_T.Last_Name_VC,
    Employee_T.Phone_Number_VC,
```

The next line of the select list contains columns from another table and again we have specified the table name as a prefix to the column names. However, the only column that *requires* a table name prefix is the Location_ID column. This is because this column exists in both the Employee_T and Location_T tables. If we did not prefix the table name to this column we would get an error message about an ambiguous column name.

```
--    Select data from the Location_T table
--
      Location_T.Location_ID, Location_T.Location_Name_VC,
```

Next we specify a single column from the System_Assignment_T table and also prefix this column with the table name:

```
--    Select data from the System_Assignment_T table
--
      System_Assignment_T.System_Assignment_ID
```

The main table that we are selecting data from is the Employee_T table and this is the table specified in our FROM clause:

```
--    From
--
      FROM Employee_T
```

Next we use a LEFT OUTER JOIN to join the Location_T table. This ensures that we get all employees from the Employee_T table even if an employee has not been assigned a location. In this case the columns specified in the select list from the Location_T table will be returned with null values:

```
--    Join the Location_T table
--
      LEFT OUTER JOIN Location_T ON Employee_T.Location_ID =
          Location_T.Location_ID
```

The next table that we want to join is the System_Assignment_T table. Again we have used a LEFT OUTER JOIN, as the employee in the Employee_T table may not have been assigned a system yet:

```
--    Join the System_Assignment_T table
--
      LEFT OUTER JOIN System_Assignment_T ON Employee_T.Employee_ID =
          System_Assignment_T.Employee_ID
```

The last thing we want to do in this stored procedure is to sort the results returned. We do this by using the ORDER BY clause, and order the results by the Last_Name_VC column followed by the First_Name_VC column. This returns the data sorted by last name first followed by first name:

```
--    Sort the results
--
      ORDER BY Last_Name_VC, First_Name_VC
```

How It Works – Locations Select Stored Procedure

The next stored procedure that we created was the procedure to select all locations that existed in the
Location_T table. This simple procedure, up_select_locations, simply selects the Location_ID
and Location_Name_VC columns and orders the results by the Location_Name_VC column:

```
CREATE PROCEDURE dbo.up_select_locations AS

SELECT Location_ID, Location_Name_VC
    FROM Location_T
    ORDER BY Location_Name_VC
```

How It Works – Employees and Locations Stored Procedure

The final stored procedure that we created, up_select_employees_and_locations, was designed
to execute the previous two stored procedures. It will return two results sets within one Recordset
object. This will allow us to process the first recordset and then use the NextRecordset method of the
Recordset object to access the second recordset within that same Recordset object.

Notice that we have specified the up_select_locations procedure to be executed first. This will
make the location data the first recordset in the Recordset object:

```
CREATE PROCEDURE dbo.up_select_employees_and_locations AS

EXEC up_select_locations
EXEC up_select_employees
```

Let's add some code to our VB project to process these new stored procedures.

Try It Out – Process the Employees and Locations Stored Procedure

1. The code to be added to the Hardware Tracking project, created in Appendix D, is presented
in the following *How It Works* section.

2. Once you have added all the code, save your project and then run the program to test it out.
When the form loads, the combo boxes on the **Employee** tab and the **Employee** combo box
on the **System Assignment** tab will be loaded. Then the **Employee** tab will be selected and
the first entry in the **Last Name** combo box will be displayed. This will cause the rest of the
fields on this tab to be populated with the corresponding data:

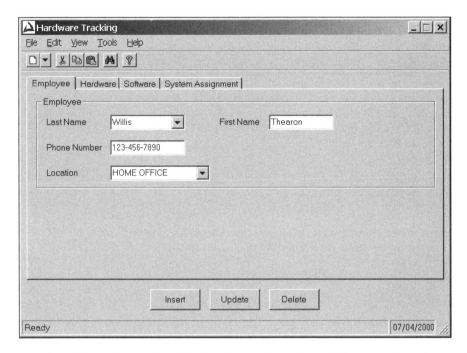

At this point the only tab that works is the Employee tab, so if you click on another tab you will receive an error.

How It Works – Process the Employees and Locations Stored Procedure

The first thing we want to do is to declare some objects in the general declarations section of the main form (frmMain). These objects will be used in various procedures in this form:

```
'Declare objects
Dim objData As clsSelectData
Dim objRSData As ADODB.Recordset
```

Then we want to add code to the Form_Load event. The first piece of code that we want to add is the code that will call the login form so we can establish a connection with the database:

```
Private Sub Form_Load()
    'Display the login form
    frmLogin.Show vbModal
```

Then we want to show the main form to give the illusion that the form is just about ready for use. We do this using the Show method of the form and then we set the mouse pointer to an arrow and hourglass so the user knows that some processing is still taking place. We have included the DoEvents function to yield execution to the processor and to allow the form to be refreshed:

```
    'Show the form and set the mouse pointer to busy
    Me.Show
    Me.MousePointer = vbArrowHourglass
    DoEvents
```

Then we call the procedure to load the **Employee** tab on the form. We'll define this procedure shortly:

```
'Load Employees
Call LoadEmployees
```

We want to handle the click event for the different tabs on the `tabData` tab control, and we do this in the `tabData_Click` procedure. To ensure that the **Employee** tab is always displayed first, we set the `Tab` property of the `tabData` tab control to the first tab. Then we call the `tabData_Click` procedure to get a recordset of employees:

```
'Initialize controls
tabData.Tab = 0
Call tabData_Click(0)
```

Once we have completed all data processing, we set the mouse pointer back to the default pointer and display a message in the status bar, indicating that we are ready:

```
'Return mouse pointer to default value
Me.MousePointer = vbDefault

'Display status
StatusBar1.Panels("pnlStatus").Text = "Ready"
End Sub
```

Having established a connection and declared some local objects, we want to clean these up as the form is unloading. By adding the following code to the `Form_Unload` procedure. The first thing we do is check to see if the `objRSData` Recordset object is active, by looking to see if it is equal to nothing. Then, if it is active, we check to see if the `Recordset` object is open by looking at the `State` property, using the `adStateOpen` constant from the `ObjectStateEnum` enumeration. If the `Recordset` object is open we close it. Regardless of whether the `Recordset` object was open or closed, we then set it to `Nothing` to remove our reference to it:

```
Private Sub Form_Unload(Cancel As Integer)
    'Dereference local objects
    If Not objRSData Is Nothing Then
        If objRSData.State = adStateOpen Then
            objRSData.Close
        End If
        Set objRSData = Nothing
    End If
```

Next we remove our reference to the `objData` object and then call the procedure to terminate our database connection:

```
    Set objData = Nothing

    'Termination the database connection
    Call TerminateConnection
End Sub
```

The LoadEmployees procedure calls the SelectEmployeesAndLocations function in the select data class (clsSelectData) so let's look at this function first. The SelectEmployeesAndLocations function should be coded in the clsSelectData class.

This function accepts a Connection object and a Recordset object as parameters and returns a Long data type as a return code. Both objects are passed by reference and the Connection object should be an active connection. The Recordset object is opened in this function and if it was opened successfully, a zero return code is returned.

When we pass a parameter by reference (ByRef) we are actually passing a pointer to the address of that parameter – this is all taken care of behind the scenes in VB. We are then able to access and modify the contents of that parameter using the address that was passed. When we pass a parameter by value (ByVal) we pass a copy of the value of the parameter. The function or procedure to which it has been passed can modify the parameter but the original data is not accessed or modified.

```
Public Function SelectEmployeesAndLocations( _
    ByRef objConn As ADODB.Connection, _
    ByRef objRS As ADODB.Recordset) As Long
```

The first thing we do in this function is to set up our error handling. This is the standard error handling that we have been using in the past few chapters. We will define the ADOError procedure next:

```
    'Setup error handling
    On Error GoTo SelectEmployeesAndLocations_Err
```

Next, we open the recordset using the Open method. We use the up_select_employees_and_locations stored procedure, which will return two recordsets in one Recordset object. We only want to read this recordset in a forward direction so we have specified the adOpenForwardOnly constant for the CursorType parameter. The LockType parameter has also been specified as read-only, as we have used the adLockReadOnly constant for this parameter:

```
    'Open the recordset object
    objRS.Open "up_select_employees_and_locations", _
        objConn, adOpenForwardOnly, adLockReadOnly, adCmdStoredProc
```

If no errors occurred we set this function to return a zero return code and then exit the function:

```
    'Set the return code
    SelectEmployeesAndLocations = 0

    'Exit Function
    Exit Function
```

Our error handler calls the ADOError procedure, passing it a couple of parameters: the Connection object that was passed to this function and the function name as a string. Once control has been returned from the error handling procedure we set this function to return a return code of 1, indicating failure:

```
SelectEmployeesAndLocations_Err:
    'Call the error handler and return a return code of 1
    Call ADOError(objConn, "SelectEmployeesAndLocations")
    SelectEmployeesAndLocations = 1
End Function
```

The `ADOError` procedure is also defined in the `clsSelectData` class. This procedure accepts two parameters: the `Connection` object and the calling procedure as a string. The first thing we do in this procedure is to declare an ADO `Error` object:

```
Private Sub ADOError(ByRef objConn As ADODB.Connection, _
    ByVal strProcedure As String)

    'Declare local objects
    Dim objError As ADODB.Error
```

We use the `Connection` object that was passed by reference and loop through the `Errors` collection. Using the `App` object in VB, we log each error to the NT event log. (On Windows 98 this method writes to the file specified in the `LogPath` property. If no file has been specified then the event is written to a file named `vbevents.log`.)

```
    'Loop through the errors collection and log all errors
    For Each objError In objConn.Errors
        App.LogEvent "The following error was encountered in the " & _
            strProcedure & " procedure:" & vbCrLf & _
            objError.Number & " : " & objError.Description, _
            vbLogEventTypeError
    Next
```

We remove our reference to the `Error` object that we defined at the beginning of this procedure and then we exit the procedure:

```
    'Dereference error object
    Set objError = Nothing
End Sub
```

The next function that we need to code in the select data class is the `ExecuteSQL` function. This function will be called from the main form and is a generic routine to execute stored procedures or in-line SQL statements that do not require parameters and that do return data. This function accepts the SQL string to be executed and opens a `Recordset` object that executes that SQL string. This function accepts four parameters: a `Connection` object, a `Recordset` object, the SQL string to be executed, and the `CommandType`. This last parameter is one of the constants from the ADO `CommandTypeEnum` enumeration that will provide a drop down list of the available constants.

```
Public Function ExecuteSQL( _
    ByRef objConn As ADODB.Connection, _
    ByRef objRS As ADODB.Recordset, _
    ByVal strSQL As String, _
    ByVal lngCommandType As ADODB.CommandTypeEnum) As Long
```

As usual we set up our error handling first. Since this function executes a SQL string that will be held open, we set the `CursorLocation` property of the `Recordset` object to use a client-side cursor. This lets us disconnect this recordset from the database so we do not have to hold an open connection between the `Recordset` object and the database, thus reducing the number of resources used.

```
    'Setup error handling
    On Error GoTo ExecuteSQL_Err

    'Use a client side cursor
    objRS.CursorLocation = adUseClient
```

Then we open the `Recordset` object using the SQL string that was passed. Notice that for the `Options` parameter of the `Recordset` we have specified the `lngCommandType` parameter that was passed to this function. This parameter should contain one of the constants from the `CommandTypeEnum` enumeration.

```
'Open the recordset object
objRS.Open strSQL, _
    objConn, adOpenStatic, adLockReadOnly, lngCommandType
```

After the recordset has been opened, we need to disconnect it, by setting the `ActiveConnection` property to `Nothing`. By doing this we remove the active `Connection` object from the recordset, disconnecting it from the database. Setting the `CursorLocation` property to `adUseClient` before the `Recordset` object is open and then setting the `ActiveConnection` property to `Nothing` after the `Recordset` object has been opened will provide us with a disconnected recordset that uses minimum resources. Then we set the return code for this function and exit:

```
'Disconnect the recordset
Set objRS.ActiveConnection = Nothing

'Set the return code
ExecuteSQL = 0

'Exit function
Exit Function
```

Our error handling for this function is the same as the error handling for the last function:

```
ExecuteSQL_Err:
    'Call the error handler and return a return code of 1
    Call ADOError(objConn, "ExecuteSQL")
    ExecuteSQL = 1
End Function
```

Switching back to the main form (`frmMain`) we need to add the code for the `LoadEmployees` procedure. This procedure will load the combo boxes on the **Employee** tab on the form. Since we coded the `up_select_employees` stored procedure to also include system assignment information, we will also use this procedure to load the **Employee** combo box on the **System Assignment** tab.

The first thing we do in this procedure is set up our error handling. Then we display a message in the status bar to indicate that we are loading employees, before declaring our local variables:

```
Sub LoadEmployees()
    'Setup error handling
    On Error GoTo LoadEmployees_Err

    'Display status
    StatusBar1.Panels("pnlStatus").Text = "Loading Employees"

    'Declare local variables
    Dim lngRC As Long
```

We then set a reference to the global `Recordset` object and to the select data class:

```
'Set a reference to the recordset object
Set g_objRS = New ADODB.Recordset

'Set a reference to the select data class
Set objData = New clsSelectData
```

We call the `SelectEmployeesAndLocations` function in the select data class, passing it the global `Connection` object and the global `Recordset` object.

After execution of the function we check the return code and, if it is not zero, we raise an error using the `Raise` method of the VB `Err` object. The first parameter of the `Raise` method is the error `Number`. Error numbers 0–512 are reserved for system errors. The range available to us is 513–65535. We have picked 513. When we set our own error number we need to add it to the `vbObjectError` constant. The next parameter of the `Raise` method is the `Source` of the error. We have specified the name of this procedure as the source. The next parameter is the error `Description` and we have specified the appropriate description:

```
'Open the recordset
lngRC = objData.SelectEmployeesAndLocations(g_objConn, g_objRS)

'Ensure we were successful
If lngRC <> 0 Then
    Err.Raise 513 + vbObjectError, "LoadEmployees", _
        "Call to SelectEmployeesAndLocations failed"
End If
```

At this point we clear the combo boxes on the **Employee** tab and the **Employee** combo box on the **System Assignment** tab. We could be executing this procedure multiple times during the execution of this program so we want to ensure we do not have any duplicate data in these combo boxes. Multiple executions will be handled in subsequent chapters as we insert and update data.

```
'Clear combo boxes
cboLocation.Clear
cboLastName.Clear
cboEmployee.Clear
```

Next, we loop through the recordset and load the **Location** combo box on the **Employee** tab. We add the location name to the combo box and the location ID to the `ItemData` property of the combo box:

```
'Load location combo box
Do While Not g_objRS.EOF
    cboLocation.AddItem g_objRS!Location_Name_VC
    cboLocation.ItemData(cboLocation.NewIndex) = g_objRS!Location_ID
    g_objRS.MoveNext
Loop
```

Once an end-of-file condition has occurred on the `Recordset` object, we execute the `NextRecordset` method of the `Recordset` object to get the next recordset:

```
'Get the next recordset
Set g_objRS = g_objRS.NextRecordset
```

This loop loads both the `cboLastName` combo box on the **Employee** tab and the `cboEmployee` combo box on the **System Assignment** tab. In the `cboLastName` combo box we only add the last name of the employee and set the `ItemData` property of the combo box to the employee ID.

In loading the `cboEmployee` combo box, we concatenate the employee's last name and first name, separated by a comma. We also add the employee ID to the `ItemData` property of the combo box:

```
'Load the last name combo box and employee combo box
Do While Not g_objRS.EOF
   'Last name combo box
   cboLastName.AddItem g_objRS!Last_Name_VC
   cboLastName.ItemData(cboLastName.NewIndex) = g_objRS!Employee_ID
   'Employee combo box
   cboEmployee.AddItem g_objRS!Last_Name_VC & ", " & g_objRS!First_Name_VC
   cboEmployee.ItemData(cboEmployee.NewIndex) = g_objRS!Employee_ID
   g_objRS.MoveNext
Loop

'Close the recordset
g_objRS.Close
```

Once all processing has been completed, we remove the references to our objects and display a ready message in the status bar. Then we exit the procedure:

```
'Remove references to objects
Set g_objRS = Nothing
Set objData = Nothing

'Display status
StatusBar1.Panels("pnlStatus").Text = "Ready"

'Exit Sub
Exit Sub
```

The error handling in this procedure calls the `ADOError` procedure in this form, so let's take a look at that code next:

```
LoadEmployees_Err:
   Call ADOError
End Sub
```

This `ADOError` procedure is called from other procedures in the main form. The first thing we do here is to declare a string variable, `strError`:

```
Sub ADOError()
   'Declare local variables
   Dim strError
```

Then we loop through the `Errors` collection and add each error to the string variable:

```
'Loop through the errors collection and display all errors
For Each g_objError In g_objConn.Errors
    strError = strError & g_objError.Number & " : " & _
        g_objError.Description & vbCrLf & vbCrLf
Next
```

We display a message box using the `MsgBox` function, using the `strError` variable as the message to be displayed. Then we unload the form to clean up and end the program:

```
'Display the error
MsgBox strError, vbCritical + vbOKOnly, "ADO Error"

'Unload the form to clean up and then end
Unload Me
End
End Sub
```

The next procedure that we want to take a look at is the `tabData_Click` event procedure. This event is fired when the user clicks on a tab on the tab control on the form. This procedure was made available when you added the **SSTab** control and it passes the previous tab as a parameter. We are not interested in the previous tab, only the current tab that the user has clicked on, so we will be referencing the `Tab` property to find out what the current tab is.

The first thing we do in this procedure is to set up our error handling. Then we display a message that we are processing data on the tab, and declare our local variables:

```
Private Sub tabData_Click(PreviousTab As Integer)
    'Setup error handling
    On Error GoTo tabData_Click_Err

    'Display status
    StatusBar1.Panels("pnlStatus").Text = "Processing Tab Data"

    'Declare local variables
    Dim lngRC As Long, strSQL As String
```

This procedure will use the `objRSData` `Recordset` object defined in this form to open and hold open a recordset. This recordset will contain data that is specific to the tab that we are on. So the first thing we need to do is to check to see if the `Recordset` object has a reference set to it. We do this by checking to see if it is equal to `Nothing`. If it is not, we look to see if it is open by checking the `State` property of the `Recordset` object. If it is open, we close it. If it has a reference to the ADO `Recordset` object then we set it to `Nothing`. Performing these checks will clean up any open recordset and references that it held and is very similar logic to what we used in the `Form_Unload` event. By using only one `Recordset` object we reduce the amount of resource that must be held and used.

```
'Close and dereference recordset if it is already open
If Not objRSData Is Nothing Then
    If objRSData.State = adStateOpen Then
        objRSData.Close
    End If
    Set objRSData = Nothing
End If
```

Then we set a new reference to the ADO `Recordset` object. Next, we use the **Tab** property of the `tabData` tab control in a `Select Case` statement to find out which tab is now the current tab. This `Select Case` statement will set the appropriate SQL string to be executed. Here we have set the SQL string to the `up_select_employees` stored procedure:

```
'Set a reference to the recordset object
Set objRSData = New ADODB.Recordset

'Set the appropriate string
Select Case tabData.Tab
    Case 0   'Employee
        strSQL = "up_select_employees"
    Case 1   'Hardware
    Case 2   'Software
    Case 3   'System Assignment
End Select
```

If the current tab is one of the first three tabs (0-2) then we set a reference to the select data class and execute the `ExecuteSQL` function. We pass this function four parameters: the global `Connection` object, the `Recordset` object defined in this form, the SQL string to be executed, and a constant from the `CommandTypeEnum` enumeration, indicating what type of SQL string we are executing. Since this is a stored procedure we have specified the `adCmdStoredProc` constant. The function returns a `Long` data type as its return code.

```
'If one of the first three tabs, open a recordset
If tabData.Tab <> 3 Then

    'Set a reference to the select data class
    Set objData = New clsSelectData

    'Open the recordset
    lngRC = objData.ExecuteSQL(g_objConn, objRSData, strSQL, adCmdStoredProc)
```

We check to ensure we received a zero return code and if not we raise an error:

```
'Ensure we were successful
If lngRC <> 0 Then
    Err.Raise 513 + vbObjectError, "tabData_Click", _
        "Call to ExecuteSQL failed"
End If

End If
```

Next we want to display the first entry in the combo box if any data exists. Using the `Select Case` statement again, we determine which tab we are on in the `tabData` tab control. Then we look to see if any entries exist in the `cboLastName` combo box, by checking the `ListCount` property of that combo box. If the `ListCount` property is not equal to −1 then at least one entry exists, and we set the `ListIndex` of the combo box to 0 so the first entry will be displayed.

Setting the `ListIndex` property of the combo box causes the `cboLastName_Click` procedure to fire, which we will code next.

```
'Show the first record if available
Select Case tabData.Tab
    Case 0  'Employee
        If cboLastName.ListCount <> -1 Then
            cboLastName.ListIndex = 0
        End If
    Case 1  'Hardware
    Case 2  'Software
    Case 3  'System Assignment
End Select
```

We remove the reference to our class object and display a ready message in the status bar. Then we exit the procedure:

```
'Remove references to objects
Set objData = Nothing

'Display status
StatusBar1.Panels("pnlStatus").Text = "Ready"

'Exit sub
Exit Sub
```

The error handling in this procedure is the same error handling we have seen before:

```
tabData_Click_Err:
    Call ADOError
End Sub
```

The `cboLastName_Click` procedure fires whenever we change the `ListIndex` property of the `cboLastName` combo box, either by selecting a new entry in the combo box or by setting the `ListIndex` property through code.

The first thing that we do in this procedure is to check the `ListIndex` property. If it is equal to −1 then no entry has been selected and we want to exit the procedure. Then we declare our local variables:

```
Private Sub cboLastName_Click()
    'Check the ListIndex property
    If cboLastName.ListIndex = -1 Then
        Exit Sub
    End If

    'Declare local variables
    Dim intIndex As Integer
```

This procedure uses the open recordset that was opened in the `tabData_Click` procedure to find the last name that was selected. The first thing we want to do is to move to the first record in the recordset.

Then, using the `Find` method of the `Recordset` object, we search for the employee ID for the last name that was selected. We look for a match between the `Employee_ID` field in the recordset and the `ItemData` property of the combo box. The `Find` method accepts several parameters but we are only using the first one, `Criteria`. The `Criteria` parameter specifies the field name in the recordset to be used in the search, the comparison operator (for example, $=$, $>$, $<$, or $>=$), and the value to be compared:

```
'Move to the first record
objRSData.MoveFirst

'Find the correct record in the recordset
objRSData.Find "Employee_ID = " & _
    cboLastName.ItemData(cboLastName.ListIndex)
```

Once a match is found we fill the form fields using the data from the open client-side recordset:

```
'Fill the form fields
txtFirstName.Text = objRSData!First_Name_VC
txtPhoneNumber.Text = objRSData!Phone_Number_VC
```

To display the correct entry in the `Location` combo box, we must loop through the `ItemData` property of the `cboLocation` combo box, looking for a match between the `ItemData` property and the `Location_ID` field in the recordset. Once a match has been found, we set the `ListIndex` property of the combo box so the correct entry is displayed, and then we exit the `For` loop and the procedure:

```
'Loop through the location combo box and find the right entry
For intIndex = 0 To cboLocation.ListCount - 1
    If cboLocation.ItemData(intIndex) = objRSData!Location_ID Then
        cboLocation.ListIndex = intIndex
        Exit For
    End If
  cboLocation.ListIndex = -1
Next
End Sub
```

There are a few little procedures that we must also add code for. The first of these is the `mnuFileExit_Click` procedure. When the **Exit** menu item in the **File** menu is clicked, we want to end the program. We do this by specifying the `Unload` statement:

```
Private Sub mnuFileExit_Click()
    Unload Me
End Sub
```

When we click on one of the menu items in the **View** menu we want to switch to that tab in the `tabData` tab control. Again we use the `Tab` property of the tab control and set it to the appropriate tab that corresponds to the menu item:

```
Private Sub mnuViewEmployee_Click()
    'Make the employee tab active
    tabData.Tab = 0
End Sub
```

```
Private Sub mnuViewHardware_Click()
    'Make the hardware tab active
    tabData.Tab = 1
End Sub

Private Sub mnuViewSoftware_Click()
    'Make the software tab active
    tabData.Tab = 2
End Sub

Private Sub mnuViewSystemAssignment_Click()
    'Make the system assignment tab active
    tabData.Tab = 3
End Sub
```

Try It Out – Hardware and CD Select Stored Procedures

Next we will create stored procedures to select data for the Hardware tab on the main form. We already have a stored procedure to select CD data, so all we need is a stored procedure to select hardware data, and a stored procedure to select both hardware and CD data to return multiple recordsets in a single Recordset object.

1. Start the Query Analyzer if it is not already running.

2. To create the hardware stored procedure enter the following code:

```
CREATE PROCEDURE dbo.up_select_hardware AS

--
--    Select data from the Hardware_T table
--
SELECT Hardware_ID, Manufacturer_VC, Model_VC, Processor_Speed_VC,
    Memory_VC, HardDrive_VC, Sound_Card_VC, Speakers_VC,
    Video_Card_VC, Monitor_VC, Serial_Number_VC, Lease_Expiration_DT,
--
--    Select data from the CD_T table which is aliased as CD_Table
--
    CD_Table.CD_ID, CD_Type_CH AS CD_DRIVE
--
--    From
--
    FROM Hardware_T
--
--    Join the CD_T table and alias it as CD_Table
--
    JOIN CD_T AS CD_Table ON Hardware_T.CD_ID = CD_Table.CD_ID
--
--    Sort the results
--
    ORDER BY Manufacturer_VC, Model_VC
```

3. Parse the code for errors, and then create the stored procedure by clicking on the Execute Query icon on the toolbar.

4. Start the Enterprise Manager if it is not already running. Grant permissions on the up_select_hardware stored procedure to the hardware users role.

5. To create the stored procedure to select hardware and CD data, first clear the current query window or open a new query window. Then enter the following stored procedure:

```
CREATE PROCEDURE dbo.up_select_hardware_and_cds AS

EXEC up_select_cd_types
EXEC up_select_hardware
```

6. You do not need to parse this code for errors but you can if you want. Create this stored procedure by clicking on the Execute Query icon on the toolbar.

7. Start the Enterprise Manager if it is not already running. Grant permissions on the up_select_hardware_and_cds stored procedure to the hardware users role.

How It Works – Hardware Select Stored Procedure

The up_select_hardware stored procedure selects the hardware data from the Hardware_T table and also the corresponding CD data from the CD_T table:

```
CREATE PROCEDURE dbo.up_select_hardware AS
```

This stored procedure also has plenty of comments to quickly identify what each line of this stored procedure does. The SELECT statement shown in the next line of this stored procedure is selecting data from the Hardware_T table and lists the individual columns that we are selecting data from:

```
--    Select data from the Hardware_T table
--
SELECT Hardware_ID, Manufacturer_VC, Model_VC, Processor_Speed_VC,
    Memory_VC, HardDrive_VC, Sound_Card_VC, Speakers_VC,
    Video_Card_VC, Monitor_VC, Serial_Number_VC, Lease_Expiration_DT,
```

Then we specify the corresponding columns from the CD_T table in the select list:

```
--    Select data from the CD_T table which is aliased as CD_Table
--
    CD_Table.CD_ID, CD_Type_CH AS CD_DRIVE
```

Then we specify the FROM clause and the main table that we are selecting data from:

```
--    From
--
    FROM Hardware_T
```

319

Next we join the CD_T table using an INNER JOIN, which can be specified as INNER JOIN or JOIN. We have chosen to use the latter as this is the most common way to specify an INNER JOIN. Remember that this type of join will only select data if data exists in both tables. This is what we want as we will not insert an entry into the Hardware_T table without specifying the CD type. We are using the column CD_ID in both tables as the join criteria.

```
--   Join the CD_T table and alias it as CD_Table
--
    JOIN CD_T AS CD_Table ON Hardware_T.CD_ID = CD_Table.CD_ID
```

Lastly, we want to sort the results, and do so by specifying the ORDER BY clause, sorting the results set first by manufacturer and then by model:

```
--   Sort the results
--
    ORDER BY Manufacturer_VC, Model_VC
```

How It Works – Hardware and CD Select Stored Procedure

The next stored procedure that we created is the stored procedure to return multiple recordsets within a single Recordset object. This stored procedure simply executes the up_select_cd_types stored procedure and the up_select_hardware stored procedure:

```
CREATE PROCEDURE dbo.up_select_hardware_and_cds AS

EXEC up_select_cd_types
EXEC up_select_hardware
```

Try It Out – Process the Hardware and CD Select Stored Procedure

1. The code for this is presented in the *How It Works* section. Once you have worked through all the additions and modifications to the code, save your project in preparation for testing.

2. Run your program and log in. The Employee tab is displayed by default so click on the Hardware tab. Once you do, the new code that was just added will be executed and the first entry in the cboManufacturer combo box will be displayed:

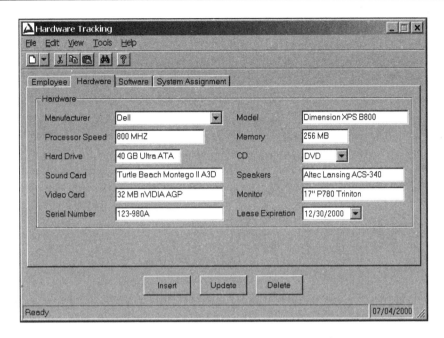

How It Works – Process the Hardware and CD Select Stored Procedure

First we will modify the VB code in the main form (frmMain). We want to have the combo boxes on the Hardware tab loaded at startup. Place the call to the LoadHardware procedure in the Form_Load event, as indicated by the code below:

```
'Load Employees
Call LoadEmployees

'Load Hardware
Call LoadHardware
```

We want to create the LoadHardware procedure next so let's take a look at its code. The first thing we do in this procedure is to set up our error handling and display a message in the status bar that we are loading the hardware. Then we declare our local variables:

```
Sub LoadHardware()
    'Setup error handling
    On Error GoTo LoadHardware_Err

    'Display status
    StatusBar1.Panels("pnlStatus").Text = "Loading Hardware"

    'Declare local variables
    Dim lngRC As Long
```

Next, we set a reference to the global `Recordset` object and then set a reference to the select data class:

```
'Set a reference to the recordset object

Set g_objRS = New ADODB.Recordset

'Set a reference to the select data class
Set objData = New clsSelectData
```

We execute the `SelectHardwareAndCDs` function, which we will define next, in the select data class. This function accepts two parameters: a `Connection` object and a `Recordset` object. It returns a `Long` data type as a return code. After we have executed the function, we check the return code and raise an error if it is not zero:

```
'Open the recordset
lngRC = objData.SelectHardwareAndCDs(g_objConn, g_objRS)

'Ensure we were successful
If lngRC <> 0 Then
    Err.Raise 513 + vbObjectError, "LoadHardware", _
        "Call to SelectHardwareAndCDs failed"
End If
```

We clear the `cboCD` and `cboManufacturer` combo boxes as we could execute this procedure more than once during the course of the program:

```
'Clear combo boxes
cboCD.Clear
cboManufacturer.Clear
```

We loop through the recordset, loading the `cboCD` combo box until an end-of-file condition occurs on the recordset. After an end-of-file condition occurs, we execute the `NextRecordset` method of the `Recordset` object to get the next recordset:

```
'Load cd combo box
Do While Not g_objRS.EOF
    cboCD.AddItem g_objRS!CD_Type_CH
    cboCD.ItemData(cboCD.NewIndex) = g_objRS!CD_ID
    g_objRS.MoveNext
Loop

'Get the next recordset
Set g_objRS = g_objRS.NextRecordset
```

Then we loop through the second recordset, loading the cboManufacturer combo box. After an end-of-file condition occurs on the recordset, we close the Recordset object:

```
'Load manufacturer combo box
Do While Not g_objRS.EOF
    'Manufacturer combo box
    cboManufacturer.AddItem g_objRS!Manufacturer_VC
    cboManufacturer.ItemData(cboManufacturer.NewIndex) = g_objRS!Hardware_ID
    g_objRS.MoveNext
Loop

'Close the recordset
g_objRS.Close
```

Then we remove our references to the global Recordset object and the class object. We display a ready message indicating that processing has been completed. Then we exit the procedure:

```
'Remove references to objects
Set g_objRS = Nothing
Set objData = Nothing

'Display status
StatusBar1.Panels("pnlStatus").Text = "Ready"

'Exit sub
Exit Sub
```

The error handling is the same error handling that we have used in the other procedures in this form:

```
LoadHardware_Err:
    Call ADOError
End Sub
```

Switching to the clsSelectData class we want to create the SelectHardwareAndCDs function. This function accepts two parameters, both by reference. The first parameter is the Connection object and the second parameter is the Recordset object. The first thing that is performed in this function is to set up the error handling:

```
Public Function SelectHardwareAndCDs( _
    ByRef objConn As ADODB.Connection, _
    ByRef objRS As ADODB.Recordset) As Long

    'Setup error handling
    On Error GoTo SelectHardwareAndCDs_Err
```

Then, using the passed `Recordset` and `Connection` objects, we open the recordset using a forward-only cursor and read-only lock. We set the return code for this function and then exit the function:

```
'Open the recordset object
objRS.Open "up_select_hardware_and_cds", _
    objConn, adOpenForwardOnly, adLockReadOnly, adCmdStoredProc

'Set the return code
SelectHardwareAndCDs = 0

'Exit function
Exit Function
```

The error handling in our *class* is slightly different from our *form*, as we saw earlier. Since this class will ultimately end up in an ActiveX DLL, we want to log all messages instead of displaying them in a message box. To that end we call the `ADOError` procedure in this class, passing it the `Connection` object and the name of this function. Then we set the return code for this function to 1 to indicate a failure:

```
SelectHardwareAndCDs_Err:
    'Call the error handler and return a return code of 1
    Call ADOError(objConn, "SelectHardwareAndCDs")
    SelectHardwareAndCDs = 1
End Function
```

Switching back to the code in our form, we need to add some code to the `tabData_Click` procedure. Remember that this procedure is fired when we click on a tab in the tab control. We need to add the stored procedure to be executed when the **Hardware** tab is clicked on. This will open the `objRSData` recordset and will obtain the hardware data. Modify the code in your procedure as shown:

```
'Set the appropriate string
Select Case tabData.Tab
    Case 0  'Employee
        strSQL = "up_select_employees"
    Case 1  'Hardware
        strSQL = "up_select_hardware"
```

We also want to display the first entry in the `cboManufacturer` combo box if one exists. Modify your code to include the code shown here:

```
'Show the first record if available
Select Case tabData.Tab
    Case 0  'Employee
        If cboLastName.ListCount <> -1 Then
            cboLastName.ListIndex = 0
        End If
    Case 1  'Hardware
        If cboManufacturer.ListCount <> -1 Then
            cboManufacturer.ListIndex = 0
        End If
```

Remember that setting the ListIndex property of a combo box will cause the click event for that combo box to fire. To that end we want to add some code to the cboManufacturer_Click procedure. The first thing we do in this procedure is to check the ListIndex property for a value of −1, which means no entry has been selected. Then we declare our local variables and move to the first record in the objRSData recordset:

```
Private Sub cboManufacturer_Click()
    'Check the ListIndex property
    If cboManufacturer.ListIndex = -1 Then
        Exit Sub
    End If

    'Declare local variables
    Dim intIndex As Integer

    'Move to the first record
    objRSData.MoveFirst
```

We use the Find method of the objRSData recordset to find the entry that was selected in the cboManufacturer combo box. Here we are using the Hardware_ID field in the recordset to match against the ItemData property of the selected entry in the cboManufacturer combo box:

```
    'Find the correct record in the recordset
    objRSData.Find "Hardware_ID = " & _
        cboManufacturer.ItemData(cboManufacturer.ListIndex)
```

Once the match has been found, we populate the fields on the **Hardware** tab using data from the opened recordset:

```
    'Fill the form fields
    txtModel.Text = objRSData!Model_VC
    txtProcessorSpeed.Text = objRSData!Processor_Speed_VC
    txtMemory.Text = objRSData!Memory_VC
    txtHardDrive.Text = objRSData!HardDrive_VC
    txtSoundCard.Text = objRSData!Sound_Card_VC
    txtSpeakers.Text = objRSData!Speakers_VC
    txtVideoCard.Text = objRSData!Video_Card_VC
    txtMonitor.Text = objRSData!Monitor_VC
    txtSerialNumber.Text = objRSData!Serial_Number_VC
    dtpLeaseExpiration.Value = objRSData!Lease_Expiration_DT
```

We must loop through the cboCD combo box to find the correct entry that matches the data in the recordset. Then we exit the procedure:

```
    'Loop through the cd combo box and find the right entry
    For intIndex = 0 To cboCD.ListCount - 1
        If cboCD.ItemData(intIndex) = objRSData!CD_ID Then
            cboCD.ListIndex = intIndex
            Exit For
        End If
    Next
End Sub
```

Try It Out – Adding the Code for the Software Tab

At this point we want to add the code to implement the functionality for the **Software** tab. There are no new stored procedures to write for this as we have written all the necessary stored procedures in previous chapters. If you recall, we wrote the `up_select_software_and_categories` stored procedure in Chapter 7 and this executes the `up_select_software` and `up_select_categories` stored procedures within it.

1. Once again, the code required for this stage in the project is presented throughout the following *How It Works* section. When you have entered the code, save your project before we begin testing this newest functionality.

2. Run your program and then click on the **Software** tab. You should see results similar to those shown in the next figure:

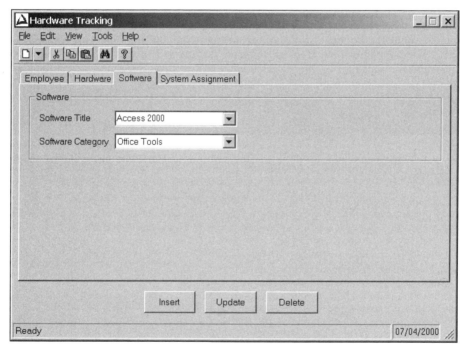

How It Works – Adding the Code for the Software Tab

Let's start with the code in the `Form_Load` event. Modify this procedure as shown:

```
'Load Hardware
Call LoadHardware

'Load Software
Call LoadSoftware
```

We want to add the `LoadSoftware` procedure next. This procedure performs double duty, as it will also load the `lstInstalledSoftware` list on the **System Assignment** tab. To start this procedure we set up our error handling and then display a message in the status bar to indicate that we are loading software. Then we declare our local variable:

```
Sub LoadSoftware()
    'Setup error handling
    On Error GoTo LoadSoftware_Err

    'Display status
    StatusBar1.Panels("pnlStatus").Text = "Loading Software"

    'Declare local variables
    Dim lngRC As Long
```

We set a reference to the global `Recordset` object next and also set a reference to the select data class:

```
    'Set a reference to the recordset object
    Set g_objRS = New ADODB.Recordset

    'Set a reference to the select data class
    Set objData = New clsSelectData
```

The `SelectSoftwareAndCategories` function in the select data class will accept two parameters: a `Connection` object and a `Recordset` object. This function will return a `Long` data type as the return code. Then we check the return code and raise an error if the return code is not zero:

```
    'Open the recordset
    lngRC = objData.SelectSoftwareAndCategories(g_objConn, g_objRS)

    'Ensure we were successful
    If lngRC <> 0 Then
        Err.Raise 513 + vbObjectError, "LoadSoftware", _
            "Call to SelectSoftwareAndCategories failed"
    End If
```

We want to clear the combo and list boxes before we load the data. Then we load the `cboSoftware` combo box on the **Software** tab and the `lstInstalledSoftware` list box on the **System Assignment** tab, using the same data for both:

```
    'Clear combo and list boxes
    cboSoftware.Clear
    cboSoftwareCategory.Clear
    lstInstalledSoftware.Clear

    'Load software combo box and software list
    Do While Not g_objRS.EOF
        'Software combo box
        cboSoftware.AddItem g_objRS!Software_Name_VC
        cboSoftware.ItemData(cboSoftware.NewIndex) = g_objRS!Software_ID
        'Software list
```

```
        lstInstalledSoftware.AddItem g_objRS!Software_Name_VC
        lstInstalledSoftware.ItemData(lstInstalledSoftware.NewIndex) = _
            g_objRS!Software_ID
    g_objRS.MoveNext
    Loop
```

After we have reached an end-of-file condition on the recordset, we execute the NextRecordset method to get the next recordset in the Recordset object. Then we loop through the new recordset and load the cboSoftwareCategory combo box:

```
    'Get the next recordset
    Set g_objRS = g_objRS.NextRecordset

    'Load software category combo box
    Do While Not g_objRS.EOF
        cboSoftwareCategory.AddItem g_objRS!Software_Category_VC
        cboSoftwareCategory.ItemData(cboSoftwareCategory.NewIndex) = _
            g_objRS!Software_Category_ID
        g_objRS.MoveNext
    Loop
```

After an end-of-file condition has been reached, we close the Recordset object and remove our references to the Recordset object and the class object:

```
    'Close the recordset
    g_objRS.Close

    'Remove references to objects
    Set g_objRS = Nothing
    Set objData = Nothing
```

Then we display a ready message in the status bar and exit the procedure. The error handling has been covered before:

```
    'Display status
    StatusBar1.Panels("pnlStatus").Text = "Ready"

    'Exit sub
    Exit Sub

LoadSoftware_Err:
    Call ADOError
End Sub
```

Switching to the select data class (clsSelectData) we want to add the code for the SelectSoftwareAndCategories function. This function will open a recordset that contains two recordsets, one that contains the software and one that contains the software categories. This function accepts a Connection object and a Recordset object by reference as input parameters. It returns a Long data type as a return code. The first thing we do in this function is to set up our error handling:

```
Public Function SelectSoftwareAndCategories( _
    ByRef objConn As ADODB.Connection, _
    ByRef objRS As ADODB.Recordset) As Long

    'Setup error handling
    On Error GoTo SelectSoftwareAndCategories_Err
```

Then we open the `Recordset` object using a forward-only cursor and read-only lock, as indicated by the `adOpenForwardOnly` constant for the `CursorType` parameter and the `adLockReadOnly` constant for the `LockType` parameter. We then set the return code for this function and exit the function:

```
    'Open the recordset object
    objRS.Open "up_select_software_and_categories", _
        objConn, adOpenForwardOnly, adLockReadOnly, adCmdStoredProc

    'Set the return code
    SelectSoftwareAndCategories = 0

    'Exit function
    Exit Function
```

The error handling code will call the `ADOError` procedure in this class and the function will return a return code of 1, indicating that it failed:

```
SelectSoftwareAndCategories_Err:
    'Call the error handler and return a return code of 1
    Call ADOError(objConn, "SelectSoftwareAndCategories")
    SelectSoftwareAndCategories = 1
End Function
```

Switching back to the code in our form, we want to modify the code in the `tabData_Click` procedure. Modify this procedure as shown below. This will set the SQL string to the stored procedure to be executed when a user clicks on the **Software** tab:

```
Case 1:  'Hardware
    strSQL = "up_select_hardware"
Case 2:  'Software
    strSQL = "up_select_software"
```

Once a client-side recordset has been opened with the software data, we want to display the first software title in the `cboSoftware` combo box. Add the following code to this procedure also:

```
Case 1:  'Hardware
    If cboManufacturer.ListCount <> -1 Then
        cboManufacturer.ListIndex = 0
    End If
Case 2:  'Software
    If cboSoftware.ListCount <> -1 Then
        cboSoftware.ListIndex = 0
    End If
```

The last piece of code we need to add is in the `cboSoftware_Click` procedure. We check the `ListIndex` property of the combo box and exit the procedure if it is equal to -1. Then we declare our local variables and move to the first record in our disconnected client-side recordset:

```
Private Sub cboSoftware_Click()
    'Check the ListIndex property
    If cboSoftware.ListIndex = -1 Then
        Exit Sub
    End If


    'Declare local variables
    Dim intIndex As Integer


    'Move to the first record
    objRSData.MoveFirst
```

Then we search the recordset using the `Find` method, looking for a match between the `Software_ID` field in the `Recordset` object and the `ItemData` property of the selected entry in the `cboSoftware` combo box.

Once a match has been found, we loop through the `cboSoftwareCategory` combo box to find the corresponding software category:

```
    'Find the correct record in the recordset
    objRSData.Find "Software_ID = " & _
        cboSoftware.ItemData(cboSoftware.ListIndex)

    'Loop through the software category combo box and find the right entry
    For intIndex = 0 To cboSoftwareCategory.ListCount - 1
        If cboSoftwareCategory.ItemData(intIndex) = _
            objRSData!Software_Category_ID Then
            cboSoftwareCategory.ListIndex = intIndex
            Exit For
        End If
    Next
End Sub
```

We have now coded three tabs in our project. Before we move on to the final one, we need to discuss temporary tables.

Temporary Tables

A **temporary table** is just that – temporary. It is created, populated, used, and then discarded. SQL Server supports two types of temporary tables: local temporary tables and global temporary tables.

❑   **Local temporary table** names are prefixed with a single pound sign (#) and are local to the user who has created them. This means that a temporary table is created in the `TempDB` database and only that user has access to that table. Unless specifically destroyed, SQL Server will drop this type of temporary table when the current user ends their session with SQL Server. Or, if the temporary table was created in a stored procedure, it is dropped when the stored procedure ends. It should be noted that temporary table names have a limit of 116 characters.

❑ A **global temporary table** name is prefixed with two pound signs (##) and is available to all users of the database in which it is created. When the last user who is referencing the temporary table ends their session, SQL Server will drop that temporary table. Global temporary tables have no security rights and therefore any user can access the table and modify the data contained in it.

Why do we use temporary tables? Sometimes there are special data needs that cannot be achieved using a single SELECT statement. Sometimes we may need to select data, manipulate it, and then select it again before passing it on to the caller. This is where a temporary table can be used. We will explore more reasons later in this chapter.

All temporary tables are stored in the TempDB database, and there are two ways to create a temporary table, either *implicitly* or *explicitly*. When SQL Server creates the temporary table for you it is created implicitly. Let's look at the following example:

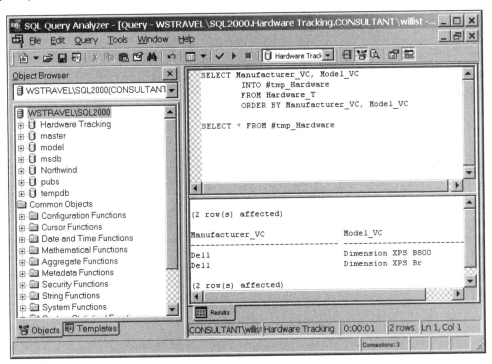

This is a local temporary table that was created implicitly. This is because we used the INTO clause in the SELECT statement, which instructs SQL Server to insert the data from the select list into a new temporary table. Notice that we specified a temporary table name and the name is prefixed with a pound sign. SQL Server will create the temporary table using the column names and data types of the columns in the select list.

After we have inserted data into the temporary table using the SELECT statement, we select all data from the temporary table using another SELECT statement, specifying the temporary table name.

Because we have not specifically instructed SQL Server to destroy the temporary table, it remains in the TempDB database until we terminate our connection.

When we explicitly create a temporary table we use the CREATE TABLE T-SQL statement to specify the attributes of the temporary table. This is just like creating a permanent table, except that the pound sign in the table name indicates to SQL Server that this is a temporary table and it is created in the TempDB database. Then we use an INSERT statement to insert data into the temporary table. Let's look at the following example:

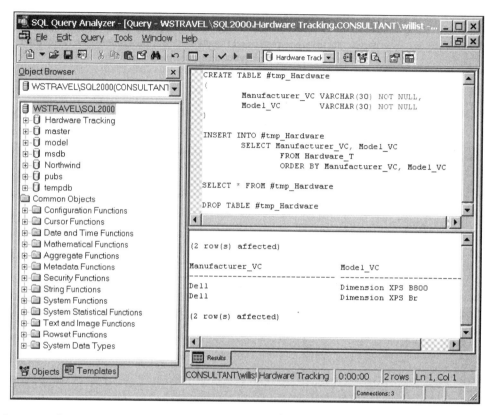

In this example we specify the CREATE TABLE T-SQL statement to create the temporary table. Like other T-SQL statements, the CREATE TABLE T-SQL statement is complex. The basic syntax of this statement is shown:

```
CREATE TABLE table-name (column-name data-type [NULL | NOT NULL] [,...n])
```

❑ The table-name argument specifies a valid table name. For temporary tables the table name must be prefixed with a pound sign.

❑ The column-name argument specifies a valid column name. The ,...n argument specifies additional column names as needed.

❑ The data-type argument specifies a valid SQL Server data type.

❑ The NULL and NOT NULL arguments are optional and specify whether or not null data can be inserted into the column.

So the example above creates a temporary table named **#tmp_Hardware** and adds two columns to that temporary table.

Then we use the INSERT statement to insert data into the temporary table. We have specified the INTO keyword instead of specifying a column list and value list. Because we have specified the same column names in the select list that exist in the temporary table, we do not have to specify a column list or the VALUES keyword.

After we have inserted the data into the temporary table, we select the data from the temporary table using a SELECT statement.

After selecting all data from the temporary table, we explicitly destroy the temporary table by specifying the DROP TABLE T-SQL statement. The DROP TABLE statement is very simple as all we need to specify is the table name to drop.

We have demonstrated two very different methods of creating a temporary table; one created implicitly and one explicitly. Each method has its place and the choice depends on the data that is being inserted and the column names that you want in the temporary table. We will be using a temporary table in a stored procedure very shortly.

Table and Column Aliases

Sometimes we need to select data from a table using two separate sets of criteria and will need to use the same table in the query or stored procedure twice. Because each table and column name in our query or stored procedure must be unique, we use a **table alias**, also known as a **correlation name**. This is where we assign another name to a table so we can use the same table more than once in the same query or stored procedure, and the table can be referenced using unique names.

A table alias can be assigned using one of two methods: with or without the AS keyword. Let's take a look at the following two examples. In both examples the table alias follows the regular table name, as shown in the JOIN clause.

The first example does not use the AS keyword and can be confusing at first glance:

```
SELECT Software_T.Software_Name_VC, Category_T.Software_Category_VC
    FROM Software_T
    JOIN Software_Category_T Category_T ON Software_T.Software_Category_ID =
        Category_T.Software_Category_ID
```

The second example uses the AS keyword which makes the code much more readable:

```
SELECT Software_T.Software_Name_VC, Category_T.Software_Category_VC,
    Category_T.Software_Category_ID
    FROM Software_T
    JOIN Software_Category_T AS Category_T ON Software_T.Software_Category_ID =
        Category_T.Software_Category_ID
```

333

Once you assign a table alias to a table, all references to the columns in that table that are duplicate column names in other tables in the select list must use the table alias, as shown in the SELECT statement of these examples. Notice that we have prefixed the column names in the select list with the table names that these columns belong to. We do not have to prefix non-duplicate column names with the table name; this was done for demonstration purposes.

Sometimes we may need to select data from multiple tables in which the column name is the same in both tables. We could do this and prefix the column names with the table name, as shown in the next example. This prevents us from receiving a message about an ambiguous column name. But look at the results that are returned. The Last_Update_DT column is listed twice, once for the Software_T table and once for the Software_Category_T table. This table has an alias of Category_T, which is evident by the table prefix on the column names:

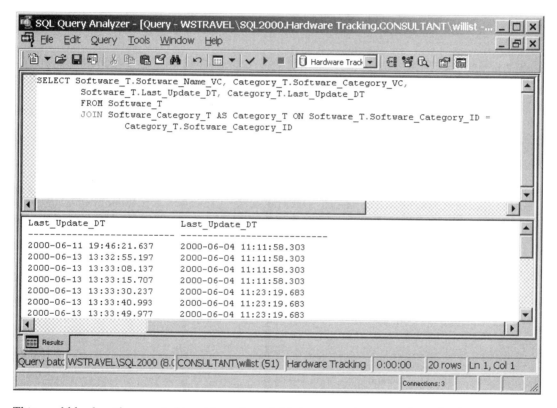

This would be fine if we wanted to address these fields in a recordset using the *ordinal position* of these fields in our VB program. But for clarity and code readability, we address fields in a recordset by *name*. This will cause problems because we have the same field name for two sets of fields in the recordset.

So how do we resolve this issue? We use a **column alias**, which is based on the same principle as a table alias. We assign a new name to the column by specifying the column name followed by the column alias. Again we have the option of specifying the AS keyword. Let's look at the next two examples.

The first example assigns a column alias to the `Last_Update_DT` column in both tables. However, we have not specified the `AS` keyword, which makes the code somewhat difficult to read:

```
SELECT Software_T.Software_Name_VC, Category_T.Software_Category_VC,
    Software_T.Last_Update_DT Software_Last_Update_DT,
    Category_T.Last_Update_DT Category_Last_Update_DT
FROM Software_T
JOIN Software_Category_T Category_T ON Software_T.Software_Category_ID =
    Category_T.Software_Category_ID
```

The second example specifies the `AS` keyword and the code is much easier to read:

```
SELECT Software_T.Software_Name_VC, Category_T.Software_Category_VC,
    Software_T.Last_Update_DT AS Software_Last_Update_DT,
    Category_T.Last_Update_DT AS Category_Last_Update_DT
FROM Software_T
JOIN Software_Category_T AS Category_T ON Software_T.Software_Category_ID =
    Category_T.Software_Category_ID
```

Let's take a look at the results of the execution of this query after we have assigned a column alias to the date columns. The date fields are now uniquely identified – we can process them by name in our recordset and know which field came from which table:

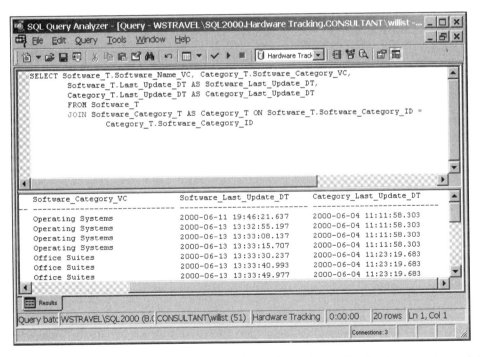

We can also concatenate data in the select list and specify a column alias for the concatenated data. Let's take a look at the following example.

This example combines the data from the `Software_Name_VC` column and the `Software_Category_VC` columns and uses a column alias of `Software`. Notice that we have used the SQL Server concatenation character, which is a plus sign, to concatenate the data. Also notice that we have included static text – a space followed by a dash followed by another space. This static text has been enclosed in single quotes. The results of the execution are shown in the results pane:

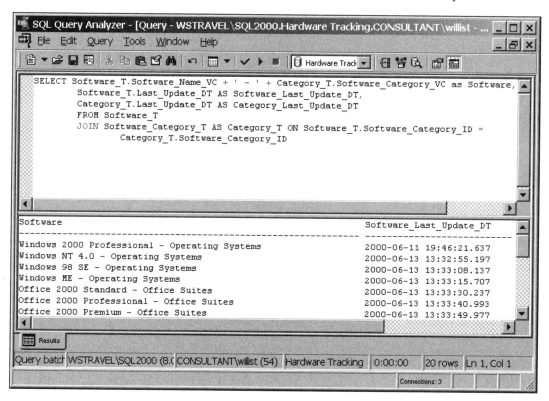

We have seen that, not only can we use a column alias for a column in the select list, but we can also concatenate data and use a column alias to identify the concatenated data.

Armed with all this new information, let's proceed to the next exercise and create a couple of stored procedures that implement table and column aliases and also temporary tables.

Try It Out – Assigned and Unassigned Systems Select Stored Procedures

On the System Assignment tab on our main form we have one combo box left to load, the System combo box. However, associated with the System combo box is the Serial Number field. We need to create a stored procedure that will select all hardware that is assigned and not assigned. This hardware will be listed in the System combo box, but how can we distinguish between systems that have been assigned and not assigned? We will need to prefix the systems that have been assigned with the letters NA for not available. Let's create the stored procedure to select this data and mark the assigned systems as NA.

1. Start the Query Analyzer if it is not already running.

2. Enter the following stored procedure:

```
SET QUOTED_IDENTIFIER ON
GO
SET ANSI_NULLS ON
GO

ALTER  PROCEDURE dbo.up_select_unassigned_and_assigned_hardware AS


--
-- Turn off row count message
--
SET NOCOUNT ON
--
-- Create temporary hardware table
--
CREATE TABLE #Tmp_Hardware
    (
    Hardware_ID        INT      NOT NULL,
    Manufacturer_VC           VARCHAR(60)      NOT NULL,
    Serial_Number_VC VARCHAR(30)     NOT NULL
    )

--
-- Insert all hardware that is not assigned
--
INSERT INTO #Tmp_Hardware
    SELECT DISTINCT Hardware_T.Hardware_ID, Manufacturer_VC + ' ' + Model_VC AS
Manufacturer_VC,
         Serial_Number_VC
         FROM Hardware_T
         JOIN System_Assignment_T ON Hardware_T.Hardware_ID <>
             System_Assignment_T.Hardware_ID
         WHERE Hardware_T.Hardware_ID NOT IN
             (SELECT Hardware_ID FROM System_Assignment_T)
--
-- Insert all hardware that is assigned and mark it as not available (NA)
--
INSERT INTO #Tmp_Hardware
    (Hardware_T.hardware_ID,Manufacturer_VC,Serial_Number_VC)
    SELECT Hardware_T.Hardware_ID,
         'NA - ' + Manufacturer_VC + ' ' + Model_VC AS Manufacturer_VC,
         Serial_Number_VC
         FROM Hardware_T
         JOIN System_Assignment_T ON Hardware_T.Hardware_ID =
             System_Assignment_T.Hardware_ID
--
-- Select all data from temporary hardware table
--
SELECT Hardware_ID, Manufacturer_VC, Serial_Number_VC
    FROM #Tmp_Hardware
    ORDER BY Manufacturer_VC
--
-- Drop temporary hardware table
--
DROP TABLE #Tmp_Hardware

GO
```

337

```
SET QUOTED_IDENTIFIER OFF
GO
SET ANSI_NULLS ON
GO
```

3. Parse the code for errors using the Parse Query icon on the toolbar.

Tip: pay careful attention to the single quote marks and plus signs in the select lists.

---

4. Create the stored procedure by clicking on the Execute Query icon on the toolbar.

5. If the Enterprise Manager is not already running, then start it and expand the Hardware Tracking database.

6. Click on the Stored Procedure group and then right-click on the up_select_unassigned_and_assigned_hardware stored procedure. Choose All Tasks and then Manage Permissions from the context menu. Grant permissions to the hardware users role.

7. Once we have populated the last combo box on the System Assignment tab, we will need to know what system is assigned to an employee. When a user selects an employee from the Employee combo box we want to display the correct system assigned to that employee. This next stored procedure will gather the required system information for a given employee; hence this stored procedure will accept one input parameter, the Employee ID.

To create this stored procedure clear the current query window in the Query Analyzer or open a new query window.

8. Enter the following stored procedure:

```
CREATE PROCEDURE dbo.up_parmsel_assigned_system
    @Employee_ID INT AS

--
-- Select data from the System_Assignment_T table
--
    SELECT System_Assignment_T.Hardware_ID,
--
-- Select data from the System_Software_Relationship_T table
--
    System_Software_Relationship_T.Software_ID
--
-- From
--
    FROM System_Assignment_T
--
-- JOIN the System_Software_Relationship_T table
--
    JOIN System_Software_Relationship_T ON
        System_Assignment_T.System_Assignment_ID =
        System_Software_Relationship_T.System_Assignment_ID
--
```

```
-- Where
--
   WHERE System_Assignment_T.Employee_ID = @Employee_ID
```

9. Parse the code for errors and then create the stored procedure by clicking on the Execute Query icon on the toolbar.

10. Right-click on the up_parmsel_assigned_system stored procedure in the Stored Procedures group in the Enterprise Manager, choose All Tasks, and then choose Manage Permissions from the context menu.

11. Grant permissions to the hardware users role.

How It Works – Unassigned Systems Select Stored Procedure

This stored procedure may look complex but we will explain every line and the code has lots of comments. The first thing we do is to specify the stored procedure name on the first line. Notice that the stored procedure name is quite long but descriptively defines what this stored procedure does.

> **Tip: a stored procedure name can contain up to 128 characters, so use as many as it takes to make the purpose of your stored procedure clear.**

```
CREATE PROCEDURE dbo.up_select_unassigned_and_assigned_hardware AS
```

We want to select all rows from the Hardware_T table that have not been assigned to an employee and place them into a temporary table. Then we want to select all rows from the Hardware_T table that have been assigned to an employee and insert them into the temporary table. However, when we select the rows from the Hardware_T table that have been assigned, we will mark them with the letters NA (Not Assigned). We'll get to that in just a moment.

First we need to create the temporary table. Using the CREATE TABLE T-SQL statement, we create a local temporary table as is evident by the single pound sign in the table name. We have also prefixed the table name with the letters tmp to indicate that it is a temporary table.

Then we specify the column names that will be contained in this temporary table, and for each column we have specified the data types. Notice that the column names and data types defined in the temporary table match those in the Hardware_T table. We have also specified that each column must contain data as we have included the NOT NULL keywords.

Also notice that the column list for the temporary table has been enclosed in parentheses:

```
-- Create temporary hardware table
--
CREATE TABLE #tmp_Hardware
    (
    Hardware_ID      INT        NOT NULL,
    Manufacturer_VC      VARCHAR(60)    NOT NULL,
    Serial_Number_VC     VARCHAR(30)     NOT NULL
    )
```

> **Tip: when building large or complex stored procedures, build and test them in small sections first.**

We now want to insert all rows from the Hardware_T table that have not been assigned to an employee. We start by specifying the INSERT statement, followed by the INTO keyword, and specify the table name that we want to insert data into.

Next, we specify the SELECT statement to select the data to be inserted. We have specified the DISTINCT keyword to eliminate duplicate rows of data. The first column in the select list is the Hardware_ID column. Then we combine the data from the Manufacturer_VC and Model_VC columns. We do this by specifying the SQL Server concatenation character, the plus sign. We concatenate the data from the Manufacturer_VC column followed by a space, which has been specified by a single quote and a space followed by another single quote. Then we concatenate the Model_VC column. We specify that this combined data should have a column alias of Manufacturer_VC, which is the column name in the temporary table. Using a column alias that matches the column name in the temporary table is not necessary but has been done for editing convenience. The last column in the select list is the Serial_Number_VC column.

So what we end up with is three columns: Hardware_ID, Manufacturer_VC, and Serial_Number_VC. The Manufacturer_VC column now contains data from two different columns: Manufacturer_VC and Model_VC.

We then include the FROM clause which is specifying that data should be selected from the Hardware_T table. The JOIN clause joins the System_Assignment_T table and we have specified that this table be joined on the Hardware_ID column from this table and the Hardware_T table. Notice that the JOIN clause is using a logical operand of not equal (<>). This ensures that we only get data that does not exist in the System_Assignment_T table.

The WHERE clause in our SELECT statement eliminates rows of data in the Hardware_T table that have matching rows in the System_Assignment_T table, as specified in the NOT IN statement. The IN statement determines if a given value in the Hardware_T.Hardware_ID column matches a value in a SELECT statement or list. We have chosen to use a nested SELECT statement to return a value list for the IN statement, and to select all the values in the Hardware_ID column in the System_Assignment_T table. This will produce a list of hardware ID values for the IN statement.

```
-- Insert all hardware that is not assigned
--
INSERT INTO #tmp_Hardware
    SELECT DISTINCT Hardware_T.Hardware_ID,
        Manufacturer_VC + ' ' + Model_VC AS Manufacturer_VC,
        Serial_Number_VC
        FROM Hardware_T
        JOIN System_Assignment_T ON Hardware_T.Hardware_ID <>
            System_Assignment_T.Hardware_ID
        WHERE Hardware_T.Hardware_ID NOT IN
            (SELECT Hardware_ID FROM System_Assignment_T)
```

This next INSERT statement inserts all assigned systems into the temporary table. Again we have specified the INSERT statement, followed by the INTO keyword, and the temporary table name. Then we specify the column list that we want to insert data into. This was not done for the last INSERT statement but is done here to demonstrate that you can specify a column list. Specifying a column list serves two purposes. First, it ensures that even if the columns in the table have been rearranged, the

INSERT statement will still work. Second, it provides self documentation as you know exactly what columns the values are being inserted into.

The first column in the select list of the SELECT statement is the Hardware_ID column. The next column starts with the letters NA followed by a dash. This has all been enclosed in single quotes, as it is static text. Then we concatenate this prefix with the data from the Manufacturer_VC column, a space, and then the Model_VC column. We then specify that all of this data should have a column alias of Manufacturer_VC.

We specify the FROM keyword next and specify that we are selecting data from the Hardware_T table.

We JOIN the System_Assignment_T using the Hardware_ID column. This time our logical operand specifies that the System_Assignment_T table be joined where the Hardware_ID column in the Hardware_T table equals the Hardware_ID in the System_Assignment_T table:

```
-- Insert all hardware that is assigned and mark it as not available (NA)
--
INSERT INTO #tmp_Hardware
    (Hardware_T.Hardware_ID, Manufacturer_VC, Serial_Number_VC)
    SELECT Hardware_T.Hardware_ID,
        'NA - ' + Manufacturer_VC + ' ' + Model_VC AS Manufacturer_VC,
        Serial_Number_VC
        FROM Hardware_T
        JOIN System_Assignment_T ON Hardware_T.Hardware_ID =
            System_Assignment_T.Hardware_ID
```

All data has now been inserted into the temporary table. The temporary table contains systems that have not been assigned and systems that have been assigned. Both types of systems have the Manufacturer_VC and Model_VC data combined to form one column named Manufacturer_VC. Also the assigned systems are prefixed with the letters NA.

We want to select all data from the temporary table to return to the caller. We have specified another SELECT statement specifying the columns that we want selected in the select list. The FROM keyword specifies the temporary table name, and we sort the results using the ORDER BY clause:

```
-- Select all data from temporary hardware table
--
SELECT Hardware_ID, Manufacturer_VC, Serial_Number_VC
    FROM #tmp_Hardware
    ORDER BY Manufacturer_VC
```

After we have selected all of the data from the temporary table we drop the temporary table, thereby freeing up resources in the database. Although the table will eventually get dropped automatically, it is good coding practice to do it explicitly:

```
-- Drop temporary hardware table
--
DROP TABLE #tmp_Hardware
```

How It Works – Assigned Systems Select Stored Procedure

This next stored procedure is a little simpler and a lot smaller. Again we have included lots of comments. This stored procedure accepts an input parameter and the name of the stored procedure reflects this, according to the standards presented in Chapter 3.

The one and only parameter to this stored procedure is the employee ID, which is a SQL Server Integer data type:

```
CREATE PROCEDURE dbo.up_parmsel_assigned_system
    @Employee_ID INT AS
```

We are only selecting two columns in the select list. The first column, Hardware_ID, is being selected from the System_Assignment_T table. The table name has been prefixed to the column name for easier reading:

```
-- Select data from the System_Assignment_T table
--
SELECT System_Assignment_T.Hardware_ID,
```

The next column that we are selecting data from is the Software_ID column in the System_Software_Relationship_T table. Again we have prefixed the column name with the table name to make it easier to read:

```
--    Select data from the System_Software_Relationship_T table
--
    System_Software_Relationship_T.Software_ID
```

We specify the main table that we are selecting data from in the FROM clause:

```
--    From
--
    FROM System_Assignment_T
```

Then we join the System_Software_Relationship_T table using the System_Assignment_ID column in both the System_Software_Relationship_T and System_Assignment_T tables:

```
--    JOIN the System_Software_Relationship_T table
--
    JOIN System_Software_Relationship_T ON
        System_Assignment_T.System_Assignment_ID =
        System_Software_Relationship_T.System_Assignment_ID
```

The WHERE clause limits the selection of data to the exact employee whose employee ID was passed as the input parameter:

```
--    Where
--
    WHERE System_Assignment_T.Employee_ID = @Employee_ID
```

It should be noted that this stored procedure will return multiple rows of data. This is because we are selecting all of the rows of `Software_ID` in the `System_Software_Relationship_T` table. Remember that this is a relationship table that contains the `Software_ID` of all software that has been installed on a single system.

Try It Out – VB Code for System Assignment Tab

We want to switch to our VB code now and implement the functionality for the **System Assignment** tab. When we display a system that has or has not been assigned, we also want to display the serial number for that system. We don't want to make another trip to the database just to get the serial number for a system that has been selected in the **System** combo box, so we will keep the serial numbers for all systems in an array.

1. To that end, add the following variable declaration in the general declarations section of the main form (`frmMain`):

```
'Declare objects
Dim objData As clsSelectData
Dim objRSData As ADODB.Recordset

'Declare variables
Dim arrSerialNumber() As String
```

2. In the `Form_Load` procedure we want to add a call to the procedure to load the rest of the combo boxes on the **System Assignment** tab. Modify the `Form_Load` procedure as shown in the code fragment below:

```
'Load Software
Call LoadSoftware

'Load Systems
Call LoadSystems
```

3. The rest of the code to be added to the project is presented in the *How It Works* section.

4. At this point you will want to save your project and you will be ready to test the final functionality that we will add in this chapter. Run your program and then select the **System Assignment** tab. The one and only employee will be selected, which will cause the appropriate system to be displayed in the **System** combo box, along with the serial number assigned to that system. Also all of the software that was installed on that system will be checked in the **Installed Software** list.

You can also test displaying the correct serial number by clicking on an entry in the **System** combo box. When you click on a new entry in this combo box, the appropriate serial number for that system is displayed. It should be noted that since we don't want the serial numbers to be changed, we set this text field up to be disabled.

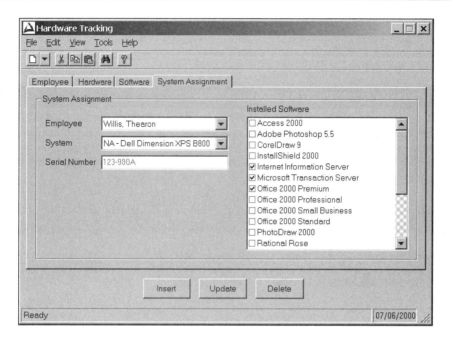

How It Works – VB Code for System Assignment Tab

Let's look at the `LoadSystems` procedure first. This procedure is created in the main form, and will retrieve the data to load into the **System** combo box and the serial number array that we just defined.

The first thing that we want to do in this procedure is to set up our error handling. Then we display a message in the status bar to indicate that we are loading system data:

```
Sub LoadSystems()
    'Setup error handling
    On Error GoTo LoadSystems_Err

    'Display status
    StatusBar1.Panels("pnlStatus").Text = "Loading Systems"
```

Next we declare our local variables and set a reference to the global `Recordset` object. We also need to set a reference to the select data class:

```
    'Declare local variables
    Dim lngRC As Long

    'Set a reference to the recordset object
    Set g_objRS = New ADODB.Recordset

    'Set a reference to the select data class
    Set objData = New clsSelectData
```

We execute the `SelectSystems` function in the select data class, passing it the global `Connection` object and the global `Recordset` object. This function returns a `Long` data type as a return value:

```
'Open the recordset
lngRC = objData.SelectSystems(g_objConn, g_objRS)
```

We check the return code from the `SelectSystems` function and if it is not equal to zero we raise an error. Then we clear the `cboSystem` combo box and re-dimension the serial number array to zero to clear any existing entries:

```
'Ensure we were successful
If lngRC <> 0 Then
    Err.Raise 513 + vbObjectError, "LoadSystems", _
        "Call to SelectSystems failed"
End If

'Clear combo boxes
cboSystem.Clear
ReDim arrSerialNumber(0)
```

We loop through the recordset, loading the **System** combo box and the serial number array. Notice that when we re-dimension the array we are using the `NewIndex` property of the `cboSystem` combo box as the number of elements to re-dimension the array with. Also we use the `Preserve` keyword to preserve the existing data in the array. This will keep the entries in the array in sync with the `cboSystem` combo box:

```
'Load system combo box
Do While Not g_objRS.EOF
    cboSystem.AddItem g_objRS!Manufacturer_VC
    cboSystem.ItemData(cboSystem.NewIndex) = g_objRS!Hardware_ID
    'Re-dimension the array and add new serial number
    ReDim Preserve arrSerialNumber(cboSystem.NewIndex)
    arrSerialNumber(cboSystem.NewIndex) = g_objRS!Serial_Number_VC
    g_objRS.MoveNext
Loop
```

After we have reached an end-of-file condition on the recordset, we close it and then remove our references from our objects to free up resources:

```
'Close the recordset
g_objRS.Close

'Remove references to objects
Set g_objRS = Nothing
Set objData = Nothing
```

We display a ready message in the status bar and then exit the procedure. The error handling is the same error handling that we have used before:

```
    'Display status
    StatusBar1.Panels("pnlStatus").Text = "Ready"

    'Exit sub
    Exit Sub

LoadSystems_Err:
    Call ADOError
End Sub
```

Switching to the code in the select data class (clsSelectData), we need to create the SelectSystems function. This function accepts two parameters, a Connection object and a Recordset object. It returns a Long data type as a return code.

The first thing we want to do in this function is to set up our error handling. Then we open the recordset, executing the up_select_unassigned_and_assigned_hardware stored procedure. Remember that this procedure will return all unassigned systems and all assigned systems. Since we only want to read the data to load a combo box, we have specified the adOpenForwardOnly constant for the CursorType parameter of the Recordset object and the adLockReadOnly constant for the LockType parameter:

```
Public Function SelectSystems( _
    ByRef objConn As ADODB.Connection, _
    ByRef objRS As ADODB.Recordset) As Long

    'Setup error handling
    On Error GoTo SelectSystems_Err

    'Open the recordset object
    objRS.Open "up_select_unassigned_and_assigned_hardware", _
        objConn, adOpenForwardOnly, adLockReadOnly, adCmdStoredProc
```

We set the return code for the function to zero and then exit the function:

```
    'Set the return code
    SelectSystems = 0

    'Exit function
    Exit Function
```

The error handling code is the same code that we have used in the other functions created in this class:

```
SelectSystems_Err:
    'Call the error handler and return a return code of 1
    Call ADOError(objConn, "SelectSystems")
    SelectSystems = 1
End Function
```

Switching back to the code in the main form we want to add one piece of code to the `tabData_Click` procedure. When the user clicks on the **System Assignment** tab we want to display the assigned system for the first employee in the **Employee** combo box, if any data exists in that combo box.

Modify the `tabData_Click` procedure as shown in the following code fragment:

```
        Case 3:  'System Assignment
            If cboEmployee.ListCount <> -1 Then
                'The Style property is set to 2 - Dropdown List and
                'will not fire the click event if the ListIndex property
                'is already set to the same number we are using here.
                'To circumvent this problem, we first set the ListIndex
                'property to -1 and then to 0 to ensure the click event
                'gets fired
                cboEmployee.ListIndex = -1
                cboEmployee.ListIndex = 0
            End If
    End Select

    'Remove references to objects
    Set objData = Nothing
```

We are not going to open a recordset in this procedure as we have done with the other tabs of the tab control. This could potentially be too much data to bring back in a recordset, as we would have to bring back each software title installed for each employee who had an assigned system. Instead, when a user selects an employee, we will execute a function in the select data class to get only the information that is pertinent to the selected employee.

To that end we want to modify the `cboEmployee_Click` procedure. This is the procedure that is fired when a user selects an employee in the **Employee** combo box.

The first thing that is done in this procedure is to check the `ListIndex` property of the combo box. If it is −1 then we exit the procedure. Then we set up our error handling and declare our local variables. We set a reference to the global `Recordset` object and also set a reference to the select data class:

```
    Private Sub cboEmployee_Click()
        'Check the ListIndex property
        If cboEmployee.ListIndex = -1 Then
            Exit Sub
        End If

        'Setup error handling
        On Error GoTo cboEmployee_Err

        'Declare local variables
        Dim lngRC As Long, intIndex As Integer

        'Set a reference to the recordset object
        Set g_objRS = New ADODB.Recordset

        'Set a reference to the select data class
        Set objData = New clsSelectData
```

Then we execute the `SelectAssignedSystem` function in the select data class; we'll cover this function next. This function accepts a `Connection` object, `Recordset` object, and the employee ID as input parameters. This function will also return a `Long` data type as a return code.

Notice that we are using the `ItemData` property of the `cboEmployee` combo box to retrieve the employee ID of the selected employee.

After the function has been executed, we check the return code and raise an error if the return code was not zero:

```
'Open the recordset
lngRC = objData.SelectAssignedSystem(g_objConn, g_objRS, _
    cboEmployee.ItemData(cboEmployee.ListIndex))

'Ensure we were successful
If lngRC <> 0 Then
    Err.Raise 513 + vbObjectError, "cboEmployee_Click", _
        "Call to SelectAssignedSystem failed"
End If
```

It is possible that the employee selected has not had a system assigned to them so we check for an end-of-file condition on the recordset. If the recordset is not at the end of the file then we loop through the entries in the `cboSystem` combo box, looking for the entry that matches the `Hardware_ID` in the recordset.

Once a match has been found we use the `intIndex` variable to set the `ListIndex` property of the `cboSystem` combo box to display the correct entry. As a result of setting the `ListIndex` property of the `cboSystem` combo box, the click event is fired for this combo box and the serial number will be set in that procedure. Then we exit the `For` loop:

```
'Select the assigned system and display serial number
If Not g_objRS.EOF Then
    For intIndex = 0 To cboSystem.ListCount - 1
        If cboSystem.ItemData(intIndex) = g_objRS!Hardware_ID Then
            'Set the index for the assigned system
            cboSystem.ListIndex = intIndex
            Exit For
        End If
    Next
End If
```

Regardless of whether or not this employee has a system assigned, we want to clear all the checkboxes for the software. To do this we loop through the **Installed Software** list and set the `Selected` property to `False`, which will uncheck the checkbox:

```
'Uncheck all software
For intIndex = 0 To lstInstalledSoftware.ListCount - 1
    lstInstalledSoftware.Selected(intIndex) = False
Next
```

If we do not have an end-of-file condition on the recordset, we loop through the recordset to process all software. Each time we process the loop for the recordset we also want to loop through the Installed Software list, searching for any instances where Software_ID in the ItemData property matches the Software_ID in the recordset. When a match has been found, we check that item and exit the For loop. Then we process the next record in the Recordset object and start all over again:

```
'Check all installed software
Do While Not g_objRS.EOF
    For intIndex = 0 To lstInstalledSoftware.ListCount - 1
        If lstInstalledSoftware.ItemData(intIndex) = g_objRS!Software_ID Then
            'Check the checkbox for the software title
            lstInstalledSoftware.Selected(intIndex) = True
            Exit For
        End If
    Next
    'Get next software title
    g_objRS.MoveNext
Loop
```

After we have checked an item in the Installed Software list it will become highlighted. This is not the look we want so we remove all highlighting by setting the ListIndex property to –1. This will leave as checked all items that have been checked, but will remove the highlighting from the row:

```
'Remove highlights from selected items
lstInstalledSoftware.ListIndex = -1
```

We close the recordset and then remove references to the objects that we have used in this procedure. Then we exit the procedure:

```
'Close the recordset
g_objRS.Close

'Remove references to objects
Set g_objRS = Nothing
Set objData = Nothing

'Exit sub
Exit Sub
```

The error handling is the same error handling we have used in previous procedures in this form:

```
cboEmployee_Err:
    Call ADOError
End Sub
```

We want to switch back to the select data class to create the SelectAssignedSystem function. This accepts a Connection object and a Recordset object by reference and an employee ID by value. Notice that the lngEmployee parameter is defined as a Long data type. However, the employee ID parameter in the up_parmsel_assigned_system stored procedure is defined as an Integer data type. This is because a Long data type in VB is equivalent to an Integer data type in SQL Server.

```
Public Function SelectAssignedSystem( _
    ByRef objConn As ADODB.Connection, _
    ByRef objRS As ADODB.Recordset, _
    ByVal lngEmployee As Long) As Long
```

As always we set up our error handling first in this function. Then we open the recordset, executing the up_parmsel_assigned_system stored procedure. Notice that as part of the Source parameter of the Open method we have specified the lngEmployee variable as the input parameter to this stored procedure. Also notice that we have enclosed the input parameter in parentheses.

Since we just want to read this recordset, and read it in a forward-only direction, we have specified the adOpenForwardOnly constant for the CursorType parameter and the adLockReadOnly constant for the LockType parameter:

```
'Setup error handling
On Error GoTo SelectAssignedSystem_Err

'Open the recordset object
objRS.Open "up_parmsel_assigned_system (" & lngEmployee & ")", _
    objConn, adOpenForwardOnly, adLockReadOnly, adCmdStoredProc
```

After the recordset has been opened we set the return code for this function and then exit:

```
'Set the return code
SelectAssignedSystem = 0

'Exit function
Exit Function
```

The error handling code for this function is the same as for the other functions in this class:

```
SelectAssignedSystem_Err:
    'Call the error handler and return a return code of 1
    Call ADOError(objConn, "SelectAssignedSystem")
    SelectAssignedSystem = 1
End Function
```

Switching back to the main form, we need to code one more procedure. If a user clicks on the **System** combo box in the **System Assignment** tab we want to display the serial number associated with that system. To that end we need to add some code to the cboSystem_Click procedure, as shown below. The first thing we want to do here is to ensure that the ListIndex property is not equal to −1. If it is then we exit the procedure.

Using the `ListIndex` property of the `cboSystem` combo box, we get the corresponding serial number from the `arrSerialNumber` array and display it in the `txtSystemSerialNumber` text box:

```
Private Sub cboSystem_Click()
    'Check the ListIndex property
    If cboSystem.ListIndex = -1 Then
     'Clear the serial number
     txtSystemSerialNumber.Text = Empty
        Exit Sub
    End If

    'Display the serial number from the array
    txtSystemSerialNumber.Text = arrSerialNumber(cboSystem.ListIndex)
End Sub
```

That completes the code for this part of the project.

Summary

We have introduced quite a few new T-SQL statements, functions, and clauses in this chapter. In particular we have introduced joins, which allow us to join data from multiple tables and to select this data. While there are many different types of join, we used the INNER JOIN (also known as JOIN) the most. This allowed us to join a table based solely on the logical operand, which only retrieved data from the joined table that matched with data in the table to which we were joining it. We also used the LEFT OUTER JOIN to join two tables and return null values for rows that did not match the table to which we were joining.

During our discussion of temporary tables, we saw how to implicitly and explicitly create temporary tables. We also had the opportunity to create a temporary table in our stored procedure first hand. This allowed us to expand our knowledge of temporary tables and the different methods used to populate them.

We can use column and table aliases to uniquely identify columns and tables in our stored procedures. This provides us the opportunity to join the same table in a query or stored procedure twice. While we did not use this technique, we did use column aliases to uniquely identify a column of data that consisted of static text and data from multiple columns. You should realize what a powerful feature this is and know that it can provide many benefits as you write more complex stored procedures.

To summarize, you should know how to:

- ❑ Create, populate, and drop temporary tables
- ❑ Use the various joins in SQL Server
- ❑ Use column aliases
- ❑ Use table aliases

Now that the framework has been built for our VB front-end and we have added code to select and display data, it's time to move forward and write stored procedures and code to insert new data into the database. In the next chapter we will cover INSERT stored procedures and introduce new topics such as logic and error handling in stored procedures.

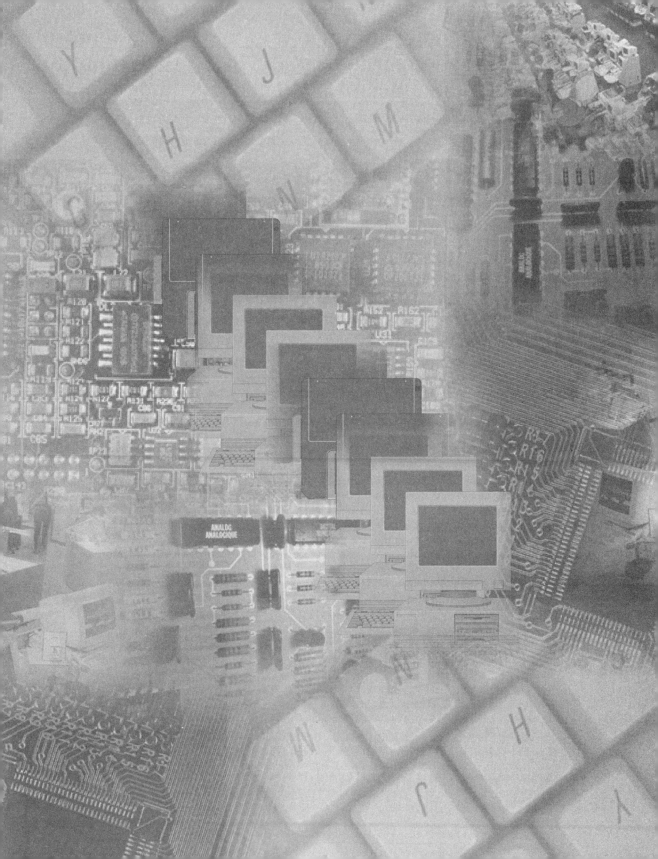

Inserting Data

In the last chapter we saw our stored procedures become more complex as we introduced terms such as joins, temporary tables, and column and table aliases. We learned that we could do a whole lot more with stored procedures than merely selecting data from a single table.

This chapter expands your knowledge of stored procedures as we introduce new terms and concepts such as using local variables, performing conditional processing, and handling errors. While the stored procedures in this chapter are not as complex as those we encountered in the last chapter, they are equally important as they implement new features.

This chapter will also allow you to take advantage of some of the features that you learned about in previous chapters, such as using return values and output parameters.

As we progress through this chapter we will be expanding the functionality of our Hardware Tracking application by implementing the stored procedures we create here. When we have finished the chapter, your VB application will be able to insert data as well as select and display it.

This chapter will cover the following stored procedure topics:

- ❑ Local variables
- ❑ Conditional processing logic
- ❑ Error handling and raising errors

Local Variables

Let's begin our discussion with local variables. A **local variable** in a stored procedure is just like a local variable in VB. We must declare the variable before we use it, and we must also specify the data type of the variable.

So why would we use local variables in stored procedures? Well, for the same reasons we use them in VB, in other words to store, manipulate, and pass data, and as counters in loops. We can do all of these things with local variables in stored procedures, as we shall see in this and coming chapters.

Local variables are just that – *local*. They belong to the stored procedure in which they are created and cannot be referenced outside of that procedure. The variable goes out of scope when the stored procedure ends.

In SQL Server there is a restriction on variable names. All variable names must begin with a single "at" sign (@). After that, the variable name must follow the rules for identifiers and can contain a total of 128 characters. When we say characters, we mean that the name can contain letters, numbers, the "at" sign (@), the pound sign (#), the dollar sign ($), and the underscore (_) character. The variable name cannot contain any dashes (-) or spaces.

Let's look at some local variables in the following code fragments. In each of these examples we have used the DECLARE T-SQL statement, followed by the variable name, and then the data type:

```
DECLARE @Hardware_ID INT      -- This is valid

DECLARE #Hardware_ID INT      -- This is NOT valid, the name begins with #

DECLARE @Hardware-ID INT      -- This is NOT valid, the name contains a dash
```

Once you have declared your variables, you can assign values to them, using either the SELECT statement or the SET statement.

The SELECT statement is usually used to assign values to your variables from data in a column. For example, suppose we want to assign the value contained in the Hardware_ID column of the Hardware_T table to the @Hardware_ID variable, where the Memory_VC column contained a value of 256 MB. We could use the following query to do this:

```
DECLARE @Hardware_ID INT

SELECT @Hardware_ID = Hardware_ID
    FROM Hardware_T
    WHERE Memory_VC = '256 MB'

PRINT @Hardware_ID
```

You should be aware that if the Hardware_T table contains more than one row that meets the condition set in the WHERE clause, the value assigned to the @Hardware_ID variable will be the *last* row of data that meets the condition. This may not produce the results you want, so you must be aware of this.

When you declare a local variable and assign a value to it, the local variable should be of the same data type as the value that you are assigning to it. Using the example above, we could not assign a string value to the @Hardware_ID local variable. Along the same lines, if you declare a local variable as a VarChar(10) data type and you assign it a value that is a VarChar(20) data type, the value will be assigned to the local variable, but SQL Server will truncate the last 10 characters.

There is a T-SQL statement in the previous example that we have not come across before; the PRINT statement accepts a character, string expression, or local variable as a parameter, and then returns the data to the client. In our case it displays the value in the @Hardware_ID variable when running these statements in the Query Analyzer. This is a common way for most developers to write and debug stored procedures. They use the PRINT statement to print out the values in their variables.

Normally, when we use the SELECT statement to assign a value to a local variable, we want to see if a specific row of data exists, and select the primary key value in a variable. Then we test the variable to see if it contains a valid number, indicating that the row of data was found.

Let's look at the previous example again, which demonstrates setting the local variable using a SELECT statement:

```
DECLARE @Hardware_ID INT

SELECT @Hardware_ID = Hardware_ID
    FROM Hardware_T
    WHERE Memory_VC = '256 MB'
PRINT @Hardware_ID
```

In this example, we are looking for a specific row of data, and assigning the data in the Hardware_ID column, if it exists, to the @Hardware_ID variable. Then we use the PRINT statement to print the value contained in the variable.

The most common way to assign a value to a variable is to use the SET statement. This assigns a value to a variable, and can be used in many forms. The basic format of the SET statement is shown here:

```
SET @variable = expression
```

In this syntax, @variable represents the local variable that you have defined, and expression can be anything from simple static text to a complex SELECT statement.

Using the previous example, we could use the SET statement instead of the SELECT statement to assign the value, as shown in the next example. Here, we use the SET statement and a SELECT statement. Notice that our SELECT statement has been enclosed in parentheses. This is because the entire SELECT statement is considered an expression, and must return a value. Therefore, it is enclosed in parentheses so this expression gets evaluated first, and then the value is returned from the SELECT statement.

```
DECLARE @Hardware_ID INT

SET @Hardware_ID = (SELECT Hardware_ID
    FROM Hardware_T
    WHERE Memory_VC = '256 MB')

PRINT @Hardware_ID
```

You should be aware that using a SELECT statement in this manner should only return a single value. If the SELECT statement finds more than one row of matching data, you will receive an error message stating that the subquery returned more than one value and that this is not permitted in a subquery.

Let's look at a simpler example, where we know the number that we want to assign to the local variable:

```
DECLARE @Hardware_ID INT

SET @Hardware_ID = 2
```

The examples that we have been dealing with have all used the `Integer` data type. We can use other data types for our local variables, with a few exceptions. We cannot use the `Text`, `nText`, and `Image` data types.

Conditional Processing Logic

In VB, we use `IF...ELSE` statements to test for certain conditions and then process, or branch to and process, another part of the code. SQL Server also provides `IF...ELSE` statements to test for conditions and then process or branch to another part of the code. The difference between SQL Server's `IF...ELSE` statements and VB's `IF...ELSE` statements is that SQL Server does not have an `END IF` statement. Instead we use the control-of-flow keywords, `BEGIN` and `END`. These keywords encapsulate a block of code in both the `IF` and the `ELSE` sections of code.

Let's take a quick look at an example that expands on our previous examples:

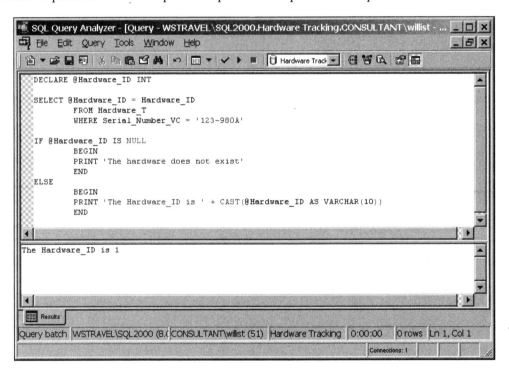

In this example we are testing the `@Hardware_ID` variable to see if it contains a null value, which means that it did not find a row of data in the `Hardware_T` table. Briefly, when we declare a `Long` variable in VB the default value is 0. In SQL Server when we declare an `Integer` variable the default value is null, so we are able to test for a null value in the `IF` statement.

After the `IF` statement, we begin a block of code, as designated by the `BEGIN` control-of-flow keyword. We then have one or more lines of code followed by the `END` keyword. Then we have the `ELSE` keyword to perform some other type of processing if the condition in the `IF` statement is not true.

The previous example uses the PRINT statement to print the results of our test, as is shown in the results pane. We have also introduced another new function, CAST. This function will convert an expression from one data type to another. In the example we are casting an Integer data type to a VarChar data type.

The IF...ELSE statements do not require the control-of-flow keywords BEGIN and END if you are only executing one SQL statement. They are only required if you are executing more than one SQL statement. Always coding the BEGIN and END keywords simply makes the code easier to read, as you know at a glance exactly what code is being executed as part of the IF...ELSE statement.

It should be noted that the ELSE statement is optional, just like it is in VB. If we do not have any code that we want executed in an ELSE condition, then we do not include it.

Let's take a look at a modified version of the previous example. This time we will not include the ELSE statement or the BEGIN and END keywords:

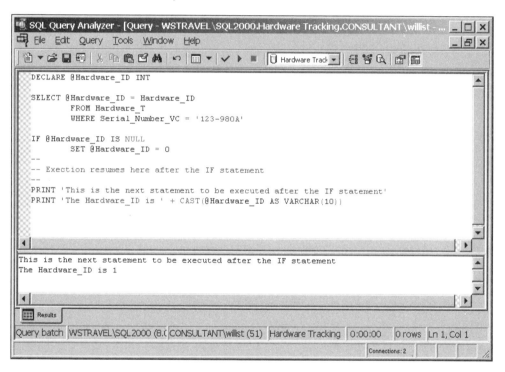

In this example, we check to see if the @Hardware_ID variable contains a null value; if it does then we set the variable to 0. The next line of code to execute after the IF condition has been marked with comments.

IF statements in SQL Server can be nested just as they are in VB. In these cases you need to include the BEGIN and END control-of-flow keywords. As a side note, there are no restrictions to the number of nested IF statements that can be included in your code.

It's time to put this newly found knowledge to practical use, as we begin to add more functionality to our Hardware Tracking application. Our Hardware Tracking application allows us to not only select data, but to insert data as well. We will be following the same format as we did in the last chapter, by adding the code for the stored procedures and VB code for each tab in the tab control on our main form.

We want to start with the **Employee** tab. This contains information about an employee and their location. We have two tables that we need to insert data into, the `Employee_T` table and the `Location_T` table. We can accomplish this with one stored procedure by using local variables and conditional processing logic to execute multiple SQL statements.

Try It Out – Employee Insert Stored Procedure

The stored procedure that we want to create will take the location name and check to see if it exists in the `Location_T` table. If it does, then it will assign the value in the `Location_ID` column to a local variable to be used when we insert the employee. If not, the stored procedure will insert the new location, and then save the identity value that was inserted into a local variable and pass it on to be used when we insert the new employee.

1. Start the Query Analyzer and log in.

2. Enter the following stored procedure:

```
CREATE PROCEDURE dbo.up_parmins_employee
    @First_Name_VC          VARCHAR(15),
    @Last_Name_VC           VARCHAR(15),
    @Phone_Number_VC   VARCHAR(20),
    @Location_VC            VARCHAR(30) AS

-- ********************************************************************
-- Declare variables
-- ********************************************************************
DECLARE @Location_ID        INT

-- ********************************************************************
-- See if the location name already exists by selecting the Location_ID
-- ********************************************************************
SELECT @Location_ID = Location_ID
    FROM Location_T
    WHERE Location_Name_VC = @Location_VC

IF @Location_ID IS NULL

    --
    -- This location does not exist so insert it
    --
    BEGIN
    INSERT INTO Location_T
        (Location_Name_VC, Last_Update_DT)
        VALUES(@Location_VC, GETDATE())

    --
    -- Save the IDENTITY value
    --
    SET @Location_ID = @@IDENTITY
    END

-- ********************************************************************
-- Insert the employee
-- ********************************************************************
```

```
INSERT INTO Employee_T
    (Location_ID, First_Name_VC, Last_Name_VC, Phone_Number_VC,
        Last_Update_DT)
    VALUES(@Location_ID, @First_Name_VC, @Last_Name_VC, @Phone_Number_VC,
        GETDATE())
--
-- Return to the caller
--
RETURN 0
```

3. Parse the code for errors by clicking on the **Parse Query** icon on the toolbar.

4. Create this stored procedure by clicking on the **Execute Query** icon on the toolbar.

5. Start the Enterprise Manager and expand the **Hardware Tracking** database, and then click on the **Stored Procedures** group.

6. Right-click on the **up_parmins_employee** stored procedure, choose **All Tasks**, and then choose **Manage Permissions** from the context menu.

7. Grant **EXEC** permissions to the **Hardware Users** role.

How It Works – Employee Insert Stored Procedure

All of the stored procedures that we create in this and the next two chapters will be parameterized stored procedures, meaning that they will accept parameters.

The first line of this stored procedure specifies the CREATE PROCEDURE statement followed by the stored procedure name, which is in accordance with the naming standards that were presented in Chapter 3.

The next four lines of this stored procedure specify the input parameters and their data types for this stored procedure. Notice that a comma separates each parameter:

```
CREATE PROCEDURE dbo.up_parmins_employee
    @First_Name_VC          VARCHAR(15),
    @Last_Name_VC           VARCHAR(15),
    @Phone_Number_VC        VARCHAR(20),
    @Location_VC            VARCHAR(30) AS
```

The first thing we want to do in our stored procedure is to declare the local variables that we will need. Here we are declaring a local variable that will hold the Location_ID from the Location_T table. We have specified the local variable along with the data type that this variable will represent.

Notice that we have used plenty of comments in this stored procedure, and that each major section of code has asterisks (***) on the comment line preceding the section to identify the section:

```
-- ************************************************************************
-- Declare variables
-- ************************************************************************
DECLARE @Location_ID          INT
```

Before we can insert an employee, we must determine if the location name passed in the `@Location_VC` input parameter already exists. We start this test by selecting the `Location_ID` from the `Location_T` table into the `@Location_ID` variable, using a `SELECT` statement. Notice that we have specified the `WHERE` clause to limit the number of rows returned to the specific location that we are looking for:

```
--  *************************************************************************
-- See if the location name already exists by selecting the Location_ID
--  *************************************************************************
SELECT @Location_ID = Location_ID
     FROM Location_T
     WHERE Location_Name_VC = @Location_VC
```

We check the `@Location_ID` variable to see if it contains a null value. If it does, then the location did not exist, and therefore we want to insert it. Since we are executing more than one SQL statement, we must use the `BEGIN` and `END` keywords to signify a block of code that belongs to the `IF` statement. Also notice that there is no `ELSE` statement included here.

We execute an `INSERT` statement to insert the new location, using the `@Location_VC` input parameter that contains the new location to be inserted in the values list of the `INSERT` statement:

```
IF @Location_ID IS NULL
     --
     -- This location does not exist so insert it
     --
     BEGIN
     INSERT INTO Location_T
          (Location_Name_VC, Last_Update_DT)
          VALUES(@Location_VC, GETDATE())
     --
     -- Save the IDENTITY value
     --
     SET @Location_ID = @@IDENTITY
     END
```

After we have inserted the new location, we want to get the identity value that was inserted into the primary key column. We use the `@@IDENTITY` function to do this, and set the `@Location_ID` variable to the value returned by the `@@IDENTITY` function, using the `SET` statement.

At this point, the `@Location_ID` variable either contains the value from the `Location_ID` column that was set using the `SELECT` statement mentioned previously, or contains the identity value that was inserted and set using the `SET` statement above. Either way, this variable now contains the primary key of the location that the caller has specified.

We now want to insert the new employee, and we'll use an `INSERT` statement to do this. We have specified the column list for the columns that we want to insert data into, and the values list containing the values to be inserted. We have used the local variable `@Location_ID` in the values list in this `INSERT` statement:

```
--  *************************************************************************
-- Insert the employee
--  *************************************************************************
INSERT INTO Employee_T
     (Location_ID, First_Name_VC, Last_Name_VC, Phone_Number_VC,
          Last_Update_DT)
     VALUES(@Location_ID, @First_Name_VC, @Last_Name_VC, @Phone_Number_VC,
          GETDATE())
```

After we have inserted the new employee, we return to the caller, passing back a return value of 0:

```
-- Return to the caller
--
RETURN 0
```

Try It Out – Process the Employee Insert Stored Procedure

At this point, we want to start adding VB code to our Hardware Tracking application. Using the same project from the last chapter as the basis for our work, we want to start implementing new functionality to insert data. This exercise will create a function to execute the stored procedure just created and add code to the Insert button on the main form. This code will insert the employee information that has been entered on the Employee tab on the form.

1. Open the `HardwareTracking.vbp` project from the last chapter so we can make the necessary additions.

2. We want to add a new class module to the project, so click on the Project menu and choose the Add Class Module menu item. Set the Name property of the class to clsInsertData. The code to be added to the project is presented in the *How It Works* section.

3. After entering all of the code you should now save your project, and then we are ready to test. Run your program and test it. First clear the fields on the Employee tab, by clicking on the File menu, choosing the New menu item, and then choosing the Employee submenu item. The fields on the Employee tab should now be cleared:

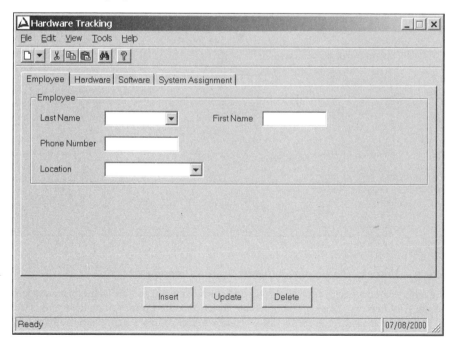

4. Click on the Hardware tab and then click back on the Employee tab. The fields on the Employee tab have been repopulated. Remember that we added code in the last chapter to the `tabData_Click` event to get a recordset of the data for the current tab and to automatically display the first entry.

5. To test the New toolbar icon functionality, click on the New icon on the toolbar. Once again, the fields on the Employee tab should have been cleared. Click on the Hardware tab and then click back on the Employee tab. Once again, the fields have been repopulated.

6. To test the drop-down menu for the New icon on the toolbar, click on the down arrow and then choose Employee on the drop-down menu. Once again the fields on the Employee tab should have been cleared.

7. We are now ready to test the insert functionality for inserting a new employee. Enter some data in the fields on this tab, and then click the Insert button at the bottom of the form. The new employee will be added, and if the last name of the employee added is less than the last employee, that employee will be listed now. This is done because we have reloaded the Last Name combo box after the insert, and the stored procedure that provides this data sorts the data by last name (as specified in the ORDER BY clause). Otherwise, you can select the new employee in the Last Name combo box to have the appropriate data added:

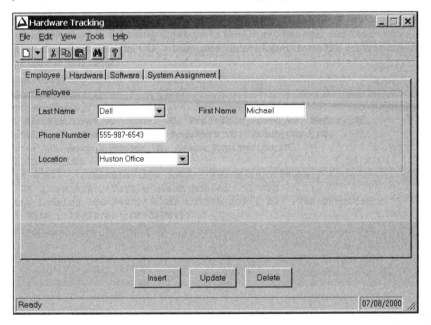

How It Works – Process the Employee Insert Stored Procedure

Starting with our new insert data class, the first thing we want to add in this procedure is a function to enumerate ADO errors. This will be a private function called internally within the class. This function should accept the `Connection` object by reference and return a string. The returned string will be formatted to contain all of the errors, separated by a carriage return line feed character. This allows each message to be displayed on a separate line so the messages don't run into one another.

The first thing that we do in this function is to declare an ADO `Error` object. This will allow us to access each error in the `Errors` collection:

```
Private Function EnumerateErrors( ByRef objConn As ADODB.Connection) As String

    'Declare local objects
    Dim objError As ADODB.Error
```

Next, we loop through the `Errors` collection and add each error number and description to the string. Notice that we are using the function name as the string variable, because this function returns a string. At the end of each message that we add, two carriage return line feed characters are also appended:

```
    'Loop through the errors collection and concatenate all errors
    For Each objError In objConn.Errors
        EnumerateErrors = EnumerateErrors & objError.Number & " : " & _
            objError.Description & vbCrLf & vbCrLf
    Next
```

After we have added all error messages, we remove our reference to the `Error` object that we declared and then exit the function:

```
    'Dereference error object
    Set objError = Nothing
End Function
```

We mentioned earlier that the business server component that we create will contain all of the business logic for our application. Since this class will ultimately end up in that component, we will need to perform the data validation here. This allows us to ensure the data meets the business needs before we pass it on to SQL Server to be inserted.

The function that we want to create to insert employees is a public function, and accepts all of the parameters required to insert a new employee. The first parameter is the `Connection` object, which is passed by reference. The next four parameters are the employee data, which are passed by value. The last parameter is a message parameter, which is passed by reference. We will append all error messages to this parameter and the caller will be able to access the errors in that string:

```
Public Function InsertEmployee( _
    ByRef objConn As ADODB.Connection, _
    ByVal strFirstName As String, _
    ByVal strLastName As String, _
    ByVal strPhoneNumber As String, _
    ByVal strLocation As String, _
    ByRef strMessage As String) As Long
```

As usual, we first set up our error handling in this function, then we declare our local variables and objects. Notice that we have declared an ADO `Command` object. We will use this to execute the `up_parmins_employee` stored procedure.

Next, we set the default value for our `blnValidated` variable:

```
'Setup error handling
On Error GoTo InsertEmployee_Err

'Declare local variables and objects
Dim blnValidated As Boolean
Dim objCmd As ADODB.Command

'Set default values
blnValidated = True
```

We perform all of the data validation next. This validation is rather simple, and you could perform more complex data validation should you choose to do so. We simply want to check to ensure each parameter passed for the employee is not a zero length string after we have trimmed the spaces, and that the parameters do not exceed the maximum length allowed.

If any validation fails, then we set the `blnValidated` variable to `False`, add a message to the message string parameter, and then continue validating the rest of the parameters:

```
'Validate First Name
If RTrim (Len(strFirstName)) = 0 Then
    strMessage = "First Name is zero length" & vbCrLf & vbCrLf
    blnValidated = False
End If
If RTrim(Len(strFirstName)) > 15 Then
    strMessage = "First Name is greater than 15 characters" & vbCrLf & vbCrLf
    blnValidated = False
End If


'Validate Last Name
If RTrim(Len(strLastName)) = 0 Then
    strMessage = strMessage & "Last Name is zero length" & vbCrLf & vbCrLf
    blnValidated = False
End If
If RTrim(Len(strLastName)) > 15 Then
    strMessage = strMessage & _
        "Last Name is greater than 15 characters" & vbCrLf & vbCrLf
    blnValidated = False
End If


'Validate Phone Number
If RTrim(Len(strPhoneNumber)) = 0 Then
    strMessage = strMessage & "Phone Number is zero length" & vbCrLf & vbCrLf
    blnValidated = False
End If
If RTrim(Len(strPhoneNumber)) > 20 Then
    strMessage = strMessage & _
        "Phone Number is greater than 20 characters" & vbCrLf & vbCrLf
    blnValidated = False
End If
```

```
'Validate Location
If RTrim(Len(strLocation)) = 0 Then
    strMessage = strMessage & "Location is zero length" & vbCrLf & vbCrLf
    blnValidated = False
End If
If RTrim(Len(strLocation)) > 30 Then
    strMessage = strMessage & _
        "Location is greater than 30 characters" & vbCrLf & vbCrLf
    blnValidated = False
End If
```

Once all data has been validated, we check the `blnValidated` variable, and if it is `False` we raise an error. This will cause us to fall into our error handling code at the bottom of this function. Notice that once again we have used the VB `Err` object to raise the error:

```
'Check validation variable
If Not blnValidated Then
    Err.Raise 513 + vbObjectError, "InsertEmployee", _
        "Data validation failed"
End If
```

If all validation has passed, we set a reference to the `Command` object. We could have used the `Connection` object to execute this stored procedure, passing it all of the parameters. But the `Command` object provides us with extra features that are not available in the `Connection` object.

For example, we can retrieve a return value from a stored procedure using the `Command` object, but we cannot do so using the `Connection` object. Similarly, we can also process output parameters using the `Command` object, but we cannot do this using the `Connection` object.

Remember that when we pass string parameters in a stored procedure, we must enclose the string in single quotes. This would be the case when using the `Connection` object. But what if the string already contained a single quote? This would cause problems, as SQL Server would interpret the string as two separate parameters, which would cause errors. We could use the VB `Replace` function, which would replace all single quotes in our string with two consecutive single quotes. This would solve the problem, but we would have to do this for every string variable that we passed to the stored procedure.

Using the `Command` object eliminates this extra processing, and it handles strings that contain a single quote automatically for us, so there is nothing that we need to do.

```
'Set a reference to the command object
Set objCmd = New ADODB.Command
```

After we have set a reference to the `Command` object, we can set the `Command` object's properties. We set the `ActiveConnection` property to the `Connection` object that was passed to this function by reference. Then we set the `CommandText` property to the stored procedure that we want to execute, and set the `CommandType` property using the `adCmdStoredProc` constant from the `CommandTypeEnum` enumeration:

```
'Set the command object properties
Set objCmd.ActiveConnection = objConn
objCmd.CommandText = "up_parmins_employee"
objCmd.CommandType = adCmdStoredProc
```

Since the up_parmins_employee stored procedure returns a return value, the first parameter that we append to the Parameters collection must be the parameter for the return value. We have chosen to give this parameter a name of RC. Then we append the rest of the parameters to the parameters collection in the same order as the stored procedure expects them:

```
'Create and append the parameters to the parameters collection
objCmd.Parameters.Append objCmd.CreateParameter("RC", _
    adInteger, adParamReturnValue)
objCmd.Parameters.Append objCmd.CreateParameter("FirstName", _
    adVarChar, adParamInput, 15, strFirstName)
objCmd.Parameters.Append objCmd.CreateParameter("LastName", _
    adVarChar, adParamInput, 15, strLastName)
objCmd.Parameters.Append objCmd.CreateParameter("PhoneNumber", _
    adVarChar, adParamInput, 20, strPhoneNumber)
objCmd.Parameters.Append objCmd.CreateParameter("Location", _
    adVarChar, adParamInput, 30, strLocation)
```

> Tip: the **Size** parameter of the **CreateParameter** method must match the size of the parameter in the stored procedure. For example, if the stored procedure specifies **VarChar(15)**, then the **Size** parameter must also be 15.

After all parameters have been appended to the Parameters collection, we execute the Command object to have the data inserted.

We then check the return value from the stored procedure in the Parameters collection. If the return value is not equal to zero we raise an error, which will cause us to fall into our error handling code at the end of this function:

```
'Execute the command object
objCmd.Execute

'Check the return value from the stored procedure
If objCmd.Parameters("RC") <> 0 Then
    Err.Raise 513 + vbObjectError, "InsertEmployee", _
        "up_parmins_employee failed"
End If
```

If everything was OK, we remove our reference to the Command object, set the return value for this function, and then exit the function:

```
'Remove references to objects
Set objCmd = Nothing
```

```
'Set the return code
InsertEmployee = 0

'Exit function
Exit Function
```

Our error handling code for this function is different from what we have seen in the past. We set the `strMessage` parameter, which was passed by reference, to contain the errors returned by the `EnumerateErrors` function. Then we append any VB errors from the `Err` object, and set the return value from this function to `1`, which indicates that this function failed:

```
InsertEmployee_Err:
    'Enumerate ADO errors
    strMessage = EnumerateErrors(objConn)
    'Append any VB errors
    strMessage = strMessage & Err.Number & " : " & Err.Description
    'Return to the caller with a RC of 1
    InsertEmployee = 1
End Function
```

Switching to the code in our main form (`frmMain`), we need to declare an object for the new class that we have added. We want to declare this object in the general declarations section of the form. Add this object, as shown in the following code fragment:

```
'Declare objects
Dim objData As clsSelectData
Dim objInsert As clsInsertData
Dim objRSData As ADODB.Recordset
```

We will want to add some code to the click event for the Insert button (`cmdInsert_Click`). Since there is only one Insert button, and four tabs on our tab control, we will need to determine which tab we are on when the Insert button is clicked.

The first thing that is done in this procedure is to set up our error handling. Then we display a message in the status bar to indicate that we are processing an insert. Next, we declare all local variables that will be needed in this procedure:

```
Private Sub cmdInsert_Click()
    'Setup error handling
    On Error GoTo cmdInsert_Click_Err

    'Display status
    StatusBar1.Panels("pnlStatus").Text = "Processing Insert"

    'Declare local variables
    Dim lngRC As Long, strMessage As String
```

We want to set a reference to the insert data class (`clsInsertData`), and this is done next. Then, using the `Tab` property of the `tabData` tab control, we determine which tab we are on, in a `Select Case` statement:

```
'Set a reference to the insert data class
Set objInsert = New clsInsertData

'Process tab data
Select Case tabData.Tab

    Case 0   'Employee
```

We call the `InsertEmployee` function, passing it the required parameters. Notice that even though we have a combo box for **Last Name**, we are using the `Text` property of the combo box to get the data for the last name. If we used the `List` property of the combo box we would only get entries that already existed in the combo box and not the new entries that the user has entered.

```
'Insert the new employee
lngRC = objInsert.InsertEmployee(g_objConn, _
    txtFirstName.Text, _
    cboLastName.Text, _
    txtPhoneNumber.Text, _
    cboLocation.Text, _
strMessage)
```

After control has returned from our function, we check the return code from the function. If it is non-zero, we raise an error, which forces us into the error handling code in this procedure.

Then we call the `LoadEmployees` procedure to reload the combo boxes on this tab, to reflect the new employee who has just been added:

```
'Ensure we were successful
If lngRC <> 0 Then
    Err.Raise 513 + vbObjectError, "cmdInsert_Click", _
        "Call to InsertEmployee failed"
End If

'ReLoad Employees
Call LoadEmployees
```

We also want to repopulate the recordset that contains the employees, so we call the `tabData_Click` procedure. Remember that this procedure expects a parameter to indicate the previous tab, so we just pass 0 for this to indicate the **Employee** tab.

The rest of the `Case` statements have been added, but contain no code. We'll take care of that as we progress through this chapter.

```
        'Re-initialize the tab control so the opened RS is reloaded
        'to reflect the new employee
        Call tabData_Click(0)

    Case 1   'Hardware

    Case 2   'Software

    Case 3   'System Assignment

End Select
```

After we have finished processing the insert, we remove our reference to the insert data class and then display a ready message. After that, we exit the procedure:

```
    'Remove reference to object
    Set objInsert = Nothing

    'Display status
    StatusBar1.Panels("pnlStatus").Text = "Ready"

    'Exit sub
    Exit Sub
```

Our error handling code for this procedure will display a message box using the `strMessage` variable that was passed to the `InsertEmployee` function. This variable will contain any errors returned in that function. This allows us to display any validation errors, and continue processing.

```
cmdInsert_Click_Err:
    'Display errors from the function call
    MsgBox strMessage, vbCritical + vbOKOnly, "Hardware Tracking"
End Sub
```

When we want to add a new employee, we usually want to start with a clean slate, so to speak. That is, we want all fields on the form cleared, and we have a submenu item to do just that. When the user clicks on the File menu and chooses the New menu item, a submenu is displayed with all of the tabs on our tab control. We'll need to add some code to the `mnuFileNewEmployee_Click` procedure to clear the fields on the Employee tab when this submenu item is chosen.

All we do in this function is set all text fields on the Employee tab to empty, and set the `ListIndex` property of the `cboLastName` combo box to −1, which clears any selected items:

```
Private Sub mnuFileNewEmployee_Click()
    'Clear the fields on the Employee tab
    txtFirstName.Text = Empty
    cboLastName.ListIndex = -1
    txtPhoneNumber.Text = Empty
    cboLocation.ListIndex = -1
End Sub
```

There is also a corresponding toolbar button for clearing the fields on the **Employee** tab. This toolbar button is a drop-down button that provides the same choices as the **New** menu item in the **File** menu.

A user can either click on the **New** icon on the toolbar, or they can click the down arrow on the drop-down portion of the **New** button. Given this, let's assign a default action to the **New** icon on the toolbar which will clear the fields on the **Employee** tab.

The `Toolbar1_ButtonClick` event is fired when a toolbar button has been clicked. Here, we use a `Select Case` statement, checking the `Key` property of the `Button` collection in the toolbar to determine which button was clicked.

Since we have already written the code to clear the fields on the **Employee** tab, we simply need to call the `mnuFileNewEmployee_Click` procedure. We'll get to the rest of the buttons later, in subsequent chapters.

```
Private Sub Toolbar1_ButtonClick(ByVal Button As MSComctlLib.Button)
    'Process the appropriate toolbar button and call the
    'corresponding menu item
    Select Case Button.Key

        Case "btnNew"
            Call mnuFileNewEmployee_Click

        Case "btnCut"

        Case "btnCopy"

        Case "btnPaste"

        Case "btnFind"

        Case "btnHelp"

    End Select
End Sub
```

When the user clicks on the down arrow on the **New** toolbar button, the drop-down menu is displayed. We need to add code to process the selected menu item in that drop-down menu. This code can be placed in the `Toolbar1_ButtonMenuClick` procedure, as this is the event that is fired when a user clicks on a button menu item.

Again, we are using a `Select Case` statement to find the correct button menu item that was chosen. This time however, instead of using the `Button` collection, we use the `ButtonMenu` collection, and check the `Key` property to identify the button menu item chosen:

```
Private Sub Toolbar1_ButtonMenuClick(ByVal ButtonMenu As MSComctlLib.ButtonMenu)
    'Process the appropriate button menu item and call the
    'corresponding menu item
    Select Case ButtonMenu.Key

        Case "btnNewEmployee"
            Call mnuFileNewEmployee_Click
```

```
        Case "btnNewHardware"

        Case "btnNewSoftware"

        Case "btnNewSystemAssignment"

    End Select
End Sub
```

Having coded the events for the menu and toolbar, we are now able to choose either one, and have the fields on the Employee tab cleared.

There's one last piece of code that we want to add before we begin testing. In the Form_Unload procedure, we want to remove our reference to the insert data class. Add the code to this procedure as shown here:

```
Set objData = Nothing
Set objInsert = Nothing


'Termination the database connection
Call TerminateConnection
```

Error Handling in SQL Server

SQL Server provides a function called @@ERROR that allows us to check the error code from the last statement executed. If no error occurred, then this function will return zero, otherwise it returns the error number of the error that occurred. The associated error messages are contained in the SysMessages table in the master database, and can be read from there should an error occur.

Because the @@ERROR function is cleared and reset with a new error number after each SQL statement is executed, you have to save the error number *immediately* after the statement that you want to check, and then to check the saved error you can reference it by that number. Consider the following example:

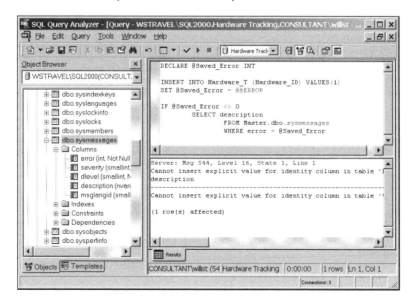

In this example we have declared a variable (`@Saved_Error`) to be used to save the error number. Then we execute the `INSERT` statement, which has been purposely set up to fail, and we set the `@Saved_Error` variable to the error number returned from the `INSERT` statement.

Next we check the saved error, and if it is not equal to zero we select the appropriate error message from the `SysMessages` table in the `master` database, using the saved error number in the `WHERE` clause.

There are two things to take notice of here. First, the `SELECT` statement shows how to access a table in another database. We specify the database name, followed by the user prefix of the owner of the object, followed by the table name.

The second thing to notice here is the message returned from our `SELECT` statement. First, SQL Server printed the message number and message description, and then our `SELECT` statement printed the same message description.

The message description in the example above is fairly straightforward, but this is not always the case. This is why we have the `RAISERROR` statement. This statement allows us to raise our own customized error messages, and these messages are returned from SQL Server to ADO and finally to our own program.

The `RAISERROR` statement has a fairly complex syntax, but we only need show the basic syntax here:

```
RAISERROR(error_message, severity, state)
```

In this syntax, the `error_message` argument is a string variable or string constant containing the error message to be returned.

The `severity` argument represents the user-defined severity level to be associated with the error. You can use severity numbers in the range of 0 through 18, but it is recommended that you use a number in the range of 11 through 16. This range indicates errors that can be corrected by the user. A severity level of 10 is an informational message caused by the information that was entered, indicating the information was incorrect. A severity level of 17 indicates insufficient resources, and a severity level of 18 indicates that a non-fatal internal error has occurred. Severity levels of 0-9 are not used by the system.

The `state` argument is a number from 1 through 127 that represents information about the invocation state of the error.

Using the previous example, let's raise our own error message instead of selecting the predefined error message from SQL Server:

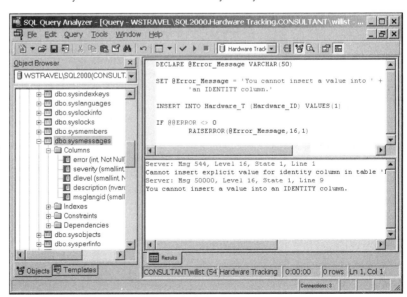

In this example we have declared a variable (@Error_Message) to hold our own error message, and then set that variable to the error message that we want displayed when we raise an error.

We then execute the INSERT statement and check for an error using the @@ERROR function. If the value returned from the @@ERROR function was not zero, we raise our own custom error using the RAISERROR statement. Notice that we have specified a string variable for the *error_message* argument, a value of 16 for the *severity* argument, and a value of 1 for the *state* argument.

Take notice of the results pane. SQL Server raised and displayed the first error; we raised the second error and SQL Server displayed it for us.

Now let's move on, and create some stored procedures that check for, and handle, errors.

Try It Out – Hardware Insert Stored Procedure

The stored procedure we want to create in this exercise will insert the data from the Hardware tab on the main form of our application. This stored procedure will only be inserting data into one table, the Hardware_T table.

1. Start the Query Analyzer if it is not already running.

2. Enter the following stored procedure.

> **Tip: since there are a lot of columns from the Hardware_T table, use the drag and drop features of the Query Analyzer, by dragging the column names from the Object Browser to the query window.**

```
CREATE PROCEDURE dbo.up_parmins_hardware
        @Manufacturer_VC         VARCHAR(30),
        @Model_VC                VARCHAR(30),
        @Processor_Speed_VC      VARCHAR(20),
        @Memory_VC               VARCHAR(10),
        @HardDrive_VC            VARCHAR(15),
        @Sound_Card_VC           VARCHAR(30),
        @Speakers_VC             VARCHAR(30),
        @Video_Card_VC           VARCHAR(30),
        @Monitor_VC              VARCHAR(30),
        @Serial_Number_VC        VARCHAR(30),
        @Lease_Expiration_DT     VARCHAR(22),
        @CD_ID            INT    AS


--  ****************************************************************************
--  Insert the hardware
--  ****************************************************************************
INSERT INTO Hardware_T
        (Manufacturer_VC, Model_VC, Processor_Speed_VC, Memory_VC,
            HardDrive_VC, Sound_Card_VC, Speakers_VC, Video_Card_VC,
            Monitor_VC, Serial_Number_VC, Lease_Expiration_DT,
            CD_ID, Last_Update_DT)
```

```
        VALUES(@Manufacturer_VC, @Model_VC, @Processor_Speed_VC, @Memory_VC,
            @HardDrive_VC, @Sound_Card_VC, @Speakers_VC, @Video_Card_VC,
            @Monitor_VC, @Serial_Number_VC, @Lease_Expiration_DT,
            @CD_ID, GETDATE())
--
-- Check for errors
--
IF @@ERROR > 0
    BEGIN
    RAISERROR('Insert of hardware failed',16,1)
    RETURN 99
    END
--
-- Return to the caller
--
RETURN 0
```

3. Parse the code for errors, by clicking on the **Parse Query** icon, and then create this stored procedure, by clicking on the **Execute Query** icon.

4. Start the Enterprise Manager if it is not already running.

5. Right-click on the up_parmins_hardware stored procedure, choose **All Tasks**, then choose **Manage Permissions** from the context menu.

6. Grant EXEC permissions on this stored procedure to the **Hardware Users** role.

How It Works – Hardware Insert Stored Procedure

The first part of this stored procedure specifies the stored procedure name and all of the input parameters. Using a VarChar field for the lease date provides us much more flexibility when working with the date field in VB and passing it to SQL Server.

Next we specify the INSERT statement, listing all of the columns that we will be inserting data into in the column list, and all of the values in the values list. Notice that for the date value to be inserted, we are using the GETDATE function, which returns the current date and time:

```
-- ********************************************************************
-- Insert the hardware
-- ********************************************************************
INSERT INTO Hardware_T
    (Manufacturer_VC, Model_VC, Processor_Speed_VC, Memory_VC,
        HardDrive_VC, Sound_Card_VC, Speakers_VC, Video_Card_VC,
        Monitor_VC, Serial_Number_VC, Lease_Expiration_DT,
        CD_ID, Last_Update_DT)
    VALUES(@Manufacturer_VC, @Model_VC, @Processor_Speed_VC, @Memory_VC,
        @HardDrive_VC, @Sound_Card_VC, @Speakers_VC, @Video_Card_VC,
        @Monitor_VC, @Serial_Number_VC, @Lease_Expiration_DT,
        @CD_ID, GETDATE())
```

Immediately following the INSERT statement, we check for errors by checking the value contained in the @@ERROR function. We check this error using an IF statement, and then place all of the code to be executed if there is an error between the BEGIN and END keywords.

Using the RAISERROR statement, we raise our own custom message that gets returned to the caller. After the RAISERROR statement, we use the RETURN statement to send a return value of 99 back to the stored procedure.

> **It should be noted that the RETURN statement is immediate and complete. No other code is executed after a RETURN statement.**

```
-- Check for errors
--
IF @@ERROR > 0
    BEGIN
    RAISERROR('Insert of hardware failed',16,1)
    RETURN 99
    END
```

If no error occurred, we execute the RETURN statement to return a return value of zero to the caller:

```
-- Return to the caller
--
RETURN 0
```

Try It Out – Process the Hardware Insert Stored Procedure

The functionality that we want to add to our VB program in this exercise will be to add the necessary code to support inserting new hardware from the Hardware tab on the main form. We want to create a function to execute the stored procedure that we just created and also add some code to the Insert button on the main form.

1. The code is provided throughout the *How It Works* section; once you have entered it you should save your project – we are then ready to test.

2. Run your program, and then click on the Hardware tab. Click on the File menu, choose the New menu item, and then choose the Hardware submenu item. The fields on the Hardware tab should be cleared:

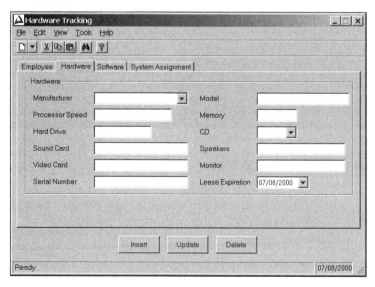

3. You will also want to test the drop-down menu for the New toolbar icon. So click on another tab and then click back on the Hardware tab. The Hardware tab is once again populated. Now click on the down arrow on the New icon on the toolbar, and then choose the Hardware menu item from the drop-down list. The Hardware tab is once again cleared.

4. You are now ready to test the newest insert functionality that you have added. Enter data in all of the fields on the Hardware tab, and then click the Insert button. The new hardware is added, and is shown in the Manufacturer combo box:

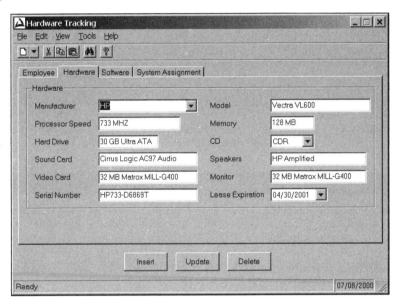

How It Works – Process the Hardware Insert Stored Procedure

We start by creating the `InsertHardware` function to call this stored procedure in the insert data (`clsInsert`) class.

This function accepts the `Connection` object by reference, and then all of the fields on the Hardware tab by value. The last parameter, `strMessage`, is passed by reference, so we can append any error message that may occur to it.

Take note of the `dteLeaseExpiration` parameter – it is being passed as a `Date` data type. This will allow us to perform a date check on it in our data validation. Other than that, most of what follows should be quite familiar to you by now:

```
Public Function InsertHardware( _
    ByRef objConn As ADODB.Connection, _
    ByVal strManufacturer As String, _
    ByVal strModel As String, _
    ByVal strProcessorSpeed As String, _
    ByVal strMemory As String, _
    ByVal strHardDrive As String, _
    ByVal strSoundCard As String, _
```

```
        ByVal strSpeakers As String, _
        ByVal strVideoCard As String, _
        ByVal strMonitor As String, _
        ByVal strSerialNumber As String, _
        ByVal dteLeaseExpiration As Date, _
        ByVal lngCDID As Long, _
        ByRef strMessage As String) As Long
```

We set up our error handling in this procedure and then declare our local variables. Again, we are going to be using the Command object to handle the execution of our stored procedure.

We then set the default value for the blnValidated variable:

```
    'Setup error handling
    On Error GoTo InsertHardware_Err

    'Declare local variables and objects
    Dim blnValidated As Boolean
    Dim objCmd As ADODB.Command

    'Set default values
    blnValidated = True
```

Data validations are performed next, checking the length of the parameter strings to ensure they are not zero length, and that they do not exceed the length as defined by the input parameters of the up_parmins_hardware stored procedure:

```
    'Validate Manufacturer
    If RTrim(Len(strManufacturer)) = 0 Then
        strMessage = "Manufacturer is zero length" & vbCrLf & vbCrLf
        blnValidated = False
    End If
    If RTrim(Len(strManufacturer)) > 30 Then
        strMessage = "Manufacturer is greater than 30 characters" & vbCrLf & vbCrLf
        blnValidated = False
    End If
```

Due to space, and because we have already covered these, the rest of the data validations have been omitted in this text, but are included in the code download, all except for the validation of the dteLeaseExpiration parameter, which is shown and explained next.

We need to point out the validation of this parameter. Here, we know that the value returned from the date picker control is a valid date, so all we need to do is to ensure that the date chosen is a date in the future, as this is the parameter representing the lease expiration. We do this by comparing the dteLeaseExpiration parameter against the current date using the Now function. This function returns the current date and time. We check the dteLeaseExpiration parameter to see if it is less than or equal to the current date, and set the blnValidated variable to False if it is:

```
    'Validate Lease Expiration
    If dteLeaseExpiration <= Now Then
        strMessage = "Lease Expiration is not a date in the future" & Chr(0)
        blnValidated = False
    End If
```

377

After all validations have been performed, we check the blnValidated variable. If it is False, then we raise an error, which will cause us to fall through to our error handling code in this function. If all validations have passed, we set a reference to the Command object:

```
'Check validation variable
If Not blnValidated Then
    Err.Raise 513 + vbObjectError, "InsertHardware", _
        "Data validation failed"
End If

'Set a reference to the command object
Set objCmd = New ADODB.Command
```

We set the Command object's ActiveConnection property next, using the Connection object that was passed as a parameter. Then we set the CommandText and CommandType properties:

```
'Set the command object properties
Set objCmd.ActiveConnection = objConn
objCmd.CommandText = "up_parmins_hardware"
objCmd.CommandType = adCmdStoredProc
```

We create and append all of the parameters to the Parameters collection. Again, it should be noted that when a stored procedure returns a return value, that this must be the first parameter in the Parameters collection:

```
'Create and append the parameters to the parameters collection
objCmd.Parameters.Append objCmd.CreateParameter("RC", _
    adInteger, adParamReturnValue)
objCmd.Parameters.Append objCmd.CreateParameter("Manufacturer", _
    adVarChar, adParamInput, 30, strManufacturer)
objCmd.Parameters.Append objCmd.CreateParameter("Model", _
    adVarChar, adParamInput, 30, strModel)
objCmd.Parameters.Append objCmd.CreateParameter("Processor", _
    adVarChar, adParamInput, 20, strProcessorSpeed)
objCmd.Parameters.Append objCmd.CreateParameter("Memory", _
    adVarChar, adParamInput, 10, strMemory)
objCmd.Parameters.Append objCmd.CreateParameter("HardDrive", _
    adVarChar, adParamInput, 15, strHardDrive)
objCmd.Parameters.Append objCmd.CreateParameter("SoundCard", _
    adVarChar, adParamInput, 30, strSoundCard)
objCmd.Parameters.Append objCmd.CreateParameter("Speakers", _
    adVarChar, adParamInput, 30, strSpeakers)
objCmd.Parameters.Append objCmd.CreateParameter("VideoCard", _
    adVarChar, adParamInput, 30, strVideoCard)
objCmd.Parameters.Append objCmd.CreateParameter("Monitor", _
    adVarChar, adParamInput, 30, strMonitor)
objCmd.Parameters.Append objCmd.CreateParameter("SerialNumber", _
    adVarChar, adParamInput, 30, strSerialNumber)
```

The lease expiration parameter was defined in the stored procedure as a `VarChar` data type. This means that the date has to be passed as a string. Here, we are passing the date in the `dteLeaseExpiration` parameter and it is automatically interpreted as a string:

```
objCmd.Parameters.Append objCmd.CreateParameter("LeaseExp", _
    adVarChar, adParamInput, 22, dteLeaseExpiration)
objCmd.Parameters.Append objCmd.CreateParameter("CDID", _
    adInteger, adParamInput, , lngCDID)
```

After we have appended all of the parameters to the `Parameters` collection, we execute the `Command` object. Then we check the return value from the stored procedure, and raise an error if it is not zero:

```
'Execute the command object
objCmd.Execute

'Check the return value from the stored procedure
If objCmd.Parameters("RC") <> 0 Then
    Err.Raise 513 + vbObjectError, "InsertHardware", _
        "up_parmins_hardware failed"
End If
```

If everything went well, we remove our reference to the `Command` object and set the return code for this function. Then we exit the function:

```
'Remove references to objects
Set objCmd = Nothing

'Set the return code
InsertHardware = 0

'Exit function
Exit Function
```

If an error occurred, we execute the code in our error handler. It should be noted that if the `RAISERROR` statement in the stored procedure raised an error, you will see the error when you enumerate the errors in the `Errors` collection.

```
InsertHardware_Err:
    'Enumerate ADO errors
    strMessage = EnumerateErrors(objConn)
    'Append any VB errors
    strMessage = strMessage & Err.Number & " : " & Err.Description
    'Return to the caller with a RC of 1
    InsertHardware = 1
End Function
```

We now want to switch back to the main form (`frmMain`) and add some more code to the `cmdInsert_Click` procedure. The code we want to add is in the `Case` statement for the **Hardware** tab.

Our `objInsert` object already has a reference set to the insert data class, so all we need to do is to execute the `InsertHardware` function:

```
Case 1  'Hardware

        'Insert the new hardware
        lngRC = objInsert.InsertHardware(g_objConn, _
            cboManufacturer.Text, _
            txtModel.Text, _
            txtProcessorSpeed.Text, _
            txtMemory.Text, _
            txtHardDrive.Text, _
            txtSoundCard.Text, _
            txtSpeakers.Text, _
            txtVideoCard.Text, _
            txtMonitor.Text, _
            txtSerialNumber.Text, _
            dtpLeaseExpiration.Value, _
            cboCD.ItemData(cboCD.ListIndex), _
            strMessage)
```

After control is returned from our function, we check the return code returned by the function, and raise an error if it is not zero:

```
        'Ensure we were successful
        If lngRC <> 0 Then
            Err.Raise 513 + vbObjectError, "cmdInsert_Click", _
                "Call to InsertHardware failed"
        End If
```

Next, we want to reload the combo boxes on the **Hardware** tab to reflect the new hardware that was just inserted. Then we need to call the `LoadSystems` procedure to have the **Systems** combo box reloaded in order to reflect the new hardware:

```
        'Reload Hardware
        Call LoadHardware

        'Reload Systems combo box on the System Assignment tab
        Call LoadSystems
```

Last, we call the `tabData_Click` procedure, passing it the number of the tab that we are on as the **Previous Tab** parameter. This will cause the recordset for this tab to also be reloaded, thus reflecting the new hardware:

```
        'Re-initialize the tab control so the opened RS is reloaded
        'to reflect the new hardware
        Call tabData_Click(1)
```

When a user clicks on the **File** menu, chooses the **New** menu item, and then the **Hardware** sub menu item, we want to clear all fields on the **Hardware** tab. To that end, we need to add some code to the `mnuFileNewHardware_Click` procedure.

This procedure sets all text fields to empty, and sets the `ListIndex` property of all combo boxes to -1, so no items in the combo boxes are selected. The `Value` property of the `dtpLeaseExpiration` control cannot be set to empty, so we set it to the current date:

```
Private Sub mnuFileNewHardware_Click()
    'Clear the fields on the Hardware tab
    cboManufacturer.ListIndex = -1
    txtModel.Text = Empty
    txtProcessorSpeed.Text = Empty
    txtMemory.Text = Empty
    txtHardDrive.Text = Empty
    txtSoundCard.Text = Empty
    txtSpeakers.Text = Empty
    txtVideoCard.Text = Empty
    txtMonitor.Text = Empty
    txtSerialNumber.Text = Empty
    dtpLeaseExpiration.Value = Now
    cboCD.ListIndex = -1
End Sub
```

We also want to modify the `Toolbar1_ButtonMenuClick` procedure. This procedure is fired when a user clicks on an item in the drop-down menu of the **New** toolbar button.

We want to add some code to the `btnNewHardware` Case statement to call the `mnuFileNewHardware_Click` procedure that we just coded:

```
        Case "btnNewEmployee"
            Call mnuFileNewEmployee_Click


        Case "btnNewHardware"
            Call mnuFileNewHardware_Click
```

Try It Out – Software Insert Stored Procedure

The stored procedure to insert new software and its assigned category has already been built in a previous chapter. However, we do want to modify this stored procedure to include our error handling code and also to return a return value to the caller.

1. To modify this stored procedure, start the Enterprise Manager if it is not already running, and expand the **Stored Procedures** group in the **Hardware Tracking** database.

2. Double-click on the **up_parmins_software** stored procedure, which will display the **Stored Procedures Properties** dialog.

3. Make the following modifications to this stored procedure:

```
ALTER PROCEDURE dbo.up_parmins_software
    @Software_Title_VC VARCHAR(30),
    @Software_Category_ID INT AS
```

```
INSERT INTO Software_T
    (Software_Name_VC, Software_Category_ID, Last_Update_DT)
    VALUES(@Software_Title_VC, @Software_Category_ID, GETDATE())
--
-- Check for errors
--
IF @@ERROR > 0
    BEGIN
    RAISERROR('Insert of software failed',16,1)
    RETURN 99
    END
--
-- Return to the caller
--
RETURN 0
GO
```

4. Check the syntax of the code added by clicking on the Check Syntax button. If the syntax is correct, you will receive a message indicating the syntax check was successful. Click OK on this informational dialog and then click OK on the Stored Procedures Properties dialog to have the changes applied.

This method of modifying a stored procedure works well with small simple code sections. If you need to add a lot of code, or more complex code, you might want to copy the SQL statements in the Stored Procedures Properties dialog and then paste them into the Query Analyzer to perform the work. This allows you to take advantage of the Query Analyzer's debugging methods discussed in Chapter 5.

You could then either drop and recreate the stored procedure, or copy the code from the Query Analyzer and paste it into the Stored Procedures Properties dialog.

How It Works – Software Insert Stored Procedure

The code that we added to this stored procedure merely checks for a successful insert, and raises an error if the insert failed. If the insert fails, a return value of 99 is returned.

If everything was successful, we return a return value of 0:

```
-- Check for errors
--
IF @@ERROR > 0
    BEGIN
    RAISERROR('Insert of software failed',16,1)
    RETURN 99
    END
--
-- Return to the caller
--
RETURN 0
```

Try It Out – Process the Software Insert Stored Procedure

This exercise will make the necessary modifications to our VB code to support inserting new software on the Software tab on the main form. We will need to add some more code to the Insert button to support inserting software. We will also need to add a new function to the insert data class to execute the stored procedure that we just created.

1. The necessary code is listed in the *How It Works* section. After you have made all of the modifications save your project in preparation for testing. Then run the program and click on the Software tab.

2. We want to test the menu functionality first, so click on the File menu and then the New menu item. Next, click on the Software submenu item and all fields on the Software tab are cleared:

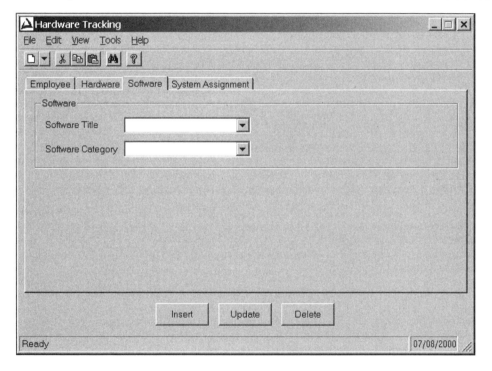

3. Click on another tab and then click back on the Software tab. The fields on the Software tab have been repopulated. Now click on the down arrow on the New icon on the toolbar and choose Software from the drop-down menu. Once again, the fields on the Software tab have been cleared.

4. We are now ready to insert a new software title. Enter a Software Title and then choose the appropriate category in the Software Category combo box. Click the Insert button to have the new software title added.

5. Once the software title has been added, it is immediately available in the Software Title combo box, as shown in the following figure:

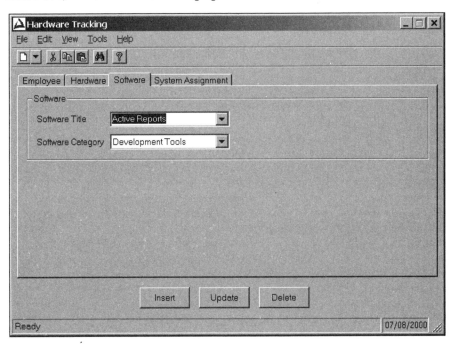

How It Works – Process the Software Insert Stored Procedure

We need to add a function in the insert data class in our VB application to execute this stored procedure. The `InsertSoftware` function accepts the `Connection` object by reference as the first parameter in this function. Then we specify the software title as a `String`, and the software category as a `Long` data type. The `strMessage` parameter is passed by reference, so we can append any error messages that we may encounter:

```
Public Function InsertSoftware( _
    ByRef objConn As ADODB.Connection, _
    ByVal strSoftware As String, _
    ByVal lngCategoryID As Long, _
    ByRef strMessage As String) As Long
```

We set up our error handling next and then declare our local variables and objects:

```
'Setup error handling
On Error GoTo InsertSoftware_Err

'Declare local variables and objects
Dim blnValidated As Boolean
Dim objCmd As ADODB.Command
```

We set the `blnValidated` variable to True, and then proceed with our data validations. The only data validation in this function is for the software title:

```
'Set default values
blnValidated = True

'Validate Software Title
If RTrim(Len(strSoftware)) = 0 Then
    strMessage = "Software Title is zero length" & vbCrLf & vbCrLf
    blnValidated = False
End If
If RTrim(Len(strSoftware)) > 30 Then
    strMessage = "Software Title is greater than 30 characters" & _
        vbCrLf & vbCrLf
    blnValidated = False
End If
```

After we have validated the data, we check the `blnValidated` variable. If it is False we raise an error, which causes us to fall into our error handling code at the bottom of this function:

```
'Check validation variable
If Not blnValidated Then
    Err.Raise 513 + vbObjectError, "InsertSoftware", _
        "Data validation failed"
End If
```

Next we set a reference to the ADO `Command` object. Then we set the `Command` object's properties and append the parameters to the `Parameters` collection:

```
'Set a reference to the command object
Set objCmd = New ADODB.Command

'Set the command object properties
Set objCmd.ActiveConnection = objConn
objCmd.CommandText = "up_parmins_software"
objCmd.CommandType = adCmdStoredProc

'Create and append the parameters to the parameters collection
objCmd.Parameters.Append objCmd.CreateParameter("RC", _
    adInteger, adParamReturnValue)
objCmd.Parameters.Append objCmd.CreateParameter("Software", _
    adVarChar, adParamInput, 30, strSoftware)
objCmd.Parameters.Append objCmd.CreateParameter("CategoryID", _
    adInteger, adParamInput, , lngCategoryID)
```

We execute the `Command` object and then check the return value from the stored procedure. If it is not zero, we raise an error and we are thrown into our error handling code:

```
'Execute the command object
objCmd.Execute

'Check the return value from the stored procedure
```

385

```
       If objCmd.Parameters("RC") <> 0 Then
           Err.Raise 513 + vbObjectError, "InsertSoftware", _
               "up_parmins_software failed"
       End If
```

If all was successful, we remove our reference to the Command object, then set the return code for this function to zero before exiting the function:

```
    'Remove references to objects
    Set objCmd = Nothing

    'Set the return code
    InsertSoftware = 0

    'Exit function
    Exit Function
```

The error handling code in this function is the same code that we have used in the last two functions in this class:

```
InsertSoftware_Err:
    'Enumerate ADO errors
    strMessage = EnumerateErrors(objConn)
    'Append any VB errors
    strMessage = strMessage & Err.Number & " : " & Err.Description
    'Return to the caller with a RC of 1
    InsertSoftware = 1
End Function
```

The next piece of code that we need to add is in the cmdInsert_Click procedure in our main form. We add our code to the appropriate Case statement for the **Software** tab. Add code as shown in the following code fragment.

Since the objInsert object already has a reference set to the insert data class, we just need to start by calling the InsertSoftware function. We pass it the Text property of the cboSoftware combo box because we are inserting new software. We then pass the ItemData property of the selected entry in the cboSoftwareCategory combo box, as we only need the primary key to this entry in the Software_Category_T table:

```
        Case 2  'Software

            'Insert the new software
            lngRC = objInsert.InsertSoftware(g_objConn, _
                cboSoftware.Text, _
                cboSoftwareCategory.ItemData(cboSoftwareCategory.ListIndex), _
                strMessage)
```

After control has been returned from the InsertSoftware function we check the return code. If it is non-zero then we raise an error:

```
            'Ensure we were successful
            If lngRC <> 0 Then
```

```
            Err.Raise 513 + vbObjectError, "cmdInsert_Click", _
                "Call to InsertSoftware failed"
        End If
```

Next we call the `InsertSoftware` procedure to have the combo boxes on the **Software** tab reloaded. Remember that this procedure also loads the `lstInstalledSoftware` list on the **System Assignment** tab.

Then we call the `tabData_Click` procedure, passing it a value of 2 for the previous tab parameter. This will reload the recordset used on this tab of our tab control.

```
        'Reload Software
        Call Loadsoftware

        'Re-initialize the tab control so the opened RS is reloaded
        'to reflect the new software
        Call tabData_Click(2)
```

We also need to add some code to the `mnuFileNewSoftware_Click` procedure to clear the fields on the **Software** tab. This procedure simply sets the `ListIndex` property of the combo boxes to −1 to deselect all items:

```
    Private Sub mnuFileNewSoftware_Click()
        'Clear the fields on the Software tab
        cboSoftware.ListIndex = -1
        cboSoftwareCategory.ListIndex = -1
    End Sub
```

The drop-down menu for the **New** toolbar button also needs some code added, so that when we click on the **Software** menu item in the drop-down menu on the toolbar button, the fields on the **Software** tab are cleared. Add the following code to the `Toolbar1_ButtonMenuClick` procedure:

```
        Case "btnNewHardware"
            Call mnuFileNewHardware_Click

        Case "btnNewSoftware"
            Call mnuFileNewSoftware_Click
```

Try It Out – System Assignment Insert Stored Procedures

When we assign a system to an employee, we not only choose the hardware assigned to them, we also choose the software that is installed on their system. Doing this causes us to write two separate stored procedures. We could do all of this processing in one stored procedure, but it would be large and overly complex. This would cause maintenance of that stored procedure to be very time consuming because of all the code it would contain, and it would expose more opportunity for errors during maintenance.

The simplest solution is to write two separate stored procedures, one to insert the system assignment and one to insert the software installed in the system. We will call the latter stored procedure for each software title installed on a system.

387

Given the multiple executions of stored procedures to assign a system to an employee, there is a greater chance of failure. On account of this, we also want to write a stored procedure to clean up the inserts should we have a failure. While we have not fully covered DELETE stored procedures yet, we will write a simple delete stored procedure and explain it in this chapter.

1. To create these stored procedures start the Query Analyzer, if it is not already running.

2. Enter the following stored procedure:

```
CREATE PROCEDURE dbo.up_parmins_system_assignment
     @Employee_ID     INT,
     @Hardware_ID     INT,
     @System_ID  INT OUTPUT AS


-- **********************************************************************
-- Insert the system assignment
-- **********************************************************************
INSERT INTO System_Assignment_T
     (Employee_ID, Hardware_ID, Last_Update_DT)
     VALUES(@Employee_ID, @Hardware_ID, GETDATE())
--
-- Check for errors
--
IF @@ERROR > 0
     BEGIN
     RAISERROR('Insert of system assignment failed',16,1)
     RETURN 99
     END
--
-- Get the IDENTITY value inserted to return to the caller
--
SET @System_ID = @@IDENTITY
--
-- Return to the caller
--
RETURN 0
```

Tip: notice that the last parameter in this stored procedure is an OUTPUT parameter.

---

3. Parse the code for errors and then click on the Execute Query icon to create this stored procedure.

4. Start the Enterprise Manager if it is not already running. Expand the Hardware Tracking database and click on the Stored Procedures group.

5. Right-click on the up_parmins_system_assignment stored procedure, choose All Tasks and then Manage Permissions from the context menu.

6. Grant EXEC access to the Hardware Users role.

7. To create the next stored procedure clear the current query window by clicking on the Clear Query Window icon, or open a new query window by clicking on the New Query icon.

8. Enter the following stored procedure:

```
CREATE PROCEDURE dbo.up_parmins_system_software
    @System_ID    INT,
    @Software_ID      INT AS

-- ************************************************************************
-- Insert the system software
-- ************************************************************************
INSERT INTO System_Software_Relationship_T
    (System_Assignment_ID, Software_ID)
    VALUES(@System_ID, @Software_ID)
--
-- Check for errors
--
IF @@ERROR > 0
    BEGIN
    RAISERROR('Insert of system software failed',16,1)
    RETURN 99
    END
--
-- Return to the caller
--
RETURN 0
```

9. Parse the code for errors, and create the stored procedure by clicking on the **Execute Query** icon.

10. In the Enterprise Manager, right-click on the **up_parmins_system_software** stored procedure and choose **All Tasks**, and then choose **Manage Permissions** from the context menu.

11. Grant **EXEC** permissions to the **Hardware Users** role.

12. To create the last stored procedure clear the current query window by clicking on the **Clear Query Window** icon, or open a new query window by clicking on the **New Query** icon.

13. Enter the following stored procedure:

```
CREATE PROCEDURE dbo.up_parmdel_failed_system_assignment
    @System_ID  INT AS

-- ************************************************************************
-- Delete any existing software
-- ************************************************************************
DELETE FROM System_Software_Relationship_T
    WHERE System_Assignment_ID = @System_ID


-- ************************************************************************
-- Delete the system assignment
-- ************************************************************************
DELETE FROM System_Assignment_T
    WHERE System_Assignment_ID = @System_ID
```

14. Parse the code for errors, and create the stored procedure by clicking on the **Execute Query** icon.

15. In the Enterprise Manager, right-click on the **up_parmdel_failed_system_assignment** stored procedure, choose **All Tasks**, and then choose **Manage Permissions** from the context menu.

16. Grant EXEC permissions to the **Hardware Users** role.

How It Works – System Assignment Insert Stored Procedures

The up_parmins_system_assignment stored procedure was the first procedure that we created. This stored procedure will insert the employee ID and hardware ID in the System_Assignment_T table. It then returns the System_Assignment_ID value inserted in the output parameter. This value will be used by the next stored procedure.

This stored procedure has two input parameters, and one output parameter:

```
CREATE PROCEDURE dbo.up_parmins_system_assignment
      @Employee_ID      INT,
      @Hardware_ID      INT,
      @System_ID   INT OUTPUT AS
```

The INSERT statement inserts the employee ID and hardware ID into the System_Assignment_T table.

Then we check for errors and raise an error if the @@ERROR function did not contain a 0. Then we return to the caller with a return value of 99. Remember that executing the RETURN statement is immediate and final; no other code is executed after a RETURN statement.

```
-- *************************************************************************
-- Insert the system assignment
-- *************************************************************************
INSERT INTO System_Assignment_T
    (Employee_ID, Hardware_ID, Last_Update_DT)
    VALUES(@Employee_ID, @Hardware_ID, GETDATE())
--
-- Check for errors
--
IF @@ERROR > 0
    BEGIN
    RAISERROR('Insert of system assignment failed',16,1)
    RETURN 99
    END
```

If everything was successful, we use the SET statement to assign the identity value that was inserted to the output parameter @System_ID. Then we return to the caller with a return value of 0:

```
-- Get the IDENTITY value inserted to return to the caller
--
SET @System_ID = @@IDENTITY
--
-- Return to the caller
--
RETURN 0
```

After we have executed the up_parmins_system_assignment stored procedure and retrieved the system ID that was inserted, we need to execute the up_parmins_system_software stored procedure once for each software title checked. We pass this stored procedure the output parameter from the up_parmins_system_assignment stored procedure.

This stored procedure needs only two parameters, the system ID of the system that was assigned, and the software ID of the software title checked:

```
CREATE PROCEDURE dbo.up_parmins_system_software
    @System_ID  INT,
    @Software_ID    INT AS
```

The INSERT statement inserts these parameters into the System_Software_Relationship_T table. Remember that this table contains a many-to-one relationship to the System_Assignment_T table.

```
-- ***********************************************************************
-- Insert the system software
-- ***********************************************************************
INSERT INTO System_Software_Relationship_T
    (System_Assignment_ID, Software_ID)
    VALUES(@System_ID, @Software_ID)
```

After the insert, we check for errors by checking the value contained in the @@ERROR function. If an error occurred, we raise an error and return to the caller with a return value of 99. If no errors occurred, we return to the caller with a return value of 0:

```
-- Check for errors
--
IF @@ERROR > 0
    BEGIN
    RAISERROR('Insert of system software failed',16,1)
    RETURN 99
    END
--
-- Return to the caller
--
RETURN 0
```

The last stored procedure is a contingency stored procedure. We hope we never have to use it, but we need to create it to clean up a partial system assignment should we receive an error somewhere. We want the process to complete entirely, or not at all.

The up_parmdel_failed_system_assignment stored procedure simply deletes all entries from the System_Software_Relationship_T table and then deletes the one entry from the System_Assignment_T table. Notice that we are deleting in the reverse order that we have inserted data. This is required because of the foreign key constraint between the System_Assignment_T and System_Software_Relationship_T tables.

This stored procedure has only one parameter, the system ID of the row or rows to be deleted:

```
CREATE PROCEDURE dbo.up_parmdel_failed_system_assignment
    @System_ID  INT AS
```

The first DELETE statement will delete all rows from the System_Software_Relationship_T table where the value in the System_Assignment_ID column equals the value in the @System_ID input parameter. If no rows are found, then the stored procedure will continue processing the next statement – no error occurs.

```
--  ********************************************************************
-- Delete any existing software
--  ********************************************************************
DELETE FROM System_Software_Relationship_T
    WHERE System_Assignment_ID = @System_ID
```

The next DELETE statement deletes the one row of data from the System_Assignment_T table where the value in the System_Assignment_ID column equals the value in the @System_ID input parameter:

```
--  ********************************************************************
-- Delete the system assignment
--  ********************************************************************
DELETE FROM System_Assignment_T
    WHERE System_Assignment_ID = @System_ID
```

Try It Out – Process the System Assignment Insert Stored Procedure

This exercise will add the necessary functionality to our VB program to allow us to insert a new system assignment on the **System Assignment** tab in the main form. To that end, we will be adding code to the Insert button and also adding a new function in the insert data class to execute the new stored procedures that we just built.

1. After adding the code, presented in the *How It Works* section, to your project, save your project and then run your program.

2. We want to test the functionality to clear the **System Assignment** tab, so click on this tab.

3. Next, click on the **File** menu, then click on the **New** menu item, and then click on the **System Assignment** submenu item. The fields on the **System Assignment** tab are then cleared:

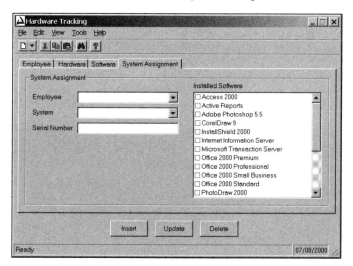

4. To test the functionality of the New toolbar button click on another tab, and then click on the System Assignment tab again, so that the fields are repopulated.

5. Next, click on the down arrow on the New icon and then on System Assignment in the drop-down menu. Once again the fields on the System Assignment tab are cleared.

6. We are now ready to test the insert functionality. Pick a new employee who has not had a system assigned and then choose an available system. Select the software check boxes for the software that is installed on the system. Click the Insert button and the assignment will be made.

7. To verify the assignment, click on the employee in the Employee combo box and then choose the employee that you just inserted the system assignment for:

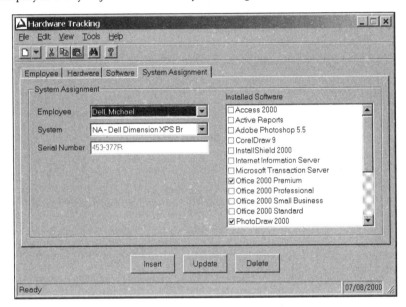

How It Works – Process the System Assignment Stored Procedure

Let's start discussing the VB code in the main form (`frmMain`) this time. We want to modify the `cmdInsert_Click` procedure, as shown in the following code. In essence what we need to do here is to build an array of all software titles that have been checked in the `lstInstalledSoftware` list on the System Assignment tab. Then we will pass this array to the function that will perform the insert of the new system assignment.

We start by modifying the `cmdInsert_Click` procedure to add some new local variables, as shown in the next code fragment:

```
'Declare local variables
Dim lngRC As Long, strMessage As String, _
    lngInstalledSoftware() As Long, intIndex As Integer, _
    intArrayIndex As Integer
```

Next we want to add some code to the `Case` statement for the **System Assignment** tab.

The first thing that we want to do is to build an array of all checked software in the `lstInstalledSoftware` list. We will use two counters in the following loop. The first counter is the `intArrayIndex` counter. This counter will be our index into the `lngInstalledSoftware` array and has been set to –1 before we enter the loop. The reason for this is that, by default, all arrays are zero-based, unless you specifically change them. The second counter is the `intIndex` variable and will be our index into the list of software.

We process the loop using the `ListCount` property of the `lstInstalledSoftware` list. The `lstInstalledSoftware` is a zero-based list, but the `ListCount` property returns the actual number of items in the list, therefore we need to subtract one from the `ListCount` property:

```
Case 3   'System Assignment

    'Build an array of installed software
    intArrayIndex = -1
    For intIndex = 0 To lstInstalledSoftware.ListCount - 1
```

The first thing we do in the loop is to check the `Selected` property of the `lstInstalledSoftware` list. If it has a value of `True`, then the item has been checked and we want to add it to our array of software:

```
        'If the selected item is checked then
        If lstInstalledSoftware.Selected(intIndex) = True Then
```

We increment the `intArrayIndex` counter and then re-dimension the array using the `Preserve` keyword to preserve the existing entries:

```
            'Increment the array index variable and redim the array
            intArrayIndex = intArrayIndex + 1
            ReDim Preserve lngInstalledSoftware(intArrayIndex)
```

Then we add the software to the array. We are using the `ItemData` property of the `lstInstalledSoftware` list, as this property contains the primary key of the software that has been checked, and is the value that we need to insert into the `System_Software_Relationship_T` table.

We continue processing the loop and process all items in the `lstInstalledSoftware` list:

```
            'Add the ItemData property value to the array
            lngInstalledSoftware(intArrayIndex) = _
                lstInstalledSoftware.ItemData(intIndex)
        End If
    Next
```

Once our array has been built, we call the `InsertSystemAssignment` function to insert the new system assignment and all checked software. The employee ID is being passed using the value in the `ItemData` property of the `cboEmployee` combo box, and the hardware ID is being passed using the value in the `ItemData` property of the `cboSystem` combo box.

The `lngInstalledSoftware` array is being passed and contains all checked software in the `lstInstalledSoftware` list:

```
'Insert the system assignment and software
lngRC = objInsert.InsertSystemAssignment(g_objConn, _
    cboEmployee.ItemData(cboEmployee.ListIndex), _
    cboSystem.ItemData(cboSystem.ListIndex), _
    lngInstalledSoftware(), _
    strMessage)
```

Once control has been returned from the `InsertSystemAssignment` function, we check the return code that has been returned and raise an error if it is non-zero:

```
'Ensure we were successful
If lngRC <> 0 Then
    Err.Raise 513 + vbObjectError, "cmdInsert_Click", _
        "Call to InsertSystemAssignment failed"
End If
```

If everything was successful we call the `LoadSystems` procedure to reload the data on the **System Assignment** tab.

Then we call the `tabData_Click` procedure, passing it a previous tab parameter of 3, which is the current tab:

```
'Reload Systems
Call LoadSystems

'Re-initialize the tab control so the opened RS is reloaded
'to reflect the new system assignment
Call tabData_Click(3)
```

Now that we know what data is passed to the `InsertSystemAssignment` function, let's build this function next. Switching to the insert data class, we create this function pretty much like the other functions in this class.

This function has five parameters, the first of which is the `Connection` object, which is passed by reference. The next two parameters are the employee ID and system ID, which are passed by value. The software ID array must be passed by reference, as this is a restriction with arrays. The last parameter is the message parameter, which is passed by reference:

```
Public Function InsertSystemAssignment( _
    ByRef objConn As ADODB.Connection, _
    ByVal lngEmployeeID As Long, _
    ByVal lngSystemID As Long, _
    ByRef lngSoftwareID() As Long, _
    ByRef strMessage As String) As Long
```

We set up our error handling and then declare our local variables and objects. The `lngAssignmentID` variable will be used to hold the system ID that was assigned and returned as an output parameter from the `up_parmins_system_assignment` stored procedure.

The `intIndex` variable will be used as an index into the `lngSoftwareID` array:

```
'Setup error handling
'On Error GoTo InsertSystemAssignment_Err

'Declare local variables and objects
Dim lngAssignmentID As Long, intIndex As Integer
Dim objCmd As ADODB.Command
```

Next we set a reference to the `Command` object and set its properties. The `CommandText` property is being set to the `up_parmins_system_assignment` stored procedure. This stored procedure inserts the employee ID and hardware ID of the system being assigned:

```
'Set a reference to the command object
Set objCmd = New ADODB.Command

'Set the command object properties
Set objCmd.ActiveConnection = objConn
objCmd.CommandText = "up_parmins_system_assignment"
objCmd.CommandType = adCmdStoredProc
```

We create and append the parameters to the `Parameters` collection. Notice that the first parameter is for our return value from the stored procedure, and the last parameter is an output parameter from our stored procedure. This last parameter will contain the `System_Assignment_ID` that was inserted:

```
'Create and append the parameters to the parameters collection
objCmd.Parameters.Append objCmd.CreateParameter("RC", _
    adInteger, adParamReturnValue)
objCmd.Parameters.Append objCmd.CreateParameter("Employee", _
    adInteger, adParamInput, , lngEmployeeID)
objCmd.Parameters.Append objCmd.CreateParameter("System", _
    adInteger, adParamInput, , lngSystemID)
objCmd.Parameters.Append objCmd.CreateParameter("Assignment", _
    adInteger, adParamOutput)
```

After all parameters have been appended to the `Parameters` collection, we execute the `Command` object. Then we check the return value from the stored procedure, and raise an error if it is not zero:

```
'Execute the command object
objCmd.Execute

'Check the return value from the stored procedure
If objCmd.Parameters("RC") <> 0 Then
    Err.Raise 513 + vbObjectError, "InsertSystemAssignment", _
        "up_parmins_system_assignment failed"
End If
```

Next, we want to save the `System_Assignment_ID` that was inserted, and get this value from the assignment output parameter. Then, we remove our reference to the `Command` object:

```
'Save the output parameter from the command object
lngAssignmentID = objCmd.Parameters("Assignment")

'Remove references to objects
Set objCmd = Nothing
```

We want to process all of the entries in the `lngSoftwareID` array. We will execute the `up_parmins_system_software` stored procedure for each entry in the `lngSoftwareID` array.

We loop through the array using the `LBound` and `UBound` functions. The `LBound` function returns the lowest subscript in the array and the `UBound` function returns the highest subscript in the array:

```
'Process all software titles selected
For intIndex = LBound(lngSoftwareID) To UBound(lngSoftwareID)
```

The first thing we do in this loop is to set a reference to the `Command` object and then set the `Command` object's properties. At the end of the loop we remove our reference to the `Command` object.

Why do we set and remove a reference to the `Command` object each time we perform the loop? The reason is to clear all properties of the `Command` object and the `Parameters` collection. This will clear the previous return value from the `Parameters` collection.

```
'Set a reference to the command object
Set objCmd = New ADODB.Command

'Set the command object properties
Set objCmd.ActiveConnection = objConn
objCmd.CommandText = "up_parmins_system_software"
objCmd.CommandType = adCmdStoredProc
```

We append all of the parameters to the `Parameters` collection. Notice the last parameter being appended. We use the value in the `lngSoftwareID` array and use the `intIndex` variable, which we are using as the index in the array:

```
'Create and append the parameters to the parameters collection
objCmd.Parameters.Append objCmd.CreateParameter("RC", _
    adInteger, adParamReturnValue)
objCmd.Parameters.Append objCmd.CreateParameter("AssignedSystem", _
    adInteger, adParamInput, , lngAssignmentID)
objCmd.Parameters.Append objCmd.CreateParameter("Software", _
    adInteger, adParamInput, , lngSoftwareID(intIndex))
```

After all parameters have been appended to the `Parameters` collection, we execute the `Command` object. Then we check the return value from the stored procedure, and raise an error if it is not zero:

```
'Execute the command object
objCmd.Execute

'Check the return value from the stored procedure
If objCmd.Parameters("RC") <> 0 Then
   Err.Raise 513 + vbObjectError, "InsertSystemAssignment", _
      "up_parmins_system_software failed"
End If
```

We remove our reference to the `Command` object, and then continue the loop:

```
'Remove references to objects
Set objCmd = Nothing

Next
```

After we have processed all items in the `lngSoftwareID` array, we set the return code for this function and then exit the function:

```
'Set the return code
InsertSystemAssignment = 0

'Exit function
Exit Function
```

The penultimate line of our error handling code is new, and is specific to this function. Here, we are using the `Connection` object to execute the `up_parmdel_failed_system_assignment` stored procedure. This stored procedure will clean up any data that was inserted in the `System_Software_Relationship_T` and `System_Assignment_T` tables:

```
InsertSystemAssignment_Err:
   'Enumerate ADO errors
   strMessage = EnumerateErrors(objConn)
   'Append any VB errors
   strMessage = strMessage & Err.Number & " : " & Err.Description
   'Clean up database
   objConn.Execute "up_parmdel_failed_system_assignment (" & lngSystemID & ")"
   'Return to the caller with a RC of 1
   InsertSystemAssignment = 1
End Function
```

We want to switch back to the main form (`frmMain`) to insert the last little bit of code required for this exercise. We need to add some code to the `mnuFileNewSystemAssignment_Click` procedure. This procedure is executed when you click on the **System Assignment** submenu item, and will clear the fields on the **System Assignment** tab.

The first thing that we do in this procedure is to declare our local variables. Then we clear the combo boxes by setting their `ListIndex` property to –1, and clear the text box by setting its `Text` property to `Empty`:

```
Private Sub mnuFileNewSystemAssignment_Click()
   'Declare variables
   Dim intIndex As Integer

   'Clear the fields on the System Assignment tab
   cboEmployee.ListIndex = -1
   cboSystem.ListIndex = -1
   txtSystemSerialNumber.Text = Empty
```

We need to loop through the `lstInstalledSoftware` list and uncheck all items in the list. We do this by setting the `Selected` property to `False`:

```
   'Uncheck all software
   For intIndex = 0 To lstInstalledSoftware.ListCount - 1
      lstInstalledSoftware.Selected(intIndex) = False
   Next
End Sub
```

If the user clicks on **System Assignment** in the drop-down menu from the **New** button on the toolbar, we want to execute the `mnuFileNewSystemAssignment_Click` procedure. To that end, we need to modify the `Toolbar1_ButtonMenuClick` procedure, as shown in the next code fragment:

```
   Case "btnNewSoftware"
       Call mnuFileNewSoftware_Click
   Case "btnNewSystemAssignment"
       Call mnuFileNewSystemAssignment_Click
```

399

Summary

This chapter has expanded your knowledge of stored procedures by showing how you can build powerful and flexible stored procedures, incorporating conditional processing logic and using variables. We have also seen how we can process multiple statements in a single stored procedure, such as selecting and inserting data all in one stored procedure.

We have also covered error handling, and have shown you how to check for errors, as well as how to raise your own errors should an error occur. The errors that you raise in a stored procedure are passed back to the calling program from SQL Server to ADO and then finally back to your program.

We have also seen how you can use the RETURN statement to halt processing after an error occurs, and to return a return value other than zero.

All in all, our stored procedures are becoming more sophisticated, and at the same time are becoming more complex.
To summarize, you should know how to:

❑ Declare and use local variables

❑ Use conditional processing to control the flow of logic

❑ Check for errors and raise your own errors

❑ Write complex stored procedures that include multiple SQL statements

In the next chapter we will implement functionality in our Hardware Tracking application to *update* the existing data. The chapter will introduce new concepts in stored procedure processing, such as transactions. We will also show you how you could implement data validation in your stored procedures, as opposed to having the data validated in your business component.

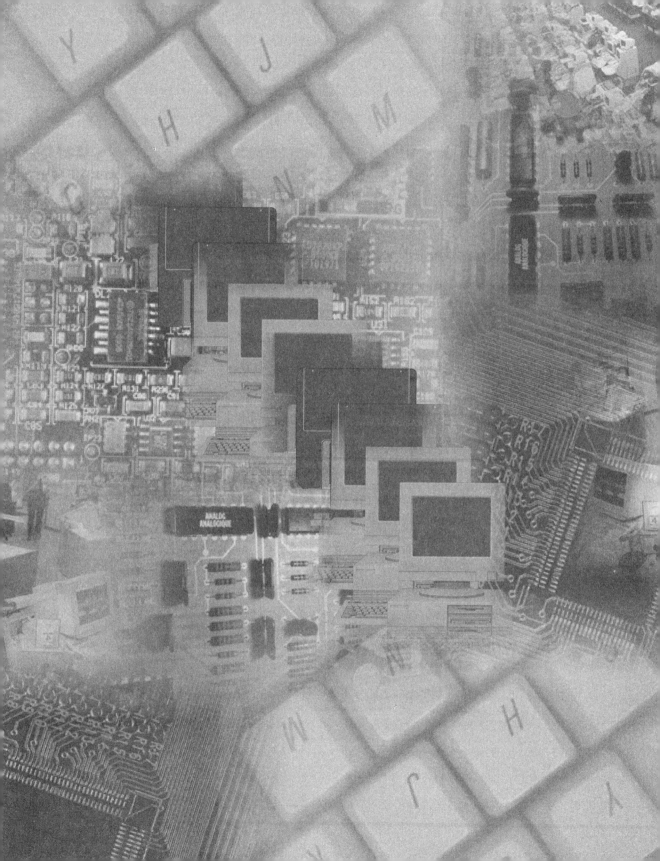

Updating Data

In the last chapter we saw how we could use local variables and conditional processing to control the flow of logic in a stored procedure. We also saw how we could use error handling to check for errors and to raise our own errors. All of these features help to make our stored procedures more sophisticated and robust. This chapter expands on that knowledge and introduces new concepts, more T-SQL statements, and further functions that will aid you in writing more sophisticated stored procedures.

Data integrity should be the main concern while writing a stored procedure that inserts, updates, or deletes data. We want to ensure that while our stored procedure executes we maintain the integrity of the data in our database. To that end, in this chapter we will introduce transactions, single units of work consisting of multiple SQL statements, and show you how to implement them in your stored procedures.

Along with data integrity is data validation. We want to ensure that the data we are inserting into our tables is valid, and that we have all of the data before attempting to run our stored procedure. To that end, this chapter will show you how you can perform data validation in your stored procedures.

As we write stored procedures to update data, we will implement the necessary functionality into our Hardware Tracking application to take advantage of these new stored procedures.

So, in this chapter we will:

- ❑ Examine the differences between SQL Server transactions and COM+ transactions
- ❑ Implement transactional support in a stored procedure
- ❑ Grant permissions on our stored procedures using SQL statements
- ❑ Validate data in a stored procedure
- ❑ Edit and delete stored procedures from the Query Analyzer

COM+ versus SQL Server Transactions

When we talk about **COM+** in this section, we are also referring to **MTS** (Microsoft Transaction Server) for the benefit of those readers who are still running on Windows NT operating systems. COM+ is a replacement for MTS, and provides many more features than were previously available. COM+ is actually a more robust service than MTS and is built into the Windows 2000 operating system. Because COM+ is built into the operating system, it is only available in the Windows 2000 environment. Operating systems prior to Windows 2000 must still use MTS.

Basically, COM+ is a service that extends the Component Object Model (COM) and provides transactional support for your components. COM+ extends COM by providing a single interface that can be used by any language. COM+ can be referenced in your Visual Basic business server components and allows you to implement transactional support that ensures the data integrity of your database.

Transactional support can be implemented in your business server component in one of two ways. If you are writing a new component, you can set a reference to COM+ and implement code to handle transactions. New and existing components that do not specifically implement transactions can be set up in COM+ using the Component Services console, and transactional support can be set through the Properties dialog for the installed component.

Basically, what COM+ provides is a method to ensure data atomicity, which means that either the entire transaction completes or none of it completes. Atomicity is explained in detail shortly.

The following diagram shows how your VB component fits into the picture when using COM+. Your component actually runs inside the confines of COM+, thus allowing you to take advantage of its services.

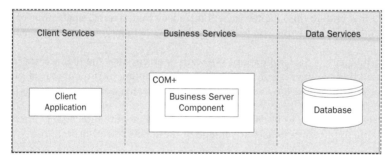

So what does all this mean? Simply put, you can execute a method in a component running in COM+ and should that method fail, all database transactions will automatically be backed out. If the method succeeds, then all database transactions are committed.

SQL Server Transactions

SQL Server provides a similar method that we can implement directly in our stored procedures – called **transactions**. A transaction is single logical unit of work, and can consist of one or more SQL statements that modify data in our tables. When a transaction is committed, all data modified since the beginning of the transaction is committed. If a transaction is rolled back, then all changes made since beginning the transaction are undone.

A logical unit of work must exhibit four properties, known as **ACID** (atomicity, consistency, isolation, and durability).

Atomicity is a term used to ensure that all transactions are completed as a group. That is, if you insert, update, or delete data in one table and move on to insert, update, or delete data in another table, and that function fails, then the entire transaction is backed out. In other words, the changes to the first table are not committed to the database. This helps to ensure the integrity of your data. SQL Server provides transactional support that provides atomicity.

> *Consistency is when a transaction completes and leaves the data in a consistent state such as completing inserts to multiple tables. **Isolation** is when a transaction isolates the modifications made from other transactions. **Durability** is when the changes made by a transaction are made a permanent part of the system when the transaction completes.*

So which do we use, SQL Server transactions or COM+? There is no standard or easy answer to this question. COM+ provides many more benefits than have been discussed here and should be considered the logical choice if you want your application to scale in an n-tier environment. If you are running a small application where your business server component either runs on the client or on a small server then SQL Server can be used. Since this book is about SQL Server, we will discuss and use SQL Server transactions.

Using SQL Server Transactions

In order to use transactions in our stored procedures, we must explicitly start and end each transaction. The BEGIN TRANSACTION T-SQL statement, like most other T-SQL statements, has a fairly complex syntax; therefore we will show only the basics here:

```
BEGIN TRANSACTION transaction-name
```

The `transaction-name` argument is the name assigned to the transaction. This name can be up to 128 characters and follows the rules for identifiers. However, SQL Server only uses the first 32 characters of a transaction name.

To commit a transaction that has successfully executed you need to specify the COMMIT TRANSACTION statement. This statement is one of the few T-SQL statements with a simple syntax, and is shown next:

```
COMMIT TRANSACTION transaction-name
```

The `transaction-name` argument is the name of the transaction that was used in the BEGIN TRANSACTION statement.

> **Once a transaction has been committed, all changes made to the database are final. The only way to recover from it is to use the transaction log for your database and perform a backward recovery. This topic is beyond the scope of this book.**

Should your code fail or receive an error message, you need to specify the ROLLBACK TRANSACTION T-SQL statement. This statement will undo all changes to your database since the transaction was started. This T-SQL statement also has a fairly complex syntax, so again we will only show the basic syntax here:

```
ROLLBACK TRANSACTION transaction-name
```

The *transaction-name* argument is the name of the transaction that was used in the BEGIN TRANSACTION statement.

> **You can only roll back a transaction that has not been committed. Therefore, you need to ensure that your ROLLBACK TRANSACTION statements come before your COMMIT TRANSACTION statement.**

Let's take a look at a simple query that uses transactions. In this query we define the local variable @CD_Type and then set its value. Next, we begin a transaction named Insert_CD and then proceed to insert the new CD type:

```
DECLARE @CD_Type CHAR(4)
SET @CD_Type = 'CDR'
--
-- Begin the transaction
--
BEGIN TRANSACTION Insert_CD

INSERT INTO CD_T
      (CD_Type_CH, Last_Update_DT)
      VALUES(@CD_Type, GETDATE())
```

Then we check for errors, and if one occurred we raise an error and roll back the transaction, specifying the transaction name. If everything was successful, we commit the transaction, again specifying the transaction name:

```
--
-- Check for errors
--
IF @@ERROR > 0
      BEGIN
      RAISERROR('Insert of CD failed',16,1)
      ROLLBACK TRANSACTION Insert_CD
      RETURN 99
      END
--
-- Commit the transaction
--
COMMIT TRANSACTION Insert_CD
```

As you can see from this simple example, using transactions is easy and helps to ensure data integrity in our database. The stored procedures that we write in this chapter will use transactions. This is especially important where we update more than one table in a single stored procedure.

Try It Out – Employee Update Stored Procedure

On the Employee tab of our hardware tracking application we have employee and location data. When we wrote the INSERT stored procedure to insert a new employee, we inserted data into both tables (Employee_T and Location_T) using the same stored procedure. The update stored procedure that we are about to write will also perform the same type of processing, as we will update the location and employee using the same stored procedure. We will also introduce a new T-SQL statement to grant execute permission on this stored procedure to the hardware users role.

To create this stored procedure:

1. Start the Query Analyzer, if it is not already running, and log in.

2. Enter the following stored procedure:

```
CREATE PROCEDURE dbo.up_parmupd_employee
    @Employee_ID          INT,
    @First_Name_VC        VARCHAR(15),
    @Last_Name_VC         VARCHAR(15),
    @Phone_Number_VC      VARCHAR(20),
    @Location_ID          INT,
    @Location_VC          VARCHAR(30) AS


-- *********************************************************************
-- Begin Transaction
-- *********************************************************************
BEGIN TRANSACTION Update_Employee


-- *********************************************************************
-- Update the location
-- *********************************************************************
UPDATE Location_T
    SET Location_Name_VC = @Location_VC,
    Last_Update_DT = GETDATE()
    WHERE Location_ID = @Location_ID
--
-- Check for errors
--
IF @@ERROR > 0
    BEGIN
    RAISERROR('Update of location failed',16,1)
    ROLLBACK TRANSACTION Update_Employee
    RETURN 99
    END


-- *********************************************************************
-- Update the employee
-- *********************************************************************
UPDATE Employee_T
    SET Location_ID = @Location_ID,
    First_Name_VC = @First_Name_VC,
    Last_Name_VC = @Last_Name_VC,
    Phone_Number_VC = @Phone_Number_VC,
```

```
        Last_Update_DT = GETDATE()
        WHERE Employee_ID = @Employee_ID
--
-- Check for errors
--
IF @@ERROR > 0
    BEGIN
    RAISERROR('Update of employee failed',16,1)
    ROLLBACK TRANSACTION Update_Employee
    RETURN 99
    END


-- ***********************************************************************
-- Commit Transaction
-- ***********************************************************************
COMMIT TRANSACTION Update_Employee


--
-- Return to the caller
--
RETURN 0

GO

GRANT EXECUTE ON up_parmupd_employee TO [Hardware Users]
```

3. Parse the code for errors by clicking on the **Parse Query** icon on the toolbar.

4. Create this stored procedure by clicking on the **Execute Query** icon on the toolbar.

We are not going to use the Enterprise Manager to grant permissions to this stored procedure as it has been done in the last line of code.

How It Works – Employee Update Stored Procedure

In order to update the employee and location data, we need not only the data to be used in the update, but we also need the primary key to the tables. This allows us to perform the update on the exact row of data that represents the employee and location. To that end, this stored procedure has the same parameters that its insert counterpart had, but in addition it also has the @Employee_ID and @Location_ID parameters:

```
CREATE PROCEDURE dbo.up_parmupd_employee
    @Employee_ID            INT,
    @First_Name_VC          VARCHAR(15),
    @Last_Name_VC           VARCHAR(15),
    @Phone_Number_VC        VARCHAR(20),
    @Location_ID            INT,
    @Location_VC            VARCHAR(30) AS
```

Because we are updating multiple tables, it becomes even more important to use transactions to ensure data integrity. Here we begin a transaction and have specified a transaction name of Update_Employee:

```
-- ****************************************************************************
-- Begin Transaction
-- ****************************************************************************
BEGIN TRANSACTION Update_Employee
```

We want to update the location name and are using a simple UPDATE statement to do this. We specify the UPDATE statement followed by the table name to be updated. Then we specify the SET keyword followed by the column name to be updated. We set the value in the column to the value in the input parameter. The next column to be updated, Last_Update_DT, is not preceded by the SET keyword; only the first column is. The WHERE clause specifies the exact row of data that should be updated, as indicated by the @Location_ID input parameter:

```
-- ****************************************************************************
-- Update the location
-- ****************************************************************************
UPDATE Location_T
    SET Location_Name_VC = @Location_VC,
    Last_Update_DT = GETDATE()
    WHERE Location_ID = @Location_ID
```

After the UPDATE statement we check for errors. If the @@ERROR function contains an error number that is not equal to zero, we raise an error that will be passed back to the caller. Then we roll back the transaction and return to the caller with a return value of 99:

```
-- Check for errors
--
IF @@ERROR > 0
    BEGIN
    RAISERROR('Update of location failed',16,1)
    ROLLBACK TRANSACTION Update_Employee
    RETURN 99
    END
```

We want to update the employee next and have specified another UPDATE statement. This time the UPDATE statement contains multiple columns that are being updated. Again we have specified the WHERE clause to limit the update to the row that contains the employee to be updated:

```
-- ****************************************************************************
-- Update the employee
-- ****************************************************************************
UPDATE Employee_T
    SET Location_ID = @Location_ID,
    First_Name_VC = @First_Name_VC,
    Last_Name_VC = @Last_Name_VC,
    Phone_Number_VC = @Phone_Number_VC,
    Last_Update_DT = GETDATE()
    WHERE Employee_ID = @Employee_ID
```

Again we check for errors immediately following the UPDATE statement. If an error has occurred we execute the same statements as earlier and specify that the transaction should be rolled back. This time, however, there was an update applied to the Location_T table. This update will be rolled back and then we will return to the caller with a return value of 99:

409

```
-- Check for errors
--
IF @@ERROR > 0
    BEGIN
        RAISERROR('Update of employee failed',16,1)
        ROLLBACK TRANSACTION Update_Employee
        RETURN 99
    END
```

If all went well, we want to commit the transaction so that all changes made in this stored procedure are made a permanent part of the database. Here we have specified the COMMIT TRANSACTION statement followed by the transaction name. Then we return to the caller with a return value of zero:

```
-- **********************************************************************
-- Commit Transaction
-- **********************************************************************
COMMIT TRANSACTION Update_Employee


--
-- Return to the caller
--
RETURN 0
```

The GO command is not a T-SQL statement; it is a command recognized by the Query Analyzer to execute a batch of SQL statements. Nothing further is processed until all of the preceding SQL statements have been executed. We specify the GO command so the stored procedure will be created before the next SQL statement is executed. If we did not specify the GO command, the Query Analyzer would execute all statements as one batch. We would get an error that the stored procedure did not exist, and we would be unable to grant permissions on it.

The GRANT T-SQL statement grants various permissions on different database objects to users and roles. The GRANT statement that is shown in the next code fragment grants EXECUTE permissions on the stored procedure that we just created, to the hardware users role. The role name has been enclosed in square brackets because it contains spaces:

```
GO

GRANT EXECUTE ON up_parmupd_employee TO [Hardware Users]
```

After having created this stored procedure in the Query Analyzer, you can verify the permissions on this stored procedure. In the Enterprise Manager right-click on this stored procedure, choose **All Tasks** and then **Manage Permissions** from the context menu. You will see that the hardware users role already has EXECUTE permissions to this stored procedure because we granted this role permission through code.

Granting Permissions Through Code

The basic syntax of the GRANT statement is shown in the next code fragment:

```
GRANT permissions ON object TO account
```

In the syntax of this statement, the *permissions* argument refers to the appropriate permissions for the object specified in the *object* argument. Some examples of the different permissions include SELECT, INSERT, UPDATE, DELETE, and EXECUTE.

The *object* argument refers to a valid object in your database such as a column, table, view, or stored procedure.

The *account* argument refers to a valid user or role in your database.

Try It Out – Process the Employee Update Stored Procedure

Now that we have built a stored procedure to update employee and location data, we need to implement the functionality in our Hardware Tracking application to execute this stored procedure. We will use the same project from the last chapter and expand on the functionality already in it.

1. So, to continue, work through the following *How It Works* section, entering the code as you go.

2. At this point you'll want to save your project before beginning testing. Run your program and log in. Choose an employee to update on the **Employee** tab, make any changes necessary, and then click the **Update** button.

3. The updates are applied and the combo boxes on this tab are reloaded. Choose the employee who was updated to verify the updates. I chose to update my personal details, and updated the phone number and the location.

When I added the location I added it all in upper case letters. Now the location contains both upper and lower case letters. This is because when the Update button is clicked, the stored procedure is called and this reloads the Location combo box with values from the database. In this case the value in the database is Home Office and not HOME OFFICE.

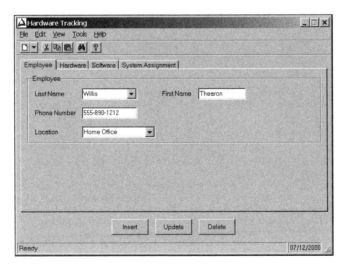

How It Works – Process the Employee Update Stored Procedure

In this exercise we will add a new class module to our project in which we will code all of our update functions. This class will handle all of the updates for our project. We will also be adding code to the Update button on the main form to update the employee information on the Employee tab. So, let's get on with it.

Open the HardwareTracking.vbp project and add a new class module to the project. Set its Name property to clsUpdateData. In the last chapter we wrote the EnumerateErrors function in the insert data class (clsInsertData) to enumerate any and all errors from the Errors collection. That seemed to work pretty well for us, so let's use that same function in this class.

Instead of duplicating code, let's modify the EnumerateErrors function in the insert data class (clsInsertData). All we want to do here is change the function from Private to Public as shown in the following code:

```
Public Function EnumerateErrors( _
    ByRef objConn As ADODB.Connection) As String
```

This will cause the insert data class to expose this function as a public method that can be executed by anyone.

Let's code a function in the update data class (clsUpdateData) to update the employee by executing the up_parmupd_employee stored procedure. This function has been modeled upon the InsertEmployee function and has the extra parameters needed to support updating an employee.

As you can see from the parameters in this function, we have added the lngEmployeeID and lngLocationID parameters so we know which row of data needs to be updated in the Employee_T and Location_T tables respectively:

```
Public Function UpdateEmployee( _
    ByRef objConn As ADODB.Connection, _
    ByVal lngEmployeeID As Long, _
    ByVal strFirstName As String, _
    ByVal strLastName As String, _
    ByVal strPhoneNumber As String, _
    ByVal lngLocationID As Long, _
    ByVal strLocation As String, _
    ByRef strMessage As String) As Long
```

Next we set up our error handling and declare our local variables and objects. Then we set the default values for our variables:

```
'Setup error handling
On Error GoTo UpdateEmployee_Err

'Declare local variables and objects
Dim blnValidated As Boolean
Dim objCmd As ADODB.Command

'Set default values
blnValidated = True
```

Even though some data already exists, we still need to validate the data coming into this stored procedure. It is the job of this class to execute the stored procedures that update data in the database, and this class needs to validate all data before passing it on to the stored procedures.

With that said, we perform the same validation routines as we did in the `InsertEmployee` function. To save space here we have listed only the first validation. The rest of the validations are listed in the code available in the download, but have been omitted here. Refer to the `InsertEmployee` function for the appropriate data validation routines and cut and paste them into this function:

```
'Validate First Name
If RTrim(Len(strFirstName)) = 0 Then
    strMessage = "First Name is zero length" & vbCrLf & vbCrLf
    blnValidated = False
End If
If RTrim(Len(strFirstName)) > 15 Then
    strMessage = "First Name is greater than 15 characters" & _
        vbCrLf & vbCrLf
    blnValidated = False
End If
```

After we have performed all of the data validations, we check the validation variable, `blnValidated`. If it is `False`, then we raise an error and are thrown into our error handling code at the bottom of this procedure:

```
'Check validation variable
If Not blnValidated Then
    Err.Raise 513 + vbObjectError, "UpdateEmployee", _
        "Data validation failed"
End If
```

We set a reference to the `Command` object and then set the `Command` object's properties. This code is no different from that which was demonstrated in the last chapter.

```
'Set a reference to the command object
Set objCmd = New ADODB.Command

'Set the command object properties
Set objCmd.ActiveConnection = objConn
objCmd.CommandText = "up_parmupd_employee"
objCmd.CommandType = adCmdStoredProc
```

We need to create and append the various parameters to the `Parameters` collection. Since our stored procedure returns a return value, we append the parameter for the return value first. Then we append the rest of the parameters to the `Parameters` collection in the same order as they are listed in our `up_parmupd_employee` stored procedure:

```
'Create and append the parameters to the parameters collection
objCmd.Parameters.Append objCmd.CreateParameter("RC", _
    adInteger, adParamReturnValue)
objCmd.Parameters.Append objCmd.CreateParameter("EmployeeID", _
    adInteger, adParamInput, , lngEmployeeID)
objCmd.Parameters.Append objCmd.CreateParameter("FirstName", _
    adVarChar, adParamInput, 15, strFirstName)
```

```
objCmd.Parameters.Append objCmd.CreateParameter("LastName", _
    adVarChar, adParamInput, 15, strLastName)
objCmd.Parameters.Append objCmd.CreateParameter("PhoneNumber", _
    adVarChar, adParamInput, 20, strPhoneNumber)
objCmd.Parameters.Append objCmd.CreateParameter("LocationID", _
    adInteger, adParamInput, , lngLocationID)
objCmd.Parameters.Append objCmd.CreateParameter("Location", _
    adVarChar, adParamInput, 30, strLocation)
```

After the last parameter has been appended to the `Parameters` collection, we execute the `Command` object.

Next we check the return value from the stored procedure in the `Parameters` collection and raise an error if it is not equal to zero:

```
'Execute the command object
objCmd.Execute

'Check the return value from the stored procedure
If objCmd.Parameters("RC") <> 0 Then
    Err.Raise 513 + vbObjectError, "UpdateEmployee", _
        "up_parmupd_employee failed"
End If
```

We remove our reference to the `Command` object to free up system resources and then set the return code for this function. Then we exit this function, returning to the caller:

```
'Remove references to objects
Set objCmd = Nothing

'Set the return code
UpdateEmployee = 0

'Exit function
Exit Function
```

Our error handling code is slightly different from that of the last chapter. Instead of executing the `EnumerateErrors` function as a local function, we must execute this function in the insert data class. To that end, we must declare an object and set a reference to that class. We have done this in one step by declaring the `objErrors` object and setting it to the `clsInsertData` class.

Then we are able to execute the `EnumerateErrors` function in that class, passing it the `Connection` object that was passed to this function. After control is returned from that function, we set the `objErrors` object to `Nothing` to free up resources.

The rest of the error handling code is the same code that we used in the last chapter:

```
UpdateEmployee_Err:
    'Enumerate ADO errors
    Dim objErrors As New clsInsertData
    strMessage = objErrors.EnumerateErrors(objConn)
    Set objErrors = Nothing
```

```
      'Append any VB errors
      strMessage = strMessage & Err.Number & " : " & Err.Description
      'Return to the caller with a RC of 1
      UpdateEmployee = 1
   End Function
```

Switching to the code in our main form (frmMain) we need to declare an object for the update data class. Modify the code in the general declarations section of the form, as shown in the following code fragment:

```
'Declare objects
Dim objData As clsSelectData
Dim objInsert As clsInsertData
Dim objUpdate As clsUpdateData
Dim objRSData As ADODB.Recordset
```

In order to update the location, we need to keep track of the location ID of the location that is or will be selected in the Location combo box. To that end we need to add another variable to the general declarations section of the form, as shown in the following code:

```
'Declare variables
Dim arrSerialNumber() As String
Dim lngLocationID As Long
```

When a user clicks on a location in the Location combo box, we want to save the location ID of that location. There are two reasons for this. Firstly, the user could select a new location which we would want to assign to the employee displayed. Secondly, we could update the text for the current location and we need the location ID to pass to the stored procedure created previously. After we change the text in the Location combo box the ListIndex property is set to −1. We therefore have no idea of the location ID of the location, which is why we need to save it.

Add the following code to the cboLocation_Click procedure. The first thing we do in this procedure is to check the ListIndex property of the Location combo box. If it is equal to −1 we want to exit the procedure and perform no further processing here:

```
   Private Sub cboLocation_Click()
      'Check the ListIndex property
      If cboLocation.ListIndex = -1 Then
         Exit Sub
      End If
```

If the ListIndex property of the Location combo box is not equal to −1 then we want to save the location ID contained in the ItemData property for the currently selected location:

```
      'Save the location id for the location selected
      lngLocationID = cboLocation.ItemData(cboLocation.ListIndex)
   End Sub
```

When the user clicks on the Update button, the cmdUpdate_Click procedure is executed. This is the procedure that we want to add code to next. Following the same principle as the cmdInsert_Click procedure, we will use a Select Case statement to determine which tab we are on and what data should be processed.

The first thing that we have done here is to set up our error handling. Then we display a message in the status bar that we are processing an update:

```
Private Sub cmdUpdate_Click()
    'Setup error handling
    On Error GoTo cmdUpdate_Click_Err

    'Display status
    StatusBar1.Panels("pnlStatus").Text = "Processing Update"
```

We declare our local variables next and set a reference to the update data class. Then we proceed to process the Select Case statement using the Tab property of the tabData tab control:

```
    'Declare local variables
    Dim lngRC As Long, strMessage As String

    'Set a reference to the update data class
    Set objUpdate = New clsUpdateData

    'Process tab data
    Select Case tabData.Tab

        Case 0  'Employee
```

We call the UpdateEmployee function passing it the appropriate parameters. Notice that for the lngEmployeeID parameter we have used the actual Employee_ID field from the objRSData recordset. Remember that this recordset is open and points to the employee that is currently displayed in the **Employee** tab.

After control is returned from the UpdateEmployee function we check the return code and if it is not equal to zero, we raise an error:

```
            'Update the employee
            lngRC = objUpdate.UpdateEmployee(g_objConn, _
                objRSData!Employee_ID, _
                txtFirstName.Text, _
                cboLastName.Text, _
                txtPhoneNumber.Text, _
                lngLocationID, _
                cboLocation.Text, _
                strMessage)

            'Ensure we were successful
            If lngRC <> 0 Then
                Err.Raise 513 + vbObjectError, "cmdUpdate_Click", _
                    "Call to UpdateEmployee failed"
            End If
```

We call the LoadEmployees procedure next to reload the combo boxes on the **Employee** tab. This ensures that the combo boxes will reflect the updates that we have just applied.

Then we call the tabData_Click procedure, passing it 0 as the previous tab parameter. This causes the first employee listed in the **Last Name** combo box to be displayed.

The rest of the Case statements have been added with comments to let you know which tab they represent:

```
        'Reload Employees
        Call LoadEmployees

        'Re-initialize the tab control so the opened RS is reloaded
        'to reflect the employee updates
        Call tabData_Click(0)

    Case 1  'Hardware

    Case 2  'Software

    Case 3  'System Assignment

End Select
```

After all processing has been completed, we set the objUpdate object to Nothing and then display a ready message in the status bar before exiting the procedure:

```
    'Remove reference to object
    Set objUpdate = Nothing

    'Display status
    StatusBar1.Panels("pnlStatus").Text = "Ready"

    'Exit sub
    Exit Sub
```

The error handling for this procedure simply displays a message box and uses the strMessage variable as the message to be displayed:

```
  cmdUpdate_Click_Err:
     'Display errors from the function call
     MsgBox strMessage, vbCritical + vbOKOnly, "Hardware Tracking"
  End Sub
```

The **Hardware** tab on the main form displays hardware data from the Hardware_T table and from the CD_T table. However, when we inserted data into the Hardware_T table we only inserted the primary key (CD_ID) from the CD_T table. We did not perform any inserts into the CD_T table itself.

Given that, our stored procedure for updating hardware will not insert data into the CD_T table. We will only be updating one table, the Hardware_T table. Since we are only updating one table, there is no need to use transactions in our stored procedure, as we would have nothing to roll back should an error occur and the insert fail.

Try It Out – Hardware Update Stored Procedure

The stored procedure that we will create here will be a simple update stored procedure. To create this procedure:

1. Open a new query window in the Query Analyzer, by clicking on the New Query icon on the toolbar or clear the current query window by clicking on the Clear Query Window icon on the toolbar.

2. Enter the following stored procedure:

```
CREATE PROCEDURE dbo.up_parmupd_hardware
        @Hardware_ID            INT,
        @Manufacturer_VC        VARCHAR(30),
        @Model_VC               VARCHAR(30),
        @Processor_Speed_VC     VARCHAR(20),
        @Memory_VC              VARCHAR(10),
        @HardDrive_VC           VARCHAR(15),
        @Sound_Card_VC          VARCHAR(30),
        @Speakers_VC            VARCHAR(30),
        @Video_Card_VC          VARCHAR(30),
        @Monitor_VC             VARCHAR(30),
        @Serial_Number_VC       VARCHAR(30),
        @Lease_Expiration_DT    VARCHAR(22),
        @CD_ID          INT     AS


-- ****************************************************************
-- Update the hardware
-- ****************************************************************
UPDATE Hardware_T
    SET Manufacturer_VC = @Manufacturer_VC,
    Model_VC = @Model_VC,
    Processor_Speed_VC = @Processor_Speed_VC,
    Memory_VC = @Memory_VC,
    HardDrive_VC = @HardDrive_VC,
    Sound_Card_VC = @Sound_Card_VC,
    Speakers_VC = @Speakers_VC,
    Video_Card_VC = @Video_Card_VC,
    Monitor_VC = @Monitor_VC,
    Serial_Number_VC = @Serial_Number_VC,
    Lease_Expiration_DT = @Lease_Expiration_DT,
    CD_ID = @CD_ID,
    Last_Update_DT = GETDATE()
    WHERE Hardware_ID = @Hardware_ID


--
-- Check for errors
--
IF @@ERROR > 0
    BEGIN
    RAISERROR('Update of hardware failed',16,1)
    RETURN 99
    END
```

```
--
-- Return to the caller
--
RETURN 0

GO

GRANT EXECUTE ON up_parmupd_hardware TO [Hardware Users]
```

3. Parse the code for errors by clicking on the **Parse Query** icon on the toolbar.

4. Create the stored procedure by clicking on the **Execute Query** icon on the toolbar.

Again we have used the GRANT T-SQL statement to grant permissions to this stored procedure to the hardware users role, so we do not have to do this in the Enterprise Manager.

How It Works – Hardware Update Stored Procedure

This is a simple update stored procedure and all of the input parameters represent data for each of the columns in the Hardware_T table:

```
CREATE PROCEDURE dbo.up_parmupd_hardware
        @Hardware_ID                INT,
        @Manufacturer_VC            VARCHAR(30),
        @Model_VC                   VARCHAR(30),
        @Processor_Speed_VC         VARCHAR(20),
        @Memory_VC                  VARCHAR(10),
        @HardDrive_VC               VARCHAR(15),
        @Sound_Card_VC              VARCHAR(30),
        @Speakers_VC                VARCHAR(30),
        @Video_Card_VC              VARCHAR(30),
        @Monitor_VC                 VARCHAR(30),
        @Serial_Number_VC           VARCHAR(30),
        @Lease_Expiration_DT        VARCHAR(22),
        @CD_ID           INT        AS
```

The UPDATE statement specifies each column to be updated along with the appropriate input parameter. The WHERE clause limits the update to the specific row where the value in the Hardware_ID equals the value in the @Hardware_ID input parameter:

```
-- ***************************************************************************
-- Update the hardware
-- ***************************************************************************
UPDATE Hardware_T
     SET Manufacturer_VC = @Manufacturer_VC,
     Model_VC = @Model_VC,
     Processor_Speed_VC = @Processor_Speed_VC,
     Memory_VC = @Memory_VC,
     HardDrive_VC = @HardDrive_VC,
     Sound_Card_VC = @Sound_Card_VC,
     Speakers_VC = @Speakers_VC,
     Video_Card_VC = @Video_Card_VC,
     Monitor_VC = @Monitor_VC,
```

```
        Serial_Number_VC = @Serial_Number_VC,
        Lease_Expiration_DT = @Lease_Expiration_DT,
        CD_ID = @CD_ID,
        Last_Update_DT = GETDATE()
        WHERE Hardware_ID = @Hardware_ID
```

After the UPDATE statement is executed, we check for errors by checking the error number in the @@ERROR function. If an error occurred, we raise an error message and return to the caller with a return value of 99:

```
    --
    -- Check for errors
    --
    IF @@ERROR > 0
        BEGIN
        RAISERROR('Update of hardware failed',16,1)
        RETURN 99
        END
```

If no errors occurred then we return to the caller with a return value of zero:

```
    --
    -- Return to the caller
    --
    RETURN 0
```

Again, we have specified the GO command to have the preceding SQL statements executed. This will create the stored procedure and then we can execute the GRANT statement to grant EXECUTE permissions on this stored procedure to the hardware users role:

```
    GO

    GRANT EXECUTE ON up_parmupd_hardware TO [Hardware Users]
```

Try It Out – Process the Hardware Update Stored Procedure

Switching to our VB code, we want to code the function that executes this stored procedure, and implement the code for the Update button on the main form to update the data on the Hardware tab.

1. To do this, enter the code as shown in the following *How It Works* section.

2. Save your project before you begin testing, then run your program and log in.

3. Click on the Hardware tab and select an entry in the cboManufacturer combo box to update and change any fields that you want, before clicking on the Update button to perform the update. The update will then be performed, the cboManufacturer combo box will be reloaded, and the first entry selected.

4. Select the entry that you updated to verify that the updates have occurred.

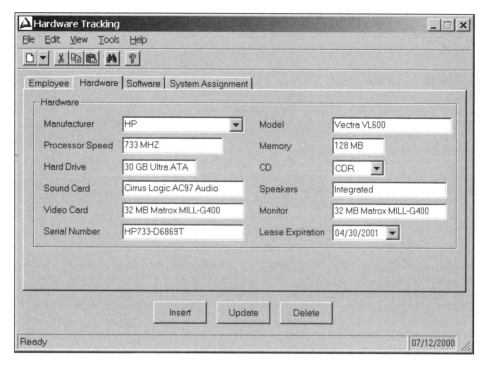

How It Works – Process the Hardware Update Stored Procedure

The `UpdateHardware` function is created in the update data class (`clsUpdateData`) and will validate all data before executing the `up_parmupd_hardware` stored procedure.

The parameters for this function list all of the data required by the stored procedure and the data and objects required by this function:

```
Public Function UpdateHardware( _
    ByRef objConn As ADODB.Connection, _
    ByVal lngHardwareID As Long, _
    ByVal strManufacturer As String, _
    ByVal strModel As String, _
    ByVal strProcessorSpeed As String, _
    ByVal strMemory As String, _
    ByVal strHardDrive As String, _
    ByVal strSoundCard As String, _
    ByVal strSpeakers As String, _
    ByVal strVideoCard As String, _
    ByVal strMonitor As String, _
    ByVal strSerialNumber As String, _
    ByVal dteLeaseExpiration As Date, _
    ByVal lngCDID As Long, _
    ByRef strMessage As String) As Long
```

Now we set up our error handling and then declare our local variables and objects. Then we set the default value for the `blnValidated` variable and proceed to validate the data.

Most of the data validation routines have been omitted here, but are included in the code download. You can copy the data validation routines from the InsertHardware function in the insert data class and paste them into your UpdateHardware function.

```
'Setup error handling
On Error GoTo UpdateHardware_Err

'Declare local variables and objects
Dim blnValidated As Boolean
Dim objCmd As ADODB.Command

'Set default values
blnValidated = True

'Validate Manufacturer
If RTrim(Len(strManufacturer)) = 0 Then
    strMessage = "Manufacturer is zero length" & vbCrLf & vbCrLf
    blnValidated = False
End If
If RTrim(Len(strManufacturer)) > 30 Then
    strMessage = "Manufacturer is greater than 30 characters" & _
    vbCrLf & vbCrLf
    blnValidated = False
End If
```

After all data validation has been performed, we check the validation variable, blnValidated, to see if it is True or False. If it is False, we raise an error and will be thrown into our error handling code at the bottom of the procedure:

```
'Check validation variable
If Not blnValidated Then
    Err.Raise 513 + vbObjectError, "UpdateHardware", _
        "Data validation failed"
End If
```

Next we set a reference to the Command object and set its properties:

```
'Set a reference to the command object
Set objCmd = New ADODB.Command

'Set the command object properties
Set objCmd.ActiveConnection = objConn
objCmd.CommandText = "up_parmupd_hardware"
objCmd.CommandType = adCmdStoredProc
```

We then proceed to create and append the required parameters to the Parameters collection in the same order as they are specified in the stored procedure. Notice that the first parameter that we have appended to the Parameters collection is for the return value from the stored procedure:

```
'Create and append the parameters to the parameters collection
objCmd.Parameters.Append objCmd.CreateParameter("RC", _
    adInteger, adParamReturnValue)
```

```
objCmd.Parameters.Append objCmd.CreateParameter("HardwareID", _
    adInteger, adParamInput, , lngHardwareID)
objCmd.Parameters.Append objCmd.CreateParameter("Manufacturer", _
    adVarChar, adParamInput, 30, strManufacturer)
objCmd.Parameters.Append objCmd.CreateParameter("Model", _
    adVarChar, adParamInput, 30, strModel)
objCmd.Parameters.Append objCmd.CreateParameter("Processor", _
    adVarChar, adParamInput, 20, strProcessorSpeed)
objCmd.Parameters.Append objCmd.CreateParameter("Memory", _
    adVarChar, adParamInput, 10, strMemory)
objCmd.Parameters.Append objCmd.CreateParameter("HardDrive", _
    adVarChar, adParamInput, 15, strHardDrive)
objCmd.Parameters.Append objCmd.CreateParameter("SoundCard", _
    adVarChar, adParamInput, 30, strSoundCard)
objCmd.Parameters.Append objCmd.CreateParameter("Speakers", _
    adVarChar, adParamInput, 30, strSpeakers)
objCmd.Parameters.Append objCmd.CreateParameter("VideoCard", _
    adVarChar, adParamInput, 30, strVideoCard)
objCmd.Parameters.Append objCmd.CreateParameter("Monitor", _
    adVarChar, adParamInput, 30, strMonitor)
objCmd.Parameters.Append objCmd.CreateParameter("SerialNumber", _
    adVarChar, adParamInput, 30, strSerialNumber)
objCmd.Parameters.Append objCmd.CreateParameter("LeaseExp", _
    adVarChar, adParamInput, 22, dteLeaseExpiration)
objCmd.Parameters.Append objCmd.CreateParameter("CDID", _
    adInteger, adParamInput, , lngCDID)
```

After all parameters have been appended to the `Parameters` collection, we execute the `Command` object. Then we check the return value from the stored procedure in the `Parameters` collection. If the return value was not zero we raise an error:

```
'Execute the command object
objCmd.Execute

'Check the return value from the stored procedure
If objCmd.Parameters("RC") <> 0 Then
    Err.Raise 513 + vbObjectError, "UpdateHardware", _
        "up_parmupd_hardware failed"
End If
```

To finish up our processing in this function, we remove our reference to the `Command` object and set the return code for this function. Then, finally, we exit the function:

```
'Remove references to objects
Set objCmd = Nothing

'Set the return code
UpdateHardware = 0

'Exit function
Exit Function
```

The error handling code is the same as the error handling code that we added to the last function we created:

```
UpdateHardware_Err:
    'Enumerate ADO errors
    Dim objErrors As New clsInsertData
    strMessage = objErrors.EnumerateErrors(objConn)
    Set objErrors = Nothing
    'Append any VB errors
    strMessage = strMessage & Err.Number & " : " & Err.Description
    'Return to the caller with a RC of 1
    UpdateHardware = 1
End Function
```

Switching to the code in our main form (frmMain) we need to modify the cmdUpdate_Click procedure to handle updating the hardware on the **Hardware** tab. Modify this procedure as shown in the next code fragment:

The first thing we do in this code is to call the UpdateHardware function that we just created. Notice that we have specified the Hardware_ID field from the open objRSData recordset for the lngHardwareID parameter.

The reason we have done this is because the Style property for the cboManufacturer combo box is set to 0 - Dropdown combo. If we update the manufacturer's name in this combo box, we lose the reference to the ItemData property which contains the hardware ID for this entry; this occurs because the ListIndex property gets set to -1. Using the Hardware_ID field from the objRSData recordset, we are able to pass the correct hardware ID value for this entry:

```
Case 1   'Hardware

    'Update the hardware
    lngRC = objUpdate.UpdateHardware(g_objConn, _
        objRSData!Hardware_ID, _
        cboManufacturer.Text, _
        txtModel.Text, _
        txtProcessorSpeed.Text, _
        txtMemory.Text, _
        txtHardDrive.Text, _
        txtSoundCard.Text, _
        txtSpeakers.Text, _
        txtVideoCard.Text, _
        txtMonitor.Text, _
        txtSerialNumber.Text, _
        dtpLeaseExpiration.Value, _
        cboCD.ItemData(cboCD.ListIndex), _
        strMessage)
```

After control is returned from the UpdateHardware function, we check the return code from this function. If it is not zero we raise an error:

```
'Ensure we were successful
If lngRC <> 0 Then
    Err.Raise 513 + vbObjectError, "cmdUpdate_Click", _
```

```
                    "Call to UpdateHardware failed"
          End If
```

If everything worked fine, we want to reload the cboManufacturer combo box on the **Hardware** tab to reflect the updates. We call the LoadHardware procedure to perform this task. Then we call the LoadSystems procedure to reload the **Systems** combo box on the **System Assignment** tab.

Finally, we call the tabData_Click procedure to select the first item in the cboManufacturer combo box. We pass a value of 1 for the previous tab parameter of the tabData_Click procedure:

```
          'Reload Hardware
          Call LoadHardware

          'Reload Systems combo box on the System Assignment tab
          Call LoadSystems

          'Re-initialize the tab control so the opened RS is reloaded
          'to reflect the hardware update
          Call tabData_Click(1)
```

Stored Procedure Data Validation

At some point you will need to perform **data validation**, not in the client or business server components, but in your stored procedure. This could be because you have to write a stored procedure that gets called from a number of different applications. You should probably not rely on those different applications to validate the data before sending it to your database; therefore, you will want to validate this data in the stored procedure. This section takes a look at what is involved in data validation in a stored procedure.

There are numerous T-SQL functions that can be used to validate numeric and string data in SQL Server. We will take a look at only a few in this section, but it should give you a good idea of the possibilities.

Let's start with a simple example where we need to validate that the value in an Integer data type falls within a certain range of numbers. We declare the variable and set its value. This would normally be an input parameter, but for demonstration purposes we are using a local variable.

In the following example we are using the BETWEEN operator to test that the value in the @Age_IN variable falls within a range of numbers. We also specify the optional NOT keyword so the results of the test are negated. This will allow us to handle only the exception where the value in the @Age_IN variable does not fall within the range. In this example, we use the PRINT statement to print a message when the test fails and when the test passes:

```
DECLARE @Age_IN INT
SET @Age_IN = 35

IF @Age_IN NOT BETWEEN 18 AND 105
     PRINT 'Age is not within the limits of 18 and 105'
ELSE
     PRINT 'Age has been validated'
```

Let's assume we have a variable that contains a numeric value and we want to ensure that the value is exactly three digits, no more and no less. We would need to check the length of the variable to ensure that it contained exactly three digits. Using the Object Browser in the Query Analyzer, you can expand the String Functions group under Common Objects and then expand the LEN function. Hover your mouse pointer over the function to get a tooltip that contains a brief description of that function.

The following figure shows how we go about coding this query to use the LEN function. After we have declared and set this variable, which is a SMALLINT data type, we check the number of digits in this variable for a length less than and greater than 3. If the variable contains less than or more than three digits, we print an error message.

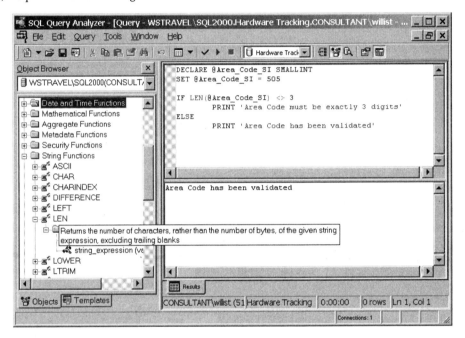

Now that we have taken a look at a couple of methods to validate numeric data types, let's look at how we can validate *string* data types. Normally we don't know what data is valid in a string variable, so the best that we can do is to check the length of the variable to ensure it is not zero. Sometimes you may have a string variable that contains codes that can be validated against a table or static text in your stored procedure.

The following example uses the LEN function to check the length of a string variable. SQL Server will automatically trim the spaces to the right of the variable, thus the following code will fail the validation:

```
DECLARE @Phone_Number_VC VARCHAR(20)
SET @Phone_Number_VC = '  '

IF LEN(@Phone_Number_VC) = 0
    PRINT 'Phone Number is empty'
ELSE
    PRINT 'Phone Number has been validated'
```

If we set the `@Phone_Number_VC` variable to a number or character followed by a space and then print the length of the variable, we will notice that the length returned is 1. This is because SQL Server has trimmed the spaces on the right side of the variable. This is done automatically to eliminate spaces in your `VarChar` columns:

```
DECLARE @Phone_Number_VC VARCHAR(20)
SET @Phone_Number_VC = '2 '

IF LEN(@Phone_Number_VC) = 0
     PRINT 'Phone Number is empty'
ELSE
     PRINT 'Phone Number has been validated'

PRINT LEN(@Phone_Number_VC)
```

If we changed the SET statement in the previous code fragment to read SET @Phone_Number_VC = ' 2 ' then we would see a length of 2 returned even though there is a space to the right of the 2 in the variable. SQL Server still trimmed the spaces on the right side of the variable.

Suppose we wanted to ensure the phone number variable was formatted correctly, by including a dash in a certain position. We could use the PATINDEX function, which will return the starting position of a pattern within a string. This function is very similar to the VB InStr function.

The pattern that you search for is a string variable or expression, and must be enclosed in percent (%) signs. Let's take a look at how we can validate that the phone number contains a dash (-) in position 4:

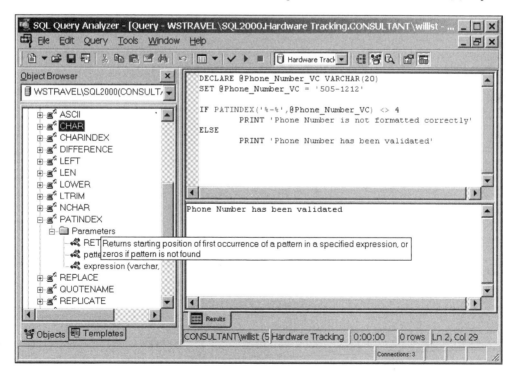

Let's expand on the previous example for a moment. Normally a phone number string (in the US) consists of a three-digit area code followed by a dash followed by a three-digit prefix followed by another dash and finally the last four digits. An example of this is shown in the next code fragment.

After we have validated that the first part of the phone number contains a dash in position 4, we need to validate the second dash in the phone number and validate that it is in the correct position.

Using the SUBSTRING function we can extract the portion of the phone number that has not been validated. The SUBSTRING function will return a portion of a string from a string expression or variable. The SUBSTRING function has the following format:

```
SUBSTRING(string-expression, start, length)
```

In this format, string-expression is a valid string expression or variable, start is the starting position in the string to start extracting, and length is the length to be extracted.

In this example we have expanded the phone number to include an area code, prefix, and number, all separated by dashes. We perform the same validation as we did earlier, to validate the area code and first dash:

```
DECLARE @Phone_Number_VC VARCHAR(20)
SET @Phone_Number_VC = '987-505-1212'

IF PATINDEX('%-%',@Phone_Number_VC) <> 4
    PRINT 'Phone Number is not formatted correctly'
ELSE
    PRINT 'Area Code has been validated'
```

Next we extract the portion of the phone number that has not been validated, using the SUBSTRING function, and pass it as the string expression in the PATINDEX function. Once we have extracted the portion of the phone number that has not been validated, LEN(@Phone_Number_VC)-4 returns the phone number minus the area code, and the dash in the phone number is once again in position 4. The value returned from the SUBSTRING function in the following code fragment is 505-1212:

```
IF PATINDEX('%-%',SUBSTRING(@Phone_Number_VC,5,LEN(@Phone_Number_VC)-4)) <> 4
    PRINT 'Phone Number is not formatted correctly'
ELSE
    PRINT 'Prefix has been validated'
```

The results returned from this validation are as shown:

```
Area Code has been validated
Prefix has been validated
```

Let's proceed by creating our next stored procedure, which validates data.

Try It Out – Software Update Stored Procedure

The stored procedure that we want to create to update the software on the Software tab of our Hardware Tracking application already exists. There are a couple of choices that we have to modify the up_parmupd_software stored procedure. We could edit the stored procedure in the Enterprise Manager as we did in the last chapter, or we could edit this stored procedure in the Query Analyzer.

However, the amount of changes that we will be making to this stored procedure does not warrant editing it. We simply want to delete it and create a new one. Since we have been demonstrating various ways to deal with stored procedures without using the Enterprise Manager in this chapter, we will continue to do so here.

1. To delete the existing up_parmupd_software stored procedure start the Query Analyzer and log in, if it is not already running.

2. Expand the Hardware Tracking database in the Object Browser.

3. Expand the Stored Procedures group and find the up_parmupd_software stored procedure.

4. Right-click on this stored procedure and choose Delete from the context menu. Notice that you could also choose Edit from the context menu if you wanted to edit this stored procedure.

5. You will be prompted with a dialog to confirm the delete, as shown in the following figure. Click the OK button to delete this stored procedure.

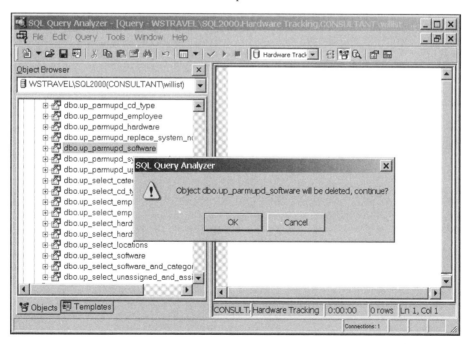

6. To create the new up_parmupd_software stored procedure open a new query window by clicking on the New Query icon on the toolbar, or clear the existing query window by clicking on the Clear Query Window icon on the toolbar.

7. Enter the following stored procedure:

```
CREATE PROCEDURE dbo.up_parmupd_software
      @Software_ID            INT,
      @Software_Title_VC      VARCHAR(30),
      @Software_Category_ID   INT AS


-- ***********************************************************************
-- Declare variables
-- ***********************************************************************
DECLARE @Validated      BIT
--
-- Set default values
--
SET @Validated = 1


-- ***********************************************************************
-- Validate data
-- ***********************************************************************
--
-- Validate Software ID
--
IF @Software_ID = 0 OR @Software_ID IS NULL

      --
      -- Set the @Validated variable to false
      --
      SET @Validated = 0
--
-- Validate Software Title
--
IF LEN(@Software_Title_VC) = 0 OR @Software_Title_VC IS NULL

      --
      -- Set the @Validated variable to false
      --
      SET @Validated = 0
--
-- Validate Software Category ID
--
IF @Software_Category_ID = 0 OR @Software_Category_ID IS NULL

      --
      -- Set the @Validated variable to false
      --
      SET @Validated = 0

-- ***********************************************************************
-- Check validation variable
-- ***********************************************************************
IF @Validated = 0
      BEGIN
      RAISERROR('Data validation of software failed',16,1)
      RETURN 99
      END
```

```
-- ************************************************************************
-- Update the software
-- ************************************************************************
UPDATE Software_T
    SET Software_Name_VC = @Software_Title_VC,
    Software_Category_ID = @Software_Category_ID,
    Last_Update_DT = GETDATE()
    WHERE Software_ID = @Software_ID
--
-- Check for errors
--
IF @@ERROR > 0
    BEGIN
    RAISERROR('Update of software failed',16,1)
    RETURN 99
    END


--
-- Return to the caller
--
RETURN 0

GO

GRANT EXECUTE ON up_parmupd_software TO [Hardware Users]
```

8. Parse the code for errors by clicking on the **Parse Query** icon on the toolbar.

9. Create this stored procedure by clicking on the **Execute Query** icon on the toolbar. You will need to refresh the Object Browser to see the stored procedure that you have just created.

How It Works – Software Update Stored Procedure

The first thing that we have done in this stored procedure is to specify the input parameters. We need the software ID to identify which row in the Software_T table should be updated and the software title to update the Software_Name_VC column. These two items have been specified as input parameters. The only thing we need for the software category is the software category ID that is used as a foreign key in the Software_T table:

```
CREATE PROCEDURE dbo.up_parmupd_software
    @Software_ID            INT,
    @Software_Title_VC      VARCHAR(30),
    @Software_Category_ID   INT AS
```

We declare our local variables next. Here we only have one, and this variable will be used as a flag to indicate whether or not the data validation has been passed. SQL Server does not provide a Boolean variable, so we use the BIT data type, which can only contain a value of 0 or 1.

We set the @Validated variable to 1 to indicate true and then proceed with the data validations:

```
-- ************************************************************************
-- Declare variables
-- ************************************************************************
```

431

```
DECLARE @Validated     BIT
--
-- Set default values
--
SET @Validated = 1
```

Notice the comments that identify each section of code in this stored procedure. Using comments is important in any language and helps to document your code.

The first validation that we are performing is to validate that the @Software_ID input parameter does not contain a value of 0 or Null. If it does, then we set the @Validated variable to false by setting it to zero:

```
-- ********************************************************************
-- Validate data
-- ********************************************************************
--
-- Validate Software ID
--
IF @Software_ID = 0 OR @Software_ID IS NULL
        --
        -- Set the @Validated variable to false
        --
        SET @Validated = 0
```

The next validation that is performed is on the @Software_Title_VC input parameter. Since this parameter is a VarChar data type we validate the length of the parameter using the LEN function and validate that this parameter is not NULL:

```
-- Validate Software Title
--
IF LEN(@Software_Title_VC) = 0 OR @Software_Title_VC IS NULL
        --
        -- Set the @Validated variable to false
        --
        SET @Validated = 0
```

The last parameter that we validate is an Integer data type. Again, we only validate that this parameter does not contain a value of 0 and is not NULL:

```
-- Validate Software Category ID
--
IF @Software_Category_ID = 0 OR @Software_Category_ID IS NULL
        --
        -- Set the @Validated variable to false
        --
        SET @Validated = 0
```

After all data validations have been performed we check our validation variable, @Validated, to see if it has a value of 0, which would indicate that the data validations failed. If they failed, we raise an error and return to the caller with a return code of 99:

```
-- ***********************************************************************
-- Check validation variable
-- ***********************************************************************
IF @Validated = 0
    BEGIN
    RAISERROR('Data validation of software failed',16,1)
    RETURN 99
    END
```

If all data validations have passed we update the `Software_T` table. Our `UPDATE` statement contains the columns to be updated and the input parameters that contain the data to be used in the update. The `WHERE` clause specifies the exact row of data to be updated:

```
-- ***********************************************************************
-- Update the software
-- ***********************************************************************
UPDATE Software_T
    SET Software_Name_VC = @Software_Title_VC,
    Software_Category_ID = @Software_Category_ID,
    Last_Update_DT = GETDATE()
    WHERE Software_ID = @Software_ID
```

After our `UPDATE` statement we check for errors by checking the value in the `@@ERROR` function. If this function does not return zero, we raise an error and return to the caller with a return value of 99:

```
-- Check for errors
--
IF @@ERROR > 0
    BEGIN
    RAISERROR('Update of software failed',16,1)
    RETURN 99
    END
```

If all went well and no errors were encountered, we return to the caller with a return value of zero:

```
-- Return to the caller
--
RETURN 0
```

Again we specify the `GO` command so the Query Analyzer executes the previous code before proceeding any further. This ensures our stored procedure gets created before we try to grant permissions on it.

Next we grant `EXECUTE` permissions on the `up_parmupd_software` stored procedure to the hardware users role:

```
GO

GRANT EXECUTE ON up_parmupd_software TO [Hardware Users]
```

433

Try It Out – Process the Software Update Stored Procedure

Switching to our VB code, we want to add functionality to our project to update the fields on the **Software** tab on the main form. This involves creating the `UpdateSoftware` function in the update data class (`clsUpdateData`) and adding code to the **Update** button on the main form. The `UpdateSoftware` function will execute the `up_parmupd_software` stored procedure that we just created.

1. The next step is to work through the following *How It Works* section, entering the VB code as you go.

2. At this point you can save your project and you will be ready for testing. Run your program and log in and then click on the **Software** tab.

3. Select a software title to change, then change the name of the software and/or select a new category for this software title.

4. Click on the **Update** button to have the update applied. Then select the changed software title from the **Software Title** combo box.

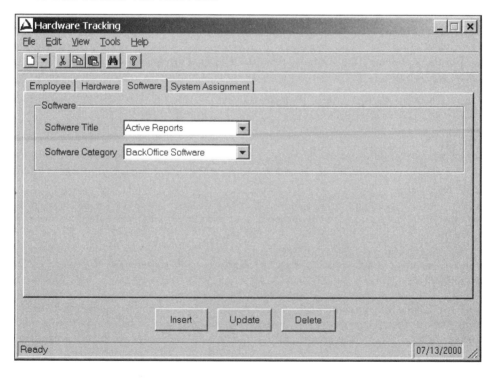

How It Works – Process Software Update Stored Procedure

We define all of the parameters in this function, which include the parameters that are input parameters to our stored procedure. We also define a parameter for the `Connection` object and one for the message string that will be used to return any error messages encountered in this function:

```
Public Function UpdateSoftware( _
    ByRef objConn As ADODB.Connection, _
    ByVal lngSoftwareID As Long, _
    ByVal strSoftware As String, _
    ByVal lngCategoryID As Long, _
    ByRef strMessage As String) As Long
```

We set up our error handling and declare our local objects, in this case a single Command object. Notice that we have not included any data validations in this function. This is because we have placed all data validations in the stored procedure:

```
'Setup error handling
On Error GoTo UpdateSoftware_Err

'Declare local objects
Dim objCmd As ADODB.Command
```

Next, we set a reference to the Command object and then set the Command object's properties:

```
'Set a reference to the command object
Set objCmd = New ADODB.Command

'Set the command object properties
Set objCmd.ActiveConnection = objConn
objCmd.CommandText = "up_parmupd_software"
objCmd.CommandType = adCmdStoredProc
```

We create and append all parameters to the Parameters collection. Again, we should point out that the first parameter to be created is the parameter that will return the return value from our stored procedure.

```
'Create and append the parameters to the parameters collection
objCmd.Parameters.Append objCmd.CreateParameter("RC", _
    adInteger, adParamReturnValue)
objCmd.Parameters.Append objCmd.CreateParameter("SoftwareID", _
    adInteger, adParamInput, , lngSoftwareID)
objCmd.Parameters.Append objCmd.CreateParameter("Software", _
    adVarChar, adParamInput, 30, strSoftware)
objCmd.Parameters.Append objCmd.CreateParameter("CategoryID", _
    adInteger, adParamInput, , lngCategoryID)
```

Next we execute the Command object and check the return value from the parameter named RC. If this parameter does not contain a zero value we raise an error:

```
'Execute the command object
objCmd.Execute

'Check the return value from the stored procedure
If objCmd.Parameters("RC") <> 0 Then
    Err.Raise 513 + vbObjectError, "UpdateSoftware", _
        "up_parmupd_software failed"
End If
```

At this point everything has executed according to plan, so we remove our reference to the `Command` object and set the return code for this function. Then we exit this function, returning to the caller:

```
        'Remove references to objects
        Set objCmd = Nothing

        'Set the return code
        UpdateSoftware = 0

        'Exit function
        Exit Function
```

Our error handling code for this function is the same code that we have included in the other functions written in this chapter:

```
    UpdateSoftware_Err:
        'Enumerate ADO errors
        Dim objErrors As New clsInsertData
        strMessage = objErrors.EnumerateErrors(objConn)
        Set objErrors = Nothing
        'Append any VB errors
        strMessage = strMessage & Err.Number & " : " & Err.Description
        'Return to the caller with a RC of 1
        UpdateSoftware = 1
    End Function
```

Switching to the code in our main form (`frmMain`) we need to modify the `cmdUpdate_Click` procedure to process an update from the **Software** tab. Add the following modifications to this procedure, as shown in the following code fragment.

The first thing that we do in this code is to execute the `UpdateSoftware` function to perform the update. We use the `Software_ID` field in the `objRSData` recordset as the software ID for this update. This ensures we have the correct software ID for the row being updated. We use the `Text` property of the `cboSoftware` combo box to get the software title, and the `ItemData` property of the `cboSoftwareCategory` combo box to get the software category ID:

```
        Case 2   'Software

            'Update the software
            lngRC = objUpdate.UpdateSoftware(g_objConn, _
                objRSData!Software_ID, _
                cboSoftware.Text, _
                cboSoftwareCategory.ItemData(cboSoftwareCategory.ListIndex), _
                strMessage)
```

After control has been returned from the `UpdateSoftware` function we check the return code from this function. If it is not equal to zero we raise an error and then fall through to our error handling code for this procedure:

```
            'Ensure we were successful
            If lngRC <> 0 Then
```

```
        Err.Raise 513 + vbObjectError, "cmdUpdate_Click", _
            "Call to UpdateSoftware failed"
    End If
```

If the update was successful, we reload the combo boxes on the **Software** tab to reflect the updated software. Then we call the `tabData_Click` procedure, passing it a value of 2 for the previous tab parameter. This procedure will display the first software title in the `cboSoftware` combo box:

```
        'Reload Software
        Call LoadSoftware

        'Re-initialize the tab control so the opened RS is reloaded
        'to reflect the software update
        Call tabData_Click(2)
```

Editing a Stored Procedure

When we develop stored procedures we try to plan ahead and include all data that might be used. This was the case when we created the `up_parmsel_assigned_system` stored procedure. We tried to include all columns in the select list that we thought we might need when processing this data. However, no matter how much we plan or try to think ahead, some things inevitably get dropped or missed.

This is the case with the `up_parmsel_assigned_system` stored procedure. In order to process an update on the **System Assignment** tab, we need to know the `System_Assignment_ID` of the system that is being updated. This column of data was not included in the stored procedure that we created in Chapter 9, so we will have to edit this stored procedure to include this data.

We can use the Query Analyzer to edit this procedure by expanding the **Hardware Tracking** database in the Object Browser and then expanding **Stored Procedures** group. To edit this stored procedure, right-click on the `up_parmsel_assigned_system` stored procedure and choose **Edit** from the context menu.

Notice that the stored procedure is opened in a query window and the original CREATE PROCEDURE statement has been replaced with an ALTER PROCEDURE statement. This has been done automatically for you and when you execute the code the stored procedure will be altered. The ALTER PROCEDURE statement alters the code in an existing stored procedure but does not alter the existing permissions on the stored procedure.

We want to modify this line of the stored procedure:

```
    -- Select data from the System_Assignment_T table
    --
    SELECT System_Assignment_T.Hardware_ID,
```

We need to add the `System_Assignment_ID` column to the select list, as shown in the next code fragment overleaf. Notice that we have prefixed this column with the table name so that it is clear from which tables the columns in the select list are coming:

```
-- Select data from the System_Assignment_T table
--
SELECT System_Assignment_T.System_Assignment_ID,
      System_Assignment_T.Hardware_ID,
```

After you have made the modifications necessary to this stored procedure, you will want to execute the code in the query window to update the stored procedure in the database. At this point you can click on the Execute Query icon on the toolbar to alter this stored procedure.

After the Query Analyzer has executed the code, you will see a message in the results pane indicating that the command completed successfully, as shown in the next figure:

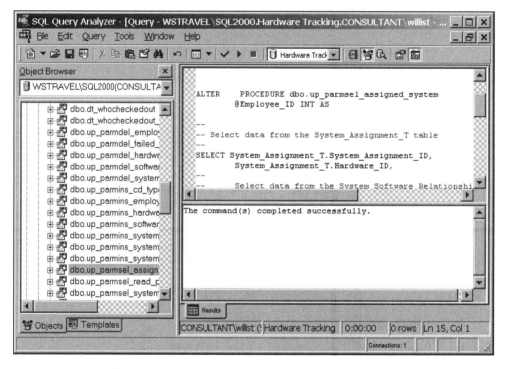

At this point you can close the current query window by clicking on the X in the upper right hand corner or clear the current query window. The code in this window is not the actual stored procedure, but a copy of the code from the stored procedure placed there by the Query Analyzer. Therefore, you do not need to save the code in this query window.

Try It Out – System Assignment Update Stored Procedure

The last stored procedure that we need to create will be used to update the data on the System Assignment tab in our Hardware Tracking application. This screen allows us to not only assign a new system to an employee, but also to change the software installed on that system.

When we think about the software installed on a system and about the changes required to determine what software was removed and what software has been added, we quickly come to realize that this could involve quite a bit of processing.

438

The easiest and most efficient solution to this dilemma is to delete all software from the `System_Software_Relationship_T` table for this system and then insert all software that has been checked.

To create this procedure:

1. Open a new query window by clicking on the New Query icon on the toolbar or clear the current query window by clicking on the Clear Query Window icon on the toolbar.

2. Enter the following stored procedure:

```
CREATE PROCEDURE dbo.up_parmupd_system_assignment
     @System_Assignment_ID    INT,
     @Employee_ID             INT,
     @Hardware_ID             INT AS

-- ****************************************************************************
-- Begin Transaction
-- ****************************************************************************
BEGIN TRANSACTION Update_System_Assignment

-- ****************************************************************************
-- Update the system assignment
-- ****************************************************************************
UPDATE System_Assignment_T
     SET Employee_ID = @Employee_ID,
     Hardware_ID = @Hardware_ID,
     Last_Update_DT = GETDATE()
     WHERE System_Assignment_ID = @System_Assignment_ID
--
-- Check for errors
--
IF @@ERROR > 0
     BEGIN
     RAISERROR('Update of system assignment failed',16,1)
     ROLLBACK TRANSACTION Update_System_Assignment
     RETURN 99
     END

-- ****************************************************************************
-- Delete all associated software
-- ****************************************************************************
DELETE FROM System_Software_Relationship_T
     WHERE System_Assignment_ID = @System_Assignment_ID
--
-- Check for errors
--
IF @@ERROR > 0
     BEGIN
     RAISERROR('Delete of associated software failed',16,1)
     ROLLBACK TRANSACTION Update_System_Assignment
     RETURN 99
     END
```

```
-- ***********************************************************************
-- Commit Transaction
-- ***********************************************************************
COMMIT TRANSACTION Update_System_Assignment


--
-- Return to the caller
--
RETURN 0

GO

GRANT EXECUTE ON up_parmupd_system_assignment TO [Hardware Users]
```

3. Parse the code for errors by clicking on the **Parse Query** icon on the toolbar.

4. Create this stored procedure by clicking on the **Execute Query** icon on the toolbar.

How It Works – System Assignment Update Stored Procedure

The first part of our stored procedure accepts the System_Assignment_ID value as an input parameter. This was the column that we just added in the up_parmsel_assigned_system stored procedure. The other two parameters are for the employee ID and hardware ID.

```
CREATE PROCEDURE dbo.up_parmupd_system_assignment
    @System_Assignment_ID    INT,
    @Employee_ID             INT,
    @Hardware_ID             INT AS
```

Since this stored procedure will modify data in multiple tables we want to begin a transaction. We have specified the BEGIN TRANSACTION statement followed by a transaction name of Update_System_Assignment:

```
-- ***********************************************************************
-- Begin Transaction
-- ***********************************************************************
BEGIN TRANSACTION Update_System_Assignment
```

Next we update the System_Assignment_T table, assigning either a new employee or a new system for this system assignment. The @System_Assignment_ID input parameter is used in the WHERE clause to limit this update to the specific row of data that was selected on the **System Assignment** tab in our application:

```
-- ***********************************************************************
-- Update the system assignment
-- ***********************************************************************
UPDATE System_Assignment_T
    SET Employee_ID = @Employee_ID,
    Hardware_ID = @Hardware_ID,
    Last_Update_DT = GETDATE()
    WHERE System_Assignment_ID = @System_Assignment_ID
```

After the update we check for errors and raise an error if the @@ERROR function returned anything other than 0. Then we roll back the transaction and return to the caller with a return value of 99:

```
-- Check for errors
--
IF @@ERROR > 0
    BEGIN
    RAISERROR('Update of system assignment failed',16,1)
    ROLLBACK TRANSACTION Update_System_Assignment
    RETURN 99
    END
```

We want to delete all rows of data from the System_Software_Relationship_T table that relate to this system assignment. This has been done by specifying the @System_Assignment_ID input parameter in the WHERE clause. This DELETE statement will be deleting multiple rows of data:

```
-- ***********************************************************************
-- Delete all associated software
-- ***********************************************************************
DELETE FROM System_Software_Relationship_T
    WHERE System_Assignment_ID = @System_Assignment_ID
```

Once again, we check for errors and roll back the transaction if an error occurred. It is important to remember that if we rolled back the transaction at this point, the update applied in the earlier UPDATE statement would also be undone.

```
-- Check for errors
--
IF @@ERROR > 0
    BEGIN
    RAISERROR('Delete of associated software failed',16,1)
    ROLLBACK TRANSACTION Update_System_Assignment
    RETURN 99
    END
```

If no errors occurred, we commit the transaction using the COMMIT TRANSACTION statement, also specifying the transaction name. Then we return to the caller with a return value of 0:

```
-- ***********************************************************************
-- Commit Transaction
-- ***********************************************************************
COMMIT TRANSACTION Update_System_Assignment


--
-- Return to the caller
--
RETURN 0
```

We specify the GO command to have the Query Analyzer create this stored procedure, followed by the GRANT statement to grant the hardware users role permissions on this stored procedure:

```
GO

GRANT EXECUTE ON up_parmupd_system_assignment TO [Hardware Users]
```

Try It Out – Process the System Assignment Update Stored Procedure

We now want to add functionality to the program by enabling the data on the **System Assignment** tab to be updated. We do this by adding new code to the **Update** button and adding a new function to the update class. Given the very nature of the data and the association of data on the **System Assignment** tab, there are quite a few modifications that are required in the program. Most of this was seen in the last chapter when we inserted a new system assignment.

1. Implement these changes by reading through the next *How It Works* section, adding the VB code as you step through it.

2. At this point save your project, run the program and log in. Click on the **System Assignment** tab and choose an employee who has an assigned system to update. You can change the system assigned to them or change the software installed on that system.

3. Click on the **Update** button to have the update performed and the fields on this tab reloaded. You can then verify the updates made.

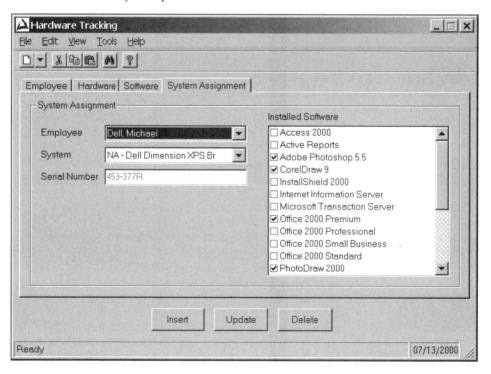

How It Works – Process the System Assignment Update Stored Procedure

We want to start these modifications in the main form (frmMain) in our VB project. In the general declarations section of the form add the following variable, as shown in the following code fragment:

```
'Declare variables
Dim arrSerialNumber() As String
Dim lngLocationID As Long
Dim lngSystemAssignmentID As Long
```

Next we want to modify the cboEmployee_Click procedure. When a user selects an employee, we want to save the system assignment ID for that employee. Modify this procedure as shown in the following code fragment:

```
    'Save the system assignment id
    lngSystemAssignmentID = g_objRS!System_Assignment_ID
End If

'Uncheck all software
For intIndex = 0 To lstInstalledSoftware.ListCount - 1
    lstInstalledSoftware.Selected(intIndex) = False
Next
```

Before we modify the cmdUpdate_Click procedure to update the system assignment, let's code the UpdateSystemAssignment procedure in the update data class (clsUpdateData). This procedure is very similar to the InsertSystemAssignment, so you could copy and then modify that code if you choose.

We start this function by specifying all of the parameters, the first of which is the Connection object. Then we specify the system assignment ID as lngAssignmentID followed by the employee ID and the system ID. The lngSoftwareID() parameter is an array of software IDs for the software installed on the system and must be passed by reference. The last parameter is the strMessage and will contain any error messages that we need to return:

```
Public Function UpdateSystemAssignment( _
    ByRef objConn As ADODB.Connection, _
    ByVal lngAssignmentID As Long, _
    ByVal lngEmployeeID As Long, _
    ByVal lngSystemID As Long, _
    ByRef lngSoftwareID() As Long, _
    ByRef strMessage As String) As Long
```

We set up our error handling for this function and then declare our local variables and objects. Next, we set a reference to the Command object:

```
    'Set up error handling
    On Error GoTo UpdateSystemAssignment_Err

    'Declare local variables and objects
    Dim intIndex As Integer
    Dim objCmd As ADODB.Command
```

```
'Set a reference to the command object
  Set objCmd = New ADODB.Command
```

We set the Command object properties and specify the up_parmupd_system_assignment stored procedure as the CommandText property of the Command object:

```
'Set the command object properties
Set objCmd.ActiveConnection = objConn
objCmd.CommandText = "up_parmupd_system_assignment"
objCmd.CommandType = adCmdStoredProc
```

We create and append all of the parameters to the Parameters collection, specifying the parameter that contains the return value from our stored procedure first:

```
'Create and append the parameters to the parameters collection
objCmd.Parameters.Append objCmd.CreateParameter("RC", _
    adInteger, adParamReturnValue)
objCmd.Parameters.Append objCmd.CreateParameter("SystemID", _
    adInteger, adParamInput, , lngAssignmentID)
objCmd.Parameters.Append objCmd.CreateParameter("Employee", _
    adInteger, adParamInput, , lngEmployeeID)
objCmd.Parameters.Append objCmd.CreateParameter("System", _
    adInteger, adParamInput, , lngSystemID)
```

After all parameters have been appended to the Parameters collection we execute the Command object. Then we check the return value from the stored procedure in the RC parameter. If it is not zero then we raise an error:

```
'Execute the command object
objCmd.Execute

'Check the return value from the stored procedure
If objCmd.Parameters("RC") <> 0 Then
    Err.Raise 513 + vbObjectError, "UpdateSystemAssignment", _
        "up_parmupd_system_assignment failed"
End If
```

We remove our reference to the Command object by setting it to nothing:

```
'Remove references to objects
Set objCmd = Nothing
```

Remember that our up_parmupd_system_assignment stored procedure deleted all rows in the System_Software_Relationship_T table that relate to the system assignment that we updated. Therefore, we need to re-insert all of the software. The software to be added could be all the same software, or it could contain new or previously deleted software. This is the cleanest and most efficient way to perform the task.

The following loop is exactly the same loop that we created in the last chapter, so we will not cover the details of the code again. But to recap, the loop processes all software IDs in the lngSoftwareID array and executes the up_parmins_system_software stored procedure to insert them into the System_Software_Relationship_T table:

```
'Process all software titles selected
For intIndex = LBound(lngSoftwareID) To UBound(lngSoftwareID)

    'Set a reference to the command object


    Set objCmd = New ADODB.Command

    'Set the command object properties
    Set objCmd.ActiveConnection = objConn
    objCmd.CommandText = "up_parmins_system_software"
    objCmd.CommandType = adCmdStoredProc

    'Create and append the parameters to the parameters collection
    objCmd.Parameters.Append objCmd.CreateParameter("RC", _
        adInteger, adParamReturnValue)
    objCmd.Parameters.Append objCmd.CreateParameter("AssignedSystem", _
        adInteger, adParamInput, , lngAssignmentID)
    objCmd.Parameters.Append objCmd.CreateParameter("Software", _
        adInteger, adParamInput, , lngSoftwareID(intIndex))

    'Execute the command object
    objCmd.Execute

    'Check the return value from the stored procedure
    If objCmd.Parameters("RC") <> 0 Then
        Err.Raise 513 + vbObjectError, "UpdateSystemAssignment", _
            "up_parmins_system_software failed"
    End If

    'Remove references to objects
    Set objCmd = Nothing

Next
```

After all software IDs have been inserted into the System_Software_Relationship_T table, we set the return code for this function and then exit the function:

```
'Set the return code
UpdateSystemAssignment = 0

'Exit function
Exit Function
```

Our error handling code is the same as for all other functions in this class:

```
UpdateSystemAssignment_Err:
    'Enumerate ADO errors
    Dim objErrors As New clsInsertData
    strMessage = objErrors.EnumerateErrors(objConn)
    Set objErrors = Nothing
    'Append any VB errors
    strMessage = strMessage & Err.Number & " : " & Err.Description
    'Clean up database
    objConn.Execute "up_parmdel_failed_system_assignment"
    'Return to the caller with a RC of 1
    UpdateSystemAssignment = 1
End Function
```

Now we want to switch back to the code in our main form (frmMain). Here we want to modify the cmdUpdate_Click procedure and add some code to call the UpdateSystemAssignment function. Modify the code in this procedure as outlined in the next code fragment.

The first thing we need to do in this procedure is to add some more variables to support updating data on the **System Assignment** tab. These variables will be used in the new code that we will add in just a moment, to build an array of all the software IDs that are checked in the lstInstalledSoftware list:

```
'Declare local variables
Dim lngRC As Long, strMessage As String, _
    lngInstalledSoftware() As Long, intIndex As Integer, _
    intArrayIndex As Integer
```

The first thing that we do in this section of code is to build the array of software IDs. This is the same code that we inserted into the cmdInsert_Click procedure in the last chapter. Basically what this code does is to loop through the lstInstalledSoftware list and look at each item to see if it has been checked. If it has, it adds the value from the ItemData property of the lstInstalledSoftware list:

```
Case 3    'System Assignment

        'Build an array of installed software
        intArrayIndex = -1
        For intIndex = 0 To lstInstalledSoftware.ListCount - 1
           'If the selected item is checked then
           If lstInstalledSoftware.Selected(intIndex) = True Then
              'Increment the array index variable and redim the array
              intArrayIndex = intArrayIndex + 1
              ReDim Preserve lngInstalledSoftware(intArrayIndex)
              'Add the ItemData property value to the array
              lngInstalledSoftware(intArrayIndex) = _
                  lstInstalledSoftware.ItemData(intIndex)
           End If
        Next
```

We now want to call the UpdateSystemAssignment procedure to have the update performed. We use the lngSystemAssignmentID variable that was set in the cboEmployee_Click procedure and get the employee ID from the ItemData property of the cboEmployee combo box. We also use the ItemData property of the cboSystem combo box to get the ID of the system being updated. The lngInstalledSoftware() variable contains an array of all software IDs that have been checked.

446

```
'Update the system assignment and software
lngRC = objUpdate.UpdateSystemAssignment(g_objConn, _
    lngSystemAssignmentID, _
    cboEmployee.ItemData(cboEmployee.ListIndex), _
    cboSystem.ItemData(cboSystem.ListIndex), _
    lngInstalledSoftware(), _
    strMessage)
```

After control has been returned from the UpdateSystemAssignment function we check the return code from this function. If it is not zero then we raise an error:

```
'Ensure we were successful
If lngRC <> 0 Then
    Err.Raise 513 + vbObjectError, "cmdUpdate_Click", _
        "Call to UpdateSystemAssignment failed"
End If
```

We call the LoadSystems procedure to have the fields on the **System Assignment** tab reloaded to reflect the updates. Then we call the tabData_Click procedure, passing it a value of 3 for the previous tab parameter:

```
'Reload Systems
Call LoadSystems

'Re-initialize the tab control so the opened RS is reloaded
'to reflect the system assignment update
Call tabData_Click(3)
```

Summary

This chapter has covered several different topics, the first of which was the difference between COM+ and SQL Server transactions. We know that COM+ should be considered for transaction handling and that it offers many more benefits than we have talked about. However, COM+ may not always be the best solution, especially when distributing an application and DLLs to the client, when SQL Server transactions are preferable.

We talked about SQL Server transactions and got first hand experience of building and using transactions. We know that we can roll back a transaction at any trouble spot in our stored procedure and SQL Server will undo all changes that have been made since the transaction was started, regardless of how many tables we have modified.

We know that sometimes data validation must be performed in a stored procedure and, having gone through several examples, we put this knowledge to use in the up_parmupd_software stored procedure. While the data validations in this stored procedure were simple, we know that we can perform more complex data validations in a stored procedure should it be necessary.

We have also learned a little more about the Query Analyzer in this chapter. We know that we can edit and delete stored procedures from within this environment. Given this knowledge and knowing how to grant permissions through code, we have come to rely on the Enterprise Manager less and less.

We completed the functionality to update data in our Hardware Tracking application and you should now have a better idea of what is involved in performing updates to a single table and multiple tables. We continue to see our stored procedures become more sophisticated as our knowledge of T-SQL and stored procedures grows.

In summary, you should know:

❑   When you should use SQL Server for transaction handling

❑   How to code transactions in a stored procedure

❑   How to validate data in a stored procedure

❑   How to edit and delete stored procedures from the Query Analyzer

❑   How to grant permissions on a stored procedure when creating it

In the next chapter we will take a look at how SQL Server deletes data using cascading referential integrity constraints, and how to create stored procedures and triggers to delete data.

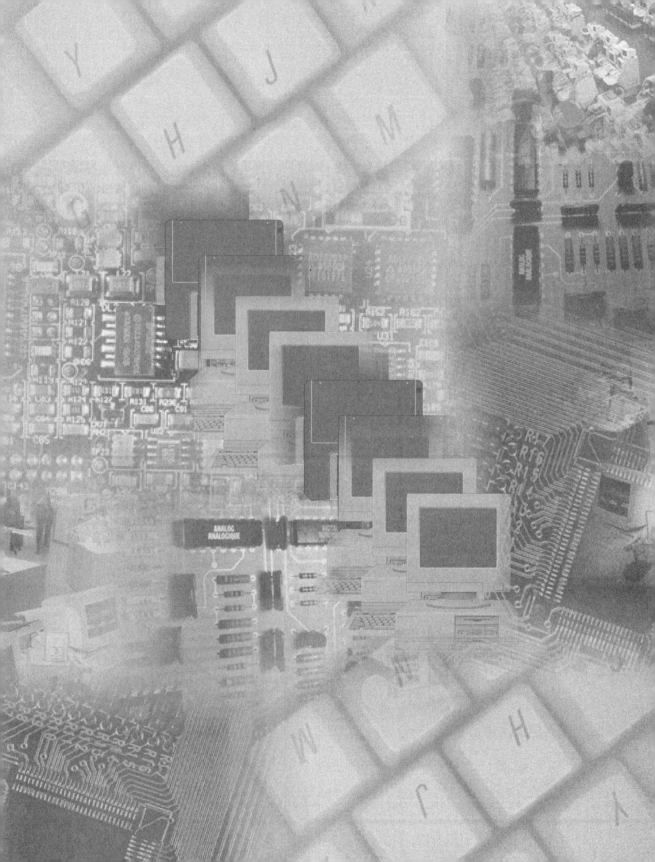

Deleting Data

In the last chapter we saw how the use of transactions helped to ensure data integrity as we modified data in multiple tables within the same stored procedure. If an error occurred, we were able to roll back all modifications to the data in our tables.

This chapter expands on data integrity; as we take a closer look at cascading referential integrity constraints, delete stored procedures, and triggers. All of these objects help to ensure that if we delete a row of data from one table, all associated rows are also deleted. For example, if we delete an employee, then we will also want to delete their assigned system.

Cascading referential integrity constraints were defined in our database in Chapter 3, when we added the foreign key constraints to our tables. As we take a look at DELETE stored procedures, we will see how these constraints are automatically executed and how they help to clean up data in our database.

Triggers can be used where more logic is required to cascade deletes that cannot be handled by cascading referential integrity constraints. We will take a closer look at triggers, and we will create our own trigger to delete data in other tables. Using a trigger will also help us to maintain data integrity in our database.

So, in this chapter we will:

❑   Examine cascading referential integrity constraints

❑   Examine and create triggers

❑   Examine and create delete stored procedures

Referential Integrity

Referential integrity is based on the relationship of data between two tables, using columns that are defined as primary and foreign keys. This ensures that the entries in each table are *unique* and that they *relate* to one another. The table that contains the foreign key cannot reference an entry in the table that contains the primary key unless that entry exists. Likewise, a row in the table that contains the primary key entry cannot be deleted until the row in the table that holds the foreign key reference is also deleted.

The referential integrity between the two tables that contain the primary and foreign keys is maintained by the primary and foreign key constraints, as mentioned in Chapter 1. When deleting data from tables that contain primary and foreign keys, we must be aware of the relationship between all the tables involved.

SQL Server automatically provides referential integrity up to a point. It will not allow us to add a foreign key to a non-existent entry. Likewise, it will not allow us to delete a primary key entry while a foreign key in another table is referencing it. What *we* must provide is atomicity. When we delete an employee from the Employee_T table, we must ensure that all related records are also deleted. Atomicity, as we saw in the last chapter, is when a transaction completes successfully or fails. Any item in the transaction that fails causes the entire transaction to fail.

We can provide atomicity in several ways. First, we can use a stored procedure that employs transactions. This ensures that if a modification to any of the tables fails, the entire transaction will be rolled back. Another method is to use triggers, which are very similar to stored procedures. We'll talk more about this later in the chapter. Another method that we can use is cascading referential integrity constraints.

Cascading Referential Integrity Constraints

At some point, the data in our database no longer serves a useful purpose and must be deleted. For example, this could be true of employee data where the employee has left our company. While it is logical to delete the employee from the employee table, we will also need to delete all other data associated with this employee from the other tables in our database. If we failed to do this we would not be able to maintain data integrity in our database, as we would still have other data that referenced the deleted employee. While foreign key constraints prevent most of this, there could be certain situations where this would not be prevented, such as an audit log table that contained the employee ID or employee name, but did not have a foreign key reference to the Employee_T table. Under such circumstances, we would not be able to delete an employee without deleting all of their associated data first.

Our System_Assignment_T table has a foreign key reference to the Employee_T table. This would normally require us to delete the row of data in the System_Assignment_T table that referenced the employee we wanted to delete, before we deleted the employee in the Employee_T table. Foreign key constraints enforce this rule to help maintain data integrity.

However, because we checked the **Cascade Delete Related Records** check box in the **Create Relationship** dialog when we defined the foreign key relationship between these two tables, we are able to delete an employee from the Employee_T table and have the associated row of data deleted in the System_Assignment_T table automatically.

This is known as **cascading referential integrity constraints**. By checking the **Cascade Delete Related Records** check box, all related rows in the table that contain a foreign key where we have defined this constraint will automatically be deleted when we delete the employee.

A single DELETE statement against a table can cause a series of cascading deletes to occur on multiple tables. This is the case when we delete an employee from the Employee_T table.

So, when we delete a row of data from the System_Assignment_T table, all associated data in the System_Software_Relationship_T table will also be deleted. This is what we want, as when we delete a system assignment, we also want to delete all of the software that was installed on that system, which is contained in the System_Software_Relationship_T table. We do not delete the hardware in the Hardware_T table, because potentially we may want to reassign that system to another employee.

So, let's look at how deleting an employee causes a chain of cascading deletes to occur. The following figure shows how this happens when we execute the following DELETE statement:

```
DELETE FROM Employee_T
    WHERE Employee_ID = 3
```

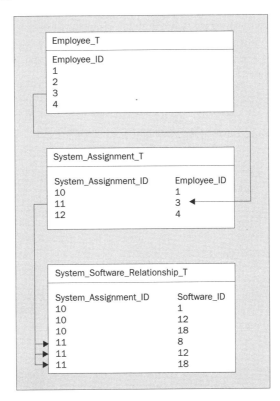

This statement causes the cascading referential integrity constraint to be executed, which then deletes the related row of data in the System_Assignment_T table where the Employee_ID = 3. The System_Assignment_ID in this table contains a value of 11. Employee_ID and System_Assignment_ID are the primary keys of their respective tables. Primary keys are used in the DELETE statement to ensure we are deleting one unique row of data.

Deleting the system assignment in the System_Assignment_T table causes another cascading referential integrity constraint to be executed, which then deletes all rows in the System_Software_Relationship_T table where the System_Assignment_ID = 11.

A single DELETE statement from the Employee_T table starts this chain of events. By defining cascading referential integrity constraints, we are better able to maintain data integrity in our database, and simplify our stored procedures that delete data. This ensures that all related data is deleted when the employee is deleted.

Try It Out – Employee Delete Stored Procedure

Now that we know that a single delete from the Employee_T table will delete all related data in the System_Assignment_T table, and that this in turn will cause all related data to be deleted in the System_Software_Relationship_T table, let's create a stored procedure to delete an employee.

This will be a simple stored procedure that will delete one row of data from the Employee_T table.

1. To create the up_parmdel_employee stored procedure start the Query Analyzer, if it is not already running, and log in.

2. Enter the following stored procedure:

```
CREATE PROCEDURE dbo.up_parmdel_employee
    @Employee_ID      INT AS


-- **************************************************************************
-- Delete the employee
-- **************************************************************************
DELETE FROM Employee_T
    WHERE Employee_ID = @Employee_ID
--
-- Check for errors
--
IF @@ERROR > 0
    BEGIN
    RAISERROR('Delete employee failed',16,1)
    RETURN 99
    END
--
-- Return to the caller
--
RETURN 0

GO

GRANT EXECUTE ON up_parmdel_employee TO [Hardware Users]
```

3. Parse the code for errors by clicking on the Parse Query icon on the toolbar and create this stored procedure by clicking on the Execute Query icon on the toolbar.

How It Works – Employee Delete Stored Procedure

This simple but effective stored procedure causes a chain of events to occur as we discussed earlier. The first line of this stored procedure specifies the one and only input parameter, @Employee_ID. This parameter will contain the ID of the employee to be deleted.

```
CREATE PROCEDURE dbo.up_parmdel_employee
    @Employee_ID      INT AS
```

The DELETE statement for this stored procedure will delete the row of data in the Employee_T table where the value in the Employee_ID column equals the value in the @Employee_ID parameter:

```
-- ****************************************************************
-- Delete the employee
-- ****************************************************************
DELETE FROM Employee_T
    WHERE Employee_ID = @Employee_ID
```

After we have executed the DELETE statement, we check for errors by checking the value returned by the @@ERROR function. If the value is non-zero, we raise an error and return to the caller with a return value of 99:

```
-- Check for errors
--
IF @@ERROR > 0
    BEGIN
    RAISERROR('Delete employee failed',16,1)
    RETURN 99
    END
```

If all went well, we return to the caller with a return value of 0:

```
-- Return to the caller
--
RETURN 0
```

We specify the GO command to have the Query Analyzer create this stored procedure before we execute any more SQL statements. Then we grant EXECUTE permissions on this stored procedure to the Hardware Users role:

```
GO

GRANT EXECUTE ON up_parmdel_employee TO [Hardware Users]
```

Before we execute this stored procedure, we need to talk about triggers, which are covered in the next section.

Triggers

Triggers are a special type of stored procedure that are automatically fired by SQL Server when a specific action is taken against a table that a trigger has been defined for. Triggers are typically used to help enforce business rules, to perform audit logging, and to help ensure data integrity.

When we say that a trigger is a special type of stored procedure, we mean that a trigger can contain any type of T-SQL statement or function. However, triggers are designed to perform some type of action, and therefore should not return data, although they can. When creating a trigger, you must ensure that any SELECT statements in your trigger do not return data, by assigning the data returned from the SELECT statement to variables.

Triggers can be created on a table to fire *after* an INSERT, UPDATE, or DELETE statement is executed against a table. Triggers can also be created to fire *instead* of the INSERT, UPDATE, or DELETE statement. Most of the time you will want a trigger to fire after an action is performed against a table, thereby allowing the trigger to help enforce data integrity or enforce some business rules.

However, you may want not to delete data in a specific table, such as a tax table. In a case like this, you could create a trigger which fires instead of a DELETE statement. This trigger could then flag the row as deleted using a BIT data type column in a table, and the user would be none the wiser. This would allow you to maintain old tax data without having to archive the data. Then when you select data from that table you could select data where the value in the BIT data type column is not turned on.

When triggers are fired after an INSERT, UPDATE, or DELETE statement, how do you know which data was changed or deleted? SQL Server provides two logical tables that only triggers can access. After an insert or update, a trigger can access the *inserted* table to find out what data has been inserted or what data has been updated. Likewise, after a delete has occurred, a trigger can access the *deleted* table to find out what data has been deleted.

> *When a row of data is inserted or updated, the information is placed into the* inserted *table for triggers to query. Likewise, when a row of data is deleted, the deleted information is placed in the* deleted *table for triggers to query. All of this happens automatically and is taken care of by SQL Server.*

It should be noted that a trigger designed to fire after completion of an INSERT, UPDATE, or DELETE statement will only be executed if that statement is successful. If for any reason the statement fails, the trigger will not be fired.

Let's take a look at the basic syntax of the CREATE TRIGGER statement:

```
CREATE TRIGGER trigger-name ON table-name
    AFTER | INSTEAD OF
    INSERT, UPDATE, DELETE
    AS
    SQL-statements
```

In this syntax, *trigger-name* refers to the name of the trigger and must conform to the rules for identifiers. Trigger names must be unique within the database.

The *table-name* argument specifies the table name on which the trigger is being created.

The *SQL-statements* argument specifies one or more SQL statements to be executed.

Let's assume we have a table called Audit_Log_T, in which we log all the inserts and updates to the Employee_T table. We could create a trigger on the Employee_T table that would log the Employee_ID that was inserted or updated, and also the user who performed the insert or update. Let's look at the following example.

The first thing that must be specified is the CREATE TRIGGER statement, followed by the trigger name. This name has been specified according to the naming standards presented in Chapter 3. If we wanted to create a second trigger on this table, we could specify a name of Employee_2_G to signify the second trigger on the Employee_T table.

Next, we specify the table name on which this trigger is to be created. This is followed by the AFTER keyword, to indicate that the trigger should be fired after the successful completion of specific SQL statements. Here, we have specified that the trigger will fire only after successful INSERT and UPDATE statements. The last keyword in the CREATE TRIGGER statement is the AS keyword. We then specify the SQL statements to be executed.

```
CREATE TRIGGER Employee_G ON Employee_T
    AFTER INSERT, UPDATE AS
```

The first thing that happens in this trigger is that we declare our local variables – in this case we only have one, @Employee_ID.

Next, we set this variable to the Employee_ID that has been inserted or updated. Notice that we are selecting this value from the logical Inserted table:

```
--
-- Declare local variables
--
DECLARE @Employee_ID INT
--
-- Get employee id inserted
--
SET @Employee_ID = (SELECT Employee_ID
        FROM Inserted)
```

Finally, we insert values into the Employee_ID and Insert_User_VC columns in the imaginary Audit_Log_T table:

```
--
-- Insert the employee id being inserted and the user who
-- performed this action, into the audit log
--
INSERT INTO Audit_Log_T
    (Employee_ID, Insert_User_VC)
    VALUES(@Employee_ID, SYSTEM_USER)
```

SYSTEM_USER is a system function that returns the current user who is logged in. For example, I am logged in using NT authentication, so the SYSTEM_USER function returns my domain name and user account as CONSULTANT\willist. If a user is logged in using SQL Server authentication, then their user account is returned, for example, stephanie.

Triggers, like stored procedures, can be as simple or as complex as necessary. The trigger that we have just shown is a simple one. Depending on your needs, you could define a trigger on a table that performs multiple actions against multiple tables.

Try It Out – Creating a Trigger on the Employee Table

When we delete an employee, we know that if they have a system assigned to them in the System_Assignment_T table, the row of data will be deleted. This happens automatically because of the cascading referential integrity constraints that were defined on that table.

There is also an associated row of data for an employee in the Location_T table. To help keep our tables clean and up to date, we want to delete the row of data for that location. However, we only want this to happen if the employee being deleted is the last employee associated with a certain location.

Given this, we know that we cannot define a cascading referential integrity constraint on the Location_T table because this would attempt to delete the location from the Location_T table and would cause an error if another employee were referencing that row of data. What we want to do is to create a trigger on the Employee_T table that will only fire when an employee is deleted.

To create this trigger:

1. Start the Query Analyzer and log in, if it is not already running.

2. Enter the following trigger:

```
CREATE TRIGGER Employee_G ON Employee_T
    AFTER DELETE AS

-- ******************************************************************
-- Declare variables
-- ******************************************************************
DECLARE @Employee_ID    INT

-- ******************************************************************
-- Select the Employee_ID to get a count of employees at this location
-- ******************************************************************
SELECT @Employee_ID = Employee_ID
    FROM Employee_T
    WHERE Location_ID = (SELECT Location_ID FROM deleted)
--
-- Check the row count, if this was the last employee at this location
-- then delete the location
--
IF @@ROWCOUNT = 0
    --
    -- Delete the location
    --
    DELETE FROM Location_T
        WHERE Location_ID = (SELECT Location_ID FROM deleted)
```

3. Parse the code for errors by clicking on the **Parse Query** icon on the toolbar, then create this trigger by clicking on the **Execute Query** icon on the toolbar.

There are no permissions to grant on a trigger.

How It Works – Creating a Trigger on the Employee Table

The first line of this trigger specifies the CREATE TRIGGER statement, followed by the trigger name and the table name for which the trigger is being created. Notice that we named this trigger according to the naming standards presented in Chapter 3.

The second line of our trigger specifies when SQL Server should fire the trigger. Here, we have specified that the trigger should fire *after* a DELETE statement has executed:

```
CREATE TRIGGER Employee_G ON Employee_T
    AFTER DELETE AS
```

Since we don't want our trigger to return any data, we declare a local variable that will be used in our SELECT statement. This way the data from the SELECT statement will be assigned to our variable.

```
-- *****************************************************************
-- Declare variables
-- *****************************************************************
DECLARE @Employee_ID    INT
```

We want to select the Employee_ID from the Employee_T table, and assign it to our variable. Since this SELECT statement could return more than one row, only the last Employee_ID selected is assigned to our variable. The WHERE clause of our SELECT statement checks the value in the Location_ID column against that of the Location_ID from the Deleted table. We have used a **subquery** to select the Location_ID from the Deleted table. A subquery statement is a SELECT statement within another SELECT statement.

```
-- *****************************************************************
-- Select the Employee_ID to get a count of employees at this location
-- *****************************************************************
SELECT @Employee_ID = Employee_ID
    FROM Employee_T
    WHERE Location_ID = (SELECT Location_ID FROM Deleted)
```

We do not care about the data in the @Employee_ID variable, as this variable was simply used to prevent this trigger from returning any data. What we do care about, however, is the number of rows that were affected by the last statement, the SELECT statement. The @@ROWCOUNT function returns the number of rows affected by the last SQL statement, in this case a SELECT statement.

If the @@ROWCOUNT function returns 0, we know that this was the last employee at this location.

```
-- Check the row count, if this was the last employee at this location
-- then delete the location
--
IF @@ROWCOUNT = 0
```

We then proceed to delete the location from the Location_T table using a DELETE statement. Notice that SELECT statement in the WHERE clause is used to return the Location_ID from the Deleted table:

```
-- Delete the location
--
DELETE FROM Location_T
    WHERE Location_ID = (SELECT Location_ID FROM Deleted)
```

Now when we delete an employee from the Employee_T table, not only will their associated assigned system be deleted if it exists, but the location will also be deleted if this employee is the last employee assigned to this location. This will ensure that our Location_T table only contains valid locations that are assigned to an employee.

Viewing Triggers

You can view all the triggers created on a table in either the Enterprise Manager or the Query Analyzer. Since we already have the Query Analyzer open, let's look at our trigger here first.

Expand the Hardware Tracking database in the Object Browser, and then expand the User Tables group. Next, expand the Employee_T table and then expand the Triggers group. You can edit and delete all triggers created for this table from here, by right-clicking on the trigger and then choosing Edit or Delete from the context menu.

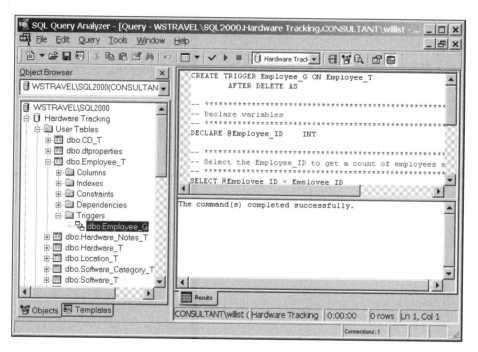

To view and manage triggers from the Enterprise Manager, expand the Hardware Tracking database, and then expand the Tables group. Right-click on the Employee_T table, choose All Tasks, and then choose Manage Triggers from the context menu.

The Trigger Properties dialog is displayed and by default has <new> in the Name combo box, and the basic syntax for a new trigger in the Text window. You could create a new trigger in this dialog if you chose to. However, while this dialog does provide syntax checking, it does not provide the debugging facilities that the Query Analyzer provides.

To view an existing trigger, select the trigger name in the Name combo box, and the code for the trigger will be displayed in the Text window. You can now edit the code for the trigger here, and then click the OK or Apply button to have the new code applied to the trigger:

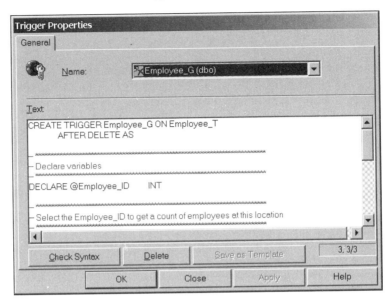

So, now that we know about cascading referential integrity constraints and triggers let's move on and try employing these methods in our database.

Try It Out – Implementing the Employee Delete Stored Procedure

From our previous discussion, we know what data will be deleted when we delete an employee from the Employee_T table. We can proceed by creating the VB code that will execute the up_parmdel_employee stored procedure to delete an employee.

Given the cascading referential integrity constraint created on the System_Assignment_T table, and the Employee_G trigger that we've just created, we now know that this stored procedure will delete one employee together with any associated system assignments, and also delete their location if they are the last employee at that location.

1. All of the required VB code is listed in the following *How It Works* section.

2. After entering the code, save your project and then run the program and log in.

3. Select an employee to delete in the Last Name combo box and click on the Delete button.

    The employee will be deleted, and if they had a system assigned to them, that system relationship will also be deleted. If this employee was the last employee at the location then the location will also be deleted.

4. You can test these different criteria by inserting an employee with a unique location and assigning a system to them. Then delete that employee and verify that the associated system assignment and location were deleted.

By performing these tests we can see at first hand how cascading referential integrity constraints and triggers work.

How It Works – Implementing the Employee Delete Stored Procedure

We will be expanding on the existing project that we have been working with in the last three chapters. Open the `HardwareTracking.vbp` and add a new class module. Set its `Name` property to `clsDeleteData`. We want to add a new function to this class in order to execute the `up_parmdel_employee` stored procedure.

The `DeleteEmployee` function is a public function that will be called from the main form. This function accepts the `Connection` object by reference, the ID of the employee to be deleted by value, and the message string by reference. These are the only three parameters that we need in order to delete an employee. The function will return a `Long` data type as the return code:

```
Public Function DeleteEmployee( _
    ByRef objConn As ADODB.Connection, _
    ByVal lngEmployeeID As Long, _
    ByRef strMessage As String) As Long
```

We set up our error handling and declare the `Command` object as a local object. Then we set a reference to the `Command` object:

```
'Setup error handling
On Error GoTo DeleteEmployee_Err

'Declare local objects
Dim objCmd As ADODB.Command

'Set a reference to the command object
Set objCmd = New ADODB.Command
```

Next, we set the various properties of the `Command` object:

```
'Set the command object properties
Set objCmd.ActiveConnection = objConn
objCmd.CommandText = "up_parmdel_employee"
objCmd.CommandType = adCmdStoredProc
```

We create and append all parameters to the `Parameters` collection. The `up_parmdel_employee` stored procedure only accepts one input parameter, but we have created two parameters, one for the return value from the stored procedure and one for the `@Employee_ID` input parameter in the stored procedure:

```
'Create and append the parameters to the parameters collection
objCmd.Parameters.Append objCmd.CreateParameter("RC", _
    adInteger, adParamReturnValue)
objCmd.Parameters.Append objCmd.CreateParameter("EmployeeID", _
    adInteger, adParamInput, , lngEmployeeID)
```

Now that our parameters have been created, we execute the Command object. Then we check the return value from the stored procedure in the RC parameter and raise an error if the return value is not 0:

```
'Execute the command object
objCmd.Execute

'Check the return value from the stored procedure
If objCmd.Parameters("RC") <> 0 Then
    Err.Raise 513 + vbObjectError, "DeleteEmployee", _
        "up_parmdel_employee failed"
End If
```

If everything was successful, we remove our reference to the Command object by setting it to Nothing. Then we set the return code for this function, and exit the function:

```
'Remove references to objects
Set objCmd = Nothing

'Set the return code
DeleteEmployee = 0

'Exit function
Exit Function
```

Our error handling is the same as we used in the last chapter. In short, we declare an object and set it to the clsInsertData class, then call the EnumerateErrors function in that class to enumerate any ADO errors that we might have. Then we append any VB errors to the strMessage variable, set the return code for this function and exit:

```
DeleteEmployee_Err:
    'Enumerate ADO errors
    Dim objErrors As New clsInsertData
    strMessage = objErrors.EnumerateErrors(objConn)
    Set objErrors = Nothing
    'Append any VB errors
    strMessage = strMessage & Err.Number & " : " & Err.Description
    'Return to the caller with a RC of 1
    DeleteEmployee = 1
End Function
```

Now that we have a function to execute the up_parmdel_employee stored procedure, we need to add some code in our main form (frmMain) to call this function. The first code that we want to add in the main form is an object for the delete data class. This object is defined in the general declarations section of the form:

```
'Declare objects
Dim objData As clsSelectData
Dim objInsert As clsInsertData
Dim objUpdate As clsUpdateData
Dim objDelete As clsDeleteData
Dim objRSData As ADODB.Recordset
```

Since we have declared an object for the delete data class, we also need to add some code to remove our reference to it. In the `Form_Unload` procedure we add the following code:

```
Set objData = Nothing
Set objInsert = Nothing
Set objUpdate = Nothing
Set objDelete = Nothing
```

Now that our `objDelete` object has been defined we want to add some code to the `cmdDelete_Click` procedure. This procedure is executed when a user clicks on the **Delete** button. This procedure is similar to the `cmdInsert_Click` and `cmdUpdate_Click` in that we use a `Select Case` statement to determine which tab is the current tab displayed.

The first thing that we do in this procedure is to set up our error handling. Then we display a message in the status bar to indicate that we are processing a delete:

```
Private Sub cmdDelete_Click()
    'Setup error handling
    On Error GoTo cmdDelete_Click_Err

    'Display status
    StatusBar1.Panels("pnlStatus").Text = "Processing Delete"
```

We declare our local variables next, and then set a reference to the delete data class:

```
    'Declare local variables
    Dim lngRC As Long, strMessage As String

    'Set a reference to the Delete data class
    Set objDelete = New clsDeleteData
```

Using a `Select Case` statement we query the `Tab` property of the `tabData` tab control to determine which tab is currently being displayed. Then, using a `Case` statement, we process the code for the correct tab:

```
    'Process tab data
    Select Case tabData.Tab

        Case 0   'Employee
```

The first thing we want to do here is to call the `DeleteEmployee` function. We pass the global `Connection` object for the first parameter and the `Employee_ID` field of the `objRSData` recordset for the employee ID parameter. The last parameter this function expects is the message string parameter. We pass the `strMessage` variable and any error message will be returned in this variable.

```
            'Delete the employee
            lngRC = objDelete.DeleteEmployee(g_objConn, _
                objRSData!Employee_ID, _
                strMessage)
```

After control has returned from the `DeleteEmployee` function, we check the return code from this function and raise an error if the return code is not zero:

```
'Ensure we were successful
If lngRC <> 0 Then
    Err.Raise 513 + vbObjectError, "cmdDelete_Click", _
        "Call to DeleteEmployee failed"
End If
```

We call the `LoadEmployees` procedure to reload the fields on the **Employee** tab to reflect the deleted employee. Remember that this function also reloads the `cboEmployee` combo box on the **System Assignment** tab. This ensures that if we clicked on this tab next, this combo box would accurately reflect the data in our database.

```
'Reload Employees
Call LoadEmployees
```

We call the `tabData_Click` procedure next, to reload the `objRSData` recordset and to select the first employee in the `cboLastName` combo box if any exists.

The rest of the `Case` statements have been coded and commented to reflect their respective tabs on the tab control:

```
        'Re-initialize the tab control so the opened RS is reloaded
        'to reflect the deleted employee
        Call tabData_Click(0)

    Case 1   'Hardware

    Case 2   'Software

    Case 3   'System Assignment

End Select
```

After all processing has been completed, we remove our reference to the delete data class and then display a ready message in the status bar. Then we exit the procedure:

```
'Remove reference to object
Set objDelete = Nothing

'Display status
StatusBar1.Panels("pnlStatus").Text = "Ready"

'Exit sub
Exit Sub
```

Our error handling routine in this procedure will simply display a message box using the `strMessage` variable as the prompt argument:

```
cmdDelete_Click_Err:
    'Display errors from the function call
    MsgBox strMessage, vbCritical + vbOKOnly, "Hardware Tracking"
End Sub
```

Try It Out – Hardware Delete Stored Procedure

The `Hardware_T` table has a foreign key reference to the `CD_T` table. However, when we delete hardware from the `Hardware_T` table we do not want to delete the entries in the `CD_T` table. There are no cascading referential integrity constraints between the `Hardware_T` table and the `System_Assignment_T` table, so trying to delete a system from the `Hardware_T` table that is assigned to an employee will cause all kinds of errors, as shown in the following figure:

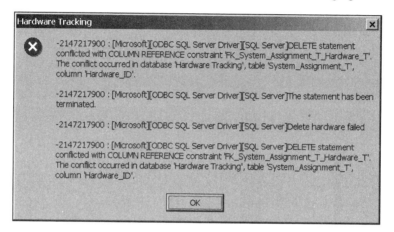

This message box was displayed from the `cmdDelete_Click` procedure using the `strMessage` variable. These messages were set in this variable using the `EnumerateErrors` function; this was called from the `DeleteHardware` function, which we will be coding in a few minutes.

Take notice of the third error message in this dialog. This is the message that we will be adding to our `DELETE` stored procedure in the `RAISERROR` statement. This demonstrates how the error messages that we raise in our stored procedure are returned to our program through ADO.

The bottom line here is that the rules of referential integrity are enforced by our foreign key constraints, and we must first delete the system assignment for a system, before we delete it from the `Hardware_T` table. This ensures that we don't accidentally delete the wrong system from the `Hardware_T` table.

To create the `up_parmdel_hardware` delete stored procedure:

1. Clear the current query window by clicking on the **Clear Query Window** icon on the toolbar, or open a new query window by clicking on the **New Query** icon on the toolbar.

2. Enter the following stored procedure:

```
CREATE PROCEDURE dbo.up_parmdel_hardware
    @Hardware_ID      INT AS


-- ****************************************************************************
-- Delete the hardware
-- ****************************************************************************
```

```
DELETE FROM Hardware_T
    WHERE Hardware_ID = @Hardware_ID
--
-- Check for errors
--
IF @@ERROR > 0
    BEGIN
    RAISERROR('Delete hardware failed',16,1)
    RETURN 99
    END
--
-- Return to the caller
--
RETURN 0

GO

GRANT EXECUTE ON up_parmdel_hardware TO [Hardware Users]
```

3. Parse the code for errors by clicking on the **Parse Query** icon on the toolbar, then create this stored procedure by clicking on the **Execute Query** icon on the toolbar.

How It Works – Hardware Delete Stored Procedure

This stored procedure needs only one input parameter, the hardware ID of the hardware to be deleted:

```
CREATE PROCEDURE dbo.up_parmdel_hardware
    @Hardware_ID      INT AS
```

Our DELETE statement simply deletes the row of data that is specified by the value in the @Hardware_ID input parameter:

```
-- ************************************************************************
-- Delete the hardware
-- ************************************************************************
DELETE FROM Hardware_T
    WHERE Hardware_ID = @Hardware_ID
```

After the DELETE statement has been executed, we check for errors and raise an error if the delete failed. The error message shown here is the same error message that was displayed in our last message box. After we raise an error, we return to the caller with a return value of 99:

```
-- Check for errors
--
IF @@ERROR > 0
    BEGIN
    RAISERROR('Delete hardware failed',16,1)
    RETURN 99
    END
```

If the delete was successful and the hardware was deleted, we return to the caller with a return value of 0:

```
-- Return to the caller
--
RETURN 0
```

We specify the GO command and then grant EXECUTE permissions to this stored procedure to the Hardware Users role:

```
GO

GRANT EXECUTE ON up_parmdel_hardware TO [Hardware Users]
```

Try It Out – Process the Hardware Delete Stored Procedure

Let's switch to the code in our VB project. All of the code is presented in the *How It Works* section below.

1. When you have made all of the necessary additions, you ought to save your project before beginning testing. Run your program and log in.

2. Click on the Hardware tab and choose a system that you know has been assigned to an employee. You can verify this information by clicking on the System Assignment tab and looking at the entries in the cboSystem combo box.

3. After you have selected a system on the Hardware tab that has been assigned to an employee, click on the Delete button. You should see a message box similar to the one that was shown in the previous error message screenshot.

4. Now click on a system that has not been assigned, and click on the Delete button. The system is deleted and the fields on the Hardware tab are reloaded.

How It Works – Process the Hardware Delete Stored Procedure

The first thing that we want to code here is the DeleteHardware function in the delete data class. This function will execute the up_parmdel_hardware stored procedure.

This function accepts three parameters, the same two parameters that we have been using for several chapters, and also the hardware ID of the system to be deleted:

```
Public Function DeleteHardware( _
    ByRef objConn As ADODB.Connection, _
    ByVal lngHardwareID As Long, _
    ByRef strMessage As String) As Long
```

The first thing that we want to do here is to set up our error handling, and then declare our local objects:

```
'Setup error handling
On Error GoTo DeleteHardware_Err

'Declare local objects
Dim objCmd As ADODB.Command
```

Next, we set a reference to the `Command` object and then set its various properties:

```
'Set a reference to the command object
Set objCmd = New ADODB.Command

'Set the command object properties
Set objCmd.ActiveConnection = objConn
objCmd.CommandText = "up_parmdel_hardware"
objCmd.CommandType = adCmdStoredProc
```

Next, we create and append our parameters to the `Parameters` collection. The first parameter is for the return value from our stored procedure, the second is the hardware ID of the row of data to be deleted:

```
'Create and append the parameters to the parameters collection
objCmd.Parameters.Append objCmd.CreateParameter("RC", _
    adInteger, adParamReturnValue)
objCmd.Parameters.Append objCmd.CreateParameter("HardwareID", _
    adInteger, adParamInput, , lngHardwareID)
```

We then execute the `Command` object, and then check the return value from our stored procedure.

This is the point in the code that failed when we saw the previous error message. We received a return value of 99 from the `up_parmdel_hardware` stored procedure in the `RC` parameter and then raised an error:

```
'Execute the command object
objCmd.Execute

'Check the return value from the stored procedure
If objCmd.Parameters("RC") <> 0 Then
    Err.Raise 513 + vbObjectError, "DeleteHardware", _
        "up_parmdel_hardware failed"
End If
```

If everything has been successful so far, we remove our reference to the `Command` object, set the return code for this function, and then exit:

```
'Remove references to objects
Set objCmd = Nothing

'Set the return code
DeleteHardware = 0

'Exit function
Exit Function
```

Our error handling code handles all errors and calls the `EnumerateErrors` function in the insert data class. This was the case when this code failed, and we received the error message shown previously. After control has returned from the `EnumerateErrors` function, we append any VB errors to the `strMessage` variable, set the return code from the function, and then exit:

```
DeleteHardware_Err:
    'Enumerate ADO errors
    Dim objErrors As New clsInsertData
```

469

```
         strMessage = objErrors.EnumerateErrors(objConn)
         Set objErrors = Nothing
         'Append any VB errors
         strMessage = strMessage & Err.Number & " : " & Err.Description
         'Return to the caller with a RC of 1
         DeleteHardware = 1
   End Function
```

Switching to the code in our main form (frmMain), we want to modify the cmdDelete_Click procedure to include the code to call the DeleteHardware function. Modify this procedure as shown in the next code fragment.

The first thing that we have done here is to execute the DeleteHardware function. We pass it the global Connection object, the Hardware_ID field from the objRSData recordset, and the strMessage variable:

```
   Case 1   'Hardware

         'Delete the hardware
         lngRC = objDelete.DeleteHardware(g_objConn, _
            objRSData!Hardware_ID, _
            strMessage)
```

After control has returned from the DeleteHardware function, we check the return code from this function and raise an error if it is not zero.

This is the point in this procedure that failed when we received the error message screenshot shown earlier. The DeleteHardware function returned a return code of 1 and we raised an error:

```
         'Ensure we were successful
         If lngRC <> 0 Then
            Err.Raise 513 + vbObjectError, "cmdDelete_Click", _
               "Call to DeleteHardware failed"
         End If
```

If everything was successful, we call the LoadHardware procedure to reload the fields on the Hardware tab and the LoadSystems procedure to reload the cboSystem combo box on the System Assignment tab.

Then we call the tabData_Click procedure to select the first system in the cboManufacturer combo box, if any still exist:

```
         'Reload Hardware
         Call LoadHardware

         'Reload Systems combo box on the System Assignment tab
         Call LoadSystems

         'Re-initialize the tab control so the opened RS is reloaded
         'to reflect the deleted hardware
         Call tabData_Click(1)
```

Try It Out – Software Delete Stored Procedure

Like the `Hardware_T` table, the `Software_T` table also has a foreign key. This table contains a foreign key to the `Software_Category_T` table, but we don't want to delete any software categories when we delete a software title. Therefore, our DELETE stored procedure will only delete a row from the `Software_T` table.

The `System_Software_Relationship_T` table contains a foreign key to the `Software_T` table, and thus will prevent you from deleting any software title that has been assigned to a system assignment in the `System_Assignment_T` table. You will receive an error message similar to the one shown earlier if you try to delete a software title that is being referenced in the `System_Software_Relationship_T` table. The error message will warn you that a foreign key constraint exists that prevents you from deleting a software title in the `Software_T` table.

To create the `up_parmdel_software` stored procedure:

1. Clear the current query window by clicking on the **Clear Query Window** icon on the toolbar, or open a new query window by clicking on the **New Query** icon on the toolbar.

2. Enter the following stored procedure:

```
CREATE PROCEDURE dbo.up_parmdel_software
    @Software_ID    INT AS

-- ********************************************************************
-- Delete the software
-- ********************************************************************
DELETE FROM Software_T
    WHERE Software_ID = @Software_ID
--
-- Check for errors
--
IF @@ERROR > 0
    BEGIN
    RAISERROR('Delete software failed',16,1)
    RETURN 99
    END
--
-- Return to the caller
--
RETURN 0

GO

GRANT EXECUTE ON up_parmdel_software TO [Hardware Users]
```

3. Parse the code for errors by clicking on the **Parse Query** icon on the toolbar, then create this stored procedure by clicking on the **Execute Query** icon on the toolbar.

How It Works – Software Delete Stored Procedure

Like the two previous stored procedures that we have created in this chapter, this stored procedure only has one input parameter. This input parameter will contain the software ID of the row of data to be deleted:

```
CREATE PROCEDURE dbo.up_parmdel_software
    @Software_ID      INT AS
```

The DELETE statement deletes the one row of data where the value in the Software_ID column matches the value in the @Software_ID input parameter as specified in the WHERE clause:

```
-- ************************************************************************
-- Delete the software
-- ************************************************************************
DELETE FROM Software_T
   WHERE Software_ID = @Software_ID
```

After our DELETE statement has executed, we check for errors using the @@ERROR function and raise an error if this function does not contain a value of zero. Then we return to the caller with a return value of 99:

```
-- Check for errors
--
IF @@ERROR > 0
   BEGIN
   RAISERROR('Delete software failed',16,1)
   RETURN 99
   END
```

If the delete was successful, we return to the caller with a return value of 0:

```
-- Return to the caller
--
RETURN 0
```

We specify the GO command to have the stored procedure created before granting permissions on this stored procedure:

```
GO

GRANT EXECUTE ON up_parmdel_software TO [Hardware Users]
```

Try It Out – Process the Software Delete Stored Procedure

1. Switching to the code in our VB project, make the amendments and additions presented throughout the *How It Works* section.

2. Save your project before you begin testing. Then run the program, log in, and click on the Software tab.

3. Choose a software title that has not been assigned to a system and then click the Delete button.

The software title is deleted, the fields on the **Software** tab are reloaded and the first software title in the **Software Title** combo box is displayed.

4. For the next test, choose a software title that is assigned and then click on the **Delete** button. You should receive an error message similar to the one shown in the following figure:

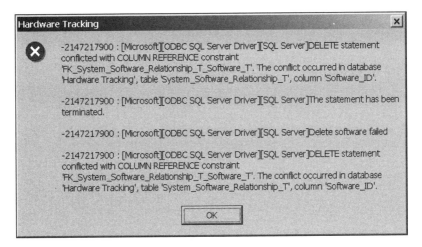

The first message in this message box tells us that there was a foreign key constraint error in the `System_Software_Relationship_T` table. This is because the software ID that we were trying to delete exists in the `System_Software_Relationship_T` as a foreign key.

The third message shown in this message box came from our `up_parmdel_software` stored procedure. This is the error message that we used in the `RAISERROR` statement.

As you can see from the message, our error handling code works well, and the error messages that we raise in our stored procedures are returned to the caller. Most importantly however, the rules of foreign key constraints ensure data integrity in our database.

How It Works – Process the Software Delete Stored Procedure

We want to code the `DeleteSoftware` function in the `Delete Data` class first. This function is very similar to the previous two functions that we have coded in this class and accepts most of the same parameters.

The `lngSoftwareID` parameter will contain the software ID of the software title to be deleted:

```
Public Function DeleteSoftware( _
    ByRef objConn As ADODB.Connection, _
    ByVal lngSoftwareID As Long, _
    ByRef strMessage As String) As Long
```

We set up our error handling in this function first. Then we declare the `Command` object that we will be using to execute the `up_parmdel_software` stored procedure:

```
'Setup error handling
On Error GoTo DeleteSoftware_Err

'Declare local objects
Dim objCmd As ADODB.Command
```

We set a reference to the `Command` object and then set the various properties of the `Command` object:

```
'Set a reference to the command object
Set objCmd = New ADODB.Command

'Set the command object properties
Set objCmd.ActiveConnection = objConn
objCmd.CommandText = "up_parmdel_software"
objCmd.CommandType = adCmdStoredProc
```

Next, we create and append the parameters to the `Parameters` collection:

```
'Create and append the parameters to the parameters collection
objCmd.Parameters.Append objCmd.CreateParameter("RC", _
    adInteger, adParamReturnValue)
objCmd.Parameters.Append objCmd.CreateParameter("SoftwareID", _
    adInteger, adParamInput, , lngSoftwareID)
```

Finally, we execute the `Command` object and then check the return value from the stored procedure in the `RC` parameter. If the return value is non-zero, we raise an error that causes us to fall into our error handling code in this function:

```
'Execute the command object
objCmd.Execute

'Check the return value from the stored procedure
If objCmd.Parameters("RC") <> 0 Then
    Err.Raise 513 + vbObjectError, "DeleteSoftware", _
        "up_parmdel_software failed"
End If
```

If the stored procedure was executed successfully, we remove our reference to the `Command` object and then set the return code for this function. Then we exit this function, returning to the caller:

```
'Remove references to objects
Set objCmd = Nothing

'Set the return code
DeleteSoftware = 0

'Exit function
Exit Function
```

Our error handling code is the same error handling code that we have seen in the last two functions:

```
DeleteSoftware_Err:
    'Enumerate ADO errors
    Dim objErrors As New clsInsertData
    strMessage = objErrors.EnumerateErrors(objConn)
    Set objErrors = Nothing
    'Append any VB errors
    strMessage = strMessage & Err.Number & " : " & Err.Description
    'Return to the caller with a RC of 1
    DeleteSoftware = 1
End Function
```

Switching to the code in our main form (frmMain) we want to modify the cmdDelete_Click procedure, as shown in the next code fragment.

We call the DeleteSoftware function, passing it the required parameters. The data for the software ID parameter is taken from the Software_ID field in the objRSData recordset. This recordset is open and points to the current software title that is displayed on the **Software** tab.

```
        Case 2   'Software

            'Delete the software
            lngRC = objDelete.DeleteSoftware(g_objConn, _
                objRSData!Software_ID, _
                strMessage)
```

We check the return code from the DeleteSoftware function to ensure it is zero. If it is not, we raise an error, which causes us to fall through to the error handling code for this procedure:

```
            'Ensure we were successful
            If lngRC <> 0 Then
                Err.Raise 513 + vbObjectError, "cmdDelete_Click", _
                    "Call to DeleteSoftware failed"
            End If
```

If everything was successful, we call the LoadSoftware procedure to reload the fields on the **Software** tab to reflect the deleted software title.

Then we call the tabData_Click procedure to display the first software title in the **Software** combo box on this tab:

```
            'Reload Software
            Call LoadSoftware

            'Re-initialize the tab control so the opened RS is reloaded
            'to reflect the deleted software
            Call tabData_Click(2)
```

Viewing Constraints

When we deleted an employee who had a system assigned to them, the system assignment was automatically deleted, which caused the associated software assigned to that system to also be deleted from the `System_Software_Relationship_T` table. This was automatically done because of the cascading referential integrity constraints that were defined on the `System_Assignment_T` and `System_Software_Relationship_T` tables.

In order to view the constraints defined on these tables, expand the Hardware Tracking database in the Object Browser in the Query Analyzer and then expand the User Tables group. Next, expand the `System_Assignment_T` table and then expand Constraints. You should see three different constraints defined for this table. One is the primary key constraint, one is a foreign key constraint to the `Hardware_T` table, and another one is a foreign key constraint to the `Employee_T` table. It is this last constraint that we are most interested in.

If you right-click on this constraint, you will see the Open and View context menu items are grayed out, meaning we cannot view this constraint in a dialog. We can, however, choose the context menu item Script Object To New Window As and then choose Create. This will cause the constraint to be scripted into a new query window, as shown in the following figure:

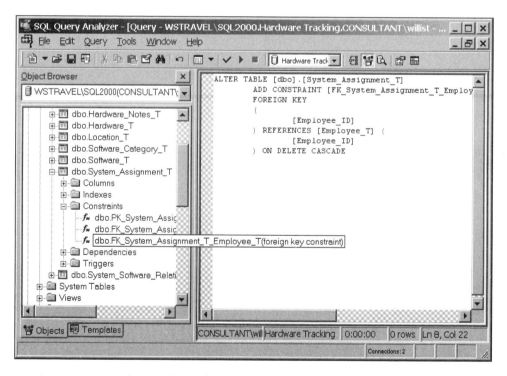

The most interesting point here is the last line of the script, `ON DELETE CASCADE`. We know that this constraint will cascade all deletes from the `Employee_T` table.

Let's look at the constraints for the `System_Software_Relationship_T` table. In particular, we want to examine the constraint to the `System_Assignment_T` table. This constraint, shown in the next figure, also has the `ON DELETE CASCADE` option, which means that when we delete a row from the `System_Assignment_T` table all foreign key entries in the `System_Software_Relationship_T` table will also be deleted.

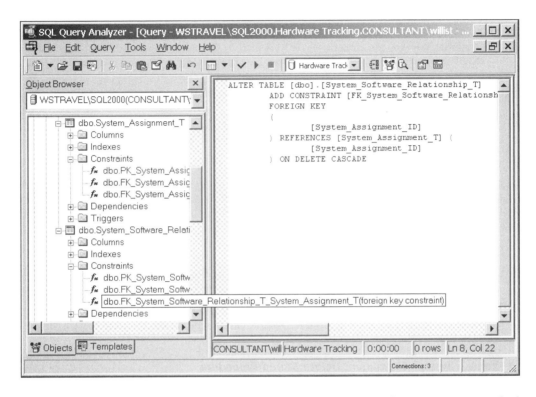

The Query Analyzer provides more than just a tool to write queries as we have come to see in the last few chapters, it is also a tool that allows us to view and edit the various objects in our database.

Try It Out – System Assignment Delete Stored Procedure

When we delete an entry from the `System_Assignment_T` table, all associated software in the `System_Software_Relationship_T` table will be automatically deleted, because of the cascading referential integrity constraints that have been defined on the `System_Software_Relationship_T` table (as we saw in the previous figure).

To create the `up_parmdel_system_assignment` stored procedure:

1. Open a new query window by clicking on the New Query icon on the toolbar, or clear the current query window by clicking on the Clear Query Window icon on the toolbar.

2. Enter the following stored procedure:

```
CREATE PROCEDURE dbo.up_parmdel_system_assignment
   @System_Assignment_ID   INT AS


-- *************************************************************************
-- Delete the system assignment
-- *************************************************************************
DELETE FROM System_Assignment_T
   WHERE System_Assignment_ID = @System_Assignment_ID
--
-- Check for errors
--
IF @@ERROR > 0
   BEGIN
   RAISERROR('Delete system assignment failed',16,1)
   RETURN 99
   END
--
-- Return to the caller
--
RETURN 0

GO

GRANT EXECUTE ON up_parmdel_system_assignment TO [Hardware Users]
```

3. Parse the code for errors by clicking on the **Parse Query** icon on the toolbar and create this stored procedure by clicking on the **Execute Query** icon on the toolbar.

How It Works – System Assignment Delete Stored Procedure

Again we have a simple delete stored procedure that uses no transactions and simply deletes one row of data from a single table. However, executing this stored procedure will cause the cascading referential integrity constraint to be fired by SQL Server and all associated rows of data in the System_Software_Relationship_T table will also be deleted.

This stored procedure accepts a single input parameter, the system assignment ID of the system assignment to be deleted:

```
CREATE PROCEDURE dbo.up_parmdel_system_assignment
   @System_Assignment_ID   INT AS
```

The DELETE statement deletes the one row of data where the value in the System_Assignment_ID column matches the value in the @System_Assignment_ID input parameter:

```
-- *************************************************************************
-- Delete the system assignment
-- *************************************************************************
DELETE FROM System_Assignment_T
   WHERE System_Assignment_ID = @System_Assignment_ID
```

After the DELETE statement is executed, we check for errors by checking the value in the @@ERROR function. If the value returned by this function is not zero, then we raise an error and return to the caller with a return value of 99:

```
-- Check for errors
--
IF @@ERROR > 0
   BEGIN
   RAISERROR('Delete system assignment failed',16,1)
   RETURN 99
   END
```

If everything was successful, we return to the caller with a return value of 0:

```
-- Return to the caller
--
RETURN 0
```

We have the Query Analyzer create this stored procedure before proceeding any further, by specifying the GO command. Then we grant permissions on this stored procedure to the Hardware Users role:

```
GO

GRANT EXECUTE ON up_parmdel_system_assignment TO [Hardware Users]
```

Try It Out – Process the System Assignment Delete Stored Procedure

1. Let's switch to our VB project now, and add the code presented in the *How It Works* section.

2. Save your project before you begin testing. Run your program and click on the System Assignment tab.

3. Choose an employee whose system assignment you want to delete. But, before clicking on the Delete button, go to the Query Analyzer and view the data in the System_Software_ Relationship_T table. You can use the following SELECT statement to do this:

```
SELECT *
   FROM System_Software_Relationship_T
```

4. Now delete the system assignment by clicking on the Delete button on your main form. Run the previous query again, and notice that the related rows of data have been deleted from the System_Software_Relationship_T table.

479

How It Works – Process the System Assignment Delete Stored Procedure

The first thing we will do is code the DeleteSystemAssignment function in the delete data class to execute this stored procedure.

This function accepts the standard parameters that we have been using for a while now, and also the system assignment ID of the system assignment to be deleted:

```
Public Function DeleteSystemAssignment( _
    ByRef objConn As ADODB.Connection, _
    ByVal lngAssignmentID As Long, _
    ByRef strMessage As String) As Long
```

We set up our error handling for this function and then declare our local objects for the function:

```
    'Setup error handling
    On Error GoTo DeleteSystemAssignment_Err

    'Declare local objects
    Dim objCmd As ADODB.Command
```

We set a reference to the Command object next and then set the various properties of the Command object:

```
    'Set a reference to the command object
    Set objCmd = New ADODB.Command

    'Set the command object properties
    Set objCmd.ActiveConnection = objConn
    objCmd.CommandText = "up_parmdel_system_assignment"
    objCmd.CommandType = adCmdStoredProc
```

Next, we create and append the necessary parameters to the Parameters collection:

```
    'Create and append the parameters to the parameters collection
    objCmd.Parameters.Append objCmd.CreateParameter("RC", _
        adInteger, adParamReturnValue)
    objCmd.Parameters.Append objCmd.CreateParameter("SystemID", _
        adInteger, adParamInput, , lngAssignmentID)
```

We then execute the Command object to have the system assignment deleted. We check the return value from the stored procedure in the RC parameter and raise an error if it is not equal to zero:

```
    'Execute the command object
    objCmd.Execute

    'Check the return value from the stored procedure
    If objCmd.Parameters("RC") <> 0 Then
        Err.Raise 513 + vbObjectError, "DeleteSystemAssignment", _
            "up_parmdel_system_assignment failed"
    End If
```

If everything was successful, we remove our reference to the Command object, set the return code for this function, and exit the function:

```
    'Remove references to objects
    Set objCmd = Nothing

    'Set the return code
    DeleteSystemAssignment = 0

    'Exit function
    Exit Function
```

Our error handling will capture and return any errors that may have occurred:

```
DeleteSystemAssignment_Err:
    'Enumerate ADO errors
    Dim objErrors As New clsInsertData
    strMessage = objErrors.EnumerateErrors(objConn)
    Set objErrors = Nothing
    'Append any VB errors
    strMessage = strMessage & Err.Number & " : " & Err.Description
    'Return to the caller with a RC of 1
    DeleteSystemAssignment = 1
End Function
```

Switching to the code in the main form (frmMain) we want to modify the cmdDelete_Click procedure to include the code to call the DeleteSystemAssignment function. Modify this procedure, as shown in the next code fragment.

The first thing that we do in this code is to call the DeleteSystemAssignment function, passing it the required parameters. Notice that we are using the lngSystemAssignmentID variable for the system assignment ID parameter. This variable contains the saved system assignment ID that was set when a user clicked on an employee in the **System Assignment** tab. This functionality was coded in the last chapter.

```
    Case 3   'System Assignment

        'Delete the system assignment and software
        lngRC = objDelete.DeleteSystemAssignment(g_objConn, _
            lngSystemAssignmentID, _
            strMessage)
```

We check the return code from our function to ensure we were successful. If the return code is not zero then we raise an error:

```
        'Ensure we were successful
        If lngRC <> 0 Then
            Err.Raise 513 + vbObjectError, "cmdDelete_Click", _
                "Call to DeleteSystemAssignment failed"
        End If
```

If everything was successful, we call the `LoadSystems` procedure to reload the data on the **System Assignment** tab to reflect the deleted system assignment.

Then we call the `tabData_Click` procedure to display the first entry in the `Employee` combo box on the **System Assignment** tab:

```
'Reload Systems
Call LoadSystems

'Re-initialize the tab control so the opened RS is reloaded
'to reflect the deleted system assignment
Call tabData_Click(3)
```

Summary

This chapter has taken a broad look at referential integrity, cascading referential integrity constraints, triggers, and DELETE stored procedures. Of all of the stored procedures that we have coded so far, these DELETE procedures have been by far the simplest. This is because we have cascading referential integrity constraints and triggers to aid us in maintaining referential integrity in our database.

We have seen at first hand how cascading referential integrity constraints can help clean up related data in tables that contain a foreign key to the table that we are deleting data from. We know that cascading deletes can be a wonderful tool that helps us to maintain referential integrity. Knowing when and how to use cascading referential integrity constraints can make your job as a developer much easier.

We have also seen how we can use triggers to automatically help us clean up data that does not fall into the category of using cascading referential integrity constraints. The trigger that we created on the `Employee_T` table was automatically fired after an employee was deleted; it checked the location data in the `Employee_T` table and, if the location was not being referenced by any employee, it was deleted from the `Location_T` table.

Because our DELETE stored procedures were simple, we had no need to use transactions. SQL Server took care of everything and would not delete the data or fire the constraints or triggers if an error occurred.

To summarize, you should know:

- ❏ What referential integrity is, and how to maintain it
- ❏ How to use cascading referential integrity constraints to delete data
- ❏ How to create triggers to help maintain referential integrity
- ❏ How to write delete stored procedures

In the next chapter we will cover the 'mysterious world' of the SQL Server `Text` data type. This data type is capable of storing vast amounts of information, but can be rather cumbersome to work with. The chapter will show you how this data type is used in SQL Server, and how you can use it in your stored procedures and VB programs.

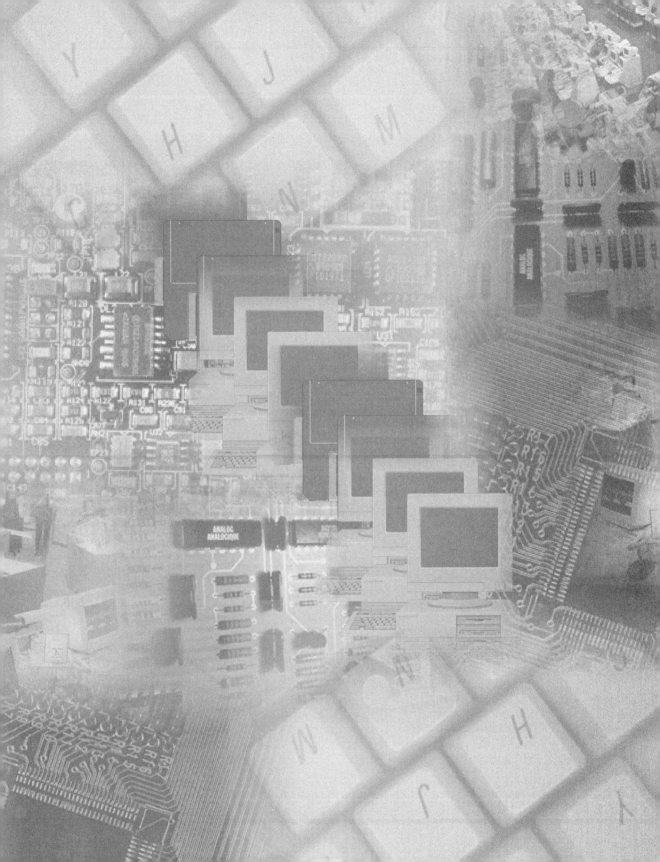

Working with Text Data

Throughout the book we have been working with SQL Server string data types of Char and VarChar. We know that both of these data types can contain up to 8,000 characters, or 8K of data. While that seems like a lot of data, there will come a time when this is simply not enough.

SQL Server provides the Text data type, which is capable of holding up to 2,147,483,647 characters, or 2 gigabytes of data. This data type should be able to handle the most demanding needs for data storage. However, working with the Text data type requires some special handling, both in SQL Server and in your VB programs.

This chapter takes a look at these special requirements. We will modify our database to include a table that contains a Text data type so that we can get first hand experience of working with it in SQL Server and Visual Basic.

So, in this chapter we will:

❑ Examine how SQL Server stores and manages text data

❑ Learn how to insert and select text data

❑ Learn how to work with text pointers to access data in a text column

❑ Learn how to read, write, and update text data

How SQL Server Manages Text Data

In this chapter when we talk about Text data types we are also referring to the nText data type. The nText data type is the Unicode data type equivalent to the Text data type. Unicode data uses the UNICODE UCS-2 character set, thus it uses two bytes to represent a single character. Therefore, an nText data type is limited to half the number of characters of a Text data type, or 1,073,741,823 characters.

SQL Server stores the data for a text column in a collection of data pages, which are 8K in size and called **text pages**. The data row for a text column contains a 16-byte **binary pointer**, which is a pointer to the **address** in the root structure. The root structure manages text pages and their addresses. The diagram overleaf shows the **B-tree** that is used to manage text data. The B-tree is made up of the root structure and data pages. The root structure is made up of a series of pointers pointing to the data pages:

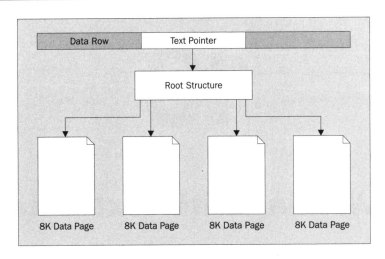

Text pages can contain text data from multiple rows in your table, and the text pages from one row of data may not necessarily reside next to each other physically. They are, however, arranged logically in the root structure. SQL Server manages the text pages so that a complete text page is filled with data even if it comes from more than one row in your table. Likewise, if your application only fills part of a page with 4K of data and then comes back later to add another 8K of data, the first page is filled with data and the remaining 4K of data is written to another page.

This type of data management provides two major benefits. Firstly, SQL Server can efficiently manage the entire text column. If you want to read data in the middle of the text column, SQL Server can quickly locate the text page that contains the data to be read. Secondly, this method of data storage is very efficient, as there is no wasted space in your database. SQL Server fills an entire 8K page before creating another, even if this means combining data from several rows in your table.

SQL Server 2000 provides a Text In Row option for storing and managing text data that is specific to each table that contains a column that has a TEXT data type. This option, which by default is turned off, allows SQL Server to store text data either in the data row or in text pages. When this option is turned off the text page method described previously is used.

If the Text In Row option is turned on, SQL Server 2000 uses a different approach to managing the text data in our tables. SQL Server will store the text data directly in the table row, provided that the length of the text string is shorter than the limit that has been set for the Text In Row option and that there is enough space available in the data row to hold the text string. When you turn this option on, you specify a maximum limit in the range of 24 to 7,000 bytes.

So when the Text In Row option is turned on for a table, SQL Server does not have to access the root structure nor the text page or pages to read the data we are after. Using this option increases performance as it reduces the number of reads required to access the data we are interested in.

What happens if the length of the text data we want to write exceeds the limit that has been set for the Text In Row option? If this occurs, SQL Server writes the pointers (which are normally stored in the root structure) in the data row, if space is available. This eliminates having to read the root structure to get the pointers to the text pages. This also reduces the number of reads required to access our text data.

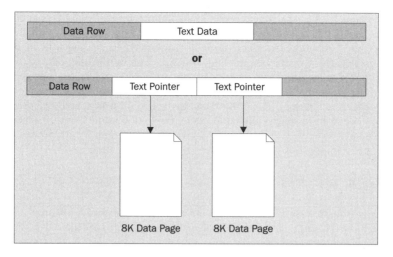

If space is not available for the pointers to be written in the data row then SQL Server will write as many pointers as it can in the data row and the rest are written in the root structure.

So how do we access the data in these text pages? Actually, we don't access them directly; SQL Server provides a text pointer to the root structure or directly to the text pages, and we use this pointer to access the data. SQL Server takes care of all this behind the scenes. We only need to use text pointers when we want to work with specific portions of the data.

SQL Server provides three functions that allow us to work with specific portions of data in a text column. They are READTEXT, WRITETEXT, and UPDATETEXT. All three of these functions require us to use a text pointer to access specific portions of the data. We will be covering these functions later in the chapter.

> **When the Text In Row option is turned on we cannot use these SQL functions.**

Setting the Text In Row Option

As we mentioned earlier, the Text In Row option is switched off by default. In order to turn this option on we must execute the system stored procedure SP_TABLEOPTION. This system stored procedure allows us to turn the Text In Row option on or off and adjust the maximum size for text stored in the table row. The range of sizes for text stored in a table row is from 24 to 7000 bytes.

In order to execute this system stored procedure you must be a member of the sysadmin, db_owner, or db_ddladmin role.

Before considering turning this option on you should examine how you plan to use the Text data type in your application and how much data you anticipate storing.

I once worked on an application where the majority of the data that we wanted to store in a Text data type was in the range of 4 to 5 K (4,000 – 5,000 bytes). However, occasionally we needed to store up to 15K worth of data, which is why we had to use the Text data type. This scenario was perfect for the Text In Row option because most of the data that we were storing fitted directly in the table row, consequently we gained an added performance increase by using this option.

If, however, the majority of your data exceeds the maximum size of 7,000 bytes and you want to access only a portion of the text data, you are better off not using this option. When you use this option you must read, insert, and update the text data in one operation. When dealing with small amounts of text data this option is ideal; however, when dealing with large amounts of text data, let's say larger than 1 MB, you will probably not want to turn this option on.

As mentioned earlier, the `Text In Row` option can be turned on using the `SP_TABLEOPTION` system stored procedure. We need to specify the table name, the option name of `text in row`, and the option value, a range between `24` and `7,000`. This represents the maximum length of data allowed in the table row. The following example shows how this stored procedure is called:

```
sp_tableoption 'Hardware_Notes_T', 'text in row', '7000'
```

When we execute this system stored procedure, the options are set and a message is returned indicating successful completion. This option can only be executed on a table that has a `Text` column defined in it. If it does not, the stored procedure will return an error.

Creating a Notes Table

In order to get practical hands-on experience of working with text data, we want to modify our database structure to include a table that contains a `Text` data type column. The hardware contained in the `Hardware_T` table seems like a logical choice for keeping notes. This would allow us to track user and technician comments on specific systems and we could then quickly identify hardware that had consistent problems or that performed poorly.

So, what we want to do is to add a table that has a text column and also a foreign key reference to the `Hardware_T` table. We are not going to use the Enterprise Manager to add this new table. Instead, we are going to use the Query Analyzer and add a table using SQL statements.

This would be a good time to use the templates in the Object Browser, as there are several useful templates provided to create tables. However, as you are not completely familiar with the syntax of creating a table, we are going to do this manually so you can become more familiar with the `CREATE TABLE` syntax. As you become familiar with this syntax you can then use the templates, which provide an efficient shortcut.

We briefly covered creating a table using T-SQL statements in Chapter 9, but let's look again at the syntax for this. The syntax for the `CREATE TABLE` T-SQL statement, as with most other T-SQL statements, is fairly complex and lengthy. To keep the learning curve short, we will only show the basic syntax here:

```
CREATE TABLE table-name
    (
    column-name data-type [NULL | NOT NULL]
          [IDENTITY(seed,increment)]
          [PRIMARY KEY] [CLUSTERED | NONCLUSTERED]
    [,...n]
```

In this syntax, the data in square brackets ([ ]) is optional. The `table-name` argument specifies the name of the table to be created.

The *column-name* argument specifies the column name and the *data-type* argument specifies the data type for the column. NULL and NOT NULL are optional keywords and specify whether or not the column will allow null values, with NULL being the default.

The optional IDENTITY argument specifies that the column is an identity column, and you can specify the *seed* value and *increment* value. The default values for the seed and increment values are both 1.

The optional PRIMARY KEY argument specifies that this column should be the primary key for this table. SQL Server will automatically create a primary key constraint for this column based on the specified argument: CLUSTERED or NONCLUSTERED.

The *...n* argument shows that you can specify more columns as needed.

Altering a Table

The ALTER TABLE statement is another complex T-SQL statement that allows us to alter the structure of a table. We can alter a column or add and drop columns and constraints. The basic syntax for our examples is as follows:

```
ALTER TABLE table-name
    ADD CONSTRAINT constraint-name
    FOREIGN KEY (column-name)
    REFERENCES table-name(column-name)
    [ON DELETE CASCADE | ON UPDATE CASCADE]
```

In the syntax above, the *table-name* argument specifies the name of the table to be altered. The *column-name* argument for FOREIGN KEY specifies the column name in the table that is being defined as a foreign key. Notice that the column name is enclosed in parentheses. We can also add constraints when we create the table.

The *table-name* argument for REFERENCES specifies the table name that the foreign key references and is followed by the *column-name* in the referenced table.

The ON DELETE CASCADE and ON UPDATE CASCADE arguments are optional and will cascade deletes or updates of the column that has been specified in the REFERENCES argument.

Try It Out – Create the Hardware Notes Table

Now that we have discussed the basic syntax for the CREATE TABLE and ALTER TABLE statements, let's start building our query to create this new table. It's usually a good idea to create a simple table and then modify the structure of the table. This is the case here, where we are specifying that the basic table be created with the primary key constraint. Then we specify the GO command to have the Query Analyzer execute the preceding SQL statements before continuing.

1. Start the Query Analyzer, log in, and start entering the query as shown in the following code fragment:

```
CREATE TABLE Hardware_Notes_T
    (
```

```
        Hardware_Notes_ID      INT IDENTITY(1,1) PRIMARY KEY CLUSTERED,
        Hardware_ID            INT      NOT NULL,
        Hardware_Notes_TX      TEXT     NOT NULL,
        Last_Update_DT         DATETIME NOT NULL
        )

GO
```

2. Knowing the basic syntax of the ALTER TABLE statement, we want to alter our new table to add a foreign key constraint. The code for this constraint is shown in the next code fragment:

```
ALTER TABLE Hardware_Notes_T
     ADD CONSTRAINT FK_Hardware_Notes_T
     FOREIGN KEY (Hardware_ID)
     REFERENCES Hardware_T(Hardware_ID)
     ON DELETE CASCADE

GO
```

3. The last line of code for this query is the GRANT statement. Here we are granting permissions on the new table to the hardware users role. Since this is a table, we have specified the SELECT, UPDATE, INSERT, and DELETE permissions:

```
GRANT SELECT, UPDATE, INSERT, DELETE ON Hardware_Notes_T TO [Hardware Users]
```

4. At this point the query is complete, so go ahead and execute it. Once the query has completed successfully, you can view the new table in the Object Browser.

5. Expand the Hardware Tracking database and then expand the User Tables group. Expand the Hardware_Notes_T table and then expand the Columns group to view the columns:

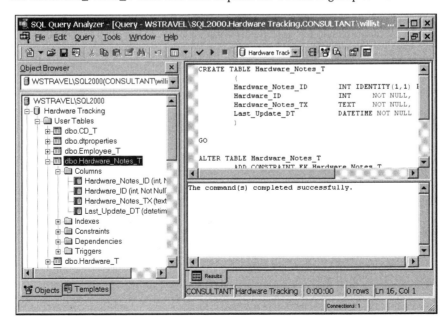

How It Works – Create the Hardware Notes Table

In the partial query shown in the first code fragment, we have specified the CREATE TABLE statement followed by the table name for our new table. Then we have specified each of the columns that we want in this table.

```
CREATE TABLE Hardware_Notes_T
    (
    Hardware_Notes_ID        INT IDENTITY(1,1) PRIMARY KEY CLUSTERED,
    Hardware_ID              INT      NOT NULL,
    Hardware_Notes_TX        TEXT     NOT NULL,
    Last_Update_DT           DATETIME NOT NULL
    )
```

Notice that the first column is an IDENTITY column and also the PRIMARY KEY of our table. Because we have specified that this column be an identity column and also the primary key, we do not specifically have to define NOT NULL, as it will be done for us by SQL Server. This is because an identity column will not allow null values nor will a primary key allow null values. We have specified that the primary key constraint be created as CLUSTERED. The Hardware_Notes_TX column in our table is the text column in this table. All columns have been defined as NOT NULL meaning that they will not allow null values to be inserted into them.

Next we have specified the new table in the ALTER TABLE statement and have specified a constraint name of FK_Hardware_Notes_T. We have also specified that the foreign key in this table is the Hardware_ID column and that it references the Hardware_ID column in the Hardware_T table. We have also specified the ON DELETE CASCADE argument so that all deletes from the Hardware_T table will be cascaded to this table. Again we have specified the GO command so the Query Analyzer will execute the preceding SQL statements and alter the table:

```
ALTER TABLE Hardware_Notes_T
    ADD CONSTRAINT FK_Hardware_Notes_T
    FOREIGN KEY (Hardware_ID)
    REFERENCES Hardware_T(Hardware_ID)
    ON DELETE CASCADE

GO
```

We will not be using the Text In Row option for our new table. The reason for this is to allow you to get first hand experience with the READTEXT, WRITETEXT, and UPDATETEXT SQL statements, which are not available for use when the Text In Row option is turned on.

Inserting Text Data

We are going to depart from the norm here, and discuss insert stored procedures first. When we initially insert data into a text column we usually have all of the data that we want to insert and we are most likely going to be dealing with a lot of data. The maximum amount of data that can be inserted into a text column is 2 gigabytes, and even though the amount of data that we will be inserting is usually a lot less than this, it is still likely to be significantly large.

2 gigabytes is a lot of data to try to manage in our programs, not to mention in a single variable. This would be nearly impossible on most workstations, since the amount of available memory is normally around 128 – 256 MB.

This is where ADO comes to the rescue. ADO provides the `AppendChunk` method for the `Parameter` object. We can insert data using the `Parameter` object by appending the data to the parameter and then appending the parameter to the `Parameters` collection. Then we can execute the `Command` object to have the data inserted.

Basically, the `AppendChunk` method allows us to append a large amount of data to the `Parameter` object in chunks. This makes the data more manageable and does not consume as many system resources. We perform this manipulation of data in a loop, calling the `AppendChunk` method each time. The first call to the `AppendChunk` method writes the data to the `Parameter` object, overwriting any existing data that may have been there. Each subsequent call to the `AppendChunk` method appends the chunk of data to the `Parameter` object.

When initially inserting data into a text column we can use the standard `INSERT` statement that we have been using all along. However, keep in mind that the `INSERT` statement is a logged operation and can quickly fill up the transaction log, if the log is not set to automatically grow, or if there is a size limit on the log. Therefore, after a large amount of text has been inserted, the transaction log should be backed up.

Try It Out – Hardware Notes Insert Stored Procedure

The insert stored procedure that we want to create here (`up_parmins_sytem_notes`) should insert data into the `Hardware_Notes_T` table. The values that we will need to insert are a foreign key to the `Hardware_T` table and the hardware notes that will be inserted into the text column of our table.

To create this stored procedure:

1. Open a new query window by clicking on the New Query icon on the toolbar, or clear the current query window by clicking on the Clear Query Window icon on the toolbar.

2. Enter the following stored procedure:

```
CREATE PROCEDURE up_parmins_system_notes
     @Hardware_ID           INT,
     @System_Notes_TX       TEXT AS


--   **********************************************************************
--   Insert system notes
--   **********************************************************************
INSERT INTO Hardware_Notes_T
     (Hardware_ID, Hardware_Notes_TX, Last_Update_DT)
     VALUES(@Hardware_ID, @System_Notes_TX, GETDATE())
--
-- Check for errors
--
IF @@ERROR > 0
     BEGIN
     RAISERROR('Insert of system notes failed',16,1)
```

```
        RETURN 99
        END
--
-- Return to the caller
--
RETURN 0

GO

GRANT EXECUTE ON up_parmins_system_notes TO [Hardware Users]
```

3. Parse the code for errors by clicking on the **Parse Query** icon on the toolbar.

4. Create this stored procedure by clicking on the **Execute Query** icon on the toolbar.

How It Works – Hardware Notes Insert Stored Procedure

The insert stored procedure to insert text data does not differ from any other insert stored procedure that we have created. Here we specify the CREATE PROCEDURE statement followed by the stored procedure name.

Then we specify the input parameters for this stored procedure. The @Hardware_ID input parameter will contain the hardware ID that this note is associated with, and the @System_Notes_TX input parameter will contain the entire system notes:

```
CREATE PROCEDURE up_parmins_system_notes
        @Hardware_ID            INT,
        @System_Notes_TX        TEXT AS
```

The INSERT statement specifies, in the columns list, the columns into which we want to insert data, and the values list contains the values to be inserted:

```
-- **********************************************************************
-- Insert system notes
-- **********************************************************************
INSERT INTO Hardware_Notes_T
    (Hardware_ID, Hardware_Notes_TX, Last_Update_DT)
    VALUES(@Hardware_ID, @System_Notes_TX, GETDATE())
```

After we have executed the INSERT statement we want to check for errors. If the @@ERROR function does not contain a value of zero then we raise an error. Then we return to the caller with a return value of 99:

```
-- Check for errors
--
IF @@ERROR > 0
    BEGIN
    RAISERROR('Insert of system notes failed',16,1)
    RETURN 99
    END
```

If the insert was successful, we return to the caller with a return value of zero:

```
-- Return to the caller
--
RETURN 0
```

We specify the GO command to have the Query Analyzer create this stored procedure before we grant permissions on it:

```
GO

GRANT EXECUTE ON up_parmins_system_notes TO [Hardware Users]
```

Now that we have a stored procedure to insert system notes, let's move on to selecting data from a text column.

Selecting Text Data

When we want to select all of the data in a text column we can use a standard SELECT statement. This allows us to return all of the data from SQL Server to our VB program. However, our VB program cannot handle and process the large amount of data that will be returned. Again, this is a limitation placed on us by the system (in this case system memory).

This is where ADO comes to the rescue again. The Field object provides a method called GetChunk that allows us to get chunks of data. This allows us to get a manageable chunk of data, process it, and then get another chunk of data, repeating the process until we have retrieved all of the data in the Field object.

When using the GetChunk method, we specify the size of the chunk of data that we want to retrieve. The first call to the GetChunk method starts reading the data in the Field object at position 1 and each subsequent call to the GetChunk method reads the data from where the last call left off. ADO manages this for you behind the scenes; there is nothing that you need to do. If the size of the remaining data is less than the size of the chunk of data you want to retrieve then the GetChunk method will simply return the remaining data.

Try It Out – Hardware Notes Select Stored Procedure

The select stored procedure that we want to create (up_parmsel_system_notes) will select all data in the text column for a specific row. Since the data in this table is related to a specific system in the Hardware_T table, we need to specify the Hardware_ID as an input parameter. This will let us know which row of data is to be selected.

To create this stored procedure:

1. Open a new query window by clicking on the **New Query** icon on the toolbar, or clear the current query window by clicking on the **Clear Query** Window icon on the toolbar.

2. Enter the following stored procedure:

```
CREATE PROCEDURE up_parmsel_system_notes
    @Hardware_ID INT AS

-- ************************************************************************
-- Select the notes for a specific system
-- ************************************************************************
SELECT Hardware_Notes_ID, Hardware_Notes_TX
    FROM Hardware_Notes_T
    WHERE Hardware_ID = @Hardware_ID
--
-- Check for errors
--
IF @@ERROR > 0
    BEGIN
    RAISERROR('Select system notes failed',16,1)
    RETURN 99
    END
--
-- Return to the caller
--
RETURN 0

GO

GRANT EXECUTE ON up_parmsel_system_notes TO [Hardware Users]
```

3. Parse the code for errors by clicking on the **Parse Query** icon on the toolbar.

4. Create this stored procedure by clicking on the **Execute Query** icon on the toolbar.

How It Works – Hardware Notes Select Stored Procedure

This stored procedure accepts one input parameter, the hardware ID of the row of data to be selected. Remember that the Hardware_ID column in the Hardware_Notes_T table is a foreign key to the Hardware_ID column in the Hardware_T table.

```
CREATE PROCEDURE up_parmsel_system_notes
    @Hardware_ID INT AS
```

Using a SELECT statement, we select two columns of data, the Hardware_Notes_ID that is the primary key to this table, and the Hardware_Notes_TX column that is the text column in this table:

```
-- ************************************************************************
-- Select the notes for a specific system
-- ************************************************************************
SELECT Hardware_Notes_ID, Hardware_Notes_TX
    FROM Hardware_Notes_T
    WHERE Hardware_ID = @Hardware_ID
```

After our SELECT statement has executed, we check for errors and raise an error if the @@ERROR function does not return a value of 0. Then we return to the caller with a return value of 99:

495

```
-- Check for errors
--
IF @@ERROR > 0
     BEGIN
     RAISERROR('Select system notes failed',16,1)
     RETURN 99
     END
```

If the SELECT statement was successful, we return to the caller with a return value of zero:

```
-- Return to the caller
--
RETURN 0
```

We specify the GO command to have the Query Analyzer create this stored procedure before continuing to process SQL statements. Then we grant permissions to this stored procedure to the members of hardware users role:

```
GO

GRANT EXECUTE ON up_parmsel_system_notes TO [Hardware Users]
```

Try It Out – Modifying the Hardware Tracking Application

At this point we want to make the necessary modifications to the Hardware Tracking application to enable us to insert and select system notes for our hardware. Because the data that we will be displaying could get quite lengthy, let's use a separate form to display and insert the system notes. We will be using the existing project from the last chapter, so open the HardwareTracking.vbp project.

1. Add a new form to this project and set its properties as shown in the following table:

Property	Value
Name	frmNotes
BorderStyle	3 – Fixed Dialog
Caption	Notes
Height	4392
Icon	none
StartUpPosition	1 – CenterOwner
Width	6984

2. Add the controls shown in the following table to this new form:

Control	Name	Properties
PictureBox	Picture1	Height = 3852, Width = 4812, BackColor = &H00FFFFFF&
Image	Image1	Picture = (your choice). This Image has been drawn inside of the PictureBox control.
Label	lblSystemNotes	BackStyle = 0 – Transparent, Caption = System Notes for , Height = 204, Left = 672, Top = 192, Width = 3948. This Label has been drawn inside the PictureBox control.
TextBox	txtNotes	BorderStyle = 0 – None, Height = 3180, Left = 10, MultiLine = True, Text = nothing, Top = 576, Width = 4716. This TextBox has been drawn inside the PictureBox control.
CommandButton	cmdReadPartialNotes	Caption = Read Partial Notes
CommandButton	cmdInsertNewNotes	Caption = Insert New Notes
CommandButton	cmdUpdatePartialNotes	Caption = Update Partial Notes
CommandButton	cmdReplaceNotes	Caption = Replace Notes
Label	Label1	Caption = Offset
Label	Label2	Caption = Length
Textbox	txtOffset	Alignment = 1 – Right Justify, Height = 288, Text = 0, Width = 492
TextBox	txtLength	Alignment = 1 – Right Justify, Height = 288, Text = 0, Width = 492
Label	lblMessage	Caption = nothing, Height = 204, Left = 4992, Top = 3744, Width = 1836

The following figure shows the position of these controls:

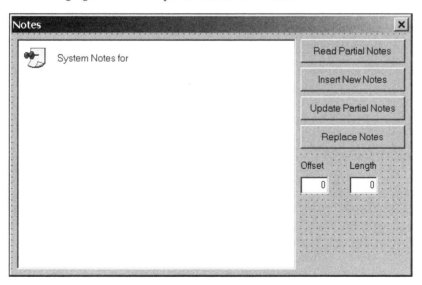

3. All of the code for this form and the new class module that is required will be explained in the *How It Works* section that follows. Enter the code before testing.

4. At this point you should save your project. Then run your program, log in and then click on the **System Assignment** tab. Next, double-click on the image control and the **Notes** form will be displayed:

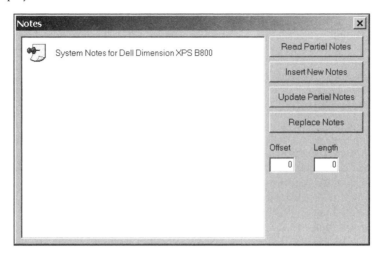

5. Notice that the system manufacturer and model are displayed on this form. We are now ready to insert some notes for this system. Enter some notes data and then click on the **Insert New Notes** button. After the notes are inserted you should see a message at the bottom of the form indicating that the insert was successful.

6. Close the form by clicking on the **X** in the upper right-hand corner. Now double-click on the image control on the **System Assignment** tab and the **Notes** form will be shown with the notes that you have entered:

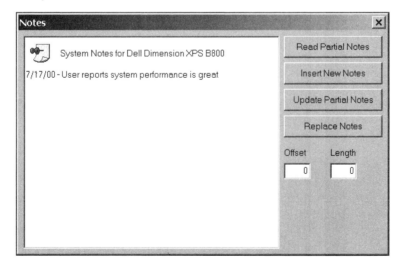

How It Works – Modifying the Hardware Tracking Application – Insert Notes Function

The first bit of code that we want to add to this project will be a couple of functions to process the
up_parmins_system_notes and up_parmsel_system_notes stored procedures that we created
earlier in this chapter. So let's add a new class module to the project that will support all of our text data
stored procedures. Set the Name property of the new class module to clsTextData.

The first function that we want to build in this new class is a function to insert new notes. The
InsertNotes function is very similar to the other functions that we have coded in our class modules.
The only difference here is that we will be appending each parameter to the Parameters collection using
the Parameter object, because we need to use the AppendChunk method of the Command object.

The InsertNotes function accepts four parameters. The first and last parameters should already be
familiar to you. The second parameter will contain the hardware ID that the system notes should be
associated with, and the strNotes parameter will contain the system notes to be inserted. Notice that
this parameter has been passed by reference. Since this parameter will contain a large amount of data,
we don't want to try to pass a copy of it as is done when we pass a parameter by value. When we pass a
parameter by reference we pass a pointer to the location of the data, rather than the data itself.

```
Public Function InsertNotes( _
    ByRef objConn As ADODB.Connection, _
    ByVal lngHardwareID As Long, _
    ByRef strNotes As String, _
    ByRef strMessage As String) As Long
```

We then set up our error handling and declare our local variables. Notice that we have included three
local variables, all of which are Long data types. Then we have declared a Parameter object in
addition to the Command object:

```
    'Set up error handling
    On Error GoTo InsertNotes_Err

    'Declare local variables and objects
    Dim lngTextSize As Long, lngOffset As Long, lngChunkSize As Long
    Dim objCmd As ADODB.Command
    Dim objParm As ADODB.Parameter
```

There is only one validation for this function. We simply want to validate that the strNotes parameter
passed to this function is not a zero length string. If it is then we raise an error, which causes us to fall
through to our error handling code:

```
    'Validate notes data
    If RTrim(Len(strNotes)) = 0 Then
        strMessage = "Notes data is zero length" & vbCrLf & vbCrLf
        Err.Raise 513 + vbObjectError, "InsertNotes", _
            "Data validation failed"
    End If
```

We set a reference to the Command object next and then set the Command object's properties:

499

```
'Set a reference to the command object
Set objCmd = New ADODB.Command

'Set the command object's properties
Set objCmd.ActiveConnection = objConn
objCmd.CommandText = "up_parmins_system_notes"
objCmd.CommandType = adCmdStoredProc
```

The first parameter that we will be appending to the Parameters collection is the parameter for the return value from our up_parmins_system_notes stored procedure. We set a reference to the Parameter object and then set the parameter's properties.

Since this is a return value we need only set three properties for this parameter. The first property is the Name property that will allow us to access this parameter in the Parameters collection by name. The second property is the Type property and has been set using the adInteger constant from the DataTypeEnum enumeration. The last property, Direction, specifies the direction of this parameter. We have set this property using the adParamReturnValue constant from the ParameterDirectionEnum enumeration:

```
'*************************************************
'First parameter - Return value
'*************************************************
'Set a reference to the parameter object
Set objParm = New ADODB.Parameter

'Set the parameter properties
objParm.Name = "RC"
objParm.Type = adInteger
objParm.Direction = adParamReturnValue
```

After we have set the properties for this parameter we append this parameter to the Parameters collection. We then remove our reference from the Parameter object to clear all properties that were set:

```
'Append the parameter to the parameters collection
objCmd.Parameters.Append objParm

'Remove reference to the parameter object
Set objParm = Nothing
```

The next parameter that we want to append is the parameter for the hardware ID. First we set a reference to the Parameter object and then proceed to set the parameter's properties. This is an input parameter and we have identified it as such by setting the Direction property to the adParamInput constant. The Value property is set using the lngHardwareID parameter that is passed to this function:

```
'*************************************************
'Second parameter - Hardware ID
'*************************************************
'Set a reference to the parameter object
Set objParm = New ADODB.Parameter

'Set the parameter properties
```

```
objParm.Name = "HardwareID"
objParm.Type = adInteger
objParm.Direction = adParamInput
objParm.Value = lngHardwareID
```

Once again we append this parameter to the `Parameters` collection and then remove our reference to the `Parameter` object:

```
'Append the parameter to the parameters collection
objCmd.Parameters.Append objParm

'Remove reference to the parameter object
Set objParm = Nothing
```

The last parameter that we want to create will contain the data for the text column. First we set a reference to the `Parameter` object and then proceed to set the parameter's properties:

```
'**************************************************
'Third parameter - Notes data
'**************************************************
'Set a reference to the parameter object
Set objParm = New ADODB.Parameter
```

Since we are dealing with a large amount of data and the input parameter for the `up_parmins_system_notes` stored procedure specifies that this parameter is a `Text` data type, we must set the `Attributes` property using the `adFldLong` constant from the `FieldAttributeEnum` enumeration. Setting this property also allows us to use the `AppendChunk` method of the `Command` object. The `Type` property is set using the `adLongVarChar` constant from the `DataTypeEnum` enumeration.

The `Size` property has been set using the VB `Len` function to set this property to the length of the `strNotes` parameter. Remember that the `strNotes` parameter is one of the parameters for this function.

```
'Set the parameter properties
objParm.Attributes = adFldLong
objParm.Name = "Notes"
objParm.Type = adLongVarChar
objParm.Direction = adParamInput
objParm.Size = Len(strNotes)
```

We set the default values for our local variables next. We set the `lngTextSize` variable to the size of the `strNotes` parameter that was input to this function. Then we set the `lngChunkSize` variable to the length of the `lngTextSize` variable divided by 10.

> *In a production application you will need to set this to a size that is appropriate for the system that the application will be running on. Remember that the size that you specify here should be a little less than the amount of physical memory available.*

This allows us to process the data in chunks. While this isn't a big deal for our little tests, imagine if you will that you are processing hundreds of megabytes of data. This can really make a big difference and allows you to manage the data in smaller chunks. The last variable is the `lngOffset` variable and this will be used to address the offset into the `strNotes` parameter:

```
'Set default values
lngTextSize = Len(strNotes)
lngChunkSize = (lngTextSize / 10)
lngOffset = 1
```

Now we want to perform a loop while the value in the lngOffset variable is less than the value in the lngTextSize variable.

The first line in the loop uses the AppendChunk method of the Parameter object. Here we are using the Mid function to get a chunk of data from the strNotes variable. Using the lngOffset variable, we specify the starting point in the strNotes variable that we want to start reading data from, and using the lngChunkSize variable we specify how much data we want to read from the starting point. We then append the chunk of data to the Parameter.

The second line in this loop increments the lngOffset variable, using the lngOffset variable plus the lngChunkSize variable:

```
'Loop through the string and append the data to the parameter object
Do While lngOffset <= lngTextSize
    objParm.AppendChunk Mid(strNotes, lngOffset, lngChunkSize)
    lngOffset = lngOffset + lngChunkSize
Loop
```

After all data has been appended to the Parameter object, we append the Parameter object to the Parameters collection. Then we remove our reference to the Parameter object by setting it to Nothing:

```
'Append the parameter to the parameters collection
objCmd.Parameters.Append objParm

'Remove reference to the parameter object
Set objParm = Nothing
```

Once all parameters have been appended to the Parameters collection we execute the Command object to have the system notes inserted. Then we check the return value from the stored procedure in the RC parameter and raise an error if it is not zero:

```
'Execute the command object
objCmd.Execute

'Check the return value from the stored procedure
If objCmd.Parameters("RC") <> 0 Then
    Err.Raise 513 + vbObjectError, "InsertNotes", _
        "up_parmins_system_notes failed"
End If
```

Finally, we remove our reference to the Command object and then set the return code for this function. Then we exit the function, bypassing the error handling function:

```
'Remove references to objects
Set objCmd = Nothing
```

```
'Set the return code
InsertNotes = 0

'Exit function
Exit Function
```

The error handling code is the same error handling that we have used in the past few chapters. Basically, we set a reference to the `clsInsertData` class and execute the `EnumerateErrors` function to enumerate the ADO errors. Then we append any VB messages to the `strMessage` parameter and set the return code for this function:

```
InsertNotes_Err:
    'Enumerate ADO errors
    Dim objErrors As New clsInsertData
    strMessage = objErrors.EnumerateErrors(objConn)
    Set objErrors = Nothing
    'Append any VB errors
    strMessage = strMessage & Err.Number & " : " & Err.Description
    'Return to the caller with a RC of 1
    InsertNotes = 1
End Function
```

This function has demonstrated the `AppendChunk` method of the `Parameter` object. While the amount of data that we are dealing with is relatively small, the `AppendChunk` method does provide a method to allow you to deal with chunks of data when dealing with large string variables. This allows your program to process more manageable chunks of data instead of trying to process the entire string at one time, which may be limited due to system resources such as memory.

How It Works – Modifying the Hardware Tracking Application – Select Notes Function

The next function that we want to code in this class is the `SelectNotes` function. This function will execute the `up_parmsel_system_notes` stored procedure.

This function accepts a `Connection` object and a `Recordset` object as parameters, both passed by reference. We also need the hardware ID, as this is the input parameter to our stored procedure. The `strMessage` parameter is passed to return any errors that might be encountered:

```
Public Function SelectNotes( _
    ByRef objConn As ADODB.Connection, _
    ByRef objRS As ADODB.Recordset, _
    ByVal lngHardwareID As Long, _
    ByRef strMessage As String) As Long
```

We set up our error handling for this function and then open the `Recordset` object. Notice overleaf that we have specified the stored procedure followed by the `lngHardwareID` parameter. We have enclosed this parameter in parentheses.

Since we only want to read this recordset to populate the text box on the `frmNotes` form, we have specified the `adOpenForwardOnly` constant for the `CursorType` parameter of the `Recordset`. We have also specified the `adLockReadOnly` constant for the `LockType` parameter of the `Recordset` object:

```
        'Setup error handling
        On Error GoTo SelectNotes_Err

        'Open the recordset object
        objRS.Open "up_parmsel_system_notes (" & lngHardwareID & ")", _
            objConn, adOpenForwardOnly, adLockReadOnly, adCmdStoredProc
```

After the recordset is open, we set the return code for this function and then exit the function:

```
        'Set the return code
        SelectNotes = 0

        'Exit function
        Exit Function
```

Our error handling code is the same code as was listed in the `InsertNotes` function:

```
SelectNotes_Err:
        'Enumerate ADO errors
        Dim objErrors As New clsInsertData
        strMessage = objErrors.EnumerateErrors(objConn)
        Set objErrors = Nothing
        'Append any VB errors
        strMessage = strMessage & Err.Number & " : " & Err.Description
        'Return to the caller with a RC of 1
        SelectNotes = 1
End Function
```

How It Works – Modifying the Hardware Tracking Application – the Notes Form

We are now ready to start adding some code in the notes form (`frmNotes`). We want to add the appropriate code to this form to enable us to retrieve and display the notes for the selected system when the form is loaded. We also want to add the functionality that will allow us to insert new notes for a system. The first thing we want to do in this form is to add some variables and objects to the general declarations section. The following code shows the variables and objects to be added:

```
        'Declare variables
        Dim lngHardwareID As Long
        Dim lngNotesID As Long

        'Declare objects
        Dim objText As clsTextData
```

In the `Form_Unload` procedure we want to remove our reference to the `objText` object, so add the following code to this procedure:

```
        Private Sub Form_Unload(Cancel As Integer)
            'Remove reference to local objects
            Set objText = Nothing
        End Sub
```

We will be calling this form from our main form and we will want to pass some variables to this form. Therefore, we have opted to code a `Public` procedure in this form that can be called from the main form. We always want to display the system notes for the system selected, so the `DisplayNotes` procedure will perform this task.

The two parameters for this procedure are: the system ID of the system selected in the **System** combo box on the **System Assignment** tab of the main form, and the text data that is displayed in the **System** combo box:

```
Public Sub DisplayNotes( _
    ByVal lngSystemID As Long, _
    ByVal strSystem As String)
```

Now we set up our error handling for this procedure and then declare our local variables. Notice that some of these variables are the same variables that we saw in the `InsertNotes` function:

```
'Setup error handling
On Error GoTo DisplayNotes_Err

'Declare local variables
Dim lngRC As Long, lngTextSize As Long, lngOffset As Long, _
    lngChunkSize As Long, strMessage As String
```

If the `strSystem` parameter contains the `NA` prefix we want to get rid of it. Using the `Right` function we return the right most portion of this parameter minus the left five characters:

```
'Trim string if necessary
If Left$(strSystem, 4) = "NA -" Then
    strSystem = Right$(strSystem, Len(strSystem) - 5)
End If
```

Then we use this parameter in the `lblSystemNotes` label to display the system, which contains the manufacturer name and model. Next we want to save the system ID for use now and later:

```
'Display system manufacturer and model
lblSystemNotes.Caption = lblSystemNotes.Caption & strSystem

'Save system id
lngHardwareID = lngSystemID
```

We set a reference to the global `Recordset` object next. Then we set a reference to the text data class:

```
'Set a reference to the recordset object
Set g_objRS = New ADODB.Recordset

'Set a reference to the text data class
Set objText = New clsTextData
```

Next, we execute the `SelectNotes` function, passing it the system ID that was passed to this procedure, and saved in the `lngHardwareID` variable:

```
'Open the recordset
lngRC = objText.SelectNotes( _
    g_objConn, _
    g_objRS, _
    lngHardwareID, _
    strMessage)
```

After control has returned from the `SelectNotes` function we check the return code from this function. If the return code is not zero, we raise an error, which causes us to fall through to the error handling code for this procedure:

```
'Ensure we were successful
If lngRC <> 0 Then
    Err.Raise 513 + vbObjectError, "DisplayNotes", _
        "Call to SelectNotes failed"
End If
```

Because we always load the system notes and may have not inserted any notes for the system being displayed, we need to check for an end-of-file condition on the `Recordset` object:

```
'Load notes text box and save the notes id
If Not g_objRS.EOF Then
```

If an end-of-file condition does not exist then we set the `lngTextSize` variable to the current size of the `Hardware_Notes_TX` field in the `Recordset` object. Notice that we are using the `ActualSize` property of the `Field` object.

Next we set the `lngChunkSize` variable to `102400`. This is the size of chunks of data that we want to read and is an arbitrary number chosen for this demonstration.

```
'Get the actual size of the text field in the RS
lngTextSize = g_objRS!Hardware_Notes_TX.ActualSize

'Set the chunk size to be retrieved
lngChunkSize = 102400
```

If the current size of the `Hardware_Notes_TX` field is greater than the chunk size we will read the data in chunks and populate our text box:

```
If lngTextSize > lngChunkSize Then
```

Using a loop similar to the loop in the `InsertNotes` function, we process the data from the `Hardware_Notes_TX` field in chunks. We process this loop while the `lngOffset` variable is less than the `lngTextSize` variable, which contains the size of the `Hardware_Notes_TX` field:

```
'Process data in chunks
Do While lngOffset <= lngTextSize
```

The first line in our loop uses the GetChunk method of the Field object. Here we are setting the text in the txtNotes text box to itself plus a chunk of data from the Hardware_Notes_TX field. The GetChunk method expects the size of the chunk to be read and we use the lngChunkSize variable for this parameter.

The GetChunk method keeps track of the offset in the Hardware_Notes_TX field automatically for us behind the scenes. Also, if we request a chunk of data that is larger than the amount of remaining data, the GetChunk method just returns the remaining data; it does not raise an error.

The second line in our loop increments the lngOffset variable, setting it to itself plus the lngChunkSize variable. This variable controls the loop so that we process all data in the Hardware_Notes_TX field:

```
'Get a chunk of data and add it to the notes text box
txtNotes.Text = txtNotes.Text & _
   g_objRS!Hardware_Notes_TX.GetChunk(lngChunkSize)

'Increment the offset counter
lngOffset = lngOffset + lngChunkSize

Loop
```

If the current size of the Hardware_Notes_TX field is less than the chunk size then we just add the data in the Hardware_Notes_TX field to the txtNotes text box. There is no need to process this small amount of data in chunks:

```
Else

    'Small amount of data, just load the text box
    txtNotes.Text = g_objRS!Hardware_Notes_TX

End If
```

Before we close our recordset we want to save the Hardware_Notes_ID field. This will allow us to process updates to these notes if the user wants to update them:

```
'Save the notes id
lngNotesID = g_objRS!Hardware_Notes_ID

End If
```

After all processing has been completed, we close the Recordset object and then remove our reference to it. We also remove our reference to the text data class object:

```
'Close the recordset
g_objRS.Close

'Remove references to objects
Set g_objRS = Nothing
Set objText = Nothing
```

At this point we want to show this form. We specify the `Show` method of the form and use the `Me` keyword, which references the `frmNotes` form. We specify the `vbModal` style so that the user cannot go back to the main form without first closing this form. Then we exit this procedure:

```
'Display the form as modal
Me.Show vbModal

'Exit sub
Exit Sub
```

Our error handling code for this procedure will simply display a message box, using the `strMessage` variable as the `Prompt` parameter:

```
DisplayNotes_Err:
    'Display errors from the function call
    MsgBox strMessage, vbCritical + vbOKOnly, "Hardware Tracking"
End Sub
```

How It Works – Modifying the Hardware Tracking Application – Inserting System Notes

We need to code the `cmdInsertNewNotes_Click` procedure to support inserting new system notes. This procedure is fired when a user clicks on the Insert New Notes button.

The first thing that we want to do here is to set up our error handling. Then we declare our local variables and set a reference to the text data class:

```
Private Sub cmdInsertNewNotes_Click()
    'Setup error handling
    On Error GoTo cmdInsertNewNotes_Click_Err

    'Declare local variables
    Dim lngRC As Long, strMessage As String

    'Set a reference to the text data class
    Set objText = New clsTextData
```

We execute the `InsertNotes` function, passing it the `lngHardwareID` variable and the text from the `txtNotes` text box:

```
'Insert the notes
lngRC = objText.InsertNotes( _
    g_objConn, _
    lngHardwareID, _
    txtNotes.Text, _
    strMessage)
```

After control has returned from the `InsertNotes` function we check the return code from this function. If the return code is not zero we raise an error:

```
'Ensure we were successful
If lngRC <> 0 Then
```

```
        Err.Raise 513 + vbObjectError, "cmdInsertNewNotes_Click", _
            "Call to InsertNotes failed"
    End If
```

If everything was successful we remove our reference to the objText object and display a message in the lblMessage label. Then we exit this procedure:

```
    'Remove references to objects
    Set objText = Nothing

    'Display message
    lblMessage.Caption = "Insert Successful"

    'Exit sub
    Exit Sub
```

Our error handling code for this procedure will simply display any error messages contained in the strMessage variable:

```
    cmdInsertNewNotes_Click_Err:
        'Display errors from the function call
        MsgBox strMessage, vbCritical + vbOKOnly, "Hardware Tracking"
    End Sub
```

Before we begin testing we need to make a couple of modifications to the main form. We want to add an image control to the **System Assignment** tab, as shown in the following figure. Set the Name property of this image control to imgNotes and set its Picture property to a suitable icon:

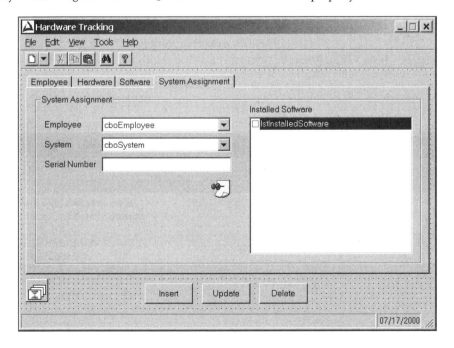

We now want to add some code for this image control to display the notes form when the user double-clicks on the image control. The code for the imgNotes_DblClick procedure is shown in the next code fragment. If you wanted, you could add this code to the imgNotes_Click procedure instead. This would fire this code on a *single* click of the image.

We execute the DisplayNotes procedure in the **Notes** form, passing it the required parameters. Notice that we are getting the system ID from the ItemData property of the cboSystem combo box for the selected system. We are using the Text property of this combo box for the System string parameter:

```
Private Sub imgNotes_DblClick()
    'Display Notes form
    frmNotes.DisplayNotes cboSystem.ItemData(cboSystem.ListIndex), _
        cboSystem.Text
End Sub
```

The INSERT and SELECT SQL statements that we have demonstrated so far have been the same INSERT and SELECT SQL statements that we have seen in the past few chapters. These SQL statements, along with the UPDATE SQL statement, can be used on text columns with the Text In Row option either turned on or off.

In fact, when the Text In Row option is turned on, these are the SQL statements that you *must* use to manage data in a text column, because text pointers are not allowed when this option is turned on.

Text Pointers

At the beginning of this chapter we covered how SQL Server manages data using the Text data type. We know that with the Text In Row option turned off SQL Server stores a text pointer to the root structure, which in turn stores pointers to the text data in the text pages.

SQL Server provides a T-SQL function (TEXTPTR) that will return the text pointer that is contained in the text column of your table. This text pointer is a 16 byte binary number. If we were to use the Query Analyzer and select all data in the Hardware_Notes_T table, SQL Server would use the text pointer stored in the Hardware_Notes_TX column and return the data that the text pointer points to.

Try It Out – Viewing a Text Pointer

1. Run the following query to see the data that you have inserted:

```
SELECT Hardware_Notes_ID, Hardware_Notes_TX
    FROM Hardware_Notes_T
```

Notice that the actual data you inserted is shown.

2. Now, using the TEXTPTR function, run the following query:

```
SELECT Hardware_Notes_ID, TEXTPTR(Hardware_Notes_TX)
    FROM Hardware_Notes_T
```

Notice now that the actual text pointer itself is displayed, such as:
0xFFFF42060000000009500000001000100.

How It Works – Viewing a Text Pointer

The TEXTPTR function accepts the text column name as the one and only parameter. In turn it returns the binary text pointer contained in the column specified. This allows us to access data in a text column using the READTEXT, WRITETEXT, and UPDATETEXT statements. We'll cover these statements shortly.

Before we use a text pointer in our code we must first retrieve a text pointer to our text data. To do this we need to declare a local variable using the VarBinary data type and specify a size for this variable of 16. The following code fragment shows this variable declaration:

```
DECLARE @Text_Pointer VARBINARY(16)
```

In order to set the text pointer variable, you need to select the text pointer for the text column in the row of data that you want to access. The next code fragment demonstrates this:

```
SELECT @Text_pointer = TEXTPTR(Hardware_Notes_TX)
    FROM Hardware_Notes_T
    WHERE Hardware_Notes_ID = @Notes_ID
```

The TEXTPTR function has a companion function called TEXTVALID. This function will validate whether a text pointer is valid or not. The TEXTVALID function has the following syntax:

```
TEXTVALID('table-name.column-name',text-pointer)
```

In the syntax above, *table-name* represents the name of the table that contains the text column, and *column-name* represents the column name of the text column. Notice that the table name and column name have been separated by a period and these arguments have been enclosed in single quotes. This is a requirement of this function.

The *text-pointer* argument specifies a text pointer variable to be validated. This pointer must have already been set using the TEXTPTR function.

If the text pointer is valid this function returns a value of 1. If the text pointer is not valid this function returns a value of 0. The following code fragment demonstrates how to validate the text pointer variable that has been set:

```
IF TEXTVALID('Hardware_Notes_T.Hardware_Notes_TX',@Text_Pointer) <> 1
    BEGIN
    RAISERROR('Text pointer is invalid',16,1)
    RETURN 99
    END
```

Text pointers are only needed when you want to read a certain portion of the text data, update a certain portion of your text data, or completely overwrite the existing text data. You use the READTEXT, UPDATETEXT, and WRITETEXT SQL statements to perform these actions. These T-SQL statements are non-logged statements, meaning that they are not logged in the transaction log. When you use these statements you will not be able to perform a backward recovery to recover data that was accidentally overwritten.

Reading Text Data

SQL Server provides the READTEXT T-SQL statement to allow you to read portions of data in a text column. This allows you to process only certain portions of the data in a text column; a text column can contain up to 2 gigabytes of data, and it is highly unlikely that you would want to select and display that much data at one time. Using the READTEXT statement you can process any portion of the data in a text column by specifying the offset and length of the data that you want to read.

The READTEXT statement has the following syntax:

```
READTEXT table-name.column-name text_pointer offset size
```

In this syntax, *table-name* represents the table name containing the text column and *column-name* represents the name of the column that the text data resides in.

The *text-pointer* argument is a valid text pointer or text pointer variable. The *offset* argument specifies the offset at which SQL Server should start reading data, meaning the number of characters from the beginning of the column. The *size* argument specifies how many characters should be read, starting from the offset value.

Suppose we wanted to skip the first 10 bytes of data and then read 20 bytes of data. The following code fragment shows how we would do this using the READTEXT statement:

```
READTEXT Hardware_Notes_T.Hardware_Notes_TX @Text_Pointer 10 20
```

Try It Out – READTEXT Stored Procedure

The stored procedure that we want to create in this section can only be used if the Text In Row option is turned off. This stored procedure will allow us to specify the offset and length of data to be read from the Hardware_Notes_TX text column in the Hardware_Notes_T table, thus returning only a portion of the available data in the Hardware_Notes_TX text column.

To create this stored procedure:

1. Clear the current query window by clicking on the Clear Query Window icon on the toolbar, or open a new query window by clicking on the New Query icon on the toolbar.

2. Enter the following stored procedure:

```
CREATE PROCEDURE up_parmsel_read_partial_system_notes
     @Notes_ID    INT,
     @Offset      INT,
     @Length      INT AS

--  ************************************************************************
--  Declare variable for the text pointer
--  ************************************************************************
DECLARE @Text_Pointer VARBINARY(16)
```

```
--  ********************************************************************
--  Initialize the text pointer
--  ********************************************************************
SELECT @Text_pointer = TEXTPTR(Hardware_Notes_TX)
    FROM Hardware_Notes_T
    WHERE Hardware_Notes_ID = @Notes_ID


--
-- Check for a valid text pointer
--
IF TEXTVALID('Hardware_Notes_T.Hardware_Notes_TX',@Text_Pointer) <> 1
    BEGIN
    RAISERROR('Text pointer is invalid',16,1)
    RETURN 99
    END


--  ********************************************************************
-- Read the text data
--  ********************************************************************
READTEXT Hardware_Notes_T.Hardware_Notes_TX @Text_Pointer @Offset @Length
--
-- Check for errors
--
IF @@ERROR > 0
    BEGIN
    RAISERROR('Reading system notes failed',16,1)
    RETURN 99
    END


--
-- Return to the caller
--
RETURN 0

GO

GRANT EXECUTE ON up_parmsel_read_partial_system_notes TO [Hardware Users]
```

3. Parse the code for errors by clicking on the **Parse Query** icon on the toolbar.

4. Create this stored procedure by clicking on the **Execute Query** icon on the toolbar.

How It Works – READTEXT Stored Procedure

This stored procedure accepts three parameters, the first of which is the hardware notes ID, the primary key in the Hardware_Notes_T table. The next two parameters specify the offset and the length of data to be read:

```
CREATE PROCEDURE up_parmsel_read_partial_system_notes
    @Notes_ID    INT,
    @Offset      INT,
    @Length      INT AS
```

513

The first thing that we do in this stored procedure is to declare a local variable to hold the text pointer:

```
-- **********************************************************************
-- Declare variable for the text pointer
-- **********************************************************************
DECLARE @Text_Pointer VARBINARY(16)
```

Next we initialize the text pointer variable, setting it to the text pointer contained in the Hardware_Notes_TX text column:

```
-- **********************************************************************
-- Initialize the text pointer
-- **********************************************************************
SELECT @Text_pointer = TEXTPTR(Hardware_Notes_TX)
    FROM Hardware_Notes_T
    WHERE Hardware_Notes_ID = @Notes_ID
```

After we have set our text pointer, we want to validate it to ensure it is valid, meaning that it contains a valid pointer. Using the TEXTVALID function we validate the text pointer and raise an error if it is not equal to 1. Remember that the TEXTVALID function returns a value of 1 if the text pointer is valid:

```
-- Check for a valid text pointer
--
IF TEXTVALID('Hardware_Notes_T.Hardware_Notes_TX',@Text_Pointer) <> 1
    BEGIN
    RAISERROR('Text pointer is invalid',16,1)
    RETURN 99
    END
```

If everything is successful at this point we want to read a portion of the data in our Hardware_Notes_TX column. Using the READTEXT statement we specify the table name and column name of the text column, along with the text pointer variable and the offset and length:

```
-- **********************************************************************
-- Read the text data
-- **********************************************************************
READTEXT Hardware_Notes_T.Hardware_Notes_TX @Text_Pointer @Offset @Length
```

We check for errors and raise an error if the @@ERROR function does not return a zero value:

```
-- Check for errors
--
IF @@ERROR > 0
    BEGIN
    RAISERROR('Reading system notes failed',16,1)
    RETURN 99
    END
```

Finally, we return to the caller with a return value of zero:

```
-- Return to the caller
--
RETURN 0
```

We specify the GO command to have the Query Analyzer create this stored procedure before we grant permissions on it:

```
GO

GRANT EXECUTE ON up_parmsel_read_partial_system_notes TO [Hardware Users]
```

Try It Out – VB Code to Use the READTEXT Stored Procedure

Now that the up_parmsel_read_partial_system_notes stored procedure has been created, let's switch to our VB code and create a function in the text data class (clsTextData) to enable us to execute this stored procedure.

1. All the code is presented in the *How It Works* section.

2. To test this newest functionality and to see the text pointer in action, save your project and then run it. Log in and then click on the **System Assignment** tab.

3. Next, select the system that you entered system notes for, or select the employee who has been assigned the system that you entered system notes for. Double-click the image control to have the system notes displayed.

4. Enter an offset value in the **Offset** text box and a length in the **Length** text box. Then click on the **Read Partial Notes** button to have the up_parmsel_read_partial_system_notes stored procedure read partial data from the Hardware_Notes_T table:

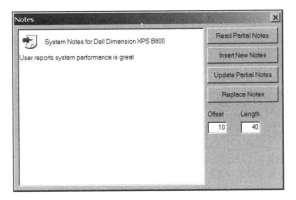

How It Works – VB Code to Use the READTEXT Stored Procedure

The SelectPartialNotes function is similar to the SelectNotes function in that it will execute a stored procedure to select data. However, as you can see in the next code fragment overleaf, this stored procedure accepts a couple more parameters than its counterpart. Because the up_parmsel_read_partial_system_notes stored procedure expects us to supply the offset and length values, this function must also specify these values as parameters to this function:

515

```
Public Function SelectPartialNotes( _
    ByRef objConn As ADODB.Connection, _
    ByRef objRS As ADODB.Recordset, _
    ByVal lngNotesID As Long, _
    ByVal lngOffset As Long, _
    ByVal lngLength As Long, _
    ByRef strMessage As String) As Long
```

We set up our error handling for this function first. Notice that there is no need to declare any local variables in this function.

```
'Setup error handling
    On Error GoTo SelectPartialNotes_Err
```

Then we open the `Recordset` object, specifying the `up_parmsel_read_partial_system_notes` stored procedure and the parameters this stored procedure expects as the `Source` parameter of the `Recordset` object. Again, we only want to read this data, so we have specified the `adOpenForwardOnly` and `adLockReadOnly` constants for the `CursorType` and `LockType` parameters:

```
'Open the recordset object
    objRS.Open "up_parmsel_read_partial_system_notes (" & _
        lngNotesID & "," & lngOffset & "," & lngLength & ")", _
        objConn, adOpenForwardOnly, adLockReadOnly, adCmdStoredProc
```

After the recordset has been opened we set the return code for this function and then exit the function:

```
'Set the return code
    SelectPartialNotes = 0

    'Exit function
    Exit Function
```

The error handling code for this function should come as no surprise as it is the same as the previous two functions coded in this class:

```
SelectPartialNotes_Err:
    'Enumerate ADO errors
    Dim objErrors As New clsInsertData
    strMessage = objErrors.EnumerateErrors(objConn)
    Set objErrors = Nothing
    'Append any VB errors
    strMessage = strMessage & Err.Number & " : " & Err.Description
    'Return to the caller with a RC of 1
    SelectPartialNotes = 1
End Function
```

Switching to the code in the notes form (`frmNotes`) we need to add some code to the `cmdReadPartialNotes_Click` procedure. This is the procedure that is executed when a user clicks on the **Read Partial Notes** button. We set up our error handling for this procedure first:

```
'Setup error handling
On Error GoTo cmdReadPartialNotes_Click_Err
```

Next, we declare our local variables and then set a reference to the global `Recordset` object. Then we set a reference to the text data class:

```
'Declare local variables
Dim lngRC As Long, strMessage As String

'Set a reference to the recordset object
Set g_objRS = New ADODB.Recordset

'Set a reference to the text data class
Set objText = New clsTextData
```

Finally we execute the `SelectPartialNotes` function, passing it the required data. Notice that we are getting the notes ID from the `lngNotesID` variable. Remember that this variable was set in the `DisplayNotes` procedure when the form was displayed. The `Offset` and `Length` parameters are being retrieved from their respective text boxes on the form:

```
'Open the recordset
lngRC = objText.SelectPartialNotes( _
    g_objConn, _
    g_objRS, _
    lngNotesID, _
    txtOffset.Text, _
    txtLength.Text, _
    strMessage)
```

After control is returned from the `SelectPartialNotes` procedure we check the return code and raise an error if it is not zero:

```
'Ensure we were successful
If lngRC <> 0 Then
    Err.Raise 513 + vbObjectError, "cmdReadPartialNotes_Click", _
        "Call to SelectPartialNotes failed"
End If
```

Since the amount of data we are dealing with is relatively small, which is the reason we use the `READTEXT` T-SQL statement, we simply set the text in the `Notes` text box directly from the `Hardware_Notes_TX` field in the `Recordset` object. We do not need to use the `GetChunk` method of the `Field` object because we have enough system resources (such as memory) to handle the amount of text that we are dealing with in this example:

```
'Load the notes text box
txtNotes.Text = g_objRS!Hardware_Notes_TX
```

Then we close the `Recordset` object and remove our references to the objects used in this procedure:

```
'Close the recordset
g_objRS.Close
```

```
'Remove references to objects
Set g_objRS = Nothing
Set objText = Nothing
```

We then clear any existing messages in the lblMessage label. There is no need to display a message, as placing the desired text in the **Notes** text box is evidence that this procedure succeeded. Then we exit the procedure, bypassing the error handling code:

```
'Clear any previous messages
lblMessage.Caption = Empty

'Exit sub
Exit Sub
```

The error handling code simply displays any error messages using the MsgBox function:

```
cmdReadPartialNotes_Click_Err:
    'Display errors from the function call
    MsgBox strMessage, vbCritical + vbOKOnly, "Hardware Tracking"
End Sub
```

Updating Text Data

At this point we can select data from the Hardware_Notes_TX text column using the SELECT statement, or we can use the READTEXT statement to read portions of the data in this text column. Now we want to examine a method that allows us to update only a portion of the text in a text column.

If you had the Text In Row option turned on, you could use the INSERT and SELECT statements that we discussed earlier. In addition, since you could not use text pointers you would use the UPDATE SQL statement to update the data in a text column. This entails replacing all of the data in a text column, as was the case with the UPDATE statements that we have used in previous chapters.

Remember that the Text In Row option, when turned on, allows you to work with Text columns but only in the same manner as with other data types, such as a Char or VarChar data type. While this does increase performance, you are limited to selecting or updating the entire column of text in a text column.

This is where the UPDATETEXT statement comes in. This T-SQL statement allows us to update only a specified portion of the data in our text column. Like its counterpart, READTEXT, the UPDATETEXT statement needs to know the offset at which to start and the length of the data to be deleted. The basic syntax for this statement is as follows:

```
UPDATETEXT table-name.column-name text-pointer
NULL | insert-offset
NULL | delete-length
insert-data
```

In this syntax, the *table-name* argument specifies the name of the table containing the text column followed by the *column-name* argument, which specifies the column name of the text column. The *text-pointer* argument specifies a valid text pointer.

The *insert-offset* argument specifies the zero-based offset at which the data will be updated. A null value indicates that the update should occur at the end of all existing data in the text column, thereby allowing you to append more text to the existing text.

The *delete-length* argument specifies the length of the data to be deleted from the offset. A value of 0 will delete no data and a Null value will delete all data from the offset to the end of the text column.

The *insert-data* argument specifies the data to be inserted.

Let's look at a quick example of the UPDATETEXT statement. This example assumes we have already declared and set a valid text pointer.

```
UPDATETEXT Hardware_Notes_T.Hardware_Notes_TX
    @Text_Pointer 10 0 'new text here'
```

In this example we have specified an offset of 10, meaning the text to be updated will start at position 11, because the offset is a zero-based offset. By specifying a length of 0 the text new text here will be inserted at this point.

To update the text at this offset we could specify the following code. This assumes the text to be deleted is only 13 characters in length:

```
UPDATETEXT Hardware_Notes_T.Hardware_Notes_TX
    @Text_Pointer 10 13 'new text here'
```

So what we have seen from these two code fragments is that we can either *insert* new text in the middle of a text column or *replace* the text in the middle of a text column.

Try It Out – UPDATETEXT Stored Procedure

The stored procedure that we want to create now will allow us to update text in the middle of the Hardware_Notes_TX text column or insert new data in the middle of this column. It will be driven off the offset and length values that we supply. If we supply a length value of 0 then the text that we specify will be inserted. If we specify a length greater than 0 then any existing text in the text column up to the specified length will be deleted first before the next text is inserted.

To create this stored procedure:

1. Clear the current query window by clicking on the Clear Query Window icon on the toolbar, or open a new query window by clicking on the New Query icon on the toolbar.

2. Enter the following stored procedure:

```
CREATE PROCEDURE up_parmupd_update_system_notes
    @Notes_ID        INT,
```

```
        @Offset          INT,
        @Length          INT,
        @System_Notes_TX  TEXT AS

-- ************************************************************************
-- Declare variable for the text pointer
-- ************************************************************************
DECLARE @Text_Pointer VARBINARY(16)


-- ************************************************************************
-- Initialize the text pointer
-- ************************************************************************
SELECT @Text_Pointer = TEXTPTR(Hardware_Notes_TX)
    FROM Hardware_Notes_T
    WHERE Hardware_Notes_ID = @Notes_ID


--
-- Check for a valid text pointer
--
IF TEXTVALID('Hardware_Notes_T.Hardware_Notes_TX',@Text_Pointer) <> 1
    BEGIN
    RAISERROR('Text pointer is invalid',16,1)
    RETURN 99
    END


-- ************************************************************************
-- Update a specific portion of text data
-- ************************************************************************
UPDATETEXT Hardware_Notes_T.Hardware_Notes_TX
    @Text_Pointer @Offset @Length @System_Notes_TX


--
-- Check for errors
--
IF @@ERROR > 0
    BEGIN
    RAISERROR('Update of system notes failed',16,1)
    RETURN 99
    END


--
-- Return to the caller
--
RETURN 0

GO

GRANT EXECUTE ON up_parmupd_update_system_notes TO [Hardware Users]
```

3. Parse the code for errors by clicking on the **Parse Query** icon on the toolbar.

4. Create this stored procedure by clicking on the **Execute Query** icon on the toolbar.

How It Works – UPDATETEXT Stored Procedure

This stored procedure needs to know the hardware notes ID of the row of data that should be updated, along with the offset and length of the text to be replaced. We also need to specify the text to be inserted. All of these have been specified as input parameters to this stored procedure:

```
CREATE PROCEDURE up_parmupd_update_system_notes
     @Notes_ID         INT,
     @Offset           INT,
     @Length           INT,
     @System_Notes_TX  TEXT AS
```

When working with the UPDATETEXT statement we need to specify a valid text pointer, so the first thing that we have done here is to declare a local variable as a text pointer:

```
-- ****************************************************************
-- Declare variable for the text pointer
-- ****************************************************************
DECLARE @Text_Pointer VARBINARY(16)
```

We initialize the text pointer next, using the TEXTPTR function:

```
-- ****************************************************************
-- Initialize the text pointer
-- ****************************************************************
SELECT @Text_Pointer = TEXTPTR(Hardware_Notes_TX)
     FROM Hardware_Notes_T
     WHERE Hardware_Notes_ID = @Notes_ID
```

Then, using the TEXTVALID function, we validate the text pointer variable to ensure it is valid. If it is not valid we raise an error and return to the caller with a return value of 99:

```
-- Check for a valid text pointer
--
IF TEXTVALID('Hardware_Notes_T.Hardware_Notes_TX',@Text_Pointer) <> 1
     BEGIN
     RAISERROR('Text pointer is invalid',16,1)
     RETURN 99
     END
```

Next, we execute the UPDATETEXT statement to update or insert text in the Hardware_Notes_TX text column:

```
-- ****************************************************************
-- Update a specific portion of text data
-- ****************************************************************
UPDATETEXT Hardware_Notes_T.Hardware_Notes_TX
     @Text_Pointer @Offset @Length @System_Notes_TX
```

We check for errors by checking the value returned by the @@ERROR function. If this function returns any value other than zero we raise an error and return to the caller with a return value of 99:

```
-- Check for errors
--
IF @@ERROR > 0
    BEGIN
    RAISERROR('Update of system notes failed',16,1)
    RETURN 99
    END
```

If everything was successful we return to the caller with a return value of zero:

```
-- Return to the caller
--
RETURN 0
```

Specifying the GO command, the Query Analyzer will execute the preceding code before continuing. Then we grant permissions on this stored procedure to the hardware users role:

```
GO

GRANT EXECUTE ON up_parmupd_update_system_notes TO [Hardware Users]
```

Try It Out – VB Code to Process the UPDATETEXT Stored Procedure

1. Switching to our VB code, the next *How It Works* section contains all of the necessary code modifications.

2. Save your project at this point in preparation for testing. Run your program and log in. Click on the **System Assignment** tab and select the employee who has system notes assigned to their system. Then double-click on the image control.

3. Select a spot in your notes to insert data and then enter some text. For this test the text will be inserted at the point that we type the text; no existing text will be replaced. Calculate the offset where the inserted text should be placed and place this number in the **Offset** text box. Then highlight the new text to be inserted. The **Length** text box should contain a value of 0. This ensures that the highlighted text will be inserted and no existing text will be deleted.

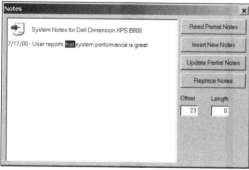

4. Click on the **Update Partial Notes** button to have the text inserted. The text will be inserted and you will receive a message in the lblMessage label on the form, indicating that the update was successful. You have now successfully inserted data in the middle of the text column.

If you want to view the entire text that includes your updates, you will need to close the dialog and then open it again.

5. To test the update functionality of the up_parmupd_update_system_notes stored procedure find some text to be deleted. Calculate the offset and the length of the text to be deleted and enter these numbers in the **Offset** and **Length** text boxes. If you want to enter some new text, enter the text and highlight it. If you do not want to insert any new text, simply highlight a blank space. Then click on the **Update Partial Notes** button to have the specified text deleted and the new text, if any, inserted in its place.

You will receive a message in the lblMessage label on the form indicating that the update was successful. You have then successfully deleted some old text and inserted new text in its place.

How It Works – VB Code to Process the UPDATETEXT Stored Procedure

We want to code the UpdateNotes function in the text data class (clsTextData) first. This function will execute the up_parmupd_update_system_notes stored procedure to update or insert data in our text column.

This function accepts all of the parameters that are required by the up_parmupd_update_system_notes stored procedure plus the Connection object and the Message string:

```
Public Function UpdateNotes( _
    ByRef objConn As ADODB.Connection, _
    ByVal lngNotesID As Long, _
    ByVal lngOffset As Long, _
    ByVal lngLength As Long, _
    ByRef strNotes As String, _
    ByRef strMessage As String) As Long
```

First, we set up our error handling in this function, and follow this by declaring a Command object:

```
'Set up error handling
On Error GoTo UpdateNotes_Err

'Declare local objects
Dim objCmd As ADODB.Command
```

We want to validate the Notes data before executing the stored procedure and only check it for a zero length. If it is zero length then we raise an error. To save space the data validation of the lngOffset and lngLength parameters has been omitted. You should provide your own validation of these parameters.

```
'Validate notes data
If RTrim(Len(strNotes)) = 0 Then
    strMessage = "Notes data is zero length" & vbCrLf & vbCrLf
    Err.Raise 513 + vbObjectError, "UpdateNotes", _
```

```
            "Data validation failed"
      End If
```

We set a reference to the Command object next and then set its properties:

```
   'Set a reference to the command object
   Set objCmd = New ADODB.Command

   'Set the command object properties
   Set objCmd.ActiveConnection = objConn
   objCmd.CommandText = "up_parmupd_update_system_notes"
   objCmd.CommandType = adCmdStoredProc
```

When using the SQL Server UPDATETEXT statement we are usually dealing with small amounts of data that are to be changed in the database and therefore do not need to use the AppendChunk method of the Parameter object. Therefore we can use the Command object to create and append the required parameters to the Parameters collection.

Notice that the last parameter we are creating uses the adLongVarChar constant for the data type parameter of the CreateParameter method. This is because this parameter is defined in the stored procedure as a TEXT data type:

```
   'Create and append the parameters to the parameters collection
   objCmd.Parameters.Append objCmd.CreateParameter("RC", _
      adInteger, adParamReturnValue)
   objCmd.Parameters.Append objCmd.CreateParameter("NotesID", _
      adInteger, adParamInput, , lngNotesID)
   objCmd.Parameters.Append objCmd.CreateParameter("Offset", _
      adInteger, adParamInput, , lngOffset)
   objCmd.Parameters.Append objCmd.CreateParameter("Length", _
      adInteger, adParamInput, , lngLength)
   objCmd.Parameters.Append objCmd.CreateParameter("Notes", _
      adLongVarChar, adParamInput, Len(strNotes), strNotes)
```

After we have created and appended all of the parameters to the Parameters collection we execute the Command object.

Then we check the return value from the stored procedure in the RC parameter. If the stored procedure did not return a return value of zero we raise an error:

```
   'Execute the command object
   objCmd.Execute

   'Check the return value from the stored procedure
   If objCmd.Parameters("RC") <> 0 Then
      Err.Raise 513 + vbObjectError, "UpdateNotes", _
         "up_parmupd_update_system_notes failed"
   End If
```

Finally, we remove our reference to the Command object and then set the return code for this function. Then we exit the function:

```
                'Remove references to objects
                Set objCmd = Nothing

                'Set the return code
                UpdateNotes = 0

                'Exit function
                Exit Function
```

We use the standard error handling code that we have used throughout this class:

```
        UpdateNotes_Err:
            'Enumerate ADO errors
            Dim objErrors As New clsInsertData
            strMessage = objErrors.EnumerateErrors(objConn)
            Set objErrors = Nothing
            'Append any VB errors
            strMessage = strMessage & Err.Number & " : " & Err.Description
            'Return to the caller with a RC of 1
            UpdateNotes = 1
        End Function
```

Switching to the code in the notes form (frmNotes) we need to add some code to the cmdUpdatePartialNotes_Click procedure. This is the procedure that gets executed when the user clicks on the Update Partial Notes button.

The first thing that is done in this procedure is to set up our error handling. Then we declare our local variables:

```
        Private Sub cmdUpdatePartialNotes_Click()
            'Setup error handling
            On Error GoTo cmdUpdatePartialNotes_Click_Err

            'Declare local variables
            Dim lngRC As Long, strMessage As String
```

Next we set a reference to the text data class and then we execute the UpdateNotes function, passing it the required parameters:

```
            'Set a reference to the text data class
            Set objText = New clsTextData

            'Update a portion of the notes
            lngRC = objText.UpdateNotes( _
                g_objConn, _
                lngNotesID, _
                txtOffset.Text, _
                txtLength.Text, _
                txtNotes.SelText, _
                strMessage)
```

After control has been returned from the UpdateNotes function we check the return code from this function. If the return code is not zero, we raise an error:

```
            'Ensure we were successful
            If lngRC <> 0 Then
                Err.Raise 513 + vbObjectError, "cmdUpdatePartialNotes_Click", _
                    "Call to UpdateNotes failed"
            End If
```

Next, we remove our reference to the text data class and display a message in the `lblMessage` label to indicate that the update was successful. Finally, we exit this procedure:

```
            'Remove references to objects
            Set objText = Nothing

            'Display message
            lblMessage.Caption = "Update Successful"

            'Exit sub
            Exit Sub
```

Our error handling code simply displays a message box that displays the errors contained in the `strMessage` variable:

```
        cmdUpdatePartialNotes_Click_Err:
            'Display errors from the function call
            MsgBox strMessage, vbCritical + vbOKOnly, "Hardware Tracking"
        End Sub
```

Writing Text Data

When working with text data we are usually working with large amounts of data. Knowing this, and knowing that the UPDATE statement is a logged statement, we need an alternative method of replacing the data in a text column.

When we say that the UPDATE statement is a logged statement, what we mean is that the data that gets updated by the UPDATE statement is logged in the transaction log. This means that the data in the column that is being updated is written to the transaction log before it gets updated, to allow for backward recovery of the data in that column.

This is not a good idea when dealing with text data as SQL Server could potentially write up to 2 gigabytes worth of data into the log. If you recall, 2 gigabytes is the maximum size of a Text data type. Fortunately SQL Server provides us with an alternative to avoid this situation.

The WRITETEXT T-SQL statement works just like its UPDATE counterpart except it only works on text columns. The WRITETEXT statement will update the data in a text column, completely replacing all existing data. Therefore, we do not need to specify an offset or length parameter. We do, however, need to provide a valid text pointer for this statement.

Let's take a quick look at the syntax for this statement:

```
    WRITETEXT table-name.text-column-name text-pointer data
```

In this syntax, the *table-name* argument specifies the name of the table that contains the text column and the *text-column-name* argument specifies the name of the text column.

The *text-pointer* argument specifies a valid text pointer.

The *data* argument specifies the new text data to be written in the text column.

Let's take a look at an example of the WRITETEXT statement at work. This example assumes we have already declared and set a valid text pointer to the data:

```
WRITETEXT Hardware_Notes_T.Hardware_Notes_TX @Text_Pointer 'This is new data'
```

Executing this statement will completely replace all existing data in the Hardware_Notes_TX column and place the new data in this column.

Try It Out – WRITETEXT Stored Procedure

The stored procedure that we want to create here will use a WRITETEXT statement and will completely replace any existing data in the Hardware_Notes_TX text column. This stored procedure only needs two input parameters, the hardware notes ID of the row to be updated and the notes data that will be written to the Hardware_Notes_TX text column.

To create this stored procedure:

1. Clear the current query window by clicking on the Clear Query Window icon on the toolbar, or open a new query window by clicking on the New Query icon on the toolbar.

2. Enter the following stored procedure:

```
CREATE PROCEDURE up_parmupd_replace_system_notes
    @Notes_ID          INT,
    @System_Notes_TX   TEXT AS

--  ********************************************************************
-- Declare variable for the text pointer
--  ********************************************************************
DECLARE @Text_Pointer VARBINARY(16)

--  ********************************************************************
-- Initialize the text pointer
--  ********************************************************************
SELECT @Text_Pointer = TEXTPTR(Hardware_Notes_TX)
    FROM Hardware_Notes_T
    WHERE Hardware_Notes_ID = @Notes_ID
--
-- Check for a valid text pointer
--
IF TEXTVALID('Hardware_Notes_T.Hardware_Notes_TX',@Text_Pointer) <> 1
    BEGIN
        RAISERROR('Text pointer is invalid',16,1)
        RETURN 99
```

```
        END

--  *********************************************************************
--  Write the text, replacing any existing text
--  *********************************************************************
WRITETEXT Hardware_Notes_T.Hardware_Notes_TX @Text_Pointer @System_Notes_TX
--
-- Check for errors
--
IF @@ERROR > 0
      BEGIN
      RAISERROR('System notes replacement failed',16,1)
      RETURN 99
      END
--
-- Return to the caller
--
RETURN 0

GO

GRANT EXECUTE ON up_parmupd_replace_system_notes TO [Hardware Users]
```

3. Parse the code for errors by clicking on the Parse Query icon on the toolbar.

4. Create this stored procedure by clicking on the Execute Query icon on the toolbar.

How It Works – WRITETEXT Stored Procedure

This stored procedure accepts the hardware notes ID of the row to be updated and the notes text to be used in the WRITETEXT statement:

```
CREATE PROCEDURE up_parmupd_replace_system_notes
      @Notes_ID         INT,
      @System_Notes_TX  TEXT AS
```

Since the WRITETEXT statement requires a valid text pointer we declare a local variable to hold the text pointer:

```
--  *********************************************************************
--  Declare variable for the text pointer
--  *********************************************************************
DECLARE @Text_Pointer VARBINARY(16)
```

Then we initialize the text pointer using the TEXTPTR function:

```
--  *********************************************************************
--  Initialize the text pointer
--  *********************************************************************
SELECT @Text_Pointer = TEXTPTR(Hardware_Notes_TX)
      FROM Hardware_Notes_T
      WHERE Hardware_Notes_ID = @Notes_ID
```

We want to validate the text pointer next, and we use the TEXTVALID function to ensure we have a valid text pointer. If this function does not return a value of 1, we raise an error and return to the caller with a return value of 99:

```
-- Check for a valid text pointer
--
IF TEXTVALID('Hardware_Notes_T.Hardware_Notes_TX',@Text_Pointer) <> 1
    BEGIN
    RAISERROR('Text pointer is invalid',16,1)
    RETURN 99
    END
```

Using the WRITETEXT statement we replace the existing data in the Hardware_Notes_TX text column with the data contained in the @System_Notes_TX input parameter:

```
-- *************************************************************************
-- Write the text, replacing any existing text
-- *************************************************************************
WRITETEXT Hardware_Notes_T.Hardware_Notes_TX @Text_Pointer @System_Notes_TX
```

After executing the WRITETEXT statement we check for errors, and if the @@ERROR function returned anything other than a zero we raise an error and return to the caller with a return value of 99:

```
-- Check for errors
--
IF @@ERROR > 0
    BEGIN
    RAISERROR('System notes replacement failed',16,1)
    RETURN 99
    END
```

Finally, we return to the caller with a return value of zero:

```
-- Return to the caller
--
RETURN 0
```

We specify the GO command so the Query Analyzer will create the stored procedure before we grant permissions on it:

```
GO

GRANT EXECUTE ON up_parmupd_replace_system_notes TO [Hardware Users]
```

Try It Out – VB Code to Process the WRITETEXT Stored Procedure

1. The code to be added to the VB project is presented and explained in the *How It Works* section.

2. At this point you will want to save your project before beginning testing. Run your program and log in.

3. Then click on the System Assignment tab and choose the employee that you entered system notes for.

4. Double-click on the Image control to display the Notes form.

5. Next, delete the existing notes in the Notes text box, enter some new notes, and then click on the Replace Notes button.

6. The notes will be replaced and you can verify this by closing the Notes form and then opening it again.

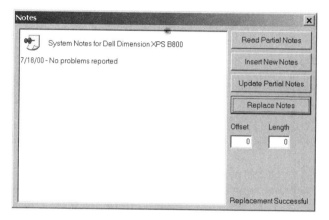

How It Works – VB Code to Process the WRITETEXT Stored Procedure

We want to create a new function in the text data class (`clsTextData`). Since this function will execute the `up_parmupd_replace_system_notes` stored procedure, which uses the `WRITETEXT` statement, let's give this new function a name of `ReplaceNotes`. This is exactly what the `WRITETEXT` statement does: it replaces the current data in a text column.

For this function to execute successfully, we need to pass not only the data that replaces the data in the `Hardware_Notes_TX` column but also the hardware notes ID. Notice that we have specified for the `strNotes` parameter to be passed by reference. This allows us to get a pointer to the large string variable containing the data instead of trying to pass a large amount of data around in the system.

```
Public Function ReplaceNotes( _
    ByRef objConn As ADODB.Connection, _
    ByVal lngNotesID As Long, _
    ByRef strNotes As String, _
    ByRef strMessage As String) As Long
```

We set up our error handling first and then declare our local variables and objects. Notice that we have declared a `Parameter` object. Since we could potentially have a large amount of data to deal with, we will perform the same type of processing in this function to append the data to the `Parameter` object as we did in the `InsertNotes` function:

```
'Set up error handling
On Error GoTo ReplaceNotes_Err

'Declare local variables and objects
Dim lngTextSize As Long, lngOffset As Long, lngChunkSize As Long
```

```
Dim objCmd As ADODB.Command
Dim objParm As ADODB.Parameter
```

We validate that some data exists in the `strNotes` parameter before continuing. If no data exists then we add a message to the `strMessage` parameter before raising an error:

```
'Validate notes data
If RTrim(Len(strNotes)) = 0 Then
    strMessage = "Notes data is zero length" & vbCrLf & vbCrLf
    Err.Raise 513 + vbObjectError, "ReplaceNotes", _
        "Data validation failed"
End If
```

Next we set a reference to the `Command` object and then set its various properties:

```
'Set a reference to the command object
Set objCmd = New ADODB.Command

'Set the command object properties
Set objCmd.ActiveConnection = objConn
objCmd.CommandText = "up_parmupd_replace_system_notes"
objCmd.CommandType = adCmdStoredProc
```

The first parameter that we create is for the return value from our stored procedure. You have seen this before and it should look familiar:

```
'*************************************************
'First parameter - Return value
'*************************************************
'Set a reference to the parameter object
Set objParm = New ADODB.Parameter

'Set the parameter properties
objParm.Name = "RC"
objParm.Type = adInteger
objParm.Direction = adParamReturnValue

'Append the parameter to the parameters collection
objCmd.Parameters.Append objParm

'Remove reference to the parameter object
Set objParm = Nothing
```

The next parameter that we create and append to the `Parameters` collection is the parameter for the hardware notes ID:

```
'*************************************************
'Second parameter - Notes ID
'*************************************************
'Set a reference to the parameter object
Set objParm = New ADODB.Parameter
```

```
'Set the parameter properties
objParm.Name = "NotesID"
objParm.Type = adInteger
objParm.Direction = adParamInput
objParm.Value = lngNotesID

'Append the parameter to the parameters collection
objCmd.Parameters.Append objParm

'Remove reference to the parameter object
Set objParm = Nothing
```

The last parameter that we want to create is the parameter that contains the notes data. Since we use the AppendChunk method of the Parameter object, let's quickly go over this again.

First we set a reference to the Parameter object. Then we set the various properties of the Parameter. Remember that we must set the Attributes property using the adFldLong constant when the Type property is set to use the adLongVarChar constant:

```
'*************************************************
'Third parameter - Notes data
'*************************************************
'Set a reference to the parameter object
Set objParm = New ADODB.Parameter

'Set the parameter properties
objParm.Attributes = adFldLong
objParm.Name = "Notes"
objParm.Type = adLongVarChar
objParm.Direction = adParamInput
objParm.Size = Len(strNotes)
```

We set the lngTextSize variable to the size of the data, the number of characters. Then we set the lngChunkSize variable to the size of the data divided by 10. This gives us a chunk size to work with when we append chunks of data to the Parameter object. Lastly, we set the starting offset value in the lngOffset variable:

```
'Set default values
lngTextSize = Len(strNotes)
lngChunkSize = (lngTextSize / 10)
lngOffset = 1
```

We perform a loop while the lngOffset variable is less than the lngTextSize variable. We use the MID function to extract portions of the data from the strNotes parameter, using the lngOffset and lngChunkSize variables for the starting position and length positions. Then, using the AppendChunk method of the Parameter object, we append that chunk of data to it:

```
'Loop through the string and append the data to the parameter object
Do While lngOffset <= lngTextSize
    objParm.AppendChunk Mid(strNotes, lngOffset, lngChunkSize)
    lngOffset = lngOffset + lngChunkSize
Loop
```

After all of the data has been appended to the `Parameter` object we append the `Parameter` object to the `Parameters` collection. Then we remove our reference to the `Parameter` object:

```
'Append the parameter to the parameters collection
objCmd.Parameters.Append objParm

'Remove reference to the parameter object
Set objParm = Nothing
```

Finally, we execute the `Command` object, which executes the `up_parmupd_replace_system_notes` stored procedure. This replaces the current hardware notes with the new notes.

We check the return value from the stored procedure in the RC parameter and raise an error if it is not zero:

```
'Execute the command object
objCmd.Execute

'Check the return value from the stored procedure
If objCmd.Parameters("RC") <> 0 Then
    Err.Raise 513 + vbObjectError, "ReplaceNotes", _
        "up_parmupd_replace_system_notes failed"
End If
```

To wrap up, we remove our reference to the `Command` object, set the return code for this function, and then exit the function:

```
'Remove references to objects
Set objCmd = Nothing

'Set the return code
ReplaceNotes = 0

'Exit function
Exit Function
```

Our error handling will execute the `EnumerateErrors` function in the `clsInsertData` class should we receive an error. Then we would append any VB error message to the `strMessage` parameter, set the return code and then exit the function:

```
ReplaceNotes_Err:
    'Enumerate ADO errors
    Dim objErrors As New clsInsertData
    strMessage = objErrors.EnumerateErrors(objConn)
    Set objErrors = Nothing
    'Append any VB errors
    strMessage = strMessage & Err.Number & " : " & Err.Description
    'Return to the caller with a RC of 1
    ReplaceNotes = 1
End Function
```

The code that we want to add in the notes form (frmNotes) will be contained in the cmdReplaceNotes_Click procedure. This is the procedure that gets fired when we click on the **Replace Notes** button.

The first thing that we do in this procedure is to set up our error handling and then declare our local variables. Then we set a reference to the text data class:

```
Private Sub cmdReplaceNotes_Click()
    'Setup error handling
    On Error GoTo cmdReplaceNotes_Click_Err

    'Declare local variables
    Dim lngRC As Long, strMessage As String

    'Set a reference to the text data class
    Set objText = New clsTextData
```

We execute the ReplaceNotes function, passing it the saved hardware notes ID in the lngNotesID variable, and also pass the notes from the txtNotes text box:

```
    'Replace existing notes
    lngRC = objText.ReplaceNotes( _
        g_objConn, _
        lngNotesID, _
        txtNotes.Text, _
        strMessage)
```

After control has returned from the ReplaceNotes function we check the return code from this function. If the return code is not zero then we raise an error:

```
    'Ensure we were successful
    If lngRC <> 0 Then
        Err.Raise 513 + vbObjectError, "cmdReplaceNotes_Click", _
            "Call to ReplaceNotes failed"
    End If
```

Next, we remove our reference to the text data class and display a message in the lblMessage label indicating that the replacement was successful. Then we exit the procedure, bypassing our error handling code:

```
    'Remove references to objects
    Set objText = Nothing

    'Display message
    lblMessage.Caption = "Replacement Successful"

    'Exit sub
    Exit Sub
```

Our error handling code for this procedure simply displays the strMessage variable in a message box. This variable contains all error messages that were returned from the ReplaceNotes function:

```
cmdReplaceNotes_Click_Err:
    'Display errors from the function call
    MsgBox strMessage, vbCritical + vbOKOnly, "Hardware Tracking"
End Sub
```

Since this is the last exercise that creates a function in our classes, we are ready to remove the classes from our project and create the Hardware Tracking business server component. Appendix E covers the details behind creating the business server component and the necessary modifications to the Hardware Tracking application to use the new component.

Reminders

Keep in mind when using the READTEXT, UPDATETEXT, and WRITETEXT statements that these statements can only be used when the Text In Row option is switched off. Also these statements require a valid text pointer, meaning that some data must have been previously inserted into the text column. These T-SQL statements are non-logged statements, meaning that they are not logged in the transaction log.

If the text column allows null values, then you could insert a null value in a text column to create a text pointer. Inserting a null value in a text column will create a valid text pointer, thus allowing you to use the statements above.

Whether the Text In Row option is on or off, you can use the SELECT, INSERT, and UPDATE statements to select, insert, and update data in a text column. However, keep in mind that you are dealing with *all* of the data in the text column at one time.

When the Text In Row option is turned on, you can only use the SELECT, INSERT, and UPDATE statements. You cannot use the READTEXT, UPDATETEXT, and WRITETEXT statements when this option is on, as text pointers are not valid.

Although we did not cover deleting data from a table that contains a text column, it is no different from deleting data from any other table. In fact, the data in the Hardware_Notes_T table will be automatically deleted when the system is deleted from the Hardware_T table. This is because we defined a cascading referential integrity constraint on this table.

Summary

This chapter has taken a look at how SQL Server manages text data. We have seen how SQL Server will place the text data in the actual data row, if it fits, when the Text In Row option is turned on. This allows for faster retrieval of the data as SQL Server has reduced the number of reads that are required to return the data.

We have also seen how SQL Server manages text data when the Text In Row option is turned off. We know that we must use text pointers to access portions of the data. This method is very efficient when working with very large text columns as it allows us to access only the data that we want to work with.

Having examined how to *retrieve* a text pointer, we also covered how to *validate* the text pointer. Then we proceeded to work with the READTEXT, UPDATETEXT, and WRITETEXT statements. The READTEXT statement allowed us to read only the portion of data that we wanted to work with. The UPDATEXT statement was the most flexible as it not only allowed us to update specific portions of text data, but also allowed us to insert data anywhere in a text column. The WRITETEXT statement allowed us to completely replace the data in a text column with new data.

So, to summarize, you should know:

❑   How SQL Server manages text data

❑   The benefits of using the Text In Row option

❑   How to initialize and validate text pointers

❑   How to select and read text data

❑   How to update and replace text data

The next chapter covers the installation of Internet Information Services (IIS) on Windows 2000 Professional and Windows NT 4.0. IIS is a prerequisite for Chapter 15 when we start working with the XML features of SQL Server 2000.

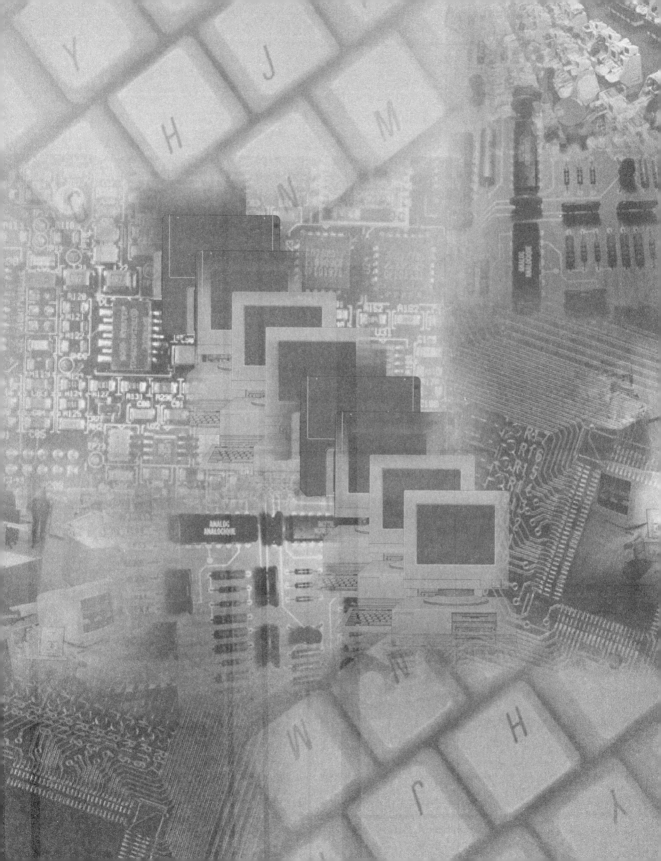

Installing Internet Information Server (IIS)

This chapter is a prerequisite for the next, where we will actually begin to work with the XML features of SQL Server 2000. Before we can begin working with XML, we need to install IIS. This chapter gives an overview of IIS explaining what it is, and how we can use it.

We will cover the installation of IIS on both Windows 2000 and Windows NT. After installation, we will walk through creating a virtual directory in IIS for the web site that we will set up and also for SQL Server. A virtual directory is a directory on your hard drive that is designated as a share point in IIS, meaning that IIS points to a directory on your hard drive that is usually shared.

It should be noted that, in order to complete this chapter and the next, you need to be running SQL Server 2000 on Windows NT 4.0 or Windows 2000 Professional. The IIS Virtual Directory Management for SQL Server utility requires one of these operating systems.

So, in this chapter we will:

- ❏ Conduct an overview of IIS
- ❏ Cover the installation of IIS on Windows 2000 and Windows NT
- ❏ Create a virtual directory for a web site
- ❏ Create a virtual directory for SQL Server

IIS Overview

Microsoft **Internet Information Server** (**IIS**) is an Internet service that can also be used on a private intranet. It allows you to view and share information using a standard protocol called **HyperText Transfer Protocol** (**HTTP**). Using this protocol you can access and view information in web pages such as those pages that end with the htm, html, shtml, and asp file extensions.

The web pages themselves can provide links to other web pages and to documents that can be viewed in a web browser such as Microsoft Internet Explorer (IE). For example, a web page can contain a link to a Microsoft Word document and when you click on the link, the Word document will be displayed in your browser (if you have Microsoft Word installed on your machine).

A web page itself can display HTML (HyperText Markup Language), DHTML (Dynamic HyperText Markup Language), and XML (Extensible Markup Language), or a combination of the three.

IIS processes HTTP requests from the URL (Uniform Resource Locator) that was entered in a browser or sent from a web page. A URL (essentially an address such as http://www.apress.com/about/ordering.html) specifies the virtual directory name of the web site and the page that you want to access. For example, assume you had a virtual directory set up called `Controls` installed on your machine, and you wanted to access the web page named `Tasks.htm`. You could enter the following URL in your browser:

```
http://localhost/Controls/Tasks.htm
```

IIS would look in the virtual directory named `Controls` for the web page named `Tasks.htm`. If IIS found the page, it would send the requested information back to the browser that requested it.

IIS runs as a service to provide web server capabilities in Windows 2000 and Windows NT; it also provides many more features than we have space to discuss. In Windows 2000 (all editions), IIS comes as part of the operating system; however, for Windows 2000 Professional edition it must be installed before it can be used. It is installed by default on the Server editions. In Windows NT 4.0 IIS comes as part of the Windows NT 4.0 Option Pack that must also be installed before IIS can be used.

Requirements

In order to be able to use the XML features of SQL Server 2000, you must install IIS 4.0 or higher, or alternatively, **Personal Web Server** (**PWS**) 4.0 or higher on Windows NT Workstation 4.0. Both IIS and PWS can be installed from the Windows NT 4.0 Option Pack, which can be found on the Visual Studio Professional and Enterprise installation CDs or can be downloaded at:

http://www.microsoft.com/ntworkstation/downloads/Recommended/ServicePacks/NT40ptPk/Default.asp

For Windows 2000 Professional edition, the Administrative Tools pack (`Adminpak.msi`) must be installed. This file can be found in the `i386` folder on all Windows 2000 Server editions' CDs only.

IIS Installation for Windows 2000

Installation of IIS on this platform is a simple process, which is performed by the Windows Component Wizard. To invoke this wizard and begin the installation of IIS:

1. Click on the Start button on the task bar, then click on Settings, and then click on Control Panel.

2. In the control, find and double-click on Add/Remove Programs.

3. In the Add/Remove Programs dialog, click on the Add/Remove Windows Components button in the explorer bar:

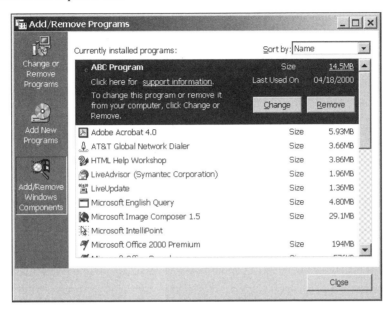

4. Once the Windows Components Wizard appears, tick the check box for Internet Information Services (IIS) and then click the Next button:

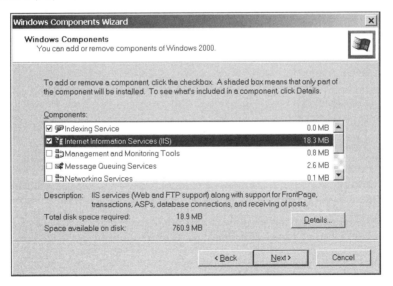

5. The Windows Components Wizard will then proceed to install and configure IIS on your machine. Depending on the speed of your machine and the amount of available memory, this may take a few minutes:

541

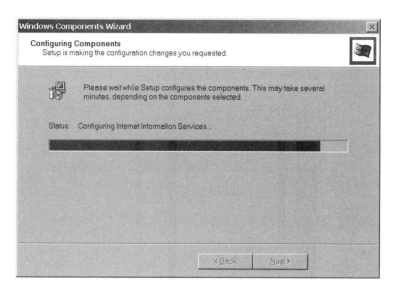

6. When the Windows Components Wizard has completed the installation, the following dialog box is displayed. Click on the Finish button to close the Windows Component Wizard.

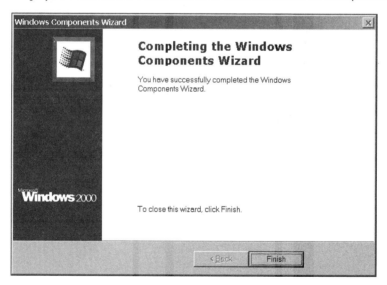

At this point, IIS has been installed and configured on Windows 2000 and is ready for use. There is one more component that is required for Windows 2000 – the Administrative Tools pack. You must have a Windows 2000 Server CD (any server edition) to install the Administrative Tools.

To install the Administrative Tools:

7. Insert the Windows 2000 Server CD and navigate to the i386 folder.

8. Double-click on Adminpak.msi to invoke the Windows 2000 Administration Tools Setup Wizard. The first step of the wizard informs you what the wizard will do. Click the Next button to proceed:

9. The wizard will perform the installation of the Administration Tools and requires no action at this point:

10. Once the wizard has completed the installation, the following dialog box is shown. Click on the Finish button to finish the installation:

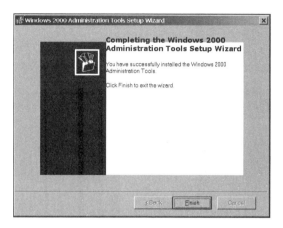

After having installed IIS and the Administration Tools, the prerequisites for Windows 2000 have been met.

IIS Installation for Windows NT 4.0

The installation of IIS on Windows 2000 was quick and easy. Unfortunately this is not the case for Windows NT. This installation requires many more steps, as IIS is not part of the Windows NT operating system. The installation steps outlined here use the Windows NT 4.0 Option Pack that comes on the Visual Studio CDs, but can be applied equally well if you download the Option Pack from Microsoft.

To begin the installation of IIS for Windows NT:

1. Insert CD1 of the Visual Studio CDs. If you do not see the following screen, then double-click on AutoRun.exe in the root of the CD. The option that should be selected is Server Applications and Tools. Click the Next button to proceed.

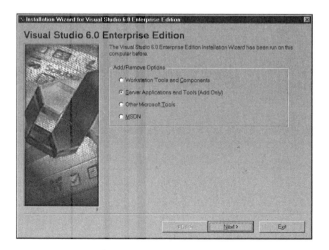

2. We want to launch the BackOffice Installation Wizard, so ensure this entry is highlighted and then click the Install button:

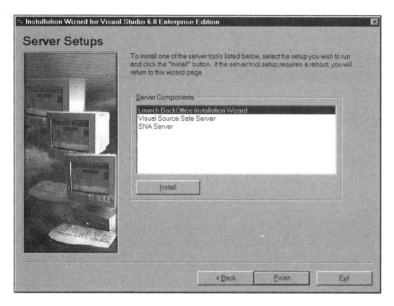

3. At this point you are prompted to insert CD 2. Insert this CD and then click on the OK button to continue:

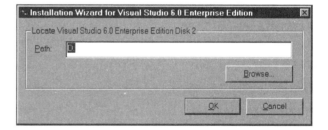

4. At this point, we are only interested in installing IIS, so we want to choose the Custom option on the next screen. Click on the Next button to proceed:

5. On the next screen you need to choose Windows NT Option Pack, since this is where IIS is installed. Click the Next button to proceed:

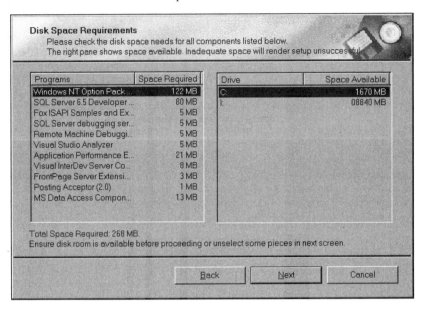

6. The next step requires us to choose MS Data Access Components when we choose Windows NT Option Pack 4.0. Since we have a newer version of MDAC, this installation will not interfere with the most recent version. This is required when installing IIS. Check both options, and then click on the plus sign next to Windows NT Option Pack 4.0 so that we can see all the available options and check those that we require.

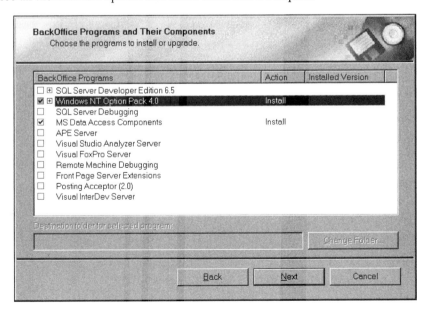

7. The following two figures show the options to be checked. Once you have checked the options as shown, click the **Next** button to proceed:

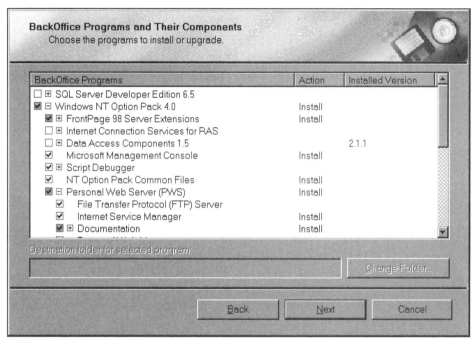

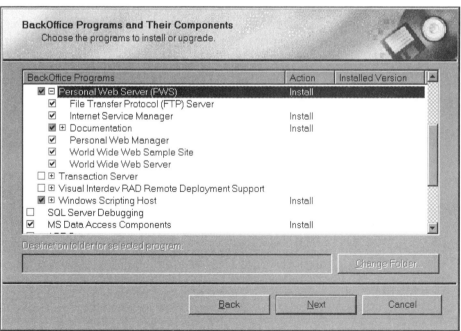

8. The next step of the installation process allows you to change the installation folder for IIS. Change this information if necessary. If you have more than one drive and more room on another drive then you can change the drive that the software is installed on. Then click the Next button to proceed.

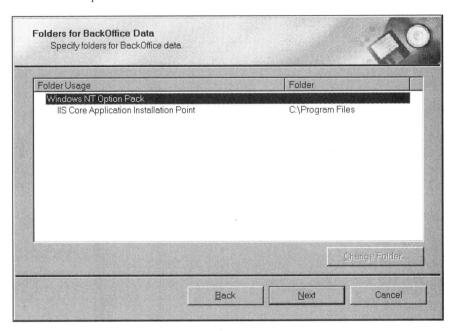

9. The next step of the process allows you to confirm your installation choices. If you want to make any changes, click on the Back button. Otherwise, click on the Next button to have IIS installed:

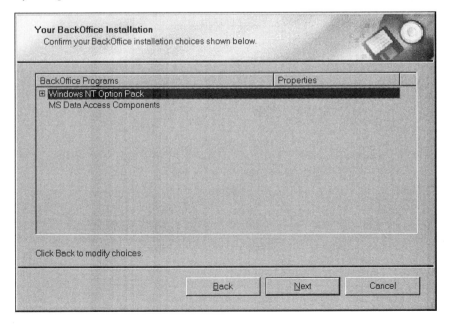

10. At this point the installation starts, so sit back and wait for it to complete. This may take a few minutes depending on the speed of your workstation and the amount of memory that you have:

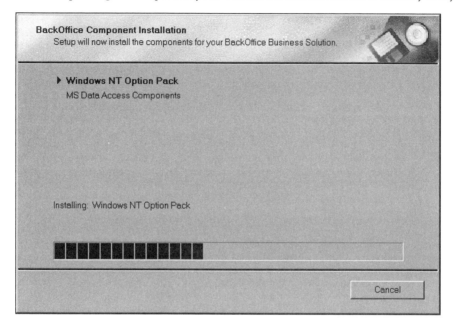

11. Once the installation of the actual files has completed, the Finish dialog is displayed. Click the Finish button to proceed:

12. You will be prompted to reboot your machine at this point, so make sure you have saved any work and then click OK in the dialog:

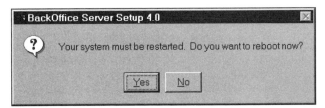

13. After your machine has restarted and you have logged in, the Installation Wizard displays the Server Setups dialog. Click the Finish button to dismiss this dialog:

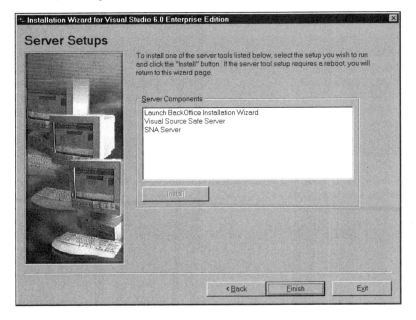

At this point the installation of IIS on Windows NT has been completed. We are now ready to move on and create a virtual directory. Since you have installed additional components on Windows NT, you will want to re-install the latest service pack that you had previously installed.

Creating a Virtual Directory for a Web Site

As we mentioned earlier, a **virtual directory** is a directory on your hard drive that is designated as a share point in IIS. So, what this means is that we need to create a directory on our hard drive somewhere, and then create the virtual directory in IIS that will point to the physical directory on our hard drive.

IIS processes the HTTP requests from the URL, then determines which virtual directory has been specified and what web page was requested. IIS uses the virtual directory specified, which has been mapped to a physical directory, and then serves up the web page requested.

To create a virtual directory in IIS:

1. Create a directory on you hard drive named `Hardware Tracking`. Most developers create the directory for web sites under the `InetPub\WWWRoot` directory. Therefore, if this directory, which is installed with IIS, is installed on your C drive you could create the `Hardware Tracking` directory as `C:\Inetpub\wwwroot\Hardware Tracking`.

2. Start the **Internet Services Manager**. In Windows 2000, this can be located in the `Administrative Tools` folder under `Programs`, and in Windows NT can be found in the `Programs\Windows NT 4.0 Option Pack\Microsoft Personal Web Server` folder.

The **Internet Services Manager** is run as a snap-in in the MMC console and displays your computer name as the default computer. If you chose to install the FTP services, you will see it listed, as shown in the following figure:

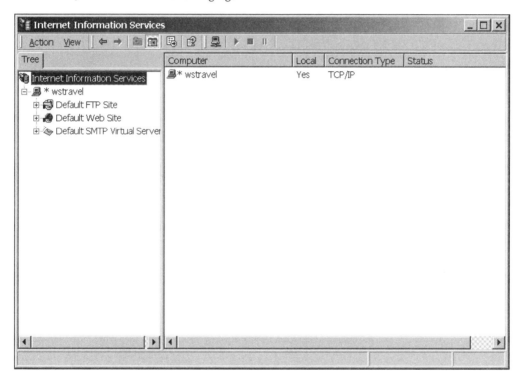

3. To set up the virtual directory in IIS, expand the **Default Web Site** group in the tree pane, then right-click on this group and choose **New** and then **Virtual Directory** from the context menu.

In Windows 2000 you will see the **Welcome** screen for the **Virtual Directory Creation Wizard**. Click the **Next** button to proceed. You will not see this welcome screen in Windows NT.

4. In both Windows 2000 and Windows NT you will see a screen that prompts you to enter a virtual directory name. Enter HardwareTracking as the virtual directory name and then click the Next button to proceed. This time we have not included a space in the name although we could have. This just makes dealing with this name in a URL easier.

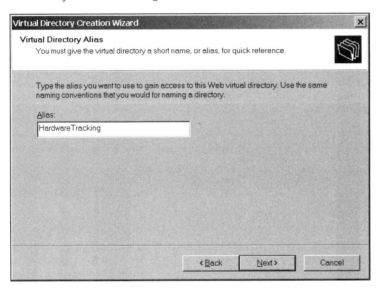

5. The next step prompts you to enter the physical directory that the virtual directory should be mapped to. You are provided with a Browse button that allows you to browse to the directory that should be used. Once the directory name has been placed in the Directory text box, click the Next button to proceed:

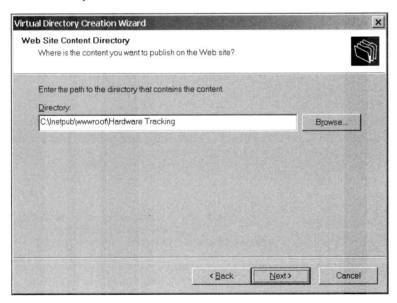

6. The next step of the wizard allows you to set the various permissions on the web site. By default, the Read and Run Scripts options are checked. This allows a user to read files located in this web site, such as a web page or a physical file located in this directory.

The Execute option is not checked, but should be if you plan to run ISAPI applications or CGI scripts. This allows us to run ISAPI applications and CGI scripts if we ever find the need to. ISAPI is an acronym for Internet Server Application Programming Interface, which is a set of APIs that allow you to take advantage of IIS features in your applications. CGI is an acronym for Common Gateway Interface, which is a mechanism that allows a web server to run a program or script on the server.

Write access allows a user or script to write data to the directory. This option is not recommended because this allows a user or script to overwrite existing files, which could lead to the destruction of your web site.

The last option, Browse, is also not recommended as this allows a user to browse the directory and directory structure of your web site through a browser, identifying all of the files in your web site.

Ensure the first three options (Read, Run scripts, and Execute) are checked. If using Windows NT, click the Finish button. On the other hand, if you are using Windows 2000, you will need to click the Next button in order to get to the final step of the wizard, and then click the Finish button.

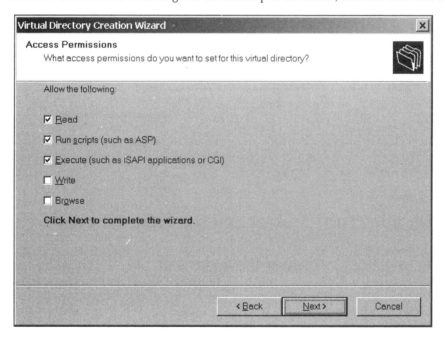

At this point your virtual directory has been set up and is ready for use. To summarize, we have created a virtual directory in IIS, which has the URL http://localhost/hardwaretracking. This actually points to the physical directory C:\Inetpub\wwwroot\Hardware Tracking. You can create a very simple web page in this directory to test your web site. Enter the following code in NotePad, or if you have an HTML editor use that. We will defer the explanation of this code until the next chapter.

```
<HTML>
<HEAD>
<TITLE></TITLE>
</HEAD>
<BODY>
<P>This is a test of our new web site.</P>
</BODY>
</HTML>
```

Save the file in the `C:\Inetpub\wwwroot\Hardware Tracking` directory as `Test.htm`. To test your web site, open Microsoft Internet Explorer and enter the URL shown in the following figure. Your results should also look similar to those shown here. It should be noted at this point that the URL that we have entered is all lower case. When entering a URL, case does not make a difference.

You have now successfully set up your own personal web site on your workstation. If you are connected to a local area network, other users can access this web site by substituting your machine name for localhost in the URL. For example, a user connected on the same local area network as I am on could enter the URL http://wstravel/hardwaretracking/test.htm and access this same page. You can, of course, also use this URL to access the test web page.

Creating a Virtual Directory for SQL Server

SQL Server 2000 provides native built-in support for XML that allows us to query the database from a web browser. We will be exploring this feature more in the next chapter. However, in order to work with the XML features of SQL Server 2000, we must create a virtual directory for SQL Server. This is slightly different from creating a virtual directory for a web site. SQL Server provides a utility called **IIS Virtual Directory Management for SQL Server**, which allows you to set up and manage virtual directories for SQL Server.

This utility works like and looks similar to the Internet Services Manager. The IIS Virtual Directory Management for SQL Server associates a virtual directory with a SQL Server instance and the physical directory on your hard drive. Since the virtual directory will be associated with SQL Server 2000, there are many more steps that are required to set up a virtual directory. For instance, you need to supply database and login information.

To set up a virtual directory for SQL Server:

1. Create a directory on you hard drive under `InetPub\WWWRoot`, calling it `htData`.

2. Start the IIS Virtual Directory Management for SQL Server utility by navigating to the Microsoft SQL Server group in Programs, and then clicking on the Configure SQL XML Support in IIS item.

3. Expand the group that contains your machine name. If you have previously set up any virtual directories, they will be displayed here:

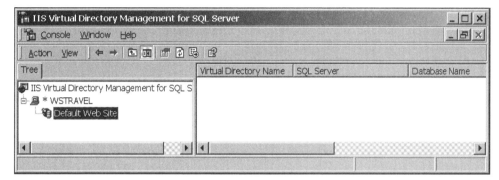

4. Right-click on the Default Web Site group, choose New and then New Virtual Directory from the context menu. The New Virtual Directory Properties dialog is displayed.

5. Enter a Virtual Directory Name of htData and place the full path for this directory in the Local Path text box:

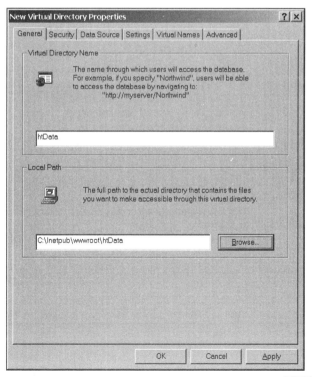

6. Next, click on the Security tab. Enter a User Name that has authority to the Hardware Tracking database. I chose to use the sa login, and since this login uses SQL Server authentication, we need to ensure the SQL Server option is checked for the Account Type. In a production environment you would want to use a User Name that had limited authority to the database. If you are using a Windows Account Type then you would not need to enter a password and that text box would be grayed out

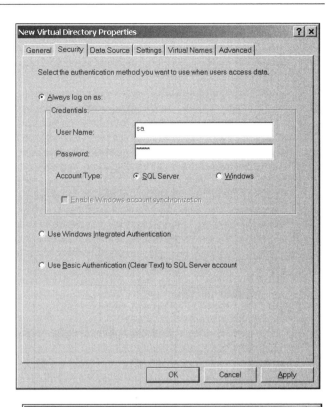

7. Click on the Data Source tab next, and enter a valid server name where SQL Server is running. This should be your machine name if you installed SQL Server 2000 on your workstation. Also, if the instance of SQL Server 2000 is not the default instance, you will need to enter the instance name, as shown in the following figure.

Once you have entered a server name, select the Hardware Tracking database from the Database combo box:

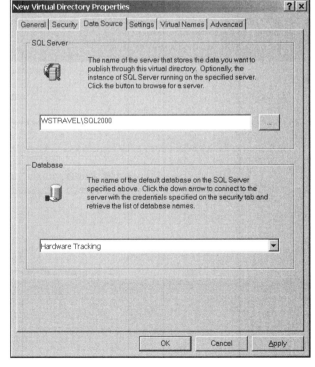

8. Click on the Settings tab next, and ensure the check boxes for Allow URL Queries, Allow Template Queries, and Allow XPath are checked. URL examples of each of these options are shown on this tab. We will be explaining and exploring these options in depth in the next chapter.

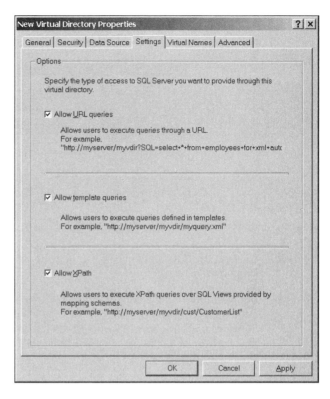

9. The last tab that we want to work with is the Virtual Names tab. Click on this tab so that we can define some virtual names. These will provide subdirectories under the `htData` directory and allow us to manage the content (such as templates and schemas) more effectively. We will also cover these in depth in the next chapter.

10. The first virtual name that we want to define is Template. Click on the New button to invoke the Virtual Name Configuration dialog. Enter a Virtual Name of Template, and select Template in the Type combo box. Next, click on the Browse button (signified by three dots) to browse for a folder for this new folder.

In the Browse For Folder dialog, browse to the drive where the `InetPub\WWWRoot` directory is, and then click on the htData directory. Next, click on the New Folder button and enter a folder name of Template, then click on the OK button.

11. The completed Virtual Name Configuration dialog should now look like the one shown in the following figure. Click the Save button in order to save the information and to close the dialog:

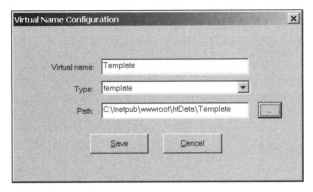

12. Click on the New button again on the Virtual Names tab of the New Virtual Directory Properties dialog.

In the Virtual Name Configuration dialog, enter a Virtual Name of Schema and select Schema in the Type combo box. Next, click on the browse button to browse to the htData directory and click on it. Then click the New Folder button to create a new folder in this directory giving the folder a name of Schema. Then click the OK button to close the Browse For Folder dialog.

Now click on the Save button in the Virtual Name Configuration dialog.

The completed Virtual Names tab of the New Virtual Directory Properties dialog should now look like the next figure:

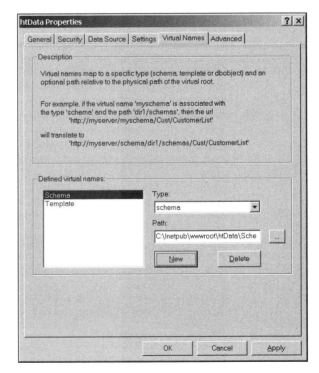

13. Click the OK button to have the virtual directory for SQL Server set up. The IIS Virtual Directory Management for SQL Server utility now shows the virtual directory for the Hardware Tracking database:

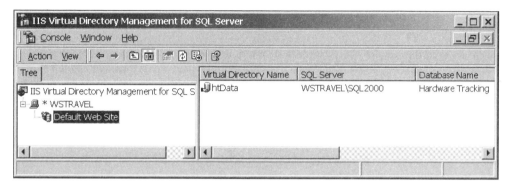

14. At this point your virtual directory for SQL Server is set up, and you are now ready to test it. Open Microsoft Internet Explorer and enter the following URL:

```
http://localhost/htdata?sql=SELECT * FROM Employee_T WHERE Employee_ID=1 FOR XML
AUTO
```

15. What we have done here is to enter the following query in the URL and use our virtual directory that has been set up for SQL Server. The full details of this query will be explained in the next chapter.

```
SELECT *
    FROM Employee_T
    WHERE Employee_ID=1
    FOR XML AUTO
```

16. Notice that when you pressed *Enter*, the browser converted all spaces in the URL and replaced them with the space character %20, as shown in the next figure. This is because spaces are not allowed in a URL and the browser handles this for you automatically.

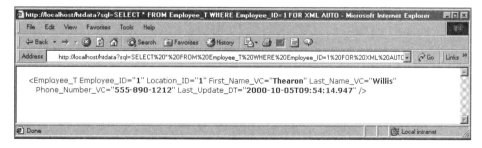

Basically what we have done here is to execute a query in the URL of the browser. What has actually happened is that IIS has taken the query that we entered and passed it off to SQL Server for execution. SQL Server then in turn executed the query and returned the data to IIS. It was then passed to the browser to be displayed.

Summary

This chapter has taken a brief look at what IIS is, and what it does. We know that IIS processes HTTP requests from URLs and displays the web pages that were requested. This is a simplistic description as it does a lot more than this, such as processing server-side scripts and Active Server Pages.

We have covered the installation of IIS in both Windows 2000 and Windows NT. We have also set up a virtual directory for a web site and a virtual directory for SQL Server. We have created a simple test page for our web site to ensure we were able to access the virtual directory that was set up. Also, we've executed a simple query to validate that our virtual directory for SQL Server was set up correctly.

To summarize, you should know how to:

❑ Install IIS on Windows 2000 and Windows NT

❑ Set up a virtual directory for a web site

❑ Set up a virtual directory for SQL Server

The next chapter introduces SQL Server 2000's XML features, and we will find out how we can employ this technology on the Web.

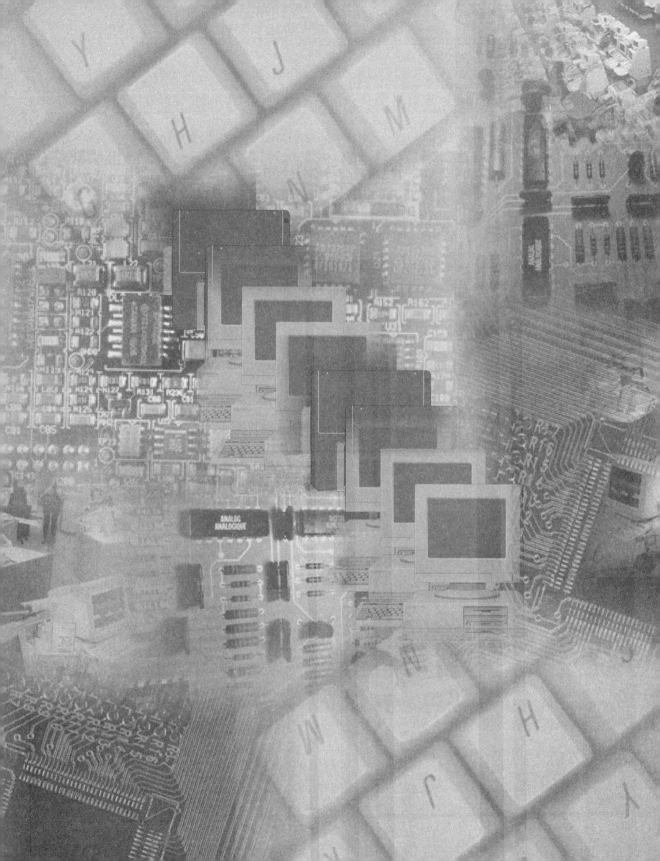

SQL Server and XML

Just a few short years ago we would display data from our database on the Web as HTML using Active Server Pages to select and format the data. We would also send and receive data as plain text files in business-to-business (B2B) applications.

XML (**Extensible Markup Language**) is changing all of that, and SQL Server 2000's XML-related features are helping to speed up the process of change. SQL Server provides native built-in support for XML that allows us to select and write XML data in SQL Server. What this means is that we can write queries and stored procedures that allow us to retrieve data in XML format. SQL Server stores data natively as XML, and when XML data is requested SQL Server formats the data selected into the required XML format. All of this happens behind the scenes and is part of SQL Server's built-in support for XML.

SQL Server also provides several features that allow us to select XML data using a URL (Universal Resource Locator) just as we would use a URL to access a web page. SQL Server also provides the XML-Data Reduced (XDR) language, which allows us to use annotated XDR schemas to describe the structure of the data in an XML document.

This chapter explores these new XML features in SQL Server 2000 and takes a look at how you can exploit them to your benefit. We will also take a look at how we can use XSL (Extensible Stylesheet Language) to format and display XML data.

So, this chapter will cover:

- ❑ A brief introduction to XML and its related technologies
- ❑ Accessing data using a URL
- ❑ Creating and using stored procedures that return XML formatted data
- ❑ Creating and using XML templates
- ❑ Creating and using XSL templates
- ❑ Creating and using annotated XDR schemas

XML Overview

XML is an acronym for **Extensible Markup Language** and is a language that is used to describe data and how it should be displayed. XML is not just for the Web, which is what it is commonly used for, as it can be used anywhere that self-describing data is needed. An example of this is in B2B (business-to-business) applications where an exchange of data is required. By using self-describing data, any recipient of that data can work with it and know what each item is. This is the great power of XML.

XML markup describes an XML document using **tags** and **attributes** in the document. The tags, also known as element names, describe the data, and the attributes describe some attribute of the actual data elements themselves. For example, consider the following element:

```
<FirstName Employee_ID="1">Thearon</FirstName>
```

The <FirstName> tag describes that the data is the first name of an employee and the attribute of Employee_ID describes the employee ID of this employee. The tag name and attribute name suggest the data structure, and the values 1 and Thearon represent the actual data itself.

In XML, unlike HTML, the developer defines the tags and attributes, so they can be given meaningful names. XML allows you to nest one element within another to represent groups of data.

Most tags in an XML document have a corresponding closing tag. The closing tag begins with a forward slash and contains the same name as the beginning tag. Using a corresponding closing tag for each defined tag creates what is known as a **well-formed document** that strictly adheres to the XML standard. Other rules for defining a well-formed XML document include ensuring that there is only one root element and that the element names do not contain spaces. We'll see more of this in just a few minutes.

To define a document as an XML document we must specify the <?XML?> element that allows any XML-compliant browser, such as Microsoft Internet Explorer, to properly parse and display the document. This element has several attributes and the syntax is shown:

```
<?XML version="version" standalone="DTDflag" encoding="encodingname" ?>
```

The version attribute specifies the version number of XML that is being used. The current version of XML is 1.0.

The DTDflag attribute is an optional argument that specifies a Boolean value (either yes or no) indicating whether or not this XML file includes a reference to an external **Document Type Definition** (**DTD**). A DTD defines the elements and attributes that can be used in an XML document and can also contain pre-defined XML data definitions. It also lays out any rules about how many of each element should be present, and in what order.

The optional encodingname attribute specifies the type of character set encoding used in the document. This argument is usually one of the character sets supported by Microsoft Internet Explorer, such as UTF-8. UTF-8 supports Unicode data that allows you to use non-ASCII characters.

Looking at the following example below we see that the <Employees> tag has a corresponding closing tag of </Employees>. This is very similar to HTML, where the closing tags for various HTML elements contain a forward slash to indicate a closing tag. Some XML tags do not require a separate closing tag as this can be accomplished in the beginning tag. For example, suppose we had a tag for middle name and the employee did not have a middle name, we could specify the tag as `<MiddleName />`. This would indicate that there was no data for the `<MiddleName>` element.

XML data can usually be structured in a hierarchical way. The `<Employees>` element in the example below is referred to as the **root element** as it is the topmost data element in the document:

```xml
<?xml version="1.0" encoding="utf-8" ?>
<Employees>
   <Employee>
      <EmployeeID>1</EmployeeID>
      <FirstName>Thearon</FirstName>
      <LastName>Willis</LastName>
   </Employee>
   <Employee>
      <EmployeeID>4</EmployeeID>
      <FirstName>Cheryl</FirstName>
      <LastName>Carson</LastName>
   </Employee>
</Employees>
```

Within the `Employees` element we have two `Employee` elements, each with three child elements, `EmployeeID`, `FirstName`, and `LastName`.

In this example, and XML in general, elements form a hierarchy of parent-child relationships. The `<Employees>` element represents a group of employees and is the root element. The `<Employee>` parent element represents a single employee. Within the `<Employee>` element we have specified each of the employee child elements and each element has a tag describing the data (for example `<FirstName>`).

> XML is case sensitive, meaning an element with a name of **EmployeeID** is not the same as an element with a name of **employeeid**. This is true for all XML elements and attributes.

When we save this file we save it with a `.xml` extension. The file can then be viewed in a browser, such as Microsoft Internet Explorer, by simply double-clicking on the file within Windows Explorer. This figure shows the example as it is displayed in IE5:

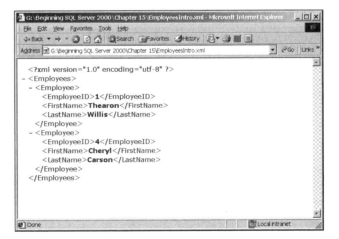

Notice that each group of data in our document is expandable and collapsible, as indicated by the dash next to the group name. This means that we can collapse the employee groups, which are children of the employees group.

> **Note: this is a feature of Microsoft Internet Explorer 5.0 and other browsers may not allow you to expand and collapse the element groups in this way.**

Now that we know what XML looks like, let's move on and see how SQL Server 2000 can help us create and display XML in a browser.

Selecting XML Data

We know that we can select data in SQL Server 2000 using the SELECT statement. We can also select data and have it formatted as XML, using the FOR XML clause. The FOR XML clause is only valid in a SELECT statement (it can not be used with INSERT, UPDATE, etc.) and returns the results of the SELECT statement in a variety of XML formats, which we will cover shortly.

Let's take a look at the following familiar SELECT statement:

```
SELECT Employee_ID, First_Name_VC, Last_Name_VC
    FROM Employee_T
```

Execution of this SELECT statement in the Query Analyzer produces the following results. These are the standard results that we are used to seeing:

```
Employee_ID First_Name_VC   Last_Name_VC
----------- --------------- ---------------
1           Thearon         Willis
2           Michael         Dell
4           Cheryl          Carson
```

If we take the same SELECT statement shown above and add the FOR XML clause:

```
SELECT Employee_ID, First_Name_VC, Last_Name_VC
    FROM Employee_T FOR XML RAW
```

we see a totally different set of results:

```
XML_F52E2B61-18A1-11d1-B105-00805F49916B
-------------------------------------------------------------------
<row Employee_ID="1" First_Name_VC="Thearon" Last_Name_VC="Willis"/><row
Employee_ID="2" First_Name_VC="Michael" Last_Name_VC="Dell"/>"/><row
Employee_ID="4" First_Name_VC="Cheryl" Last_Name_VC="Carson"/>
```

Notice that our data now looks similar to our XML example that we displayed earlier. In the output above, row is an element and the remaining data has been specified as attributes of that element. Each row of data in our Employee_T table has been specified as a separate row element.

The actual amount of data that is displayed in the results window of the Query Analyzer is limited. To increase the display limit click on the Tools menu and select the Options menu item. Then click on the Results tab and enter a large value, such as 1000, in the Maximum characters per column text box. Then click the OK button to close the Options dialog.

The syntax for the FOR XML clause is shown next:

```
FOR XML mode [,XMLDATA] [,ELEMENTS][,BINARY Base64]
```

In the syntax above the *mode* argument specifies the shape of the XML data returned. There are three possible values for *mode*: RAW, AUTO, and EXPLICIT. The RAW mode produces XML results that are formatted using default element names, while AUTO mode produces results using the table and column names as the element and attribute names. EXPLICIT mode is much more complex and you must specify the element names and nesting required. In short, you must specify the shape of the XML document in your query.

The partial results shown below (for just one row in the table) represent data formatted using RAW and AUTO modes respectively:

```
<row Employee_ID="1" First_Name_VC="Thearon" Last_Name_VC="Willis"/>
```

```
<Employee_T Employee_ID="1" First_Name_VC="Thearon" Last_Name_VC="Willis"/>
```

The optional XMLDATA, ELEMENTS, and BINARY Base64 arguments can only be used with the AUTO mode. These arguments further define how the XML data should be formatted. For example, the XMLDATA argument specifies that an XML-Data schema should be returned with your XML data, while the ELEMENTS argument specifies that your XML data be returned in elements, instead of as attributes on a single element. The BINARY Base64 argument specifies that binary data be returned in the binary base64-encoded format, and this is the default argument for AUTO mode. Binary base64 is a standard content transfer encoding method used to encode data to be sent to a browser. The browser then decodes the data and displays it in a readable form.

Try It Out – Using the FOR XML Clause

To illustrate the points discussed so far, let's create and execute some simple queries in the Query Analyzer that use the FOR XML clause. We will use the SELECT query that we saw earlier. If you have not already done so, increase the maximum characters that are displayed in the results window in the Query Analyzer.

1. The first query that we want to run will use the AUTO mode in the FOR XML clause. Enter and execute the following query:

```
SELECT Employee_ID, First_Name_VC, Last_Name_VC
   FROM Employee_T FOR XML AUTO
```

You should see results similar to those shown overleaf. Due to limited space, only partial results are shown. Depending on the amount of data in your Employee_T table, you should be able to see most, if not all, of the data in the results window by scrolling the window:

567

```
XML_F52E2B61-18A1-11d1-B105-00805F49916B
-------------------------------------------------------------------------
<Employee_T Employee_ID="1" First_Name_VC="Thearon"
Last_Name_VC="Willis"/><Employee_T Employee_ID="2" First_Name_VC="Michael"
Last_Name_VC="Dell"/>
```

Each element in the results represents one row from the Employee_T table, and the element name is the table name. This has been done automatically for you because you specified the AUTO argument.

2. Now enter and execute the following query. It might be useful to open a new query window instead of clearing the current query window. This will allow you to switch between the various query windows to view the different results that are generated.

```
SELECT Employee_ID, First_Name_VC, Last_Name_VC
    FROM Employee_T FOR XML AUTO, XMLDATA
```

This example not only displays the XML data but it also returns a schema that further defines the elements and attributes of your XML data. When you run your query, the schema is displayed first, followed by the ElementType and then the AttributeType.

Notice in the partial results below, taken from the schema, that the AttributeType for each of the columns specified in the SELECT statement is displayed. Each AttributeType has a name assigned and the data type specified. We'll be discussing AttributeType later in this chapter.

```
<AttributeType name="Employee_ID" dt:type="i4"/><AttributeType
name="First_Name_VC" dt:type="string"/><AttributeType name="Last_Name_VC"
dt:type="string"/>
```

3. The next query that we want to execute is shown below and uses the ELEMENTS argument. Enter and execute this query:

```
SELECT Employee_ID, First_Name_VC, Last_Name_VC
    FROM Employee_T FOR XML AUTO, ELEMENTS
```

This query displays all of the XML data as elements and looks very similar to the first example that we saw in this chapter:

```
XML_F52E2B61-18A1-11d1-B105-00805F49916B
-------------------------------------------------------------------------
<Employee_T><Employee_ID>1</Employee_ID><First_Name_VC>Thearon</First_Name_VC><Last
_Name_VC>Willis</Last_Name_VC></Employee_T>
```

So what we have seen here is that by using the FOR XML clause on a SELECT statement, we can return XML formatted data directly in the Query Analyzer. We can also display XML data formatted in a variety of ways depending on the intended use of the data, such as displaying it in a browser or sending it through a B2B application.

Selecting XML Data in a URL

When we set up a virtual directory for SQL Server in the last chapter, we selected data from the database in a URL to test the successful implementation of our virtual directory. This is where the real power of SQL Server and XML comes into play. This section takes a look at the basics of using the URL to return XML data from SQL Server.

As we saw in the last chapter, we can execute queries from a browser using the virtual directory that we set up. The query that we executed in the last chapter was entered in the URL as:

```
http://localhost/htdata?sql=SELECT * FROM Employee_T WHERE Employee_ID=1 FOR XML
AUTO
```

When we pressed the *Enter* key, Internet Explorer replaced all spaces in the URL with a hexadecimal value of %20. This is because we cannot use spaces in a URL. This makes the URL cluttered and hard to read. What we can do is use the special character of a plus sign (+) to represent a space. The browser will not replace this special character with its equivalent hexadecimal value and our URL is much easier to read.

There are also a few other special characters that we should look at before continuing. The following table lists the special characters that will be used throughout the rest of this chapter:

Special Character	Hexadecimal Value	Meaning
+	%20	Indicates a space.
/	%2F	Separates directories and subdirectories.
?	%3F	Separator between the actual URL and the parameters.
%	%25	Specifies special characters. Anytime that you need to use a character in your query that is a reserved character, you specify a percent sign followed by the hexadecimal value for that character.
&	%26	Separator between parameters specified in the URL.

When we display XML data, a top-level element, known as a root element or root node, is required. The example shown in the figure earlier indicates that Employees is the root element and under Employees there were many Employee elements that each represented a single employee. XML is like a tree – we start with a single root and then we grow and branch out from there.

The example URL above only extracted one record (where the employee ID = 1) and displayed it in the browser. Let's take a look at an example that will select certain columns and all rows from the Employee_T table and display the results in a browser.

Try It Out – SELECT Statement in a URL

In this exercise we want to enter a query in a URL that will select the `Employee_ID`, `First_Name_VC`, and `Last_Name_VC` columns for all rows in the `Employee_T` table.

1. To illustrate our point about the root element in an XML document, enter the following URL in a browser:

```
http://localhost/htData?SQL=SELECT+Employee_ID,+First_Name_VC,+Last_Name_VC+FROM+E
mployee_T+FOR+XML+AUTO
```

You will receive this error message, "*Only one top level element is allowed in an XML document. Line 1, Position 77*, and your XML data will be displayed as one continuous line of data. This error indicates that the XML is not well-formed and that a root element is required.

2. In order to resolve this problem we can specify the Root keyword as a parameter in our URL. The name that you assign to the Root keyword should describe the data being displayed.

Enter the following URL in a browser:

```
http://localhost/htData?SQL=SELECT+Employee_ID,+First_Name_VC,+Last_Name_VC+FROM+E
mployee_T+FOR+XML+AUTO&Root=Employees
```

You should now see the data from the `Employee_T` table displayed as XML in the browser, as shown in the following screenshot. Notice that `Employees` is the name of the root element. You can experiment with this by giving the root a different name and running the query again.

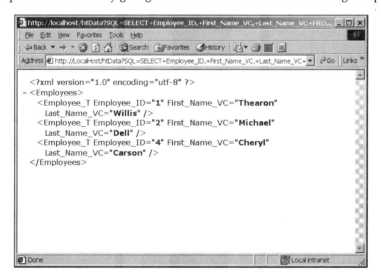

Now that we have executed a query in a URL and displayed XML data in a browser, let's take a more detailed look at the URL syntax. The syntax below shows the basic URL that can be executed:

```
http://iisserver/virtualroot?{sql=SQLString | template=XMLTemplate}
[&param=value[&param=value]...n]
```

In this syntax, *iisserver* represents the machine name that IIS is installed on. If IIS is installed on your local machine then you can specify localhost for *iisserver*, otherwise you would specify the machine name where IIS is installed.

The *virtualroot* argument specifies the virtual directory. In our case this virtual directory was set up, in the last chapter, with a name of htData.

The optional ?sql argument specifies that a SQL string or stored procedure is to be executed. This is followed by the *SQLString* argument, which specifies the actual SQL string or stored procedure that will be executed.

The optional argument, ?template, specifies an XML document that contains a query string to be executed. The query string can be a SQL statement, stored procedure, or a table name. This is a more secure way of allowing users access to our data and we'll cover this later in the chapter.

The optional ?param arguments represent parameter names or keywords. Valid keywords are ContentType, OutputEncoding, Root, and XSL. ContentType specifies the content type of the returned documents. There are various options for this but the one that we will be using is text/XML, which identifies the document as text and HTML. OutputEncoding indicates what character set is to be used for the output. The encoding used by default is UTF-8. The Root keyword, as we have seen, allows us to specify the root element for our XML document. The XSL keyword allows us to specify an XSL document that will be used to format the results of our XML document. We'll be using this keyword in the next section.

XSL Stylesheets

XML documents can contain actual XML data or a query that will be executed to retrieve the XML data from SQL Server. We have seen how XML data is displayed in a browser from the examples that we have executed. While the data displayed is well formed and we can identify the various elements in the XML document, it really does not provide the type of data that we would want to display in a browser.

XSL helps solve this problem; it is an acronym for **Extensible Stylesheet Language** and describes the way that XML data should be formatted and displayed. Like XML, XSL also uses tags to describe and format the XML data. Each tag has a corresponding closing tag that begins with a forward slash (/). XSL, like XML, uses strict formatting standards to create well-formed documents.

Using XSL we can define a **stylesheet**. This can contain an entire HTML document within the XSL document. The HTML is intermixed with XSL elements and will be merged with the resulting XML data to form a completed HTML document that will be displayed in a browser.

An XSL file is like an XML file, but for stylesheets, and must begin with the XML declaration. The following code fragment shows the beginning of an XSL stylesheet:

```
<?xml version="1.0" encoding="UTF-8"?>
<xsl:stylesheet xmlns:xsl="http://www.w3.org/TR/WD-xsl">
    <xsl:template match = "/">
```

The first line of code here is the XML declaration, which is included as the first line of every XML document.

The next line of code is the `<xsl:stylesheet>` element that defines this XML document as an XSL stylesheet. It should be noted here that your XSL stylesheets will have a `.xsl` file extension. Within the `<xsl:stylesheet>` element we have declared a **namespace** of `xmlns:xsl=http://www.w3.org/TR/WD-xsl`. This is the standard namespace supported by Microsoft Internet Explorer 5.0. A namespace allows you to declare elements of a certain namespace and differentiate these elements from others of the same name. In other words you can specify a collection of names that can be used as element or attribute names in your document.

> **At this point it is worth noting that, like XML, XSL is also case sensitive. This includes the elements themselves and their attributes.**

Following the `<xsl:stylesheet>` element we declare the `<xsl:template>` element to indicate that the stylesheet **template** corresponds to the root element of the XML document. We are going to look at how to use templates in a little while.

These three lines of code are the standard beginning of every XSL stylesheet that you will create. Keep in mind that the `<xsl:stylesheet>` and `<xsl:template>` elements require a closing tag at the end of the stylesheet, as shown:

```
    </xsl:template>
  </xsl:stylesheet>
```

The XSL language provides many elements that help us to process and display XML data. We can even include VBScript or JScript/JavaScript in our XSL stylesheets, although that is beyond the scope of this chapter. At the core of XSL is the `<xsl:for-each>` element that sets up a loop for processing XML data.

This element accepts the `select` attribute, which specifies the XSL pattern for the **node** of XML data to be iterated. A node is an element in the XML tree structure that has links to one or more nodes below it. An example of this is shown in the next code fragment:

```
<xsl:for-each select="Employees/Employee_T">
```

The nodes that we have specified in the `select` attribute specify the root node of Employees and a sub node of Employee_T. Let's take a look again at the figure we saw earlier. The root node is listed as Employees and the sub-node under the root is listed as Employee_T, which is the name of our table. SQL Server placed this node name here automatically for us and derived the name from the table name.

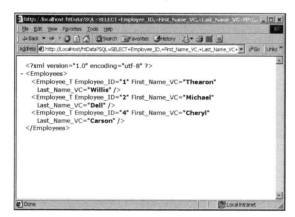

Notice that for each `Employee_T` node there are several XML attributes that we want to process, such as `Employee_ID`, `First_Name_VC`, and `Last_Name_VC`. These are processed using the `<xsl:value-of>` element.

The code fragment below shows how we use the `<xsl:value-of>` element. The `select` attribute specifies the pattern to match and the data from this match is then inserted as a text string into your document. Because our data is being generated from SQL Server we must specify the 'at' sign (@) before the element name to be matched. After the pattern name we include a forward slash to indicate the closing of this element.

```
<xsl:value-of select="@Employee_ID "/>
<xsl:value-of select="@First_Name_VC"/>
<xsl:value-of select="@Last_Name_VC"/>
```

This demonstrates the point made earlier; remember that while all XML and XSL elements require a closing tag, we can sometimes specify a forward slash at the end of the element to indicate a closing tag for that element, such as we have done in the previous code fragment.

Try It Out – XSL Stylesheet

Now that we know the basic elements that make up an XSL stylesheet, let's create one to display the first and last name of all employees from the `Employee_T` table.

1. To create this stylesheet you can use any text editor you want; the complete code for this XSL stylesheet is listed below:

```
<?xml version="1.0" encoding="UTF-8"?>
<xsl:stylesheet xmlns:xsl="http://www.w3.org/TR/WD-xsl">
    <xsl:template match = "/">
        <HTML>
        <HEAD>
        <STYLE>
        TH
        {
            background-color: #CCCCCC;
        }
        </STYLE>
        </HEAD>
        <BODY>
        <TABLE Border="1">
            <TR>
                <TH ColSpan="2">Hardware Tracking Employees</TH>
            </TR>
            <TR>
                <TH>First Name</TH>
                <TH>Last Name</TH>
            </TR>
            <xsl:for-each select="Employees/Employee_T">
                <TR>
                    <TD><xsl:value-of select="@First_Name_VC"/></TD>
                    <TD><xsl:value-of select="@Last_Name_VC"/></TD>
                </TR>
            </xsl:for-each>
```

```
            </TABLE>
          </BODY>
        </HTML>
     </xsl:template>
  </xsl:stylesheet>
```

2. Once you have entered the code save the stylesheet in the `htData` directory as `Employee.xsl`. On my machine I created the `htData` directory under the `\Inetpub\wwwroot\` directory.

3. We can test this XSL stylesheet by running another query in the URL of our web browser. Enter the following URL in your browser and press the *Enter* key:

```
http://localhost/htData?SQL=SELECT+First_Name_VC,+Last_Name_VC+FROM+Employee_T+FOR
+XML+AUTO&XSL=Employee.xsl&ContentType=Text/HTML&Root=Employees
```

You should now see results similar to those shown in the following screenshot:

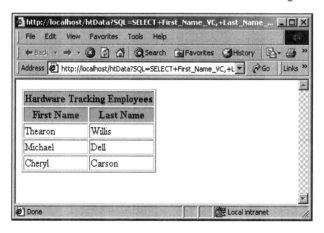

How It Works – XSL Stylesheet

As we mentioned earlier, the first three lines of our stylesheet are standard. The first line is the XML declaration and is required to identify this as an XML document so it can be parsed correctly by the browser. The second line is the `<xsl:stylesheet>` element that defines this XML document as an XSL stylesheet. The third line contains the `<xsl:template>` element and specifies that the stylesheet should match all elements starting at the root element of the XML document:

```
<?xml version="1.0" encoding="UTF-8"?>
<xsl:stylesheet xmlns:xsl="http://www.w3.org/TR/WD-xsl">
   <xsl:template match = "/">
```

Now we start defining an HTML document within our XSL stylesheet. This will cause an HTML document to be generated using HTML elements and XML data. The first thing we do here is to specify the `<HTML>` tag, which signifies the beginning of an HTML document. Then we specify the `<HEAD>` tag, which specifies information about the HTML document:

```
<HTML>
<HEAD>
```

The `<STYLE>` element defines an in-line **cascading stylesheet** within the HTML document. A cascading stylesheet is a set of styles (such as font size, font color) that are defined in the HTML document and that can be applied to any HTML element. So we can use the styles we define here throughout our HTML document.

```
<STYLE>
```

The first style that is defined is one that is automatically applied to the table header, `<TH>`, element. The style object is given a name of `TH` and the properties of this style are enclosed in curly brackets (`{}`). Here we have set the `background-color` property to a color of `#CCCCCC`, a light shade of gray. This property has been terminated with a semicolon. Each property that we set in our style object must be terminated with a semicolon.

When setting properties that change the color of the background or text, we can specify the RGB (Red-Blue-Green) value, as we have done here, or specify the color name. However, be aware that not all browsers recognize color names, while they should recognize all the RGB value for a color, so it is a good habit to specify the RGB value.

```
TH
{
    background-color: #CCCCCC;
}
```

Since this is the only style that we want to define we specify the closing tags for the `<STYLE>` and `<HEAD>` elements. Then we begin the body of the HTML document by specifying the `<BODY>` tag:

```
</STYLE>
</HEAD>
<BODY>
```

The first thing that we specify in the body of our HTML document is a table. Using a table helps keep the data that we want to display aligned correctly in rows and columns. Using the `<TABLE>` element we specify that a table should be drawn and we set the `Border` attribute to a value of 1. This specifies that a one-pixel border is to be drawn in and around the table.

We define a row in a table by specifying the `<TR>` tag, which begins a row of data in a table. Then we specify that a column header be placed in this row by specifying the `<TH>` tag. We set the `ColSpan` attribute to a value of 2, which indicates that this column header will span two columns of the table. Then we place the text to be displayed in the column header and close the column header by specifying the closing tag for the `<TH>` element. Next we specify the closing tag for the table row:

```
<TABLE Border="1">
  <TR>
    <TH ColSpan="2">Hardware Tracking Employees</TH>
  </TR>
```

The next row in our table specifies the column headers for each column. The first column in our table will contain the employee's first name and the second column in our table will contain the employee's last name:

```
<TR>
    <TH>First Name</TH>
    <TH>Last Name</TH>
</TR>
```

Now we want to iterate through the nodes in our XML data. Using the XSL <xsl:for-each> element we iterate through the Employees/Employee_T node of our XML data. For each iteration through the Employees/Employee_T node we specify that a row of HTML data be built, by specifying the opening <TR> tag:

```
<xsl:for-each select="Employees/Employee_T">
    <TR>
```

Within the table row we want to specify two columns as indicated by the <TD> element. This HTML element specifies that a cell in the table be built. Within this cell we have specified the XSL <xsl:value-of> element to select the data in the First_Name_VC element of our XML data. The <xsl:value-of> element will place the data contained in the element that it selects in the table cell. Then we close the table cell using the closing tag of the <TD> element.

We end the row of data in our table by specifying the closing tag of the table row and the closing tag of the XSL <xsl:for-each> element, which defines the end of the code within the loop:

```
        <TD><xsl:value-of select="@First_Name_VC"/></TD>
        <TD><xsl:value-of select="@Last_Name_VC"/></TD>
    </TR>
</xsl:for-each>
```

Next, we end the table and the body of our HTML document and then the HTML document itself. We have done this by specifying the appropriate closing tags:

```
    </TABLE>
    </BODY>
    </HTML>
```

Finally, we end our XSL stylesheet by specifying the closing tags for the XSL </xsl:template> element and the </xsl:stylesheet> element. It should be noted that the <?xml> element is the only element that does not have a corresponding closing tag.

```
    </xsl:template>
</xsl:stylesheet>
```

Let's take a look at the URL that we entered to produce the results shown earlier. The first part of this URL should look familiar as it is the same data that we that we entered before, except that we have not included the Employee_ID column in the SELECT statement:

```
http://localhost/htData?SQL=SELECT+First_Name_VC,+Last_Name_VC+FROM+Employee_T+FOR
+XML+AUTO
```

The last part of this URL is new, as we have specified the XSL keyword and the XSL stylesheet that we created. We have also specified the ContentType keyword and specified that our results should be displayed as Text/HTML. The Root keyword is the same that we used in the last URL.

```
&XSL=Employee.xsl&ContentType=Text/HTML&Root=Employees
```

If you are curious, you can right-click in the browser window and choose View Source from the context menu to view the HTML that was generated by the XSL stylesheet.

Sorting Data Using XSL

The results that were displayed in the last example were not sorted. They were displayed in the same order as they were entered in the Employee_T table. We have a choice when sorting data; either use the ORDER BY clause in our SELECT statement, or use the order-by attribute of the <xsl:for-each> element.

Since we are already familiar with the ORDER BY clause in SQL Server let's examine the order-by attribute of the XSL <xsl:for-each> element. Using this attribute allows us to sort the XML data that has been returned by SQL Server in our XSL stylesheet.

The order-by attribute allows us to specify the sort criteria using one or more XSL patterns, in other words nodes in our XML data. An XSL pattern provides a mechanism to identify nodes in our XML document based on their type, name or values. The sort criterion is a string value enclosed by quotes and each XSL pattern to be sorted is separated by a semicolon. To indicate the direction of the sort, ascending or descending, you must include a plus sign (+) or a minus sign (–) respectively. Like most sorts that you have dealt with, ascending is the default and need not be specified if this is the sort order required.

Suppose we want to sort our data by ascending order of first names, and then by descending order of last names. We could specify the order-by attribute as shown in the code fragment below. The first names would be sorted first in ascending order and then, if there were two identical first names, the last names for the identical first name would be sorted in descending order:

```
<xsl:for-each select="Employees/Employee_T"
    order-by="+@First_Name_VC; -@Last_Name_VC">
```

It should be noted that the order-by attribute is set to become an obsolete standard, although it will still be supported. Future releases of XSL by the **W3C** (**World Wide Web Consortium**) will supply the <xsl:sort> element in its place. Until the next release of XSL we should continue to use the order-by attribute of the <xsl:for-each> element.

Using XSL Templates

We used a template in the last section, and we are going to look at templates in more detail here. XSL templates provide a convenient method that allows us to provide any special formatting of the data that is returned by an XML node. That is, we can select the data for a specific node and apply any special formatting or manipulation of the data before we display it.

We define templates in XSL using the `<xsl:template>` element. If you are going to use scripting functions in the template to manipulate the data you can specify the `language` attribute and the scripting language (`JScript` or `VBScript`). Using the `match` attribute we specify the node in the XML data to be matched. Let's look at the following example:

```
<xsl:template match="@Last_Name_VC">
   <TD><B><xsl:value-of/></B></TD>
</xsl:template>
```

In this example we have specified that the template should match the `Last_Name_VC` node in the XML data. When a match has been found and applied, the data in that node will be placed inside a table cell as specified by the `<TD>` HTML element and the XSL `<xsl:value-of/>` element. We have also specified that the data should be rendered in bold text as indicated by the `<B>` HTML element. The `<xsl:value-of/>` element inserts the value of the selected node as text.

Just because we have specified a template to format our data doesn't mean that the formatting will be applied to our document. In order to apply the formatting supplied by the template we must use the XSL `<xsl:apply-templates>` element. This element will apply the template that matches the node in the `select` attribute. The following example demonstrates this:

```
<xsl:apply-templates select="@Last_Name_VC"/>
```

What happens here is that we select the data in the `Last_Name_VC` node of our XML data and the `<xsl:apply-templates>` element will apply the template that we have defined for this node. The text that is produced by the template will be inserted at this point.

Assuming the `Last_Name_VC` node in our XML data contains a value of `Willis`, the template, when applied, would produce the following line of data:

```
<TD><B>Willis</B></TD>
```

Try It Out – XSL Sorting and Templates

Let's put all of this new knowledge to use in an XSL stylesheet that will sort our data and use templates to format it. We want to format the first name by changing the font color to navy, and we want to change the font for the last name to a bold font. We will sort the data in our XML document in ascending order by last name and then by first name.

1. The complete text for the XSL stylesheet is listed below. After you enter the text for this XSL stylesheet, using any text editor, save the file as `EmployeeMatch.xsl` in the `htData` directory:

```
<?xml version="1.0" encoding="UTF-8"?>
<xsl:stylesheet xmlns:xsl="http://www.w3.org/TR/WD-xsl">
   <xsl:template match="/">
      <HTML>
      <HEAD>
      <STYLE>
      TH
      {
         background-color: #CCCCCC;
      }
      </STYLE>
```

```
        </HEAD>
        <BODY>
        <TABLE Border="1">
           <TR>
              <TH ColSpan="2">Hardware Tracking Employees</TH>
           </TR>
           <TR>
              <TH>First Name</TH>
              <TH>Last Name</TH>
           </TR>
           <xsl:for-each select="Employees/Employee_T"
              order-by="@Last_Name_VC; @First_Name_VC">
              <TR>
                 <xsl:apply-templates select="@First_Name_VC"/>
                 <xsl:apply-templates select="@Last_Name_VC"/>
              </TR>
           </xsl:for-each>
        </TABLE>
        </BODY>
        </HTML>
   </xsl:template>

   <xsl:template match="@First_Name_VC">
      <TD><FONT Color="#000080"><xsl:value-of/></FONT></TD>
   </xsl:template>

   <xsl:template match="@Last_Name_VC">
      <TD><B><xsl:value-of/></B></TD>
   </xsl:template>
</xsl:stylesheet>
```

2. To test this XSL stylesheet enter the following URL in your browser. This is the same URL that you entered last time, except that we have specified the new XSL stylesheet:

```
http://localhost/htData?SQL=SELECT+First_Name_VC,+Last_Name_VC+FROM+Employee_T+FOR
+XML+AUTO&XSL=EmployeeMatch.xsl&ContentType=Text/HTML&Root=Employees
```

After executing the URL above you should see results similar to those shown below. The text in the First Name column is navy in color and the text in the Last Name column is bold. All data has been sorted by the last name first and then by first name:

How It Works – XSL Sorting and Templates

The first three lines of our XSL stylesheet are the standard lines of code defining this document as an XSL stylesheet.

Next, using the same code as we did in our last XSL stylesheet, we specify the HTML elements that define an HTML document. This includes the `<HEAD>` and `<STYLE>` elements:

```
<HTML>
<HEAD>
<STYLE>
TH
{
    background-color: #CCCCCC;
}
</STYLE>
</HEAD>
```

The body of our HTML document starts out the same; we define the same column headers as before:

```
<BODY>
<TABLE Border="1">
    <TR>
        <TH ColSpan="2">Hardware Tracking Employees</TH>
    </TR>
    <TR>
        <TH>First Name</TH>
        <TH>Last Name</TH>
    </TR>
```

We specify the same XSL `<xsl:for-each>` element as in the last example and have included one additional attribute, `order-by`. We are specifying that this element should iterate through the `Employees/Employee_T` nodes in our XML data and that it should also sort the data by the `Last_Name_VC` attribute first and then by the `First_Name_VC` attribute, which is different from the sort we performed earlier:

```
<xsl:for-each select="Employees/Employee_T"
    order-by="@Last_Name_VC; @First_Name_VC">
```

Now, when we build a row of data in our table we apply the `<xsl:apply-templates>` elements, defined via the matching XSL templates at the end of the stylesheet, to the data which is returned by the `<xsl:for-each>` element:

```
<TR>
    <xsl:apply-templates select="@First_Name_VC"/>
    <xsl:apply-templates select="@Last_Name_VC"/>
</TR>
```

We end our loop by specifying the closing tag `</xsl:for-each>`. We end the table in our HTML code and the HTML code itself by specifying the appropriate HTML closing tags. The last thing we do is close the template that applies to the root node of our XML data:

```
            </xsl:for-each>
        </TABLE>
        </BODY>
        </HTML>
    </xsl:template>
```

Using the XSL `<xsl:template>` element we define a template to format the data contained in the `First_Name_VC` element of our XML data. The `match` attribute specifies the element to be matched in the XML data.

This template will build the HTML to display a cell in our table as specified by the HTML `<TD>` element. We change the color of the text that will be displayed by specifying the HTML `<FONT>` element. The `Color` attribute listed here is using the RGB value of `#000080`, which represents the color navy. Then we specify the XSL `<xsl:value-of/>` element to insert the value of the selected node as text. Lastly, we specify the appropriate closing HTML tags and close this template element:

```
    <xsl:template match="@First_Name_VC">
        <TD><FONT Color="#000080"><xsl:value-of/></FONT></TD>
    </xsl:template>
```

The template that formats the data from the `Last_Name_VC` elements of our XML data uses the HTML `<B>` element to render the text in a bold font:

```
    <xsl:template match="@Last_Name_VC">
        <TD><B><xsl:value-of/></B></TD>
    </xsl:template>
```

We then end our XSL stylesheet by specifying the `</xsl:stylesheet>` closing tag.

Try It Out – Hardware XSL Stylesheet

Now that we have worked with some employee data from the `Employee_T` table and created a couple of XSL stylesheets for employee data, let's recap and practice these skills again. In this exercise we want to create a simple XSL stylesheet for hardware data that will simply display all manufacturers and models listed in the `Hardware_T` table.

1. The code for the XSL stylesheet is listed below. Once you have entered the code save it in the `htData` directory as `Hardware.xsl`.

```
<?xml version="1.0" encoding="UTF-8"?>
<xsl:stylesheet xmlns:xsl="http://www.w3.org/TR/WD-xsl">
    <xsl:template match = "/">
        <HTML>
        <HEAD>
        <STYLE>
        TH
        {
            background-color: #CCCCCC;
        }
        </STYLE>
        </HEAD>
```

```
        <BODY>
        <TABLE border="1">
          <TR>
            <TH ColSpan="2">Hardware</TH>
          </TR>
          <TR>
            <TH>Manufacturer</TH>
            <TH>Model</TH>
          </TR>
          <xsl:for-each select="Hardware/Hardware_T">
            <TR>
              <TD><xsl:value-of
                    select="@Manufacturer_VC"/></TD>
              <TD><xsl:value-of select="@Model_VC"/></TD>
            </TR>
          </xsl:for-each>
        </TABLE>
        </BODY>
        </HTML>
    </xsl:template>
</xsl:stylesheet>
```

2. To test this XSL stylesheet you need to enter the following URL in your browser. Notice that our SELECT statement in the URL specifies the Manufacturer_VC and Model_VC columns from the Hardware_T table. We have also specified the Hardware.xsl stylesheet and a root element of Hardware:

```
http://localhost/htData?SQL=SELECT+Manufacturer_VC,+Model_VC+FROM+Hardware_T+FOR+X
ML+AUTO&XSL=Hardware.xsl&ContentType=Text/HTML&Root=Hardware
```

The results of your execution should look similar to this:

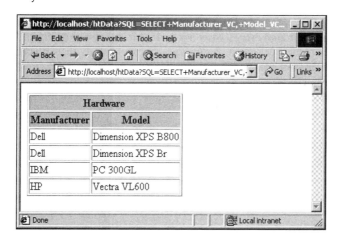

How It Works – Hardware XSL Stylesheet

This XSL stylesheet looks very similar to the Employee.xsl stylesheet that you created. In fact, it works in the same fashion, but it uses XML data from the Hardware_T table.

The first three lines of our stylesheet are the standard lines of code that define this as an XSL stylesheet.

Next, we start defining the HTML elements that define our HTML document. Notice that we are using the same style for our column headers:

```
<HTML>
<HEAD>
<STYLE>
TH
{
    background-color: #CCCCCC;
}
</STYLE>
</HEAD>
```

We start the body of our HTML document by specifying the HTML <BODY> tag. Then we start the table definition and define the column headers in the table:

```
<BODY>
<TABLE border="1">
    <TR>
        <TH ColSpan="2">Hardware</TH>
    </TR>
    <TR>
        <TH>Manufacturer</TH>
        <TH>Model</TH>
    </TR>
```

Using the XSL <xsl:for-each> element we iterate through all of the XML data in the Hardware_T elements under the root element of Hardware.

For each row of data in our table we use the <xsl:value-of> element to select the Manufacturer_VC and Model_VC attributes from our XML data. We display these values in our table cells.

We end our loop using the closing tag for the <xsl:for-each> element:

```
<xsl:for-each select="Hardware/Hardware_T">
    <TR>
        <TD><xsl:value-of
                select="@Manufacturer_VC"/></TD>
        <TD><xsl:value-of select="@Model_VC"/></TD>
    </TR>
</xsl:for-each>
```

We then close our table and end the HTML document. Next we end the template and stylesheet by specifying the appropriate XSL elements:

```
        </TABLE>
        </BODY>
        </HTML>
    </xsl:template>
</xsl:stylesheet>
```

583

Calling Stored Procedures in URLs

The SELECT statements that we have entered so far in the URL of our browser have been relatively short. But you should be able to see how they could quickly become cumbersome as we start to enter more complex queries and use joins. Also, we really don't want to have a user learn the SQL language just to display some data in a browser. This is where stored procedures can be very useful.

Using a stored procedure we can use the same SELECT statements that we entered into the URL of the browser and reduce the length of the URL that needs to be entered. We can then just execute the stored procedure in the URL instead of having to specify the entire SELECT statement.

As we have discovered in past chapters, using a stored procedure is more efficient because it is optimized in SQL Server and is compiled and cached on its first execution. This, and the fact that we can easily write more complex queries in a stored procedure, makes using them ideal.

When we execute a stored procedure in the URL we need to specify the EXECUTE keyword and the stored procedure name, just as we would in the Query Analyzer. An example of this is shown:

```
http://localhost/htData?SQL=EXECUTE+up_select_xml_hardware&XSL=Hardware.xsl&Conten
tType=Text/HTML&Root=Hardware
```

The only difference between this URL and the last is that this URL executes a stored procedure instead of the SELECT statement. All other keywords such as SQL, XSL, ContentType, and Root must still be specified.

Try It Out – Hardware Select Stored Procedure

Let's put this knowledge to use by creating a stored procedure to select the hardware data that is required by our Hardware.xsl template.

1. The stored procedure that we want to create is listed below. Enter the code for this stored procedure in the Query Analyzer and execute it:

```
CREATE PROCEDURE up_select_xml_hardware AS

SELECT Manufacturer_VC, Model_VC
    FROM Hardware_T
    FOR XML AUTO

GO

GRANT EXECUTE ON up_select_xml_hardware TO [Hardware Users]
```

2. To test this stored procedure enter the following URL in your browser:

```
http://localhost/htData?SQL=EXECUTE+up_select_xml_hardware&XSL=Hardware.xsl&Conten
tType=Text/HTML&Root=Hardware
```

The results of executing this stored procedure should be the same as you saw in the last exercise. The only difference here is that we have just executed a stored procedure in the URL instead of a SELECT statement.

How It Works – Hardware Select Stored Procedure

This stored procedure looks just about like every other SELECT stored procedure that we have created. We start the stored procedure by specifying the CREATE PROCEDURE statement followed by the stored procedure name and the AS keyword.

Then we specify the SELECT statement, which selects two columns from the Hardware_T table. We have also included the FOR XML clause so the results of the stored procedure will be returned as XML data to the browser:

```
SELECT Manufacturer_VC, Model_VC
    FROM Hardware_T
    FOR XML AUTO
```

We specify the GO command to have the Query Analyzer create this stored procedure before we grant permissions on it to the hardware users role:

```
GO

GRANT EXECUTE ON up_select_xml_hardware TO [Hardware Users]
```

> It is important to note that you cannot execute just any stored procedure in a URL. It must be a **SELECT** stored procedure, and it must return XML data. The **SELECT** statement must, therefore, contain the **FOR XML** clause.

Stored Procedure Parameters

Now that we know we can execute a stored procedure in the URL, it stands to reason that we could also execute a stored procedure that accepts parameters. This is true, and not as difficult as it may seem. This section will walk through a couple of examples that illustrate executing stored procedures that accept parameters, and point out what is needed to pass parameters to a stored procedure.

When we execute a parameterized stored procedure in the Query Analyzer, we simply specify the EXECUTE statement followed by the stored procedure name and any parameters that it might expect. Looking at the following example, the up_parmsel_assigned_system stored procedure accepts one parameter, the Employee_ID. Execution of this code produces the desired results:

```
EXECUTE up_parmsel_assigned_system 1
```

Assuming this stored procedure returned the results as XML data we would execute this same stored procedure in a browser using the following code fragments in place of the SQL statements.

The first code fragment demonstrates executing this stored procedure by only passing the parameter as we do in the Query Analyzer:

```
EXECUTE+up_parmsel_assigned_system+1
```

The second code fragment demonstrates specifying the parameter name and its value. When using this method the parameter name specified must exactly match the parameter name in the stored procedure:

```
EXECUTE+up_parmsel_assigned_system+@Employee_ID=1
```

Let's assume for a moment that we have a stored procedure named up_parmsel_employee. This stored procedure expects the employee's last name as the first input parameter and the employee's location ID as the second input parameter. To execute this stored procedure in a URL we would specify the code as shown in the following code fragments in place of the usual SQL statements.

The first example simply specifies the parameter values. Notice that we have included a comma between the two input parameters and, since the first parameter is a string value, it has been enclosed in single quotes:

```
EXECUTE+up_parmsel_employee+'Willis'+,+1
```

The second example specifies the parameter names and parameter values. Again we have enclosed the first parameter in single quotes and used a comma to separate the parameters:

```
EXECUTE+up_parmsel_employee+@Last_Name_VC='Willis'+,+@Location_ID=1
```

Try It Out – Parameterized Stored Procedure

Now that we know that we can execute a parameterized stored procedure in a URL we want to create a stored procedure that accepts parameters so we can experience this first hand. The stored procedure that we want to create should select most of the columns in the Hardware_T table. The input parameter to this stored procedure will be the Hardware_ID, which will point to the row of data that we want to select.

1. The code for this stored procedure is listed below. Enter this code in the Query Analyzer and execute it:

```
CREATE PROCEDURE up_parmsel_xml_hardware
    @Hardware_ID INT AS

SELECT Manufacturer_VC, Model_VC, Processor_Speed_VC,
    Memory_VC, HardDrive_VC, Sound_Card_VC,
    Speakers_VC, Video_Card_VC, Monitor_VC,
    Serial_Number_VC, Lease_Expiration_DT,
    CD_Type_CH

    FROM Hardware_T
    JOIN CD_T ON Hardware_T.CD_ID = CD_T.CD_ID

    WHERE Hardware_ID = @Hardware_ID

    FOR XML AUTO

GO

GRANT EXECUTE ON up_parmsel_xml_hardware TO [Hardware Users]
```

2. Before you execute this stored procedure in a browser, you will need to obtain a valid number for the hardware ID. You can do this by right-clicking on the Hardware_T table in the Object Browser of the Query Analyzer and choosing Open from the context menu.

3. Once you have a valid hardware ID enter the following URL in your browser, replacing the hardware ID specified with one that is valid in your `Hardware_T` table:

```
http://localhost/htData?SQL=EXECUTE+up_parmsel_xml_hardware+1+&Root=Hardware
```

You should see results similar to those shown in the next figure. Notice that we have not used an XSL stylesheet to format the data in this example, so it is just returned as XML data:

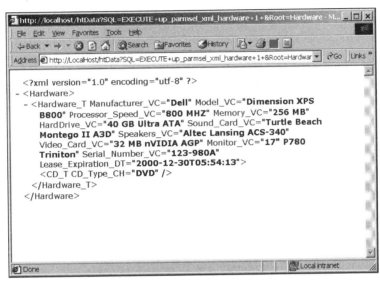

4. You can further test this stored procedure and see the different results by substituting the `@Hardware_ID` parameter with different values. If you use a value that does not exist, you will not receive an error message but just an empty XML document, as shown in the next figure:

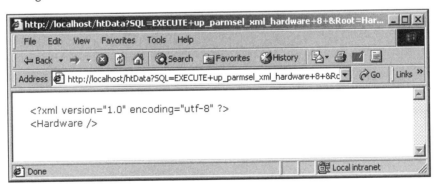

How It Works – Parameterized Stored Procedure

This stored procedure accepts one input parameter, the hardware ID of the row of data to be selected. The `SELECT` statement selects the various columns from the `Hardware_T` table and the `CD_T` table. The results are returned as XML, as indicated by the `FOR XML` clause. We specify the `GO` command to have the stored procedure created before permissions are granted on it.

Try It Out – XSL Stylesheet for Stored Procedures

We now have a couple of stored procedures that we can execute in the URL of the browser. The first stored procedure, `up_select_xml_hardware`, already has an XSL stylesheet that we can use to display the data. The second stored procedure, `up_parmsel_xml_hardware`, does not have an XSL stylesheet so let's create one for it.

The previous XSL stylesheets that we created have displayed the XML data in a table using columns and rows. While this is fairly standard practice, this is not required as part of creating an XSL stylesheet. We can use whatever HTML formatting we need to get the desired results. An XSL stylesheet merely provides a means to build an HTML document and to select and format the XML data. The XSL stylesheet that we will build here will not use tables. Instead we will use a variety of HTML elements to format the data for display.

1. Here is the stylesheet, which you should save in the `htData` directory as `SystemSpecs.xsl`:

```xml
<?xml version="1.0" encoding="UTF-8"?>
<xsl:stylesheet xmlns:xsl="http://www.w3.org/TR/WD-xsl">
    <xsl:template match = "/">
        <HTML>
        <HEAD>
        <STYLE>
        .Title
        {
            background-color: #CCCCCC;
        }
        .NormalText
        {
            font-family: Arial;
            font-size: 10pt;
        }
        </STYLE>
        </HEAD>
        <BODY>
            <P Width="100%">
                <CENTER Class="Title">Hardware Specifications</CENTER>
            </P>
            <xsl:for-each select="Hardware/Hardware_T">
            <P Class="NormalText">
                <B Style="color: #000080;">
                    <xsl:value-of select="@Manufacturer_VC"/>
                    <xsl:value-of select="@Model_VC"/> with
                    <xsl:value-of select="@Memory_VC"/> of memory.
                </B>
            </P>
            <P Class="NormalText">
                Comes with a
                <xsl:value-of select="@HardDrive_VC"/>
                hardrive and
                <xsl:for-each select="CD_T">
                    <xsl:value-of select="@CD_Type_CH"/>.
                </xsl:for-each>
```

```
      </P>
      <P Class="NormalText">
              <xsl:value-of select = "@Video_Card_VC"/>
              video card and a <xsl:value-of select="@Monitor_VC"/>
              monitor comes as standard equipment.
      </P>
      <P Class="NormalText">
              <xsl:value-of select="@Sound_Card_VC"/>
              sound card and <xsl:value-of select="@Speakers_VC"/>
              speakers for true stereo sound.
      </P>
      <P Class="NormalText">
              Serial number for this model is
              <xsl:value-of select="@Serial_Number_VC"/>
              and the lease expires on
              <xsl:value-of select="@Lease_Expiration_DT"/>.
      </P>
      </xsl:for-each>
    </BODY>
    </HTML>
  </xsl:template>
</xsl:stylesheet>
```

2. To test this XSL stylesheet enter the following URL in your browser:

```
http://localhost/htData?SQL=EXECUTE+up_parmsel_xml_hardware+@Hardware_ID=1+&XSL=Sy
stemSpecs.xsl&ContentType=Text/HTML&Root=Hardware
```

This URL specifies that we want to execute the `up_parmsel_xml_hardware` stored procedure and we have specified the `@Hardware_ID` input parameter and its value. We have also specified the `XSL`, `ContentType`, and `Root` keywords in the URL.

The results that you see should look similar to those shown in the following figure. Notice that our data is displayed in complete paragraphs and the text is formatted using the styles defined in the in-line stylesheet:

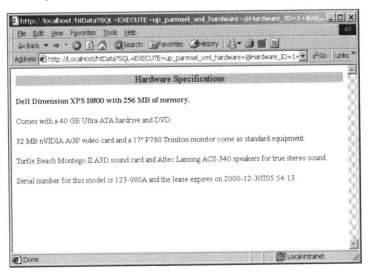

589

How It Works – XSL Stylesheet for Stored Procedures

We start this stylesheet as we have the others by including the standard lines of code that start every XSL stylesheet. This lets the browser know that this is an XSL stylesheet and it should parse the data as XML. We start the HTML portion of this XSL stylesheet by specifying the <HTML> and <HEAD> tags.

Then we define an in-line stylesheet for our HTML document. These styles will be used in our HTML to format the text. The first style that we want to define is a style for the title text that will be displayed in our HTML document. Notice that we must begin user-defined styles with a period, and we have done so here followed by the style name:

```
<STYLE>
.Title
{
    background-color: #CCCCCC;
}
```

The second style that we have defined will be used for most of the other text in our HTML document. This style specifies the font name to be used, as indicated by the font-family property. We have also specified that the text is to be displayed using a 10 point font, as indicated by the font-size property.

We then end our in-line stylesheet for our HTML document and end the <HEAD> element:

```
.NormalText
{
    font-family: Arial;
    font-size: 10pt;
}
</STYLE>
</HEAD>
```

We start the body of our HTML document by specifying the <BODY> tag. Then we start a paragraph in our HTML document by specifying the <P> tag. We set the Width attribute of the paragraph so that it will span across the entire HTML document.

Within the paragraph we specify the text that should be displayed. However, since we want this text displayed in the center of the document we have enclosed the <CENTER> element, which will cause the text to be centered. Notice that we have also specified the Class attribute of the <CENTER> element. This attribute specifies the style that should be used to format the text within the beginning and ending tags of the <CENTER> element. This is the style that we have defined in our in-line stylesheet for our HTML document.

We end the paragraph by specifying the </P> tag. It should be noted here that a closing tag is not required in HTML for a paragraph element. However, to conform to XML standards and to ensure that our XSL stylesheet is well-formed, all elements must include a closing tag. If you do not specify a closing tag, you will receive an error message and the data will not be displayed.

```
<BODY>
    <P Width="100%">
        <CENTER Class="Title">Hardware Specifications</CENTER>
    </P>
```

We want to start retrieving some XML data next so we have specified the XSL `<xsl:for-each>` element. We are specifying that we want to select data from the `Hardware/Hardware_T` elements in our XML data, as given in the `select` attribute:

```
<xsl:for-each select="Hardware/Hardware_T">
```

Next, we start another paragraph in our HTML document and specify the `Class` attribute of the `<P>` element. Here we indicate that the class to be used from our in-line stylesheet is the `NormalText` class. The next line specifies that we want the text to be rendered in bold as we have specified the `<B>` element. We have also coded the `Style` attribute and have set the color of the text to the RGB value of `#000080`, which is navy.

Using the XSL `<xsl:value-of>` element we select the appropriate elements from our XML data. Notice that after the second and third `<xsl:value-of>` elements we have included some static text. This will cause the data from the `<xsl:value-of>` elements to be displayed in between our static text to form a complete sentence.

We then end the bold text and the paragraph by specifying the appropriate closing tags:

```
<P Class="NormalText">
   <B Style="color: #000080;">
   <xsl:value-of select="@Manufacturer_VC"/>
   <xsl:value-of select="@Model_VC"/> with
   <xsl:value-of select="@Memory_VC"/> of memory.
      </B>
    </P>
```

The next paragraph that we define also uses the `NormalText` style which has been specified in the `Class` attribute of the `<P>` element. We specify some static text and then specify the XSL `<xsl:value-of>` element to select the `HardDrive_VC` element from our XML data.

The `CD_Type_CH` element is a child of the `CD_T` element and not the `Hardware_T` element. Therefore we need to specify a nested `<xsl:for-each>` element and specify that it should select elements from the `CD_T` parent element. Then we specify the `<xsl:value-of>` element to select the `CD_Type_CH` element, and the closing `</xsl:for-each>` tag for the `CD_T` element:

```
<P Class="NormalText">
   Comes with a
   <xsl:value-of select="@HardDrive_VC"/>
   hardrive and
   <xsl:for-each select="CD_T">
      <xsl:value-of select="@CD_Type_CH"/>.
   </xsl:for-each>
</P>
```

The next paragraph uses the `<xsl:value-of>` element to select the elements that we need to build this paragraph. Again we have specified static text and the `<xsl:value-of>` elements to build a complete sentence:

```
<P Class="NormalText">
    <xsl:value-of select = "@Video_Card_VC"/>
    video card and a <xsl:value-of select="@Monitor_VC"/>
    monitor come as standard equipment.
    </P>
```

The next two paragraphs perform the same function as the last by using the `<xsl:value-of>` element and static text to build complete sentences:

```
<P Class="NormalText">
    <xsl:value-of select="@Sound_Card_VC"/>
    sound card and <xsl:value-of select="@Speakers_VC"/>
    speakers for true stereo sound.
    </P>

<P Class="NormalText">
    Serial number for this model is
    <xsl:value-of select="@Serial_Number_VC"/>
    and the lease expires on
    <xsl:value-of select="@Lease_Expiration_DT"/>.
    </P>
```

After all of the paragraphs have been built we specify the closing tag for the XSL `<xsl:for-each>` element and the closing tags for the HTML `<BODY>` and `<HTML>` elements. Then we end the XSL stylesheet by specifying the closing tags for the `<xsl:template>` and `<xsl:stylesheet>` elements:

```
            </xsl:for-each>
        </BODY>
        </HTML>
    </xsl:template>
</xsl:stylesheet>
```

XML Templates

In previous chapters we saw that our SELECT statements have the potential to become very large, so we can also see the potential for our stored procedure statements to become large. This increases as we add more and more parameters, especially if we use string parameters such as an employee name. All of this leads to more data that needs to be entered into the URL of the browser.

To help reduce the amount of data that needs to be entered into the URL we can use **XML templates**. XML templates are simply XML files that contain the query string or stored procedure to be executed. We can also specify the root element for our XML data, thus eliminating the need to specify the Root keyword in the URL.

Templates also provide security. When we use templates the query string, or stored procedure name, is stored in the template and not exposed in the URL of the browser. This hides the details of our columns and tables that were exposed when we included a SELECT statement in the URL.

As we mentioned above, templates are XML documents, thus they must conform to the XML standards and be well-formed. Also all elements must conform to the XML standards set out by the W3C.

Let's take a look at a simple template. This template starts with the `<?XML?>` element, identifying it as an XML document. This ensures that the browser parses the document correctly:

```
<?xml version="1.0" encoding="UTF-8"?>
    <Employees xmlns:sql="urn:schemas-microsoft-com:xml-sql"
        sql:xsl="../Employee.xsl">
        <sql:query>
            SELECT First_Name_VC, Last_Name_VC FROM Employee_T
                FOR XML AUTO
        </sql:query>
    </Employees>
```

The second line of code in this template specifies the `Root` element and we have named it `Employees`. The namespace, which is required, is `xmlns:sql="urn:schemas-microsoft-com:xml-sql"`. A namespace specifies a collection of names that can be used as element or attribute names in your XML document. This namespace describes the data in this XML document as SQL Server XML data.

The `sql:xsl` attribute specifies the XSL stylesheet that should be used. Our template resides in the `Template` directory, which is a sub-directory of the `htData` directory. Our XSL stylesheet resides in the root of the `htData` directory. Given this, we specify two consecutive periods and then a forward slash before the XSL stylesheet name. This ensures that IIS goes up one directory to look for the `Employee.xsl` stylesheet.

The third element defined in the template, `<sql:query>`, specifies the query string to be executed. The query string can consist of SQL statements or a stored procedure name. We then have the closing tags for the `<sql:query>` element and the root element of `<Employees>`. If you were to save this template as `Employee.xml` in the `Template` directory of the `htData` directory you could execute this template using the following URL:

```
http://localhost/htData/Template/Employee.xml?ContentType=Text/HTML
```

Notice that the amount of data that needs to be entered into the URL has been reduced by the use of the template. Here we have specified the machine name that IIS is running on, followed by our virtual directory name and the directory that contains our template, before finally identifying our template name.

To have the results displayed as *formatted* XML, we have specified the `ContentType` keyword. (If this keyword is not specified, the resulting XML will be returned as *raw* XML.)

The results that would be displayed are shown below:

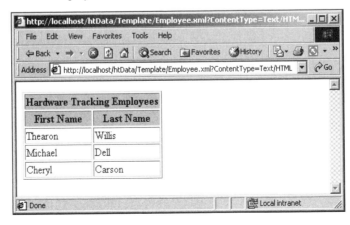

Try It Out – Hardware XML Template

Let's create a template to execute our up_select_xml_hardware stored procedure and use the
Hardware.xsl stylesheet to format the results.

1. The code below shows the Hardware.xml template. Enter this code using your favorite text
editor and save the file in the Template directory as Hardware.xml. (The Template
directory is a sub-directory of the htData directory.)

```xml
<?xml version="1.0" encoding="UTF-8"?>
    <Hardware xmlns:sql="urn:schemas-microsoft-com:xml-sql"
        sql:xsl="../Hardware.xsl">
        <sql:query>
            EXECUTE up_select_xml_hardware
        </sql:query>
    </Hardware>
```

2. To execute this XML template, enter the following URL in your browser. This URL specifies
that the Hardware.xml template should be executed and that this template resides in the
Template directory in the htData virtual directory. We have specified the ContentType
keyword to have the results formatted as HTML.

```
http://localhost/htData/Template/Hardware.xml?ContentType=Text/HTML
```

The results of the execution of this template are shown in the following figure. Notice that the
results of the execution are formatted using the Hardware.xsl stylesheet that we specified in
our template:

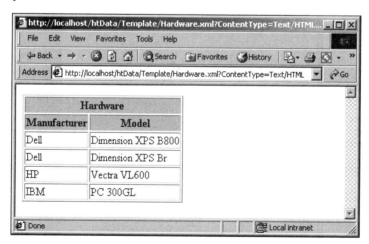

How It Works – Hardware XML Template

We start this template off with the standard XML declaration. Then we specify the root element and
give it a name of Hardware. We specify the standard SQL namespace of
xmlns:sql="urn:schemas-microsoft-com:xml-sql" and then include the sql:xsl attribute
to point to the Hardware XSL stylesheet. Notice that since this stylesheet resides in the root of the
htData directory we have specified two periods followed by a forward slash to indicate that IIS should
go up one directory level from where the template resides to find the stylesheet.

```
<?xml version="1.0" encoding="UTF-8"?>
    <Hardware xmlns:sql="urn:schemas-microsoft-com:xml-sql"
        sql:xsl="../Hardware.xsl">
```

We then specify the `<sql:query>` element, the `EXECUTE` statement, and then the stored procedure name to be executed.

We then terminate the `<sql:query>` element and the root element.

```
<sql:query>
    EXECUTE up_select_xml_hardware
</sql:query>
</Hardware>
```

XML Templates that Accept Parameters

We know that we can create a template that executes a SQL string and we can also create a template that executes a stored procedure. We have seen how using templates cuts down on the amount of text that needs to be included in a URL to get the XML data that we want.

Now let's examine how to create a template that executes a stored procedure that accepts parameters. When we create a template that executes these stored procedures, we must define those parameters in the template also. This is because we will pass the parameters to the template when we execute it. The XML inside the template will in turn pass these parameters to the stored procedure being executed.

In order to define parameters in a template we must include the `<sql:header>` element. Within this element we define one `<sql:param>` element for each parameter that our stored procedure expects. The `<sql:param>` element has a `name` attribute that we use to assign the name of the parameter. If we want, we can even specify a default value for the parameter.

The following code fragment shows the parameters for the `up_parmsel_employee` stored procedure. This stored procedure does not actually exist and is used for illustration purposes only. Notice that we have specified a default value for each parameter between the beginning `<sql:param>` tag and the closing tag for this element:

```
<sql:header>
    <sql:param name="Last_Name_VC">Willis</sql:param>
    <sql:param name="Location_ID">1</sql:param>
</sql:header>
```

Let's assume the completed template has been saved with a name of `EmployeeLocation.xml`. We would then be able to execute this template without any parameters by specifying the following URL. This URL would cause the default values defined in our template to be passed to the stored procedure.

```
http://localhost/htData/Template/EmployeeLocation.xml?ContentType=Text/HTML
```

Assuming we now wanted to execute this same template and pass it some parameters that were in turn to be passed to the stored procedure, we would then specify a URL such as the one shown below. Here we have listed the parameter names and values:

```
http://localhost/htData/Template/EmployeeLocation.xml?Last_Name_VC='Carson'+,+Loca
tion_ID=1&ContentType=Text/HTML
```

Try It Out – XML Template with Parameters

Since we now know how to create parameters within a template, let's put this knowledge to use. The template that we want to create now will execute the `up_parmsel_xml_hardware` stored procedure. Since this stored procedure accepts one input parameter we will define one parameter in our template.

1. The code for the `SystemSpecs.xml` template is listed below. Create this template and save it in the `Template` directory of the `htData` virtual directory:

```xml
<?xml version="1.0" encoding="UTF-8"?>
    <Hardware xmlns:sql="urn:schemas-microsoft-com:xml-sql"
        sql:xsl="../SystemSpecs.xsl">
        <sql:header>
            <sql:param name="Hardware_ID"></sql:param>
        </sql:header>
        <sql:query>
            EXECUTE up_parmsel_xml_hardware @Hardware_ID
        </sql:query>
    </Hardware>
```

2. To execute this template enter the following URL in your browser. You will need to substitute the value for the `Hardware_ID` parameter with a valid hardware ID from your `Hardware_T` table.

```
http://localhost/htData/Template/SystemSpecs.xml?Hardware_ID=1&ContentType=Text/HT
ML
```

The results you see should resemble the results shown in the next figure. This template uses the `SystemSpecs.xsl` stylesheet to format the results:

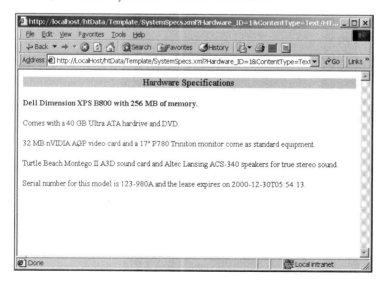

How It Works – XML Template with Parameters

We start this template with the standard XML declaration. Then we include the `Hardware` root element, which contains the SQL namespace and the XSL stylesheet to be used to format the XML data:

```
<?xml version="1.0" encoding="UTF-8"?>
    <Hardware xmlns:sql="urn:schemas-microsoft-com:xml-sql"
        sql:xsl="../SystemSpecs.xsl">
```

Next, we include the `<sql:header>` element. Within this element we define the `<sql:param>` element and set its `name` attribute to the parameter name in our stored procedure. We have not specified a default value here but if you wanted to, you could assign a default value between the beginning `<sql:param>` element and the closing tag for this element.

```
<sql:header>
    <sql:param name="Hardware_ID"></sql:param>
</sql:header>
```

We include the `<sql:query>` element next which contains the stored procedure to be executed followed by the input parameters for this stored procedure. Then we have the closing tag for the root element:

```
<sql:query>
    EXECUTE up_parmsel_xml_hardware @Hardware_ID
</sql:query>
</Hardware>
```

XML Template Summary

This section has taken a look at XML templates. We have seen how we can code and execute SQL statements and stored procedures in templates. This helps to provide better security, as the code that retrieves the data is hidden from the end user.

We have also seen how using templates reduces the amount of data that needs to be entered in the URL of the browser.

There is an added benefit that has not yet been discussed. Like stored procedures, templates reside in one central place; this allows us to enhance the templates and have them immediately available to everyone who executes them. This helps to reduce our maintenance costs and the time spent updating our code, because we need only make the change in one place.

Annotated XDR Schemas

XDR is an acronym for **XML-Data Reduced** and is a language used to create schemas. Normally a Data Type Definition (DTD) is used to describe the structure of the data in an XML document. This is generally fine, except that in the DTD and XML document all data is character data. **XDR schemas** provide you with a way to map the elements to their respective fields in a SQL Server table.

Annotations to the XDR schema allow you to map different elements to the fields in the database and assign your own element name attributes. Using annotations to the XDR schema is an alternative to using the XML FOR EXPLICIT mode, which is quite complex.

A schema file is built to perform the mapping of columns in your database table to the elements in an XML document. This file has a .xml extension and is in fact an XML document itself. The browser will parse a schema file as an XML document and execute any queries contained in your document.

Let's take a look at the basics for an XML schema file. As with all XML and XSL documents the first line in a schema file is the XML declaration:

```
<?xml version="1.0" encoding="UTF-8"?>
```

Annotations for an XDR schema are specified in the namespace. There are actually three different namespaces that we need to include in a schema document and these namespaces are defined in the <Schema> element of the schema document.

The first of these namespaces is the Microsoft schema namespace. This defines this document as a Microsoft XDR schema document:

```
xmlns="urn:schemas-microsoft-com:xml-data"
```

The next line of code defines the namespace for data types. Using this namespace allows us to specify the data type of an element or attribute:

```
xmlns:dt="urn:schemas-microsoft-com:datatypes"
```

The final namespace allows us to map SQL fields to attribute types in our schema document. This namespace is defined as shown in the code below:

```
xmlns:sql="urn:schemas-microsoft-com:xml-sql"
```

After all of the namespaces have been specified we define the <ElementType> element. This element provides the mapping to a table in your database. An example of this mapping is shown in the next code fragment. We specify the name attribute for this element and specify the table that this element is mapped to using the sql:relation annotation:

```
<ElementType name="Employee_T" sql:relation="Employee_T">
```

Within the <ElementType> element we specify the <AttributeType> element. This element defines an attribute type for use within the schema. We can optionally specify the data type and a default value for this attribute. In the example below the <AttributeType> element has been assigned a name of FirstName and an XML data type of bin.base64, which maps to a VarChar data type in SQL Server. The *Data Type Coercions* topic in the SQL Books Online provides a complete cross-reference between SQL Server data types and XML data types.

```
<AttributeType name="FirstName" dt:type="bin.base64" />
```

We use the `<attribute>` element to define the actual attribute and specify how it should be mapped to the database. Using the `sql:field` annotation, we specify the physical mapping between this element and a column in the table specified in the `<ElementType>` element above. The code below demonstrates how this is done:

```
<attribute type="FirstName" sql:field="First_Name_VC"/>
```

These are the basic elements required to create an annotated XDR schema. Let's move on and see how this actually works.

Try It Out – Create an Annotated XDR Schema

The schema that we want to create here will display the `Software_ID` and `Software_Name_VC` columns from the `Software_T` table. We will be using the `sql:field` annotation to map the `Software_ID` and `Software_Name_VC` columns to attributes that we define.

1. The code for the schema is listed below. Using your favorite text editor, enter the following code and save it as `SoftwareSchema.xml`. This XML document should be saved in the `htData\Schema` directory.

```
<?xml version="1.0" encoding="UTF-8"?>
<Schema xmlns="urn:schemas-microsoft-com:xml-data"
    xmlns:dt="urn:schemas-microsoft-com:datatypes"
    xmlns:sql="urn:schemas-microsoft-com:xml-sql">

    <ElementType name="Software_T" sql:relation="Software_T">
        <AttributeType name="ID"/>
        <AttributeType name="Software"/>

        <attribute type="ID" sql:field="Software_ID"/>
        <attribute type="Software" sql:field="Software_Name_VC"/>
    </ElementType>
</Schema>
```

2. To test this schema, enter the following URL in the browser. After the schema name we specify the table name that will supply the data to this schema. Since we have not defined a root element in the schema we must specify the root element here; in this case we have chosen a root element name of `Software`:

```
http://localhost/htData/Schema/SoftwareSchema.xml/Software
_T?Root=Software
```

Note the forward slash after the schema name – the syntax for calling a schema is slightly different from that for calling a template. When we execute a schema template we must specify the schema directory instead of a template directory, followed by a forward slash and then the schema name, which is just another XML document. We follow this with another forward slash followed by the table name that the schema is applied to. Finally, a question mark is inserted, followed by the parameter name `Root`, then an equals sign, then the name of the root element that we want to use.

599

The results that are displayed should be similar to those shown in the following figure. Notice that the Software_T element contains the ID attribute instead of Software_ID and the Software attribute is specified instead of Software_Name_VC:

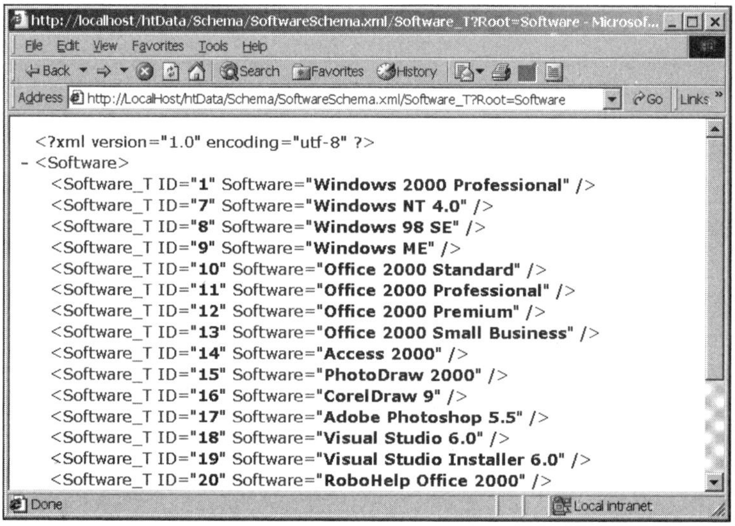

How It Works – Create an Annotated XDR Schema

The first line of code in this schema is the XML declaration and is standard in all XML and XSL documents that we create.

The <Schema> element defines the namespaces for this schema and includes the three namespaces that we have just discussed.

```
<Schema xmlns="urn:schemas-microsoft-com:xml-data"
    xmlns:dt="urn:schemas-microsoft-com:datatypes"
    xmlns:sql="urn:schemas-microsoft-com:xml-sql">
```

We have defined the <ElementType> element next and it provides a mapping between this element and a table in the database. Here we have specified that the <attributes> defined for this element will be mapped to the Software_T table:

```
<ElementType name="Software_T" sql:relation="Software_T">
```

Next, we specify the <AttributeType> element. We have no special data types that we want these fields to represent so we take the default XML data type of bin.base64:

```
<AttributeType name="ID"/>
<AttributeType name="Software"/>
```

We specify the <attribute> elements next and use the sql:field annotation to map these attributes. Notice that the first attribute is the ID attribute and this has been mapped to the Software_ID column in the Software_T table. The second attribute has been mapped to the Software_Name_VC column:

```
<attribute type="ID" sql:field="Software_ID"/>
<attribute type="Software" sql:field="Software_Name_VC"/>
```

We specify the closing tags for the `<ElementType>` and `<Schema>` elements:

```
    </ElementType>
</Schema>
```

Try It Out – Create a Schema Template

Having coded and executed our XDR schema we see that we are getting back to entering a lot of data in the URL. However, we can eliminate this by creating a template to execute the schema for us. This will reduce the amount of text that must be entered into the URL of the browser.

1. The template that we must code is very similar to our previous templates. The complete code for this template is listed below. Enter this code and save it as `Software.xml` in the `Template` directory:

```
<?xml version="1.0" encoding="UTF-8"?>
  <Software xmlns:sql="urn:schemas-microsoft-com:xml-sql">
     <sql:xpath-query mapping-schema="../Schema/SoftwareSchema.xml">
         Software_T
</sql:xpath-query>
  </Software>
```

2. To execute this template enter the following URL in your browser:

```
http://localhost/htData/Template/Software.xml
```

The results that you see are the same as for the last exercise, except that now we have executed a template that has executed a query to execute the schema. The results are shown in the following figure:

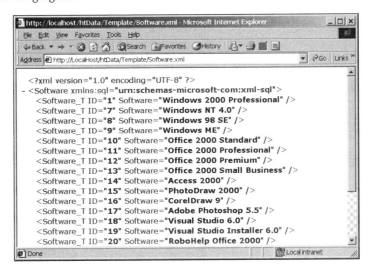

How It Works – Create a Schema Template

The first line of code in the template is the standard XML declaration. The second line of code is the root element to which we have assigned a name of `Software`. Within this element is the standard namespace for templates, which we have seen before:

```
<?xml version="1.0" encoding="UTF-8"?>
    <Software xmlns:sql="urn:schemas-microsoft-com:xml-sql">
```

Using the `<sql:xpath-query>` element we specify the mapping to the schema file. Notice that since the `Schema` directory is at the same level as the `Template` directory we have specified two periods to get back to the root level of the `htData` virtual directory. Then we specify a forward slash and the `Schema` directory followed by another forward slash and the schema file.

Within the `<sql:xpath-query>` element we have specified the query to be executed, and the table name of `Software_T`. This will cause the data from the entire table to be returned.

```
<sql:xpath-query mapping-schema="../Schema/SoftwareSchema.xml">
    Software_T
</sql:xpath-query>
```

Lastly we close the root element by specifying the closing tag for the `<Software>` element:

```
</Software>
```

Summary

By now you should realize that working with XML is not all that hard. Hopefully this chapter has dispelled some of the mystique surrounding XML, and you have a better feel for what XML can do and what you can do with XML.

We have introduced some of the more common XML features of SQL Server 2000 and have shown how easy it is to access data in SQL Server using the URL of your web browser. We have displayed data in the browser as unformatted well-formed XML data and, through the use of XSL stylesheets, we have also formatted XML data.

By now you should feel comfortable using XSL stylesheets to format XML data and to display it in a web page. While we have only touched on the basics of XSL stylesheets, be aware that XSL provides many different elements that will aid you in formatting the XML data to suit your needs. Appendix F provides some links and places to go for more information on XSL and XML.

We have seen how we were able to reduce the amount of data that needs to be entered into the URL through the use of templates. We also know that templates provide better security, as we have hidden the details of the queries and the details of our database from the end user. The maintenance aspects of templates are self-evident, as we need only make the necessary changes in one place and they are immediately effective for everyone who uses the templates.

We have also seen that we can execute SQL statements directly in our templates or execute stored procedures. We have demonstrated how to do both of these and how to define and pass parameters to a template that executes a parameterized stored procedure. In the last example we also saw how a template can execute a query and use an annotated XDR schema document to process and display the results.

Having executed various queries and stored procedures in the URL you should now feel comfortable with this. You should also realize that this could be a good method of creating ad hoc queries to retrieve data formatted as XML, because a browser is available to everyone whereas the client tools for SQL Server are not.

To summarize, you should know how to:

❏   Execute queries and stored procedures in the URL to return XML data

❏   Execute queries and stored procedures in a template to return XML data

❏   Create and use XSL stylesheets to format XML data

❏   Create and use templates

❏   Create and use an annotated XDR schema

In the next chapter we will continue to work with XML as we take a look at generating XML reports in a web browser.

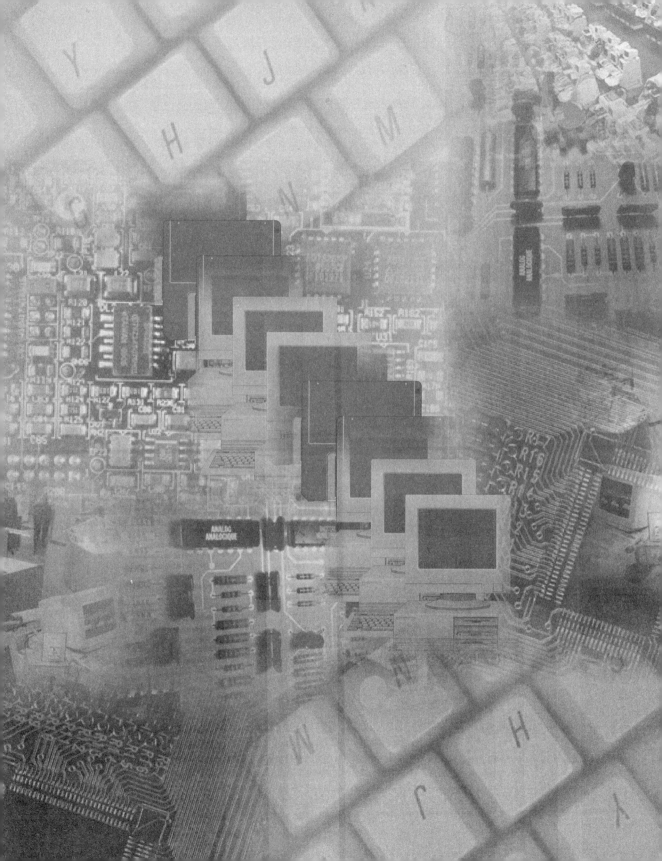

XML Web Reports

Having just completed the last chapter on XML and XSL, you are probably hungry for more and want to learn how you can use XML on the Web to generate more sophisticated reports. This chapter will help you do just that as we work through some exercises to create **XML web reports**. Web reports are nothing more than data formatted and displayed in such a manner as to make the information useful. There are many third-party tools that you can purchase to create web reports; but why go to the expense when XML and XSL are free and perfectly adequate for our needs?

Not only will we generate more sophisticated XML reports but, as we go along, we will also learn more about various XSL elements. HTML and DHTML (Dynamic HTML) will provide the report framework; their use will be explained, so you don't need any previous knowledge of these languages. We will also introduce a little JavaScript along the way as it provides the best functionality to perform the tasks at hand. JavaScript offers more flexibility and functionality over VBScript and has been chosen to perform the tasks that are better suited to JavaScript.

> *The reports that will be produced in this chapter all stem from data that is currently in the tables. There will be no table modifications required. However, it may be prudent to ensure you have an adequate amount of data in them. For example, ensure you have at least three rows of data in the* Employee_T *and* Hardware_T *tables.*

So, in this chapter we will explore:

- ❏ Further XSL elements
- ❏ Including script in XSL
- ❏ Using client-side scripts
- ❏ Handling browser events
- ❏ Using DHTML

More XSL Elements

XSL is just like any programming language; the more sophisticated your program becomes the more sophisticated your code becomes. This is the case as we start to work further with XSL and create more sophisticated web reports. Remember that XSL is an acronym for Extensible Stylesheet Language and, as a language, XSL provides many features to manipulate and control how XML data is used and displayed.

There are a variety of XSL elements that can help to control the *flow* of processing of our XSL stylesheets, as well as elements that apply various *styles* to the output. There are even elements that execute XSL *scripts*. All of these elements help us evaluate and process data in our XSL stylesheet. This chapter introduces some of these XSL elements, and we start with the `<xsl:script>` element.

> **As we start to look at new XSL elements, remember that these elements and their attributes are case sensitive.**

XSL Scripts

The `<xsl:script>` element provides the functionality that allows us to include **script** in our XSL stylesheet to process XML and HTML elements. The scripts that we define in an `<xsl:script>` element are only valid while the XML and XSL elements are being processed on the server. This element does not apply to client-side HTML. When we talk about server-side processing and client-side processing we are referring to where the processing of XML, XSL, and script data takes place. In server-side processing all processing is done on the web server and the results of the processing are sent to the client. In client-side processing the processing is done on the client by the browser, and the results are displayed in the browser.

The `<xsl:script>` element supports the `language` attribute that allows us to specify the scripting language in use. The default language is JScript but you can specify any scripting language supported by your browser. Common values for the language attribute are `JScript`, `JavaScript`, and `VBScript`.

JScript is Microsoft's version of JavaScript, which itself is a subset of the Java language. Likewise, VBScript is a subset of the VB language. These scripts only include limited functionality and a small subset of the keywords, functions, and statements found in their parent languages.

The code fragment below shows a typical `<xsl:script>` element:

```
<xsl:script language="JavaScript">
```

Just as with a script block in HTML, you can define variables and functions within the `<xsl:script>` element. The `<xsl:script>` element can appear anywhere in the `<xsl:stylesheet>` or `<xsl:template>` elements. It is common practice to place scripts either at the beginning of the document or at the end of the document.

The code in your script usually contains symbols, such as the less than (<) and greater than (>) characters which you use to compare values. These characters and many more are XML **reserved characters** and will cause a validation error in your XSL stylesheet. The way to get around this is to use the `<![CDATA[...]]>` section. This is used inside your `<xsl:script>` element to make the code contained in your script opaque to the XML parser. The `<![CDATA[...]]>` section instructs the parser to ignore the code contained within its bounds. The following example illustrates how this section is used:

```
<xsl:script language="JavaScript">
<![CDATA[
  ...your script code here...
]]>
</xsl:script>
```

Now you can use any XML reserved characters that you need in your script and no errors will occur when the XML parser parses your XSL stylesheet.

Evaluating Data – Making Decisions

There are several different XSL elements that evaluate data, but the one we want to concentrate on here is the `<xsl:choose>` element. This element provides conditional testing in conjunction with the `<xsl:when>` and `<xsl:otherwise>` elements. This is like an IF..THEN..ELSE statement in Visual Basic.

The `<xsl:when>` element evaluates an expression or tests an XSL pattern. The expression or pattern must return a true or false value. When the expression or pattern returns true the code inside the `<xsl:when>` element is executed.

The `<xsl:otherwise>` element is like the ELSE statement in a VB IF..THEN..ELSE statement. If the tests for the `<xsl:when>` element or elements return false then the code contained in the `<xsl:otherwise>` element is executed.

You can include as many `<xsl:when>` elements as required and they are evaluated from top to bottom. That is, they are evaluated in the order they are coded. The inclusion of the `<xsl:otherwise>` element is totally optional – it is only included when you want something to happen if all the tests fail for the `<xsl:when>` elements.

The `<xsl:choose>` and `<xsl:otherwise>` elements have no attributes. However, the `<xsl:when>` element has the expr and test attributes to specify whether an expression should be evaluated or a test for an XSL pattern should be made. It also has the optional language attribute that allows you to specify the scripting language for the expr attribute.

Using the test Attribute

Let's take a look at an example that uses the test attribute. We will assume that we are selecting data from the CD_T table and we want to print some special text in an HTML document when a system has a DVD drive. Using the test attribute of the `<xsl:when>` element we test the value in the CD_Type_CH element in our XML data:

```
<xsl:choose>
    <xsl:when test="@CD_Type_CH [.='DVD']">
        8X DVD w/Free Movie Offer
```

```
    </xsl:when>
        <xsl:otherwise>
            <xsl:value-of select="@CD_Type_CH "/>
        </xsl:otherwise>
    </xsl:choose>
```

When the @CD_Type_CH element contains a value of DVD, the text 8X DVD w/Free Movie Offer will be displayed, as indicated by the test attribute of the <xsl:when> element.

Notice that since we are getting our XML data from SQL Server we still need to prefix the CD_Type_CH element with an at sign (@). We enclose the value to test for in square brackets ([ ]) and precede the value with a period (.) and equal sign (=). Since we are testing a string value we also must enclose the value in single quotes ('). As with all XML and XSL elements, the value being tested is case sensitive, so the value DVD is not the same as the value dvd.

Let's now suppose we are testing the value in the CD_ID element, which contains a numeric value, and we are checking for a value greater than 1. We could specify the comparison operator using an alternative syntax. For example, to specify the comparison operator of greater than we specify a dollar sign ($), followed by the characters gt, followed by another dollar sign. This ensures that our XSL document is well formed and does not use any reserved XML characters, such as the greater than sign (>).

```
<xsl:when test="@CD_ID[.$gt$ 1]">
```

The following table lists some of the more common comparison operators used in XSL:

Operator	Alternative Syntax	Description
and	and	Logical and
or	or	Logical or
=	eq	Equality
!=	ne	Not equal
<	lt	Less than
<=	le	Less than or equal
>	gt	Greater than
>=	ge	Greater than or equal

Using the expr Attribute

When we use the expr attribute of the <xsl:when> element we are executing a function in an XSL script. The following example executes a function called even, which tests whether the numeric value is an even number, and passes the current object by specifying the this keyword. If the expression is evaluated to true then the code in the <xsl:when> element is executed. If the expression is evaluated to false then the code in the <xsl:otherwise> expression is executed:

```
<xsl:choose>
   <xsl:when expr="even(this)">
      <xsl:attribute name="Class">EvenRow</xsl:attribute>
   </xsl:when>
   <xsl:otherwise>
      <xsl:attribute name="Class">OddRow</xsl:attribute>
   </xsl:otherwise>
</xsl:choose>
```

The even function is a user-defined function that we will be creating later in this chapter.

Creating Web Reports

We now have enough knowledge to create a web report. Our first series of exercises will implement the topics that were just discussed to build a report that consists of all employees and their locations. The report will display, in a web browser, a table listing the employees' first and last names along with their phone number and location:

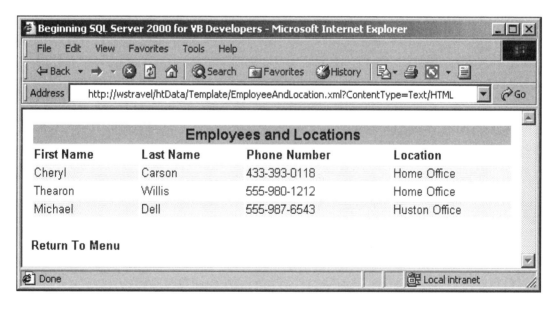

We will need to code a stored procedure to retrieve the employee and location data from the database, and return the results as XML data. We will also need to create an XML template and an XSL stylesheet to display the employee information. The XSL stylesheet that we code will contain a mix of XSL and HTML to produce the web pages that will display our reports. We will use an external cascading stylesheet for our HTML, so we will need to code this also.

We will also need to code a default web page that the user can access in the `HardwareTracking` virtual directory to link to our XML report:

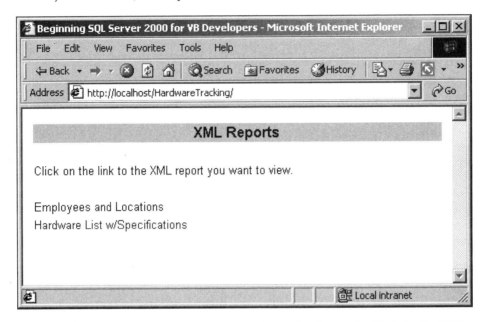

This will enable the user to view each report without the need to key in the URL for the XML template. This web page will be created in the `HardwareTracking` virtual directory that we set up in Chapter 14. As we create more web reports throughout this chapter we will add links from this default page to each of the reports.

Finally, we will add the necessary code to the Hardware Tracking program to display this web page that will contain the links to our web reports.

Try It Out – Employees and Locations Report – Stored Procedure

1. The first task is to create the stored procedure that will return the XML data for employees and locations. Create this stored procedure by entering the following code in the Query Analyzer:

```
CREATE PROCEDURE dbo.up_select_xml_employees_and_locations AS

SELECT First_Name_VC, Last_Name_VC, Phone_Number_VC, Location_Name_VC
    FROM Employee_T
    JOIN Location_T ON Employee_T.Location_ID = Location_T.Location_ID
    ORDER BY Location_Name_VC, Last_Name_VC, First_Name_VC
    FOR XML AUTO

GO

GRANT EXECUTE ON up_select_xml_employees_and_locations TO [Hardware Users]
```

2. Once you have created the stored procedure you can execute it in the Query Analyzer to see how the XML data is formatted. This will come in useful once you start building the XSL stylesheet. To execute the stored procedure in the Query Analyzer enter the following code in a new query window:

```
EXECUTE up_select_xml_employees_and_locations
```

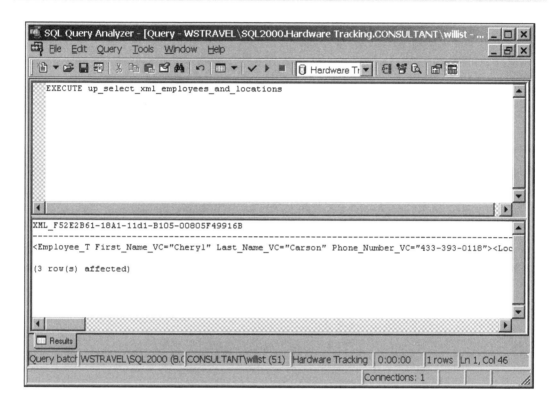

How It Works – Employees and Locations Report – Stored Procedure

The first line of code in this stored procedure is the CREATE PROCEDURE statement followed by the stored procedure name. In case you haven't noticed, there is a pattern in our stored procedure names. Not only are we following the naming standards presented in Chapter 3 but we have also been adding _xml after the standard prefix to indicate that the stored procedure returns XML data:

```
CREATE PROCEDURE dbo.up_select_xml_employees_and_locations AS
```

This serves two purposes, the first of which, as we just mentioned, identifies this stored procedure as a stored procedure that returns XML data. Secondly, it keeps all of our XML stored procedures grouped together in the Enterprise Manager.

The SELECT statement selects the employees' names and phone numbers from the Employee_T table and the location names from the Location_T table. The Location_T table is joined to the Employee_T table using the Location_ID:

```
SELECT First_Name_VC, Last_Name_VC, Phone_Number_VC, Location_Name_VC
    FROM Employee_T
    JOIN Location_T ON Employee_T.Location_ID = Location_T.Location_ID
```

We want the results sorted so we include the ORDER BY clause. Notice that we are sorting the data by location first, then by the employees' last name, and then by their first name:

```
ORDER BY Location_Name_VC, Last_Name_VC, First_Name_VC
```

We specify the FOR XML clause so the results are returned as XML:

```
FOR XML AUTO
```

Next, we code the GO command to have the Query Analyzer create the stored procedure before we grant permissions on it to the hardware users role:

```
GO

GRANT EXECUTE ON up_select_xml_employees_and_locations TO [Hardware Users]
```

Try It Out – Employees and Locations Report – XML Template

1. Let's build the XML template to execute this stored procedure next. Enter the following code in your text editor:

```
<?xml version="1.0" encoding="UTF-8"?>
    <Employees xmlns:sql="urn:schemas-microsoft-com:xml-sql"
        sql:xsl="../EmployeeAndLocation.xsl">
        <sql:query>
            EXECUTE up_select_xml_employees_and_locations
        </sql:query>
    </Employees>
```

2. Save this file as EmployeeAndLocation.xml in the htData/Template directory.

How It Works – Employees and Locations Report – XML Template

The first line of code in this template specifies the standard XML declaration. Then we assign a root element of Employees to our XML data and specify the SQL namespace. The sql:xsl attribute has been set to the EmployeeAndLocation.xsl XSL stylesheet that we have yet to create:

```
<?xml version="1.0" encoding="UTF-8"?>
    <Employees xmlns:sql="urn:schemas-microsoft-com:xml-sql"
        sql:xsl="../EmployeeAndLocation.xsl">
```

The <sql:query> element executes our stored procedure that we just created:

```
        <sql:query>
            EXECUTE up_select_xml_employees_and_locations
        </sql:query>
```

612

Try It Out – Employees and Locations Report – Cascading Stylesheet

In order for the XML data to be formatted when we display it in the browser, we need an XSL stylesheet. Before we dive in and create this stylesheet, let's create a cascading stylesheet that will be used to format the HTML data in our web reports.

1. Using NotePad or your favorite text or HTML editor create the styles listed below:

```
TH
{
   background-color: #CCCCCC;
   font-family: Arial, Verdana, Helvetica;
   font-size: 12pt;
}

.NormalText
{
   font-family: Arial, Verdana, Helvetica;
   font-size: 10pt;
}

.BlueText
{
   font-family: Arial, Verdana, Helvetica;
   font-size: 10pt;
   color: #000080;
   cursor: hand;
}

A.BlueText
{
   text-decoration: none;
}

A.BlueText:Hover
{
   color: #FF0000;
}

.EvenRow
{
   font-family: Arial, Verdana, Helvetica;
   font-size: 10pt;
   background-color: #FFFFFF;
}

.OddRow
{
   font-family: Arial, Verdana, Helvetica;
   font-size: 10pt;
   background-color: #F5F5F5;
}
```

2. Since we will be using this stylesheet in the XSL templates and the default web page in the HardwareTracking virtual directory, we will save the stylesheet in the HardwareTracking virtual directory. Save this stylesheet with a name of htPageStyles.css. Notice the extension for this file. Since this is a cascading stylesheet we use the .css extension.

How It Works – Employees and Locations Report – Cascading Stylesheet

The first style that we want to create is the standard style that we have been using for the table header (<TH>) element. However, we have expanded this style from the last chapter. Just as a reminder, when you create a style that should be applied to *all* elements, use the element name as the style name and do not precede the style name with a period. This is what we have done for the TH style listed below and this causes this style to be automatically applied to all <TH> elements in our HTML document:

```
TH
{
    background-color: #CCCCCC;
    font-family: Arial, Verdana, Helvetica;
    font-size: 12pt;
}
```

We set the background-color attribute using the RGB value of #CCCCCC, which is a light shade of gray. Then we set the font-family attribute using several different fonts. Using several different fonts ensures that if the first font is not installed on the user's machine then the second font will be used. If that font is not installed then the third font is used. Finally, if that font is not installed then the default font for the browser will be used. Specifying several different fonts ensures that for at least 99% of the time your HTML document will have the look and feel that you want.

The last attribute that we have specified in this style is the font-size attribute. Here we have specified that a 12-point font be used.

Just as a reminder, the attributes are enclosed within the style using braces ({}), each attribute name is separated from its value using a colon (:), and each value is terminated with a semicolon (;).

The next style that we want to define is the NormalText style. This style is a user-defined style and thus the style name is preceded by a period. The style will not be applied to any elements unless we specifically request so, by setting the Class attribute on the HTML elements where we want the style applied.

```
.NormalText
{
    font-family: Arial, Verdana, Helvetica;
    font-size: 10pt;
}
```

Again we have specified the font-family attribute and have specified three different fonts for this attribute. We have also specified a font size to be used when this style is applied.

The next user-defined style that we want to create is a style that will render the text displayed in a blue color. Given this, we have named this style BlueText and start this style by coding the font-family attribute, again listing three different fonts. We also set the font-size attribute and the color attribute. We use the RGB value to specify the color that should be displayed. The cursor attribute will cause the mouse pointer to use the hand cursor when the cursor hovers over the text where this style has been applied. This gives the illusion that the text is a hyperlink when it actually is not.

```
.BlueText
{
    font-family: Arial, Verdana, Helvetica;
    font-size: 10pt;
    color: #000080;
    cursor: hand;
}
```

When we do use the BlueText class for a hyperlink we want some special things to happen. A hyperlink is defined in the <A> element, thus we have specified that element here, followed by a period and the style name of BlueText. We will apply the BlueText style inside the <A> element; the styles defined in this class will also be applied. Here we have specified that we do not want any text decoration applied to our hyperlink. Normally the hyperlink would be displayed in the default color set in your browser and would be underlined.

```
A.BlueText
{
    text-decoration: none;
}
```

When the mouse pointer hovers over a hyperlink defined with the BlueText style we want the color of the text to be displayed in red. We have again defined the style for the <A> element and have specified the element, followed by the style name of BlueText. We have also specified a colon and the Hover pseudo-class. In this style we have specified the attributes that should be set when the mouse pointer hovers over a hyperlink:

```
A.BlueText:Hover
{
    color: #FF0000;
}
```

Given the nature of the BlueText style we want to create a corresponding style using red text, and we name this style RedText. This style will perform the same features as the previous style except that it will render the text using the color red. This style will only be used when we have not defined an actual hyperlink in the HTML document:

```
.RedText
{
    font-family: Arial, Verdana, Helvetica;
    font-size: 10pt;
    color: #FF0000;
    cursor: hand;
}
```

Given the potential that there may be a lot of data, and the fact that we will be displaying the employee information in rows, we want to alternate the color of each row. This will help the user looking at the data to follow the data along the row, without dropping to the row below or the row above.

We define a style for all even numbered rows and have specified the font-family attribute and the font-size. We are setting the background-color attribute for this row to white:

```
.EvenRow
{
    font-family: Arial, Verdana, Helvetica;
    font-size: 10pt;
    background-color: #FFFFFF;
}
```

The style for the odd numbered rows will use the same font and size. However, for the `background-color` attribute of this style we will use an off white color called `WhiteSmoke`. This provides just enough contrast between the even numbered rows and the odd numbered rows.

```
.OddRow
{
    font-family: Arial, Verdana, Helvetica;
    font-size: 10pt;
    background-color: #F5F5F5;
}
```

Try It Out – Employees and Locations Report – XSL Stylesheet

Next we need to create the XSL stylesheet. The code for this is presented in the *How It Works* section below. Save it in the root of the `htData` virtual directory as `EmployeeAndLocation.xsl`.

How It Works – Employees and Locations Report – XSL Stylesheet

The code in the XSL stylesheet processes and displays the employee and location data.

We start this XSL stylesheet using the standard three lines of code that identify this as an XSL stylesheet and specify that this stylesheet should process all data from the root element of the XML data:

```
<?xml version="1.0" encoding="UTF-8"?>
<xsl:stylesheet xmlns:xsl="http://www.w3.org/TR/WD-xsl">
    <xsl:template match = "/">
```

We start building the HTML document next by specifying the standard lines of code that begin every HTML document. The `<TITLE>` element specifies the title of the document and this is the title that is displayed in the title bar of the browser:

```
<HTML>
<HEAD>
<TITLE>Beginning SQL Server 2000 for VB Developers</TITLE>
```

We code the `<LINK>` element next, which will link in our stylesheet. The `<LINK>` element can be used to link any external document into the HTML document. Common uses are linking in cascading stylesheets and scripts.

The `Rel` attribute specifies that we are linking in a stylesheet and the `Type` attribute specifies what type of data is contained in the document that we are linking in. The `Href` attribute specifies the location and the name of the document.

616

Since we could be requesting this data from another machine on the network, we have specified the **fully qualified name** where the stylesheet exists. This means that we have specified the machine name (WSTravel) where the HardwareTracking virtual directory exists, as opposed to just using localhost. You will need to change this to the name of your machine. Since the stylesheet exists in the HardwareTracking virtual directory we have also specified this as part of the URL in the Href attribute:

```
<LINK Rel="StyleSheet" Type="Text/CSS"
      Href="http://WSTravel/HardwareTracking/htPageStyles.css"/>
```

We end the <HEAD> element and start the <BODY> element to begin building the body of our HTML document.

The first thing that we do in this HTML document is to build a table. We have specified that the table should have no border around it, by setting the Border attribute to a value of zero. We also specify that the table should stretch to fill 100 percent of the document window by setting the Width attribute using a value of 100%. This allows the table to expand and contract as the user resizes the browser window.

```
</HEAD>
<BODY>
<TABLE Border="0" Width="100%">
```

The first row of data in the table contains the table header, as specified by the <TH> element. Here we have specified that the table header should span across four columns in our table by setting the ColSpan attribute to 4:

```
<TR>
    <TH ColSpan="4">
        <CENTER>Employees and Locations</CENTER>
    </TH>
</TR>
```

The next row of data in our table contains the text that identifies the columns of data. By coding the Class attribute on this row, the style specified, NormalText, will be applied to all columns in this row unless overridden by another style specified on a particular cell. This is the style that is defined in our cascading stylesheet. We have made all text in these columns bold, by coding the <B> element:

```
<TR Class="NormalText">
    <TD>
        <B>First Name</B>
    </TD>
    <TD>
        <B>Last Name</B>
    </TD>
    <TD>
        <B>Phone Number</B>
    </TD>
    <TD>
        <B>Location</B>
    </TD>
</TR>
```

Knowing how your data is returned from your stored procedure will be helpful here. If you take a look at the results from the execution of the stored procedure in the Query Analyzer you will see that `Employee_T` is a top-level element. You will also find that `Location_T` is a sub-element of `Employee_T`, which we will address shortly. We start our loop to process all the XML data by specifying the `<xsl:for-each>` element. In the `<TR>` element we have specified a couple of events to be handled:

```
<xsl:for-each select="Employees/Employee_T">
    <TR onMouseOver="this.style.color='#FF0000'"
        onMouseOut="this.style.color='#000000'">
```

We enter code for the onMouseOver event and the action it should take when the mouse pointer is placed over this row of text. Here we are specifying that the color of the text should be changed to red. This is done using the `this` keyword which represents the current object, in this case the entire row. We specify that the `style` be changed, and the style attribute that should be changed is the `color` attribute. We set this to the RGB value of #FF0000, which represents the color red.

We enter the same code for the onMouseOut event, except that we are changing the color of the text back to black when the mouse pointer moves out of the row.

We will use the `<xsl:choose>` element in conjunction with the `<xsl:when>` element to test for even and odd rows. Notice that the `<xsl:when>` element uses the `expr` attribute and executes a function, passing it the current object, which in this case is the `<TR>` element:

```
<xsl:choose>
    <xsl:when expr="even(this)">
        <xsl:attribute
        name="Class">EvenRow</xsl:attribute>
    </xsl:when>
    <xsl:otherwise>
        <xsl:attribute
        name="Class">OddRow</xsl:attribute>
    </xsl:otherwise>
</xsl:choose>
```

If the expression evaluates to `true` then we execute the code within the `<xsl:when>` element. This code uses the `<xsl:attribute>` element to set the `Class` attribute of the `<TR>` element. We have specified `Class` in the `name` attribute of this element. The actual style that should be used is specified as the value in the `<xsl:attribute>` element.

If the expression evaluated to `false` then we execute the code contained in the `<xsl:otherwise>` element. This code sets the `Class` attribute of the `<TR>` element to the `OddRow` style.

Now that the row element, `<TR>`, has been built, the style set, and the events handled, we define the code for the columns in this row. Using the `<xsl:value-of>` element we populate the data in these columns:

```
<TD>
    <xsl:value-of select="@First_Name_VC"/>
</TD>
<TD>
    <xsl:value-of select="@Last_Name_VC"/>
```

```
        </TD>
        <TD>
            <xsl:value-of select="@Phone_Number_VC"/>
        </TD>
```

Since the location name came from the Location_T table, it is assigned a sub-element name of Location_T within the Employee_T element, meaning that the Location_T element falls between the beginning and ending tag of the Employee_T element. Thus we must address this element in the XML data using a nested <xsl:for-each> element. We use the <xsl:value-of> element to populate the data in this column and then close the nested <xsl:for-each> element:

```
            <xsl:for-each select="Location_T">
                <TD>
                    <xsl:value-of select="@Location_Name_VC"/>
                </TD>
            </xsl:for-each>
```

It should be noted that an employee is only assigned to a single location, thus the <xsl:for-each> element will only loop once to process the single location. Then we end the row of data, the <xsl:for-each> element, and the table:

```
            </TR>
        </xsl:for-each>
    </TABLE>
```

After the table has been completed we define a paragraph in our HTML document by specifying the <P> element. We also want to render the text in a bold font so we have specified the <B> element. Within this element we have set the Class attribute to BlueText style, as this should be applied to the text. We have also specified the events that we want to handle:

```
    <P>
        <B Class="BlueText" onMouseOver="this.className='RedText'"
           onMouseOut="this.className='BlueText'"
           onClick="window.history.back();">Return To Menu</B>
```

The first event is the onMouseOver event. Again we use the this keyword, enter the className attribute, and sets its value to RedText. This will cause the text to be rendered using the attributes defined in the RedText style in our cascading stylesheet.

The onMouseOut event specifies that the ClassName attribute for this text be changed back to the BlueText style and the text rendered using the attributes defined in this style. Using the onMouseOver and onMouseOut events give the illusion that this text is a hyperlink when actually it is not.

The last event that is handled in the <B> element is the onClick event. This event allows us to specify what action should be taken when a user clicks on the text. Using the window object we specify that we want to execute the back method of the history property. The history property contains information about the URLs that have been visited by the client, and in essence we specify that the browser should navigate to the last page in the history list.

619

We end the paragraph and the HTML document by entering the appropriate closing tags. We then end the template by entering the closing element for the <xsl:template> tag:

```
        </P>
        </BODY>
        </HTML>
    </xsl:template>
```

Next, we define the XSL script that is used by the <xsl:when> XSL element. We have specified the language attribute and specified that the language in this script is JavaScript. Then we code the <![CDATA[...]]> section so the code is opaque to the XML parser:

```
    <xsl:script language="JavaScript">
    <![CDATA[
        function even(oRow)
        {
            return ChildNumber(oRow)%2 == 0;
        }
    ]]>
```

> **JavaScript is like XML and XSL in that all keywords and values are case sensitive.**
> **When you enter the code for this script, you must enter it exactly as it appears.**

We have defined one function in this script: the even function. This function accepts the object of the row as a parameter to the function. This function uses the ChildNumber method to calculate if the row passed was an even or odd row. The ChildNumber method returns the item number of the element within the collection of elements with the same name. In other words, for our <TR> element the ChildNumber method returns the number of the row that has been created, thus allowing us to calculate whether the row number is even or odd.

Using the modulo operator (%) we divide the number returned by the ChildNumber method by 2. The modulo operator returns the remainder of the division of two numbers. We then return the results of the comparison of the modulo operator and the value of zero. If they are equal then a value of true is returned, if not then a value of false is returned. The return statement exits the function and returns the specified value, in our case either true or false.

We then end our script and the stylesheet by entering the appropriate closing tags:

```
        </xsl:script>
    </xsl:stylesheet>
```

Try It Out – Employees and Locations Report – Web Page

Now that our XML and XSL documents are complete we want to create a web page that the user can use to navigate to this report without having to key in the URL. This page will be placed in the HardwareTracking virtual directory. This is our main web site that the users will go to for the reports.

1. You can use your favorite text editor or an HTML editor to create this web page:

```
<HTML>
<HEAD>
<TITLE>Beginning SQL Server 2000 for VB Developers</TITLE>
<LINK Rel="StyleSheet" Type="Text/CSS" Href="htPageStyles.css"/>
</HEAD>
<BODY>
<TABLE Border="0" Width="100%" Class="NormalText">
    <TR>
        <TH><CENTER>XML Reports</CENTER></TH>
    </TR>
    <TR>
        <TD> </TD>
    </TR>
    <TR>
        <TD>Click on the link to the XML report you want to view.</TD>
    </TR>
    <TR>
        <TD> </TD>
    </TR>
    <TR>
        <TD><A Href="http://WSTravel/htData/Template/
          EmployeeAndLocation.xml?ContentType=Text/HTML" Class="BlueText"
          onMouseOver="window.status='Employees and Locations';return true;"
          onMouseOut="window.status='';return true;">
          Employees and Locations</A></TD>
    </TR>
</TABLE>
</BODY>
</HTML>
```

2. At this point save your HTML document as `Default.htm` in the HardwareTracking virtual directory.

How It Works – Employees and Locations Report – Web Page

The web page starts with the standard HTML elements defining this as a HTML document. Notice that we have used the same title in the <TITLE> element that we used in the XSL stylesheet. You can change this title to display the text that you want in the title bar of the browser:

```
<TITLE>Beginning SQL Server 2000 for VB Developers</TITLE>
```

Using the <LINK> element we can now link in our cascading stylesheet. Notice that since the stylesheet will be residing in the same directory as this web page, all we need to include in the Href attribute is the stylesheet name. We do not have to create a fully qualified URL for this as we did in the XSL stylesheet.

```
<LINK Rel="StyleSheet" Type="Text/CSS" Href="htPageStyles.css"/>
```

We then end the heading section of our document and start the body by entering the <BODY> tag.

This will be a very simple web page that merely lists the reports that can be accessed. We will use a table to keep the data elements in our page aligned. The <TABLE> element has the Border attribute set to zero so no lines will be displayed in the table. We have specified the Width attribute so the table will expand and contract when the browser window is resized. We have specified that the NormalText style be applied to all elements within the table, by setting the Class attribute:

```
<TABLE Border="0" Width="100%" Class="NormalText">
```

The first row in our table contains the table header and we specify that the text be centered on the page. The second row in our table is merely a separator row that contains nothing but a blank space in the column, as specified by the   space character:

```
<TR>
    <TH><CENTER>XML Reports</CENTER></TH>
</TR>
<TR>
    <TD> </TD>
</TR>
```

The next row in our table specifies the instructions to the user. Then we code another row that contains a blank space to again provide the appropriate spacing between the rows in our table:

```
<TR>
    <TD>Click on the link to the XML report you want to view.</TD>
</TR>
<TR>
    <TD> </TD>
</TR>
```

The last row in our table contains the hyperlink to the URL that contains the XML template to execute. We have specified this hyperlink using the <A> tag. We have specified the URL that the browser should navigate to in the Href attribute. When the user clicks on the text contained between the <A> element and its closing tag the browser will navigate to the URL specified in the Href attribute. Notice that we have used the actual machine name in this URL instead of LocalHost. This will allow this page to be accessed by another machine on the network and the hyperlink will navigate to the correct virtual directory.

> **Note: ensure that you specify the name of the machine on which SQL Server is running.**

```
<TR>
    <TD><A Href="http://WSTravel/htData/Template/
        EmployeeAndLocation.xml?ContentType=Text/HTML" Class="BlueText"
        onMouseOver="window.status='Employees and Locations';return true;"
        onMouseOut="window.status='';return true;">
        Employees and Locations</A></TD>
</TR>
```

We have specified that this element uses the `BlueText` style, indicated by the `Class` attribute.

The `onMouseOver` event will set the `status` property of the `window` object. When this happens the text in the status bar of the browser will display the text **Employees and Locations**. We terminate this statement with a semicolon, as this is actually JavaScript that we are coding in this event. We code the return statement next and specify the value of `true` so the `status` property of the `window` object gets updated.

The `onMouseOut` event contains the same code except that we are clearing the text in the status bar in the browser, by simply entering two consecutive single quotes.

Then we display the text that should be displayed in the document, between the `<A>` tag and its closing tag.

We then end the table, the body of the HTML document, and the document itself, by coding the appropriate HTML tags.

Try It Out – Modifying the Hardware Tracking Application

We want to modify our Hardware Tracking application from Chapter 13 so that it will display the default web page for our reports. Remember that we added a menu item under the **Tools** menu to display the online reports. Now we want to add the code to that menu item to display the `Default.htm` web page in a browser.

1. Add the following code to the general declarations section of the main (`frmMain`) form:

```
'Declare Windows API
Private Declare Function ShellExecute Lib "shell32.dll" Alias _
    "ShellExecuteA" ( _
    ByVal hwnd As Long, _
    ByVal lpOperation As String, _
    ByVal lpFile As String, _
    ByVal lpParameters As String, _
    ByVal lpDirectory As String, _
    ByVal nShowCmd As Long) As Long
```

2. Add the following code to the `mnuToolsOnlineReports_Click` procedure, also in the `frmMain` form:

```
Private Sub mnuToolsOnlineReports_Click()
    'Invoke a browser with the following URL
    ShellExecute Me.hwnd, "open", _
        "http://wstravel/hardwaretracking/default.htm", _
        vbNullString, vbNullString, 1
End Sub
```

3. Save your VB project and we will be ready to test.

How It Works – Modifying the Hardware Tracking Application

In order to display the Default.htm web page we need to execute a browser and pass it the URL that we want it to display. The ShellExecute Windows API provides us with a means to do this.

This API will find the program name that is associated with the file that we pass. In our case the file is an actual URL. Because this API uses the associations defined in the registry, this method will open your default browser, whether it is Microsoft Internet Explorer or Netscape Navigator:

```
'Declare Windows API
Private Declare Function ShellExecute Lib "shell32.dll" Alias _
    "ShellExecuteA" ( _
    ByVal hwnd As Long, _
    ByVal lpOperation As String, _
    ByVal lpFile As String, _
    ByVal lpParameters As String, _
    ByVal lpDirectory As String, _
    ByVal nShowCmd As Long) As Long
```

The code in the mnuToolsOnlineReports_Click procedure is executed when we click on the **Online Reports** menu item. We simply want to execute the ShellExecute API and pass it some parameters.

The first parameter that we pass is a handle to the window that is invoking this API. We do this by coding the Me keyword and the hwnd property, which contains a handle to the main form. The next parameter that we pass specifies the operation to be performed. Since we want to open a new window, in this case a browser, we code a string value of open.

The next parameter is the file to be opened, in our case a URL. We enter the fully qualified URL for the Default.htm web page just as we would enter it in a browser.

The next parameter specifies the parameters that we want to pass to the program that is being invoked. Since we have none, we have entered a null string value using the vbNullString constant. The next parameter is the default directory that should be used by the program invoked. Again we have none, so we have coded the vbNullString constant again.

The last parameter that we have entered is the show command. This parameter specifies how the window should be opened. To open the window using its normal size and position we code a value of 1, which is what we have done here. To open a window that is maximized we would code a value of 3, and to open a window that is minimized we would code a value of 6.

```
Private Sub mnuToolsOnlineReports_Click()
    'Invoke a browser with the following URL
    ShellExecute Me.hwnd, "open", _
        "http://wstravel/hardwaretracking/default.htm", _
        vbNullString, vbNullString, 1
End Sub
```

Try It Out – Running the Employees and Locations Report

1. To test all of our code, run your Hardware Tracking program and login. Select the Online Reports menu item on the Tools menu. Your default browser will be opened and the `Default.htm` web page will be displayed in the browser, as shown:

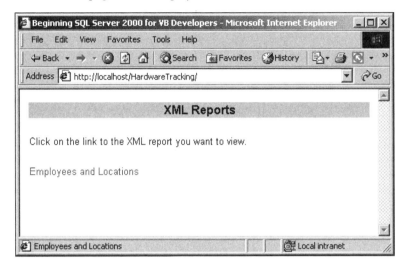

2. Hover your mouse pointer over the hyperlink and notice that the color of the text turns red and Employees and Locations is displayed in the status bar of the browser, as shown in the figure. Now, move your mouse pointer away from the hyperlink and notice that the text turns back to blue and the text in the status bar is cleared.

3. To test the XML template and XSL stylesheet click on the Employees and Locations text. The XML template is executed, which causes the XSL stylesheet to be executed to format the XML data. Notice that every other row of data is highlighted using the styles in our cascading stylesheet. Also, when you hover your mouse pointer over a row, the text turns to red. The mouse pointer does not use the hand cursor as this would indicate a hyperlink, which this row of data is not.

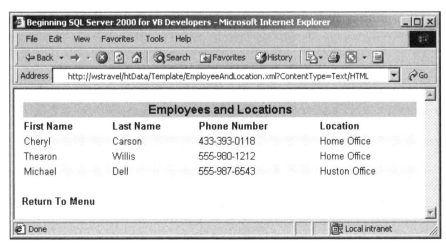

4. Take notice of the URL in your browser. This is the URL to the `EmployeeAndLocation.xml` template. Notice that when we click on the words **Return To Menu** the text turns red and the mouse pointer turns into a hand. Even though this text is not actually a hyperlink we were able to simulate the appearance so the user thinks that it is.

When you click on this text the browser will return to the previous document that was displayed, in our case the `Default.htm` web page.

Dynamic HTML

When we talk about dynamic HTML (DHTML) most people have the perception that this is some special kind of HTML. In fact it really isn't, we are just using more of the properties and attributes of the HTML elements that we define in our HTML document. Using a scripting language we manipulate these attributes and properties to change the appearance of the HTML document on the client-side.

Let's assume that we have so much data to be displayed it will not all fit on one screen. Using a `<SPAN>` or `<DIV>` element we can break this data up into smaller portions that fit onto one screen without the user having to scroll to see the rest of the information. We display one element while hiding the rest. We then provide the user with some sort of navigation method, such as buttons or text, which allows them to display the various pieces of data. All of this happens without the user having to navigate to another web page or make a trip back to the server to retrieve more data.

The scenario that we just described is the most common use of DHTML. But don't let this fool you, as DHTML can be more detailed than the scenario described above. Using DHTML, we can actually create new elements *dynamically* on the client-side and send those dynamically created elements back to the server for processing. However, that is beyond the scope of this book. For more information on this topic check out *Writing Cross-Browser Dynamic HTML* published by Apress, ISBN 1-893115-05-4.

The next report that we create will use DHTML. What we will do is build an HTML document that contains all of the data that we want to display. The data elements that we don't want to display right away will have their `Style` attribute set to hide the elements. Using client-side script we will show and hide the elements when the user clicks on some text.

Let's see how this works. We will be using the `<SPAN>` element, which acts as an in-line text container. This means that we can include any type of text or HTML elements inside the `<SPAN>` element. When we hide the `<SPAN>` element all text and elements defined inside the `<SPAN>` element are also hidden. The following two examples show how we use the `Style` attribute of the `<SPAN>` element to show and hide the text and elements contained in a `<SPAN>` element.

The first example does not have the `Style` attribute set so the `<SPAN>` element will be displayed in the HTML document:

```
<SPAN Name="spnExample">
```

The second example has its `Style` attribute coded to set the `display` property to `none`. This causes the `<SPAN>` element to not be displayed in the HTML document and to not take up any space in the document.

```
<SPAN Name="spnExample" Style="display:none;">
```

This means that the text following this <SPAN> element will be displayed directly below the text preceding the <SPAN> element. When we change the Style attribute so the <SPAN> element is displayed, the text following the <SPAN> element gets displaced, and pushed down in the document.

We mentioned earlier that we would manipulate the Style attribute through the use of client-side script. The examples below show how we can show and hide the <SPAN> element using JavaScript. Before we can access the <SPAN> element we need to set a reference to it.

Using the var statement we declare a variable called oSpan and set it to the <SPAN> element in the document. We do this using the document object and its all collection. Then we specify the item (element) that we want to access, and specify its Name attribute, in this case spnExample:

```
var oSpan = document.all.item("spnExample");
```

The first example sets the display property of the style attribute to nothing by specifying two consecutive quotes. This will cause the <SPAN> element to be displayed in the document:

```
oSpan.style.display = "";
```

The second example sets the display property to none, which causes the <SPAN> element to be hidden in the document:

```
oSpan.style.display = "none";
```

Using the style attribute of the <SPAN> element allows us to create DHTML. When the user wants to see the data they click on some text or a button and the text and HTML elements are displayed. When they click on some other text or button the previous text and elements are hidden and the new text and HTML elements are displayed.

Web Report with Hidden Details

We are going to put this into practice and create another web report that will display a list of all hardware. We will display the manufacturer, model, processor speed, and memory. All other details of the system will be hidden in a <SPAN> element:

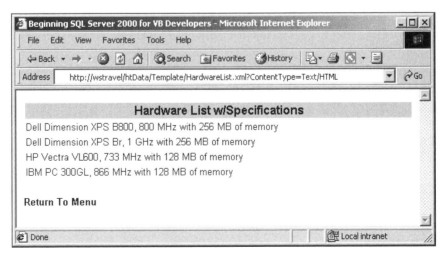

When the user clicks on a specific system, we will show the details for that system:

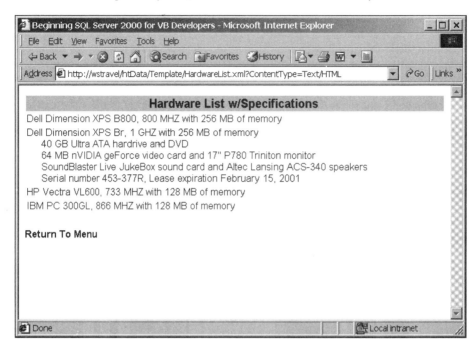

This allows us to display all of the hardware in the `Hardware_T` table without cluttering up the screen with the details of every system. This also allows the user to view the details for the system that they want to see, and makes it easier to find the system they are looking for.

Again we will need to create an XML and XSL file to retrieve the XML data and to format the XML data for display. The stored procedure that we want to use already exists, but we need to alter it to add some more columns.

Try It Out – Hardware List Report – Stored Procedure

The first thing that we want to do is to alter the `up_select_xml_hardware` stored procedure.

1. In the Object Browser of the Query Analyzer expand the **Hardware Tracking** database and then expand the **Stored Procedures** group. Scroll down to the bottom of the list of stored procedures to find the **up_select_xml_hardware** stored procedure. Right-click on this stored procedure and choose **Edit** from the context menu.

2. The only columns that are listed in the select list are `Manufacturer_VC` and `Model_VC`. We still want to include these columns, but we also want some additional columns. The columns listed in the code fragment below all come from the `Hardware_T` table. You can expand this table and drag and drop the columns into your query:

```
SELECT Hardware_ID, Manufacturer_VC, Model_VC, Processor_Speed_VC,
    Memory_VC, HardDrive_VC, Sound_Card_VC, Speakers_VC,
    Video_Card_VC, Monitor_VC, Serial_Number_VC,
```

```
            DATENAME(MONTH,Lease_Expiration_DT) + ' ' +
            DATENAME(DAY,Lease_Expiration_DT) + ', ' +
            DATENAME(YEAR,Lease_Expiration_DT) AS 'Lease_Expiration_DT',
            CD_Type_CH
            FROM Hardware_T

            JOIN CD_T ON Hardware_T.CD_ID = CD_T.CD_ID

            ORDER BY Manufacturer_VC, Model_VC

            FOR XML AUTO
```

3. When you have completed making these changes click on the Execute Query icon on the toolbar to update the stored procedure. You do not need to save the changes in the current query window once you have executed the code.

You can test this stored procedure by entering the stored procedure name in a query window and executing it. You see all of the new columns that you have just added:

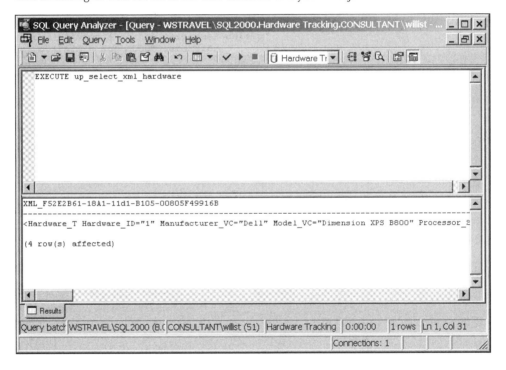

How It Works – Hardware List Report – Stored Procedure

Let's look first at the select list – in the last chapter the date and time were displayed from the Lease_Expiration_DT column. All we really need is the date so we are using the DATENAME function in SQL Server to extract the date name portions from the Lease_Expiration_DT column. The first line extracts the MONTH name and then concatenates a space behind the name. The second line is concatenated to the first line and extracts the DAY from the date. It then concatenates a comma and a space. The third line extracts the YEAR from the date and it is concatenated to the MONTH and DAY. We have specified that the concatenated date should be assigned a name of Lease_Expiration_DT:

```
DATENAME(MONTH,Lease_Expiration_DT) + ' ' +
DATENAME(DAY,Lease_Expiration_DT) + ', ' +
DATENAME(YEAR,Lease_Expiration_DT) AS 'Lease_Expiration_DT',
```

We still select the data from the `Hardware_T` table but we also need to join the `CD_T` table so we can select the `CD_Type_CH` column:

```
JOIN CD_T ON Hardware_T.CD_ID = CD_T.CD_ID
```

Since we will be displaying this data in a web report we want some semblance of order. Thus we have specified that the results are to be sorted by the `Manufacturer_VC` and `Model_VC` columns, as specified in the `ORDER BY` clause:

```
ORDER BY Manufacturer_VC, Model_VC
```

Finally, we leave the last line as is because we want this data returned as XML.

Try It Out – Hardware List Report – XML Template

1. Let's move on now and create the XML template that will execute this stored procedure. This XML template is just about like every other XML template that we have created:

```
<?xml version="1.0" encoding="UTF-8"?>
   <Hardware xmlns:sql="urn:schemas-microsoft-com:xml-sql"
      sql:xsl="../HardwareList.xsl">
      <sql:query>
         EXECUTE up_select_xml_hardware
      </sql:query>
   </Hardware>
```

2. Save this template in the `Template` directory under the `htData` virtual directory, with a name of `HardwareList.xml`.

How It Works – Hardware List Report – XML Template

We start this template with the standard XML declaration and then specify a root element of `Hardware`. We enter the SQL namespace and the XSL stylesheet to be used. This stylesheet has not been created yet, but it will reside in the root `htData` virtual directory with the name `HardwareList.xsl`.

```
<?xml version="1.0" encoding="UTF-8"?>
   <Hardware xmlns:sql="urn:schemas-microsoft-com:xml-sql"
      sql:xsl="../HardwareList.xsl">
```

Then we code the `<sql:query>` element and specify the stored procedure to be executed to return the XML data:

```
<sql:query>
   EXECUTE up_select_xml_hardware
</sql:query>
```

We then code the appropriate closing tags and we are done with this XML template.

Try It Out – Hardware List Report – XSL Stylesheet

Moving on, we want to create our XSL stylesheet next. This is where the heart of the code is for our XSL and our HTML document. The code is presented in the *How It Works* section below.

How It Works – Hardware List Report – XSL Stylesheet

We start this stylesheet with the three standard lines of code that define this as a stylesheet, and specify that we want to process data from the root element of our XML data:

```
<?xml version="1.0" encoding="UTF-8"?>
<xsl:stylesheet xmlns:xsl="http://www.w3.org/TR/WD-xsl">
   <xsl:template match = "/">
```

Then we begin our HTML document, coding the standard HTML elements that start every HTML document. Again we have used a fully qualified URL to point to our cascading stylesheet in the `HardwareTacking` virtual directory:

```
<HTML>
<HEAD>
<TITLE>Beginning SQL Server 2000 for VB Developers</TITLE>
<LINK Rel="StyleSheet" Type="Text/CSS"
    Href="http://WSTravel/HardwareTracking/htPageStyles.css"/>
</HEAD>
```

We then begin the body of our HTML document, and the first thing we define in here is a table. We have specified that the table contains no border lines, and that the table should expand and contract with the browser window.

The first row of data in our table is the table header, and the header text will be centered in the browser window:

```
<BODY>
<TABLE Border="0" Width="100%">
   <TR>
      <TH>
         <CENTER>Hardware List w/Specifications</CENTER>
      </TH>
   </TR>
```

We start the processing of data with the `<xsl:for-each>` element that sets up a loop so we can process all elements in the `Hardware/Hardware_T` element of our XML data. Our table only has one column, and all of the data that will be displayed for a specific system will be displayed in this column.

```
<xsl:for-each select="Hardware/Hardware_T">
   <TR>
      <TD>
```

We have chosen to display the manufacturer, model, processor speed, and memory in a label. To that end we have defined the <LABEL> element and set the Class attribute to the BlueText style defined in our cascading stylesheet, created previously. This will cause all text defined in this label to be rendered using this style.

We have set up some events to be handled in this label. The first one is the onMouseOver event and this will change the className of the style in use. When the mouse pointer hovers over this text the RedText style will be used, causing the text to turn red.

The onMouseOut event also changes the className attribute, and changes the style in use back to the BlueText style. Remember that both the BlueText and RedText styles have the cursor attribute set to hand, which causes the mouse pointer to use the hand cursor when it hovers over the text.

The last event that we want to handle is the onClick event. When the user clicks on the text in this label we want to execute the HideShow function, which we will be covering shortly.

```
<LABEL Class="BlueText"
    onMouseOver="this.className='RedText'"
    onMouseOut="this.className='BlueText'"
    onClick="HideShow()">
```

Within the confines of the <LABEL> element we have specified that the manufacturer, model, processor speed, and memory be displayed by using the <xsl:value-of> element. Notice that we have also intermixed some static text here so the data is not all run together, giving some semblance of order:

```
<xsl:value-of
    select="@Manufacturer_VC"/>
<xsl:value-of select="@Model_VC"/>,
<xsl:value-of
    select="@Processor_Speed_VC"/>
with
<xsl:value-of select="@Memory_VC"/> of
    memory
</LABEL>
```

Using the <SPAN> element with the display property of the Style attribute set to none, we build the hidden details for the system. Notice that we have set the Class attribute of the <SPAN> element so that all HTML inside the <SPAN> element will have the NormalText style applied to it.

We use the <DIV> element to format the text into individual lines of HTML. The <DIV> element is a container that renders HTML, and is the perfect choice for use inside the <SPAN> element. We have set the margin-left property of the Style attribute so the text inside the <DIV> element will be indented by 25 pixels.

We then code the <xsl:value-of> elements to populate the data inside the <DIV> element. Notice that once again we have intermixed static text with our XML data to form readable sentences:

```
<SPAN Class="NormalText" Style="display:none;">
    <DIV Style="margin-left:25px">
<xsl:value-of select="@HardDrive_VC"/>
hardrive and
<xsl:for-each select="CD_T">
```

```
        <xsl:value-of
            select="@CD_Type_CH"/>
        </xsl:for-each>
</DIV>
```

We repeat the process of using the <DIV> element and the <xsl:value-of> elements to form each line of HTML that we want displayed inside the <SPAN> element:

```
<DIV Style="margin-left:25px">
    <xsl:value-of select = "@Video_Card_VC"/>
    video card and <xsl:value-of select="@Monitor_VC"/>
    monitor
</DIV>

<DIV Style="margin-left:25px">
    <xsl:value-of select="@Sound_Card_VC"/>
    sound card and <xsl:value-of select="@Speakers_VC"/>
    speakers
</DIV>

<DIV Style="margin-left:25px">
    Serial number
    <xsl:value-of select="@Serial_Number_VC"/>,
    Lease expiration
    <xsl:value-of select="@Lease_Expiration_DT"/>
</DIV>
```

We close the <SPAN> element and the table column and row, and then iterate the rest of the elements in our XML data, building a new row of data for each pass through the loop:

```
            </SPAN>
        </TD>
    </TR>
</xsl:for-each>
```

Once we have processed all of the data we close the table and code a paragraph, as indicated by the <P> element. This is the same code that we used in the last XSL stylesheet – it provides a means for the user to get back to the web page that contains the menu choices for the XML reports:

```
</TABLE>
<P>
    <B Class="BlueText" onMouseOver="this.className='RedText'"
        onMouseOut="this.className='BlueText'"
        onClick="window.history.back();">Return To Menu</B>
</P>
```

We now come to the code for our client-side script. This script is coded using JavaScript, thus we have specified this in the Language attribute. In addition to the <![CDATA[]]> section we have also included the <xsl:comment> element. The <xsl:comment> element will render the text inside this element as a comment to the XML parser. Thus the code in our script will not be interpreted as XML data and we will not receive any errors.

```
<SCRIPT Language="JavaScript" TYPE="Text/JavaScript">
    <xsl:comment><![CDATA[
```

The `HideShow` function accepts no parameters to perform its processing. Instead it relies on the collection of the `<SPAN>` and `<LABEL>` elements and uses the `className` attribute to determine the correct item in the collection.

The first thing that we do in this function is to declare a variable each for the `<SPAN>` and `<LABEL>` elements. Notice that we access these elements using the `tags` member of the `all` collection of the `document` object. We specify which tag (element) that we want to access, in this case the `<SPAN>` and `<LABEL>` elements:

```
function HideShow()
{
    // Declare an object for the collection of Span
    // and Label elements
    var oSpan = document.all.tags("SPAN");
    var oLabel = document.all.tags("LABEL");
```

The `length` property of the object tells us how many items are in the collection. Using this, we set up a `for` loop and process all items in the `<SPAN>` collection.

The `for` statement accepts four arguments, the first of which is the `initialization` argument. This statement is only executed before the loop begins and initializes the i variable to 0. The second argument is the `test` argument and as long as the test returns `true` the loop is executed. The third argument is the `increment` argument and increments the counter every time we process a loop. The last argument, which is not used in our example here, is the `statement` to be executed if the test is `true`. Since we have more than one statement to be executed these are enclosed inside the `for` statement in brackets (`{}`):

```
    // Loop through the span elements collection
    for (i=0; i<oSpan.length; i++)
    {
```

The first statement to be executed is the `if` statement. Here we are checking the `className` of the item specified by the i variable in the `<LABEL>` collection. If the `className` attribute is equal to the style of `RedText` then we know this is the row of data that the user is on. Notice that we use two consecutive equal signs in the test. When we compare for *equality* we use two equal signs, but if we want to *assign* a value we use just one equal sign.

```
        // If the className attribute is RedText then
        // process the Span object
        if (oLabel[i].className == "RedText")
        {
```

If the `if` statement above evaluates to `true` then we execute the code below. Notice that all of our code for the `if` statements is enclosed in sets of braces – these segregate the code for each `if` statement. The first thing that we do is to check the `display` property of the `style` attribute of the `<SPAN>` element. If the `style` is set to nothing, as indicated by the two consecutive quotes, we know that the `<SPAN>` element is currently being displayed:

```
        // If the display style is on
        if (oSpan[i].style.display == "")
        {
```

If the <SPAN> element is currently being displayed and the user has clicked on the label again we want to hide the <SPAN> element for the label, so we set the display property of the style attribute to none:

```
            // Hide it
            oSpan[i].style.display = "none";
        }
```

Otherwise the <SPAN> element is hidden and we want to show it, so we set the display property of the style attribute to an empty string:

```
        else
        {
            // Show it
            oSpan[i].style.display = "";
        }
```

The else statement for the outer if statement will hide the <SPAN> element by setting its display property to none. This is done so that if one <SPAN> element is displayed and the user clicks on another <LABEL> element we will show the current <SPAN> element and hide the previous <SPAN> element.

```
        }
        else
        {
            // Otherwise hide it
            oSpan[i].style.display = "none";
        }
    }
}
```

We terminate our script by coding the ending section and tags:

```
        ]]></xsl:comment>
    </SCRIPT>
```

We then end our HTML document and the XSL stylesheet by coding the appropriate ending tags:

```
        </BODY>
        </HTML>
    </xsl:template>
  </xsl:stylesheet>
```

Try It Out – Hardware List Report – Web Page and Testing

We want to modify the Default.htm web page to add a hyperlink for this new report.

1. Add the following line of code after the last hyperlink that we defined for the Employees and Locations report. The URL in the <A> element specifies that we want to execute the HardwareList.xml template:

```
<TR>
    <TD><A Href="http://WSTravel/htData/Template/
    HardwareList.xml?ContentType=Text/HTML" Class="BlueText"
    onMouseOver="window.status='Hardware List w/Specifications';return true;"
```

635

```
  onMouseOut="window.status='';return true;">
  Hardware List w/Specifications</A></TD>
</TR>
```

2. After you have saved the `Default.htm` web page, run your Hardware Tracking application and click on the **Online Reports** menu item on the **Tools** menu to have a browser window opened and the `Default.htm` web page displayed.

Your `Default.htm` web page should now show a hyperlink for the **Hardware List** report, as shown in the following figure:

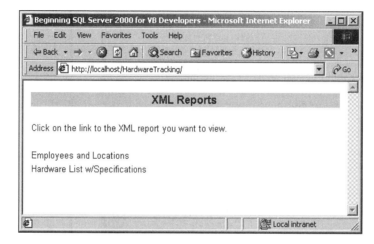

If you hover the mouse pointer over the **Hardware List w/Specifications** text, this text should turn red and should also be displayed in the status bar of the browser.

3. Now click on this link so the **Hardware List** report is displayed. Your hardware list should contain a list of all rows of data in the `Hardware_T` table. All of the text is blue and as you hover your mouse pointer over the text itwill turn into a cursor and the text will turn red. If you move your mouse pointer off the row the text will turn blue, and if you are not on another row of data the mouse pointer will return to its default cursor type.

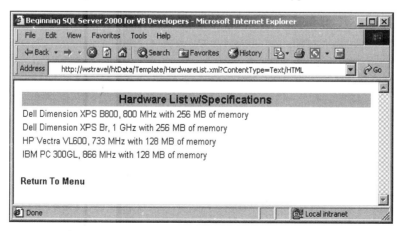

4. You'll want to test the functionality of your JavaScript now by clicking on a row of data. The `<SPAN>` element for that row of data will be displayed, listing the specifications of the hardware chosen:

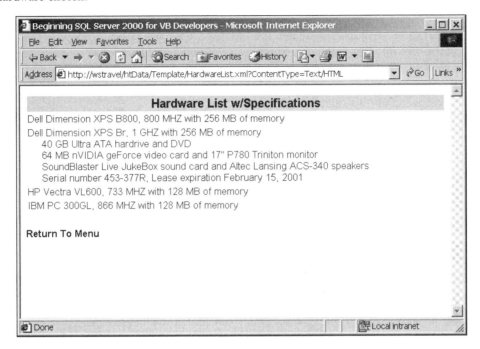

5. If you click on another row of data the `<SPAN>` element that is currently displayed will be hidden and again the correct `<SPAN>` element will be shown. To further test your script, click on the same label that currently has the `<SPAN>` element shown. The `<SPAN>` element will again be hidden and no other `<SPAN>` elements will be shown.

Organizing Your SELECT Statement

In the last exercise we saw how we could hide the extra data in the HTML document until the user wanted to see it. This becomes even more important as we start to display more and more data. As we start to build more sophisticated XML reports our stored procedures start to become more sophisticated also. This means that we are beginning to use more joins and selecting columns from different tables to retrieve the data that we need.

When building more complex stored procedures it helps to build them as a query first. Then you can test the SELECT statement to ensure you are getting all of the data that you need, and that the data is in the desired order.

After you have executed the query and are satisfied with the results, you can add the FOR XML clause and then run the query again. Viewing the resulting XML output enables you to ensure the XML data is structured the way you want it. If it is not then you may need to rearrange the columns in your select list.

Once you are satisfied with the results then you can create the stored procedure. Finally, you can test the stored procedure by executing it through the URL. This will give a better idea of how the data will be structured. You can view the nesting of the elements and see the relationships between them.

Let's take our last stored procedure as a case in point. Suppose that you thought that formatting the lease expiration date clutters up the select list, and you want to move it to the end of the select list, as shown in this code fragment:

```
SELECT Hardware_ID, Manufacturer_VC, Model_VC, Processor_Speed_VC,
    Memory_VC, HardDrive_VC, Sound_Card_VC, Speakers_VC,
    Video_Card_VC, Monitor_VC, Serial_Number_VC,
    CD_Type_CH,
    DATENAME(MONTH,Lease_Expiration_DT) + ' ' +
    DATENAME(DAY,Lease_Expiration_DT) + ', ' +
    DATENAME(YEAR,Lease_Expiration_DT) AS 'Lease_Expiration_DT'
```

In a normal SELECT statement this would be fine as the lease expiration date would simply be displayed after the CD type, as shown in the results pane:

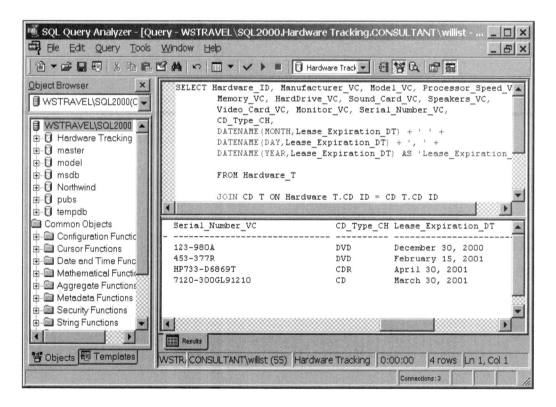

But look what happens when we add the FOR XML clause. The lease expiration date becomes part of the CD_T element, which is not what we want:

Therefore you need to specify the order of the columns in your select list carefully and keep them grouped by the tables that they are being selected from. This becomes even more important as you start to select columns from multiple tables and have multiple joins in your query. Testing the final stored procedure in the browser also becomes important as you start to code your XSL stylesheet, as this gives you a better idea of how the elements are nested.

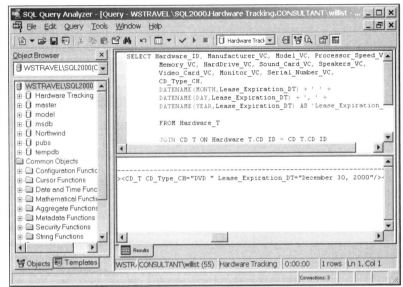

The next XML web report that we want to create is a report that lists all assigned systems. This report should list the employee to whom the system is assigned as well as the hardware details of the system. We also want to list all of the software that has been installed on that system.

Building upon the last exercise, this report will hide the hardware and software details until the user wants to display them. However, in this report we want to make the software a sub-element of the hardware. In other words, we want to be able to hide and show the hardware details. When we show the hardware details we want to be able to drill down further and show the software that is installed on the hardware. We will not be able to view the software until we have viewed the hardware:

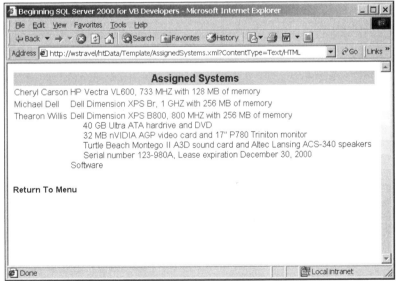

Try It Out – Assigned Systems Report – Stored Procedure

The `up_select_xml_assigned_systems` stored procedure will select all of the data for the **Assigned Systems** report. This stored procedure will be selecting data from multiple tables and thus will include multiple joins.

1. The code to be entered in the Query Analyzer is as shown:

```
CREATE PROCEDURE dbo.up_select_xml_assigned_systems AS


--
-- Select columns from the Employee_T table
--
SELECT First_Name_VC, Last_Name_VC,
--
-- Select columns from the Hardware_T table
--
    Manufacturer_VC, Model_VC, Processor_Speed_VC, Memory_VC,
    HardDrive_VC, Sound_Card_VC, Speakers_VC, Video_Card_VC,
    Monitor_VC, Serial_Number_VC,
--
-- Format the Lease_Expiration_DT column as month dd, yyyy
--
    DATENAME(MONTH,Lease_Expiration_DT) + ' ' +
    DATENAME(DAY,Lease_Expiration_DT) + ', ' +
    DATENAME(YEAR,Lease_Expiration_DT) AS 'Lease_Expiration_DT',
--
-- Select columns from the CD_T table
--
    CD_Type_CH,
--
-- Select columns from the Software_T table
--
    Software_Name_VC
--
-- From the System_Assignment_T table
--
    FROM System_Assignment_T
--
-- Join the supporting tables
--
    JOIN Employee_T ON System_Assignment_T.Employee_ID =
        Employee_T.Employee_ID

    JOIN Hardware_T ON System_Assignment_T.Hardware_ID =
        Hardware_T.Hardware_ID

    JOIN CD_T ON Hardware_T.CD_ID = CD_T.CD_ID

    JOIN System_Software_Relationship_T ON
        System_Assignment_T.System_Assignment_ID =
        System_Software_Relationship_T.System_Assignment_ID
```

```
    JOIN Software_T ON System_Software_Relationship_T.Software_ID =
       Software_T.Software_ID
--
-- Sort the results
--
    ORDER BY Last_Name_VC, First_Name_VC
--
-- Return the results as XML data
--
    FOR XML AUTO

GO

GRANT EXECUTE ON up_select_xml_assigned_systems TO [Hardware Users]
```

2. After your stored procedure has been created you can test it in the Query Analyzer by entering the stored procedure name. You can examine the XML data in the results pane, but this really doesn't give you a complete, top-down view of how the data will look.

3. We want to execute this stored procedure in the URL of a browser to fully get an idea of how our XML data is formatted and how the elements are nested. Enter the following URL in your browser:

```
http://localhost/htData?SQL=EXECUTE+up_select_xml_assigned_systems&ContentType=Tex
t/HTML&Root=Systems
```

The results that we see are not quite what we expected:

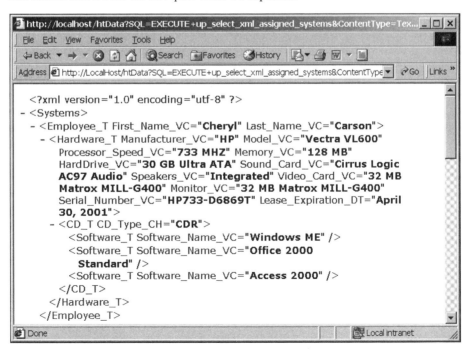

We expected to see that the data from the `Hardware_T` table would be a sub-element under `Employee_T`, and we expected to see that the data from the `CD_T` table would be a sub-element under the `Hardware_T` element. This appears as expected.

What we didn't expect to see is that the data from the `Software_T` table would be a sub-element of `CD_T` element. This is the reason why it is important that you view the structure of the XML data in the Query Analyzer before creating the stored procedure, and also view it in the browser before you start coding your XSL stylesheet. This gives you a better idea of how to set up the `<xsl:for-each>` elements in your XSL stylesheet. We will see how to resolve this issue in a few moments.

How It Works – Assigned Systems Report – Stored Procedure

Keeping in mind the order of the data and how we want it to be displayed, we will select the employees' first and last names first. This will create the top-level element in our XML data.

```
SELECT First_Name_VC, Last_Name_VC,
```

The next set of data that we want to select is from the `Hardware_T` table and will be all of the hardware details that will be displayed in our report. Notice the use of comments in the select list. This is especially useful when dealing with XML data as we can quickly identify how the elements will be nested in the XML output.

We have added comments to the code that formats the lease expiration date to include the format in which the formatted date will be returned:

```
-- Select columns from the Hardware_T table
--
    Manufacturer_VC, Model_VC, Processor_Speed_VC, Memory_VC,
    HardDrive_VC, Sound_Card_VC, Speakers_VC, Video_Card_VC,
    Monitor_VC, Serial_Number_VC,
--
-- Format the Lease_Expiration_DT column as month dd, yyyy
--
    DATENAME(MONTH,Lease_Expiration_DT) + ' ' +
    DATENAME(DAY,Lease_Expiration_DT) + ', ' +
    DATENAME(YEAR,Lease_Expiration_DT) AS 'Lease_Expiration_DT',
```

The next table that we are selecting data from is the `CD_T` table. Here we only need one column of data, the `CD_Type_CH` column.

The last table that we need to select data from is the `Software_T` table. Remember that our system assignment will contain many software titles that have been installed on a particular system. Given this we know that we will need to process all software titles for a particular system and employee, so we select the `Software_Name_VC` column.

The main table that we are selecting data from is the `System_Assignment_T` table. This table contains all of the systems that have been assigned.

The first table that we want to join is the `Employee_T`. This will provide us with the employees' first and last names. This table is joined on the `System_Assignment_T` table:

```
JOIN Employee_T ON System_Assignment_T.Employee_ID =
    Employee_T.Employee_ID
```

The next table to be joined is the `Hardware_T` table. This is where all of our hardware data exists and this table is joined on the `System_Assignment_T` table also:

```
JOIN Hardware_T ON System_Assignment_T.Hardware_ID =
    Hardware_T.Hardware_ID
```

The `CD_T` table is joined to the `Hardware_T` table to retrieve the CD type that is installed on a system:

```
JOIN CD_T ON Hardware_T.CD_ID = CD_T.CD_ID
```

In order to retrieve all of the software titles that have been installed on a system we must join two additional tables. First, in order to get the software title we must first get the `Software_ID` that has been associated with this system. This can be found in the `System_Software_Relationship_T` table, which is joined to the `System_Assignment_T` table:

```
JOIN System_Software_Relationship_T ON
    System_Assignment_T.System_Assignment_ID =
    System_Software_Relationship_T.System_Assignment_ID
```

Then we join the `Software_T` table to the `System_Software_Relationship_T` table using the `Software_ID` in order to get the software title:

```
JOIN Software_T ON System_Software_Relationship_T.Software_ID =
    Software_T.Software_ID
```

We will want to sort the results and we do so using the `ORDER BY` clause. We have specified that the results should be sorted by last name first and first name last.

Finally we specify that the results should be returned as XML data, by including the `FOR XML` clause. Then we code the `GO` command to have the Query Analyzer create this stored procedure before we grant permissions on it.

Try It Out – Assigned Systems Report – XML Template

1. Let's move on now and create the template to execute this stored procedure:

```
<?xml version="1.0" encoding="UTF-8"?>
    <Systems xmlns:sql="urn:schemas-microsoft-com:xml-sql"
        sql:xsl="../ AssignedSystems.xsl">
        <sql:query>
            EXECUTE up_select_xml_assigned_systems
        </sql:query>
    </Hardware>
```

2. Save this XML template as `AssignedSystems.xml` in the `Template` directory under the `htData` virtual directory.

How It Works – Assigned Systems Report – XML Template

Our template starts with the standard XML declaration and then we define the root element, which also contains the SQL namespace and the XSL stylesheet. We have not created the stylesheet yet but we will give it a name of `AssignedSystems.xsl` and place it in the root of the `htData` virtual directory:

```
<?xml version="1.0" encoding="UTF-8"?>
  <Hardware xmlns:sql="urn:schemas-microsoft-com:xml-sql"
      sql:xsl="../ AssignedSystems.xsl">
```

The `<sql:query>` element specifies that we should execute the `up_select_xml_assigned_systems` stored procedure. Then we end the XML template by coding the appropriate closing tags:

```
<sql:query>
    EXECUTE up_select_xml_assigned_systems
</sql:query>
</Hardware>
```

Try It Out – Assigned Systems Report – XSL Stylesheet

Moving on to our XSL stylesheet, the code is presented in the *How It Works* section that follows.

Save this file in the root of the `htData` virtual directory as `AssignedSystems.xsl`.

How It Works – Assigned Systems Report – XSL Stylesheet

We start our stylesheet by including the three standard lines of code that identify this as an XSL stylesheet and that indicate we should process all data from the root of the XML data stream:

```
<?xml version="1.0" encoding="UTF-8"?>
<xsl:stylesheet xmlns:xsl="http://www.w3.org/TR/WD-xsl">
    <xsl:template match = "/">
```

We start building our HTML document within the XSL stylesheet by coding the standard HTML elements that start every HTML document. Once again notice that we have fully qualified the URL to our cascading stylesheet in the `Href` attribute of the `<LINK>` element. You will need to ensure that you replace `WSTravel` with the name of the machine where your SQL Server is running, as explained in earlier chapters:

```
<HTML>
<HEAD>
<TITLE>Beginning SQL Server 2000 for VB Developers</TITLE>
<LINK Rel="StyleSheet" Type="Text/CSS"
Href="http://WSTravel/HardwareTracking/htPageStyles.css"/>
</HEAD>
```

We start the body of our HTML document by coding the `<BODY>` element and then start building a table by entering the `<TABLE>` element. We have specified that the table should display no border lines and that it should stretch to fit the browser window.

The first row in our table contains the table header, which is centered in the browser window. Notice that we have specified that the header should span across two columns in the table by assigning the ColSpan attribute a value of 2:

```
<BODY>
<TABLE Border="0" Width="100%">
    <TR>
        <TH ColSpan="2">
            <CENTER>Assigned Systems</CENTER>
        </TH>
    </TR>
```

We start our processing loop by coding the <xsl:for-each> element and setting the select attribute to select data from the Systems/Employee_T element. We will iterate through all of the XML data in this element. The first column in our table will contain the employees' first and last names.

Notice that we have specified the Nowrap attribute in the <TD> element. This attribute accepts no parameters and would normally be coded without the equal sign. However, to conform to XML standards we must set it to nothing by entering two quote marks. We have also specified that the data in this column be aligned vertically with the top of the column, as indicated by the Valign attribute. Finally we have specified that the HTML in this column be formatted using the NormalText style from our cascading stylesheet, as indicated by the Class attribute.

The employees' first and last names will be placed in this column because we have specified the <xsl:value-of> elements to select the First_Name_VC and Last_Name_VC elements from the XML data:

```
<xsl:for-each select="Systems/Employee_T">
    <TR>
        <TD Nowrap="" Valign="Top" Class="NormalText">
            <xsl:value-of select="@First_Name_VC"/>
            <xsl:value-of select="@Last_Name_VC"/>
        </TD>
```

The second column in our table will contain all of the data that will be displayed and hidden. The first thing that we do in this column is to define a label, using the <LABEL> element. Just as we did in the last exercise we will handle the onMouseOver, onMouseOut, and onClick events.

The onMouseOver and onMouseOut events will change the className to alternate between the RedText style and the BlueText style as the mouse pointer is moved in and out of the <LABEL> element. The onClick event will execute the HideShow function in our client-side script:

```
<TD>
    <LABEL Class="BlueText"
        onMouseOver="this.className='RedText'"
        onMouseOut="this.className='BlueText'"
        onClick="HideShow()">
```

Because the Hardware_T element is a sub-element of Employee_T we must include another <xsl:for-each> element to process this data, which we have done here. The <xsl:value-of> elements will place data for the manufacturer, model, processor speed, and memory in the <LABEL> element. We then end the <xsl:for-each> element and the <LABEL> element:

```
            <xsl:for-each select="Hardware_T">
              <xsl:value-of select="@Manufacturer_VC"/>
              <xsl:value-of select="@Model_VC"/>,
              <xsl:value-of select="@Processor_Speed_VC"/>
              with
              <xsl:value-of select="@Memory_VC"/> of memory
            </xsl:for-each>

          </LABEL>
```

The data that will be initially hidden is placed inside a <SPAN> element just as it was in the last exercise. We have specified that the HTML displayed inside the <SPAN> element be formatted using the NormalText style, as indicated by the Class attribute. We have also set the display property of the Style attribute so the <SPAN> element is initially hidden.

Again we have specified the <xsl:for-each> element to display the rest of the data from the Hardware_T element:

```
          <SPAN Class="NormalText" Style="display:none;">

            <xsl:for-each select="Hardware_T">
```

The first <DIV> element that we define inside the <SPAN> element will contain the first line of HTML that we want to display. This will consist of data from the <xsl:value-of> element and static text. Notice that we have included another <xsl:for-each> element here to select the data for the CD type, and have terminated the element after selecting the CD type:

```
            <DIV Style="margin-left:25px">
              <xsl:value-of select="@HardDrive_VC"/>
               hardrive and
              <xsl:for-each select="CD_T">
                 <xsl:value-of select="@CD_Type_CH"/>
              </xsl:for-each>
            </DIV>
```

The next several <DIV> elements are a repeat of the <DIV> elements from the last exercise. These elements simply format the data to be displayed and use the <xsl:value-of> elements to select the XML data:

```
            <DIV Style="margin-left:25px">
              <xsl:value-of select = "@Video_Card_VC"/>
              video card and <xsl:value-of select="@Monitor_VC"/>
              monitor
            </DIV>

            <DIV Style="margin-left:25px">
              <xsl:value-of select="@Sound_Card_VC"/>
              sound card and <xsl:value-of select="@Speakers_VC"/>
              speakers
            </DIV>
```

```
<DIV Style="margin-left:25px">
   Serial number
   <xsl:value-of select="@Serial_Number_VC"/>,
   Lease expiration
   <xsl:value-of select="@Lease_Expiration_DT"/>
</DIV>
```

We mentioned earlier that we would display the software titles as a sub-element of the hardware. Given that, we define a new <LABEL> element that will identify the software. This element will handle the onMouseOver, onMouseOut, and onClick events just as we did in the last <LABEL> element that we defined.

```
<LABEL Class="BlueText"
    onMouseOver="this.className='RedText'"
    onMouseOut="this.className='BlueText'"
    onClick="HideShow()">
Software</LABEL><BR/>
```

The <SPAN> element for this label is also hidden by default, as indicated by the Style attribute.

The <DIV> element for this label includes the <xsl:for-each> element so we can iterate through the Software_T elements in the CD_T element. Notice that we have qualified the select attribute with CD_T to ensure that we iterate through all of the Software_T elements.

Lastly we code the closing tag for the <SPAN> element:

```
<SPAN Class="NormalText" Style="display:none;">

    <DIV Style="margin-left:25px">
       <xsl:for-each
       select="CD_T/Software_T">
           <xsl:value-of select="@Software_Name_VC"/>,
       </xsl:for-each>
    </DIV>

</SPAN>
```

We code the closing tags for the <xsl:for-each> element that selects hardware data and then close the <SPAN> element for the hardware:

```
</xsl:for-each>
</SPAN>
```

We then code the closing tag for the column, the row, and the <xsl:for-each> element that was used to iterate through the Employee_T element. Then we close the table:

```
</TD>
</TR>
</xsl:for-each>
</TABLE>
```

647

Just as we have done in the last two exercises, we include a paragraph that allows the user to navigate back to the `Default.htm` web page so that they may select other reports:

```
<P>
    <B Class="BlueText" onMouseOver="this.className='RedText'"
       onMouseOut="this.className='BlueText'"
       onclick="window.history.back();">Return To Menu</B>
</P>
```

We start the code for our client-side script next. Again we have enclosed the actual code inside the `<xsl:comment>` element and the `<![CDATA[]]>` section. Remember that this makes the code opaque to the XML parser so no errors will be encountered in this code.

```
<SCRIPT Language="JavaScript" TYPE="Text/JavaScript">
    <xsl:comment><![CDATA[
```

The `HideShow` function in this script is a little different from that which was shown in the last exercise. This time we will not automatically hide the `<SPAN>` elements that are visible. This allows the user to compare the software installed on one machine against the software that is installed on another machine.

The first thing that we do in this function is to declare a couple of variables that access the `<SPAN>` element collection and the `<LABEL>` element collection:

```
function HideShow()
{
    // Declare an object for the collection of Span
    // and Label elements
    var oSpan = document.all.tags("SPAN");
    var oLabel = document.all.tags("LABEL");
```

Next, we loop through all of the elements in the `<LABEL>` element collection. The first thing that we do in this loop is to check the `className` of each label in the collection. If the `className` of the label is set to the `RedText` style then we know that this is the label that is highlighted and has been clicked. This check applies to both the label that displays the `Hardware` and the label that displays the `Software`.

```
    // Loop through the label elements collection
    for (i=0; i<oLabel.length; i++)
    {
        // If the className attribute is RedText then
        // process the Span object
        if (oLabel[i].className == "RedText")
        {
```

If the `display` property of the `style` attribute for the `<SPAN>` element is currently set to nothing, meaning it is being displayed, then we set the `display` property to `none`, which will cause the `<SPAN>` element to be hidden. Otherwise we set the `display` property to nothing, as indicated by two quotes, causing the `<SPAN>` element to be shown.

```
            // If the display style is on
            if (oSpan[i].style.display == "")
            {
```

```
                // Hide it
                oSpan[i].style.display = "none";
            }
            else
            {
                // Show it
                oSpan[i].style.display = "";
            }
        }
    }
}
```

We end our script code by coding the closing tags:

```
    ]]></xsl:comment>
</SCRIPT>
```

We then end our HTML document and our stylesheet:

```
</BODY>
</HTML>
    </xsl:template>
</xsl:stylesheet>
```

Try It Out – Assigned Systems Report – Web Page and Testing

We now want to move on and modify the `Default.htm` web page and add the URL to this newest report.

1. Add the following code after that for the hardware report. We have once again used the `onMouseOver` and `onMouseOut` events to display the report name in the status bar of the browser. Remember to substitute your machine name in the URL.

```
<TR>
    <TD><A Href="http://WSTravel/htData/Template/
        AssignedSystems.xml?ContentType=Text/HTML" Class="BlueText"
        onMouseOver="window.status='Assigned Systems';return true;"
        onMouseOut="window.status='';return true;">
        Assigned Systems</A></TD>
</TR>
```

2. Save your `Default.htm` web page and then run the Hardware Tracking program. Select the Online Reports menu item on the Tools menu to display the `Default.htm` web page. Your `Default.htm` web page should now look like the one shown in the next figure. Notice that when the mouse pointer hovers over the Assigned Systems text this text is also displayed in the status bar:

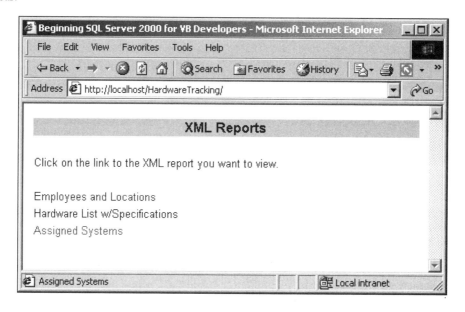

3. Click on the Assigned Systems text to view this report. The screen below appears and lists all employees that have a system assigned to them:

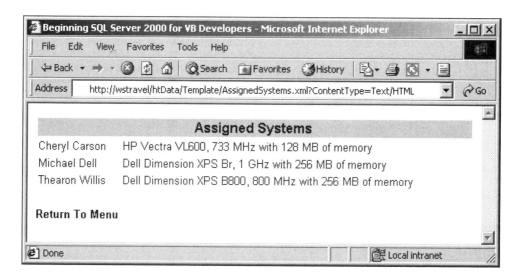

4. If you hover your mouse pointer over the blue text, the text will turn red, and if you click on it the hardware details will be displayed. The figure below shows the hardware details for one of the employees:

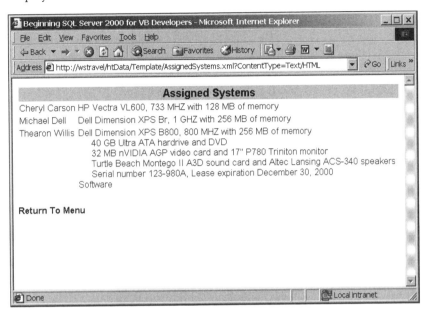

5. Notice that the text **Software** is now displayed and is rendered using the `BlueText` style. Clicking on this text will display the software that has been installed on this system, as shown in the next figure:

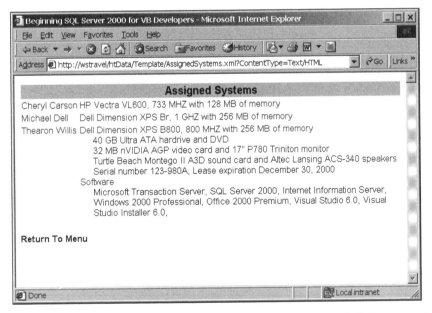

Listing the **Software** under the **Hardware** details gives the user a means to drill down into the data.

The <xsl:for-each> Element

The XSL <xsl:for-each> element is like an ADO recordset that has a static cursor. Remember that a static cursor allows us to navigate the recordset both forwards and backwards and to process it as many times as necessary. The <xsl:for-each> element allows us to process all of the elements in the XML data. The <xsl:for-each> element handles the beginning-of-file and end-of-file conditions automatically behind the scenes. All we need to do is specify this element and process the XML data. To terminate the loop we code the closing tag of </xsl:for-each>.

So where does the analogy of a static ADO recordset come into play? After we have iterated through all of the XML data using the <xsl:for-each> element we can turn around and use exactly the same <xsl:for-each> element statement to process the data again. Using ADO we would have processed the data in the Recordset object until an end-of-file condition occurred. We would then have to execute the MoveFirst method of the Recordset object before processing the data in the Recordset object again.

The <xsl:for-each> element handles all of this for us behind the scenes, allowing us to process all of the XML data and then code an identical <xsl:for-each> element and process the data again. We will get a chance to see this first hand in the next and last XML web report that we create.

The Software report that we want to create now will display a list of all software categories in a combo box. When the user selects a category in the combo box we will display the appropriate software titles associated with that category. The following screenshot shows this:

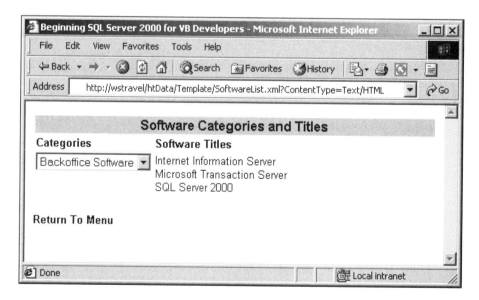

Once again we will use the <SPAN> element to build the various lists of software titles and these elements will be hidden until the appropriate category has been chosen.

Try It Out – Software Report – Stored Procedure

The stored procedure that we need to create to select the software titles and categories is listed below:

```
CREATE PROCEDURE dbo.up_select_xml_software AS

SELECT Software_Category_T.Software_Category_ID, Software_Category_VC,
    Software_Name_VC
FROM Software_Category_T

    JOIN Software_T ON Software_Category_T.Software_Category_ID
        = Software_T.Software_Category_ID

    ORDER BY Software_Category_VC, Software_Name_VC

    FOR XML AUTO

GO

GRANT EXECUTE ON up_select_xml_software TO [Hardware Users]
```

How It Works – Software Report – Stored Procedure

Remember our discussion from the last section? We talked about the order of the columns in the select list. In this stored procedure we are selecting the software category data first and then the software titles. This is the reverse of the relationship between the `Software_T` and `Software_Category_T` tables. Your first instinct would be to select the software first and all associated categories.

However, when you do this and view the XML data produced you see that the data is not presented in the order that you want. So you need to experiment with the order of the columns in your select list and view the XML data produced until you have the desired results.

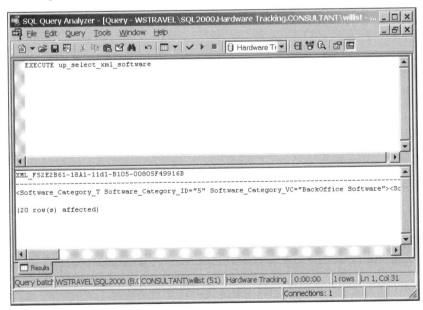

The main table that we are selecting data from is the `Software_Category_T` table. We then join the `Software_T` table to get all software titles assigned to the categories that are specified first in the select list:

```
JOIN Software_T ON Software_Category_T.Software_Category_ID
    = Software_T.Software_Category_ID
```

The `ORDER BY` clause will sort the results by the category name first and the software title last. We have also specified that the data be returned as XML data by coding the `FOR XML` clause.

We code the `GO` command to have the Query Analyzer create the stored procedure before applying permissions on it.

Try It Out – Software Report – XML Template

Moving on, we want to create our XML template next. This template is like every other XML template that we have created.

1. The first line of code in the template is the XML declaration. The second line of code specifies the root element of `Software`, the SQL namespace, and the XSL stylesheet, which we will create next. The `<sql:query>` element specifies the stored procedure that will be executed:

```
<?xml version="1.0" encoding="UTF-8"?>
    <Software xmlns:sql="urn:schemas-microsoft-com:xml-sql"
        sql:xsl="../SoftwareList.xsl">
        <sql:query>
            EXECUTE up_select_xml_software
        </sql:query>
    </Software>
```

2. Save this template as `SoftwareList.xml` in the `Template` directory of the `htData` virtual directory.

Try It Out – Software Report – XSL Stylesheet

The XSL stylesheet to process the XML data and produce our HTML document is very straightforward. The code is presented throughout the *How It Works* section.

Save this file in the root `htData` virtual directory as `SoftwareList.xsl`.

How It Works – Software Report – XSL Stylesheet

The first three lines of our XSL template are the standard lines that we have seen before and simply specify that this is an XSL stylesheet and should process all data from the root element:

```
<?xml version="1.0" encoding="UTF-8"?>
<xsl:stylesheet xmlns:xsl="http://www.w3.org/TR/WD-xsl">
    <xsl:template match = "/">
```

We start our HTML code in this XSL stylesheet by coding the standard HTML elements and header information. We set the title to be displayed in the browser's title bar and link in the cascading stylesheet. Remember to substitute your machine name.

```
<HTML>
<HEAD>
<TITLE>Beginning SQL Server 2000 for VB Developers</TITLE>
<LINK Rel="StyleSheet" Type="Text/CSS"
Href="http://WSTravel/HardwareTracking/htPageStyles.css"/>
</HEAD>
```

We start the body of the HTML document by building a table. Again we have specified that this table should expand and contract to fill 100 percent of the browser window.

The first row of data in this table is the table header. Notice that this header will span across three columns in the table, as specified by the `ColSpan` attribute:

```
<BODY>
<TABLE Border="0" Width="100%">
    <TR>
        <TH ColSpan="3">
            <CENTER>Software Categories and Titles</CENTER>
        </TH>
    </TR>
```

The second row of our table identifies the columns and uses the `NormalText` style. We have, however, specified the `<B>` element so the text will be rendered bold:

```
    <TR Class="NormalText">
        <TD>
            <B>Categories</B>
        </TD>
        <TD>
            <B>Software Titles</B>
        </TD>
    </TR>
```

The third row of data in our table is where the core of our code is. The first column in this row will contain a combo box, as indicated by the HTML `<SELECT>` element. The `<SELECT>` element can be used as a combo box that has a dropdown list that only allows one selection, or a list box that allows multiple selections. Without the `Size` attribute set the `<SELECT>` element represents a combo box, which is what we are using here. We have specified the `Name` attribute so we can access this element by name in our client-side script. We have also specified that we want to handle the `onChange` event for this HTML element and that we want to execute the `HideShow` function when the item selected changes:

```
    <TR>
        <TD VAlign="Top">
            <SELECT Name="cboCategories" onChange="HideShow()">
```

The `<xsl:for-each>` element will iterate through all of the XML data:

```
            <xsl:for-each select="Software/Software_Category_T">
```

655

Inside of the `<xsl:for-each>` element we have defined the `<OPTION>` HTML element. This element represents an option in the `<SELECT>` element. We can assign a numeric value to the `<OPTION>` element and specify the text that it should display.

Using the `<xsl:attribute>` element we are able to specify that this element should represent the `Value` attribute of the `<OPTION>` element. Then using the `<xsl:value-of>` element and setting the `select` attribute for this element to select the data from the `Software_Category_ID`, we are able to set the `Value` attribute of the `<xsl:attribute>` element.

Using the next `<xsl:value-of>` element we are able to set the text for the `<OPTION>` element. Then, conforming to XML standards, we code the closing tag for the `<OPTION>` element. In normal HTML this element does not require a closing tag.

```
<OPTION>
    <xsl:attribute name="Value">
        <xsl:value-of select="@Software_Category_ID"/>
    </xsl:attribute>
    <xsl:value-of select="@Software_Category_VC"/>
</OPTION>
```

We then terminate the `<xsl:for-each>` element, the `<SELECT>` element, and then finally this column. At this point we have iterated through all of the data in the XML `Software/Software_Category_T` element.

```
        </xsl:for-each>
        </SELECT>
    </TD>
```

Having iterated through all of the data in the XML `Software/Software_Category_T` element to load the combo box, we want to perform this loop again and process all of the software. This is the beauty of XSL, as it will take care of all of the details of repositioning the pointers back to the first element in our XML data, so we can process the data again without having to do anything.

We enter another `<xsl:for-each>` element and specify the same attributes as we did above:

```
    <TD>
        <xsl:for-each select="Software/Software_Category_T">
```

For each pass through the loop we build a `<SPAN>` element that has its `Class` attribute set to the `NormalText` style and the `display` property of the `style` attribute set to `none`. This will cause the `<SPAN>` element to be hidden.

Within the `<SPAN>` element we code a `<DIV>` element that has its `NoWrap` attribute specified. We then code another `<xsl:for-each>` element, this time selecting data from the `Software_T` element. This allows us to select all software titles for this category.

We place each software title in the `<DIV>` element and enter the `<BR>` element after the software title to cause a line break. This ensures that each software title is on its own line. Notice that we have specified the `<BR>` element and its closing tag all in one element. This can be accomplished by including a forward slash at the end of the element:

```
        <SPAN Class="NormalText" Style="display:none;">
            <DIV NoWrap="">
                <xsl:for-each select="Software_T">
                    <xsl:value-of select="@Software_Name_VC"/><BR/>
```

We end the `<xsl:for-each>` element that is the inner loop that is displaying our software titles for this category. We then code the closing tags for the `<DIV>` and `<SPAN>` elements. Next we end the outer loop by coding the closing tag for the `<xsl:for-each>` element that is processing our categories. Finally we end the column:

```
                    </xsl:for-each>
                </DIV>
            </SPAN>
            </xsl:for-each>
        </TD>
```

Because we have so little text to be displayed and we have specified that the table should expand and contract as the browser is resized, we need to code a filler column. If we did not, the little text that we do have for the software would move to the left and right in the browser window.

By coding a filler column that has the `Width` attribute set to `100%`, this column will act as a filler and will not allow the software displayed in the `Software` column to move from left to right. We also need to enter some data in this column, otherwise HTML and XSL will remove the white space, leaving us with an empty column. In that case this column would not have the effect that we desire.

To that end we have inserted a line break in the column by coding the `<BR>` element.

One last note about the `Width` attribute on the `<TD>` element: by entering a width of `100%`, this column will fill up any unused space in the table row.

We end this column, the row, and finally the table, by coding the appropriate tags:

```
        <TD Width="100%"><BR/></TD>
    </TR>
</TABLE>
```

We include the standard paragraph that contains the navigation for the user to return to the `Default.htm` web page:

```
<P>
    <B Class="BlueText" onMouseOver="this.className='RedText'"
        onMouseOut="this.className='BlueText'"
        onclick="window.history.back();">Return To Menu</B>
</P>
```

Our client-side JavaScript is a little different again. We have used the same function name as it accurately describes what this function is doing. We have specified the `<xsl:comment>` element and the `<![CDATA[]]>` section so the XML parser will ignore our script and not cause any errors:

```
<SCRIPT Language="JavaScript" TYPE="Text/JavaScript">
    <xsl:comment><![CDATA[
    function HideShow()
    {
```

We have defined two variables and set them. The first is for the collection of <SPAN> elements, which we have seen before. The second variable is for the combo box. Here we have specified the item collection of the document.all collection and have specified an item name of cboCategories, which is the name assigned to our combo box:

```
// Declare an object for the collection of Span elements
// and an object for the cboCategories element
var oSpan = document.all.tags("SPAN");
var oSelect = document.all.item("cboCategories");
```

The first thing that we want to do is to loop through the collection of <SPAN> elements and hide them, by setting the display property of the style attribute to none. Since we don't know which <SPAN> element is shown we simply process them all. This is the most efficient method, and uses less code than trying to identify which <SPAN> element is visible and only setting that element's style attribute.

```
// Loop through the span elements collection
// and hide all span elements
for (i=0; i<oSpan.length; i++)
{
    oSpan[i].style.display = "none";
}
```

The selectedIndex property of the combo box returns an integer value of the index for the item selected in the combo box. This means that if the first item is selected then the selectedIndex property will be set to 0, if the second item is selected it will return a 1 in the selectedIndex property, and so on.

Using the selectedIndex property of the combo box we are able to access the correct item in the <SPAN> element array because it is also a zero-based array and the <SPAN> elements match the items in the combo box one-for-one. We then set the display property of the style attribute to nothing, as indicated by the two quotes.

We then end our script by coding the appropriate tags:

```
    // Display the correct span element
    oSpan[oSelect.selectedIndex].style.display = "";
    }
  ]]></xsl:comment>
</SCRIPT>
```

The next client-side script that we have will execute when the window loads and will only execute once. By specifying the For attribute of the <SCRIPT> element we bind this script to a specific object, in this case the window object. The Event attribute specifies the event the script is written for, in this case the onload event. The onload event gets fired immediately after the browser loads the window. This means that the window completes loading first and then the onload event is fired.

```
<SCRIPT Language="JavaScript" TYPE="Text/JavaScript"
    For="window" Event="onload">
    <xsl:comment><![CDATA[
```

By default the first `<OPTION>` element in the `<SELECT>` element is displayed. This is fine, however, all of our `<SPAN>` elements are hidden. What we want to do here is to call the `HideShow` function, which will show the software for the first option.

```
      // Show the correct Span element for the first Option
      // in the cboCategories Select element
      HideShow();
      ]]></xsl:comment>
   </SCRIPT>
```

We end our XSL stylesheet by coding the appropriate closing HTML and XSL tags:

```
   </BODY>
   </HTML>
      </xsl:template>
   </xsl:stylesheet>
```

Try It Out – Software Report – Web Page and Testing

We want to make one final change to the `Default.htm` web page in the `HardwareTracking` virtual directory.

1. Add the code shown below between that for the hardware list and assigned systems reports:

```
   <TR>
      <TD><A Href="http://WSTravel/htData/Template/
      SoftwareList.xml?ContentType=Text/HTML" Class="BlueText"
      onMouseOver="window.status='Software Categories and Titles';return true;"
      onMouseOut="window.status='';return true;">
      Software Categories and Titles</A></TD>
   </TR>
```

2. Save the `Default.htm` web page and then run the Hardware Tracking program. Again select the **Online Reports** menu item on the **Tools** menu to display the `Default.htm` web page in a browser. Your final `Default.htm` web page should now look like this:

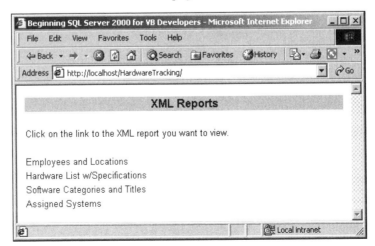

3. Click on the Software Categories and Titles hyperlink to view the software report. The first category in the combo box should be displayed along with the appropriate software titles for this category:

The appropriate software titles are displayed as you click on an entry in the combo box or use the up and down arrow keys to select entries. This is because we used the onChange event instead of the onClick event. The onClick event would not handle the changes when the user used the arrow keys to navigate through the entries in the combo box.

This completes the four web reports. We now have a useful application that can be used to allow users to view the formatted data from the hardware tracking database on an intranet site.

Summary

This chapter has taken a broader look at creating XML web reports using some of the more robust features of XSL, HTML, and DHTML. Having gone through the various exercises we have created more sophisticated reports than we did in the last chapter.

Through the use of a cascading stylesheet we have defined and applied various styles to our HTML. You should have a better appreciation of how to create the various styles, and what can be accomplished with them. We have seen how, through the use of styles, we can have regular text look and act like an actual hyperlink.

Through the use of cascading styles and XSL script we were able to alternate styles in the HTML elements as they were being built. We saw this in the Employees and Locations report. Through the use of client-side script we saw how we could manipulate our HTML, thus making a dynamic web page. We used the various properties and attributes of the HTML elements to hide and show the correct elements on our page.

We saw how we could use XSL elements to evaluate and test data, to control what data was displayed, and to control the use of styles in our HTML. You should now be familiar with these elements and know how they can be applied in various situations to make your XML reports more sophisticated.

In summary, you should know:

- ❑ How to code and use XSL and client-side script
- ❑ How to use the `<xsl:choose>` element to perform conditional processing
- ❑ How to code and use styles in a cascading stylesheet
- ❑ That you need to test your stored procedures to ensure the columns in the select list are in the order that you need and expect them to be
- ❑ How to handle HTML element events, such as the `onMouseOver` event
- ❑ How to create and handle DHTML

This concludes the chapters in this book, but the learning process will continue in the case study that follows. The first part of the case study takes a look at how you can use English Query to implement a friendly web interface that allows your users to use natural English statements to ask questions. The questions are translated by the English Query engine and turned into SQL statements that are executed. The results are then returned to the user and displayed in a web page. The second part of the case study ties into this and shows you how to deploy your English Query application on the Web.

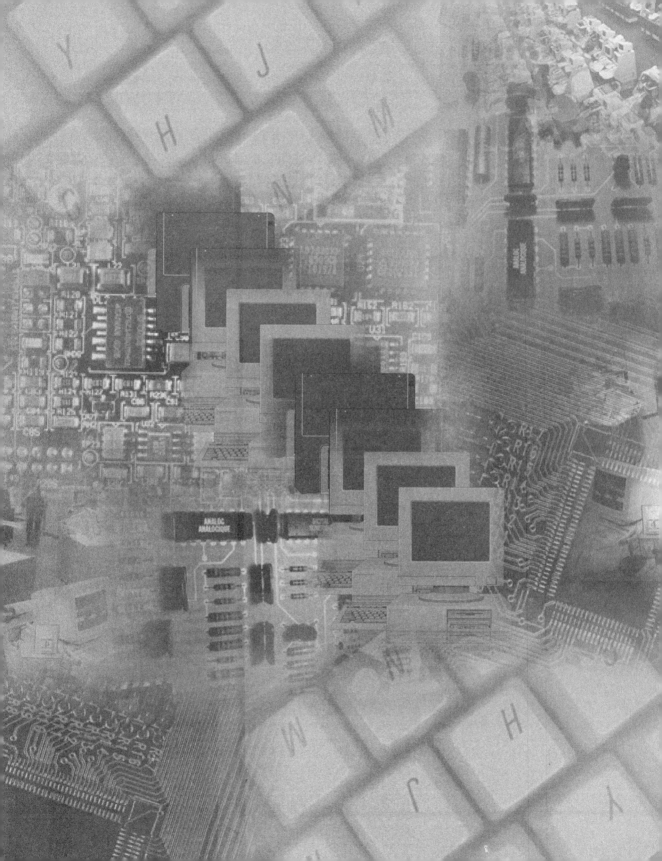

Case Study Part 1
Building an English Query Application

With all the technology that we as developers have at our disposal, we often still find it hard to provide our end users with an ad hoc reporting tool that meets their needs. Microsoft **English Query** helps to solve this problem. It provides us with a tool that enables us to build models from our SQL Server databases, which allow the end users to query the database using natural English statements.

A user can ask a question such as *"Who works at the Home Office?"* and they will get the appropriate data returned and formatted for them. The end user no longer has to learn complicated SQL statements to query the database in order to get the information that they need, because with English Query they can use natural English statements that form a statement or question.

This case study takes a look at the development of an English Query application using entities and relationships, which we will define shortly. As we walk through the development of this application, we will be performing regular tests so that you can obtain a deeper understanding of entities and relationships.

So, in this part of the case study we will:

- ❑   Install English Query
- ❑   Examine how English Query works
- ❑   Examine entities and relationships
- ❑   Build and test an English Query model

English Query Installation

The installation process for English Query is fairly quick and straightforward. You will need your SQL Server installation CD to install English Query. The prerequisites for installing English Query are simple. You need Windows 9x, Windows NT 4.0 (with Service Pack 6 or later), or Windows 2000, 40 MB of free disk space, and Microsoft Internet Explorer 5.0 or later.

To install English Query:

1. Insert the SQL Server 2000 installation CD. If AutoRun is not enabled, or if you are installing from a network, double-click on the AutoRun.exe program in the root of the CD or installation folder to start the installation process.

The following screen appears:

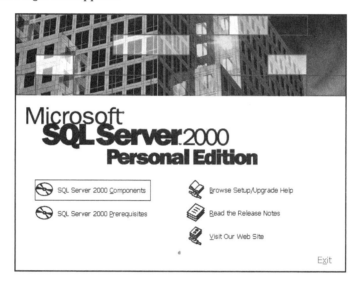

2. Click on the SQL Server 2000 Components option, the following screen will then appear:

3. Click on the Install English Query option to proceed. You are then prompted with the following Welcome screen:

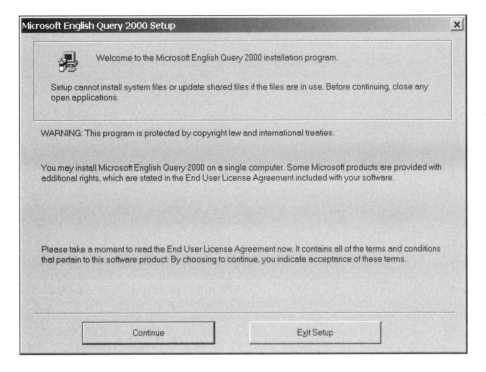

4. Click on the Continue button to proceed with the installation.

5. Read the license agreement – if you agree and want to continue with the installation, click on the I Agree button:

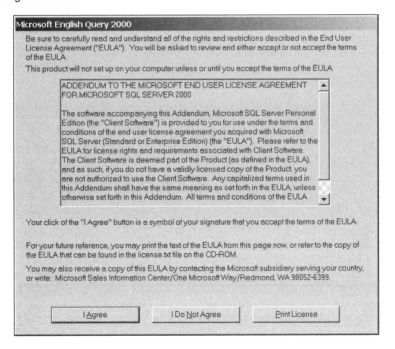

6. The setup screen prompts you for the type of installation to be performed and the location where you want the files to be installed:

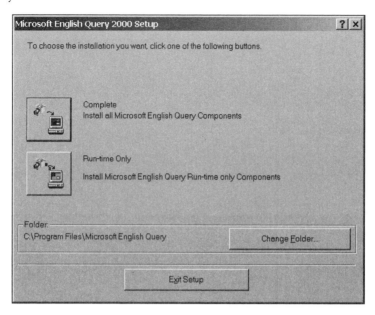

Clicking on the **Complete** button will start the installation and perform a complete installation. Clicking on the **Run-time Only** button will start the installation, but will only install the run-time files. This would be the option to select if you wanted to install English Query on a web server or client machine.

If you wanted to change the installation folder for English Query, you would click on the **Change Folder** button and choose the appropriate drive and/or folder.

At this point we want to perform a complete installation so click on the **Complete** button.

7. Once the installation starts, you just need to sit back and wait.

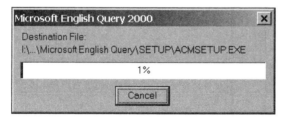

While you are waiting, it should be noted that Microsoft is moving towards integrating all development tools into a single development environment. To that end it has integrated this release of English Query in the Visual InterDev IDE. The Visual InterDev IDE is the development environment that is used to create HTML web pages, Active Server Pages, and cascading style sheets. The Visual InterDev IDE is not a prerequisite for installing English Query, because if it is not already installed, it will be installed and the appropriate menu items will be added for English Query.

8. Once the installation is complete, you will see the following completion dialog:

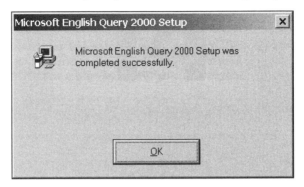

9. Click OK to dismiss the dialog – at this point the installation is complete. Then click the Exit hyperlink on the Install Components dialog.

English Query Overview

As we mentioned earlier, English Query is a tool that allows you to create a model that represents the **entities** and **relationships** in your database. Using this model the end user can ask questions using natural English to get the answers that they need.

When we talk about an entity we are referring to an object that is a noun (in other words, a person, place, or thing). The tables in your database represent entities of this sort. For example, suppose we had a Customer table. We could define an entity called customer and use that entity to represent the customers in the Customer table. Sometimes entities refer to the columns in your table. In the case of a Customer table we could define an entity called Customer Name, to represent the first and last name of a customer.

In order to tie the Customer and Customer Name entities together, we define what is called a relationship. Relationships are defined as concise statements, such as "*Customer Names are the names of Customers*". This forms the relationship between the Customer Name entity and the Customer entity.

Each relationship that you define uses a **phrase**, which expresses how the relationship defines the entities. These phrases define how the questions asked, such as "*What are the names of customers?*", will be answered. This question would use the relationship defined between the Customer Name and Customer entities to list all customer names.

In the figure overleaf, we see how the Customer and Customer Name entities are represented, and also the relationship between these entities. We also see that an entity of City has been defined, and that two separate relationships between the Customer entity and the City entity have also been defined:

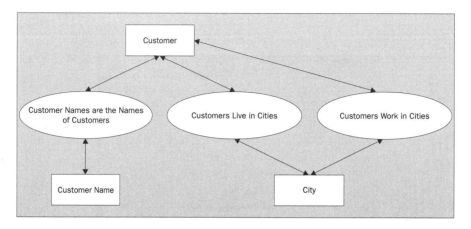

We define as many relationships as are necessary to answer the types of questions that a user may ask. Here we have defined a relationship of `Customers Live in Cities`, which will help to answer the question "*Which customers live in Paris?*". With `Paris` being the city name, English Query would look for the customers who have `Paris` listed as their city.

We have also defined the relationship `Customers Work in Cities`, which would then allow us to ask a question such as "*Which customers work in Paris?*".

When we choose a phrasing for a relationship there are several options to choose from:

❑ If we are choosing a name type relationship, we would choose the **Name/ID Phrasing** phrase, which allows us define the relationship for the `Customer Name` entity that was shown in the previous figure.

❑ If we wanted to specify that customers have something, we could use the **Trait Phrasing** phrase to define a relationship, such as `Customers have Addresses`. This would define a relationship between the `Customer` entity and the `Address` entity, which is not shown in the previous figure.

❑ Using the **Preposition Phrasing** phrase we can define a relationship between two entities that defines one entity as the subject and the other entity as the preposition of the subject. For example, we could define a relationship such as `Cities are in States`.

❑ The **Adjective Phrasing** phrase creates a relationship in which an entity is described by an adjective. An example of this would be `City is hot`. You could use this type of phrasing to describe the climate for each city.

❑ **Subset Phrasing** is used to describe the relationship in which one entity or word is a subset of another entity. Using the phrasing `Some customers are doctors`, we define that doctors are a subset of customers.

❑ To create a relationship where an entity acts, we use the **Verb Phrasing** phrase. Using verb phrasing, we can define a relationship such as `Customers buy products`, which defines a relationship between `Customers` and `Products`.

❑ Finally, **Command Phrasing** can be used to define custom phrasings where entities are not always defined by a table or column in the database. For example, you could create a command phrasing that prints a file, by specifying `Print <file>`.

What we have seen here is that we define our entities from the tables and columns in our database. We then use the different types of phrasings to define the relationships between entities that will answer the questions asked by the user.

English Query and Visual InterDev Integration

As we mentioned during the installation of English Query, the English Query development environment is integrated into Visual InterDev, so let's take a look at how English Query operates in the development environment. The following figure shows all of the various components that make up the English Query development environment:

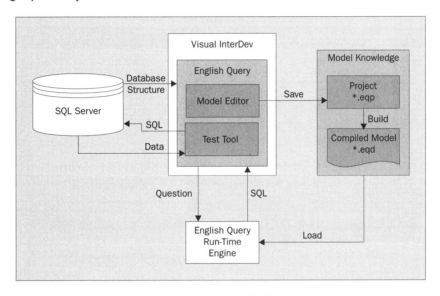

English Query retrieves the database structure from SQL Server so that it has information about your tables and columns and also about the relationships between your tables.

Using the **Model Editor**, you can build the entities and relationships that will answer the questions that the users are most likely to ask. In order to test your English Query project you must save it and compile it. This is done automatically when you run the English Query **Test Tool**. The compilation of your project produces a compiled model that is loaded by the English Query run-time engine.

When you use the Test Tool and ask a question, the question is sent to the English Query run-time engine, which loads the compiled model. It translates the question into SQL statements, which are passed back to the Test Tool. In turn, the Test Tool passes the SQL statements to SQL Server for execution. The results are then passed back from SQL Server to the Test Tool and the results are then displayed.

Having covered the basics of English Query, let's move on and create an English Query application for the Hardware Tracking database. This will give you a greater appreciation of what English Query can do, and will also allow you to gain a greater understanding of entities, relationships, and phrasings.

Creating an English Query Application

The English Query application that we will create here will answer basic questions about our employees, hardware, assigned systems, and software (using the project that we have been developing throughout the book). As we walk through the process of building the application, we will periodically stop and test the entities and relationships that we have defined.

This allows us to create entities and relationships and then see how they are actually used by English Query to answer the questions that you ask. It will also help you to better understand how relationships are used to relate two separate entities.

To begin creating this application:

1. Start Visual InterDev. If you already have Visual InterDev installed, it will be in the program folder that you installed it in. If not, you can go to **Programs** from the **Start** button and then to **Microsoft SQL Server**. Then go to the **English Query** folder and click on **Microsoft English Query**.

2. Depending on your settings, Visual InterDev may or may not prompt you for a new project. If it does not, then click on the **New Project** icon on the toolbar. Next, click on **English Query Projects** in the **New Project** dialog:

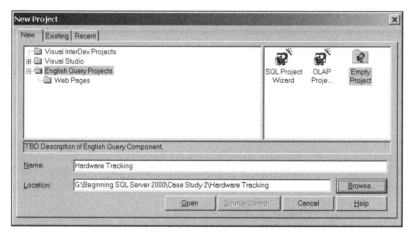

We could choose the **SQL Project Wizard**, shown in the right-hand pane of the **New Project** dialog, which would automatically read the database structure for our database, and create the entities and relationships for us. Then we could go in and modify or add new entities and relationships as we see fit.

The second option is the **OLAP Project Wizard**, which would automatically create an English Query application from your OLAP data stores.

The third option, which is the one we want, creates an empty English Query project. This allows us to define and create our own entities and relationships. Click on the **Empty Project** option.

3. Enter a project name in the Name text box and then choose the location where this English Query project should be created in the Location text box. Once you are done, click on the Open button.

4. Your project window in Visual InterDev should now look like the one shown in the following figure. The first thing that we want to do is to change the project properties. Right-click on the project name in the Project Explorer window and choose Hardware Tracking Properties from the context menu, or click on the Project menu and then choose the Hardware Tracking Properties menu item.

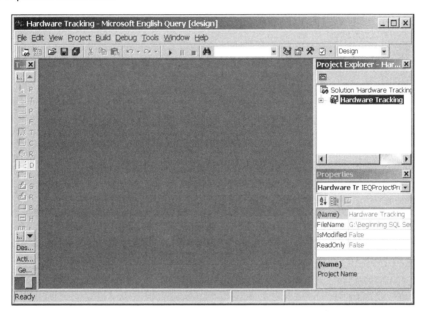

5. The Project Properties dialog has three tabs, the first being the Data Connection tab. This is where we want to focus our attention right now. If you notice, in this figure, we have no connection defined to SQL Server at this point. We need to define a connection so that English Query can read the structure of our database. Click on the Change button for SQL Connection to invoke the Data Link Properties dialog:

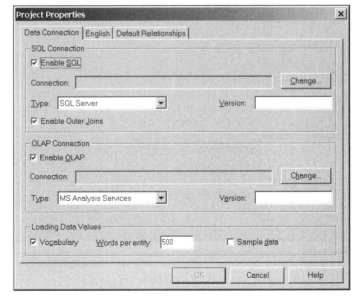

6. On the Provider tab we need to choose the appropriate provider for our connection, so choose the Microsoft OLE DB Provider for SQL Server as shown in the figure. Once you have chosen this provider, click on the Next button at the bottom of the dialog:

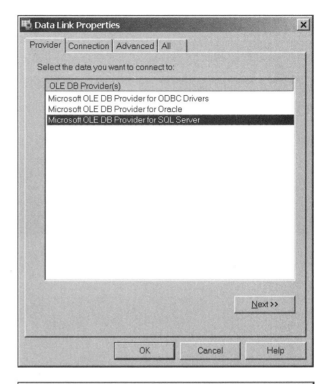

7. There are three points or steps on the Connection tab. The first step enables us to choose the instance of SQL Server that contains our Hardware Tracking database. If you select the drop down button and no SQL Servers are listed in the drop down list, you will need to manually enter the SQL Server name. This is the machine name where SQL Server is installed. Notice in the figure that I have also specified the instance name of SQL Server as I have multiple instances of SQL Server installed on the same machine. If you are running Windows 9x you will not see any SQL Servers listed in the drop down list.

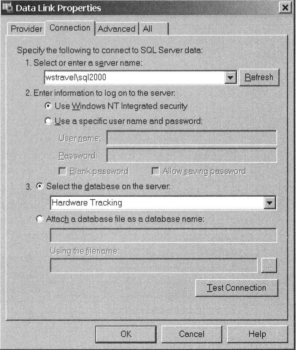

8. The second step of this tab prompts you for your login to SQL Server. If you are using Windows NT authentication, then check the first option. If you are using SQL Server authentication then check the second option and enter your User name and Password. Use the User name and Password that you have been using throughout the book.

9. The third step is to select the Hardware Tracking database.

10. Once you have completed these steps, you can test the connection by clicking on the Test Connection button. You should receive a message indicating that the test connection succeeded.

The Attach a database file as a database name option is used when using a database from SQL Server versions 7.0 and 6.5. If the database were from version 7.0 you would enter the database name in the first text box, and if you wanted to use a database from version 6.5 you would use the Using the filename option and enter the database file name in the second text box.

11. The Advanced tab contains information about network settings, connection timeouts, and access permissions. We do not want to enter or change any information on this tab.

The All tab lists all of the settings that have been chosen in this dialog and allows you to edit the values. We do not want to change any of the settings here.

Click the OK button to close this dialog, and return to the Project Properties dialog. At this point the connection to SQL Server will be established.

12. The next step that we want to perform on the Data Connection tab of the Project Properties dialog is to disable the OLAP connection since we are not working with OLAP data stores. Uncheck the Enable OLAP check box. The completed Data Connection tab should look like the one shown in the following figure:

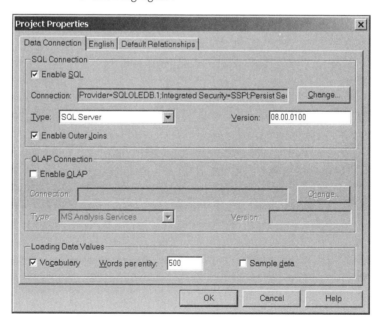

13. Also on the Data Connection tab, there are three options in the Loading Data Values section. The first of these options is the Vocabulary option. This option specifies that the values for the entities should be loaded from the database, and this is what we want.

The second option is Words per entity, which is set to a value of 500. This option specifies the maximum number of words that should be added to the dictionary for each field.

The third option specifies whether Sample Data should be provided for the entity. This option is useful if we want to use subset phrasing when defining relationships. Since we will not be using subset phrasing, we will leave this option off. Leaving this option turned off will make the model compile faster.

The English tab provides general information about our English Query application and we will accept all default values specified here.

The Default Relationships tab allows us to specify default relationships for vague questions about entities. We have no relationships defined, so we will skip this tab.

Click the OK button on this dialog to close it.

14. At this point, double-click on Module1.eqm in the Project Explorer window to display this module:

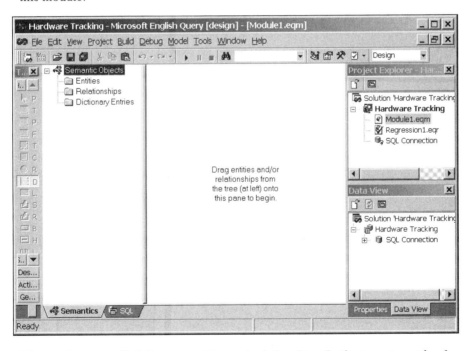

This is where we will define our entities and relationships. In the tree-view side of our Module1 window we see two tabs at the bottom. The tab currently being displayed is the Semantics tab. This tab will contain all the entities and relationships that we define. Notice in the tree pane that there are three folders, Entities, Relationships, and Dictionary Entries. The first two folders are where we will add the entities and relationships that we define. The Dictionary Entries folder is where special words are defined.

English Query comes with thousands of common English words already in the dictionary. However, your line of business may contain special words and terms that are not recognized by English Query. Using the New Dictionary Entry dialog, you can define your own words and terms that will be used by English Query.

The second tab is the SQL tab, which will contain a list of all tables that we add to our English Query project.

In the middle of the screen is the canvas pane – we'll be using this when we create relationships.

To recap, so far we've established and configured an outline for our application. The next stage is to furnish our application with some content, so let's move on and give our application some substance.

Try It Out – Adding Tables, Entities, and Relationships

1. This is a good time to add our tables, so let's click on the SQL tab. We then see that there are no tables currently listed in this tab. Click on the Model menu and then click on the Import Tables menu item. The New Database Tables and Views dialog is displayed, listing all of the tables in our database:

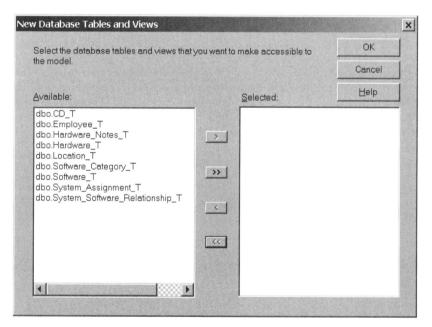

2. Click on the double right arrows to add all tables to the Selected list. Then click on the OK button to close the dialog.

The tables from our database are now shown in the SQL tab. By clicking on the + signs we can expand each table, and view the Fields in the table and the Joins that were automatically made by English Query.

Double-clicking on a table or field will display all of the fields in a table and the field data type. Double-clicking on a join will display the join and the tables involved in the join:

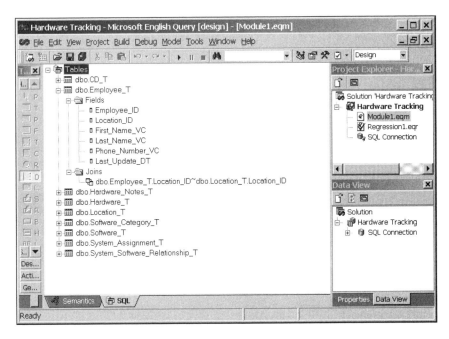

3. Back on the Semantics tab, we want to create the first entity in our project. There are a couple of methods that you can use to create a new entity. One method is to right-click on the Entities folder and choose Add Entity from the context menu. The other method is to click on the Model menu and choose the Add Entity menu item. After you have executed one of these methods, the New Entity dialog appears:

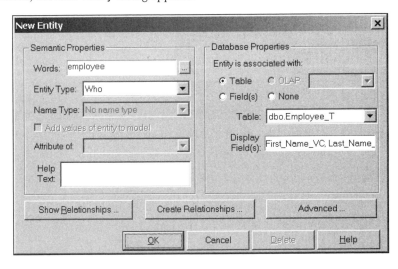

4. Click on the blue area in the Words text box and enter the entity name of employee. Since an employee is a person, we need to choose Who as the Entity Type. This allows us to ask a question such as "*Who has a computer?*". The words that you enter should be in the singular form.

Other entity types are available. The first is the **None** entity type, which indicates that there are no additional language features available for this entity. Also available is the **Where** entity type, which refers to a location of an entity, while the **When** entity type refers to an action for the entity, such as start time or date. The **Measure** entity type indicates a unit of measure, such as how much or how many.

5. The `employee` entity will be associated with the `Employee_T` table, so we want to choose the **Table** option in the **Database Properties** section of this dialog, and then choose the `Employee_T` table from the **Table** drop down list.

6. Click on the **Display Field(s)** text area and then choose the **First_Name_VC** and **Last_Name_VC** fields. These are the fields that we want displayed. Once you are done, click the **OK** button to close this dialog. At this point you can see the **employee** entity under the **Entities** folder.

7. The next entity that we want to create is the `employee name` entity. This entity will allow us to ask questions about a specific employee, such as "*What is Thearon's phone number?*". Again, either right-click on the **Entities** folder and choose **Add Entity** from the context menu, or click on the **Model** menu and choose the **Add Entity** menu item.

8. Enter **employee name** in the **Words** text box and choose an **Entity Type** of **None**.

9. In the **Database Properties** section of this dialog, click on the **Field(s)** option. Notice that the **Name Type** and **Attribute of** drop-down lists in the **Semantic Properties** section are now enabled. Now choose the **Employee_T** table in the **Table** drop-down list and choose the **First_Name_VC** and **Last_Name_VC** fields in the **Field(s)** text area.

10. Back in the **Semantic Properties** section, we want to choose a **Name Type** of **Proper Name**. This option will specify a proper name for this entity.

Another option available here is **No name type**, which is the default, which does not associate a unique name or ID with the entity being defined. Also available is the **Common Name** option, which is used for a general term such as a hard drive.

The **Classifier Name** option is used to associate a name with the entity name. For example, if we defined the `Location_T` table as a `department` entity then we could use the **Classifier Name** option and refer to an entry in the `Location_T` table as the `finance department`, where `finance` was contained as a location in the `Location_T` table.

The **Model Name** option is used to refer to brand names. This would be useful in the `Hardware_T` table to refer to the specific models in the `Model_VC` column.

The **Unique ID** option is used to represent an entity with a special type of name, such as an entry in the `Employee_ID` column in the `Employee_T` table.

The **Add values of entity to model** option is used to load values from your table to the model so references to instances of the entity can be recognized out of context. Checking this option can take several minutes to load depending on the size of your table. We will not use this option, as it provides no value to our small project.

11. We want to make this entity an attribute of the `employee` entity, so we need to choose **employee** in the drop down list of the **Attribute of** combo box. Click **OK** to have this entity created.

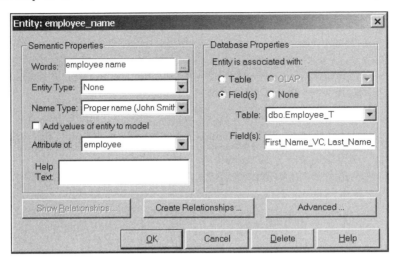

At this point you can expand the **employee** entity and see that the **employee name** entity is an attribute of the **employee** entity.

12. We now need to modify the `Employee_T` table in our English Query project and assign a name structure to the employee's name. A name structure associates the individual columns in our table with a part of the employee's name. For example, we need to define that the `First_Name_VC` column in our table represents the employee's first name.

Click on the **SQL** tab at the bottom of the editor to view a list of all our tables. Next, right- click on the **Employee_T** table and choose **Edit** from the context menu.

13. Click on the First_Name_VC Field Name and then in the **Basic** tab at the bottom of the dialog choose **First** from the **Name Structure** combo box, as shown:

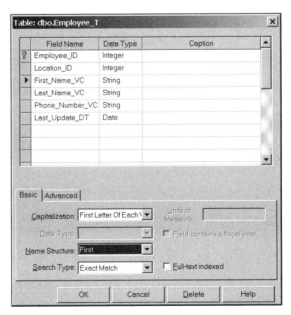

We need to repeat this process for the last name so click on the Last_Name_VC Field Name and then select Last in the Name Structure combo box.

Click the OK button to close the dialog and then click back on the Semantics tab at the bottom of the editor.

14. We need to create a relationship between the employee and employee name entities. There are several methods that can be used to do this; we will cover one method here, and then the other methods as we go along.

The first method that we want to explore is the drag and drop method of creating a relationship. First, drag and drop the employee entity from the tree pane to the canvas pane. Then drag the employee name entity from the tree pane and drop it onto the employee entity in the canvas pane. This will cause the New Relationship dialog to be invoked:

15. The Entities section of this dialog is where you add, edit, and delete the entities that are involved in the relationship. The Phrasings section of this dialog is where you can add one or more phrasings using the entities that are listed in the Entities section. Each phrasing that you add creates a separate relationship. We want to add a phrasing, so click on the Add button in the middle right of this dialog (not the Add button near the entity names) for this section.

16. The Select Phrasing dialog is displayed and lists the available phrasing. Notice that as you click on each phrase type, a sample is displayed. This helps you to choose the appropriate phrasing.

We want to add the Name/ID Phrasing to identify the relationship between employee names and employees, so click on this phrasing and then click on the OK button.

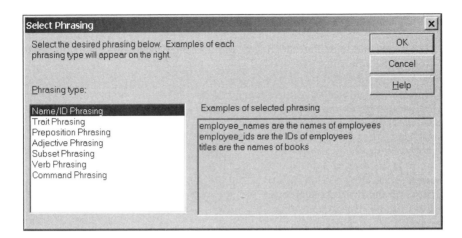

17. The Name/ID Phrasing dialog appears and allows you to enter or confirm the order of the entities that are used in this phrasing. This dialog also gives examples that help you to determine that this is the correct phrasing to be used. Since the entities have been pre-selected and the order of the entities is correct, we want to click the OK button to have this phrasing applied to our relationship.

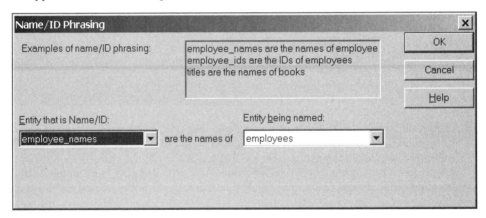

18. You are then returned to the New Relationship dialog and the phrasing that we just added is shown in the Phrasings section. Click the OK button to have the relationship created.

Notice that the relationship has been created and placed in the Relationships folder in the tree pane (you may need to expand the Relationships folder to see this). The canvas pane also displays a graphical representation of the relationship that we created.

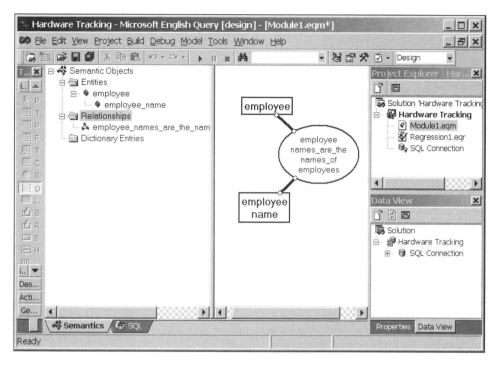

19. At this point, let's test the relationship that we have just added. In order to do so we must compile the English Query project so that the English Query run-time engine can load the compiled model. This can be done manually by clicking on the Build menu and choosing the Build menu item, or can be done automatically by clicking on the Debug menu and then clicking the Start menu item, or by clicking on the Start icon on the toolbar.

Clicking on the Start icon on the toolbar (or the Start menu item) will cause a build to be performed, and will then invoke the Test Tool. At this point, go ahead and click the Start icon or Start menu item.

20. The Model Test dialog is invoked; this is the English Query Test Tool. This dialog has a series of icons on the toolbar. The first icon allows you to Save the query that you execute. The second icon is Submit Query, which submits the query for processing. The next icon is Cancel Query, which stops an executing query. The next icon is View Results and should be clicked before you execute your query. This causes the query results to be displayed. The next icon is Suggest Relationships, and is used when the Test Tool cannot answer the question asked in the query; it allows you to go back and add additional relationships. The Test Properties icon displays the time-out value for a query and the maximum number of rows to be returned in the results. Both of these values are adjustable. Finally, the Help icon displays the English Query Books Online help.

Enter the statement: Show all employees in the Query combo box, then click on the View Results icon, and then click on the Submit Query icon on the toolbar. You should see results similar to the ones shown in the figure overleaf.

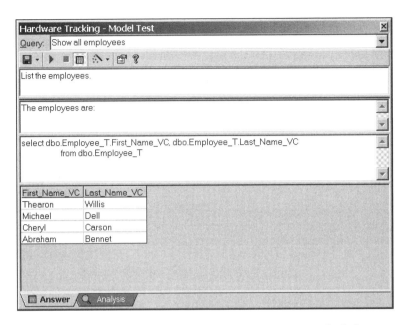

The English Query run-time engine will rephrase the question asked if necessary, and then translate the rephrased question into a SQL statement that gets executed by SQL Server. The restatement in our case is List the employees. The dialog then displays the answer, The employees are: followed by the SQL statement that gets passed to SQL Server for execution. Finally the results are displayed.

21. The Analysis tab will display the entities and relationships that were used in the query, and will allow you to modify them if necessary. If you take a look at this tab, you will notice that only the employee entity was used to answer the query that we have specified.

22. A regression file was automatically added to your project when you created the English Query project. This file can be used to retest your application after modifying it or moving it to production (the file has a .eqr extension and can be seen in the Project Explorer). The regression file contains the questions that you ask only if you add them to it. On the toolbar of the Model Test dialog, click on the Save Query icon to have the current query saved in the regression file.

Each query that you execute needs to be saved to the regression file if you plan to use this file for subsequent tests or production testing when you move your application to production. This file is saved as an XML file, and we'll be taking a brief look at it in a moment.

23. Using the entities and relationships that we have defined so far, there is another question we can ask. Given any employee who is listed, you can query for their last name. This is useful if you remember their first name but not their last name. This can also be used in reverse, that is, if you remember their last name, but not their first name, you can use the last name in the query.

Enter the following question, substituting a first name value from your Employee_T table: What is Thearon's last name. You should see the employee's last name displayed as shown in the following figure. You should note that when referring to data in your tables, such as an employee name, you must use the proper case (for example, capitalize the first letter).

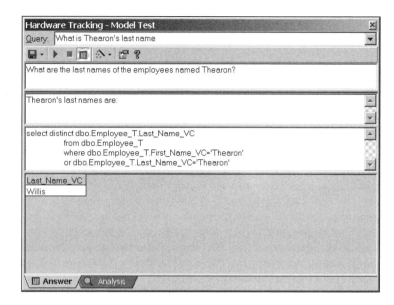

24. Now take a look at the **Analysis** tab again. You should see the entity and relationship used by English Query to answer the question that you asked.

25. Back on the **Answer** tab, click on the **Save Query** button to save the query in the regression file, and then close the **Model Test** dialog by clicking on the **X** in the upper right-hand corner.

Notice that the regression file is displayed, and is an XML document. Here you will see the question that was asked, the restatement of the question, the answer and the SQL statement that was executed:

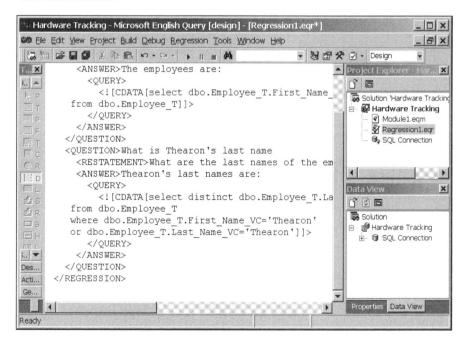

26. Close the regression file by clicking on the X in the upper right hand corner of the file window. We are not going to use this file again so you don't have to save it.

Let's recap what we've just covered. In the previous exercise we've imported tables into our application, and we've also defined a couple of new entities, namely `employee` and `employee name`. We added the name structure to the employee's first and last names in the `Employee_T` table and then established relationships between the two entities that we defined. Finally, we tested the implementation of the relationships that we had specified by querying our application in a manner that invoked the relationships we had just set up.

We'll continue now by adding a few more entities to our application, setting up relationships between these entities (employing various methods to do so), and then testing our implementation of these modifications using the Test Tool again.

Try It Out - Adding Location Related Entities and Relationships

The next entity that we want to define is for phone numbers. We want to be able to query about an employee's phone number and have the phone number returned.

1. So, either right-click on the Entities folder and choose Add Entity from the context menu, or click on the Model menu and choose the Add Entity menu item.

2. In the New Entity dialog, we want to enter phone number in the Words text box. Because a phone number is not really associated with any Entity Type that is available, we want to choose an Entity Type of None. Click on Fields in the Database Properties section of the dialog, and choose the Employee_T table in the Table combo box. Now, choose the Phone_Number_VC field in the Field(s) text area.

3. Switching back to the Semantic Properties pane, we want to choose the Name Type for this entity. Since there really is no associated name type for a phone number, we want to choose No name type in this combo box. Finally, we want to associate a phone number with an employee, so we need to choose the employee entity in the Attribute of combo box. At this point click the OK button to close this dialog.

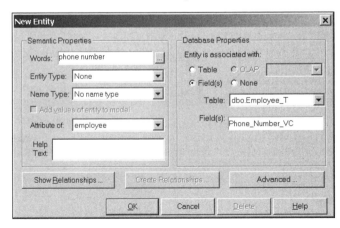

If you expand the employee entity in the semantics tree, you will see the employee name and phone number entities listed.

4. We now need to create a relationship between the `employee` and `phone number` entities. We know that we can drag the `phone number` entity and drop it onto the `employee` entity in the canvas pane to invoke the **New Relationship** dialog. However, we want to explore other methods of adding a new relationship.

This time we want to click on the **Model** menu, and choose the **Add Relationship** menu item. This will cause the **New Relationship** dialog to be invoked, but this time it will be completely empty. This means that we will have to add the entities ourselves.

5. In the **Entities** section of the dialog, click on the **Add** button to invoke the **Select Entities** dialog. In this dialog, we want to select the **employee** and **phone number** entities. You can select multiple entities by clicking on the first entity and then holding down the *Ctrl* key and selecting the next required entity. Click the **OK** button to have these entities added to the **New Relationship** dialog.

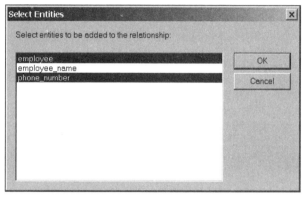

6. Click on the **Add** button in the **Phrasings** section to invoke the **Select Phrasing** dialog. Click on **Trait Phrasing**, and notice the samples that are displayed. This is the phrasing that we want, as employees have phone numbers. Click the **OK** button to invoke the **Trait Phrasing** dialog, as shown in the following figure. Notice that the appropriate entities have already been selected in the **Subject** and **Object** combo boxes. If you needed to adjust these, you could. Click the **OK** button to have the phrasing applied to the relationship.

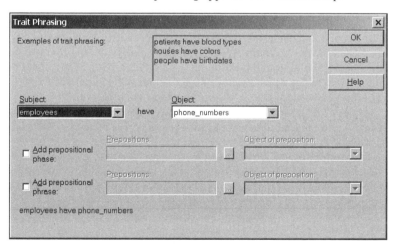

7. Click on the OK button in the New Relationship dialog to have the relationship created. Notice that the phone number entity and the new relationship were automatically added to your relationship diagram in the canvas pane.

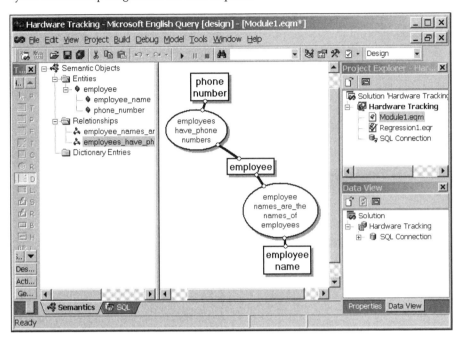

You can manually arrange the relationship diagram by dragging the entities and relationships in the canvas pane. You can also right-click on an empty area of the canvas pane and choose Float All from the context menu. This will automatically arrange the diagram in the space available.

8. Let's create one more entity and relationship before we run the Test Tool again. We want to add an entity for location, and a relationship between the location and employee entities. To add the new entity, click on the Model menu and choose the Add Entity menu item, or right-click on the Entities folder and choose Add Entity from the context menu.

9. In the Words text box, we want to enter location. Because a location is a place, we want to choose an Entity Type of Where. We only want to display the field for location, so we need to choose the Field(s) option in the Database Properties section of the dialog, since this entity represents a field in the table. Then we want to choose the Location_T table in the Table combo box, and Location_Name_VC in the Field(s) text area.

10. Switching back to the Semantic Properties section of this dialog, we want to choose a Name Type of Classifier name, because a location can be classified, such as the home office. We want to make this entity an attribute of the employee entity, so we choose employee in the Attribute of combo box. Click the OK button to close this dialog.

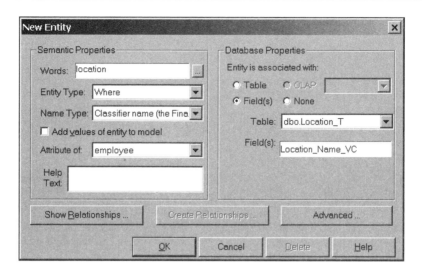

You should now see the location entity listed under the employee entity in the tree pane.

11. The final method of creating a relationship that we want to demonstrate is to right-click on the Relationships folder and choose Add Relationship from the context menu. Again the New Relationship dialog that is invoked is blank.

We need to add the entities, so click on the Add button in the Entities section of this dialog. This time, we want to select the employee and location entities in the Select Entities dialog. Click the OK button to return to the New Relationship dialog.

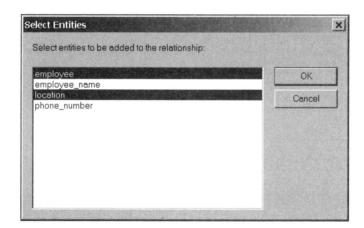

12. We now need to add the appropriate phrasing for the relationship that we want to define, so click on the Add button in the Phrasings section of the New Relationship dialog. Once again, we want to choose the Trait Phrasing, as employees have phone numbers. Click on Trait Phrasing and then click the OK button to invoke the Trait Phrasing dialog. This dialog already has the appropriate entities selected in the Subject and Object combo boxes, so click OK to close this dialog.

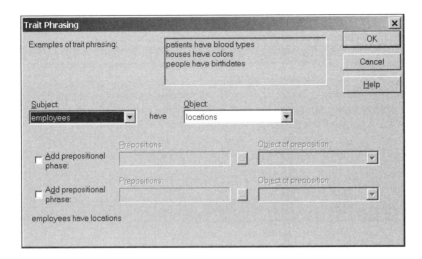

13. Click the OK button in the New Relationship dialog to have this relationship created. Again the new entity and relationship have been added to the canvas pane.

14. At this point, we want to test the new entities and relationships that we have added. Click on the Start icon on the toolbar to have English Query build our model and invoke the Model Test dialog.

We want to test the phone number entity first, so enter the query: Show employees and phone numbers, and click on the Submit Query icon. Notice that the employees and their phone numbers are listed:

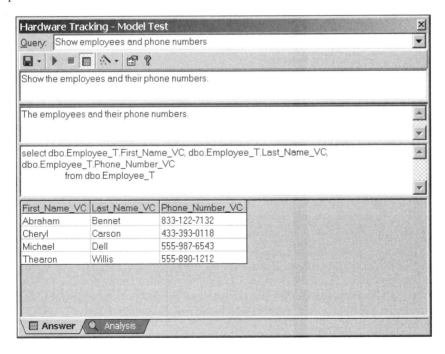

15. Now take a look at the Analysis tab to view the entities and relationships that were used by English Query to answer the query and display the results. In the analysis view, the green boxes represent entities, and the speech bubble ("a") denotes a relationship/phrasing. In this simple example, English Query used the `employee` and `phone number` entities, and the relationship "`employees have phone numbers`".

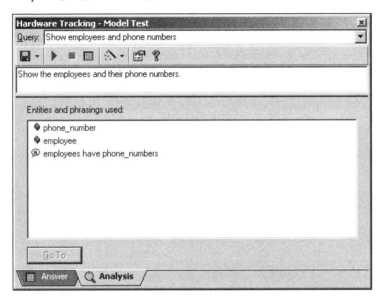

16. In order to see the phone number for one particular employee, we can also ask a more specific question, for example, What is Thearon's phone number. As you might realize, this would be a great tool for an employee directory on your intranet.

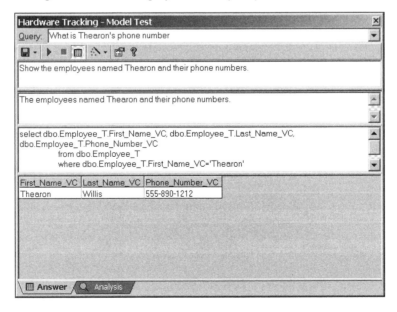

17. In order to test the `location` entity, enter a new query, Show employees and locations. Click on the Submit Query icon to view the results:

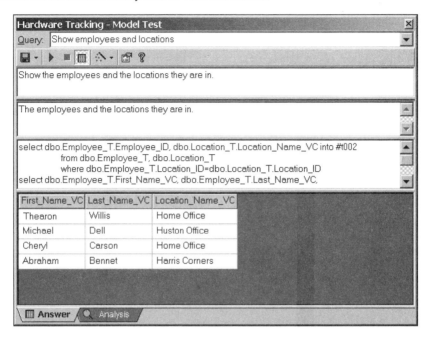

18. Notice that employees and their locations are displayed. What if we just wanted to view the locations listed in the `Location_T` table? We could enter the question Show locations, and the locations are displayed without the employees:

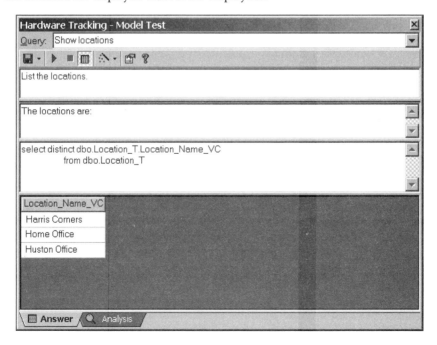

In the first question, each employee is listed along with his or her location. In the second question, just the locations are listed.

19. We can expand on location information by adding another relationship between the `employee` and `location` entities. Close the Model Test dialog and drag the location entity from the tree pane and drop it onto the employee entity in the canvas pane to invoke the New Relationship dialog. Notice that the location and employee entities are already listed in the Entities section of this dialog.

20. We want to choose a phrase for this relationship, so click on the Add button in the Phrasings section of this dialog to invoke the Select Phrasing dialog. We want to define a relationship between the `employee` and `location` entities so that we can determine where an employee works. A verb expresses some action or function of our entities, and so we want to choose Verb Phrasing. Choose this option and click the OK button.

The Verb Phrasing dialog presents us with many choices about the sentence type. In the Sentence Type combo box we can choose from five different types.

❑ The first of these is **Subject Verb**, which defines the verb type, such as *employees work at locations*. The *employees work* part is the subject verb, the *at locations* part is the prepositional clause, which will be discussed in a few moments.

❑ The second option is **Subject Verb Object**, which defines the verb as an object of the employee entity, such as an employee buys products.

❑ The third option, **Subject Verb Object Obje**ct, defines an object for both entities such as employees donate time to charity.

❑ The next option is **Object are Verb,** and defines an entity as an object, such as products are tested by employees.

❑ The last option, **Object are Verb Object,** defines an entity as an object and references the second entity as an object such as *products are tested*.

21. We want to choose the Subject Verb option as the Sentence Type. We also want to select employees as the subject in the Subject combo box, and we want to enter the word work as the verb in the Verb text box.

22. We now need to define a prepositional phrase that defines where an employee works. To that end we want to check the Add prepositional phrase check box.

We know that the Object of preposition is locations, so select that in this combo box. Now we can accurately define the preposition using the word at.

Your completed dialog should now look like this:

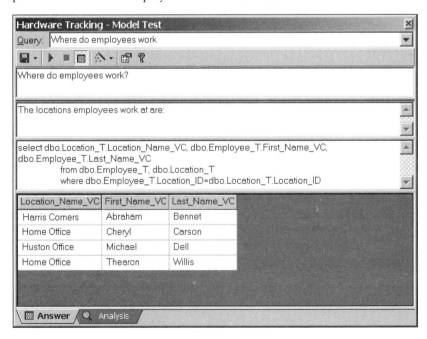

23. At this point, click the OK button to have the phrasing added to the relationship, and then click the OK button in the New Relationship dialog to have the relationship created. The new relationship has automatically been added to the relationship diagram in the canvas pane.

24. To test this new relationship, click on the Start icon to have a new model compiled and to invoke the Model Test dialog. We can now enter the question Where do employees work and expect to see a list of all employees and their locations:

25. We can also find out where a specific employee works by asking the question Where does Thearon work. Again, we can use the first or last name of an employee, and the employee and their location will be displayed:

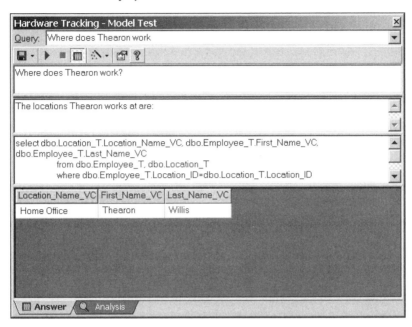

26. If you wanted to know all employees that worked at a specific location, you could ask the question Who works at the Home Office. Note that you need to match case when using specific entries in a field, just as was the case with employees earlier. In other words, Home Office works, but Home office will not. The results that you would see from raising this question would be all of the employees who work at this location, as shown in the following figure:

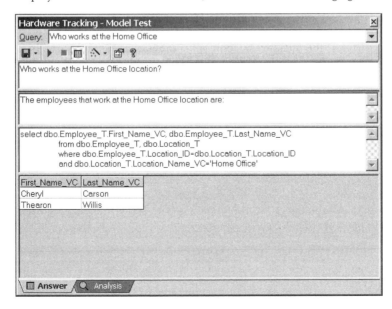

You should examine the Analysis tab for each of the three questions that you have just asked, to see the entities and relationships that were used to produce the results that you saw. Using the drop-down portion of the Query combo box you can see a list of all questions that you have asked, and can then re-execute those queries again.

Now, moving on, we'll add some more entities and relationships to further enhance the functionality of our application.

Try It Out – Adding Hardware Related Entities and Relationships

1. We want to add some additional entities and relationships, so close the Model Test dialog. The next entity that we want to add is an entity that will be an attribute of the `employee` entity, and will let us know which employees have a system assigned to them.

To that end, create a new entity by right-clicking on the Entities folder and choosing Add Entity from the context menu. In the Words text box of the New Entity dialog enter the word system. This will name this entity `system`, and allows us to refer to this entity as a system. But what if we also wanted to refer to this entity as a computer?

The Words text box allows us to enter **words**, **phrases**, or **synonyms** that identify the entity. This means that we can enter many words, phrases, or synonyms that can and will be used to refer to this entity.

2. Having already entered a word, you can click on the browse button next to the Words text box to see a list of synonyms that have been suggested by English Query. You do not have to use them, but this feature is available in case you want to identify this entity with as many words, phrases, and synonyms as possible.

Since it isn't in the list of synonyms, we want to manually enter the word computer as well as system, so click back on the Words text box; a new text box appears in which you can enter your own synonym, in this case, computer. Since a computer does not really fall into any of the categories for Entity Type, choose the None entry.

3. In the Database Properties section of the dialog choose the Field(s) option. Once you have done this choose the System_Assignment_T table in the Table combo box. In the Field(s) text area choose the System_Assignment_ID field.

4. We want to choose the No name type option in the Name Type combo box in the Semantics Properties section of this dialog. We also want to make this entity an attribute of the `employee` entity, so choose employee in the Attribute of combo box.

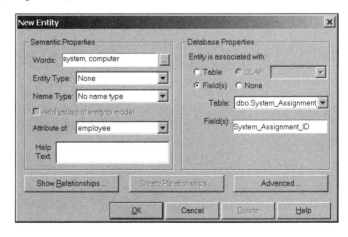

5. Click the OK button to close this dialog and have the entity created. You should now see this entity listed under the `employee` entity.

6. We now want to create a relationship between the `system` and `employee` entities. Drag the `system` entity and drop it onto the `employee` entity in the relationship diagram in the canvas pane to invoke the New Relationship diagram.

7. The appropriate entities are already added in the Entities section of this dialog, so we do not have to add any here. We do need to choose the appropriate phrasing that will describe this relationship, so click on the Add button in the Phrasings section of this dialog.

8. Since a system or computer is something an employee has, we want to choose the Trait Phrasing option in the Select Phrasing dialog. In the Trait Phrasing dialog the employees entity has already been selected in the Subject combo box, and systems has already been selected in the Object combo box. Click the OK button to accept this phrasing and to have it assigned to this relationship.

9. Finally, click the OK button in the New Relationship dialog to have the new relationship created. Again, the new entity and relationship have automatically been added to your relationship diagram.

10. Let's test this newest relationship. Click on the Start icon to have a new model compiled and to invoke the Model Test dialog. Then enter the question Which employees have a system to view the employees and the system assignment IDs:

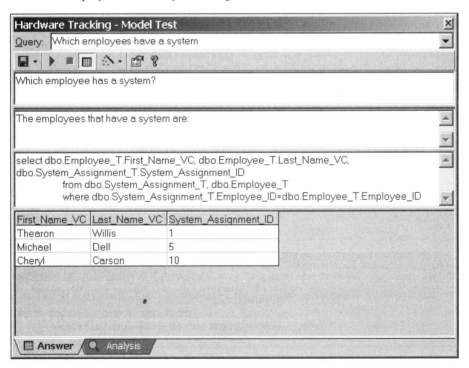

11. Because we also defined a synonym for "system", we can ask the question another way. Enter the question Which employees have a computer and you should see exactly the same results:

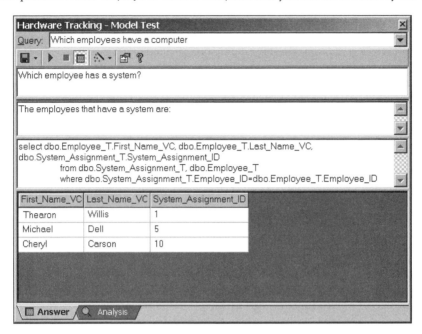

12. Like the rest of the entities that we defined as an attribute of the employee entity, we can use the employee's name to see if they have a computer. Enter the query Show Thearon's computer, to view the results that list the employee's name and their system assignment ID:

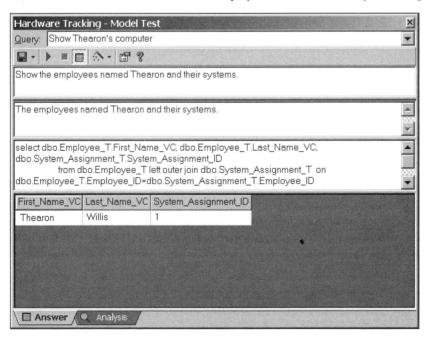

13. The next entity that we want to define is an entity that will display the hardware listed in the `Hardware_T` table. To that end, close the Model Test dialog, right-click on Entities, and choose Add Entity from the context menu.

14. Enter hardware in the Words text box of the New Entity dialog. Hardware does not fall into any of the categories listed in the Entity Type combo box, so we want to select the None option.

15. In the Database Properties section of this dialog, ensure that the Table option is selected, and then select the Hardware_T table in the Table combo box. In the Display Field(s) text area, select all fields except the CD_ID and the Last_Update_DT fields.

16. Because we have selected the Table option, the Name Type and Attribute of combo boxes in the Semantic Properties section of the dialog have been disabled. At this point click the OK button to have this entity created.

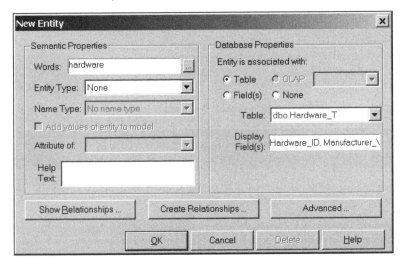

As we just want to display all hardware, we do not need to define a relationship for it. We can now just raise the query Show hardware in order to see a list of all hardware.

Because the `hardware` entity is not related to the `employee` entity, it does not need to be added to the relationship diagram.

Try It Out – Adding Software Related Entities and Relationships

1. The next entity that we want to create is an entity for software. This will allow us to view all available software in the `Software_T` table. Right-click on the Entities folder and choose Add Entity from the context menu.

2. In the New Entity dialog, enter the word software in the Words text box and choose an Entity Type of None.

3. Ensure the Table option is selected in the Database Properties section of the dialog. Then select the Software_T table in the Table combo box and select the Software_ID and Software_Name_VC fields in the Display Field(s) text area.

697

4. Let's have this entity sort the results that will be displayed. Click on the Advanced button near the bottom of the dialog to invoke the Advanced Entity Properties dialog. Click on the Sort by field in the Display Properties section of the dialog and then choose the Software_Name_VC field:

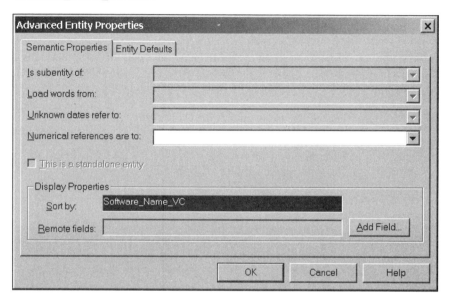

5. Click OK to close the Advanced Entity Properties dialog and then click OK to close the New Entity dialog and have the entity created:

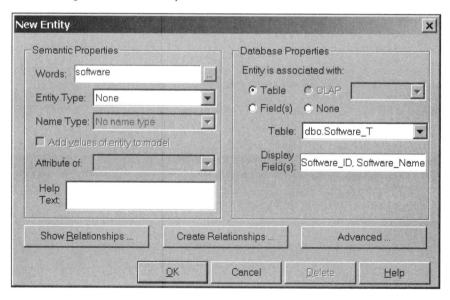

Again, we do not need to create any relationships in order to display the data for this entity. Using this entity alone, we can ask the question Show software to see a list of all software, which will sorted by name.

Because the software entity is not related to the employee entity it does not need to be added to the relationship diagram.

6. If we want to view a list of all software, it stands to reason that we would also want to view a list of all software categories. It also stands to reason that we would also want to view a list of software and categories, and just the software for a given category. We can do all of this with the introduction of another entity and two relationships.

Create another entity by right-clicking on the Entities folder, and choosing Add Entity from the context menu. In the Words text box, enter the word category. Select an Entity Type of None, because software category does not really fall into any of the categories listed in this combo box.

7. In the Database Properties section of this dialog, choose the Field(s) option and select the Software_Category_T table in the Table combo box. Then choose the Software_Category_VC field in the Field(s) text area.

8. Switching back to the Semantic Properties section of the dialog, we want to choose the Proper Name option in the Name Type combo box. This allows us to address any category by name in this entity, and since a software category really is a proper name, this fits nicely.

9. We want to make this entity an attribute of the software entity, so select software in the Attribute of combo box. Then click the OK button to have this new entity created:

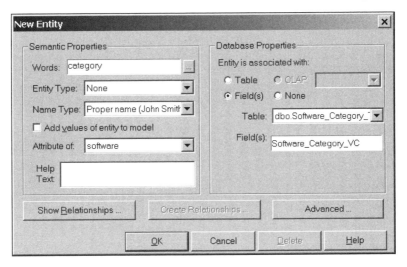

10. We want to create two relationships between the software and category entities. To start this process, drag the software entity to any white space in the relationship diagram. Because the software entity is not related to any of the entities in the relationship diagram, we can just drop it in any white space available.

Then drag the category entity and drop it onto the software entity to invoke the New Relationship dialog. Because we want to add two different relationships using the same entities, we can do it here with just this one dialog.

11. In order to list all of the software titles and their categories, we need to define a relationship that defines software as having categories. In the Phrasing section of the New Relationship dialog, click on the Add button.

We want to select the Trait Phrasing option in the Select Phrasing dialog, and then click the OK button. The softwares entity (plural of our `software` entity) has already been selected in the Subject combo box and the categories entity has already been selected in the Object combo box. Click the OK button to associate this phrasing with the relationship.

12. The next relationship that we want to add is a relationship that defines that software titles are in categories. To do this, click on the Add button in the Phrasings section of the New Relationship dialog, choose Preposition Phrasing in the Select Phrasing dialog, and then click the OK button.

The softwares entity has already been selected in the Subject combo box, and the categories entity has already been selected in the Object combo box. All we need to do is to fill in the preposition that defines the relationship.

The preposition that most accurately defines this relationship is the word "in". So, we need to click in the Prepositions text box and enter the word in. Then click the OK button to have this phrasing associated with this relationship:

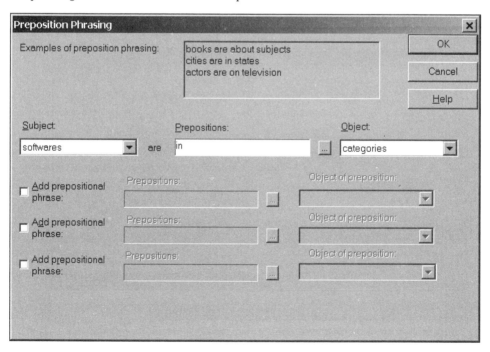

13. Now click the OK button in the New Relationship dialog to have these relationships created.

At this point, let's stop and test the new entities and relationships that we have defined.

Try It Out – Testing the Hardware and Software Entities and Relationships

1. Click on the Start icon to have a new model compiled and to invoke the Model Test dialog.

The first entity that we want to test is the hardware entity. We enter the query Show hardware, which will list all of the hardware in the Hardware_T table:

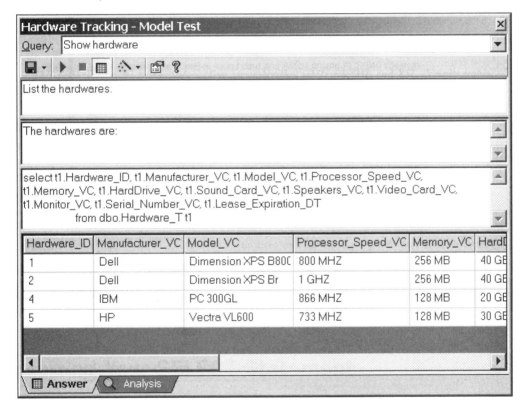

2. To test the `software` entity in the same manner, we can enter the query Show software, which will display all software titles in the `Software_T` table, sorted by name:

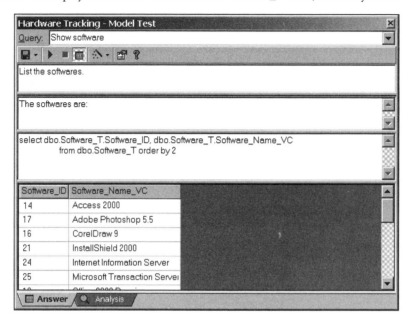

3. To test the `category` entity, we can enter the query Show categories to see a list of all software categories:

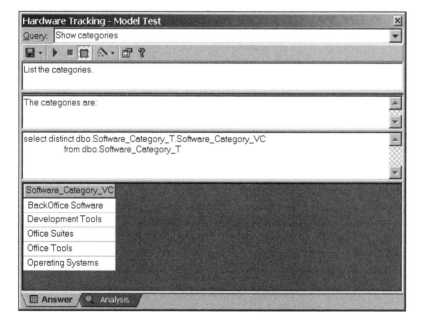

All three of these tests use only the entities that we have defined. You can verify this by looking at the Analysis tab to see the entities and relationships used to answer the question.

4. We now want to test the first relationship that we defined, `software have categories`. In order to do this, enter the query Show software and categories to see a list of all software titles and their associated categories:

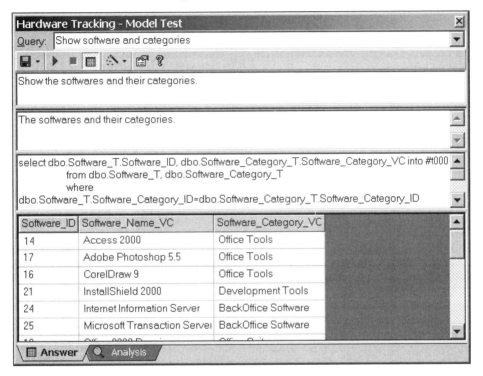

5. To test the `software are in category` relationship enter the question What software is in Office Suites. This will cause all of the software titles that have a foreign key reference to the `Office Suite` row in the `Software_Category_T` table to be displayed, as shown in the following figure:

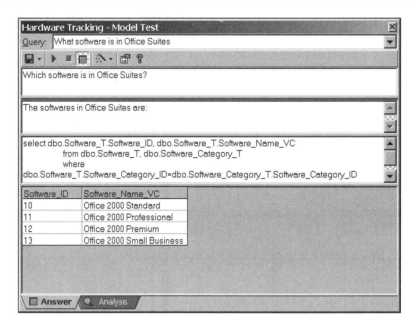

6. At this point, close the **Model Test** dialog, and let's add some more entities and relationships. We want to create an entity that will show installed software. To create this entity, right-click on the **Entities** folder and choose **Add Entity** from the context menu.

   In the **Words** text box, enter the words **installed software** and select an **Entity Type** of **None**.

   Then, in the **Database Properties** section of the **New Entity** dialog, ensure that the **Table** option is selected and choose the **System_Software_Relationship_T** table. This is the table that contains all of the software IDs of software titles that have been installed on a system. In the **Display Field(s)** text area, choose the **Software_ID** field.

7. This information alone will not give us the result we desire – which is to display the software titles that have been installed on the various systems. We need to associate the `Software_T` table with this entity in order to get the software titles. To do this, we need to click on the **Advanced** button in this dialog to invoke the **Advanced Entity Properties** dialog.

   In this dialog we want to click on the **Add Field** button at the bottom of the **Semantic Properties** tab to invoke the **Select Remote Fields** dialog. This dialog knows about the foreign key relationships between our tables, and will only display the tables that can be joined to the table that was selected in the **New Entity** dialog.

We want to select the Software_T table in the Table combo box and the Software_Name_VC in the Field combo box. Then click the Add button to add this field. Once the field has been added to the Selected fields list, click the OK button to close this dialog.

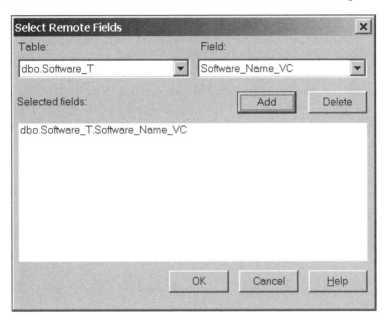

8. Click the OK button in the Advanced Entities Properties dialog to close this dialog and finally click the OK button in the New Entity dialog to have the entity created.

Having created this entity, you are now able to raise the query Show installed software to view a list of all installed software that is listed in the System_Software_Relationship_T table.

Try It Out – Adding the Assignment Entities and Relationships

1. Now that we can list all software that has been assigned, let's create an entity that will list assigned system information. Right-click on the Entities folder and choose Add Entity from the context menu.

   In the New Entity dialog, enter the words assigned system in the Words text box. Then choose an Entity Type of None.

   In the Database Properties section of this dialog, ensure the Table option is selected and select the System_Assignment_T table in the Table combo box. In the Display Field(s) text area, select the System_Assignment_ID field.

2. Of course, this is not enough information for our purposes, because we want to display more information about a system that has been assigned, such as the make and model, so we must click on the Advanced button at the bottom of this dialog to invoke the Advanced Entity Properties dialog. In the Advanced Entity Properties dialog, click the Add Field button to invoke the Select Remote Fields dialog.

3. Since the `System_Assignment_T` table has foreign key relationships to the `Hardware_T` and `Employee_T` tables, we will want to select fields from both of these tables to be displayed.

Select the Employee_T table in the Table combo box, and then select the First_Name_VC field in the Field combo box. Click the Add button to have this field added to the Selected fields list. Now select the Last_Name_VC field in the Field combo box, and click the Add button to have this field added to the Selected fields list.

4. We also want to display some fields from the Hardware_T table, so select this table in the Table combo box. We want to display basic information about the hardware, so you will need to select the Manufacturer_VC, Model_VC, Processor_Speed_VC, and Memory_VC fields, and add them to the Selected fields list, as shown in the following figure:

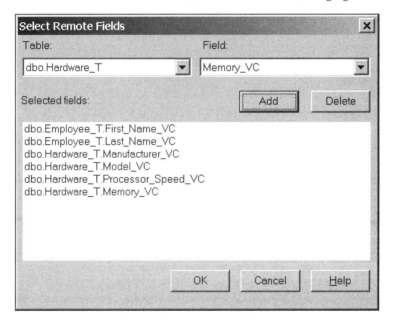

5. Click the OK button to close the Select Remote Fields dialog, and then click the OK button to close the Advanced Entity Properties dialog. Finally, click the OK button in the New Entity dialog to have the entity created.

Having created this entity we are able to make the query Show assigned systems, to view a list of all assigned systems. This will display the employee name and basic hardware information.

6. Let's create a relationship between the `assigned systems` and `installed software` entities that will allow us to view the installed software on the assigned system. To create this relationship, drag the assigned systems entity into any white space in the relationship diagram. Next, drag the installed software entity and drop it on the assigned systems entity in the relationship diagram. This action will invoke the New Relationship dialog.

7. In the New Relationship dialog, click on the Add button in the Phrasings section of this dialog. Because software is installed on assigned systems, we want to select the Trait Phrasing option in the Select Phrasing dialog. Select this option and then click on the OK button.

This time the Trait Phrasing dialog does not have any pre-selected entries in the Subject and Object combo boxes. In the Subject combo box we need to select the assigned systems entity, and in the Object combo box we want to select the installed softwares entity.

8. Click the OK button in the Trait Phrasing dialog to have this trait associated with this relationship. Then click the OK button in the New Relationship dialog to have this relationship created.

9. At this point we can test the new entities and relationships that we have just created. Click on the Run icon to have a new model compiled and to invoke the Model Test dialog.

Enter the query Show installed software to see a list of all software that has been installed on all of the systems. This is a good question to ask in order to find out what software is being used.

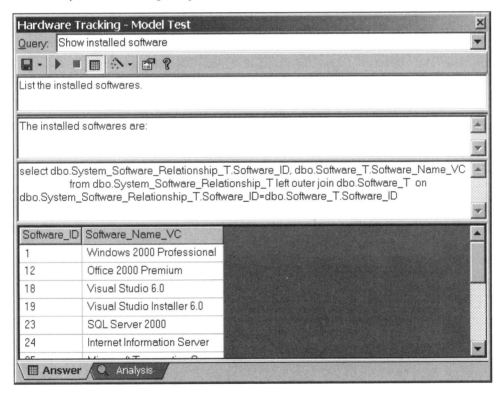

10. To test the `assigned systems` entity, enter the query **Show assigned systems**. This test will yield all of the employees who have a system assigned to them, and will also list the basic hardware information for each system, as shown in the next figure:

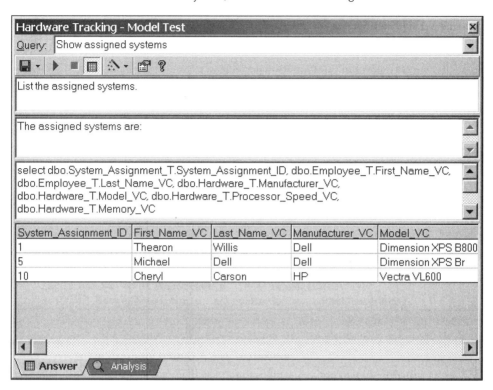

11. To view a list of all software installed on the employee's system, enter the query **Show assigned systems' installed software**. This question will list each system that is assigned to an employee, and display the basic hardware information and all installed software on that system:

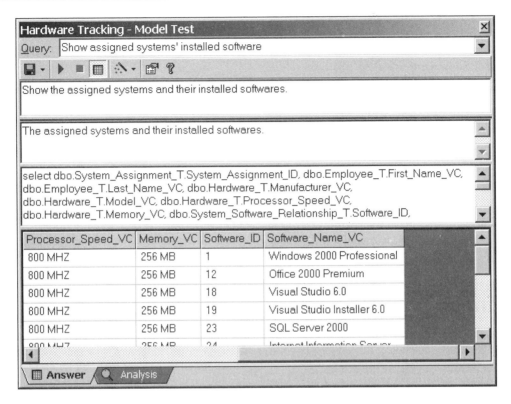

12. At this point we have created all of the entities and relationships that we need, so close the Model Test dialog. You can always come back later and create more entities and relationships. Save your project and close Visual InterDev.

The following list details the statements and questions that our English Query application now supports. Where an employee name appears, you will need to substitute the name of the employee that you want information for.

- ❏ Show all employees.
- ❏ What is Thearon's last name?
- ❏ Show employees and phone numbers.
- ❏ What is Thearon's phone number?
- ❏ Show employees and locations.
- ❏ Show locations.
- ❏ Where do employees work?
- ❏ Where does Thearon work?
- ❏ Who works at the Home Office?

- ❏ Which employees have a system?

- ❏ Show Thearon's computer.

- ❏ Show hardware.

- ❏ Show software.

- ❏ Show categories.

- ❏ Show software and categories.

- ❏ What software is in Office Suites?

- ❏ Show installed software.

- ❏ Show assigned systems.

As you can see, we have a fairly comprehensive list of questions that can be asked in order to determine information about our tables and our database. This list is by no means complete, but you can expand on this list when you have a chance or when the need arises.

Summary

This case study has taken a look at English Query, and covered the installation procedures necessary to install it. The installation of English Query was very straightforward, and there were only a small number of dialogs that we had to go through. We now know which option is required to install English Query on a workstation and which option is required to install English Query on a server such as a web server.

Having defined entities and relationships, and having actually gone through creating entities and relationships, you should now have a better understanding of these. You should also be aware of the various phrasings that define a relationship between two entities.

You should also be aware that we could use a single entity by itself to ask basic questions about the data that the entity represents. Using relationships we can define how two separate entities relate, and can ask questions about the relationship of the entities.

To summarize, you should know how to:

- ❏ Install English Query

- ❏ Create an entity

- ❏ Create a relationship between two entities

- ❏ Use the Test Tool to test the entities and relationships that you create

- ❏ Use the relationship diagram to quickly create relationships between entities

The next part of the case study will guide you through the process of deploying your English Query application on your intranet. There are several methods that you can use for deployment, including VB and VC++, but we will focus on deployment using the Web.

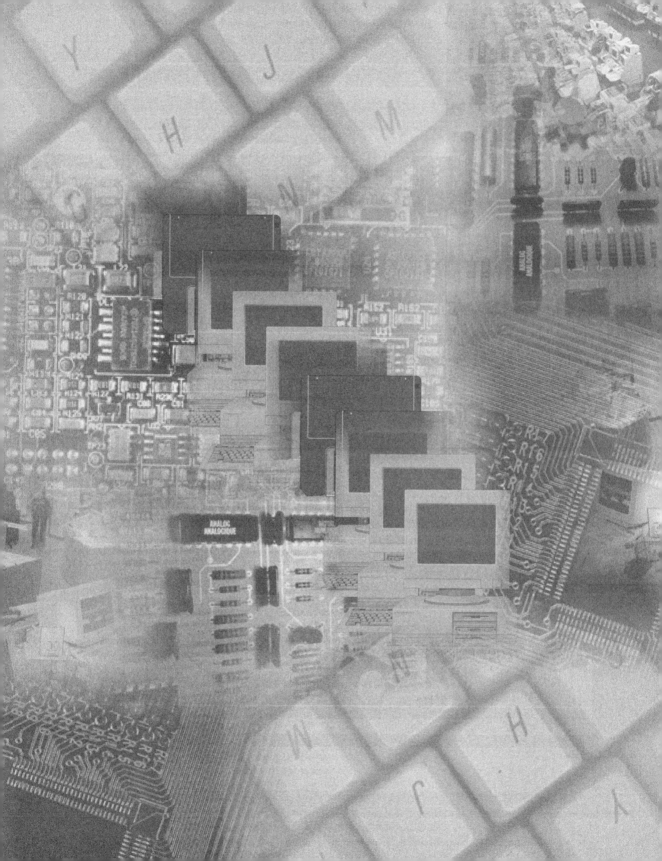

Case Study Part 2
Deploying an English Query
Application

In the last part of the case study we covered the installation of English Query and built an English Query application. There are three methods that you can use to deploy your English Query application. You can use IIS to deploy it to the Web, or you can use Visual Basic or Visual C++ to deploy it in a Windows environment. This part of the case study will walk you through the necessary steps of deploying your compiled English Query application on the Web.

We will examine what is needed to get your English Query model ready for deployment, and what is needed on the web server that will host your English Query application. We will also walk through the process of building the web pages that will run your English Query application.

When we have completed this chapter you will have gained the necessary skills, and will have developed the web pages required, to deploy your English Query application on your local intranet.

So, in this case study we will cover:

- ❏ Web deployment methods
- ❏ Distributing the run-time engine
- ❏ Building a question web page
- ❏ Building an answer web page

Web Deployment Methods

By far the easiest method of deployment is to use the **Web Project Wizard** that is part of Visual InterDev. This wizard will walk you through a series of four steps and will deploy your English Query application to the web server and virtual directory that you supply.

The only drawback to this method is that the FrontPage 98 Server Extensions must be installed on the web server that you want to deploy your application on. This is a restriction of Microsoft Visual InterDev and not English Query. Most companies do not allow these server extensions to be installed on test and production web servers. This prevents anyone with Microsoft FrontPage from just publishing a project and creating a web site. This is a matter of controlling who can create web sites on the web servers, more than anything else.

You can invoke the Web Project Wizard by clicking on the Project menu in Visual InterDev, then choosing the Deploy menu item and then choosing the Web sub menu item. The Web Project Wizard is then invoked and will walk you through a series of steps in order to deploy your English Query application.

The other method of deployment is to manually set up a virtual directory on the IIS server and copy your compiled English Query model to that virtual directory. Then you need to build your web pages to support the asking and answering of questions. This is the method that we will explore and use, as it will show you the details of creating these pages, and you will also gain a better understanding of how the English Query run-time engine works.

We set up our virtual directory for `HardwareTracking` in Chapter 14 and this is the virtual directory that we will use. This was also the virtual directory in which we deployed the `Default.htm` web page, which contains the links to our XML reports.

Before we dive in and start creating these web pages, let's ensure that we know how to distribute the English Query run-time engine.

Distributing the Run-Time Engine

As we saw in the previous part of the case study, the installation of English Query involved a step to install the run-time client components. The installation of English Query should be performed on the web server that will be hosting the English Query application, and the Run-time Only option should be selected.

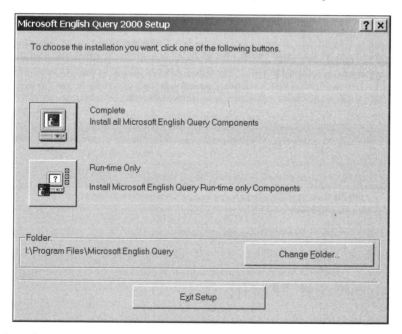

This ensures that all necessary English Query components are installed on the web server, and also ensures that you can run your English Query application using Active Server Pages in IIS. Of course, we will be testing and running our English Query application on our local machines, so we already have all of the necessary components installed.

If you are distributing an English Query application that uses Visual Basic or Visual C++ as the host, then you can manually redistribute and register the English Query DLLs. SQL Server Books Online covers the necessary DLLs that need to be redistributed, and also the steps to be performed in order to register these DLLs.

> **Keep in mind that each user to whom you distribute these DLLs must have a SQL Server client access license, because English Query accesses SQL Server.**

For our purposes here, everything that we need has already been installed, so let's move on.

Setting Up

We already have a web site that we can use to host our web pages, recall that it was set up in Chapter 14. The `Hardware Tracking` directory was created and the `HardwareTracking` virtual directory was set up in IIS.

We are also going to use this same virtual directory to host our English Query application. Other than the web pages that we are going to create, there are a couple of files that need to be copied to the `Hardware Tracking` directory.

The first of these files is the compiled English Query model for our application. This file has a `.eqd` file extension and is located in the directory where you created the `Hardware Tracking` English Query project. When we ran our last test, the model was compiled so it had all of the latest entities and relationships that we had defined. Copy this file from the project directory to the `Hardware Tracking` directory.

Since we are also going to be using ADO to access SQL Server, we need to get the **ADO constants include file**, `adovbs.inc`, so that we can include it in our Active Server Page. The ADO constants include file contains all of the ADO constants for the ADO objects and was installed when MDAC was installed, which was part of the SQL Server installation.

The location of the `adovbs.inc` include file is `C:\Program Files\Common Files\System\ADO`. This assumes that the `C` drive is the default drive that you boot from. Copy this file to the `Hardware Tracking` directory.

We now have all of the supporting files needed to deploy our English Query application. All we have left to do now is to create our web pages.

Building the Web Pages

Before we jump right in and start building the web pages that will support our English Query application, let's take a look at how the English Query run-time engine interfaces with our web pages. The following diagram shows how all of the components work together:

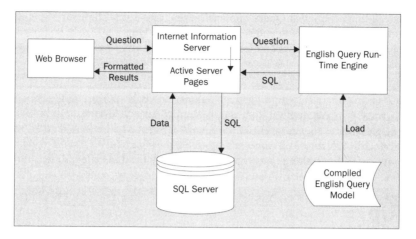

We start with the web browser, which has already received the web page which requests that the user enter a question. The browser submits the question to IIS, and IIS in turn calls the Active Server Page which will process the question and send back the response. The Active Server Page will in turn send the question to the English Query run-time engine.

The English Query run-time engine loads our `Hardware Tracking` English Query model, which is used to answer the question. The run-time engine translates the question into the form of SQL statements, which are then passed back to the Active Server Page.

The Active Server Page then passes the SQL statements to SQL Server via ADO. The data results set from the query is returned from SQL Server to the Active Server Page. The Active Server Page then formats the results, and sends them back to the web browser through IIS.

The scenario described above is of course high level, and does not cover all of the details. But, from the diagram we can see all of the various components involved in answering the question that has been submitted. Let's move on now, and start building the web pages.

We can see from the scenario above that we will need two web pages, one that will prompt the user for the question they want to ask, and one to answer the question and send back the results to the user.

Try It Out – Creating the Question Web Page

The first web page interacts with the user and prompts them to enter a question. Since this web page accesses no resources on the web server, it can be a simple HTML web page. The job of this web page is to prompt the user for a question, and to send the results back to the web server for processing.

1. Enter the code using your favorite HTML editor or text editor:

```
<HTML>
<HEAD>
<TITLE>Beginning SQL Server 2000 for VB Developers</TITLE>
<LINK Rel="StyleSheet" Type="Text/CSS" Href="htPageStyles.css"/>
</HEAD>
<BODY>
```

```
<FORM Action="Response.asp" Method="Post" Name="frmQuestion">
    <TABLE Border="0" Width="100%" Class="NormalText">
        <TR>
            <TH>
                <CENTER>
                    Hardware Tracking English Query Application
                </CENTER>
            </TH>
        </TR>
        <TR>
            <TD> </TD>
        </TR>
        <TR>
            <TD>
                Enter your question
                <SMALL>(e.g. <EM>Show all employees.</EM> or
                    <EM>Who works at the Home Office?</EM>)
                </SMALL>
            </TD>
        </TR>
        <TR>
            <TD>
                <INPUT Type="Text" Name="txtQuestion" Size="75">
            </TD>
        </TR>
        <TR>
            <TD>
                <INPUT Type="Button" Name="btnSubmit"
                    Value="Submit Question">
            </TD>
        </TR>
    </TABLE>
</FORM>
<SCRIPT Language="VBScript">
Sub Window_OnLoad()
    'Set focus to the question field
    frmQuestion.txtQuestion.focus()
End Sub
Sub btnSubmit_OnClick()
    'Validate that some text exists in the txtQuestion field
    If Len(Trim(frmQuestion.txtQuestion.value)) = 0 Then
        'Display a message box
        MsgBox "Please enter a question to be asked.", _
            vbInformation + vbOKOnly, "Hardware Tracking EQ"
        'Set focus to the field in error
        frmQuestion.txtQuestion.focus()
        'Exit the procedure without submitting the form
        Exit Sub
    End If
    'Submit the form
    frmQuestion.submit()
End Sub
</SCRIPT>
</BODY>
</HTML>
```

2. Save this file in the `Hardware Tracking` directory with a file name of `EQ.htm`.

3. There are only limited tests that we can perform until we create the next web page that will process the data sent from this web page.

To test this web page, enter the following URL in your web browser:
`http://LocalHost/HardwareTracking/EQ.htm`

4. The first test is a visual test, in that we want to ensure the web page appears and that it is formatted correctly. That is, does the page have the look that we wanted?

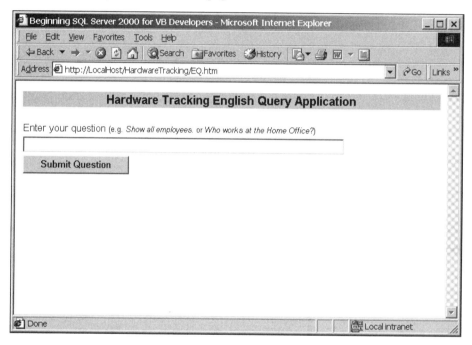

5. The next test that we want to perform is to validate that the code in the `btnSubmit_OnClick` procedure is being executed, so click on the Submit Question button. The code in the `btnSubmit_OnClick` procedure should be executed and you should receive the following message:

We can't actually enter a question and submit it until we build the response web page.

How It Works – Creating the Question Web Page

We start this web page with the standard HTML elements that define the start of every web page. We have included the <HTML> and <HEAD> elements. Remember that the <HEAD> element provides information about the document.

Within the <HEAD> element we have included the <TITLE> element. The text contained in the title element will be displayed in the title bar of the web browser. The <LINK> element links in the stylesheet that we have specified. This is the stylesheet that we built in Chapter 15.

```
<HTML>
<HEAD>
<TITLE>Beginning SQL Server 2000 for VB Developers</TITLE>
<LINK Rel="StyleSheet" Type="Text/CSS" Href="htPageStyles.css"/>
</HEAD>
```

We start the body of our HTML document by specifying the <BODY> element. Then, within the body we have defined a form, as indicated by the <FORM> element. A form allows us to gather data from the user and send the data back to the web server for processing. All of the data from the controls in the form will be placed in a collection and sent back to the server. We are then able to process the data in the collection by ordinal reference (position 0, position 1, etc.) or by name.

The Action attribute specifies the URL that the form contents should be submitted to for processing. This URL can be a fully qualified URL in which the web server, IIS virtual directory, and the web page name are specified, or can contain just the web page name as we have specified here. Normally, if the web page to which you want the form results sent is in the same directory, you just specify the web page name as we have done here.

The Method attribute specifies how we want the form data to be sent to the server. There are two choices here, Get and Post. The Get method appends the form data to the Action URL while the Post method sends the form data through the HTTP post transaction. The Post method is the most widely used, and provides for easier processing of the form data. It is also more secure, as it does not display the data being sent to the user.

The Name attribute assigns a name to our form, which in this case we have set to frmQuestion. This allows us to access the controls on this form in client-side code, which we will see shortly.

```
<BODY>
<FORM Action="Response.asp" Method="Post" Name="frmQuestion">
```

Within the form, we have specified that a table be built. This helps us to present the form to the user while keeping the controls and text aligned. We have specified that the table contains no border and that it should expand or contract to fill 100 percent of the browser window. We have also specified that all text in the form should use the NormalText style, as indicated by the Class attribute.

The first row of data in our table contains the header row for the table. This row will span across the entire browser window.

The next row of data is a filler row; this row will simply provide the appropriate white space between the header row and the first row of text in our form:

```
<TABLE Border="0" Width="100%" Class="NormalText">
    <TR>
        <TH>
            <CENTER>
                Hardware Tracking English Query Application
            </CENTER>
        </TH>
    </TR>
    <TR>
        <TD> </TD>
    </TR>
```

In the first row of data in our table, we have specified the text Enter your question. Then, using the <SMALL> element, we specify that the next section of text be rendered one font size smaller that what is currently being displayed. Here we provide some examples for the user. Using the <EM> element we emphasize the text, which renders it in italics. Notice that all of the elements that we have specified have a corresponding closing element.

```
    <TR>
        <TD>
            Enter your question
            <SMALL>(e.g. <EM>Show all employees.</EM> or
                <EM>Who works at the Home Office?</EM>)
            </SMALL>
        </TD>
    </TR>
```

The next row of data contains the first control in our form. The <INPUT> element defines multiple types of input controls that allow the user to enter or select data. The type of control being generated is controlled by the Type attribute, and here we have specified that the type of control to be generated is a text box control, as indicated by the value Text.

We assign a name to this control so that we can access it in client-side code and also in server-side code. If we did not assign a name to this control, we would have to use the ordinal reference number to access this control in the Request.Form collection. We'll cover this collection when we build the next page, but basically this collection contains all of the controls in a form.

To control the size of the text box generated, we specify the Size attribute. This specifies the size of the text box in characters; in this instance we have specified a value of 75:

```
    <TR>
        <TD>
            <INPUT Type="Text" Name="txtQuestion" Size="75">
        </TD>
    </TR>
```

The last control that we want to generate is a button control. Again, we use the <INPUT> element and specify a Type value of Button. Once again, we assign a name to this control so we can access it in client-side code. The Value attribute specifies the text that is displayed on the button.

We then end our table and end our form by specifying the appropriate closing elements:

```
<TR>
    <TD>
        <INPUT Type="Button" Name="btnSubmit"
            Value="Submit Question">
    </TD>
</TR>
</TABLE>
</FORM>
```

Our client script is next, as indicated by the `<SCRIPT>` element, and we have specified that this script is VBScript, as indicated by the Language attribute. It should be noted here, that you could place your client-side script anywhere in the HTML document. I personally like to have all of my server-side script at the top of the HTML document and all of my client-side script at the end of the document after the form.

The Window_OnLoad procedure will run immediately after the Window object loads. When we code events in VBScript, we specify the object name followed by an underscore and then the event that is fired. So, in this case, Window is the object and OnLoad is the event.

All we are doing in this procedure is setting focus to the field that we want the cursor to be in when the HTML document loads in the browser. Because we have assigned a name to our form and our controls, we are able to reference them by name in our client-side script.

We specify the form name followed by a period, and then the control name followed by another period. Then we specify the method to be executed, which in this case is the focus() method. We could also set properties of the control in the same manner by specifying the property in place of the method and then specifying the value that it should be set to.

```
<SCRIPT Language="VBScript">
Sub Window_OnLoad()
    'Set focus to the question field
    frmQuestion.txtQuestion.focus()
End Sub
```

The next event that we want to handle is the OnClick event for the button control that we have defined. Again, we have specified the object name, the name assigned to the control, followed by an underscore character and then the event name.

Within this procedure, we want to validate that some data has been entered into the question text box before we submit the form. We do this by trimming any spaces from the text box and then checking the length of the object. Once again, we have specified the form name followed by a period and then the control name followed by the value property. This property contains the text that the user has entered.

Using the VBScript Trim function, we trim all spaces from this control and then, using the VBScript Len function, we check the length of the trimmed control. If the length is equal to zero, we know that the user has not entered any data.

```
Sub btnSubmit_OnClick()
    'Validate that some text exists in the txtQuestion field
    If Len(Trim(frmQuestion.txtQuestion.value)) = 0 Then
```

We then want to display a message box for the user indicating that they must enter a question, and we do this using the VBScript MsgBox function. The MsgBox function works in the exact same way in VBScript as it does in VB. We specify the text that we want displayed and then specify that the Information icon and the OK button be displayed in the message box. We also set the title that should be displayed in the title bar of the message box. We do not need to check the response from the MsgBox function because we have only displayed one button.

Next we set the focus to the field in error, which in this case is the question field. Then we exit the procedure:

```
'Display a message box
MsgBox "Please enter a question to be asked.", _
    vbInformation + vbOKOnly, "Hardware Tracking EQ"
'Set focus to the field in error
frmQuestion.txtQuestion.focus()
'Exit the procedure without submitting the form
Exit Sub
End If
```

If the validation of the question field passed, we find ourselves here in our code and want to submit the form for processing. Here we execute the submit() method of the form by specifying the form name followed by a period and the method name. This will cause the form and its data to be submitted back to the server for processing.

We then end our script, end the body of our HTML document, and finally end the HTML document:

```
'Submit the form
frmQuestion.submit()
End Sub
</SCRIPT>
</BODY>
</HTML>
```

The response web page will be responsible for getting the answer to the question that the user has asked, and displaying the resulting data from SQL Server. We want to apply some special formatting to the table header so that the column names of the columns stand out.

Try It Out – Adding Additional Styles to the Cascading Stylesheet

Add the following style to the htPageStyles.css cascading style sheet in the Hardware Tracking directory:

```
.TableHeader
{
    background-color: #000080;
    font-family: Arial, Verdana, Helvetica;
    font-size: 10pt;
    font-weight: bold;
    color: #FFFFFF;
}
```

This user-defined style will be applied to the row of data in our table that will contain the column headers. The first line of this style specifies that the background color of the column be rendered using the color navy, as defined by its RGB value of #000080. The font for the text used will be Arial, Verdana, or Helvetica and the font size will be 10 points. The text will be rendered in a bold font, and will be white in color, as specified by the RGB value of #FFFFFF.

Try It Out – Creating the Response Web Page

The response web page will be responsible for sending the question that was submitted to the English Query run-time engine for processing. It will receive the SQL statements from the run-time engine, and then submit them to SQL Server for processing. The response web page will also format the resulting data from SQL Server in a table and display it to the user.

Since this web page performs server-side processing, and interacts with English Query and SQL Server, it will need to be an Active Server Page.

The complete code for this page (Response.asp) is listed in the following *How It Works* section. Once you have entered all the code, save the file in the Hardware Tracking directory.

How It Works – Creating the Response Web Page

You can use your favorite HTML editor to enter the code that follows, but if you have Visual InterDev it would be helpful if you used that. Visual InterDev provides intellisense and will provide you with a drop-down list of methods and properties for the English Query and ADO objects.

This web page contains mostly server-side script to process the question and answer. There is actually very little HTML code in this web page.

We begin our server-side script with the <% delimiter. To end the script we specify the %> delimiter. IIS treats all code between these two delimiters as server-side VBScript. Server-side script can also be specified using the <SCRIPT> element and specifying the RunAt attribute, for example, <SCRIPT RunAt="Server">.

The very first thing that we want to do in this web page is to code the VBScript Option Explicit statement. This statement performs the same function in VBScript as it does in VB, which is to require all variables to be declared. This ensures that we have declared our variables, so if we mistype one, this mistake will be picked up.

```
<%
'Make all variable declarations required
Option Explicit
%>
```

The #INCLUDE directive is a server-side directive which allows us to include files that contain common code. These files can contain anything from server-side or client-side script, to HTML that is common to all of our web pages. This allows us to write this code once, and then include it in other pages.

There are two keywords that can be used with the #INCLUDE directive, Virtual or File. The Virtual keyword is used when you want to include a file from another virtual directory. This is useful when you have a shared web site that contains common files that are shared among all web sites, for example, copyright information.

The File keyword is used to specify files that are local to the web site that this page is running in, or those that are located in another directory on the web server. Both the Virtual and File keywords can include a path. The difference between the two is that the Virtual keyword uses a virtual path, and the File keyword uses a relative path.

What we have done here is to include the ADOVBS.inc file, using the File keyword of the #INCLUDE directive. This file contains all of the constants that are used by the various ADO objects:

```
<!-- #INCLUDE File="ADOVBS.inc" -->
```

Next, we begin our HTML by specifying the <HTML> element and then specifying the <HEAD> element. Again, we have included a title to be displayed and linked in our cascading stylesheet:

```
<HTML>
<HEAD>
<TITLE>Beginning SQL Server 2000 for VB Developers</TITLE>
<LINK Rel="StyleSheet" Type="Text/CSS" Href="htPageStyles.css"/>
</HEAD>
```

Switching back to server-side script using the server-side script delimiter (<%), we use comments defined just like they are in VB to describe this section of code. Then we declare our global variables. Variables defined outside of a procedure or function are considered global, just like they are in VB. This allows these variables to be used by all the procedures and functions that we define.

The variables declared here will be used by the various procedures and functions that we will be coding. The first two variables are general-purpose variables that will allow us to perform loops and control the processing of data. The variables prefixed with objEQ will be used to set a reference to the English Query objects, and the variables on next line, prefixed with obj, will be used to access some of the English Query objects, and the ADO Recordset object. The last line of variables will be used to hold the English Query question, the restatement of the question, the response, and the input.

The Main process has two functions. First it will determine if this is the first time that we are processing this page or if we are processing this page after a clarification has been requested and submitted. If this is the first time that we are processing this page then we will set up our English Query objects and process the question, calling the appropriate procedures and functions.

If this page is being processed as a result of a clarification being submitted then we call the appropriate procedures and functions to process the clarification.

```
<%
'**************************************************************
'* Main process starts here
'**************************************************************

'Declare global variables
Dim intIndex
Dim blnProcessData
Dim objEQCommand, objEQCommands, objEQSession, objEQResponse
Dim objInput, objInputs, objRS
Dim strQuestion, strRestatement, strResponse, strInputName, strInput
```

This web page will process the question from the EQ.htm web page and then display the results. It will also process the question to check if it needs clarification. If it does, a clarification form will be displayed. This clarification form will post the results back to our server-side page for processing.

Given that, we need to check to see if we are processing the question from the EQ.htm web page, or the results from the clarification form. The clarification form has a field called FormAction, which contains a value of Clarify. The form from the EQ.htm web page does not have a field by this name, so we will know which form posted results to this web page.

So, we check the Request object, which contains the Form collection. We specify the field name in the Form collection that we want to process, in this case FormAction. We compare the results of the field to the static text Clarify. If they are not equal, then we know that this is the first time that we have processed this page, and that the EQ.htm web page has posted the data, so we want to follow this path of logic.

```
'Determine the path of processing
If Request.Form("FormAction") <> "Clarify" Then
```

The first thing that we want to do is to save the question from the EQ.htm web page. We do this by accessing the txtQuestion field in the Form collection of the Request object. We save the value contained in the txtQuestion field in the strQuestion variable. Remember that this is a global variable, and will be accessible to all of our procedures and functions.

```
'Process normal path, first time into the page

'Save the question from the request form
strQuestion = Request.Form("txtQuestion")
```

We need to initialize our English Query session. This next command is a two-step process, the first of which is to create the English Query session. The function GetEQSession function accepts the English Query model as a parameter and returns an English Query session, which is set in the objEQSession object. We'll see this function very shortly.

The next thing that we want to do is to have the objEQSession object parse the question and return the resulting SQL string. The resulting SQL string is set in the objEQResponse object. The objEQResponse object will now contain the response sent from the English Query run-time engine along with the restatement of the question.

```
'Initialize the English Query session
Set objEQSession = GetEQSession("Hardware Tracking.eqd")

'Set the EQ response object to the question
Set objEQResponse = objEQSession.ParseRequest(strQuestion)
```

If the FormAction field is equal to the static text value Clarify, then we know that the Clarify form in this web page has posted a clarification to the question, and this is the path of logic that we want to follow.

The first thing that we want to do here is to retrieve the saved English Query Response object, which was saved in the Session object. A Session object is used to store information for a user, and is persisted throughout the user's session. The user can go from one web page to another in the site and the Session object contains the information that was saved in it. The information that you save in a Session object can be accessed from any web page in the site.

The next section of code will process the clarification needed in case English Query needs the question to be clarified. The following figure shows what this form looks like:

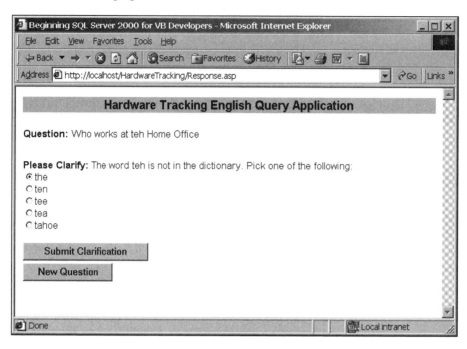

Next, we set the `objInputs` object to the `UserInputs` object of the `objEQResponse` object. The `UserInputs` object contains a collection of user clarifications:

```
Else

    'Process clarification of question

    'Set the EQ Response object and Inputs object
    Set objEQResponse = Session("EQResponse")
    Set objInputs = objEQResponse.UserInputs
```

We then declare three local constants and begin to process the clarifications contained in the `objInputs` object. The `Count` property contains the number of user clarifications contained in the `objInputs` object:

```
    'Declare constants
    Const eqListInput = 0
    Const eqTextInput = 1
    Const eqStaticInput = 2

    'Process all user clarifications
    For intIndex = 0 to objInputs.Count - 1
```

The first thing that we do in this loop is to set the `objInput` object to the user clarification contained in the `objInputs` object. Then we set the string variables to the number of the user clarification and the input from the `Clarify` form:

```
'Set the Input object
Set objInput = objInputs(intIndex)

'Set the string variables
strInputName = "Input" & intIndex
strInput = Request.Form(strInputName)
```

Using a `Select Case` statement, we determine the type of user clarification that is contained in the `objInput` object. The `Type` property can contain three different types of clarification from the user. The first is **list input**, in which the user selected an option from a list of options to clarify their question. The second is **text input**, in which the user entered text to clarify their question, and the third is **static text**, which was displayed to the user for clarification.

Our `Select Case` statement will only handle the first two options and we have also included a `Case Else` statement to handle unknown errors, should one occur:

```
'Process the appropriate clarification
Select Case objInput.Type
    Case eqListInput
        'Input selection chosen
        objInput.Selection = strInput
    Case eqTextInput
        'Input text entered
        objInput.Text = strInput
    Case eqStaticInput
        'Handle static input
    Case Else
        'Handle unknown errors
        Response.Write "Error: Unknown input type"
End Select
Next
```

Next, we resubmit the question for processing by using the `Reply()` method of the `objEQResponse` object. The `Reply()` method will reprocess the original question using the clarifications that the user submitted, and will return a new `objEQResponse` object.

We then save the question from the `Session` object in our global `strQuestion` variable for processing in the next section of code.

```
'Resubmit the question by replying to the clarification response
Set objEQResponse = objEQResponse.Reply()

'Save the question
strQuestion = Session("Question")

End If
```

Regardless of whether we are processing the question directly from the user, or after having the user clarify their question, we call the ProcessResponse procedure. This procedure will determine what type of processing should take place on the objEQResponse object:

```
'Process the response
Call ProcessResponse

'##############################################################
'# Main process ends here
'##############################################################
```

The next section of code contains all of our procedures and functions and has been clearly identified by comments. The descriptions for these procedures and functions are:

❑   CheckForErrors – This procedure performs the error checking for ADO. This procedure is called after executing a method for any ADO object such as opening a database connection or opening a Recordset object.

❑   GetEQSession – This function will either initialize a new English Query session or retrieve the saved English Query session from the Session variable.

❑   ProcessResponse – This procedure will process the response from English Query and call the appropriate procedure to actually process the commands, or set a flag requesting clarification.

❑   ProcessCommands – This procedure will process the commands from the English Query Response object and call the procedure to execute the SQL statement, or display the answer if the command is an answer command.

❑   ProcessSQLCommands – This procedure will establish a connection with SQL Server and execute the SQL string provided by the English Query Command object.

❑   RequestClarification – This procedure will display the clarification form with the options provided by the English Query Response object.

❑   BuildResultsTable – This procedure will process the Recordset object. It will process the answer to the question and display the results in a table.

CheckForErrors Procedure

The first procedure that we have defined is a procedure to check for and process errors returned in the ADO Errors collection. This procedure accepts the ADO Connection object as an input parameter, and is used to access the Errors collection.

The first thing that we do in this procedure is to declare some local variables:

```
'*************************************************************
'* Subroutines start here
'*************************************************************
Sub CheckForErrors(objConn)
'*************************************************************
'* Check for and handle ADO errors
'*************************************************************
```

```
'Declare local variables
Dim blnDisplayErrMsg
Dim objErr
```

We then check the `Count` property of the `Errors` collection to determine if there are any errors. If there are, then we process them.

To do this, the first thing that we do is to set a reference to the ADO `Error` object. The `Error` object will allow us to access the errors in the `Errors` collection and will represent a single error in this collection:

```
If objConn.Errors.Count > 0 Then

    'Create an error object to access the ADO errors collection
    Set objErr = Server.CreateObject("ADODB.Error")
```

Using a `For Each` statement, we enumerate through the errors in the `Errors` collection.

Sometimes when you establish a connection to SQL Server, you receive informational messages back about the default language that has been set. This depends on how your login was defined, and if the `Language` setting was set to a specific language. A message of this type has an error number of zero, indicating that it is purely informational. We want to ignore these types of messages, so we will only process errors that have an error number not equal to zero.

If the error number is not equal to zero, we display the error information using the `Response` object and the `Write` method. The `Response` object is used to send information to the client, and the `Write` method will write a string to the current HTTP output.

We use the `Write` method to display the various properties of the ADO `Error` object. Then we set the `blnDisplayErrMsg` variable to `True`, to indicate that we have a true error:

```
'Display all errors
For Each objErr In objConn.Errors
    'Only process errors that are not zero
    If objErr.Number <> 0 Then
        Response.Write objErr.Number & "<br>"
        Response.Write objErr.Description & "<br>"
        Response.Write objErr.Source & "<br>"
        Response.Write objErr.SQLState & "<br>"
        Response.Write objErr.NativeError & "<br><br>"
        blnDisplayErrMsg = True
    End If
Next
```

If the `blnDisplayErrMsg` variable has been set to `True`, we know that we have a serious error, so again we use the `Write` method of the `Response` object to send another message to the client. Then we use the `End` method to stop all processing. The `End` method stops all processing in our Active Server Page and sends the results that have been generated up to this point to the client.

```
If blnDisplayErrMsg Then
    'Display a message to the user
    Response.Write "An unforseen error has occurred and " & _
        "processing must be stopped."
```

```
              'Halt Execution
              Response.End
         End If
     End IF
End Sub
```

GetEQSession Function

The GetEQSession function accepts the domain file (our compiled English Query model) as the one and only input parameter. This function will in turn return a reference to the English Query Session object.

The English Query Session object is stored in an ASP Session object after the first time it has been created. This allows subsequent calls to this web page to process faster, because we do not incur the extra overhead of creating the English Query Session object; we just retrieve it from the user's ASP Session object.

```
Function GetEQSession(strDomainFile)
'*****************************************************************
'* Get the current English Query Session
'* or
'* Initialize a new English Query Session
'*****************************************************************
```

The first thing we do is to check to see if the ASP Session object, EQSession, is still valid. We do this by using the IsObject function. This function will return a value of True if the EQSession object is still valid, and False if it is not.

There is an automatic timeout value for user sessions. IIS has a default value of 900 seconds (15 minutes) and the web administrator can adjust this value. Assuming the default, if there is no activity within that 15 minutes time interval, IIS will destroy the Session object for the user. This removes all variables and objects that the ASP Session object was holding for a user.

If the EQSession object is still valid, then we set it to a local object defined in our web page:

```
If IsObject(Session("EQSession")) Then
    'Get the existing session
    Set objEQSession = Session("EQSession")
```

Otherwise, we must create the English Query Session object, either because this is the first time processing this page, or the timeout period has elapsed.

Using the Server object in ASP, we execute the CreateObject method to create an instance of the English Query Session object. We set the English Query Session object to our local object, objEQSession:

```
Else
    'Initialize a new session
    'Create the EQ object
    Set objEQSession = Server.CreateObject("MSEQ.Session")
```

Using the `InitDomain` method of the English Query `Session` object, we attach the English Query domain (our compiled English Query model) to the English Query `Session` object. Using the `MapPath` method of the `Server` object, we translate the virtual or relative path specified into a physical directory on the server.

The `ClarifySpellingErrors` property indicates to the English Query run-time engine whether or not to request clarification of spelling errors. When set to `False`, English Query will not prompt the user for clarification of misspelled words; instead it will automatically correct them. If they are not recognizable then the user will be prompted for clarification.

Next, we save the `objEQSession` object in a `Session` object that can be retrieved later if necessary:

```
    'Initialize the domain
    objEQSession.InitDomain(Server.MapPath(strDomainFile))

    'Automatically correct spelling errors when set to False
    objEQSession.ClarifySpellingErrors = False

    'Save the EQ session in the Session object for
    'faster access on subsequent calls
    Set Session("EQSession") = objEQSession
End If
```

Finally, we assign the value stored in English Query `Session` object to a variable of the same name as the function, which returns the stored value to the caller:

```
    'Return the EQ session
    Set GetEQSession = objEQSession
End Function
```

ProcessResponse Procedure

The next procedure that we want to create will process the response from the English Query run-time engine. The first thing that we do in this procedure is to declare some local constants.

At this point if we needed the `EQResponse` object that was stored in the ASP `Session` object, we would have already processed it. To that end, we want to free up the resources being held by the `Session` object, so we set it to `Nothing`:

```
Sub ProcessResponse()
'***************************************************************
'* Process the response from English Query
'***************************************************************

    'Declare response type constants
    Const eqCommandResponse   = 0
    Const eqErrorResponse = 2
    Const eqUserClarifyResponse = 3

    'Remove reference to existing Session EQ Response object
    Set Session("EQResponse") = Nothing
```

The `Type` property of the English Query `Response` object represents the type of response that the object represents. There are three possible values: 0, 2, and 3. A value of 0 indicates that this is a **command response**, whereas a value of 2 indicates that this is an **error response**, and a value of 3 indicates that this is a **user clarification response**.

Using a `Select Case` statement, we process the appropriate response:

```
'Process EQ response type
Select Case objEQResponse.Type
```

If this is a command response (a normal response), then we call the `ProcessCommands` procedure. Then we set the Boolean variable, `blnProcessData`, to `True`. This variable will be used later in our code.

```
Case eqCommandResponse
    'Normal response
    Call ProcessCommands
    blnProcessData = True
```

If this is an error response, we write its description in the web page using the `Description` property of the `Response` object. Then we execute the `End` method of the `Response` object and all processing stops here:

```
Case eqErrorResponse
    'Error response
    Response.Write objEQResponse.Description & "<BR>"
    Response.End
```

If this is a user clarification response, we simply set the `blnProcessData` variable to `False` and perform no further processing:

```
Case eqUserClarifyResponse
    'Clarify response
    blnProcessData = False
```

Finally, just in case there is some unforeseen error, we handle it here:

```
        Case Else
            'Unknown response
            Response.Write "Error: Unknown response type<BR>"
            Response.End
    End Select
End Sub
```

ProcessCommands Procedure

The `ProcessCommands` procedure processes each command in the `Commands` collection of the `Response` object. The first thing that we do in this procedure is to declare some local constants.

Remember that the English Query run-time engine will not only interpret our question and send back the appropriate SQL statements, but it will also send back the restatement and answer text to our question.

Here we are saving the restatement of the question asked by the user, in the `strRestatement` variable. As we do this, we are actually building a variable that contains HTML and text. We build the HTML and text, and then use the `Restatement` property of the `Response` object:

```
Sub ProcessCommands()
'****************************************************************
' Process all EQ Responses
'****************************************************************

    'Declare command type constants
    Const eqQueryCmd = 1
    Const eqAnswerCmd  = 2

    'Set the strRestatement variable
    strRestatement = "<B>Restatement: </B>" & objEQResponse.Restatement
```

Next we set the `objEQCommands` object to the `Commands` collection in the `Response` object. We then proceed to process all of the commands in the `objEQCommands` object and use the `Count` property to determine how many commands there are:

```
    'Set the EQ Commands object
    Set objEQCommands = objEQResponse.Commands

    'Process the EQ commands
    For intIndex = 0 To objEQCommands.Count - 1
```

The first thing that we do in this loop is to set the `objEQCommand` object to the appropriate command contained in the `Commands` collection.

Then, using a `Select Case` statement, we perform the appropriate processing based on the value contained in the `CmdID` property of the `Command` object. The `CmdID` property contains an integer value, indicating what type of command is contained in the `Command` object. There are numerous values, but we are only going to handle the query and answer commands here.

```
        'Set the Command object to the current EQ command
        Set objEQCommand = objEQCommands(intIndex)

        'Select and process the appropriate CmdID
        Select Case objEQCommand.CmdID
```

If the `Command` object contains a query then we call the procedure to process the SQL statements:

```
        Case eqQueryCmd
            Execute the SQL statement
            Call ProcessSQLCommands
```

If the `Command` object contains an answer, then we write the answer in the web page using the `Write` method of the `Response` object:

```
        Case eqAnswerCmd
            'Process the answer
            Response.Write objEQCommand.Answer
```

Otherwise, we handle all unknown values here, and write an error:

```
            Case Else
                'Process unknown errors
                Response.Write "Error: Unknown command type<BR>"
        End Select
    Next
End Sub
```

ProcessSQLCommands Procedure

The `ProcessSQLCommands` procedure will actually process the SQL statements returned from the English Query run-time engine. The first thing that we want to do in this procedure is set up our error handling.

In VBScript, all we can do is ignore the error and process the next statement, by using the `On Error Resume Next` statement. To turn off error handling we use the `On Error Goto 0` statement. These are the only two error handling statements that we currently have in VBScript.

After we have set up our error handling we declare our local variables. These variables will be used to set the maximum number of rows to be returned from SQL Server in our recordset and for the ADO `Connection` object:

```
Sub ProcessSQLCommands()
'***************************************************************
'* Process SQL Command
'***************************************************************

    'Ignore errors - we'll handle them
    On Error Resume Next

    'Declare local variables
    Dim intMaxRows
    Dim objConn
```

The first thing that we want to do here is to set a reference to the ADO `Connection` object by using the `CreateObject` method of the `Server` object. This will set an instance of the ADO `Connection` object in our `objConn` variable, which now becomes an object.

```
    'Create the Command object
    Set objConn = Server.CreateObject("ADODB.Connection")
```

We want to build a DSN-less connection string that uses SQL Server authentication. We covered the details of this in Chapter 6; however, let's recap. We want to use the OLE DB provider for SQL Server, so we have specified this as `SQLOLEDB`. This provider will provide improved performance and features over and above an ODBC driver.

We specify the `Data Source`, which is the server that SQL Server is running on. If you are running multiple instances of SQL Server, then you also need to specify the instance name as we have done here. The `Initial Catalog` is the database that you want to access, in this case we have specified the `Hardware Tracking` database.

In Chapter 4 we created a login specifically for our web pages. Now is the time that we want to use this login. This login has read-only rights to the database, meaning that it can only read data; it cannot insert, update, or delete data. In the User ID parameter of the connect string we have specified this login, and the password associated with this login in the Password parameter.

This connect string is used as the ConnectString parameter to the Open method of the Connection object. The information that you see here will not be visible or returned to the client's browser.

It should also be noted that you will need to substitute your own machine name and SQL Server instance, if required, for the Data Source argument. If you chose a different User ID and Password you will need to substitute them also.

```
'Open the connection to SQL Server using a DSN-Less
'connection w/SQL Server authentication
objConn.Open "Provider=SQLOLEDB;" & _
             "Data Source=WSTRAVEL\SQL2000;" & _
             "Initial Catalog=Hardware Tracking;" & _
             "User ID=HardwareApplication;" & _
             "Password=hardware; "
```

We check for errors by calling the CheckForErrors procedure and pass it the Connection object. This was the first procedure that we defined earlier, and will display all errors and end all processing of the web page. If it finds no errors, then it simply returns and we can then continue processing.

```
'Check for errors
Call CheckForErrors(objConn)
```

The DisplayRows property of the objEQCommand object specifies how many rows of data that the user requested in their query, for example, *Show the top 5 employees*. If the user has not asked a specific row-returning query such as this, then the DisplayRows property will contain a zero value.

We set the intMaxRows variable using the DisplayRows property and then check the value in the intMaxRows variable. If it is equal to zero, then we only want to return a maximum number of 25 rows, which we set as shown in the following code fragment. Setting a maximum of 25 rows prevents this page from returning all of the data from the tables. You can adjust this number as you see fit or as the needs of the users dictate.

```
'Set the intMaxRows variable
intMaxRows = objEQCommand.DisplayRows
If intMaxRows = 0 Then
    intMaxRows = 25
End If
```

We create an instance of the ADO Recordset object next, using the CreateObject method of the Server object. Then we specify that this Recordset object should use a client-side cursor, by setting the CursorLocation property of the Recordset object. The constant used here, adUseClient, is one of the constants defined in the ADOVBS.inc include file.

735

Remember our discussions on cursors? Well, a client-side cursor allows us to disconnect our `Recordset` object from the `Connection` object, thereby freeing up resources and the connection to SQL Server. This is especially important in a web environment, as you never know how many users will be hitting your web site at any one time. Therefore, you want to disconnect from the database as soon as possible, so that someone else can use the connection.

Using the `MaxRecords` property of the `Recordset` object, we limit the number of rows that will be returned in the recordset. We set this property using the `intMaxRows` variable, which was set in the previous code fragment.

```
'Create the Recordset object
Set objRS = Server.CreateObject("ADODB.Recordset")

'Use a client-side cursor
objRS.CursorLocation = adUseClient

'Set the maximum number of records to be returned
objRS.MaxRecords = intMaxRows
```

We now open the `Recordset` object using the `Open` method, and use the SQL statements contained in the `objEQCommand` object as the `Source` parameter to the `Open` method. We only want to read this recordset in a forward direction, so we have specified the `adOpenForwardOnly` constant for the `CursorType` parameter and the `adLockReadOnly` constant for the `LockType` parameter. Since we are executing SQL statements and not a stored procedure, we have specified the `adCmdText` constant for the `Options` parameter.

All of the constants used here are defined in the `ADOVBS.inc` include file.

After we open the recordset, we check for errors by calling the `CheckForErrors` procedure:

```
'Open the recordset objRS.Open objEQCommand.SQL, objConn, _
    adOpenForwardOnly, adLockReadOnly, adCmdText
'Check for errors
Call CheckForErrors(objConn)
```

Before we continue any further or do any other processing, we want to disconnect our `Recordset` object from the `Connection` object. We do this by setting the `ActiveConnection` property of the `Recordset` object to `Nothing` which releases the connection.

Then we are able to close the `Connection` object and release the reference to it by setting it to `Nothing`:

```
'Disconnect the Recordset object from the Connection object
Set objRS.ActiveConnection = Nothing

'Close and remove the reference to the Connection object
objConn.Close
Set objConn = Nothing
```

We want to save the response returned from the English Query run-time engine, so we set the `strResponse` variable to a string that contains a mixture of HTML and text. We use the `TableCaption` property of the `objEQCommand` object to retrieve the response. Finally we end the procedure:

```
      'Save the response from the EQ Command object
      strResponse = "<B>Response: </B>" & objEQCommand.TableCaption
   End Sub
```

RequestClarification Procedure

The `RequestClarification` procedure is called when the English Query run-time engine cannot answer your question. This procedure will display a form asking for clarification of your question.

The first thing that we want to do in this procedure is to declare our local variables and to define the constants that we will need:

```
   Sub RequestClarification()
   '*****************************************************************
   '* Request clarification of question
   '*****************************************************************

      'Declare local variables
      Dim intItemIndex, intSelection
      Dim strChecked
      Dim arrItems

      'Declare UserInput type constants
      Const eqListInput = 0
      Const eqTextInput = 1
      Const eqStaticInput = 2
```

Using the `Write` method of the `Response` object, we build a form by writing the HTML to the web page. This method provides faster processing than ending the script, then coding the HTML, and then starting the script again.

In the first `Write` statement we have specified the HTML `<FORM>` element and have specified the various attributes. Notice that we have specified that the form should post the results back to this same page, as this page contains the necessary logic to process the clarification that the user chooses.

In the second `Write` statement we have specified a hidden input field which will be used in the code at the beginning of this page to determine whether this is the first time we are processing a question, or if we are processing a clarification to a question.

Using the third `Write` statement, we display the text `Please Clarify`:

```
      'Ask for clarification and begin the form
      Response.Write "<FORM Action=""Response.asp"" Method=""POST"" " & _
         "Name=""frmClarify"">"
      Response.Write "<INPUT Type=""Hidden"" Name=""FormAction"" " & _
         "Value=""Clarify"">"
      Response.Write "<B>Please Clarify:</B> "
```

We set the object, objInputs, to the UserInputs collection in the Response object. Then we begin a loop to process all inputs in the UserInputs collection:

```
'Set the inputs object to the EQ response user inputs
Set objInputs = objEQResponse.UserInputs

'Process all user inputs from EQ
For intIndex = 0 to objInputs.Count - 1
```

The first thing that we do in this loop is to set the objInput object to a single UserInput object in the UserInputs collection. Then we set the strInputName variable to the word Input and assign the number contained in the intIndex variable.

Next, we display the caption contained in the objInput object using the Caption property. This data is written to the web page using the Write method of the Response object:

```
'Set the input object to the user inputs
Set objInput = objInputs(intIndex)

'Set the input name for the radio button
strInputName = "Input" & intIndex

'Display the clarification text
Response.Write objInput.Caption
```

Using a Select Case statement we process the type of clarification request that the run-time engine has provided in the Type property of the objInput object. The first Case statement handles the ListInput type, which provides a list of input options that the user can select from in order to clarify their question.

We set the arrItems variable to the items contained in the Items property of the objInput object. Then we set the intSelection variable to the default selection provided in the Selection property of the objInput object.

We check the value now contained in the intSelection variable, and if it is less than zero we set a default value of zero:

```
Select Case objInput.Type
    Case eqListInput
        'Get an array of items (items are suggested words)
        arrItems = objInput.Items

        'Get the default selection
        intSelection = objInput.Selection

        'If its less than zero then set it to zero
        If intSelection < 0 Then
            intSelection = 0
        End If
```

We loop through the arrItems array and build a list of options that the user can select from to clarify their question.

The first thing that we do in this loop is to check to see if the item that we are processing is the item that should be selected as the default item. This is done by comparing the intItemIndex variable to the intSelection variable. If the result of this comparison is that the variables are equal, then we set the strChecked variable to the word Checked. This variable will be used in our HTML string that we will write next.

```
'Build the options of suggested words
For intItemIndex = 0 To UBound(arrItems, 1)

    'Set the strChecked variable to Checked or
    'nothing
    If intItemIndex = intSelection Then
        strChecked = "Checked"
    Else
        strChecked = ""
    End If
```

Using the Write method, we write an HTML string to the web page. This string contains the HTML <INPUT> element, which is a radio (option) button, as specified by the Type attribute. The Name attribute of the element being built is set using the strInputName variable and the Value attribute is set using the intItemIndex variable. The strChecked variable is used to set the item as the default item if the variable contains the word Checked.

Finally, the arrItems array is used to display the text for this option button. The intItemIndex variable is used to get the correct item in the array to be added to this option button.

```
'Build the option button
Response.Write "<BR><INPUT Type=""Radio"" " & _
    "Name=""" & strInputName & """ Value="" " & _
    intItemIndex & """ " & strChecked & ">" & _
    arrItems(intItemIndex)
Next
```

The next type of request that we want to handle from the run-time engine is for text input. Here we use the Write method to build an HTML <INPUT> element that will prompt the user to enter some text to clarify their question. The Name attribute is being set using the strInputName variable:

```
Case eqTextInput
    Response.Write "<BR><INPUT Type=""Text"" Name=""" & _
        strInputName & """ Size=""40"">"
```

If we receive any other type of response, it is unknown to us and we display a message indicating an error:

```
Case Else
    'Handle unknown errors
    Response.Write "Error: Unexpected input type"
End Select
Next
```

We write two consecutive line breaks to the web page using the HTML `<BR>` elements. Then we create a submit button by using the HTML `<INPUT>` element and setting the `Type` attribute to `Submit`. The text that is displayed on the button is set in the `Value` attribute:

```
'Write two line breaks
Response.Write "<BR><BR>"

'Build the submit button
Response.Write "<INPUT Type=""Submit"" Value=""Submit Clarification"">"
```

Finally, we save the question that the user has submitted in a `Session` variable for processing after the user has submitted the clarification. We also save the `objEQResponse` object in a `Session` variable for later use:

```
'Save the question and response for the clarification page
Session("Question") = strQuestion
Set Session("EQResponse") = objEQResponse
End Sub
```

BuildResultsTable Procedure

The `BuildResultsTable` procedure is responsible for building the results table. This is the table that contains the data returned from SQL Server. The first thing that we do in this procedure is to declare our local variables.

The `intCol` variable will be used to access each `Field` object in the `Fields` collection in the `Recordset` object. The `blnEven` variable will be used to track which rows in the table are even and which rows are odd. We will then apply the appropriate style to the row so that each even row has the same style and each odd row has the same style.

```
Sub BuildResultsTable()
'***************************************************************
' Build a table with the results
'***************************************************************

    'Declare local variables
    Dim intCol
    Dim blnEven
```

The next thing that we do is to ensure we have a valid `Recordset` object. This is accomplished using the `IsObject` function. Remember that this function returns a `True/False` value indicating whether or not the object is a valid object.

We only want to process the `Recordset` object if it contains data, so we check for an end-of-file condition using the `EOF` property of the `Recordset` object:

```
'Check for a valid object first
If IsObject(objRS) Then

    'If results exist then process them
    If Not objRS.EOF Then
```

If we have data, we start building a table to contain the results. Again, we are using the `Write` method to write the HTML to our web page. The `Write` method expects a string, and a string must be enclosed in quote marks. Where we want a quote mark to appear in our HTML, we have used two consecutive quote marks. This will cause a single quote mark to appear in our final HTML output without causing an error in our string.

We loop through the `Fields` collection to build the header row for our table. Using the `Count` property of the `Fields` collection, we are able to determine how many `Field` objects are contained in the `Fields` collection.

We create a column in the table for each `Field` in the `Fields` collection. Using the `Name` property of the `Field` object, we are able to display the `Field` name that was returned by SQL Server. The `Field` name corresponds to the column name in SQL Server.

Notice that we are using the `TableHeader` class in our cascading stylesheet for these columns.

```
Response.Write "<TABLE Border=""0"" Class=""NormalText"">"

Response.Write "<TR>"
For intCol = 0 To objRS.Fields.Count - 1
    Response.Write "<TD Class=""TableHeader"">" & _
            objRS.Fields.Item(intCol).Name & "</TD>"
Next
Response.Write "</TR>"
```

We set the `blnEven` variable to `True` before we begin our loop to build the data rows in our table. Then we enter a loop to process all records in the `Recordset` object until an end-of-file condition is encountered:

```
'Build the rows of data
blnEven = True

Do While Not objRS.EOF
```

The first thing that we do in this loop is to check the `blnEven` variable. If this variable contains a value of `True`, then we use the `EvenRow` style in this row and we flip the switch for the variable by setting it not equal to itself. This will cause the variable to now contain a value of `False`.

If the value is `False`, then we use the `OddRow` style in the row and again we flip the switch for the `blnEven` variable:

```
        If blnEven Then
            'Use EvenRow style
            Response.Write "<TR Class=""EvenRow"">"
            'Flip the blnEven variable
            blnEven = Not blnEven
        Else
            'Use OddRow style
            Response.Write "<TR Class=""OddRow"">"
            'Flip the blnEven variable
            blnEven = Not blnEven
        End If
```

We now want to process each `Field` object in the `Fields` collection. Again we use the `Count` property of the `Fields` collection to determine how many `Field` objects are in the `Fields` collection. Each `Field` object in the `Field` collection is written to a separate column in the table.

Since we do not know the name of the `Field` object in the `Fields` collection, we access each `Field` object by ordinal reference, meaning that we use the index number to access each `Field` object. We check to see if the `Value` property of the `Field` object contains a `Null` value. If it does, we simply use the `Write` method of the `Response` object to write a column that contains no data.

If the `Value` property does not contain a `Null` value, we use the `Write` method to build a column that contains data. The column is populated by data from the `Value` property of the `Field` object:

```
            'Process all fields in the Record object
            For intCol = 0 To objRS.Fields.Count - 1

                'Check for a null value
                If IsNull(objRS.Fields(intCol).Value) Then
                    'If null then write nothing
                    Response.Write "<TD></TD>"
                Else
                    'If not null then write the data
                    Response.Write "<TD>" & _
                        objRS.Fields(intCol).Value & "</TD>"
                End If
            Next
```

We end the row of data in our table by writing the closing row element. Then we move to the next record in our `Recordset` object and start the loop all over again:

```
            'Write the closing element for the table row
            Response.Write "</TR>"

            'Move to the next record
            objRS.MoveNext
        Loop
```

After our loop has finished processing, we end the table by writing the closing element for the table:

```
            'Write the closing element for the table
            Response.Write "</TABLE>"
```

If the `Recordset` object returned was empty, we write a message indicating that no data was found:

```
        Else
            'Display a message that no data was found
            Response.Write("No data was found")
        End If
```

At the end of this procedure, we close the `Recordset` object and remove our reference to it by setting it to `Nothing`.

Since this is the last procedure in our server-side script we end the script:

```
        'Close and remove the reference to the Recordset object
        objRS.Close
        Set objRS = Nothing

    End If
End Sub


'#################################################################
'# Subroutines end here
'#################################################################
%>
```

Main Body of Web Page

This is the start of the body of our HTML web page. Here we start building a table and build the header column in the first row. The second row in our table contains a blank space, which is used to build an empty row that serves as a spacer between the header row and the first row of data in our table:

```
<BODY>
<TABLE Border="0" Width="100%" Class="NormalText">
    <TR>
        <TH>
            <CENTER>
                Hardware Tracking English Query Application
            </CENTER>
        </TH>
    </TR>
    <TR>
        <TD> </TD>
    </TR>
```

The first data row in our table will contain the question that the user asked, and the question is populated using the strQuestion variable. Since we need to use a server-side variable in our HTML, we must enclose the variable in the server-side script tags and precede the variable name with an equal sign.

The next row of data in our table contains the restatement of the user's question. Remember that this restatement came from the English Query run-time engine, and when we saved it in this variable we built HTML into it. This HTML will be applied here.

The next row of data contains the response, which also came from the English Query run-time engine. Again, we saved this response in a variable and also built HTML in the variable, which will be applied here.

The next row serves as a spacer row to separate the data here from the data in the table that we are getting ready to build:

```
    <TR>
        <TD><B>Question: </B><%=strQuestion%></TD>
    </TR>
    <TR>
```

743

```
        <TD><%=strRestatement%></TD>
    </TR>
    <TR>
        <TD><%=strResponse%></TD>
    </TR>
    <TR>
        <TD> </TD>
    </TR>
```

The next row in our table will contain either the data returned from SQL Server if the question was answered, or the clarification data if the English Query run-time engine requested clarification of the question. We start this row and column in the table using an HTML element.

Then we switch to server-side script to determine if we should call the `BuildResultsTable` procedure to build the results table, or call the `RequestClarification` procedure to build a form requesting clarification.

```
    <TR>
        <TD>
<%
    If blnProcessData Then
        'Build the results table
        Call BuildResultsTable
    Else
        'Request clarification
        Call RequestClarification
    End If
%>
```

After we have called the appropriate procedure, we switch back to HTML and then end the column and end the row.

The next row in our table contains a button that will allow the user to return to the EQ.htm web page to ask another question.

We then end this column and row, and then end the table:

```
        </TD>
    </TR>
    <TR>
        <TD>
            <INPUT Type="Button" Name="btnNewQuestion"
                Value="New Question">
        </TD>
    </TR>
</TABLE>
```

This page contains a small amount of client-side script. This script is written using VBScript as specified in the Language attribute of the <SCRIPT> element.

The `btnNewQuestion_OnClick` procedure will be executed when the user clicks on the `btnNewQuestion` button in the form. Here we are using the `Window` object to send the user to the `EQ.htm` web page. We set the `Href` property of the `Location` property to the `EQ.htm` web page and this will cause the browser to display the `EQ.htm` web page when this code is executed:

```
<SCRIPT Language="VBScript">
Sub btnNewQuestion_OnClick()
    Window.Location.Href = "EQ.htm"
End Sub
</SCRIPT>
```

We finally end the body of our web page and then end the web page itself, by specifying the appropriate closing HTML elements:

```
</BODY>
</HTML>
```

Save this web page as `Response.asp` in the `Hardware Tracking` directory.

Try It Out – Testing the English Query Web Application

We are now ready to test the response web page.

1. To begin testing, navigate to the `EQ.htm` web page in your browser. Enter the question Show all of teh employees in the `EQ.htm` web page and then click on the **Submit Question** button. (Note the deliberate typo.)

The `Response.asp` page is processed and the results are displayed as shown in the following figure. Because we set the `ClarifySpellingErrors` property of the English Query `Session` object to `False`, the run-time engine took care of correcting our error in the spelling of the word the.

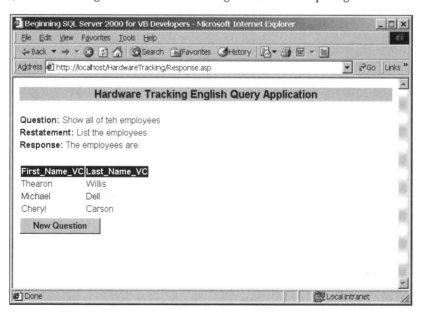

Notice in the figure that our new style has been applied to the header row of our table that contains the results. Also, every other row in the results table uses the EvenRow style.

2. To test the script for the New Question button, click on the button and you should be taken to the EQ.htm web page.

3. To test the code that prompts for clarification of a question, set the ClarifySpellingErrors property to True. Save the Response.asp page and shut down your browser. Because the English Query Session object is saved in an ASP Session variable, we need to shut down the browser. Otherwise, we will use the same English Query Session object, which has the ClarifySpellingErrors property set to False.

4. Start the browser again and navigate to the EQ.htm web page. Then enter the same question again with the misspelled word. This time when you click on the Submit Question button, a clarification request is displayed, as shown in the following figure:

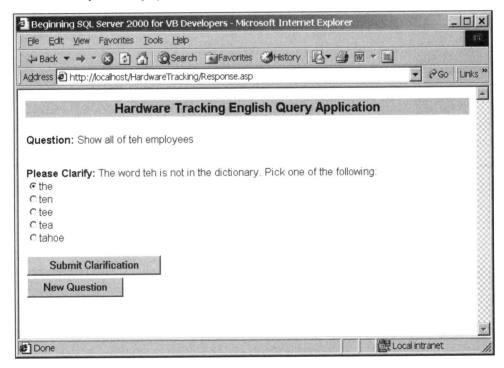

Once you choose the correct clarification option and click on the Submit Clarification button, you will see the same results that were displayed in the last figure. The question will contain the misspelled word and the restatement will contain the correct spelling of the word.

5. Change the ClarifySpellingErrors property back to False, then close the browser and open a new browser window. You can then proceed to enter all of the questions that were presented at the end of the last case study, such as Where do employees work. The next figure shows the results of this question:

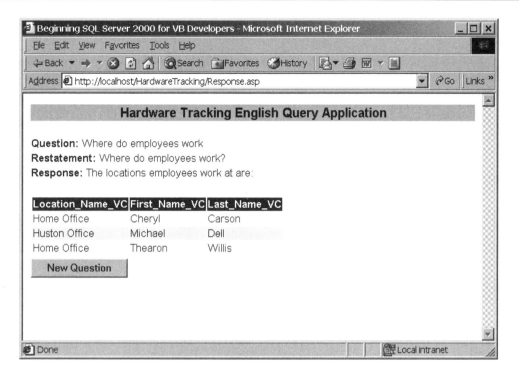

Using VB for Deployment

While we have covered deployment of your English Query application using the Web, some readers may choose to use VB instead. Although we do not have space here to cover this, we can point you to the source code that achieves this.

When you installed English Query it installed sample source code to distribute your English Query application using ASP, VB, and VC++. It also installed sample English Query application models for the FoodMart, Northwind, and pubs databases. The FoodMart database is installed when you install the optional Analysis Services.

To locate the source code and sample models, go to the folder that you chose to install English Query in. If you took the default installation then this folder will be located on your C drive under Program Files, and will be called Microsoft English Query. Under this folder there is a folder called Samples and then a folder for Applications and a folder for Models. The Applications folder contains the sample source code for distribution and the Models folder contains the sample English Query models.

Summary

This part of the case study has taken a look at one of the available deployment methods to deploy your English Query application. We could have used Visual Basic or Visual C++, but we chose to use the Web to deploy our application.

We covered the various options for redistributing the English Query run-time engine and you should now know that the best way to deploy the run-time engine is to run the installation program for English Query and choose the Run-time Only option.

Having built the question and response web pages, you should now have a better feel for what is involved in deployment over the Web. We only covered the basics in our response web page and there are many more features that you could incorporate, for instance, question building. The Question Builder can help your users by constructing simple and complex questions that they can choose from.

Our response web page can handle answering a question that needs no clarification. It can also handle questions that do need clarification, and in this case will prompt the user for clarification before processing the clarification. It displays the results of all questions answered using an HTML table.

By specifying the question that the user asked, and the restatement from the English Query run-time engine, the users can get a better feel for how to ask more appropriate questions.

To summarize, you should know:

❑   What deployment methods are available

❑   How to install the English Query run-time engine

❑   How to build a question page and post the results to the response page

❑   How to build a response page to answer questions, prompt for clarifications, and answer those clarifications

While this is the end of this book it should not be the end of your learning. To learn more about SQL Server 2000, check out *SQL: Access to SQL Server* published by Apress, ISBN 1-893115-30-5 and visit the Apress web site at http://www.apress.com for other SQL Server titles.

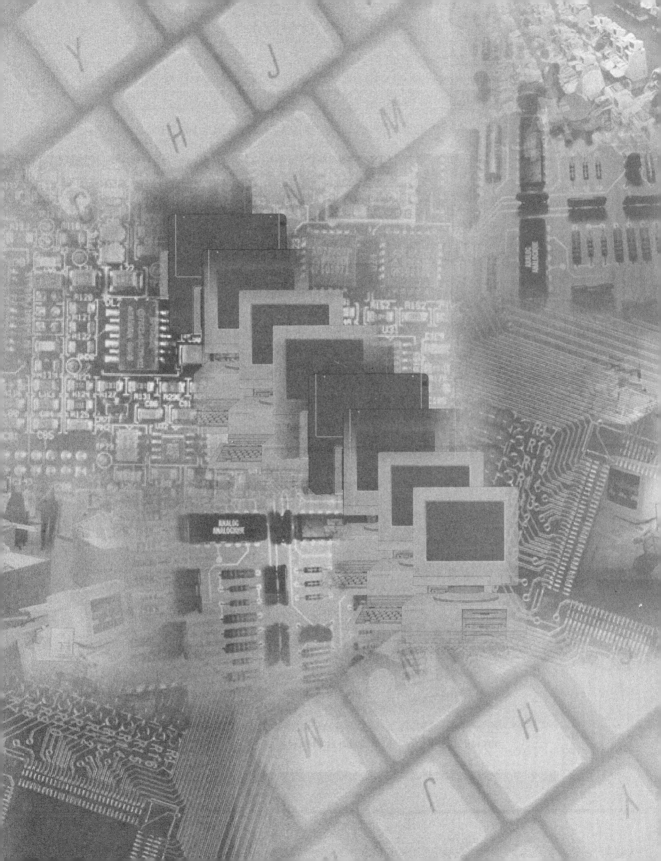

SQL Server and VB Data Types

There are some subtle differences in the SQL Server data types versus the Visual Basic data types. This table provides a side-by-side comparison of these data types:

SQL Data Type	Range	VB Data Type	Range
Bit	1 or 0	Boolean	True/False
TinyInt	0 to 255	Byte	0 to 255
Money	-922,337,203,685,477.5808 to 922,337,203,685,477.5807	Currency	-922,337,203,685,477.5808 to 922,337,203,685,477.5807
DateTime	1/1/1753 to 12/31/9999	Date	1/1/100 to 12/31/9999
Decimal	$-10^{\wedge}38\text{-}1$ to $10^{\wedge}38\text{-}1$	Decimal	+/- 79,228,162,514,264,337,593,543,950,335 with no decimal +/- 7.9228162514264433759354395 0335 with 28 places to the right of the decimal
Float	-1.79E + 308 to 1.79E + 308	Double	4.94065645841247E-324 to 1.79769313486232E308 for positive values
SmallInt	-32,768 to 32,767	Integer	-32,768 to 32,767
Int	-2,147,483,648 to 2,147,483,647	Long	-2,147,483,648 to 2,147,483,647
Real	-3.40E+38 to 3.40E+38	Single	1.401298E-45 to 3.402823E38 for positive values
Char and Varchar	Up to 8,000 characters	String	0 to 2,147,483,647
Text	Up to 2,147,483,647 characters	String	0 to 2,147,483,647

The following table lists, by type, all Transact-SQL data types:

SQL Data Type	Range
Integers	
BigInt	-9223372036854775808 to 9223372036854775807
Int	-2,147,483,648 to 2,147,483,647
SmallInt	-32,768 to 32,767
TinyInt	0 to 255
Bit	
Bit	1 or 0
Decimal and Numeric	
Decimal	-10^38-1 to 10^38-1
Numeric	Synonym for decimal
Money	
Money	-922,337,203,685,477.5808 to 922,337,203,685,477.5807
SmallMoney	-214,748.3648 to 214,748.3647
Approximate Numerics	
Float	-1.79E+308 to 1.79E+308
Real	-3.40E+38 to 3.40E+38
Date and Time	
DateTime	January 1, 1753 to December 31, 9999
SmallDateTime	January 1, 1900 to June 6, 2079
Character Strings	
Char	Fixed length character up to 8,000 characters
VarChar	Variable length character up to 8,000 characters
Text	Variable length character up to 2,147,483,647 characters

SQL Data Type	Range
Unicode Character Strings	
nChar	Fixed length data up to 4,000 characters
nVarChar	Variable length data up to 4,000 characters
nText	Variable length data up to 1,073,741,823 characters
Binary Strings	
Binary	Fixed length binary data up to 8,000 bytes
VarBinary	Variable length binary data up to 8,000 bytes
Image	Variable length binary data up to 2,147,483,647 bytes
Other	
Cursor	Reference to a cursor
RowVersion	Database-wide unique number (formerly known as a Timestamp)
SQL_Variant	Stores values of various SQL Server-supported data types, except Text, nText, Timestamp
Table	Special data type used to store a result set for later processing
UniqueIdentifier	Global unique identifier

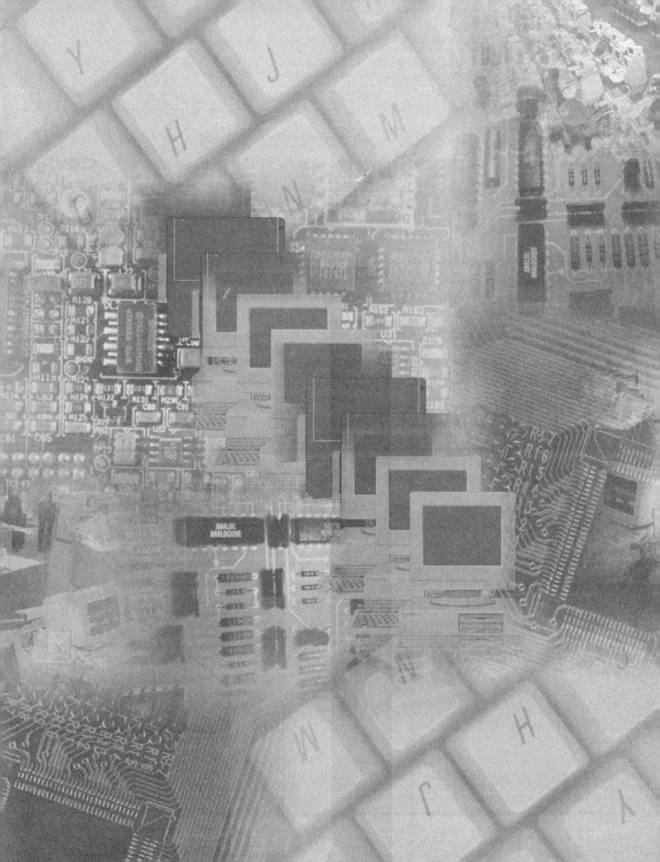

ADO 2.6 Object Model

This appendix lists the objects, methods, and properties of the Microsoft ActiveX Data Objects library version 2.6.

Objects

Name	Description
Command	A Command object defines a specific command that you intend to execute against a data source.
Connection	A Connection object represents an open connection to a data source.
Error	An Error object contains details about a single data access error pertaining to a single operation involving the provider. The provider is the driver used to access the database such as SQLOLEDB.
Errors	A collection of all the Error objects created in response to a single failure involving the provider.
Field	A Field object represents a column of data.
Fields	A collection of all the Field objects of a Recordset or Record object.
Parameter	A Parameter object represents a parameter or argument associated with a Command object based on a parameterized query or stored procedure.
Parameters	Contains all the Parameter objects of a Command object.
Property	A Property object represents a characteristic of an ADO object that is defined by the provider.
Properties	A collection of all the Property objects for a specific instance of an object.

Table continued on following page

Name	Description
Record	The Record object represents a row in a recordset, or a file or directory in a file system.
Recordset	A Recordset object represents the entire set of records from a base table or the results of an executed command. At any time, the Recordset object refers to only a single record within the set as the current record.
Stream	A Stream object represents a stream of binary data or text.

Command Object

A Command object is a definition of a specific command that you intend to execute against a data source.

Methods

Name	Returns	Description
Cancel		Cancels execution of a pending, asynchronous Execute or Open method call.
CreateParameter	Parameter object	Creates a new Parameter object with the specified properties.
Execute	Recordset object reference	Executes the query, SQL statement, or stored procedure specified in the CommandText property.

Properties

Name	Returns	Description
ActiveConnection	Variant	Indicates to which Connection object the specified Command, Recordset, or Record object currently belongs.
CommandText	String	Contains the text of a command that you want to issue against a provider.
CommandTimeout	Long	Indicates how long to wait while executing a command before terminating the attempt and generating an error.
CommandType	CommandTypeEnum	Indicates the type of a Command object.
CommandStream	Stream	Indicates the stream used as the input for a Command object.

Name	Returns	Description
Dialect	GUID	The dialect defines the syntax and general rules that the provider uses to parse the string or stream.
Name	String	Indicates the name of an object.
NamedParameters	String	Indicates whether parameter names should be passed to the provider.
Prepared	Boolean	Indicates whether to save a compiled version of a command before execution.
State	ObjectStateEnum	Indicates, for all applicable objects, whether the state of the object is open or closed.

Connection Object

A Connection object represents an open connection to a data source.

Methods

Name	Returns	Description
BeginTrans	Long	Manages transaction processing within a Connection object by beginning a new transaction.
CommitTrans		Manages transaction processing within a Connection object by committing any changes and ending the current transaction. It may also start a new transaction.
RollBackTrans		Manages transaction processing within a Connection object by canceling any changes made during the current transaction and ending the transaction. It may also start a new transaction.
Cancel		Cancels execution of a pending, asynchronous Execute or Open method call.
Close		Closes an open object and any dependent objects.
Execute	Recordset object	Executes the specified query, SQL statement, stored procedure, or provider-specific text.
Open		Opens a connection to a data source.

Table continued on following page

Name	Returns	Description
OpenSchema	Recordset object	Obtains database schema information from the provider.
Save		Saves (persists) the recordset in a file or Stream object.

Properties

Name	Returns	Description
Attributes	Long	Indicates one or more characteristics of an object.
CommandTimeout	Long	Indicates how long to wait while executing a command before terminating the attempt and generating an error.
ConnectionString	String	Contains the information used to establish a connection to a data source.
ConnectionTimeout	Long	Indicates how long to wait while establishing a connection before terminating the attempt and generating an error.
CursorLocation	CursorLocationEnum	Sets or returns the location of the cursor . A cursor can be on the client or the server.
DefaultDatabase	String	Indicates the default database for a Connection object.
IsolationLevel	IsolationLevel Enum	Indicates the level of isolation for a Connection object. Isolation specifies how transactions are isolated from one another.
Mode	ConnectMode Enum	Indicates the available permissions for modifying data in a Connection, Record, or Stream object.
Provider	String	Indicates the name of the provider for a Connection object.
State	ObjectState Enum	Indicates, for all applicable objects, whether the state of the object is open or closed.
Version	String	Indicates the ADO version number.

Error Object

An `Error` object contains details about data access errors pertaining to a single operation through the ADO provider.

Properties

Name	Returns	Description
Description	String	Describes an `error`.
HelpContext	Long	Indicates the context ID of the help topic associated with an `error`.
HelpFile	String	Indicates the help file associated with an `error`.
NativeError	Long	Indicates the provider-specific error code for a given `error`.
Number	Long	Indicates the number that uniquely identifies an `error`.
Source	String	Indicates the name of the object or application that originally generated an error.
SQLState	String	Indicates the SQL state for a given `error`. `SQLState` is a five character error code returned from SQL Server indicating the error that occurred.

Errors Collection

Contains all the `Error` objects created in response to a single failure involving the provider.

Methods

Name	Returns	Description
Clear		Removes all of the objects in a collection.
Refresh		Updates the objects in a collection to reflect objects available from and specific to the provider.

Properties

Name	Returns	Description
Count	Long	Indicates the number of objects in a collection.
Item	Object reference	Returns a specific member of the errors collection, by name or ordinal number, which is zero based.

Field Object

A `Field` object represents a column of data with a common data type.

Methods

Name	Returns	Description
AppendChunk		Appends data to a large text or binary data `Field` or `Parameter` object.
GetChunk	Variant	Returns all, or a portion of the contents, of a large text or binary data `Field` object.

Properties

Name	Returns	Description
ActualSize	Long	Indicates the actual length of a field's value.
Attributes	Long	Indicates one or more characteristics of an object.
DefinedSize	Long	Indicates the defined size of a `Field` object.
Name	String	Indicates the name of an object.
NumericScale	Byte	Indicates the scale of numeric values in a `Parameter` or `Field` object.
Original Value	Variant	Indicates the value of a field that existed in the record before any changes were made.
Precision	Byte	Indicates the degree of precision for numeric values in a `Parameter` object or for numeric `Field` objects.
Status	FieldStatus Enum	Indicates the status of a `Field` object. This status gets updated after the `Update` method has been executed for a `Record` or `Recordset` object.
Type	DataType Enum	Indicates the operational type or data type of a `Parameter`, `Field`, or `Property` object.
Underlying Value	Variant	Indicates a `Field` object's current value in the database.
Value	Variant	Indicates the value assigned to a `Field`, `Parameter`, or `Property` object.

Fields Collection

Contains all the Field objects of a Recordset or Record object.

Methods

Name	Returns	Description
Append		Appends an object to a collection. If the collection is Fields, a new Field object may be created before it is appended to the collection.
CancelUpdate		Cancels any changes made to the current or new row of a Recordset object or the Fields collection of a Record object.
Delete		Deletes an object from the Fields collection.
Refresh		Updates the objects in a collection to reflect objects available from and specific to the provider.
Resync		Refreshes the data in the current Recordset object or Fields collection of a Record object from the database.
Update		Saves any changes you make to the current record of a Recordset object.

Properties

Name	Returns	Description
Count	Long	Indicates the number of objects in a collection.
Item	Object reference	Returns a specific member of a collection by name or ordinal number.

Property Object

A Property object represents a dynamic characteristic of an ADO object that is defined by the provider.

Properties

Name	Returns	Description
Attributes	Long	Indicates one or more characteristics of an object.
Name	String	Indicates the name of an object.
Type	DataTypeEnum	Indicates the operational type or data type of a Parameter, Field, or Property object.

Table continued on following page

761

Name	Returns	Description
Value	Variant	Indicates the value assigned to a `Field`, `Parameter`, or `Property` object.

Properties Collection

Contains all the `Property` objects for a specific instance of an object.

Methods

Name	Returns	Description
Refresh		Updates the objects in a collection to reflect objects available from and specific to the provider.

Properties

Name	Returns	Description
Count	Long	Indicates the number of objects in a collection.
Item	Object reference	Returns a specific member of a collection by name or ordinal number.

Parameter Object

A `Parameter` object represents a parameter or argument associated with a `Command` object based on a parameterized query or stored procedure.

Methods

Name	Returns	Description
AppendChunk		Appends data to a large text or binary data `Field` or `Parameter` object.

Properties

Name	Returns	Description
Attributes	Long	Indicates one or more characteristics of an object.
Direction	Parameter Direction Enum	Indicates whether the parameter represents an input parameter, an output parameter, or both, or if the parameter is the return value from a stored procedure.
Name	String	Indicates the name of an object.

Name	Returns	Description
NumericScale	Byte	Indicates the scale of numeric values in a Parameter or Field object.
Precision	Byte	Indicates the degree of precision for numeric values in a Parameter object or for numeric Field objects.
Size	Long	Indicates the maximum size, in bytes or characters, of a Parameter object.
Type	DataType Enum	Indicates the operational type or data type of a Parameter, Field, or Property object.
Value	Variant	Indicates the value assigned to a Field, Parameter, or Property object.

Parameters Collection

Contains all the Parameter objects of a Command object.

Methods

Name	Returns	Description
Append		Appends an object to a collection. If the collection is Fields, a new Field object may be created before it is appended to the collection.
Delete		Deletes an object from the Parameters collection.
Refresh		Updates the objects in a collection to reflect objects available from and specific to the provider.

Properties

Name	Returns	Description
Count	Long	Indicates the number of objects in a collection.
Item	Object reference	Returns a specific member of a collection by name or ordinal number.

Record Object

The Record object represents a row in a recordset, or a file or directory in a file system.

Methods

Name	Returns	Description
Cancel		Cancels execution of a pending, asynchronous Execute or Open method call.
Close		Closes an open object and any dependent objects.
CopyRecord	String	Copies a file or directory, and its contents, to another location.
DeleteRecord		Deletes a file, or a directory and all its files and subdirectories.
GetChildren	Recordset object	Returns a Recordset object whose rows represent the files and subdirectories in the directory represented by this Record.
MoveRecord	String	Moves a file, or a directory and its contents, to another location.
Open		Opens an existing Record object, or creates a new file or directory.

Properties

Name	Returns	Description
Active Connection	String	Indicates to which Connection object the specified Command, Recordset, or Record object currently belongs.
Mode	Connect ModeEnum	Indicates the available permissions for modifying data in a Connection, Record, or Stream object.
ParentURL	String	Returns an absolute URL string pointing to the parent record of the current Record object.
RecordType	Record TypeEnum	Indicates the type of Record object.
Source	Variant	Indicates the entity represented by the Record object.
State	Object StateEnum	Indicates, for all applicable objects, whether the state of the object is open or closed.

Recordset Object

A `Recordset` object represents the entire set of records from a base table or the results of an executed command. At any time, the `Recordset` object refers to only a single record within the set as the current record.

Methods

Name	Returns	Description
AddNew		Creates a new record for an updateable `Recordset` object.
Cancel		Cancels execution of a pending, asynchronous `Execute` or `Open` method call.
CancelBatch		Cancels a pending batch update.
CancelUpdate		Cancels any changes made to the current record, or to a new record, prior to calling the `Update` method.
Clone	Recordset object	Creates a duplicate `Recordset` object from an existing `Recordset` object. Optionally, specifies that the clone be read-only.
Close		Closes an open object and any dependent objects.
CompareBook marks	Compare Enum	Compares two bookmarks and returns an indication of their relative values.
Delete		Deletes the current record or a group of records.
Find		Searches a recordset for the row that satisfies the specified criteria. Optionally, the direction of the search, starting row, and offset from the starting row may be specified. If the criteria are met, the current row position is set on the found record; otherwise, the position is set at the end (or start) of the recordset.
GetRows	Variant	Retrieves multiple records of a `Recordset` object into an array.
GetString	Variant	Returns the recordset as a string variant.
Move		Moves the position of the current record in a `Recordset` object.
MoveFirst		Moves to the first record in a specified `Recordset` object and makes that record the current record.
MoveLast		Moves to the last record in a specified `Recordset` object and makes that record the current record.

Table continued on following page

765

Name	Returns	Description
MoveNext		Moves to the next record in a specified Recordset object and makes that record the current record. If the current record is the last record, ADO sets the EOF property to True.
MovePrevious		Moves to the previous record in a specified Recordset object and makes that record the current record. If the current record is the first record, ADO sets the BOF property to True.
NextRecordset	Recordset object	Clears the current Recordset object and returns the next Recordset by advancing through a series of commands.
Open		Opens a cursor.
Requery		Updates the data in a Recordset object by re-executing the query on which the object is based.
Resync		Refreshes the data in the current Recordset object from the underlying database.
Save		Saves (persists) the recordset in a file or Stream object.
Seek		Searches the index of a recordset to quickly locate the row that matches the specified values, and changes the current row position to that row.
Supports	Boolean	Determines whether a specified Recordset object supports a particular type of functionality.
Update		Saves any changes you make to the current record of a Recordset object.
UpdateBatch		Writes all pending batch updates to disk.

Properties

Name	Returns	Description
AbsolutePage	Long	Specifies on which page the current record resides.
Absolute Position	Long	Specifies the ordinal position of a Recordset object's current record.
Active Command	Variant	Indicates the Command object that created the associated Recordset object.
Active Connection	String	Indicates to which Connection object the specified Command, Recordset, or Record object currently belongs.

Name	Returns	Description
BOF	Boolean	Indicates that the current record position is before the first record in a Recordset object.
EOF	Boolean	Indicates that the current record position is after the last record in a Recordset object.
Bookmark	Variant	Returns a bookmark that uniquely identifies the current record in a Recordset object, or sets the current record in a Recordset object to the record identified by a valid bookmark.
CacheSize	Long	Indicates the number of records from a Recordset object that are cached locally in memory.
CursorLocation	Cursor Location Enum	Sets or returns the location of the cursor service.
CursorType	CursorType Enum	Indicates the type of cursor used in a Recordset object.
DataMember	String	Specifies the name of the data member to retrieve from the object referenced by the DataSource property.
DataSource		Specifies an object containing data to be represented as a Recordset object.
EditMode	EditMode Enum	Indicates the editing status of the current record.
Filter	Variant	Specifies a filter for data in a recordset.
Index	String	Indicates the name of the index currently in effect for a Recordset object.
LockType	LockType Enum	Indicates the type of locks placed on records during editing. A lock is how the provider controls the updates to a record. For example, if you use pessimistic locking the provider will lock the record as soon as you start editing it.
MarshalOptions	Marshal OptionsEnum	Indicates which records are to be marshaled back to the server.
MaxRecords	Long	Indicates the maximum number of records to return to a recordset from a query.
PageCount	Long	Indicates how many pages of data the Recordset object contains.
PageSize	Long	Indicates how many records constitute one page in the recordset.

Table continued on following page

Name	Returns	Description
RecordCount	Long	Indicates the current number of records in a Recordset object.
Sort	String	Specifies one or more field names on which the recordset is sorted, and whether each field is sorted in ascending or descending order.
Source	String	Indicates the source for the data in a Recordset object (Command object, SQL statement, table name, or stored procedure).
State	ObjectState Enum	Indicates, for all applicable objects, whether the state of the object is open or closed.
Status	RecordStatus Enum	Indicates the status of the current record with respect to batch updates or other bulk operations.
StayInSync	Boolean	Indicates, in a hierarchical Recordset object, whether the reference to the underlying child records changes when the parent row position changes. This property applies to hierarchical recordsets such as those used by the Microsoft Data Shaping Service.

Stream Object

A Stream object represents a stream of binary data or text.

Methods

Name	Returns	Description
Cancel		Cancels execution of a pending, asynchronous Execute or Open method call.
Close		Closes an open object and any dependent objects.
CopyTo		Copies the specified number of characters or bytes (depending on Type) in the stream to another Stream object.
Flush		Forces the contents of the stream remaining in the ADO buffer to the underlying object with which the stream is associated.
LoadFrom File		Loads the contents of an existing file into a stream.
Open		Opens a Stream object to manipulate streams of binary or text data.

Name	Returns	Description
Read	Variant	Reads a specified number of bytes from a binary Stream object.
ReadText	String	Reads a specified number of characters from a text Stream object.
SaveToFile		Saves the binary contents of a stream to a file.
SetEOS		Sets the position that is the end of the stream.
SkipLine		Skips one entire line when reading a text stream.
Write		Writes binary data to a Stream object.
WriteText		Writes a specified text string to a Stream object.

Properties

Name	Returns	Description
Charset	String	Specifies the character set into which the contents of a text stream should be translated.
EOS	Boolean	Identifies whether the current position is at the end of the stream.
Line Separator	LineSeparators Enum	Specifies the character to be used as the line separator in a text stream.
Mode	ConnectMode Enum	Indicates the available permissions for modifying data in a Connection, Record, or Stream object.
Position	Long	Specifies the current position within a Stream object.
Size	Long	Indicates the total size of the stream in bytes.
State	ObjectState Enum	Indicates, for all applicable objects, whether the state of the object is open or closed.
Type	StreamType Enum	Identifies the type of data contained in the stream (binary or text).

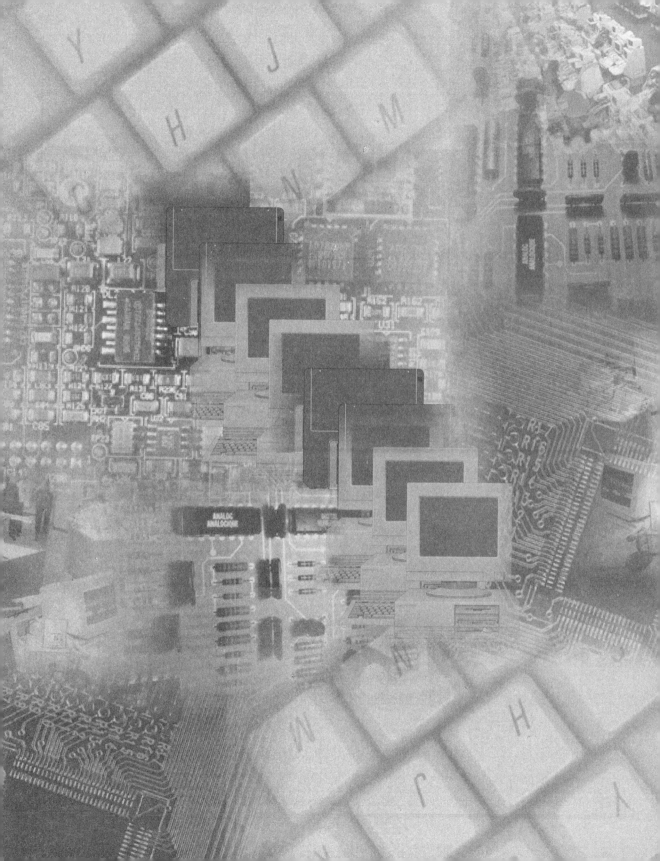

SQL Server Functions

This appendix provides a handy reference to the functions provided by SQL Server, categorized into:

❏ String functions

❏ Date and Time functions

❏ Aggregate functions

A definition, an explanation of the syntax, and an example of how each of the functions is used are provided.

String Functions

ASCII

Returns the ASCII value for the first character of a string.

```
ASCII(string_expression)
```

`string_expression` is a column name that contains character data or a character variable such as a VarChar data type.

The following example contains the name `Michael` in the `First_Name_VC` column and returns the integer value shown:

```
SELECT ASCII(First_Name_VC)
    FROM Employee_T
    WHERE Employee_ID = 2
```

```
-----------
```

CHAR

Converts an integer ASCII value to a character.

```
CHAR(integer_expression)
```

`integer_expression` is any numeric value or numeric variable.

The following example converts the value contained in the variable and returns the results shown below:

```
DECLARE @Variable INT
SELECT @Variable = 77
SELECT CHAR(@Variable)

----
M
```

CHARINDEX

Finds the starting position of an expression in a string.

```
CHARINDEX(expression1, expression2, starting_position)
```

`expression1` is the string to search for.

`expression2` is the string to be searched.

`starting_position` is an optional starting position to start the search. If not present, the search starts at position 1.

The following code searches the `First_Name_VC` column, which contains the name `Michael`, for the starting position of the string `ael`. The results are listed below:

```
SELECT CHARINDEX('ael',First_Name_VC)
    FROM Employee_T
    WHERE Employee_ID = 2

-----------
5
```

DIFFERENCE

Returns an integer value indicating the difference between two Soundex values. Soundex is used to convert an alphabetic string to a four character code to find similar sounding words or names.

```
DIFFERENCE(string_expression1, string_expression2)
```

`string_expression1` is a Char or VarChar string.

`string_expression2` is a Char or VarChar string.

A return value of 0 through 4 is returned, with 4 indicating the highest possible match.

The following code example shows three DIFFERENCE functions. The first example compares the two string expressions, which are identical, and the result of 4 is returned. The second example returns a value of 3, which indicates the string expressions are very similar. The last example returns a value of 2, which indicates there is a slight match between the two strings. The two strings compared in this example contain the string Michael in the First_Name_VC column and the string Dell in the Last_Name_VC column. Notice that two characters in each column match.

```
SELECT DIFFERENCE('michael','michael')
SELECT DIFFERENCE('michael','mike')
SELECT DIFFERENCE(First_Name_VC,Last_Name_VC)
    FROM Employee_T
    WHERE Employee_ID = 2


-----------
4
-----------
3
-----------
2
```

LEFT

Returns the left portion of a string expression.

```
LEFT(string_expression, integer_expression)
```

string_expression is a variable or string expression that contains the text.

integer_expression is the number of characters on the left side of the string to be returned.

The following example returns the left 5 characters of the First_Name_VC column and the results are shown below:

```
SELECT LEFT(First_Name_VC,5)
    FROM Employee_T
    WHERE Employee_ID = 2


-----
Micha
```

LEN

Returns the number of characters in a string.

```
LEN(string_expression)
```

string_expression is a variable or string expression that contains the text.

The following example returns the length of the string contained in the First_Name_VC column, which contains the name Michael:

```
SELECT LEN(First_Name_VC)
    FROM Employee_T
    WHERE Employee_ID = 2


-----------
7
```

LOWER

Converts a string to all lower case letters.

```
LOWER(string_expression)
```

string_expression is a variable or string expression that contains the text.

The following example converts the name Michael that is contained in the First_Name_VC column to all lower case letters. The results are displayed below:

```
SELECT LOWER(First_Name_VC)
    FROM Employee_T
    WHERE Employee_ID = 2


---------------
michael
```

LTRIM

Returns the string expression passed after trimming all spaces on the left side of the string.

```
LTRIM(string_expression)
```

string_expression is a variable or string expression that contains the text.

The following example declares a variable and assigns a string that contains spaces to it. The LTRIM function is then called to remove all spaces on the left side of the variable. The results are listed below:

```
DECLARE @Name VARCHAR(15)
SELECT @Name = '    Michael'
SELECT LTRIM(@Name)


---------------
Michael
```

NCHAR

Returns a Unicode character for the integer value passed.

```
NCHAR(integer_expression)
```

integer_expression is a number ranging from 0 to 65535.

The following example displays the Unicode character for the value 77:

```
SELECT NCHAR(77)


----
M
```

PATINDEX

Returns the starting position of a pattern in a string.

```
PATINDEX('%pattern_expression%',string_expression)
```

pattern_expression is a string expression of the pattern to search for.

string_expression is a variable or string expression that contains the text.

The example below searches the First_Name_VC column for the pattern of ha. The results are listed below, with the first occurrence of the pattern found.

```
SELECT PATINDEX('%ha%',First_Name_VC)
    FROM Employee_T
    WHERE Employee_ID = 2


-----------
4
```

REPLACE

Searches for a specific string in a string expression and replaces that string with another.

```
REPLACE(string_expression1, string_expression2, string_expression3)
```

string_expression1 is a variable or string expression that contains the text to be searched.

string_expression2 is a variable or string expression that contains the search string to be replaced.

string_expression3 is a variable or string expression that contains the text that will replace string_expression2.

The following example searches the First_Name_VC column for the characters chael and replaces them with ke, which changes the name from Michael to Mike:

```
SELECT REPLACE(First_Name_VC,'chael','ke')
    FROM Employee_T
    WHERE Employee_ID = 2


-----------
Mike
```

QUOTENAME

Returns a Unicode string with delimiters added to make the string expression a valid SQL Server delimited identifier.

```
QUOTENAME(string_expression, quote_character)
```

string_expression is a variable or string expression that contains text.

quote_character is a single character that is to be used as the identifier. This character can be a single quote mark ('), a double quote mark ("), or a left or right square bracket ([ ]).

The following example uses a single quote mark to enclose the selected quote characters, which in this case is two repeated single quote marks - so that the string doesn't produce an error:

```
SELECT QUOTENAME(First_Name_VC,'''')
    FROM Employee_T
    WHERE Employee_ID = 2


------------------------------
'Michael'
```

REPLICATE

Repeats a string expression a specified number of times.

```
REPLICATE(string_expression, integer_expression)
```

string_expression is a variable or string expression that contains text.

integer_expression is an integer number.

The following example repeats the First_Name_VC column two times and the results are displayed below:

```
SELECT REPLICATE(First_Name_VC,2)
    FROM Employee_T
    WHERE Employee_ID = 2


------------------------------
MichaelMichael
```

REVERSE

Reverses the order of characters in a string expression.

```
REVERSE(string_expression)
```

string_expression is a variable or string expression that contains text.

The following example uses the First_Name_VC column as the string expression and returns the name in reverse order:

```
SELECT REVERSE(First_Name_VC)
    FROM Employee_T
    WHERE Employee_ID = 2


---------------
leahciM
```

RIGHT

Returns the specified number of characters on the right side of a string expression.

```
RIGHT(string_expression, integer_expression)
```

string_expression is a variable or string expression that contains text.

`integer_expression` is an integer number.

The following example returns the right-most three characters from the `First_Name_VC` column:

```
SELECT RIGHT(First_Name_VC,3)
    FROM Employee_T
    WHERE Employee_ID = 2


----
ael
```

RTRIM

Removes the trailing spaces from a string expression.

```
RTRIM(string_expression)
```

`string_expression` is a variable or string expression that contains text.

The following example declares a string variable, assigns a string with spaces to it, and then uses the RTRIM function to remove the trailing spaces:

```
DECLARE @String VARCHAR(15)
SET @String = 'Michael     '
SELECT RTRIM(@String)

---------------
Michael
```

SOUNDEX

Returns a four-character (Soundex) code to evaluate the similarity of two strings.

```
SOUNDEX(string_expression)
```

`string_expression` is a variable or string expression that contains text.

The following example converts the data in the `First_Name_VC` column to a Soundex code:

```
SELECT SOUNDEX(First_Name_VC)
    FROM Employee_T
    WHERE Employee_ID = 2

-----
M240
```

SPACE

Returns a string of repeated spaces.

```
SPACE(integer_expression)
```

`integer_expression` is an integer number that specifies how many spaces to return.

The following example selects the `First_Name_VC` and `Last_Name_VC` columns and concatenates them together with two spaces between them:

```
SELECT First_Name_VC + SPACE(2) + Last_Name_VC
   FROM Employee_T
   WHERE Employee_ID = 2


--------------------------------
Michael  Dell
```

STR

Returns a string expression converted from a numeric expression.

```
STR(float_expression, length, decimal)
```

`float_expression` is a numeric variable or expression that evaluates to a Float data type.

`length` is the total length of the expression, including the decimal point and digits to the right of the decimal, that should be returned.

`decimal` is the number of digits to the right of the decimal point that should be returned.

The following example declares a Float data type variable and a VarChar data type variable. Using the STR function, the numeric variable is converted to a string variable:

```
DECLARE @Numeric FLOAT,
        @String VARCHAR(15)
SELECT @Numeric = 190.5
SELECT @String = STR(@Numeric,6,2)
PRINT @String


------
190.50
```

STUFF

Deletes a specified number of characters in a string expression and replaces them with another set of characters.

```
STUFF(string_expression, start, length, character_expression)
```

`string_expression` is a variable or string expression that contains text.

`start` is an integer value indicating the starting position in the string to start deleting characters.

`length` is an integer value indicating the number of characters to be deleted.

`character_expression` is a variable or string expression that contains the characters that are to replace the deleted characters.

The following example deletes four characters starting at position four in the `First_Name_VC` column. The character expression is inserted into the deleted characters, position.

```
SELECT STUFF(First_Name_VC,4,4,'aela')
   FROM Employee_T
   WHERE Employee_ID = 2


---------------
Micaela
```

SUBSTRING

Returns part of a string, text, binary, or image expression.

```
SUBSTRING(expression, start, length)
```

expression is a string, text, binary, or image variable or expression.

start is an integer value indicating the starting position in the string to start extracting data.

length is an integer value indicating the number of characters to be extracted.

The following example returns the first four characters from the First_Name_VC column:

```
SELECT SUBSTRING(First_Name_VC,1,4)
   FROM Employee_T
   WHERE Employee_ID = 2


----
Mich
```

UNICODE

Returns an integer value representing a Unicode character.

```
Unicode('ncharacter_expression')
```

ncharacter_expression is an NChar or NVarChar expression

The following example declares an NVarChar variable and assigns a Unicode character to it. Then we execute the Unicode function to return the integer value representing that character:

```
DECLARE @Nstring NVARCHAR(15)
SELECT @Nstring = 'Å'
SELECT UNICODE(@Nstring)


-----------
197
```

UPPER

Converts a string to all upper case letters.

```
UPPER(string_expression)
```

string_expression is a variable or string expression that contains the text.

779

The following example converts the name Michael that is contained in the First_Name_VC column to all upper case letters. The results are displayed below:

```
SELECT UPPER(First_Name_VC)
    FROM Employee_T
    WHERE Employee_ID = 2


---------------
MICHAEL
```

System Functions

APP_NAME

Returns the application name for the current session if one has been set by the application.

```
APP_NAME()
```

The APP_NAME() function returns an NVarChar(128) data type. The following example demonstrates that the application that initiated the session is a Query Analyzer session:

```
PRINT APP_NAME()

---------------
MS SQL Query Analyzer
```

CASE

Evaluates a list of conditions and returns one result.

```
CASE input_expression
When when_expression Then result_expression
Else else_result_expression
End
```

input_expression is the expression to be evaluated.

when_expression is an expression to which the input_expression is compared.

result_expression is the expression that is returned when the input_expression matches the when_expression.

else_result_expression is the expression returned when no match has been found.

The following example uses the CASE function to display the data from the Location_Name_VC column if data exists in the Location_ID column or to display Not Yet Assigned when a Location_ID is null. The results are listed after the query:

```
SELECT First_Name_VC, Last_Name_VC, 'Employee Location' =
    CASE
        WHEN Employee_T.Location_ID IS NOT NULL THEN Location_Name_VC
```

```
        ELSE 'Not Yet Assigned'
    END
    FROM Employee_T
    LEFT OUTER JOIN Location_T ON Employee_T.Location_ID = Location_T.Location_ID


-----------------------------------------------------------------
First_Name_VC    Last_Name_VC    Employee Location
--------------   --------------  -----------------------------
Abraham          Bennet          Not Yet Assigned
Cheryl           Carson          Home Office
Michael          Dell            Huston Office
Thearon          Willis          Home Office
```

CAST

Explicitly converts one data type to another.

```
CAST(expression As data_type)
```

expression is any single variable, constant, column, or function.

data_type is any valid SQL Server data type.

The following example uses the CAST function to convert the Location_ID to a Char data type and the results are listed below:

```
SELECT CAST(Location_ID AS CHAR(4))
    FROM Employee_T
    WHERE Employee_ID = 2

----
7
```

CONVERT

Explicitly converts one data type to another.

```
CONVERT(data_type[(length)], expression, [style])
```

data_type is any valid SQL Server data type.

length is an optional parameter for the NChar, NVarChar, Char, VarChar, Binary, or VarBinary data types.

expression is any single variable, constant, column, or function.

style is the style of date format you want when converting DateTime or SmallDateTime data to character data.

A style of 0 or 100 returns the date and time in mon dd yyyy hh:miAM (or PM) format, while a style of 9 or 109 returns the date and time in mon dd yyyy hh:mi:ss:mmmAM (or PM) format. A style of 13 or 113 returns the date and time in a dd mon yyyy hh:mm:ss:mmm(24h) format and a style of 20 or 120 returns a format of yyyy-mm-dd hh:mi:ss(24h). Finally, a style of 21 or 121 returns the date and time in a format of yyyy-mm-dd hh:mi:ss.mmm(24h).

781

Other styles are available to return just the date or just the time in various formats. See the SQL Server Books Online for more styles.

The following example uses the CONVERT function to convert the Last_Update_DT column to a VarChar data type using a style of 100, the default format:

```
SELECT CONVERT(VARCHAR(22),Last_Update_DT,100)
    FROM Employee_T
    WHERE Employee_ID = 2


----------------------
Jul 29 2000 10:15AM
```

COALESCE

Returns the first non-null argument among its expressions.

```
COALESCE(expression[,...n])
```

expression is any single variable, constant, column, or function.

n is a placeholder indicating that multiple expressions can be specified.

The following example uses the COALESCE function to display a zero when a Null value is encountered in the Location_ID column:

```
SELECT First_Name_VC, Last_Name_VC,
    'Employee Location' = COALESCE(Location_ID,0)
    FROM Employee_T


-----------------------------------------------
First_Name_VC    Last_Name_VC     Employee Location
---------------  ---------------  -----------------
Abraham          Bennet           0
Cheryl           Carson           1
Michael          Dell             2
Thearon          Willis           1
```

CURRENT_TIMESTAMP

Returns the current date and time in a DateTime data type and is the equivalent to the GETDATE() function.

```
CURRENT_TIMESTAMP
```

The following example demonstrates the results returned from the CURRENT_TIMESTAMP function:

```
SELECT CURRENT_TIMESTAMP


---------------------------
2000-08-03 06:58:46.360
```

CURRENT_USER

Returns the current user who is logged on.

```
CURRENT_USER
```

The following example shows the results of the CURRENT_USER function:

```
SELECT CURRENT_USER

---------------------
Stephanie
```

DATALENGTH

Returns the number of bytes in an expression.

```
DATALENGTH(expression)
```

expression is any single variable, constant, column, or function.

This example shows how you can use the DATALENGTH function to determine how many bytes are in a column:

```
SELECT First_Name_VC, DATALENGTH(First_Name_VC) AS Length_Of_First_Name
   FROM Employee_T
   WHERE Employee_ID = 2

First_Name_VC    Length_Of_First_Name
--------------   --------------------
Michael          7
```

@@ERROR

Returns the error number of the last SQL statement executed.

```
@@ERROR
```

This example shows the error number returned after a SELECT statement has been executed:

```
SELECT First_Name_VC, Last_Name_VC
   FROM Employee_T
   WHERE Employee_ID = 2
SELECT @@ERROR AS Last_Error

First_Name_VC    Last_Name_VC
--------------   ---------------
Michael          Dell

(1 row(s) affected)

Last_Error
-----------
0
```

FORMATMESSAGE

Allows you to construct a pre-defined message from the SysMessages table.

```
FORMATMESSAGE(msg_number, parameter_value[,...n])
```

msg_number is the number of the message from the SysMessages table.

parameter_value is the value to be substituted in the parameter of the message.

n is a placeholder indicating that multiple parameter values can be specified if available in the message.

The example demonstrated here uses the following message from the SysMessages table. Notice the parameter value placeholder in the message:

```
Error    Description
-----    --------------------------------
14043    The parameter %s cannot be NULL.
```

This example uses the above message and substitutes a column name for the parameter value placeholder in the message:

```
DECLARE @My_Message VARCHAR(100)
SELECT @My_Message = FORMATMESSAGE(14043,'''First_Name_VC''')
Print @My_Message

-----------------------------------------------------------------------
The parameter 'First_Name_VC' cannot be NULL.
```

GETANSINULL

Returns the default nullability for the database specified.

```
GETANSINULL('database_name')
```

database_name is the name of the database to be queried.

The following example returns the nullability for the Hardware Tracking database. GETANSINULL returns 1 if the database allows nulls.

```
SELECT GETANSINULL('Hardware Tracking')

------
1
```

HOST_ID

Returns the workstation identification number.

```
HOST_ID()
```

The following example returns the workstation identification number for the workstation running the query:

```
SELECT HOST_ID()

--------
1340
```

HOST_NAME

Returns the workstation name.

```
HOST_NAME()
```

The following example returns the name of the workstation running the query:

```
SELECT HOST_NAME()

----------------------------
WSTRAVEL
```

IDENT_INCR

Returns the increment value for the identity column of a table that was specified when the table was created.

```
IDENT_INCR('table_name')
```

table_name is the name of the table whose increment value for the identity column should be returned.

The following example returns the identity increment value for the identity column in the Employee_T table:

```
SELECT IDENT_INCR('Employee_T')

----------------------------------------
1
```

IDENT_SEED

Returns the seed value for the identity column of a table that was specified when the table was created.

```
IDENT_SEED('table_name')
```

table_name is the name of the table whose increment value for the identity column should be returned.

The following example returns the identity seed value for the identity column in the Employee_T table:

```
SELECT IDENT_SEED('Employee_T')

----------------------------------------
1
```

@@*IDENTITY*

Returns the last inserted identity value.

```
@@IDENTITY
```

This example inserts a new location into the `Location_T` table and returns the identity value that was inserted:

```
INSERT INTO Location_T
    (Location_Name_VC, Last_Update_DT)
    VALUES('Harris Corners',GetDate())
SELECT @@IDENTITY


-----------------------------------------
5
```

IDENTITY

This function is used only in a `SELECT` statement with an `INTO table` clause to insert an identity column into a new table.

```
IDENTITY(data_type[, seed, increment]) AS column_name
```

`data_type` is the data type for the identity column and must be a numeric data type, such as Integer.

`seed` is the seed value for the identity column.

`increment` is the increment value for the identity column.

`column_name` is the name of the column that is being inserted into the new table.

The following example selects the first and last names from the `Employee_T` table and inserts them into a temporary table created as a result of the `INTO` keyword. The `IDENTITY` function is used to insert an identity column into the temporary table. After the temporary table has been populated, all the rows in the temporary table are selected and the temporary table is dropped.

```
SELECT IDENTITY(INT,1,1) AS Employee_ID, First_Name_VC, Last_Name_VC
    INTO #tmp_Customer
    FROM Employee_T
SELECT * FROM #tmp_Customer
DROP TABLE #tmp_Customer

(4 row(s) affected)

Employee_ID First_Name_VC   Last_Name_VC
----------- --------------- ---------------
1           Thearon         Willis
2           Michael         Dell
3           Cheryl          Carson
4           Abraham         Bennet
```

ISDATE

Determines if an expression is a valid date and returns 1 if it is.

```
ISDATE(expression)
```

expression is an expression to be validated as a date.

This example declares a variable and then sets a value into that variable. The ISDATE function is used to determine if the date we selected into the variable is valid:

```
DECLARE @Date VARCHAR(22)
SET @Date = '1/1/2000'
SELECT ISDATE(@Date)

-----------
1
```

ISNULL

Replaces a Null value with the value specified.

```
ISNULL(expression, replacement_value)
```

expression is any single variable, constant, column, or function.

replacement_value is the value that should replace a Null value.

This example tests whether or not the Location_ID column in the Employee_T table is Null and replaces the Null value with a zero:

```
SELECT First_Name_VC, Last_Name_VC,
    ISNULL(Location_ID,0) AS 'Location_ID'
    FROM Employee_T
    WHERE Employee_ID = 7

First_Name_VC    Last_Name_VC     Location_ID
---------------  ---------------  -----------
Abraham          Bennet                 0
```

ISNUMERIC

Tests whether an expression is a valid numeric data type and returns 1 if it is.

```
ISNUMERIC(expression)
```

expression is any single variable, constant, column, or function.

The following example tests the Location_ID column in the Employee_T table to see if it contains a valid numeric value:

```
SELECT ISNUMERIC(Location_ID)
    FROM Employee_T
    WHERE Employee_ID = 2
```

787

```
-----------
1
```

NEWID

Creates a unique value of type uniqueidentifier.

```
NEWID()
```

This example creates a unique identifier that can be used wherever a unique identifier number is needed:

```
DECLARE @Unique_ID UNIQUEIDENTIFIER
SET @Unique_ID = NEWID()
PRINT @Unique_ID


-------------------------------------
890E4FF2-3138-4A81-9579-D7DD5ACF1A30
```

NULLIF

Returns a Null value if two expressions are equal otherwise the first expression is returned.

```
NULLIF(expression,expression)
```

expression is any single variable, constant, column or function.

This example demonstrates both scenarios for the NullIf function using the First_Name_VC and Last_Name_VC columns from the Employee_T table:

```
SELECT NULLIF(First_Name_VC,Last_Name_VC)
    FROM Employee_T
    WHERE Employee_ID = 2


---------------
Michael
```

```
SELECT NULLIF(First_Name_VC,First_Name_VC)
    FROM Employee_T
    WHERE Employee_ID = 2


---------------
NULL
```

PARSENAME

Returns the specified part of an object name.

```
PARSENAME('object_name',object_part)
```

object_name is partially or fully qualified object name. If a fully qualified object name is used, this object name consists of four parts: the server name, the database name, the owner name, and the object name.

object_part is an integer value indicating the part of the object name to return. A value of 1 specifies that the object name is returned and a value of 2 specifies that the owner name is returned. Values of 3 and 4 specify that the database name and the server name are to be returned.

If the object name is not fully qualified and an object part is requested for a part that does not exist in the object_name, then a Null value is returned.

The following example shows the various object parts that can be extracted from a fully qualified object name:

```
SELECT PARSENAME('WSTravel.Hardware Tracking.dbo.Employee_T',1)

------------------
Employee_T


SELECT PARSENAME('WSTravel.Hardware Tracking.dbo.Employee_T',2)

------------------
dbo


SELECT PARSENAME('WSTravel.Hardware Tracking.dbo.Employee_T',3)

------------------
Hardware Tracking


SELECT PARSENAME('WSTravel.Hardware Tracking.dbo.Employee_T',4)

------------------
WSTravel
```

PERMISSIONS

Returns an integer value containing a bitmap that indicates the statement, object, or column permissions for the current user.

```
PERMISSIONS ([objectid [, 'column']])
```

objectid is the ID of an object. If objectid is not specified, the bitmap value contains statement permissions for the current user; otherwise, the bitmap contains object permissions on the object ID for the current user. The object specified must be in the current database. Use the OBJECT_ID function with an object name to determine the objectid value.

column is the optional name of a column for which permission information is being returned. The column must be a valid column name in the table specified by objectid.

The permissions information returned is a 32-bit bitmap. The lower 16 bits reflect permissions granted to the security account for the current user, as well as permissions applied to Microsoft Windows NT groups or Microsoft SQL Server roles of which the current user is a member. For example, a returned value of 66 (hex value 0x42), when no objectid is specified, indicates the current user has permissions to execute the CREATE TABLE (decimal value 2) and BACKUP DATABASE (decimal value 64) statement permissions. The upper 16 bits reflect the permissions that the current user can GRANT to other users. The upper 16 bits are interpreted exactly as those for the lower 16 bits described in the following tables, except they are shifted to the left by 16 bits (multiplied by 65,536). For example, 0x8 (decimal value 8) is the bit indicating INSERT permissions when an objectid is specified. Whereas 0x80000 (decimal value 524,288) indicates the ability to GRANT INSERT permissions, because $524,288 = 8 \times 65,536$. Due to membership in roles, it is possible to not have permission to execute a statement, but still be able to grant that permission to someone else.

This table shows the bits used for statement permissions (objectid is not specified):

Bit dec)	Bit (hex)	Statement permission
1	0x1	CREATE DATABASE (master database only)
2	0x2	CREATE TABLE
4	0x4	CREATE PROCEDURE
8	0x8	CREATE VIEW
16	0x10	CREATE RULE
32	0x20	CREATE DEFAULT
64	0x40	BACKUP DATABASE
128	0x80	BACKUP LOG
256	0x100	Reserved

This table shows the bits used for object permissions that are returned when only objectid is specified:

Bit (dec)	Bit (hex)	Statement permission
1	0x1	SELECT ALL
2	0x2	UPDATE ALL
4	0x4	REFERENCES ALL
8	0x8	INSERT
16	0x10	DELETE
32	0x20	EXECUTE (procedures only)
4,096	0x1000	SELECT ANY (at least one column)
8,192	0x2000	UPDATE ANY
16,384	0x4000	REFERENCES ANY

This table shows the bits used for column-level object permissions that are returned when both objectid and column are specified:

Bit (dec)	Bit (hex)	Statement permission
1	0x1	SELECT
2	0x2	UPDATE
4	0x4	REFERENCES

The following example shows the permissions set on the `Employee_T` table:

```
SELECT PERMISSIONS(OBJECT_ID('Employee_T'))

-----------
1881108543
```

@@ROWCOUNT

Returns the number of rows affected by the last statement.

```
@@ROWCOUNT
```

This example selects all first names from the `Employee_T` table that begin with the letter m. The `@@RowCount` function returns the number of rows affected by this `SELECT` statement:

```
SELECT First_Name_VC
    FROM Employee_T
    WHERE First_Name_VC LIKE 'm%'
SELECT @@ROWCOUNT

First_Name_VC
---------------
Michael


-----------
1
```

SESSION_USER

Returns the current session's username.

```
SESSION_USER
```

This example displays the current session's username:

```
PRINT 'The current user for this session is ' + SESSION_USER

-------------------------------------------------
The current user for this session is Stephanie
```

STATS_DATE

Returns the date that the statistics for the specified index were last updated on.

```
STATS_DATE(table_id, index_id)
```

table_id is the ID of the table.

index_id is the ID of the index.

The example uses sysobjects and sysindexes to retrieve the ID of the Employee_T table and indexes and then uses the STATS_DATE function to display the indexes and the last date and time the indexes were updated:

```
SELECT OBJINDEX.NAME AS 'Index Name',
    STATS_DATE(OBJINDEX.ID, OBJINDEX.INDID) AS 'Statistics Date'
    FROM SYSOBJECTS OBJTABLE, SYSINDEXES OBJINDEX
    WHERE OBJTABLE.NAME = 'Employee_T' AND OBJTABLE.ID = OBJINDEX.ID

Index Name                                      Statistics Date
----------------------------------------------- ---------------------------
IX_Employee_T                                   NULL
PK_Employee_T                                   NULL
_WA_Sys_Location_ID_20C1E124                    2000-07-07 18:44:51.273
_WA_Sys_First_Name_VC_20C1E124                  2000-08-04 05:56:19.407
```

SYSTEM_USER

Returns the current system username.

```
SYSTEM_USER
```

This example displays the current system user:

```
PRINT 'The current system user is ' + SYSTEM_USER

-----------------------------------
The current system user is stephanie
```

@@TRANCOUNT

Returns the number of active transactions for the current connection.

```
@@TRANCOUNT
```

The BEGIN TRANSACTION statement increments @@TRANCOUNT by 1. ROLLBACK TRANSACTION decrements @@TRANCOUNT to 0, except for ROLLBACK TRANSACTION savepoint_name, which does not affect @@TRANCOUNT. COMMIT TRANSACTION or COMMIT WORK decrement @@TRANCOUNT by 1.

This example begins a transaction, selects some data and displays the transaction count using the @@TRANCOUNT function before committing the transaction:

```
BEGIN TRANSACTION Demo_Tran
SELECT First_Name_VC
    FROM Employee_T
    WHERE Employee_ID = 2
SELECT @@TRANCOUNT
COMMIT TRANSACTION Demo_Tran

First_Name_VC
---------------
```

```
Michael

-----------
1
```

USER_NAME

Returns a user database username from a given identification number.

```
USER_NAME([user_id])
```

user_id is the optional identification number of the username to return.

The following example demonstrates two methods to return the username. The first method specifies the ID of the user and the second method returns the name of the user who is currently logged on:

```
SELECT USER_NAME(5)

-------------------
willist

SELECT USER_NAME()

-------------------
dbo
```

Date and Time Functions

DATEADD

Returns a new datetime value based on adding an interval to the specified date.

```
DATEADD(datepart, number, date)
```

datepart is the parameter that specifies on which part of the date to return a new value. Available date parts are Year, Quarter, Month, DayOfYear, Week, Day, Hour, Minute, Second, and Millisecond.

number is the number used to increment the datepart.

date is an expression that evaluates to a valid date.

The following example selects the date from the Last_Update_DT column in the Employee_T table and adds one year to it:

```
SELECT Last_Update_DT, DATEADD(YEAR,1,Last_Update_DT) AS 'New_Date'
    FROM Employee_T
    WHERE Employee_ID = 2

Last_Update_DT                  New_Date
--------------------------      --------------------------
2000-07-07 10:15:20.063         2001-07-07 10:15:20.063
```

DATEDIFF

Returns the difference between two dates.

```
DATEDIFF(datepart, startdate, enddate)
```

datepart is the parameter that specifies on which part of the date to return a new value. Available date parts are Year, Quarter, Month, DayOfYear, Week, Day, Hour, Minute, Second, and Millisecond.

startdate is an expression that evaluates to a valid date.

enddate is an expression that evaluates to a valid date.

The example returns the number of days between the date in the Last_Update_DT column in the Employee_T table and the current date:

```
SELECT Last_Update_DT, DATEDIFF(DAY,Last_Update_DT, GETDATE()) AS 'Date
Difference'
    FROM Employee_T
    WHERE Employee_ID = 2

Last_Update_DT              Date Difference
--------------------------  ----------------
2000-07-07 10:15:20.063     28
```

DATENAME

Returns a character string representing the specified datepart of the specified date.

```
DATENAME(datepart, date)
```

datepart is the parameter that specifies on which part of the date to return a new value. Available date parts are Year, Quarter, Month, DayOfYear, Week, Day, Hour, Minute, Second, and Millisecond.

date is an expression that evaluates to a valid date.

The following example returns the month name of the date contained in the Last_Update_DT column of the Employee_T table:

```
SELECT Last_Update_DT, DATENAME(MONTH,Last_Update_DT) AS 'Date Name'
    FROM Employee_T
    WHERE Employee_ID = 2

Last_Update_DT              Date Name
--------------------------  ------------------------------
2000-07-07 10:15:20.063     July
```

DATEPART

Returns an integer representing the specified datepart of the specified date.

```
DATEPART(datepart, date)
```

datepart is the parameter that specifies on which part of the date to return a new value. Available date parts are Year, Quarter, Month, DayOfYear, Week, Day, Hour, Minute, Second, and Millisecond.

`date` is an expression that evaluates to a valid date.

This example returns the month number of the date contained in the `Last_Update_DT` column of the `Employee_T` table:

```
SELECT Last_Update_DT, DATEPART(MONTH,Last_Update_DT) AS 'Date Part'
    FROM Employee_T
    WHERE Employee_ID = 2

Last_Update_DT                 Date Part
------------------------------ -----------
2000-07-07 10:15:20.063        7
```

DAY

Returns an integer representing the day part of the specified date.

```
DAY(date)
```

`date` is an expression that evaluates to a valid date.

This example returns the day of the date contained in the `Last_Update_DT` column of the `Employee_T` table:

```
SELECT Last_Update_DT, DAY(Last_Update_DT) AS 'Day'
    FROM Employee_T
    WHERE Employee_ID = 2

Last_Update_DT                 Day
------------------------------ -----------
2000-07-07 10:15:20.063        7
```

GETDATE

Returns the current date and time.

```
GETDATE()
```

This example returns the current date and time:

```
SELECT GETDATE() AS 'Current Date and Time'

Current Date and Time
---------------------------
2000-08-04 05:30:03.227
```

MONTH

Returns an integer that represents the month part of a specified date.

```
MONTH(date)
```

`date` is an expression that evaluates to a valid date.

This example returns the month of the date contained in the `Last_Update_DT` column of the `Employee_T` table:

```
SELECT Last_Update_DT, MONTH(Last_Update_DT) AS 'Month'
    FROM Employee_T
    WHERE Employee_ID = 2

Last_Update_DT              Month
--------------------------  -----------
2000-07-07 10:15:20.063     7
```

YEAR

Returns an integer that represents the year part of a specified date.

```
YEAR(date)
```

`date` is an expression that evaluates to a valid date.

This example returns the year of the date contained in the `Last_Update_DT` column of the `Employee_T` table:

```
SELECT Last_Update_DT, YEAR(Last_Update_DT) AS 'Year'
    FROM Employee_T
    WHERE Employee_ID = 2

Last_Update_DT              Year
--------------------------  -----------
2000-07-07 10:15:20.063     2000
```

Aggregate Functions

AVG

Returns the average of the values in a group.

```
AVG([ALL | DISTINCT] expression)
```

`ALL` applies the aggregate function to all values and is the default.

`DISTINCT` specifies that `AVG` be performed only on each unique instance of a value, regardless of how many times the value occurs.

`expression` is an expression of the exact numeric or approximate numeric data type category, except for the Bit data type.

This example selects the average discount in the `Discounts` table in the `Pubs` database:

```
SELECT AVG(Discount) AS 'Average Discount Given'
    FROM Discounts

Average Discount Given
----------------------
7.400000
```

COUNT

Returns the number of items in a group.

```
COUNT({[ALL | DISTINCT] expression] | *})
```

ALL applies the aggregate function to all values and is the default.

DISTINCT specifies that COUNT be performed only on each unique instance of a value, regardless of how many times the value occurs.

expression is an expression of any type except Uniqueidentifier, Text, Image, or Ntext.

* specifies that all rows should be counted to return the total number of rows in a table. COUNT(*) takes no parameters and cannot be used with DISTINCT. COUNT(*) does not require an expression parameter because, by definition, it does not use information about any particular column. COUNT(*) returns the number of rows in a specified table without eliminating duplicates. It counts each row separately, including rows that contain Null values.

The following example selects a count of system assignments in the System_Assignment_T table:

```
SELECT COUNT(System_Assignment_ID) AS 'Total Systems Assigned'
    FROM System_Assignment_T

Total Systems Assigned
----------------------
3
```

GROUPING

An aggregate function that causes an additional column to be output with a value of 1 when the row is added by either the CUBE or ROLLUP operator, or 0 when the row is not the result of CUBE or ROLLUP.

```
GROUPING(column_name)
```

column_name is a column in a GROUP BY clause to check for CUBE or ROLLUP Null values.

Grouping is allowed only in the select list associated with a GROUP BY clause that contains either the CUBE or ROLLUP operator. Grouping is used to distinguish the Null values returned by CUBE and ROLLUP from standard null values. The NULL returned as the result of a CUBE or ROLLUP operation is a special use of NULL. It acts as a column placeholder in the result set and means "all".

The following example demonstrates the GROUPING function to rollup the Null values in the Location_ID column in the Employee_T table. The results show two NULL values in the Location_ID column. The first NULL value represents the group of NULL values from the column and the second NULL value represents the summary row, which was added by the ROLLUP clause.

```
SELECT Location_ID, GROUPING(Location_ID) AS 'Group'
    FROM Employee_T
    GROUP BY Location_ID WITH ROLLUP

Location_ID Group
----------- -----
```

```
NULL        0
1           0
2           0
NULL        1
```

MAX

Returns the maximum value in the expression.

```
MAX([ALL | DISTINCT] expression)
```

`ALL` applies the aggregate function to all values and is the default.

`DISTINCT` specifies that `MAX` be performed only on each unique instance of a value, regardless of how many times the value occurs – this is not meaningful with `MAX`, and is only present for backwards compatibility.

`expression` is a constant, column name, or function, and any combination of arithmetic, bitwise, and string operators. `MAX` can be used with numeric, character, and datetime columns, but not with bit columns.

The following example uses the `MAX` function to return the maximum discount listed in the `Discount` column in the `Discounts` table in the `Pubs` database:

```
SELECT MAX(Discount) AS 'Maximum Discount'
    FROM Discounts

Maximum Discount
----------------
10.50
```

MIN

Returns the minimum value in the expression.

```
MIN([ALL | DISTINCT] expression)
```

`ALL` applies the aggregate function to all values and is the default.

`DISTINCT` specifies that `MIN` be performed only on each unique instance of a value, regardless of how many times the value occurs – this is meaningless in the `MIN` statement.

`expression` is a constant, column name, or function, and any combination of arithmetic, bitwise, and string operators. `MIN` can be used with numeric, character, and datetime columns, but not with bit columns.

The following example uses the `MIN` function to return the minimum discount listed in the `Discount` column in the `Discounts` table in the `Pubs` database:

```
SELECT MIN(Discount) AS 'Minimum Discount'
    FROM Discounts

Minimum Discount
----------------
5.00
```

SUM

Returns the sum of all the values in a numeric column ignoring Null values.

```
SUM([ALL | DISTINCT] expression)
```

ALL applies the aggregate function to all values and is the default.

DISTINCT specifies that SUM be performed only on each unique instance of a value, regardless of how many times the value occurs.

expression is a constant, column, or function, and any combination of arithmetic, bitwise, and string operators. expression is an expression of the exact numeric or approximate numeric data type category, except for the Bit data type.

The following example uses the SUM function to return the total of the discounts listed in the Discount column in the Discounts table in the Pubs database:

```
SELECT SUM(Discount) AS 'Total Discounts'
    FROM Discounts

Total Discounts
---------------
22.20
```

STDEV

Returns the statistical standard deviation of all values in the given expression.

```
STDEV(expression)
```

expression is a numeric expression.

This example returns the standard deviation for the discounts listed in the Discount column in the Discounts table in the Pubs database:

```
SELECT STDEV(Discount) AS 'Standard Deviation'
    FROM Discounts

Standard Deviation
----------------------------------------------------
2.8160255680657436
```

STDEVP

Returns the statistical standard deviation for the population for all values in the given expression.

```
STDEVP(expression)
```

expression is a numeric expression.

This example returns the standard deviation for the population for the discounts listed in the Discount column in the Discounts table in the Pubs database:

```
SELECT STDEVP(Discount) as 'Standard Deviation for the Population'
   FROM Discounts

Standard Deviation for the Population
-------------------------------------------------------
 2.299275248130737
```

VAR

Returns the statistical variance of all values in the given expression.

```
VAR(expression)
```

expression is an expression of the exact numeric or approximate numeric data type category, except for the Bit data type.

This example returns the variance for the discounts listed in the Discount column in the Discounts table in the Pubs database:

```
SELECT VAR(Discount) AS 'Variance'
   FROM Discounts

Variance
-------------------------------------------------------
7.9299999999999926
```

VARP

Returns the statistical variance for the population for all values in the given expression.

```
VARP(expression)
```

expression is an expression of the exact numeric or approximate numeric data type category, except for the Bit data type.

This example returns the variance for the population for the discounts listed in the Discount column in the Discounts table in the Pubs database:

```
SELECT VAR(Discount) AS 'Variance for the Population'
   FROM Discounts

Variance for the Population
-------------------------------------------------------
7.9299999999999926
```

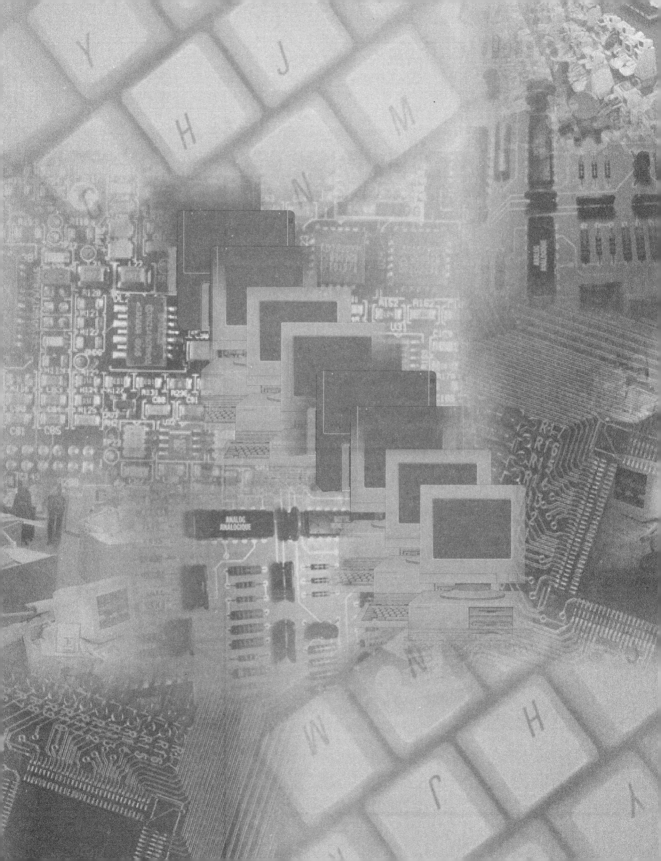

Building the Hardware Tracking Framework

In Chapters 9 to 13 we develop numerous stored procedures and call these from VB code. As the purpose of this book is to learn about SQL Server, and not to learn the basics of VB, the framework for the VB application is provided in the code download from the Apress web site. If you want to create the project yourself, or see an explanation of how the code works, this appendix provides step-by-step instructions.

We know from Chapter 3 that we want to build a three-tiered client-server application. Our client-side code will contain all of the presentation logic, and our business server component will contain all of the business logic. The database will contain the stored procedures that implement the logic needed to manage the data in SQL Server.

Because we develop this application over several chapters, it does not make sense to code the business logic into a COM component and try to test with it at this point. What we will do instead is use classes in our VB program. All of the business logic that will be implemented in our business server component will be contained in classes – we can build and test these classes in our VB program before rolling them out into a business server component at a later stage.

We know from the database design, and the inserts that took place, that we have several groups of data that we need to maintain:

❑   When dealing with employees we need to maintain data in the Employee_T and Location_T tables. Thus we will need to display data from both these tables on the same screen.

❑   When we deal with hardware we will be dealing with the Hardware_T and CD_T tables, thus we need to display data from both of these tables on the same screen.

❑   Similarly, when we deal with software we are using the Software_T and Software_Category_T tables, and both of these should be shown on the same screen.

❑   When we assign a system we are dealing with employees, hardware, and software. This screen will need to display data from all of these tables, as well as the System_Assignment_T table.

We can display all of this data in one form. We will use a tab control to display the separate groups of data. This is what the finished form will look like:

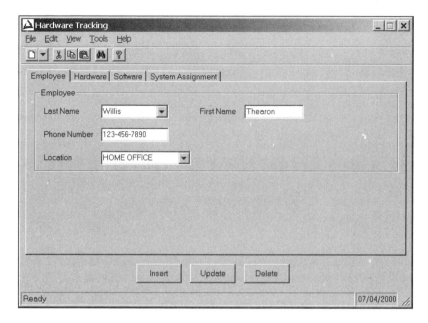

The data for each tab will be loaded when the form is loaded. When a tab is clicked we will load a recordset for that tab and this recordset will be used to tie the data together. Using the Employee tab as an example, when this is clicked on we will load a recordset that includes the employee ID and location ID. Thus, when the user clicks on a name in the Last Name combo box, the appropriate Location will be displayed.

The buttons at the bottom of the form will apply to each tab, thus we will need to include the appropriate code for each button to determine which tab we are on. This way we can execute the appropriate INSERT, UPDATE, or DELETE statements.

The menus and toolbar will provide the user with a means of clearing the fields on the current tab for inserting new data, and an alternative way to navigate between the tabs.

So let's begin building the VB front-end.

Try It Out – Building the VB Front-end

This section will walk you through the steps of building the VB front-end for our application. There is no code added in this part, so there will be no *How It Works* section. What we are interested in here is building the shell of our program so we that can identify the data our stored procedures need in order to support the front-end.

1. Start a new Standard EXE VB project.

2. Set a reference to the Microsoft ActiveX Data Objects 2.6 Library.

3. Change the project name to HardwareTracking.

4. Set the form properties as shown in the following table:

Property	Value
Name	frmMain
Caption	Hardware Tracking
Height	6048
Icon	Your choice or use the default
MaxButton	False
StartUpPosition	2 – CenterScreen
Width	8424

5. Open the Project Properties dialog by clicking on the Project menu and then clicking on the HardwareTracking Properties menu item. On the General tab we want to add a project description of Hardware Tracking Application in the Project Description text box. All the other options on this tab are fine:

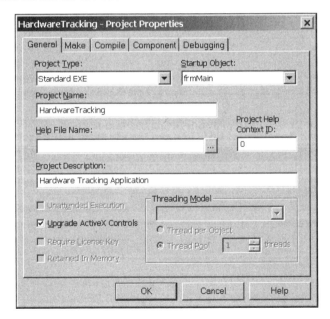

6. The Make tab contains all of the information that gets compiled with your program and is available in the Properties dialog of your compiled program. This information is also available to your program through the App object in Visual Basic. We want to automatically increment the Version Number each time we compile the program so ensure the Auto Increment checkbox has been selected.

7. The Application Title was automatically retrieved from the project name. You can change this if you want, or use the default. Notice that the Application Icon was automatically retrieved from the main form (frmMain) and this form is selected in the Icon combo box. If your project has more than one form you can choose the form that has the icon you want displayed. The icon listed here is the one associated with your executable program. When you compile your program and browse to its location using Windows Explorer, you'll see the icon listed here as the icon associated with your program. In this case we want to take the defaults for the Application information.

8. The Version information part of the screen in the dialog will also be compiled with your program. The first item in the Type list is Comments and these will be associated with your program. Enter some meaningful comments that describe what your program does. The comment that I chose to enter is: This application allows you to maintain and assign hardware in your organization.

9. The Company Name should be the name of your company.

10. Next in the Type list is File Description. This should be a one-liner as this information is displayed at the top of the Version tab of the Properties dialog for your compiled program, and the amount of text space is limited to 43 characters. The text I entered here is: Maintains and assigns hardware and software.

11. Next in the Type list is Legal Copyright. You should provide any legal copyright information for your program.

12. Legal Trademarks is next in the Type list and you should enter any trademark information for your company.

13. Product Name is next in the list. You can enter a product name here or leave this field blank. By default, the project name is inserted into this field when the component is compiled. We will accept the defaults for the rest of the options on this tab.

The Command Line Arguments text box is used to pass additional arguments to the program that would have normally been passed when the program was started from the command line. The Conditional Compilation Arguments text box is used to specify constant declarations for conditional compilation. The Remove information about unused ActiveX Controls check box allows you to remove information about the controls in the toolbox from your program if they are not referenced in your code.

For a standard EXE project, there is no information to be changed on the Compile, Component, or Debugging tabs.

14. Click OK to close the Project Properties dialog and to have the information saved.

15. The first control that we want to add to the main form is a menu. The menu will provide common functions and navigation for our program. To add a menu to your form, click on the Menu Editor from the Tools menu, or right-click on the body of the form and choose Menu Editor from the context menu. Either method invokes the Menu Editor dialog:

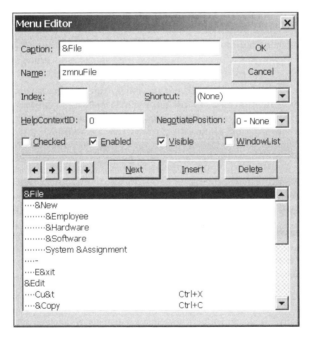

16. Menu *controls* in the table below are the top-level menus listed on your form, such as File and Edit, while menu *items* are the items of the top-level menus. Submenu items are the items of the menu items, that is, they are one more level down from the top-level menus. Use the right arrow key in the Menu Editor dialog to indent menu items. Add the menu controls and menu items as listed:

Control	Name	Properties
Menu	zmnuFile	Caption = &File
Menu Item	mnuFileNew	Caption = &New

Table continued on following page

Control	Name	Properties
Sub Menu Item	mnuFileNewEmployee	Caption = &Employee
Sub Menu Item	mnuFileNewHardware	Caption = &Hardware
Sub Menu Item	mnuFileNewSoftware	Caption = &Software
Sub Menu Item	mnuFileNewSystemAssignment	Caption = System &Assignment
Menu Item	zmnuSep1	Caption = -
Menu Item	mnuFileExit	Caption = E&xit
Menu	zmnuEdit	Caption = &Edit
Menu Item	mnuEditCut	Caption = Cu&t, Shortcut = Ctrl+X
Menu item	mnuEditCopy	Caption = &Copy, Shortcut = Ctrl+C
Menu Item	mnuEditPaste	Caption = &Paste, Shortcut = Ctrl+V
Menu Item	zmnuSep2	Caption = -
Menu Item	mnuEditFind	Caption = &Find, Shortcut = Ctrl+F
Menu	zmnuView	Caption = &View
Menu Item	mnuViewEmployee	Caption = &Employee
Menu Item	mnuViewHardware	Caption = &Hardware
Menu Item	mnuViewSoftware	Caption = &Software
Menu Item	mnuViewSystemAssignment	Caption = System &Assignment
Menu	zmnuTools	Caption = &Tools
Menu Item	mnuToolsOnlineReports	Caption = Online &Reports
Menu	zmnuHelp	Caption = &Help
Menu Item	mnuHelpContents	Caption = &Contents

Notice that all the menu names and separators are prefixed with **z**. This makes these items appear at the bottom of the Object combo box in VB. This is done for convenience because we will not be adding any code to the menus or separators, only to the menu items.

Your final File menu should look like the one shown in the figure. This menu has menu items of Exit and New, and submenu items of Employee, Hardware, Software, and System Assignment:

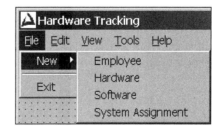

17. Now that we have built our menu, we want to add a toolbar and status bar. First however, we need to add some components to our toolbox in VB. On the Project menu click on the Components menu item to invoke the Components dialog. Add the components shown in the following figure and then click OK to close the dialog:

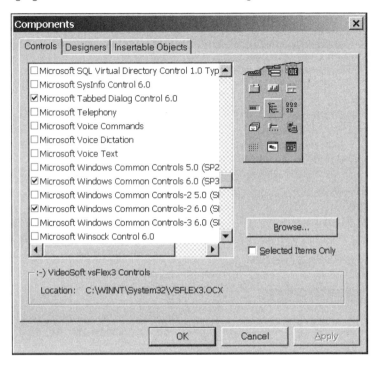

We will be using the Microsoft Tabbed Dialog Control on the form. The Microsoft Windows Common Controls 6.0 (SP3) provides the toolbar, status bar, and image list. The Microsoft Windows Common Controls-2 6.0 (SP3) provides the date/time picker that we will be using later.

18. Now that we have a reference to all the controls that we will need, add a toolbar to your form. For now, accept all the defaults for this toolbar.

19. Add an image list to your form and set its Name property to imlToolbarIcons, then right-click on it and choose Properties from the context menu, to view the Property Pages dialog. On the General tab we want to enter a value of 16 for the Height and Width of the icons.

20. On the Images tab, we want to insert a few images. Assuming you chose a default installation for VB or Visual Studio and the product is installed on your C drive, the images can be found at C:\Program Files\Microsoft Visual Studio\Common\Graphics\Bitmaps\TlBr_W95. Click on the Insert Picture button and browse to this folder.

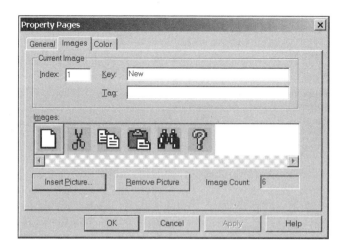

21. Select the images and assign the Key property, as shown in the following table. Click on the OK button to dismiss the dialog once you have inserted these images:

Image File Name	Key Property
New.bmp	New
Cut.bmp	Cut
Copy.bmp	Copy
Paste.bmp	Paste
Find.bmp	Find
Help.bmp	Help

22. Right-click on the toolbar and choose Properties from the context menu to invoke the Property Pages dialog. On the General tab, click on the ImageList combo box and choose imlToolbarIcons. Accept all other defaults on this tab.

23. Click on the Buttons tab and then click the Insert Button button. The first button on our toolbar is a separator button, so set the Style property to 3 – tbrSeparator.

24. Click on the Insert Button button again to insert the next button and set the Key property to btnNew. This button will be a drop-down button that displays choices, so set the Style property to 5 – tbrDropdown. Set the ToolTip Text property to New Employee and the Image index to New.

25. To insert menu items for this button, click on the Insert ButtonMenu button at the bottom of this dialog. Set the Text property to Employee and the Key property to btnNewEmployee. Click on the Insert ButtonMenu button again, then set the Text property to Hardware and the Key property to btnNewHardware. Click on the Insert ButtonMenu button again, then set the Text property to Software and the Key property to btnNewSoftware. Insert one last button menu, setting the Text property to System Assignment and the Key property to btnNewSystemAssignment.

26. Using the table below, insert the rest of the buttons for the toolbar:

Key	Style	Tool Tip	Image Index
	3 – tbrSeparator		
btnCut	0 - tbrDefault	Cut	Cut
btnCopy	0 - tbrDefault	Copy	Copy
btnPaste	0 - tbrDefault	Paste	Paste
	3 – tbrSeparator		
btnFind	0 - tbrDefault	Find	Find
	3 – tbrSeparator		
btnHelp	0 - tbrDefault	Help	Help

27. After inserting the last button click OK to close the Property Pages dialog.

28. We want to insert the status bar next. Select the StatusBar icon in the toolbox and drag it onto the form. Set its Height property to 300, then right-click on the status bar and choose Properties from the context menu. On the Panels tab, set the Key property of the first panel to pnlStatus and set the AutoSize property to 1 – sbrSpring. Next, click on the Insert Panel button at the top of the dialog to insert the next panel. After inserting a new panel you will need to click on the right arrow button at the top of the dialog to advance to the new panel that was inserted. Set its Minimum Width property to 900 and its Style property to 6 – sbrDate. Click OK to close the dialog.

At this point your form should look like this:

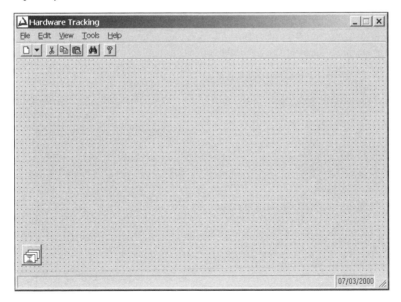

29. Select the SSTab icon in the toolbox and draw it on your form. Set its Name property to tabData, its Top property to 480, its Left property to 96, its Height property to 3852, and its Width property to 8148. Next, right click on the tab control and choose Properties from the context menu. Set the Tab Count and TabsPerRow properties to 4. Set the Style property to 1 – ssStylePropertyPage and uncheck the ShowFocusRect check box. Ensure the Current Tab property is 0 and then set the TabCaption property to Employee.

30. Click on the right arrow next to Current Tab to navigate to the next tab. Then set the TabCaption property to Hardware. Click on the arrow again to navigate to the next tab and set its TabCaption property to Software. Click on the arrow again to navigate to the last tab and set its TabCaption property to System Assignment. Click OK to close the dialog.

31. On the form click on the Employee tab of the tab control. Add to this tab the controls listed in the table below:

Control	Name	Properties
Frame	Frame1	Caption = Employee, Height = 1740, Width = 7788
Label	lblEmployee(0)	Create the labels as a control array. Caption = Last Name
ComboBox	cboLastName	Style = 0 – Dropdown Combo, Text = nothing
Label	lblEmployee(1)	Caption = First Name
TextBox	txtFirstName	Text = nothing
Label	lblEmployee(2)	Caption = Phone Number
TextBox	txtPhoneNumber	Text = nothing
Label	lblEmployee(3)	Caption = Location
ComboBox	cboLocation	Style = 0 – Dropdown Combo, Text = nothing

The correct placement of these controls is as shown:

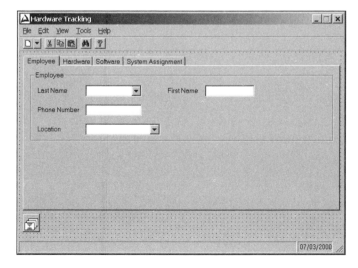

32. Click on the Hardware tab on the tab control next and add the following controls:

Control	Name	Properties
Frame	Frame2	Caption = Hardware, Height = 2700, Width = 7788
Label	lblHardware(0)	Create the labels as a control array. Caption = Manufacturer
ComboBox	cboManufacturer	Style = 0 – Dropdown Combo, Text = nothing
Label	lblHardware(1)	Caption = Model
TextBox	txtModel	Text = nothing
Label	lblHardware(2)	Caption = Processor Speed
TextBox	txtProcessorSpeed	Text = nothing
Label	lblHardware(3)	Caption = Memory
TextBox	txtMemory	Text = nothing
Label	lblHardware(4)	Caption = Hard Drive
TextBox	txtHardDrive	Text = nothing
Label	lblHardware(5)	Caption = CD
ComboBox	cboCD	Style = 2 – Dropdown List, Text = nothing
Label	lblHardware(6)	Caption = Sound Card
TextBox	txtSoundCard	Text = nothing
Label	lblHardware(7)	Caption = Speakers
TextBox	txtSpeakers	Text = nothing
Label	lblHardware(8)	Caption = Video Card
TextBox	txtVideoCard	Text = nothing
Label	lblHardware(9)	Caption = Monitor
TextBox	txtMonitor	Text = nothing
Label	lblHardware(10)	Caption = Serial Number
TextBox	txtSerialNumber	Text = nothing
Label	lblHardware(11)	Caption = Lease Expiration
DTPicker	dtpLeaseExpiration	CalendarTitleBackColor = &H8000000D& (System color: Highlight), CalendarTitleForeColor = &H8000000E& (System color: Highlight Text), Format = 1 – dtpShortDate, Height = 288, Width = 1260

When finished, the Hardware tab should look like this:

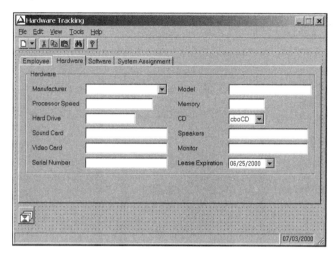

33. Click on the Software tab on the tab control next and add the following controls:

Control	Name	Properties
Frame	Frame3	Caption = Software
Label	lblSoftware(0)	Create the labels as a control array. Caption = Software Title
ComboBox	cboSoftware	Style = 0 – Dropdown Combo, Text = nothing
Label	lblSoftware(1)	Caption = Software Category
ComboBox	cboSoftwareCategory	Style = 2 – Dropdown List

The finished result is as follows:

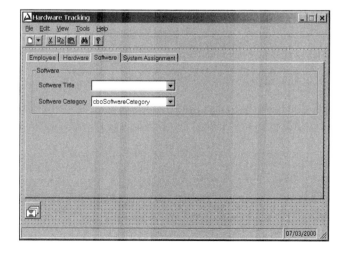

34. Click on the System Assignment tab on the tab control next and add the following controls:

Control	Name	Properties
Frame	Frame4	Caption = System Assignment
Label	lblSystemAssignment(0)	Create the labels as a control array. Caption = Employee
ComboBox	cboEmployee	Style = 2 – Dropdown List
Label	lblSystemAssignment(1)	Caption = System
ComboBox	cboSystem	Style = 2 – Dropdown List
Label	lblSystemAssignment(2)	Caption = Serial Number
TextBox	txtSystemSerialNumber	Text = nothing, Enabled = False
Label	lblSystemAssignment(3)	Caption = Installed Software
ListBox	lstInstalledSoftware	Height = 2640, Width = 3276, Style = 1 - Checkbox

This is how the System Assignment tab should look:

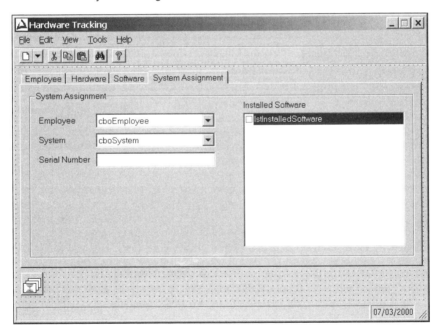

35. The last controls we want to add to this form are three Command buttons. Set their Name properties to cmdInsert, cmdUpdate, and cmdDelete and their Caption properties to Insert, Update, and Delete respectively. Your completed form should look like the one shown in the following figure:

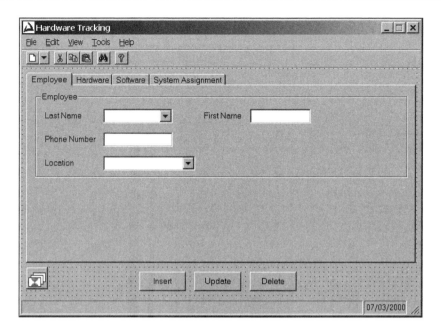

36. We want to add the login form (frmLogin, which was last updated in Chapter 7) to our project so add this form now, via the **Project, Add Form** menu. Also add the connect module (modConnect). This will allow us to connect to SQL Server.

37. Add a new class module to the project and set its **Name** property to clsSelectData. After we have inserted all of the functions and procedures and tested them thoroughly we will remove the class from our project and add it to an ActiveX DLL. This will be done in a later chapter.

This completes the framework for our front-end program. We will be adding the code to this framework to make it fully functional in Chapters 9 to 13.

Creating the Hardware Tracking Business Server Component

In Chapter 13 we added the last class to our Hardware Tracking application and fully tested the application. Now that we know the classes that we have added to this application are functioning the way we want them to, we can create our Hardware Tracking business server component.

Creating this component will allow us to share the code within it with multiple applications that need any of the functionality that the component provides. This includes other VB applications and even web applications, as this component can be called from an Active Server Page.

This appendix will detail:

❑ The steps necessary to create the Hardware Tracking business server component

❑ The modifications necessary to the Hardware Tracking application to enable it to use this new component

Removing the Classes

While Chapter 13 provided the last bit of functionality for our classes, Chapter 16 provided the last bit of functionality that we provided to our application. Therefore we want to work with the code from Chapter 16.

When we created the various classes in the Hardware Tracking application, they were created as Private. This means the Instancing property of the class was set to 1 - Private. The VB IDE did this automatically, as we cannot share a class defined in a Standard EXE with another program.

The first thing that we need to do is to remove all the classes from our Hardware Tracking application. To remove these classes:

1. Open the HardwareTracking.vbp project.

2. Remove each class by right-clicking on each class and then choosing Remove x.cls from the context menu, where x.cls represents the class name that you have clicked on.

3. Save your Hardware Tracking project and then close it.

Creating the Component

Since our application has a name of `HardwareTracking`, and our classes provide all data access to SQL Server for our application, we should probably give our component a name of `htDataAccess`. The abbreviation `ht` in the name represents a two-letter prefix for our application. I find it useful when creating components for an application to always use a two or three letter prefix for all components created for an application.

This serves a couple of purposes. Firstly, it keeps your components grouped together. Let's assume there is a standard directory that your customer/company wants all components installed in. When viewing that directory, your application's components are always grouped together. Secondly, it provides easy identification for your components. This is especially true if your shop uses standard application prefixes. For instance, you could look at the name of `htDataAccess` and immediately know that this component belongs to the Hardware Tracking application.

There are two choices when creating a server component to encapsulate our business rules. We can build an ActiveX EXE or an ActiveX DLL:

❑ An ActiveX EXE is an out-of-process component that can run as a standalone component, meaning that is does not need a client to run. When we say that this type of component is an out-of-process component we mean that this component runs in its own address space. Given this, there is extra overhead associated with using this type of component because the communications between the client and this type of component must cross process boundaries.

❑ An ActiveX DLL, on the other hand, requires a client in order to run. This type of component is instantiated by the client and runs in the same address space as the client, thus there is no extra overhead of communicating across process boundaries. This is the type of component that we want to create here.

So, with all that being said, let's get on and create the business server component for this application. To create this component:

1. Start a new ActiveX DLL project:

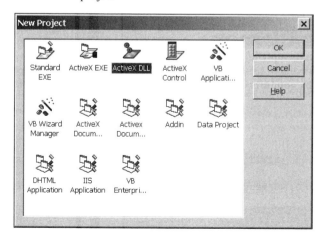

2. Invoke the Project Properties dialog by clicking on the Project menu and then choosing the Project Properties menu item. The Project Properties dialog has five tabs: General, Make, Compile, Component, and Debugging. We are only interested in the first four tabs, so this is where we will be spending our time.

3. Since we have already determined that our project name should be `htDataAccess`, let's place that name in the Project Name text box on the General tab. Since we have no help file for this component, we will not enter a help file name.

4. The name that we enter in the Project Description text box will be the project description that is displayed in the References dialog. It is important to choose and enter a proper description here to make it easy to find in the References dialog and to clearly explain what the component does.

5. When creating an ActiveX DLL it is important to check the Unattended Execution check box. Checking this check box will force any errors that would normally pop up in a message box to be logged to the Event Log.

The Upgrade ActiveX Controls checkbox will automatically check the version numbers of any ActiveX controls used in this project and upgrade the controls if a newer version of the control is found. The Retained In Memory check box retains the component in memory. If performance of a component is important and it is frequently used, then this would be a good option to check.

The completed tab should look like this:

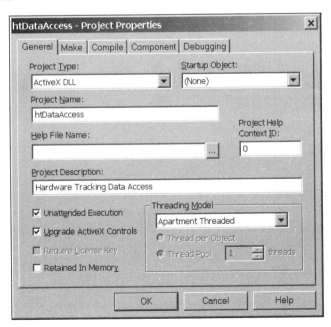

6. Switching to the Make tab, we want to check the Auto Increment check box. When checked, the VB IDE will automatically increment the Revision number each time we compile our component. You should manually change the Major version number whenever you make a major change to your component, and also change the Minor version number whenever you make minor changes to your component. An example of a major change would be the implementation of *new* functions, whereas an example of a minor change would be the enhancement of an *existing* function.

7. The application title in the Title text box has automatically been set for you. This is the title that is displayed in the App object; it is also the title used by the Package and Deployment Wizard and the Visual Studio Installer.

Unless you have forms in your component, there will be no icons to choose from. In this case, your component will have the standard icon associated with DLLs.

8. The Version Information part of the screen in this dialog will be compiled with your program. The first item in the Type list is Comments and these will be associated with your program. In the accompanying text box, enter some meaningful comments that describe what your program does.

9. The second item in the Type list is Company Name, and should be set to the name of your company.

10. Next in the Type list is File Description. This should be a one-liner here, as this information is displayed at the top of the Version tab of the Properties dialog for your compiled program, and the amount of space for text is limited to 43 characters.

11. The next item in the Type list is Legal Copyright. Here you should provide any legal copyright information for your program.

12. Legal Trademarks is next in the Type list, and it is here that you should enter any trademark information for your company.

13. Product Name is next in the list. You can enter a product name here or leave this field blank. By default, the project name is inserted into this field when the component is compiled. We will accept the defaults on the rest of the options on this tab:

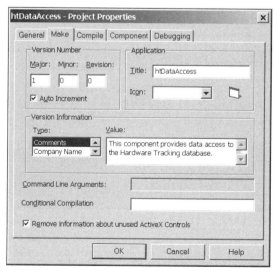

14. Switching to the Compile tab, we want to change the DLL Base Address. When the operating system loads a DLL, it tries to load it in memory at its base address, in other words the address specified in the DLL. If the memory address already contains another component, the system must go through what is called a fix-up process, whereby it finds another free address space in memory to place your DLL, and then performs the necessary steps to place it there. This process slows down the loading of your component.

To avoid this, we want to assign a unique base address to our component. In order to do this you must keep track of the addresses of all your components. The range of addresses available for VB components (ActiveX DLLs and OCXs) is from &H11000000 to &H80000000. These addresses are on 64K boundaries, and even if your component is less than 64K in size, the entire address space is reserved for your component. Likewise, if your component is 65K then your component will reserve two consecutive address spaces.

With this is mind we want to change the address for the DLL Base Address property to &H1AE00000. This is a random hexadecimal number that I chose that falls on a 64K-address boundary. To calculate an address on a 64K-address boundary, start with a base address of &H11000000 and add &H10000. Each increment of &H10000 falls on a 64K-address boundary.

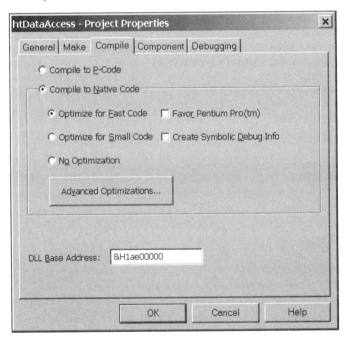

15. The last tab that we want to take a look at in the Project Properties dialog is the Component tab. The only thing we are concerned with on this tab is the Version Compatibility. There are three levels of compatibility and the first is No Compatibility. As its name implies, this option provides no compatibility whatsoever. Each time you compile your project, new class IDs and interface IDs are generated.

A class ID is a unique number assigned by VB to each class in your component, and an interface ID is a unique number assigned to each public function that you have defined in your class.

Project Compatibility maintains the type library identifier and class IDs from previous versions when you recompile your project. Interface IDs are only changed for classes that are no longer binary compatible with the previous version.

Binary Compatibility is a bit more complicated, but overall is probably the best choice once we leave the development stage and move into production. Binary compatibility maintains the same class IDs and interface IDs when you recompile your component. This does, however, impose several restrictions on changes. You cannot change (or remove) the public method interfaces (function parameters) of your component in any way without breaking binary compatibility, but you can add new interfaces to your project. If you break binary compatibility, Visual Basic will warn you when you recompile your project – heed this warning. The major benefit that choosing Binary Compatibility provides is the ability to add new or enhanced functionality to your component without having to recompile the programs or other ActiveX DLLs that use this component. This functionality cannot be achieved if you use No Compatibility or Project Compatibility.

For now however, we will use Project Compatibility, which is already set as the default.

It should be noted that the Remote Server Files option applies only to ActiveX EXEs, and is used to create a file that is used by remote systems accessing an ActiveX EXE.

16. Click OK, to save the changes we have made in the Project Properties dialog and to close the dialog itself:

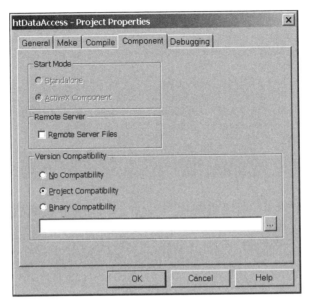

17. At this point the project name has been changed to the name that was set in the Project Name text box on the General tab of the Project Properties dialog. We now want to set a reference to the Microsoft ActiveX Data Objects 2.6 Library. We need this reference to work with the ADO `Connection`, `Command`, `Recordset`, and `Parameter` objects. Open the References dialog and set a reference to this library.

18. We are now ready to start working with the classes in our component. Remove the current class, `Class1`, by right-clicking on the class in the Project Explorer window and then choosing Remove Class1 from the context menu. You will then be prompted to save your changes to this class – click No in this dialog.

19. The first class that we want to add to our component is the delete class. To add an existing class you can right-click on a blank space in the Project Explorer window, choose Add, then choose Class Module from the context menu, or click on the Project menu and then choose the Add Class Module menu item. In the Add Class Module dialog, click on the Existing tab and navigate to the directory where your class modules are located. Then double-click on the clsDeleteData.cls class.

20. Once the class has been added, you will need to change the class properties. Click on the class module in the Project Explorer window and then click on the Instancing property for this class in the Properties window. Change the Instancing property to 5 – MultiUse. This will make this a public class, therefore its public methods are exposed in order to be called by any program that references this DLL.

21. Repeat the last two steps, adding the insert data, select data, text data, and update data classes.

22. The next step is to compile the component. Click on the File menu and then choose the Make htDataAccess.dll menu item.

23. In the Make Project dialog, click on the Create New Folder icon and create a new folder called Compatibility. Then double-click on that folder to get into it and click on the OK button to compile your component in this folder.

24. At this point we have a compiled component in the Compatibility folder. This is the component that will serve as our compatibility component. Now bring up the Project Properties dialog again, and click on the Component tab. Click on the Binary Compatibility option button and ensure that Compatibility\htDataAccess.dll is displayed in the text box below this option:

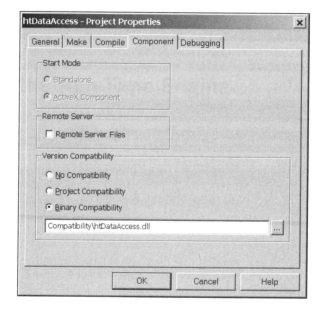

25. Click on the File menu and then choose the Make htDataAccess.dll menu item.

26. In the Make Project dialog, click on the Up One Level icon to navigate up one directory, and then compile your component again.

27. Save and close your project.

28. Note that you can view all of the properties that you set in the Project Properties dialog by right-clicking on the compiled component, htDataAccess.dll, in Windows Explorer and choosing Properties from the context menu:

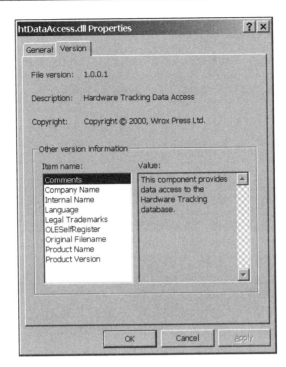

What we have done here is to create a compatibility component and a component that will be referenced by our Hardware Tracking application. Any changes we make to this component will be checked against the compatibility component files by VB and it will warn you if you try to break compatibility.

Because binary compatibility maintains the same class IDs and interface IDs when we recompile our component, we are able to make any changes necessary to our component, but only on the proviso that we do not break binary compatibility. Thus, provided we do not break binary compatibility, we are able to implement enhancements to our component without having to change the programs that access our component. What this means is that we can enhance the functionality of the component as long as we do change any of the parameters to any existing methods or add any parameters to the existing methods.

If we do need to break binary compatibility then we will have to recompile our front-end programs that access this component. At the same time we would also want to perform the same set of steps as shown previously: create a new binary compatibility component, and then compile the component that will be accessed by our front-end programs.

Front-end Modifications

Because we added the classes to our Hardware Tracking application when we developed and tested these classes, the modifications required to our front-end program to access the htDataAccess component are very minor.

To make the required modifications:

1. Open the HardwareTracking.vbp project.

2. Open the References dialog by clicking on the Project menu and choosing the References menu item.

3. Set a reference to the htDataAccess.dll component. You will find this component in the References dialog with the description that you entered for the project description when you created this component:

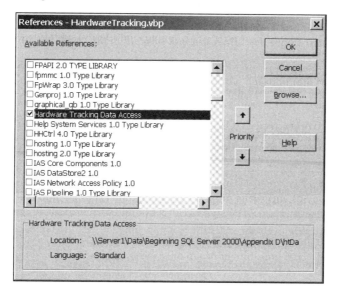

4. Click OK to close the References dialog.

5. In the general declarations section of the main form (frmMain) you should modify the objects by including the component name, as shown in the following code fragment. While this step is not necessary, it does improve the readability of the code and does not leave it open to interpretation as to where the references to these classes are coming from.

```
'Declare objects
Dim objData As htDataAccess.clsSelectData
Dim objInsert As htDataAccess.clsInsertData
Dim objUpdate As htDataAccess.clsUpdateData
Dim objDelete As htDataAccess.clsDeleteData
```

6. In the general declarations section of the notes form (`frmNotes`) you will also need to modify the object declaration, as shown in the following code fragment:

```
'Declare objects
Dim objText As htDataAccess.clsTextData
```

7. These are all the modifications necessary for this project. At this point you need to compile your program. Click on the File menu and choose the Make HardwareTracking.exe menu item.

8. In the Make Project dialog, verify or navigate to the directory where you want the program to be compiled and then click on the OK button.

9. Save your project and then close VB.

Summary

This appendix has shown how easy it can be to convert the classes in your front-end program to a business server component. We have demonstrated the steps required to create the `htDataAccess` component and then use this component in the Hardware Tracking front-end application.

We have covered some important topics when creating a component. The most important being that you should set your component to use binary compatibility once you are ready to implement your component in a production environment. This ensures that any changes you make do not break compatibility without any warning. This prevents you from having to recompile your front-end program(s).

We have also seen how setting the various properties in the Project Properties dialog affects how the component is displayed in the References dialog.

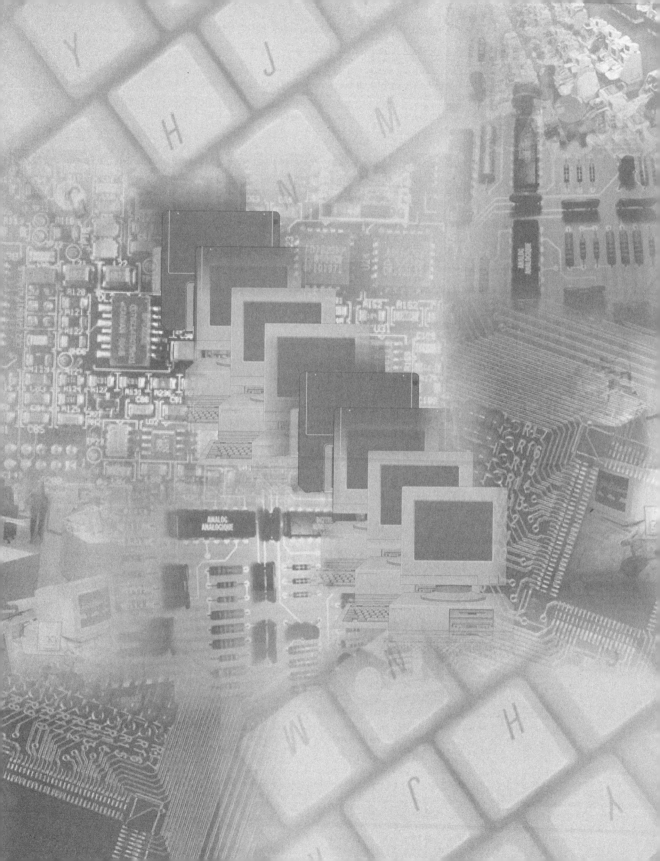

References

This appendix provides some useful references for SQL Server and XML.

SQL Server References

SQL Server: Common Problems, Tested Solutions by Neil Pike, Apress (1-893115-81-X)

SQL: Access to SQL Server by Susan Sales Harkins and Martin Reid, Apress (1-893115-30-5)

For information and tips on SQL Server check out:

```
http://www.sql-zone.com/
http://www.swynk.com
http://www.pinnaclepublishing.com/sq
http://www.mssqlserver.com/
http://www.microsoft.com/sql/
http://msdn.microsoft.com/library/default.asp
http://msdn.microsoft.com/sqlserver/
```

XML References

For information and tips on XML check out:

```
http://www.xml-zone.com/
http://www.xmldevelopernewsletter.com/
http://www.xml.com/xml/pub
http://msdn.microsoft.com/library/default.asp
http://msdn.microsoft.com/xml/default.asp
```

For the latest XML and XSL standards:

```
http://www.w3.org/
```

For more on the latest XML and SQL Server books check out:

```
http://www.apress.com
http://www.amazon.com/
```

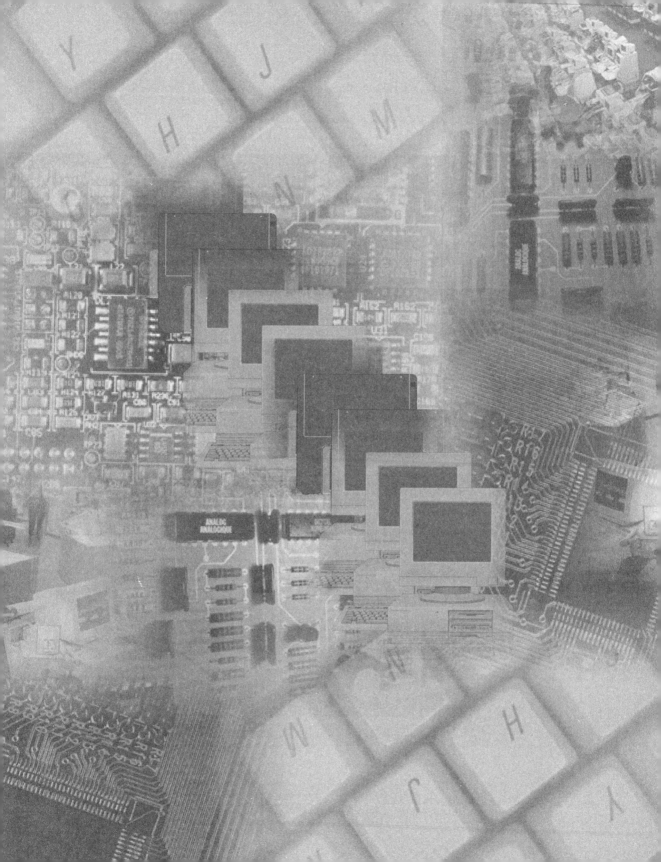

Support, Errata, and forums.apress.com

One of the most irritating things about any programming book is when you find that bit of code you've just spent an hour typing simply doesn't work. You check it a hundred times to see if you've set it up correctly and then you notice the spelling mistake in the variable name on the book page. Of course, you can blame the authors for not taking enough care and testing the code, the editors for not doing their job properly, or the proofreaders for not being eagle-eyed enough, but this doesn't get around the fact that mistakes do happen.

We try hard to ensure no mistakes sneak out into the real world, but we can't promise that this book is 100% error free. What we can do is offer the next best thing by providing you with immediate support and feedback from experts who have worked on the book, and try to ensure that future editions eliminate these gremlins.

We also now commit to supporting you not just while you read the book, but once you start developing applications as well, through our online forums, where you can put your questions to the authors, reviewers, and fellow industry professionals.

In this appendix we'll look at how to:

❑   Post and check for errata on our main site, http://www.wrox.com

❑   E-Mail support with a query or feedback on our books in general

❑   Enroll in the peer-to-forums at http://forums.apress.com

Between all three support procedures, you should get an answer to your problem very quickly.

Support and Errata on www.apress.com

We understand that errors can destroy the enjoyment of a book and can cause many wasted and frustrated hours, so we seek to minimize the distress that they can cause. The following section will explain how to find and post errata to our web site to get book-specific help.

Finding Errata

Before you send in a query, you might be able to save time by finding the answer to your problem on our web site – http://www.apress.com. Locate this book in the Online Catalog or within the book's category and go to the book's web page. Check to see if there is a Corrections link. If there is, click the link to see the posted errata.

Adding an Erratum to the Web Site

If you wish to point out an erratum or directly query a problem in the book, then on the book's web page, click the Submit errata link. Please be sure to include your name and email, and the chapter, page number, and a brief description of the problem, as requested.

We won't send you junk mail. We need the details to save your time and ours.

Queries will be forwarded to the author and editor. You may receive a direct e-mail reply, and/or the erratum will be posted to the web site for all readers to benefit from.

Customer Support

We always value hearing from our readers, and we want to know what you think about this book: what you liked, what you didn't like, and what you think we can do better next time. You can send us your comments by e-mailing support@apress.com. Please be sure to mention the book's ISBN and title in your message.

What We Can't Answer

Obviously with an ever-growing range of books and an ever-changing technology base, there is an increasing volume of data requiring support. While we endeavor to answer all questions about the book, we can't solve bugs in your own programs that you've adapted from our code. However, do tell us if you're especially pleased with the routine you developed with our help.

How to Tell Us Exactly What You Think

You might just wish to tell us how much you liked or loathed the book in question. Or you might have ideas about how this whole process could be improved. In either case you should e-mail support@apress.com. You'll always find a sympathetic ear, no matter what the problem is. Above all you should remember that we do care about what you have to say and we will do our utmost to act upon it.

The Peer-to-Peer Forums at forums.apress.com

For author and peer discussion, join the Apress discussion groups. If you post a query to our forums, you can be confident that many Apress authors, editors, and industry experts are examining it. At forums.apress.com you will find a number of different lists that will help you, not only while you read this book, but also as you develop your own applications. To sign up for the Apress forums, go to forums.apress.com and select the New User link.

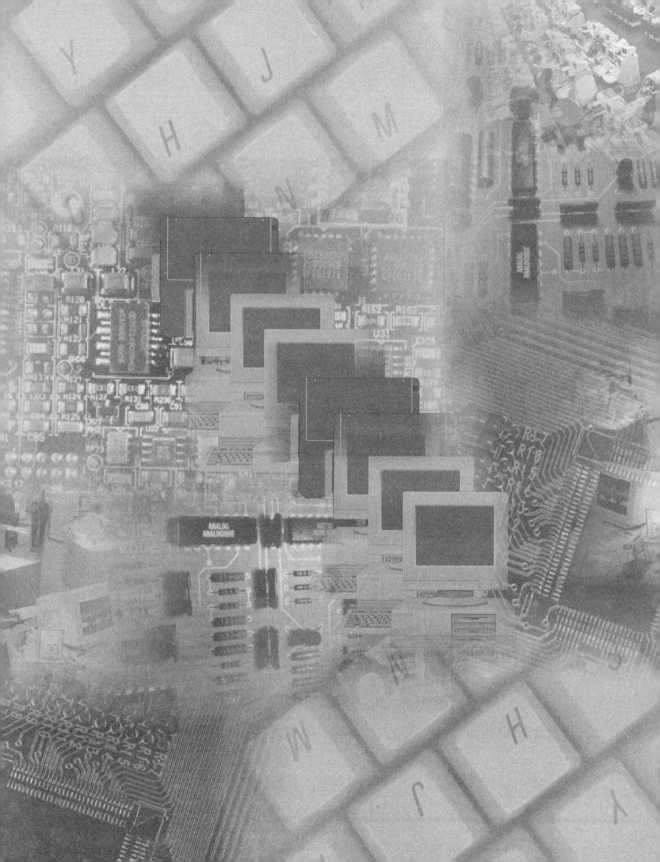

Index

A Guide to the Index

The index is arranged hierarchically, in alphabetical order, with symbols preceding the letter A. Most second-level entries and many third-level entries also occur as first-level entries. This is to ensure that users will find the information they require however they choose to search for it. Italicizing is used for fourth-level entries and to differentiate non-capitalized names from the surrounding text.

B

C

848

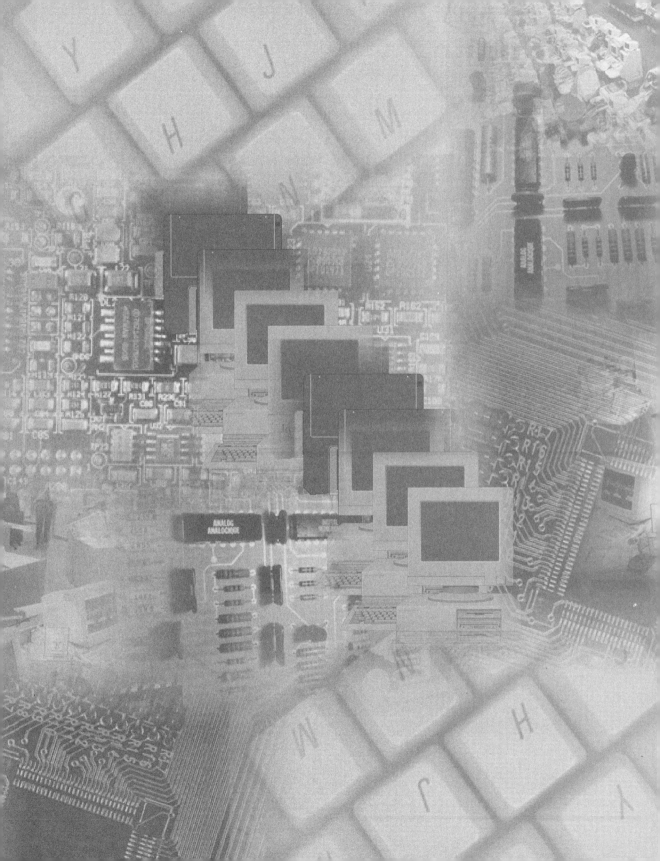